McAllister's Scottisł

Fifth Edition

McAllister's Scottish Law of Leases

Fifth Edition

Lorna Richardson
Senior Lecturer in Law at the University of Edinburgh,
Solicitor (non-practising)

Craig Anderson
Lecturer in Law at Robert Gordon University

Bloomsbury Professional

LONDON · DUBLIN · EDINBURGH · NEW YORK · NEW DELHI · SYDNEY

BLOOMSBURY PROFESSIONAL
Bloomsbury Publishing Plc
9–10 St Andrew Square, Edinburgh, EH2 2AF, UK
50 Bedford Square, London, WC1B 3DP, UK
1385 Broadway, New York, NY 10018, USA
29 Earlsfort Terrace, Dublin 2, Ireland

BLOOMSBURY and the Diana logo are trademarks
of Bloomsbury Publishing Plc

First published in Great Britain 2021

British Library Cataloguing-in-Publication Data

A catalogue record for this book is available from the British Library.

ISBN:	Print	978 1 52651 391 5
	Epub	978 1 52651 392 2
	Epdf	978 1 52651 393 9

Typeset by Evolution Design & Digital Ltd (Kent)
Printed and bound by CPI Group (UK) Ltd, Croydon, CR0 4YY

To find out more about our authors and books visit
www.bloomsburyprofessional.com. Here you will find
extracts, author information, details of forthcoming events
and the option to sign up for our newsletters

Preface

This new edition introduces a new author team. We are delighted to have been asked to take over the updating of this book. The Scottish legal community is indebted to Angus McAllister for creating this much loved and well-used work, and for his dedication in producing four editions. We have endeavoured to do it justice.

There have been a number of significant developments in the law as it relates to leases, which are dealt with in this edition. In the seven years since the last edition the Long Leases (Scotland) Act 2012, the Land Registration (Scotland) Act 2012, the Consumer Rights Act 2015 and the Private Housing (Tenancies)(Scotland) Act 2016 have come into force. The changes made by this, and related subordinate legislation, are dealt with in some detail in the relevant chapters. As the residential tenant's right to buy has been abolished we have removed that chapter from the book.

There has continued to be a steady stream of case law, in the First Tier Tribunal, the Sheriff Courts and the Court of Session on matters pertaining to the landlord / tenant relationship. We have attempted to reflect all significant developments on the matters covered in this book. This has ranged from questions such as whether there is a valid contract between parties for the renting of a property notwithstanding that it does not meet the form requirements for a lease; to the difficult question of requisite notice periods for serving a notice to quit to bring a lease to an end. Case law from the Supreme Court on matters such as the principles that should be used to interpret a lease are also incorporated into this edition.

We have also highlighted the recent work by the Scottish Law Commission on matters relating to terminating leases. It is to be hoped that some of the Commission's recommendations result in legislative change to improve the law and remove unnecessary complexities.

We have tried to state the law as at 1 November 2020.

Lorna Richardson and Craig Anderson
25 November 2020

Bibliography

(a) General texts on landlord and tenant

WM Gloag and RC Henderson *The Law of Scotland* (14th edn, 2017) Edinburgh: W Green, ch 35.

WM Gordon and S Wortley *Scottish Land Law, Vol 1* (3rd edn 2009) Edinburgh: W Green, ch 18.

GCH Paton and JGS Cameron *The Law of Landlord and Tenant in Scotland* (1967) Edinburgh: W Green.

J Rankine, *A Treatise on the Law of Leases in Scotland* (3rd edn, 1916) Edinburgh: W Green.

R Rennie S Brymer, T Mullen, M Blair and F McCarthy *Leases* (2015) Edinburgh: W Green.

(b) Specialist books on landlord and tenant

D Cockburn and R Mitchell *Commercial Leases* (2nd edn 2011) London: Bloomsbury Professsional.

AGM Duncan *The Agricultural Holdings (Scotland) Act 1991* (1991) Edinburgh: W Green.

D Flyn and K Graham *Crofting Law* (2017) Edinburgh: Edinburgh University Press.

DJ Garrity and L Richardson, *Dilapidations and Service Charge* (2019) Edinburgh: Edinburgh University Press.

K Gerber *Commercial Leases in Scotland* (3rd edn 2016) Edinburgh: W Green.

Rt Hon Lord Gill *Agricultural Tenancies* (4th edn 2016) Edinburgh: W Green.

SM Notley *Scottish Agricultural Law* (2009) Edinburgh: Avizandum Publishing.

P Robson and MM Combe *Residential Tenancies: Private & Social Renting in Scotland* (4th edn, 2019) Edinburgh: W Green.

MJ Ross and DJ McKichan *Drafting and Negotiating Commercial Leases in Scotland* (2nd edn, 1993) Edinburgh: Butterworth.

(c) Human Rights Act 1998

Mullen and Brown *The Human Rights Act 1998 and Scots Law* (2001).

R Reed and JL Murdoch *Human Rights Law in Scotland* (4th edn, 2017) London: Bloomsbury Professional.

(d) Other relevant textbooks

C Anderson *Property: A Guide to Scots Law* (2016) Edinburgh: W Green.

WM Gloag *The Law of Contract* (2nd edn, 1929) Edinburgh: W Green.

G Gretton and AJM Steven *Property, Trusts and Succession* (3rd edn, 2017) London: Bloomsbury Professional.

H MacQueen *MacQueen and Thomson's Contract Law in Scotland* (5th edn, 2020) London: Bloomsbury Professional.

WW McBryde *The Law of Contract in Scotland* (3rd edn, 2007) Edinburgh: W Green.

DM Walker *The Law of Contracts and Related Obligations in Scotland* (3rd edn, 1995) London: Butterworth.

Abbreviations

AB(S)A 2004	Antisocial Behaviour etc (Scotland) Act 2004
AC	Appeal Cases (Law Reports)
AFT(S)A 2000	Abolition of Feudal Tenure etc (Scotland) Act 2000
AH(S)A 1991	Agricultural Holdings (Scotland) Act 1991
AH(S)A 2003	Agricultural Holdings (Scotland) Act 2003
All ER	All England Law Reports
A(S)A 2010	Arbitration (Scotland) Act 2010
BADE(S)A 2007	Bankruptcy and Diligence etc (Scotland) Act 2007
CA	Court of Appeal
Ch	Chancery (Law Reports)
Cr App R	Criminal Appeal Reports
CLY	Current Law Yearbook
CSIH	Court of Session, Inner House
CSOH	Court of Session, Outer House
CRA	Consumer Rights Act 2015
CR(S)A 2010	Crofting Reform (Scotland) Act 2010
C(S)A 1991	Crofters (Scotland) Act 1993
D	Dunlop (Court of Session Reports, 2nd Series, 1838–62)
EG	Estates Gazette
EGCS	Estates Gazette Case Summaries
EGLR	Estates Gazette Law Reports
EHRR	European Human Rights Reports
ELR	Edinburgh Law Review
Env LR	Environmental Law Reports
EPA 1990	Environmental Protection Act 1990
EWHC	England and Wales High Court
F	Fraser (Court of Session Reports, 5th Series, 1898–1906)
Fam LR	Family Law Reports (Scotland)
FLR	Family Law Reports
FSR	Fleet Street Reports
GWD	Green's Weekly Digest
HL	House of Lords
HLR	Housing Law Reports

Hous LR	Greens Housing Law Reports
HRA 1998	Human Rights Act 1998
H(S)A 1987	Housing (Scotland) Act 1987
H(S)A 1988	Housing (Scotland) Act 1988
H(S)A 2001	Housing (Scotland) Act 2001
H(S)A 2006	Housing (Scotland) Act 2006
H(S)A 2010	Housing (Scotland) Act 2010
Hume Baron	Hume's Reports of Decisions, 1781–1822
JLSS	Journal of the Law Society of Scotland
Jur Rev	Juridical Review
KB	King's Bench (Law Reports)
LC(S)A 2001	Leasehold Casualties (Scotland) Act 2001
LJ	Law Journal Newspaper
LL(S)A 2012	Long Leases (Scotland) Act 2012
Lloyds LR	Lloyd's Law Reports
LR(MP)(S)A 1985	Law Reform (Miscellaneous Provisions) (Scotland) Act 1995
LR(S)A 1979	Land Registration (Scotland) Act 1979
LR(S)A 2003	Land Reform (Scotland) Act 2003
LR(S)A 2012	Land Registration etc (Scotland) Act 2012
LR(S)A 2016	Land Reform (Scotland) Act 2016
L & TR	Landlord and Tenant Reports
L & T Review	Landlord & Tenant Review
LTR(S)A 1974	Land Tenure Reform (Scotland) Act 1974
LW(CD)(S)A 2015	Legal Writings (Counterparts and Delivery) (Scotland) Act 2015
MH(FP)(S)A 1981	Matrimonial Homes (Family Protection) (Scotland) Act 1981
M	Macpherson (Court of Session Reports, 3rd Series, 1862–73)
Mor	Morison's Dictionary of Decisions
NLJ	New Law Journal
NPC	New Property Cases
OL(S)A 1960	Occupiers' Liability (Scotland) Act 1960
PA 1890	Partnership Act 1890
P & CR	Property, Planning and Compensation Reports
PRH(S)A 2011	Private Rented Housing (Scotland) Act 2011
PH(T)(S)A 2016	Private Housing (Tenancies)(Scotland) Act 2016
Prop LB	Greens Property Law Bulletin
QB	Queen's Bench (Law Reports)
R Rettie	(Court of Session Reports, 4th Series, 1873–98)
Rep LR	Reparation Law Reports

ROL(S)A 1857	Registration of Leases (Scotland) Act 1857
ROW(S) 1995	Requirements of Writing (Scotland) Act 1995
R(S)A 1984	Rent (Scotland) Act 1984
RT(S)A 1886	Removal Terms (Scotland) Act 1886
RVR	Rating and Valuation Reporter
S	Shaw (Court of Session Reports, 1st Series, 1821–38)
SC	Session Cases
SCCR	Scottish Criminal Case Reports
Sc Jur	Scottish Jurist
SCLR	Scottish Civil Law Reports
SCOLAG	Journal of Scottish Legal Action Group
Sh Ct Rep	Sheriff Court Reports
SJ	Solicitors' Journal
SLCR	Scottish Land Court Reports
SLPQ	Scottish Law and Practice Quarterly
SLR	Scottish Law Reporter
SLT	Scots Law Times
SN	Session Notes
S(S)A 1964	Succession (Scotland) Act 1964
TC(S)A 2003	Title Conditions (Scotland) Act 2003
TLR	Times Law Reports
TOCE(S)A 1997	Transfer of Crofting Estates (Scotland) Act 1997
TOS(S)A 1949	Tenancy of Shops (Scotland) Act 1949
UCTA 1977	Unfair Contract Terms Act 1977
UKSC	United Kingdom Supreme Court
WLR	Weekly Law Reports

Contents

Contents

Contents

Table of Statutes

[References are to paragraph number]

xix

Table of Statutory Instruments

[References are to paragraph number]

Table of European and International Materials

[References are to paragraph number]

Table of Cases

B

C

E

F

G

I

M

P

Q

Table of Cases

PART 1
INTRODUCTION

Chapter 1

Introduction

MAIN CHARACTERISTICS OF LEASES[1]

1.1   A lease is a contract by which a person, known as a tenant, is allowed to occupy someone else's heritable property for a finite period. In return for this the tenant pays to the person granting this right, ie the landlord, a periodical payment known as rent. Rent usually takes the form of money but may also (though not commonly) be paid in goods.[2]

Several points from this require to be developed:

1 Rankine *Leases* (3rd edn, 1916) Introduction; Paton and Cameron *Landlord and Tenant* (1967) pp 3-5.
2 For more traditional definitions see Rankine p 1 and Paton and Cameron p 5.

Subject matter of leases

1.2   The subject matter of a lease is heritable property. This means, broadly speaking, land and buildings and rights pertaining to them. In a strict sense it means land and its pertinents, including buildings and any other fixtures attached to the land; however, although it is subsidiary in legal theory, it is often a building rather than its site that is the most valuable element in a lease, and therefore the main subject of the contract. Although the term 'lease' is sometimes used loosely in connection with the hire of moveable property, such contracts are not leases.

Exclusive possession

1.3   The tenant (or tenants where there is a joint tenancy) must normally be given exclusive possession of the leased subjects. Where the landlord has reserved the right to share occupation in some way, the contract may not be a lease at all but a licence (or right of occupancy). Exclusive possession is an essential requirement for a lease in England. However, although it is undoubtedly a normal requirement in Scotland, the principle is not quite so absolute in relation to Scottish leases.

In particular, there are certain exceptional types of contract that do not involve exclusive possession by the tenant, but nevertheless have been traditionally considered to be leases. These include leases of shooting rights, salmon fishings and the right to extract minerals and are briefly considered later in the chapter.[1]

We will examine the issue of exclusive possession further when considering the difference between a lease and a licence.[2]

1 See para 1.16.
2 See para 2.50 et seq.

Occupation finite

1.4   A lease may confer only a short temporary right of occupation or its duration may be much longer. In either case the right of ownership remains with the landlord to whom possession will normally revert at the expiry of the lease. The expiry or termination date of a lease is known in Scotland as the ish.

1.5   M*aximum length of leases*   Leases entered on or after 9 June 2000 have a maximum length of 175 years.[1]

Leases entered prior to that date could be very long indeed. Durations of up to 999 years were not uncommon and even a perpetual lease was possible; in *Carruthers v Irvine*,[2] a lease was stated to endure 'perpetually and continually as long as the grass groweth up and the water runneth down'. Because of their extraordinary length, many of these older leases are of course still in existence. Under the Long Leases (Scotland) Act 2012 the tenants' interests in some of these ultra-long leases converted into ownership on 28 November 2015.[3]

1 Abolition of Feudal Tenure etc (Scotland) Act 2000, s 67; see also para 8.4 et seq.
2 (1717) Mor 15195.
3 See para 8.38 et seq.

Lease as a contract

1.6   A lease is a contract. This means that, as well as the special legal rules relating to landlord and tenant, the general law of contract also applies to leases. It is not within the scope of this book to look in any detail at the law of contract, for which there are a number of suitable textbooks at various levels.[1] However, reference to contract law will be made from time to time where relevant.

1 See the textbooks listed in the bibliography.

Lease as conferring a right of property

1.7   While it is right to regard a lease as a contract for the reasons stated above, this does not tell the full story. It is appropriate for leases of short duration, which may seem to be not unlike other types of business contract. However, where a lease is of long duration the rights conferred on a tenant may be much more substantial than one would normally expect from a contract. In many cases the tenant will be enjoying not just a temporary right of occupation, but something that, from a practical point of view, is closer to a right of property or ownership. There are several ways in which a tenant's rights may transcend those enjoyed under a contract:

1.8   *A lease confers a real right*[1]   Generally we would expect a contract only to legally bind the original parties to it. However, if the ownership of a tenanted property changes hands, the new owner will normally have to recognise the leases of any sitting tenants, despite not having been a party to their leases.

1 See para 2.30 et seq.

1.9   *Security of tenure*   If a lease's duration confers a sufficiently long period of tenure, the tenant may erect and pay for some or all of the buildings. Even where this is not the case, and the lease is not quite so long, eg 20 or 30 years, the tenant's legal interest, because of the lease's length, will acquire a capital value and become a marketable asset; in other words, a tenant may be able to charge a substantial sum of money for an assignation (transfer) of the lease to a new tenant. In the case of very long leases, eg 99 years or more, such a transaction will, in market terms, be similar to an outright sale of heritable property.[1]

1 Though the tenant's legal title may be not quite so secure as that of an owner. See Ch 5 and para 8.2.

1.10   *Registered leases*   A lease of more than 20 years may be registered in the Land Register of Scotland. Registering a lease strengthens the tenant's rights considerably; in particular it allows the tenancy to be used as security for a loan.[1]

1 See para 8.11 et seq, particularly 8.19.

1.11   *Statutory protection*   There are a number of statutes which (depending on the type of lease) may strengthen further a tenant's rights. These will be noted as we go along. In particular, we will see that in agricultural and residential tenancies a tenant may have statutory security of tenure, ie the right to stay on in the leased property even though the termination date in the lease has arrived and the landlord wants possession.[1] Generally, such statutory rights cannot be contracted out of, ie any provision in the lease purporting to deprive the tenant of them will not be given effect by the courts.

1 See generally Parts 4 and 5.

TYPES OF LEASE

Urban and rural leases

1.12   The distinction between urban and rural leases in Scots law is traditional, operating independently of the other classifications described below. It does not quite mean what these words suggest. Where the main subject of let is a building, and either there is no land attached or the land is subsidiary, eg garden ground, there is an urban lease. However, where the main subject is land it is a rural lease. An agricultural lease is therefore a rural lease: there may be farm buildings, but they are subsidiary to the land as part of the subjects of let.

The distinction between urban and rural leases is still important where the common law of landlord and tenant applies. For example, whether or not a lease is urban or rural may determine the nature of the landlord's repairing obligation[1] or whether or not it can be assigned without the landlord's consent.[2]

1 See paras 3.12, 3.26 et seq and 3.40 et seq.
2 See para 7.20 et seq.

Commercial leases

1.13   Commercial leases are urban leases, as they relate to the let of buildings. 'Commercial lease' is the term generally applied to leases of shops, offices, factories or other business premises. Commercial leases in Scotland (though not in England) are almost free of statutory regulation.[1] Commercial subjects are generally the most valuable types of heritable property, and are commonly acquired by large financial institutions for the purpose of investment. It is in this area, because of the amount of money that is often at stake, that the complex law relating to rent reviews is most pertinent.[2]

1 The main exceptions are the Law Reform (Miscellaneous Provisions)(Scotland) Act 1985 – see para 5.22 et seq and the Tenancy of Shops (Scotland) Act 1949 – see Ch 14.
2 See Ch 12.

Agricultural leases

1.14   Agricultural leases are, naturally, rural leases. Leases of farmland are closely regulated by statute, notably by the Agricultural Holdings (Scotland) Acts 1991 and 2003.[1] In the case of smaller holdings, the lease may instead be governed by the legislation relating to crofts and small landholdings.[2]

1 See Ch 15.
2 See Ch 16.

Residential leases

1.15   Residential leases are leases of dwellinghouses, including flats, and they are of course urban leases. Like agricultural leases, they are extensively regulated by statute. Until early in the 20th century, the most common types of residential let were those from private landlords. Over the course of the 20th century, the incidence of private house lets gradually decreased along with the rise in social tenancies granted by local authorities and, in more recent years, by housing associations.

Lets from private landlords are now likely to be private residential tenancies, which are governed by the Private Housing (Tenancies) (Scotland) Act 2016.[1] Tenants under such tenancies have a statutory right to security of tenure.

The main statutes relating to social tenancies (known as Scottish secure tenancies) are the Housing (Scotland) Act 2001, the Housing (Scotland) Act 2010 and the Housing (Scotland) Act 2014. Scottish secure tenants also enjoy security of tenure.[2]

1 See Ch 17, and also Chs 19, 20 and 21.
2 See Ch 18.

Leases of certain uses of land: mineral and sporting leases

1.16   Scots law has traditionally given the status of lease to certain types of agreement under which the tenant does not have an exclusive right to occupy the property, but the right to use it for certain purposes only. Many of these have fallen into disuse in modern times, but others still occur, mainly in rural areas. They include mineral leases, which logically should really be regarded as a type of sale, as the subjects are gradually removed by the tenant. For this reason, instead of rent, the mineral tenant generally pays a lordship or royalty, based on the amount of minerals taken. Other special uses of land that may be leased include salmon fishings and other sporting rights.[1]

1 For further details, see Paton and Cameron pp 73–84.

Long leases[1]

1.17   There is no prescribed length that determines whether a lease should be regarded as a long lease or not. Twenty years is perhaps as good a figure as any, as it is the limit above which leases may be registered in the Land Register.

Long leases of commercial property used to be standard, and are still to be found, though the trend in recent years is for commercial leases to be very much shorter.[2]

1 See generally Ch 8.
2 See paras 11.3 and 12.2.

1.18   *Ground leases*   This is a common type of long lease whereby the landlord leases the ground only, for a relatively modest rent, and the tenant either buys the buildings outright or is responsible for building them; obviously, a tenant will normally only agree to this if given a reasonable length of tenure, eg 99 years, which will at least match the useful life of the buildings.

Other types of lease tenure

1.19   *The Crown's kindly tenants of the four towns of Lochmaben*
This used to be a local phenomenon found in Dumfriesshire near the border, originating historically from grants by King Robert the Bruce to vassals on the lands of his castle there. It was a strange hybrid of tenancy and ownership, under which the 'tenants' had a potentially perpetual right along with an absolute right to sell, but could be removed if they failed to pay their rent.[1]

On 28 November 2004 (the appointed day for the abolition of the feudal system) the interests of kindly tenants were converted to ownership. This included any right of salmon fishing which could not be severed from the kindly tenancy.[2]

1 Rankine Ch VII; Paton and Cameron pp 69–70.
2 AFT(S)A 2000, s 64.

1.20   *Tenancy-at-will*   A tenancy-at-will is an informal type of ground lease to be found particularly in fishing and rural villages on the north-east coast, in highland villages, and in a mining village in Lanarkshire.[1] The tenant rents the land from the landowner in order to build a house, but is given no formal title and can be removed for non-payment of rent.

The Land Registration (Scotland) Act 1979 gave tenants-at-will the right to purchase the tenant's interest,[2] and defined a tenant-at-will as a person, other than a tenant under a lease or a tenant or occupier by virtue of any enactment:

'(a) who ... is by custom and usage the occupier (actual or constructive) of land on which there is a building or buildings erected or acquired for value by him or any predecessor of his;

(b) who is under an obligation to pay a ground rent to the owner of the land in respect of the said land but not in respect of the building or buildings on it, or would have been under such an obligation if the ground rent had not been redeemed; and

(c) whose right of occupancy is without ish.'[3]

1 Paton and Cameron pp 68–69.
2 Land Registration (Scotland) Act 1979, ss 20–22.
3 LR(S)A 1979 s 20(8). For the meaning of ish see para 1.4.

1.21   The nature of tenancies-at-will was considered in some depth by the Inner House in *Allen v MacTaggart*[1] in which the occupiers of eight beach huts appealed unsuccessfully against the finding of the Lands Tribunal that they were not tenants-at-will. It was held, inter alia, that:

(1) for the purposes of the 1979 Act it must be possible to identify and delineate, with adequate precision, the locality in question, and to describe, in sufficient detail, the nature and terms of the 'custom and usage' which the inhabitants of that locality generally recognise as having the force of law in place of the system of land tenure applying elsewhere in Scotland;

(2) subject to possible local customary variation, the ground rent payable under a tenancy-at-will is fixed for all time, and changes in the amount of ground rent (as in the present case) point to the existence of a lease rather than a tenancy-at-will; and

(3) the facts as averred indicated the existence of informal leases from year to year, not tenancies-at-will without ish.

1 2007 SC 482, 2007 SLT 387; see also the commentary on this case by David Cabrelli in 'Tenancies-at-will: *Allen v McTaggart*' 2007 Edin LR 436; and see also *McCann v Anderson, More v Anderson* 1981 SLT (Lands Tr) 13; *Ferguson v Gibbs* 1987 SLT (Lands Tr) 32; *Duthie v Watson* 1997 Hous LR 129; and *Wright v Shoreline Management Ltd* 2009 SLT (Sh Ct) 83, 2009 GWD 25-411.

TERM AND QUARTER DAYS

1.22   The four quarter days in Scotland are Candlemas, Whitsunday, Lammas and Martinmas. Whitsunday and Martinmas are also known as term days. The traditional dates for these were 2 February (Candlemas), 15 May (Whitsunday), 1 August (Lammas) and 11 November (Martinmas), but were changed by the Term and Quarter Days (Scotland) Act 1990 to the 28th day of the month in each case. The change applies for the purpose of any enactment or rule of law and in relation to any lease agreement or undertaking.

The purpose of the change was to divide up the year more evenly and also to sort out the confusion caused by certain statutes which, for their own limited purposes, had already defined Whitsunday and Martinmas as the 28th of the month.[1]

Although the new definitions apply generally and may affect any type of legal document, they are particularly important in relation to leases, which have always made wide use of the term and quarter days. For example, it is common in commercial and agricultural leases for the rent to be payable quarterly at the traditional quarter days (or half yearly at the term days). And where leases contain provisions for periodic rent reviews, it was normal for the review dates to be Whitsunday or Martinmas in stated years.

It is therefore essential in any lease using the term and quarter days for there to be no ambiguity regarding which days are meant. And it is equally important to avoid any confusion resulting from the transition from the old to the new definitions, since there will still be leases in force that were entered into prior to 1991 (when the Act came into force). In such cases (for example) should the Martinmas rent be paid at 11 or 28 November? Should a notice to quit be sent 40 days prior to 15 or 28 May?[2] Such questions are particularly vital in relation to rent reviews where (as we will see later) the narrow missing of a deadline can sometimes have disastrous consequences for either a landlord or tenant.[3]

1 Eg the Removal Terms (Scotland) Act 1886, s 4; see para 10.32.
2 See *Barns-Graham v Boyd* 1995 Hous LR 39, which illustrates the consequences of a slip up in this respect.
3 See Ch 12.

1.23   The Term and Quarter Days (Scotland) Act 1990 tackles such problems by operating retrospectively, and also by allowing its effect to be contracted out of. This means that where a lease refers to Candlemas, Whitsunday, Lammas or Martinmas, without assigning a date to these expressions, they will each be the 28th day of the appropriate month, whether the lease was entered into before or after the Act came into force. On the other hand, if a lease (and this also applies to those entered both before and after the entry into force of the Act) specifically assigns the traditional dates (or any other dates) to the term and quarter days, then it is these substituted dates that will take effect. Thus if a lease (old or new) merely refers to Whitsunday, this will be 28 May, but if it refers to 'Whitsunday (15 May)', then the latter date will apply.

In *Forbes v Cameron*[1] the entry clause of an agricultural lease stated that the lease ran from Whitsunday, without specifying a date, but there were other references to Whitsunday later in the lease which specified Whitsunday as being 15 May. It was held that, on the basis of the first reference, the 1990 Act operated to make Whitsunday 28 May, with the result that a notice to quit served on the tenant (which would have been too late if the ish had been 15 May) had actually been served on time.

1 2010 SLT 1017, 2010 GWD 15-300; but see also *Provincial Insurance plc v Valtos Ltd* 1992 SCLR 203, which was, however, decided while transitional arrangements were in force.

Transitional arrangements

1.24   In order to make the transition easier, the Act did not come into force until a year after it had been passed, ie until 13 July 1991. Until then, the parties to a lease could apply to the sheriff court to have any anomalies resolved.[1]

1 See eg *Provincial Insurance plc v Valtos Ltd* 1992 SCLR 203, which was decided somewhat differently from *Forbes v Cameron* referred to above – see para 1.23.

LEASES AND THE COMMON LAW

1.25   We have already noted that for certain types of lease, mainly those relating to farmland and dwelling-houses, the common law of landlord and tenant has been greatly modified by statute. In the field of commercial leases, there is not the same statutory presence, but the common law, unlike many statutory provisions, can generally be contracted out of, and often is; this means that the legal relationship between the parties is mainly governed by the terms of the lease document itself.

1.26   However, the common law of landlord and tenant remains important for a number of reasons. Some common law requirements are so fundamental that no lease can feasibly be without them, and these are considered in the next chapter. The common law will also be required to fill in any gaps that occur when statute or the terms of the lease document are silent. Thirdly, the party most likely to try and contract out of the common law is the landlord, who is generally in the stronger negotiating position when the lease contract is being drawn up; however, it is unlikely that landlords will readily give up powerful traditional rights, such as irritancy.[1]

Finally, it is salutary for parties drawing up lease documents to have in mind what might be the consequences of failing to create a clear and unambiguous contractual agreement, covering all important areas. The common law is liable to plug any gap with something that may be confused or ambiguous or contrary to modern lease trends.[2] A good example of the latter is the common law provision which confers significant repairing obligations upon a landlord, the general modern practice in commercial leases being to pass these on to the tenant in an FRI (tenant's full repairing and insuring) lease. Therefore, if a tenant is to be responsible for all repairs, this must be clearly stated in the lease, or much of the repairing obligation will revert back to the landlord.

1 See Ch 5.
2 For an example see *Little Cumbrae Estate Ltd v Island of Cumbrae Ltd* [2007] CSIH 35; 2017 SC 525.

HUMAN RIGHTS ACT 1998

Introduction

1.27   The Human Rights Act 1998 (subject to certain exceptions) adopted the European Convention on Human Rights into the domestic law of the United Kingdom. This means that most of the rights under the Convention can now be enforced in the British courts without the person whose rights have been infringed having to undertake the protracted and expensive process of taking the case to the European Court of Human Rights in Strasbourg.[1] This has profound implications for virtually all areas of UK and Scots law, including property law in general and landlord and tenant in particular.

It is not the intention here to add to the considerable literature that has grown up around human rights issues.[2] Instead there is offered an overview of the subject, identifying those Convention rights that may apply in landlord and tenant situations. Further consideration will be given to those areas affected (or potentially affected) at appropriate parts of the book.

1 In 1997 it was estimated that it took on average five years to get an action into the European Court of Human Rights once all domestic remedies had been exhausted, and that it cost on average £30,000 (Home Department *Rights Brought Home: the Human Rights Bill* (Cmnd 3782, 1997) para 1.14.
2 See the brief selection of relevant texts in the bibliography.

Relation to United Kingdom legislation[1]

1.28   The British courts must interpret primary and subordinate legislation, so far as it is possible to do so, in a way that is compatible with Convention rights. Westminster statutes are the main form of primary legislation, and secondary legislation includes delegated legislation and (significantly) Acts of the Scottish parliament.[2] If primary legislation is incompatible with the Convention, it will still be valid; however, it may be subject to a declaration of incompatibility by a superior court (in Scotland, the Court of Session for civil cases) which will not invalidate it but will allow it to be appropriately amended by a 'fast track' procedure. However, an interpretation of the legislation that is compliant with the Convention is the normal remedial measure, and declarations of incompatibility are the exception and should rarely arise.[3]

Subordinate legislation which is in conflict with the Convention will only be valid if the incompatibility was unavoidable in order to give effect to the terms of primary legislation. This means that subordinate legislation, including Acts of the Scottish Parliament and Westminster and Scottish statutory instruments may be declared invalid by the courts on the ground of such incompatibility.[4]

1 HRA 1998, ss 3 & 4.
2 HRA 1998 s 21(1).
3 *Ghaidan v Godin-Mendoza* (*sub nom Godin-Mendoza v Ghaidan, Ghaidan v Mendoza and Mendoza v Ghaidan*) [2004] 2 AC 557, [2004] 3 WLR 113.
4 Home Department *Rights brought home: the Human Rights Bill* (Cmnd 3782, 1997) para 2.21. See also *Salvesen v Riddell* [2013] UKSC 22, 2013 GWD 14-304, in which s 72(10) of the Agricultural Holdings (Scotland) Act 2003 (an Act of the Scottish Parliament) was declared to be incompatible with Protocol 1 Art 1 of the European Convention – see para 1.36.

Acts of public authorities[1]

1.29   The main purpose of the Convention and the Human Rights Act is to prevent encroachment upon the rights of citizens by the State and other public institutions. It is therefore made unlawful for a public authority to act in a way that is incompatible with a Convention right, unless it is compelled to do so by primary legislation. 'An act' includes a failure to act.

A public authority significantly includes a court or tribunal, as well as any person who has functions of a public nature, though only while in the course of exercising a public function. In the present context it should be noted that the latter may include social landlords, other than local authorities, while exercising their housing function.[2] The Inner House in *Ali v Serco Ltd,*[3] in holding that a private company contracted by the Home Office to provide temporary accommodation for asylum seekers was not a public authority, noted that there was a fundamental distinction between the entity charged with the public law responsibility and the private operator contracting with that entity to provide a service.

1 HRA 1998 s 6.
2 *R (on the application of Weaver) v London & Quadrant Housing Trust (sub nom London & Quadrant Housing Trust v Weaver)* [2010] 1 WLR 363, [2009] 4 All ER 865; see also paras 18.8 and 18.9.
3 [2019] CSIH 54; 2020 SC 182.

'Vertical' effect[1]

1.30 A person who claims that a public authority has acted (or proposes to act) in contravention of a Convention right may bring proceedings against the authority in the appropriate court or tribunal. The proceedings can be by judicial review. Alternatively, the person can rely on the Convention right in any legal proceedings, as a defence or a counterclaim in an action brought by the public authority, eg an eviction action by a local authority landlord,[2] or as the basis of an appeal against a judgment in the public authority's favour.

The person concerned must be a victim of the unlawful act, and may be an individual human being, a non-governmental organisation or a group of individuals.[3] This means that companies or other corporate bodies, and not only natural persons, can be victims and raise proceedings for infringement of their human rights.

In the above cases, the Convention has a direct or 'vertical' effect; in other words, the public authority is one of the parties to the action, either as pursuer or defender.

1 HRA 1998 s 7.
2 See *Manchester City Council v Pinnock (sub nom Pinnock v Manchester City Council)* [2010] 3 WLR 1441, [2011] 1 All ER 285; see also para 18.13 et seq.
3 Convention for the Protection of Human Rights and Fundamental Freedoms, Article 34 (incorporated by the HRA 1998, s 7(7)).

'Horizontal' effect

1.31 When the party responsible for the infringement is not a public authority but a private individual or body, the victim is not entitled to raise proceedings solely because there has been breach of a Convention right or rights. However, the Human Rights Act may have an indirect (or 'horizontal') effect in actions between private parties based on some other legal ground. This is because the court or tribunal deciding the case is itself a public body that must not act in contravention of Convention rights, unless compelled to do so by primary legislation, such as a Westminster statute.[1] There are several ways in which this horizontal influence may occur:

(1)　As noted above, a court must interpret legislation as far as possible in a way that is compatible with the Convention.[2] This is particularly relevant where the legislation gives the court a discretionary power. For example, in the case of a private residential tenancy leased by a private landlord, a number of the statutory eviction grounds are discretionary (ie the First Tier Tribunal may only grant the landlord possession when satisfied that it is reasonable to do so).[3] (There are similar discretionary eviction grounds in relation to a Scottish secure tenancy granted by a social landlord under the Housing (Scotland) Act 2001; however, in that case there will generally be a vertical effect because the landlord is a public authority, or exercising a public function.)[4]

(2)　Where there is a direct conflict between primary legislation and a convention right, a superior court may grant a declaration of incompatibility. This *may* lead to an amendment of the offending legislation, which could (eventually) give the victim a direct ground of action. If the case was originally raised in the sheriff court, it would have to be appealed to the Court of Session before a declaration of incompatibility could be made in the first place.[5]

(3)　Where the ground of action rests solely on the common law, and there is no legislation that may be in conflict with the Convention, it is thought that the courts have a duty to develop the law in a way that is compatible with Convention rights. This means that judicial precedents that pre-date the Human Rights Act 1998 may no longer be completely authoritative to the extent that they conflict with the Convention. Also, the Act imposes a general duty upon the courts to take into account judgments of the European Court of Human Rights, as well as opinions and decisions of the European Commission and the Committee of Ministers.[6]

1　See para 1.28.
2　HRA 1998, s 3; see also para 1.28.

3 See para 17.86 et seq.
4 See para 18.52.
5 See eg *Salvesen v Riddell* [2013] UKSC 22, 2013 GWD 14-304 and *South Lanarkshire Council v McKenna* 2013 SLT 22, 2012 GWD 34-693, discussed at para 18.17.
6 HRA 1998, s 2.

Landlord and tenant cases

1.32   In a landlord and tenant context, most disputes will be between private parties, and so any Convention rights can only have a horizontal application. A major exception is the case of local authorities, and also other social landlords, when the latter are exercising their housing function.[1] Also, local authorities and other public bodies often lease commercial properties and therefore could incur direct liability.

1 See para 18.7 et seq.

Relevant convention rights

1.33   Below is a brief consideration of the Convention rights that may apply in a landlord and tenant situation. In some of these cases, this is supported by case law, but in others the Convention's application remains speculative.

While some Convention rights are absolute (such as the prohibition of torture or slavery), most of those considered here are generally qualified in some way. In some cases they may conflict with each other. In a landlord and tenant context, both the landlord and the tenant have a right of property in the leased subjects that may be protected under Protocol 1, Article 1, and a balance has to be struck between these competing rights.

1.34   *Right to a fair hearing (Article 6)*   In civil as well as criminal cases, everyone is entitled to a fair and public hearing within a reasonable time by an independent and impartial tribunal established by law. This could, for example, potentially apply in relation to the remedy of summary diligence, under which a tenant's property may be seized by the landlord without the necessity of court action; on the other hand, since the tenant's consent is required (usually in the form of a lease term) it could be argued that this right has been waived.[1]

1 See para 6.24.

1.35   *Right to respect for private and family life (Article 8)*   Everyone has the right to respect for his or her private and family life, home and correspondence. This right is qualified in a number of ways that allow it to be infringed in the public interest, including the prevention of disorder or crime, or the protection of the rights and freedoms of others.

This may justify the eviction of a residential tenant, for example, because of a conviction for drug dealing or because of other anti-social behaviour. In such a case the rights of the offending tenant may be outweighed by the rights of other people in the neighbourhood under the same Article, or under Protocol 1, Article 1. This right has been widely pleaded in residential eviction cases, particularly in the case of social tenancies.[1]

1 See para 18.12 et seq.

1.36 *Protection of property (Protocol 1, Article 1)* Everyone is entitled to the peaceful enjoyment of his or her possessions and may not be deprived of them. This is also qualified in a number of ways, mainly in the public interest, eg by the State's need to control the use of property under planning law. Also the property rights of people may conflict; as noted above, the rights of the tenant have to be balanced against those of the landlord in the same leased subjects, and the property rights of an anti-social tenant have to be balanced against the property (and family) rights of a neighbouring tenant.

1.37 *Right to life* One of the fundamental Convention rights is that everyone's right to life is protected by law under Article 2. The possible relevance of this right in a landlord and tenant context was not immediately obvious until the major Scottish case of *Mitchell v Glasgow City Council*,[1] where an anti-social council tenant murdered a neighbouring tenant. The House of Lords held that the council did not have a duty under Article 2 to warn the victim of the danger, but the possibility of Article 2 liability by social landlords in different circumstances, eg where a failure to repair creates a life-threatening danger was acknowledged. This case is discussed in more depth in chapter 18, in relation to Scottish secure tenancies.[2]

1 [2009] 1 AC 874, 2009 SC (HL) 21; see also *R (on the application of AP) v HM Coroner for Worcestershire* [2011] EWHC 1453 (Admin), [2011] BLGR 952.
2 See para 18.11 et seq.

1.38 *Freedom from discrimination* Under Article 14 of the Convention it is provided that the other Convention rights should be secured without discrimination on a number of stated grounds. Article 14 does not apply independently, but only in connection with other Convention rights.[1] For example, in relation to a social tenant's Article 8 right to a home, it has been held by the House of Lords that, under article 14, a same-sex partner should have the same right as a spouse to inherit the tenancy.[2]

1 See eg *R (on the application of Erskine) v Lambeth London Borough Council* [2003] NPC 118, EWHC 2479; see also para 19.8.
2 *Ghaidan v Godin-Mendoza (sub nom Godin-Mendoza v Ghaidan, Ghaidan v Mendoza and Mendoza v Ghaidan)* [2004] 2 AC 557, 3 WLR 113. But now see the Civil Partnership Act 2004 and para 18.81 et seq.

Proportionality

1.39 In relation to those rights that are qualified rather than absolute, (ie most of those considered above) every interference with a right must be proportionate to the legitimate aim pursued. In other words, there must be a fair balance between the protection of individual rights and the interests of the community at large.[1]

1 See Reed and Murdoch *Human Rights Law in Scotland* (4th edn 2017) paras 3.81–3.84; see in particular the discussion regarding the eviction of social tenants at para 18.12 et seq.

Waiver

1.40 It is established that some of the convention rights may be waived by the alleged victim, provided that the waiver has been made in an unequivocal manner and does not run counter to an important public interest.[1] This issue can arise in landlord and tenant situations if the lease signed by the tenant contains provisions that may amount to a waiver of certain rights (eg in relation to the landlords' remedies of irritancy or summary diligence).[2]

1 See Reed and Murdoch *Human Rights Law in Scotland* (4th edn 2017) paras 3.36–3.38.
2 See paras 5.42 and 6.21.

Particular applications

1.41 The above account provides a brief introduction to the impact of human rights on the law of leases.[1] Elsewhere in the book, the application of the Human Rights Act is considered in relation to a number of specific topics, including irritancy[2] and summary diligence.[3] There are also considerable implications for residential tenancies, particularly in relation to Scottish secure tenancies, where the landlord is exercising a public function and the Human Rights Act has a direct, vertical effect.[4] In the case of residential tenancies, human rights issues can arise, inter alia, in relation to eviction or to the landlord's obligation to maintain a house in a tenantable or habitable condition.

1 For further discussion see R Rennie *et al*, *Leases* (2015), Ch 16.
2 See para 5.40 et seq.
3 See para 6.24.
4 See para 18.7 et seq.

PART 2
GENERAL LANDLORD AND TENANT LAW

Chapter 2

Basic legal requirements

FORM OF LEASE

Need for writing

2.1   A lease, if it is for more than a year, should be in writing. This has always been the case, though in other respects the relevant law was changed substantially by the Requirements of Writing (Scotland) Act 1995. That Act contains the current law on the subject; however, since it does not apply to documents executed before 1 August 1995[1] (some examples of which are still around)[2] it is necessary to consider the earlier law as well. We will also see that, under both the old and the new law, a lease that fails to meet the necessary legal requirements can sometimes be validated by the actings of one or both of the parties.

1 ROW(S)A 1995 s 14(3).
2 See para 1.5.

Leases executed prior to 1 August 1995

2.2   Contracts relating to heritable property traditionally belonged to a category known as the *obligationes literis*.[1] This meant that they had to be entered into in writing, had to be signed by the parties concerned and, in addition, certain formalities had to be observed. The latter requirement was satisfied if the writing took *one* of the three following forms:

(1)   *An attested document.* This was a formal deed, which had to be signed by both landlord and tenant on the last page, each before two witnesses who signed opposite the main party's signature. An attested deed was known as a probative document.

(2)   *A holograph document.* This was a document written entirely in the handwriting of the party concerned and signed by that party. A holograph lease, therefore, might consist of an offer handwritten and signed by the landlord followed by an acceptance handwritten and signed by the tenant. Such a lease would be perfectly valid but,

for obvious reasons, professionally drawn-up lease documents did not normally take this form.

(3) *A document adopted as holograph.* This was a variant of (2). The document was not in the handwriting of the party concerned, but was handwritten by someone else or, more commonly, printed or typewritten. The party signed it, writing above his or her signature the words 'adopted as holograph'. This meant that the person signing was accepting the document as if it were in his or her own handwriting and, as a result, it had the same legal effect as a holograph document.

If a lease was signed *before* 1 August 1995, it will normally need, in order to be valid, to have observed one of the above three *alternative* formalities. Leases subscribed on or after that date must conform to the requirements of the 1995 Act.[2]

1 See Gloag *The Law of Contract* (2nd edn 1929) pp 162–179 and other law of contract references in the bibliography.
2 See para 2.3 et seq.

Leases executed on or after 1 August 1995

2.3 Under the Requirements of Writing (Scotland) Act 1995, the general rule is that contracts do not require to be in writing.[1] However, as was the case before, there are exceptions.

Writing is required for the creation, transfer, variation or extinction of a real right in land, or for the constitution of a contract in relation to any of these.[2] A 'real right in land' does not include tenancies for a year or less.[3] Writing will normally be required to constitute a lease for more than a year except in the case of private residential tenancies.[4]

A 'real right in land' also includes 'any right to occupy or use land', which means that writing will also be required for a licence for more than one year.[5] However, in *Gray v MacNeil's Excr*[6] the Sheriff Appeal Court found that there was a valid contract between the parties for the occupation of a property for a period of 15 years despite the agreement not being in writing. For the court there could not be a lease given the lack of writing but there could be a personal contract between the original parties, breach of which would give rise to damages.[7]

1 ROW(S)A 1995 s 1(1).
2 ROW(S)A 1995 s 1(2).
3 ROW(S)A 1995 s 1(7), see also para 2.13.
4 Private Housing (Tenancies)(Scotland) Act 2016 s 3. These types of lease are discussed in Ch 17.

5 ROW(S)A 1995 s 1(7) (as amended by the Abolition of Feudal Tenure, etc (Scotland) Act 2000 Sch 12, para 58); see *Caterleisure Ltd v Glasgow Prestwick International Airport Ltd* 2006 SC 602, 2005 SLT 1083. The AFT(S) Act substituted the expression 'real right in land' for 'interest in land'. It should be noted that 'real right' in this context is not synonymous with its use elsewhere in the law of leases. The Leases Act 1449 may confer a real right valid against the landlord's singular successors upon a tenant for a year or less, but not upon the occupant under a licence of any length – see also para 2.30 et seq.

6 [2017] SAC (Civ) 9, 2017 SLT (Sh Ct) 83.

7 This decision has been convincingly criticised: see KGC Reid and GL Gretton, *Conveyancing 2017* (2018), p 175.

2.4 *Traditional and electronic documents* Part 10 of the Land Registration (Scotland) Act 2012 amended the Requirements of Writing (Scotland) Act 1995 so that the above requirements can be met either by a hard copy document (referred to as a 'traditional document') or by an electronic document. The requirements under the 1995 Act for both traditional and electronic documents are discussed in the following paragraphs.

2.5 *Traditional documents* A lease taking the form of a traditional document should be signed by both the landlord and the tenant.[1] This can take the form of an offer, signed by either the landlord or the tenant, followed by an acceptance signed by the other party.[2] For leases entered into from 1 July 2015 the lease can be signed in counterpart.[3] This means that the parties can sign separate copies of the lease document, which will become effective when the counterparts are delivered either to the party who did not sign that counterpart,[4] (ie the tenant sends the counterpart lease he has signed to the landlord and vice versa) or to a person nominated to receive delivery of the various counterparts.[5] On signing in counterpart the counterpart documents are treated as a single document made up of all of the counterpart documents or one counterpart document in its entirety together with the signing pages of the other counterparts.[6]

The requirements for signing a lease are the same whether it is one document signed by both parties, multiple documents signed in counterpart or made up of an offer and acceptance. The signature or signatures should appear at the end of the last page of the relevant document.[7] However, as long as at least one party signs on the last page, any others may sign on an additional page, eg where there is insufficient room for all signatures on the last page.[8] No witnesses are required merely to constitute the lease but a witness is required to make a document self-proving, ie to create a presumption of validity.[9] The document must be self-proving if it is to be registered in the Land Register.[10]

An annexation to the lease, eg an appendix, schedule or plan, has to be referred to in the main document and identified on its face as being the annexation referred to.[11] If the annexation describes or shows any part of the property leased it also requires to be signed; if it is a visual representation, such as a plan, drawing or photograph, it must be signed on each page, otherwise the last page will suffice.[12]

The above provisions relate to subscription by natural persons. The rules for subscription by companies and other public bodies, and for other special cases, are set out in Schedule 2 to the Act.

1 ROW(S)A 1995 s 2(1); but see also para 2.15.
2 ROW(S)A 1995 s 2(2).
3 Legal Writings (Counterparts and Delivery)(Scotland) Act 2015 s 1. It may be noted that the provisions of this Act apply to both traditional and electronic documents (s 3). However, given that electronic documents can be signed by all of the parties easily the use of counterpart signature has more of an impact on signing traditional documents.
4 LW(CD)(S)A 2015 s 1(5) and (6).
5 LW(CD)(S)A 2015 s 1(5) and (7).
6 LW(CD)(S)A 2015 s 1(3) and (4).
7 ROW(S)A 1995 s 7(1).
8 ROW(S)A 1995 s 7(3).
9 ROW(S)A 1995 s 3(1).
10 ROW(S)A 1995 s 6(1) and (2); see also also para 8.11 et seq.
11 ROW(S)A 1995 s 8(1).
12 ROW(S)A 1995 s 8(2).

2.6 *Electronic documents* The changes made to the Requirements of Writing (Scotland) Act 1995 by the Land Registration (Scotland) Act 2012 in relation to electronic documents are in force for all contracts and documents which the 1995 Act requires to be in writing, with the exception of wills, codicils and other testamentary writing.[1] As such, leases can be 'signed', ie authenticated electronically. The equivalent of a traditional document being self-proving is an electronic document being authenticated and certified.[2]

To be validly executed an electronic document must be authenticated by the granter (or by each granter if there is more than one).[3] This occurs when it is signed by means of an electronic signature. The electronic signature must be incorporated into, or be logically associated with, the electronic document, and it must have been created by the person by whom it purports to have been created.[4] The 1995 Act leaves many technical details to Regulations. The Electronic Documents (Scotland) Regulations 2014[5] provide that an advanced electronic signature must be used for an electronic document to be validly executed in terms of the 1995 Act.[6] An advanced electronic signature is one that (a) is uniquely related to the signatory; (b) is capable of identifying the signatory; (c) is created using electronic signature creation data that the signatory can, with a high level of confidence use under his sole control; and (d) is linked to the data in such a way that any later change to the data is detectable.[7] As may be apparent not all landlords and tenants are likely to have access to an advanced electronic signature. Agents can sign on their clients' behalf.[8]

As with traditional documents an offer and acceptance, eg in missives, may be in separate electronic documents, as long as each is authenticated by its granter or granters.[9] An annexation to an electronic document must be referred to in the document; identified on the face of the annexation that it is the annexation referred to in the document; and be annexed to the electronic document before the electronic signature is incorporated or logically associated with the document.[10]

The 1995 Act provides that an electronic signature is certified by means of a statement, incorporated or logically associated with the document, that the signature is a valid means of establishing the document's authenticity or integrity.[11] Further detail is provided in the Electronic Documents Regulations which require that certification is by a qualifying certificate.[12] A qualifying certificate must be issued by a qualified trust service provider[13] and must contain:[14] (a) an indication, at least in a form suitable to automated processing, that the certificate has been issued as a qualifying certificate for electronic signature; (b) a set of data unambiguously representing the qualified trust service provider issuing the certificate, including the Member State in which the provider is established and the provider's name and registration number where applicable; (c) at least the name of the signatory; (d) electronic signature validation data that corresponds to the electronic signature creation data; (e) details of the beginning and end of the certificate's period of validity; (f) the certificate identity code, which must be unique for the service provider; (g) the advanced electronic signature or the advanced electronic seal of the service provider; (h) the location where the certificate supporting the electronic signature or seal mentioned at (g) is available; (i) the location of the services that can be used to enquire about the validity status of the qualified certificate; and (j) where the electronic signature creation data related to the electronic signature validation data is located in a qualified electronic signature creation device, an appropriate indication of this, at least in a form suitable for automated processing.[15]

An electronic document may be delivered electronically, eg by e-mail, or by such other means as are reasonably practical, eg physically, by handing over a memory stick. Such a document must be in a form, and the delivery must be by a means, which the intended recipient has agreed to accept, or which it is reasonable in all the circumstances for the intended recipient to accept.[16]

2.6 *Basic legal requirements*

Section 9G of the 1995 Act provides that an electronic document will not be registered in the Land Register unless the document is presumed under sections 9C, 9D or 9E to have been authenticated by the granter and the document, the electronic signature and the certificate, where applicable, are in the form and of the type prescribed by Regulations. The Electronic Documents Regulations provide that a document is presumed to have been authenticated by a granter under section 9C of the 1995 Act where the signature is an advanced electronic signature which is certified by a qualified certificate.[17]

Having set out the requirements for authenticating and certifying an electronic lease it may be some time before parties enter into leases, especially those for more than 20 years, in this way. This is because, at the time of writing, electronic leases are not yet being accepted for registration by the Keeper.[18]

1 Land Registration etc (Scotland) Act 2012 (Commencement No 2 and Transitional Savings Provisions) Order 2014, SSI 2014 No 41, Sch Pt 2.

2 Although it may be noted that unlike signing and witnessing a traditional document there is no order in which authentication and certification need take place.

3 ROW(S)A 1995 s 9B(1).

4 ROW(S)A 1995 s 9B(2).

5 SSI 2014 No 83.

6 ED(S)R 2014 reg 2.

7 ED(S)R 2014 reg 1, by reference to art 3 of Reg (EU) No 910/2014 of the European Parliament and the Council on electronic identification and trust services for electronic transactions in the internal market.

8 RW(S)A 1995 s12(3).

9 ROW(S)A 1995 s 9B(3).

10 ED(S)R 2014 reg 4.

11 RW(S)A s 12(1), definition of 'certification'.

12 ED(S)R 2014 reg 3.

13 In Scotland the Law Society and the Keeper of the Registers of Scotland are certification service providers.

14 ED(S)R 2014 reg 3(b) with reference to Art 3 of Reg (EU) No 910/2014 of the European Parliament and the Council on electronic identification and trust services for electronic transactions in the internal market.

15 For a useful account of authentication, certification and the practicalities of both see KGC Reid and GL Gretton, *Conveyancing 2014* (2015), p 140.

16 ROW(S)A 1995 s 9F.

17 That this is the case was not clear from RW(S)A 1995 s 9C itself which provides that a document will be presumed to have been authenticated by the granter where the electronic signature incorporated or logically associated with the document is of such type and satisfies such requirements as the Scottish Ministers prescribe and *either or both* (i) the electronic signature is used in such circumstances as may be so prescribed, (ii) bears to be certified. This wording suggests that an electronic signature when used in prescribed circumstances would be enough for the electronic document to be self-proving without the need for certification. See also para 221 of the Explanatory Notes to the Land Registration (Scotland) Act 2012.

18 See para 8.12.

2.7 *Anomalies in relation to leases* When considering the above requirements in relation to leases, a close examination of the 1995 Act reveals some anomalies that will be considered later.[1]

1 See para 2.15 et seq.

Normal forms of lease

2.8 A lease is commonly constituted by missives of let, ie an offer signed by either the landlord or the tenant followed by an acceptance signed by the other party. It is common for either the offer or acceptance, or both, to be signed by a solicitor as agent for the party concerned. If a lease is of relatively short duration and/or the rent is relatively low, the contract may be allowed to rest on the missives alone.

For a lease of longer duration and/or higher rental value (which will normally be the case with commercial leases) missives of let will commonly only be used as a temporary measure, to hold the parties contractually bound until a more formal document is drawn up, in accordance with the requirements described above.[1]

A lease may have to be enforced by either the landlord or the tenant, and so it is good practice (though not legally essential) that each of them should have the documentation necessary to achieve this. This may be done by having the lease completed in duplicate, so that both the landlord and the tenant can have their own principal copy. Alternatively, the lease may be registered for preservation in the Books of Council and Session and each party issued with an extract.

1 See para 2.4 et seq.

Informal leases

2.9 *Leases defective in form* Under the old law, if a lease for more than a year (or any other contract relating to heritable property) was entered into without observing one of the required formalities, it was considered defective in form and (theoretically) either party was entitled to back out of the contract.[1]

Under the Requirements of Writing Act there are fewer formalities to be overlooked, but it is still possible for parties to enter into a landlord and tenant situation, eg where the tenant takes possession of the property and pays rent, without the requirements of the Act having been observed. For example, the document may be improperly signed, or not signed at all, eg if a draft has been drawn up but not finalised, or the parties may have gone ahead without there being anything in writing at all. In such a situation, the lease may still be enforceable because one of the parties has demonstrated a desire for the contract to continue by his or her actions which were known about and acquiesced in by the other party.[2]

Where there is a traditional document that is unsigned or improperly signed, although it is not valid on its own, it may nevertheless be used as evidence in relation to any right or obligation to which it relates.[3] The same is the case with an electronic document that has not been authenticated[4] or not authenticated with an advanced electronic signature.[5]

1 See eg *Goldston v Young* (1868) 7 M 188.
2 See para 2.10.
3 ROW(S)A 1995 s 2(3).
4 ROW(S)A 1995 s 9B(5).
5 Reg 2 of the Electronic Documents (Scotland) Regulations 2014 (SSI No 83) provides that an advanced electronic signtuare is required; as to which see para 2.6.

2.10   *Statutory remedy*   The Requirements of Writing Act provides for a situation where a contract has not been constituted either in a traditional or electronic document that complies with the statutory requirements, but one of the parties to the contract has acted or refrained from acting in reliance on the contract. In such a case the other party (provided that he or she knew and acquiesced in the situation) is not entitled to withdraw from the contract, and the contract will not be regarded as invalid.[1]

For the purpose of this provision it is not sufficient that party A merely knew generally that party B was arranging his or her affairs in reliance on the contract. It is necessary to point to specific actings or examples of refraining from acting of party B which were known to and acquiesced in by party A.[2] It is also necessary that party B has been affected to a material extent, and would be so affected if party A withdrew.[3] Such a situation could arise, for example, if a tenant took possession of a property and, on the understanding that there was a lease for a number of years, spent a substantial amount of money improving the property with the landlord's knowledge; in such circumstances, it would be unjust if the landlord could take back possession of the property simply because the lease was not in the required form. This requirement was satisfied where, in reliance upon an informal contract for the purchase of heritable property, the purchaser entered a building contract and the builder in turn incurred substantial expenditure as a result.[4] It could also include actings such as the setting up of bank accounts and the placing of supply and employment contracts, though whether the party concerned has been affected to a material extent will always be a matter of degree which will depend upon the circumstances of the particular case.[5]

The actings in reliance upon an informal contract must occur after the contract was entered,[6] and where it is sought to prove that the contract has been varied it will not be sufficient if the actings could equally be attributed to the contract in its original terms.[7]

Under the old law, a very similar doctrine operated by the application of the principles of *rei interventus* and homologation (actings of the parties that could validate an informal contract).[8] These principles have been replaced by the new statutory doctrine (though only in relation to the constitution of a contract and certain other matters covered by the 1995 Act).[9]

1 ROW(S)A 1995 s 1(3). It has been suggested that when seeking to utilise s 1(3) and (4) the party seeking to uphold the contract depsite its lack of form must give full notice of the facts and circumstances which demonstrate how, and in what way, that party has acted or refrained from acting with the full knowledge and acquiescence of the other party. Details of how the party seeking to uphold the contract has been adversely affected to a material extent must also be provided: see *Reilly v Brodie* [2016] SC EDIN 36, 2016 GWD 15-280.

2 *Mitchell v Caversham Management Ltd* [2009] CSOH 26, 2009 GWD 29-465.

3 ROW(S)A 1995 s 1(4).

4 *Tom Super Printing and Supplies Ltd v South Lanarkshire Council (No 1)* 1999 GWD 31-1496; see also *Tom Super Printing and Supplies Ltd v South Lanarkshire Council (No 2)* 1999 GWD 38-1853.

5 *Caterleisure Ltd v Glasgow Prestwick International Airport Ltd* 2006 SC 602, 2005 SLT 1083.

6 *The Advice Centre for Mortgages v McNicoll* 2006 SLT 591, 2006 SCLR 602.

7 *Tom Super Printing and Supplies Ltd v South Lanarkshire Council (No 1)* 1999 GWD 31-1496; see also *Tom Super Printing and Supplies Ltd v South Lanarkshire Council (No 2)* 1999 GWD 38-1853; *Coatbridge Retail No 1 Ltd v Oliver* 2010 GWD 19-374.

8 See eg Gloag pp 167–175, as well as more modern law of contract references in the bibliography.

9 ROW(S)A 1995 s 1(5).

2.11 *Difficulties with statutory remedy* The apparent intention of the legislators was that the new statutory doctrine would apply to leases and operate in a similar way to the old law in correcting informalities. Unfortunately, the wording of s 1(2)(a)(i), drafted with the sale of heritable property in mind, is ambiguous regarding whether it applies to leases. In the light of this and of the decision in *The Advice Centre for Mortgages v McNicoll*[1] the possibility of lease informalities being corrected by the application of the statutory remedy must now be considered to be less certain.

1 2006 SLT 591, 2006 SCLR 602; see also para 2.17 et seq.

2.12 *Older case law* There have been many cases in the past of informal leases being validated by the actings of the parties. For example, in *Wight v Newton*[1] a draft lease of a farm, approved by both parties but unsigned, was held to constitute a valid lease because the tenant had entered into possession. In *Forbes v Wilson*[2] an offer by the tenant which was not accepted in writing by the landlord was held to be sufficient, having been followed by actings of the tenant that amounted to *rei interventus*.

It was clear from these authorities that a lease for more than a year could not be validated by *rei interventus* or homologation unless there was something in writing, however informal, and even if the writing was only by one of the parties. There is no such requirement for the statutory doctrine introduced by the Requirements of Writing Act.[3] However, if a lease is entered without writing it is likely to be difficult to prove that it was intended to be for more than a year, unless there is clear evidence to this effect. If all we have is a situation where a tenant has taken possession and started paying rent, it seems unlikely that this will constitute a lease for more than a year.

1 1911 SC 762; 1911 1 SLT 335.
2 (1873) 11 M 454, 45 Sc Jur 276; see also *Errol v Walker* 1966 SC 93, 1966 SLT 159, *Ferryhill Property Investments Ltd v Technical Video Productions* 1992 SCLR 282; and *Nelson v Gerrard* 1994 SCLR 1052.
3 ROW(S)A 1995 s 1(3).

Leases for a year or less

2.13   Under the Requirements of Writing Act, a tenancy for a year or less is excluded from the definition of a real right in land, which means that it does not have to be constituted in writing.[1]

Such leases have traditionally been in a privileged position and, under the old law, could be entered either orally or by an informal document.[2] The existence of a lease for a year or less could be inferred from the actings of the parties (amounting to *rei interventus* or homologation) even where these actings were the only evidence that an agreement had been reached.[3]

On the other hand, if the circumstances preclude the possibility of there having been an agreement, it has been held that there is no lease. For instance, where a landlord continued to accept rent from a deceased tenant's son and his wife without knowing that the original tenant had died. In that case it was held that a new lease with the deceased tenant's successors could not be implied from the continued acceptance of rent alone.[4]

The authorities cited here continue to be relevant to leases for a year or less entered into on or after 1 August 1995.

1 ROW(S)A 1995 s 1(7). As explained above, such a tenant may nevertheless have a 'real right' in the sense of a right that can be enforced against the landlord's singular successors – see paras 2.3 and also 2.30 et seq.
2 Rankine pp 116–119; Paton and Cameron pp 19–21.

3 *Morrison-Low v Paterson (No 1)* 1985 SC(HL) 49, 1985 SLT 255, HL.
4 *Pickard v Ritchie* 1986 SLT 466.

2.14 *Recurring tenancies* Tenancies for a recurring period or periods do not qualify as leases for a year or less if they are spread over a period of more than one year. Even if the initial period is for less than one year, writing will be required if more than a year has elapsed by the end of the last such period.[1] This could include leases with consecutive recurring periods of a year or less, such as a lease with a break or breaks;[2] it could also apply to leases with non-consecutive periods, such as in a shooting lease or in a time share, where there is a right to a certain part of the year, over a number of years.[3]

Leases for a year or less may continue for much longer than that by the operation of the principle of tacit relocation.[4] It need hardly be said that it is good practice to have a written lease, even in the case of leases for a year or less.[5]

1 ROW(S)A 1995 s 1(7).
2 See para 10.2.
3 Kenneth G C Reid *Requirements of Writing (Scotland) Act 1995*, (2nd edn, 2015) p 9.
4 See para 10.18 et seq.
5 For an example of the evidential difficulties that can be created by the lack of a written lease see *Ali v Khosla (No 1)* 2001 SCLR 1072, 2001 GWD 25-917.

1995 Act anomalies: The parties signing

2.15 It was stated above that a lease should be signed by both the landlord and the tenant. However, the Requirements of Writing Act consistently refers to subscription by the 'granter', which is not defined. The normal interpretation of this word would include a landlord, who grants a tenancy, but not the tenant, who would more typically be referred to as the 'grantee'. Reference in the Act to subscription by more than one granter is consistent with a situation where a lease is granted by joint proprietors. The only sensible interpretation is to assume that, for the purposes of the Act, the requirement for subscription by a granter or granters should include subscription by the tenant as well as the landlord. This is perhaps implied by the provision allowing offers and acceptances to be granted in separate documents,[1] but the situation is not exactly clear.

1 ROW(S)A 1995 s 2(2).

1995 Act anomalies: Creation of lease

2.16 We saw above that writing is required not only for the creation etc of a real right in land, but also for the constitution of a contract for that purpose.[1] This distinction mainly has relevance to the sale of heritable property, where the disposition which actually creates or transfers an owner's interest is normally preceded by a contract (the missives of sale). However, although leases are commonly constituted by missives of let, which may or may not be followed by a more formal document, the situation is not analogous. Whereas missives of sale merely create a contractual obligation on the part of the seller to make the purchaser the owner at a later date, missives of let *actually create* the tenant's interest. Also, in cases where a more formal lease follows, it generally takes the form of a bilateral contract.

Arguably, therefore, both of the above forms of lease could fall under either s 1(2)(a)(i) or 1(2)(b) of the Act, as both may simultaneously constitute a contract and actually create a tenant's interest. And while it could be argued that a formal lease that follows later is not a contract for the *creation* of a right in land if the right has already been created by the missives of let, the formal deed may elaborate upon the terms of the missives; in that case it could be considered as a contract for the *variation* of that right, and fall within the same provision.

This seemingly arcane distinction is of practical importance, since the provisions of the Act that allow informalities to be corrected by actings of the parties only apply to s 1(2)(a)(i) (the constitution of a contract).[2] If the above analysis is correct, therefore, the relevant party's actings could validate not only informalities in missives of let, but also a formal lease with a defect in execution.

An alternative interpretation is that not even missives of let could be described as a 'contract for the' creation of a tenant's right, since they actually create the right rather than set up a contract for its creation in another document, as in missives of sale. The consequence of this would be to exclude leases from the application of s 1(2)(a)(i), thereby preventing informal leases being validated by the actings of the parties. This would amount to a substantial change in the law and to long-established lease practice. However, this interpretation should now be considered the correct approach given the case law on this issue.

1 ROW(S)A 1995 s 1(2).
2 ROW(S)A 1995 s 1(3).

Advice Centre for Mortgages v McNicoll

2.17   In *The Advice Centre for Mortgages v McNicoll*[1] the pursuers claimed (a) that they were tenants under a 10-year lease of a shop in Edinburgh, which by the time of the hearing they had actually been occupying for several years, and (b) that they had an option to purchase the property at year 5 from the landlords' singular successors. Their action failed on both counts. The implications of the decision in relation to the enforceability of options to purchase against singular successors will be considered later in the chapter;[2] here our concern is with the first part of the judgment.

In arriving at its decision that there was no lease the court was faced with the formidable task (which hardly reflected well upon the agents of either party) of disentangling the mess created by incomplete missives, two lost drafts (one revised, one not), an unsigned engrossment (also lost), and substantial delays between each of these stages, during all which time the tenants were occupying the property, paying rent, and making improvements to the subjects. The court considered in some depth the doctrine of personal bar and the statutory replacements of *rei interventus* that were discussed earlier,[3] with potentially far-reaching implications for their application to leases.

Lord Drummond Young held that there was no *consensus in idem*, mainly because the missives consisted only of an offer and qualified acceptance, but no final acceptance, and because the actings being relied upon to constitute personal bar preceded the qualified acceptance, as well as the later unsuccessful attempts to complete a formal lease. This made the missives irrelevant to the final decision.[4]

1 2006 SLT 591, 2006 SCLR 602; cited with approval in *Gyle Shopping Centre General Partners Ltd v Marks and Spencer plc* [2014] CSOH 122, 2014 GWD 26-527 where the court took the view that subsections 1(3) and (4) of the RW(S)A 1995 could apply to an agreement to vary the terms of a lease but not to the lease variation itself. See also Elspeth Reid 'Personal Bar: Three Cases' 2006 10 Edin LR 437.

2 See para 2.41.

3 See para 2.10.

4 This is perhaps the only result that could have been reached from the pursuers' pleadings, but there is an alternative approach to the facts of this extremely complex case that could arguably have led to the conclusion that informal missives had in fact been created – see Angus McAllister 'Leases and the Requirements of Writing' 2006 SLT (News) 254 at 257.

2.18   It was observed above that, drawing upon the sale of heritable property as a model, the Requirements of Writing (Scotland) Act 1995 distinguished between contracts for the purpose of constituting a real right in land on the one hand, and, on the other hand, the actual creation of a real right in land, and that the statutory form of personal bar only applied to the first of these. It was argued that, in the case of leases, both missives of let and the formal lease that sometimes followed could arguably fall into either category. On this basis, the statutory form of personal bar could operate to cure not only informal missives of let but also formal leases that were defective in some way.[1]

However, Lord Drummond Young took the opposite view, namely that both missives of let and the subsequent formal lease are documents intended to create a real right in land, to which the statutory form of personal bar does not apply. In the case of formal leases, this is part of the ratio of the case. However, since the missives here were considered irrelevant, on the basis that there was no consensus in idem, his lordship's views regarding the applicability of the statutory personal bar to missives of let should be regarded as obiter. Nevertheless, the thrust of his argument was that they too would normally be denied this protection. At one point he seemed to suggest that the personal bar provisions 'would be potentially applicable to the missives'; however, he also went to some length to suggest the opposite:

> 'On one hand, a lease is itself a contract for the creation of an interest in land. On the other hand, it creates an interest in land, which will give rise to real rights when possession is taken or the lease is registered. For present purposes it is not necessary to determine any general criteria for allocating leases to one or other of the two categories. It is sufficient to hold that, where it can be inferred that the intention of the parties to a lease is that possession should be taken by the tenant on the faith of the lease document, or the lease document should be registered, thus creating real rights in the tenant, that document will create an interest in land and will accordingly fall within subs (2)(c) of s 1. In that event the personal bar provisions contained in subss (3) and (4) will not apply. In my view that is the clear intention of subs (2). That subsection draws a fundamental distinction between documents that create property rights on one hand and mere contracts on the other hand. That distinction must be given effect in the case of leases. While that task may in some cases be difficult, if the document in question is one that is clearly intended, objectively speaking, to create a right of property in the tenant, it must be treated as falling within para (b) of the subsection and not para (a)(i).'

Since it is difficult to envisage missives of let that are *not* intended to create a real right in land, it follows, on this analysis, that the statutory form of personal bar cannot operate to cure informalities in missives of let.

Lord Drummond Young took the view that the relevant statutory provisions should not be given a liberal interpretation. If parties entered an informal, unwritten lease arrangement, eg by the granting of possession, payment of rent etc, this could still operate to create a lease for a year or less that was potentially renewable indefinitely by the process of tacit relocation.[2] This provided a sufficient safety net, and if they chose to enter a longer lease, particularly when they were legally represented, then they should be required to conform to the formalities of the 1995 Act.

1 See para 2.16.
2 See paras 2.13 and 10.18 et seq.

2.19   There is much logic to Lord Drummond Young's position; however it is submitted that his judgment can be criticised on several counts:

(1)   There is a huge body of pre-1995 authority, going back several centuries, to the effect that informal leases for more than a year can be cured by *rei interventus*, and very little of this authority was considered by the court.[1] If the line taken in *The Advice Centre for Mortgages* is followed, this would represent a major policy change which was signalled neither in the 1995 Act itself nor in the Scottish Law Commission report which it implemented.[2] Instead the provisions in the 1995 Act seem to have sprung from adhering too closely to the sale of heritable property model, mistakenly equating missives of let with missives of sale, and failing to think through the position in relation to leases.

(2)   While it is tempting to sympathise with Lord Drummond Young's strict line in the context of a valuable commercial lease between parties who are legally represented, it should be remembered that this law potentially applies to all types of lease for a year or more.

(3)   While the possibility remains of creating an informal lease for a year or less, it should be kept in mind that such a lease is not an automatic default situation in cases where the parties have purported to enter a longer lease and failed to observe the necessary formalities. *The Advice Centre for Mortgages* shows that a bungled attempt at a longer lease does not necessarily result in a lease for a year, but very possibly in no lease at all.

1 For some of this earlier authority, see para 2.12. For a more extensive review of the authority, see Angus McAllister 'Leases and the Requirements of Writing' 2006 SLT (News) 254.
2 Scottish Law Commission *Report on Requirements of Writing* (Scot Law Com No 112, April 1988).

Conclusion

2.20   The above analysis only scratches the surface of this very difficult case. The issues it raises in relation to leases and the requirements of writing are considered in more depth elsewhere.[1]

It is suggested that any future judicial consideration of this issue should take into account that Lord Drummond Young's opinion is obiter in relation to missives of let, and should also keep in mind the vast body of prior authority which it would seek to overturn. There would appear to be scope for a more liberal interpretation of provisions that seem to have been based upon a basic misunderstanding of the nature of leases. Meanwhile, however, practitioners should be cautious and make sure that they properly conform to the requirements of the 1995 Act.

1 Angus McAllister 'Leases and the Requirements of Writing' 2006 SLT (News) 254.

Dangers of resting on missives of let

2.21   In *Gilcomston Investments Ltd v Speedy Hire (Scotland) Ltd*,[1] the parties entered into missives of let in 2006. The missives included a formal draft lease. The tenant entered into possession and paid rent. No formal lease was signed by the parties. The missives of let provided for a ten-year lease. Five years following conclusion of the missives the tenant gave notice to the landlord that it did not wish to continue with the lease and gave up possession of the premises. The landlord raised an action of declarator that the lease was for ten years. The tenant successfully founded on the two year supercession clause contained in the missives of let. The sheriff held that the missives of let had ceased to be operative in 2008. The tenant's possession of the premises since then had not been based on the missives of let but on a yearly tenancy, renewed each year by tacit relocation.

1 2013 GWD 15-322.

ESSENTIAL ELEMENTS IN LEASES

2.22   Having seen the form that a lease should take, we will now look briefly at its content. A modern lease is typically a complex and lengthy document, almost as formidable to the lawyer as to the layman. In order to constitute a valid lease at common law, however, only four essential elements are required.[1] They are:

(1)   the parties;
(2)   the subjects;
(3)   the rent; and
(4)   the duration.

These elements are implicit in the very concept of a lease. It is difficult to think of a lease, as we have described it, without all of these basic ingredients; without the first two (the people involved and the subject matter), it is difficult to envisage having any kind of contract at all.

1 Rankine pp 114–116; Paton and Cameron pp 5–8.

The parties

2.23   A lease must have both a landlord and a tenant. Not only must they both be named, but they also must be designed (properly identified) usually by the addition of an address. Either landlord or tenant may be an individual or two or more individuals acting jointly, eg where a husband and wife are joint tenants. Also, either a landlord or tenant may be a group of people having separate legal identity, eg a limited company or other corporate body.[1]

The landlord must have the legal right to grant a lease. The most obvious and common example of a person with this right is the owner of the property. However, other parties can have a right to grant leases, such as a tenant who grants a sublease. Another example is the right of a heritable creditor under a standard security, when the debtor is in default, to enter into possession of the security subjects and lease them out, as a method of recouping part of the loss.[2] A lease granted by an undischarged bankrupt is valid but challengeable at the instance of his trustee in sequestration.[3]

1 There is a proposal for information to be collected and made publicly available (via Companies House) in relation to overseas entities with certain interests in land, including where such an entity is party to a registrable lease: draft Registration of Overseas Entities Bill (UK Parliament), likely to come into force in 2021. There is also a proposal for information to be collected and made available (via Registers of Scotland) on who actually has the beneficial interest in land, including registrable leases: see draft Land Reform (Scotland) Act 2016 Register of Persons Having a Controlled Interest in Land (Scotland) Regulations 2021 (Scottish Parliament), likely to come into force in 2022.
2 Conveyancing and Feudal Reform (Scotland) Act 1970, Sch 3 para 10(3) and (4).
3 *Iqbal v Parnez* [2017] SAC (Civ) 2, 2017 GWD 6-81.

2.24   Since it is a fundamental principle of the law of contract that a person cannot contract with himself or herself, it follows that the landlord and the tenant of a lease must be separate persons. However, this apparently self-evident distinction has become blurred in several decided cases, discussed below. The difficulty appears to stem from the fact that while it is clear that personal obligations will be extinguished by *confusio* when the debtor and creditor are the same person, it is much less clear whether a lesser real right (such as a lease) will be automatically absorbed into the greater real right (ownership) should tenant and landlord be the same person.[1]

In *Kildrummy (Jersey) Ltd v Commissioners of Inland Revenue,*[2] although the tenant company was, in theory, a separate legal person, it was, in fact, a trustee and nominee of the landlords and the lease was held to be a nullity. In *Pinkerton v Pinkerton*[3] it was held that a lease granted by a sole proprietor in favour of himself and three members of his family was valid.

On the other hand, in *Clydesdale Bank v Davidson*[4] the House of Lords held that a lease granted by three *pro indiviso* proprietors to one of their number was a nullity. In the latter case, the House of Lords did not overrule *Pinkerton* but distinguished it. In the words of Lord Clyde:[5]

'A right of sole occupation cannot co-exist with a right of ownership, albeit co-ownership, in the same person. The greater right must absorb and extinguish the lesser right. The narrow path which Lord Mackay of Clashfern identified in *Pinkerton v Pinkerton* whereby a lease could validly be constituted between a sole proprietor and several persons including himself as tenants is not available where the greater right is held in its entirety by the landlord. By virtue of that right he can grant the lesser right of occupation to others along with himself. But the co-proprietors in the present case can grant nothing to the sole tenant when he already has a right of occupation to the whole lands.'

The ratio of *Clydesdale Bank v Davidson* appears to be that it is possible for co-proprietors to enter into a contract with one of their number, eg for the management of the property or, as in that case, restricting the right of occupation to one of them. However (except in the particular circumstances of *Pinkerton* where the lease was granted to third parties as well as the proprietor) such an arrangement will not be a lease and will not be valid in any question with a third party.

The convoluted arrangements featured in the above cases perhaps make more sense when it is realised that they were generally attempts (which met with mixed success) to get round the rights of a third party, such as the then Inland Revenue or a heritable creditor.

1 For a useful discussion of how *confusio* and *consolidatio* may apply to leases see Scottish Law Commission *Discussion Paper on Aspects of Leases: Termination* (Scot Law Com No 165, May 2018), Ch 8.
2 1991 SC 1, 1992 SLT 787.
3 1986 SLT 672.
4 1998 SC (HL) 51, 1998 SLT 522; see also *Bell's Executors v Inland Revenue* 1986 SC 252, 1987 SLT 625; and *Serup v McCormack* 2012 SLCR 189.
5 *Clydesdale Bank v Davidson* 1998 SLT 522 at 529 per Lord Clyde.

2.25   *'Landord's' interest*   It was noted above that the landlord under a lease is typically the owner of the subjects.[1] However, although the tenant has a separate right (generally known as the 'tenant's interest') which is distinct and can have value, it has been held that there is no such thing as a 'landlord's interest' separate from the owner's title to the subjects (or presumably, separate from the interest of any other category of person, such as a head tenant or heritable creditor, who has the right to grant a lease).[2]

This arose in the unusual circumstances of *Crewpace Ltd v French*,[3] in which land which was the subject of an agricultural lease was divided in two and fell into the ownership of two different parties. The rent for the two parts was apportioned between the two landlords. One of these owners, without the other's consent, later resumed part of the leased subjects that was in their ownership, sold off two parts and granted a new lease of another part. The other owner claimed that the landlord's interest in the whole of the leased subjects was the common property of both owners, and that their right had been infringed without their consent.

It was held that the landlord of one part of the leased subjects did not have some incorporeal heritable interest over the part of the subjects owned by the other landlord, but only an owners' title to their own part of the subjects. The other landlord in the present case was therefore entitled to dispose of his part as he had done. The pursuers' claim of unjustified enrichment also failed, not only because they had no heritable interest which the defender had benefited from, but also because they had suffered no loss as a result of the defender's transactions.[4]

It should be noted, however, that there is another context, not mentioned in *Crewpace,* where a 'landlord's interest' *can* have a separate existence from the ownership title. This is when a landlord interposes a lease by assigning the 'landlord's interest' to a new head tenant, thereby demoting the existing tenant to the status of subtenant.[5]

1 See para 2.23.
2 See para 2.23.
3 2012 SLT 126, 2011 SCLR 730.
4 For more about unjustified enrichment in a landlord and tenant context see paras 2.63 and 5.29.
5 See para 7.40 et seq.

The subjects

2.26   There must be some property that is being leased. Furthermore, the subjects of let must be properly identified. Sometimes the postal address may be all that is necessary, except in the case of flatted properties where several subjects may share the same address. It is usually better, however, to describe the property at greater length and to provide a plan. This is particularly desirable in the case of a long lease, if it is to be registered in the Land Register.[1] It should be noted that the subjects may include areas that are not visible, for instance, that are underground.

This may be agreed between the parties and expressly provided for in the lease, however, it may occur when the landlord leases his entire interest in a property to the tenant given the property law rule, that land is owned *a coelo usque as centrum*.[2]

If the subjects of let are not properly identified, this is not necessarily fatal, as it is possible that they can be established by other evidence of what the parties have agreed[3] or, if the tenant is already in occupation, by the extent of the tenant's possession.[4] However, this should not be relied upon as a method of identification.[5]

1 See para 8.11 et seq.
2 From the heavens to the centre of the earth. This was held to be the case in *Beatsons Building Supplies Ltd v Trustees of the Alex F Noble & Son Ltd Executive Benefits Scheme* 2015 GWD 15-271, Sh Ct.
3 *Affleck v Bronsdon* [2019] UT 49, 2019 GWD 30-473; see also *Affleck v Bronson* [2020] UT 44.
4 *Piggott v Piggott* 1981 SLT 269; see also *Andert Ltd v J & J Johnston* 1987 SLT 268, where not only the subjects but also the rent and duration were allegedly uncertain.
5 For an example of the unreliability of this approach see *Ali v Khosla (No 1)* 2001 SCLR 1072, 2001 GWD 25-917.

Rent

2.27   Without the above two elements, we would arguably have nothing that could be called a contract at all. However, it is possible to create a legally binding contract allowing a person to occupy a property rent free. However, such a contract would not be a lease, but a licence.[1] This means that it would not enjoy the benefit of any of the special legal rules relating to leases, notably the provisions of the Leases Act 1449. In other words, the occupant would not obtain a real right enforceable against the granter's singular successors.[2]

While the rent is typically a sum of money it need not be. It could be the provision of a service by the tenant or the offsetting by the tenant of sums due to him by the landlord.[3]

1 *Mann v Houston* 1957 SLT 89; *Whillock v Henderson* 2007 SLT 1222, 2007 GWD 38-663; see also *Gloag v Hamilton* 2004 Hous LR 91, where both the rent and the duration were uncertain, and para 2.51 et seq. Although it seems that a Scottish secure tenancy does not require rent – see para 18.27.
2 See para 2.30.
3 Rankine, p 114.

Duration

2.28   The period of the lease should be stated.[1] However, if it is omitted for any reason (usually by accident), this may not be fatal. Provided that there is agreement on the other three essential elements mentioned above, and provided that the tenant has entered into possession or expressly agreed to enter into possession of the subjects, a duration of one year will be implied.[2] Thereafter, if neither party takes steps to terminate the lease, it can be continued indefinitely on a year to year basis by the principle of tacit relocation.[3]

In *Shetland Islands Council v BP Petroleum Development Ltd*,[4] the parties had agreed on the main terms of a long lease of over 20 years, with the exception of the rent, and the tenants were in possession of the property. It was argued on behalf of the landlords that, since the other three essential elements were present, the court could apply a similar rule to the above one (where there was no duration) and fix the rent. It was held that the court could not fix a rent for a long lease (such as the one being negotiated), but might fix a rent for an annual tenancy.

The ratio of this case is not entirely clear, but seems to be authority for a rule that, where rent is the only essential element not agreed, a lease for a year may be created, irrespective of the proposed duration, at a rent fixed by the court. This situation (where the parties intended there to be a rent, but failed to agree about its amount) should be distinguished from the one mentioned above where the parties agreed that there should be no rent; as we saw, in the latter case we do not have a lease but a licence.

1 No duration will be provided in a private residential tenancy as such tenancies are open ended: private residential tenancies are discussed in Chapter 17; it seems that a Scottish secure tenancy need not state a duration: see para 18.27.
2 *Gray v Edinburgh University* 1962 SC 157, 1962 SLT 173; *P v O* 2014 Hous LR 44, Sh Ct.
3 *Cinema Bingo Club v Ward* 1976 SLT (Sh Ct) 90; for tacit relocation, see para 10.18 et seq.
4 1990 SLT 82, 1989 SCLR 48.

OTHER REQUIREMENTS UNDER THE LAW OF CONTRACT

2.29   It naturally follows from the fact that a lease is a contract that its validity depends on the same common law rules as any other contract. There must be *consensus in idem* (agreement as to the same thing), and intention to be legally bound.

In addition, the parties must have contractual capacity. A contract will be void (invalid) if either party, at the time of entering it, was under sixteen,[1] was drunk, or was suffering from mental illness so as not to understand the nature of the obligation entered into. Also, neither party must have entered into the contract under duress, or under an error as to what was agreed, induced by the other party's misrepresentation. All these factors undermine the consent of the parties that is fundamental to the validity of a lease, or any other contract. A full account of the general requirements for contractual validity can be obtained elsewhere.[2]

1 Age of Legal Capacity (Scotland) Act 1991.
2 See the textbooks on law of contract listed in the bibliography.

ACQUISITION OF A REAL RIGHT BY THE TENANT

Leases Act 1449

2.30   We noted in Chapter 1 several respects in which a lease could confer upon a tenant rights beyond those normally enjoyed under a contract.[1] One of these derives from an important early enactment, the Leases Act 1449. Compared with most modern statutes, the 1449 Act is admirably concise, and is worth quoting in full:

Of Takis of Landis for Termes

'Item it is ordanit for the sauftie and fauour of the pure pepil that labouris the grunde that thai and al vtheris that has takyn or sal tak landis in tym to cum fra lordis and has termes and yeris thereof that suppose the lordis sel or analy thai landis that the takeris sal remayn with thare tackis on to the ische of thare termes quhais handis at euer thai landis cum to for sik lik male as thai tuk thaim of befoir.'

1 See para 1.7 et seq.

2.31   In case the meaning of the above is not immediately self-evident, let us attempt to clarify. 'Analy' means 'alienate' (transfer ownership). A 'tack' is the old Scottish term for a lease. 'Ische' (or 'ish') means 'expiry date'. 'Male' (or 'Maill') means 'rent'.[1]

The underlying theory is fairly straightforward. By its nature, a contract usually creates only personal rights and obligations (ie those which affect only the parties entering into it and not third parties). We would, therefore, expect the landlord and the tenant to be the only people bound by a lease. However, in the context of leases, the application of this theory could have unfortunate consequences. If a landlord granted a lease for (say) five years, then sold the property after two years, the new owner, not being a party to the original lease, would in theory not be bound by it and therefore able to evict the tenant immediately, without waiting until the lease expired. The tenant would be entitled to sue the original owner for damages for breach of contract, but would have no right to remain in occupation of the property.

This consequence will normally be avoided by the operation of the 1449 Act. The Act's effect is that, where a property subject to a sitting tenancy changes hands, the new owner will require to recognise the lease and allow the tenant, not only to remain in possession until the lease expires, but to do so at the original rent. The tenant has obtained not just a *personal right*, enforceable against the original landlord, but a *real right*, enforceable against the original landlord's *singular successors*. A singular successor is someone who becomes the owner of heritable property by any means other than inheritance, for example a purchaser or a heritable creditor exercising the power of sale. Someone who inherited the property on the landlord's death, although not classed as a singular successor, would also be bound to recognise the rights of sitting tenants, by virtue of the 1449 Act, and probably under the law of contract as well.[2]

1 The following is a literal translation of the Act: 'It is ordained for the safety and favour of the poor people that labour the ground that they and all others that have taken or shall take lands in time to come from lords and have terms and years thereof, that suppose the lords sell or alienate these lands, that the tenants shall remain with their leases until the end of their terms, no matter into whose hands that ever the lands come to, for the same rent as they took them for before.'
2 McBryde para 26.01 et seq.

Criteria for application

2.32   In the centuries since the 1449 Act was passed, it has naturally come before the courts for interpretation on many occasions. As a result, it has been established that several conditions, implicit in the Act's wording, must be fulfilled before it applies and a real right is conferred upon the tenant:[1]

1 Rankine Ch 5; Paton and Cameron Ch 7.

2.33   *The lease, if for more than a year, must be in writing.*   This is, in fact, the same as the common law rule that formerly applied to all leases and has now been re-enacted in the Requirements of Writing (Scotland) Act 1995.[1]

1 See para 2.3 et seq.

2.34   *The subjects of the lease must be land.*   This includes all kinds of heritable property, including buildings. Leases that only give the tenant a right to certain uses of land, eg sporting leases may not qualify, though the case authority on this is complex.[1]

1 See Paton and Cameron pp 105–106; see also para 2.39.

2.35   *There must be a specific, continuing rent*   As we saw above, this is also a basic common law requirement for all leases.[1] It is not necessary for there to be a fair or market rent, but a nominal one may not qualify.[2] It makes no difference if a capital sum (grassum) is payable at the beginning of the lease in addition to a continuing rent. However, if a grassum has been paid instead of a rent the situation is less clear.

In *Mann v Houston*[3] the owner of a garage granted occupancy of it to the defender for a period of ten years in return for a single lump sum of £200. The agreement provided that no rent should be payable, but the occupant had the right to terminate the contract prematurely, in return for which the owner was bound to refund a sum calculated at a rate of £20 per annum for the unexpired portion of the occupancy. Before the end of the ten-year term, the owner sold the property and the new owner was successful in an action to evict the occupant; it was held that the latter did not have a real right valid against the new owner, because no rent was payable. In fact, since one of the four essential elements for a lease was lacking, the contract was not a lease at all.

On the face of it, this case may seem to be authority for the proposition that, in the absence of a rent, a grassum alone is not enough either to create a lease or to bring the 1449 Act into operation. However, the contract made no mention of the lump sum (which was alleged to be a payment of rent in advance) and in fact stated that no rent was payable. On the basis of the contract's terms, therefore, no lease and no real right had been created. This seems to leave open the possibility that a grassum which the lease explicitly stated to be an advance payment of the full rent for the entire term would qualify as a rent under the 1449 Act; on the other hand, it has been thought that a singular successor is entitled to some sort of return for yielding possession to the tenant,[4] and this would not be achieved by such an arrangement.

As noted above, a contract lacking only a rent will be a licence, which will be valid and enforceable against the original granter.[5] However, a licence does not confer a real right valid against the original granter's singular successors.

1 *Mann v Houston* 1957 SLT 89; *Wallace v Simmers* 1960 SC 255, 1961 SLT 34; see
   para 2.27.
2 Rankine p 144; Paton and Cameron p 109.
3 1957 SLT 89.
4 Rankine p 146; Paton and Cameron p 109.
5 See para 2.50 et seq.

2.36   *There must be an ish (ie a term of expiry of the lease)*   As we saw in Chapter 1,[1] it was formerly possible under the common law for a lease to be in perpetuity, as a result of which this criterion would not have been met. However, as leases have now been given a maximum length by statute of 175 years,[2] the above criterion should now be met automatically.

1 See para 1.5.
2 Abolition of Feudal Tenure, etc (Scotland) Act 2000 s 67; see also paras 1.5 and 8.4 et seq.

2.37 *The tenant must have entered into possession* This condition is satisfied not only if the tenant physically occupies the property (natural possession), but also where someone else legitimately occupies it in the tenant's place (civil possession). For example, where a property has been sublet, it is not necessary for the tenant to be in physical occupation, provided that the subtenant is.

However, in a case where an owner granted a lease and then sold the property prior to the date of entry, it was held that the new owner was not bound to recognise the lease, even though the tenant had been allowed to occupy part of the property in advance of the entry date; it was only the exclusive possession granted at the date of entry that counted.[1] In the course of his judgment, Lord President Cooper usefully summed up the rationale for this criterion:

> 'It has been well established for centuries that possession under a lease is the equivalent of sasine in relation to feudal property. Without possession the tenant is merely the personal creditor of the lessor. By entering into possession the lessee publishes to the world in general, and to singular successors in particular, the fact of his lease ...'[2]

1 *Millar v McRobbie* 1949 SC 1, 1949 SLT 2.
2 1949 SC 1 at 6 per Lord Cooper.

2.38 *A landlord who is the owner of the property must be infeft* In order to be infeft, a title deed in the landlord's favour (normally a disposition) must have been registered in the Land Register (or, in the case of some older leases, in the Register of Sasines). Under this rule, the landlord should be infeft at the time the lease was granted, although if a deed in the landlord's favour is registered after the lease has begun, the lease will be validated retrospectively under the principle of accretion. The requirement for infeftment does not apply where the landlord is not the owner, the most obvious case being a tenant who has sublet the property.

Effect of registration[1]

2.39 A real right is also conferred upon a tenant where a lease has been registered in the Land Register of Scotland (or, in the case of some older leases, in the Register of Sasines). In such a case, therefore, it is not essential for the conditions of the 1449 Act to be complied with. In particular, registering a lease is legally equivalent to possession (see condition (5) above).

Registration may confer a real right upon a tenant in cases, eg some sporting leases, where the 1449 Act does not apply or where there is some doubt as to whether it applies.[2]

For all registrable leases, ie all new leases of more than 20 years, the 1449 Act has been superseded and registration in the Land Register is now the only way for a tenant to acquire a real right.[3]

1 For more about registration of leases see para 8.11 et seq.
2 *Palmer's Trustees v Brown* 1989 SLT 128, 1988 SCLR 499.
3 Registration of Leases (Scotland) Act 1857 s 20B and 20C.

TRANSMISSION OF CONDITIONS[1]

2.40 When the Leases Act 1449 has operated, or the lease has been registered, it will not only have the effect of compelling the landlord's singular successors to recognise the existence of the lease, but the conditions of the lease will generally transmit as well. In other words, they will become real conditions and will run with the land, ie they will apply not only to the original landlord and tenant but to their successors under the same lease.

However, for this to be so, the conditions must be *inter naturalia* of a lease, ie of the sort normally found in a lease. If they are personal in nature, they will not transmit and will bind only the original parties. Examples of such personal conditions include the right of a farm tenant to take peat from a moss in another part of the landlord's estate, a rent abatement in return for personal services by the tenant to the landlord, and a right by the tenant of a 999-year lease at any time to demand a feu charter of the property from the landlord, ie to be granted ownership.[2]

In modern times, transmissability issues have arisen in relation to:

(1) options in favour of the tenant to purchase the property;
(2) guarantees by third parties in favour of the landlord; and
(3) exclusivity agreements binding a landlord not to let nearby premises to a tenant's business rival.

Such agreements have sometimes been contained in separate documents, with the result that two issues arise:

(a)   is the document, if separate, framed in such a way that singular successors will be bound, or, as the case may be, will benefit?

(b)   if the undertaking is contained in the lease document, is it personal in nature or is it *inter naturalia* of a lease and therefore transmissable?

1 See generally Stewart Brymer 'Enforcing Commercial Lease Terms Against Successor Landlords' (2000) Prop LB 4 and (2001) 50 Prop LB 3; and Gretton and Reid *Conveyancing 2000* (2001), pp 56–62; see also Ian Quigley 'On the Wrong Track' 2007 JLSS 52(2) 48, in which a practitioner argues persuasively that court decisions in this area have been made without sufficient regard to the context of modern commercial lease practice.

2 Paton and Cameron pp 95–97; see also *Bisset v Magistrates of Aberdeen* (1898) 1 F 87 and *Duncan v Brooks* (1894) 21 R 760, 2 SLT 28.

Options to purchase

2.41   In *Davidson v* Zani[1] missives of let contained an option to purchase in favour of the tenant but the formal lease that followed did not contain the provision. It was held that the landlord's singular successor, who had been made aware of the tenant's option at the time of purchase, was bound by it.

However, in *The Advice Centre for Mortgages v McNicoll*[2] it was held, in broadly similar circumstances, that an option to purchase contained in the missives did *not* bind the original landlords' singular successor. The view was taken that *Davidson v Zani* was wrongly decided, and this would appear to be supported by the weight of academic opinion.[3]

Even if contained in the lease, options to purchase are thought to be personal in nature and not *inter naturalia* of a lease. This means that they are not normally enforceable by a tenant against the landlord's singular successors.[4]

1 1992 SCLR 1001.
2 2006 SLT 591, 2006 SCLR 602.
3 See Stewart Brymer 'Enforcing Commercial Lease Terms Against Successor Landlords' (2000) Prop LB 4 and (2001) 50 Prop LB 3; and Andrew J M Steven 'Options to Purchase and Successor Landlords' 2006 10 Edin LR 432.
4 *Bisset v Magistrates of Aberdeen* (1898) 1 F 87; *The Advice Centre for Mortgages v McNicoll* 2006 SLT 591, 2006 SCLR 602.

Guarantees

2.42   A guarantee of the tenant's obligations by a third party, if contained in a separate document, may nevertheless be enforceable by the landlord's singular successor against the guarantor, if the wording makes it clear that an assignation of the right to the landlord's singular successors is intended. The law on this was developed in a series of cases, involving a badly worded guarantee, between Waydale Ltd and DHL Holdings (UK) Limited.[1]

Presumably a properly worded guarantee, which is contained in a lease to which the guarantor is a party, will also transmit, and it may be enough to achieve this if the landlord is defined in the lease as including the landlord's singular successors.[2]

A third possibility is that a guarantee, which is not worded so as to include the landlord's singular successors, is nevertheless contained within the lease which the guarantor has signed as a party. It will then only transmit if considered to be *inter naturalia* of a lease. This seems doubtful, since the guarantee is not a contract between the landlord and the tenant, but is a unilateral obligation granted to the landlord by a third party. However, there is no direct authority on this.

1 *Waydale Ltd v DHL Holdings (UK) Limited (No 1)*1996 SCLR 391, *Waydale Ltd v DHL Holdings (UK) Limited (No 2)* 2000 SC 172, 2001 SLT 224 (see also 1999 SLT 631, 1999 SCLR 23) and *Waydale Ltd v DHL Holdings (UK) Ltd (No 3)* 2001 SLT 224, 2000 GWD 38-1434.
2 *Waydale Ltd v DHL Holdings (UK) Ltd (No 1)* 1996 SCLR 391, per Lord Penrose at p 399.

Exclusivity agreements

2.43   *The Optical Express case*   An exclusivity agreement is an undertaking by a landlord not to undermine a tenant's business by leasing a nearby unit (perhaps in the same shopping centre) to a tenant who is in the same line of business.[1] As with options and guarantees, such an agreement may be contained either in a separate document or in the lease.

Both of these possibilities were considered in *Optical Express (Gyle) Ltd v Marks & Spencer plc.*[2] The landlords' predecessors (Edinburgh Council) had granted a back letter agreeing that, while the tenants remained in occupation of the leased property, theirs would be the only unit in the same shopping centre that would be principally used as an opticians.

The hearing related to whether there was a *prima facie* case for granting interim interdict against a rival optician who had been granted a lease in the same centre by the original landlord's successor, and the case does not seem to have proceeded to a final judgment. However, Lord McFadyen's opinion includes a valuable consideration of the relevant principles:[3]

'In my view the pursuer's case that the first and second defenders are bound by the provisions of the back letter not to let unit 56 to the third defenders for use as an optician's shop depends on their showing both (1) that the back letter forms part of the contract of lease originally entered into between the pursuers and the council, and (2) that the obligation undertaken by the council in the back letter was of such a nature as to run with the land and thus transmit automatically against the singular successors of the council as landlords. Both must be shown because ... it is only as a provision of the lease that the exclusivity clause could run with the land and become binding on them as singular successors of the council in the landlord's interest, while it is possible for an obligation to form part of a lease yet remain personal to the original contracting parties.'

Regarding the first part of the test, his lordship suggested that the back letter being granted in a separate document pointed away from the conclusion that it was intended as an integral part of the lease rather than as a separate collateral obligation. In his opinion, the back letter also failed the second part of the test:

'Although [the back letter] was entered into as a matter of contract between the council as landlords and the pursuers as tenants of unit 41 at the Gyle centre, its effect was nothing directly to do with the lease of unit 41, but rather was to restrain the way in which the council as owners or landlords of the other units in the centre might let those other units. In my opinion such an obligation is prima facie not inter naturalia of a lease. I do not consider that that prima facie conclusion is displaced by the fact that unit 41 is one unit of a shopping centre and the land in respect of which the landlord's freedom of action is restrained is the remainder of the centre. Nor, in my view, does the close practical connection which the exclusivity clause has with the economic judgement which the tenant had to make in deciding whether or not to take the tenancy go to make the case that it is an obligation which runs with the land.'

In other words, even if the exclusivity provision had been contained in the lease, such a condition is not *inter naturalia* of a lease and therefore not binding upon singular successors.

1 Such covenants have recently been held by the Supreme Court not to engage the doctrine of restraint of trade: see *Peninsula Securities Ltd v Dunnes Stores (Bangor) Ltd* [2020] UKSC 36, [2020] 3 WLR 521.
2 2000 SLT 644, 2000 GWD 7-264.
3 *Optical Express (Gyle) Ltd v Marks & Spencer plc* 2000 SLT 644 at 649 per Lord McFadyen.

2.44   *Older case law*   There is, however, older case law which was not considered in *Optical Express*, and which took a different view of the same issue.

In *Campbell v Watt*[1] the lease of an inn contained a clause under which the landlord undertook to prohibit the sale of alcohol in any smithy to be leased by him. The landlord's singular successor later erected a new inn on his own land nearby. In an action by the tenant for an abatement of rent, the court held that the exclusivity provision could not only be enforced against the landlord's singular successor, but that the scope of its terms could be widened to include a rival inn as well as a smithy selling alcohol:

> 'The Lords were of opinion, that Mrs Watt had a good claim of abatement of rent. Observed on the Bench, ... It is true, a purchaser is not affected by pactions extrinsic to the nature of a tack, such as those for retention of rent. But the restraint here is a natural incident of a tack of such a subject; and, whether conditional or not, it was in the *bona fides* of the transaction that the landlord should not set up a rival inn to the prejudice of his own tenant in the old one. If Mrs Watt had applied timefully, she might perhaps have obtained an interdict against the new building; but in any event she is entitled to an abatement of rent.'[2]

This case is discussed again in the next chapter in relation to derogation from the landlord's grant.[3] It should be noted that the court's second observation in *Campbell* (that the scope of the exclusivity could be widened on the basis of *bona fides*) must be regarded as controversial in the light of later authority; however, in relation to the transmission of the exclusivity in its original terms, it can still be regarded as good authority.

1 (1795) Hume 788.
2 *Campbell v Watt* (1795) Hume 788 at 790.
3 See para 3.20.

2.45 In *Davie v Stark*[1] the lease of a shop contained a condition that an adjoining shop, also owned by the landlord, should not be let to a person in the same trade. Some time later, the landlord's singular successor began to sell articles in the adjoining shop which the tenant claimed fell within his monopoly. It was held that this was a material breach of contract and that the tenant was entitled to rescind.

The fact that the landlord was the singular successor of the original landlord was not an issue between the parties and the court seems to have taken it for granted that he would be bound by the undertaking. The only real consideration of the point was given by Lord Gifford:

> '[A]lthough the present respondent, Mr Davie, is a singular successor of the original lessors, it is not now contested, and indeed could not well be, that he is bound by the missives of lease granted by his authors, and clothed with possession. ... I am of opinion that

this condition and stipulation was one which might legally and competently be made – that it was binding upon the contracting parties and on the singular successors of the lessors as an integral part of the appellant's lease.'[2]

Although that precise expression was not used, both of these cases appear effectively to be saying that an exclusivity provision is *inter naturalia* of a lease. However, since the decision in *Davie v Stark* did not turn upon whether or not the singular successor was bound, the opinion in that case is obiter.

1 (1876) 3 R 1114.
2 *Davie v Stark* (1876) 3 R 1114 at 1122 per Lord Gifford.

2.46   More recently, in *Warren James (Jewellers) Ltd v Overgate GP Ltd*[1] an exclusivity provision again came under judicial scrutiny. The case was between the original parties to the lease and did not involve singular successors, and the judgment turned upon the construction of the clause. However, in the course of his judgment, Lord Drummond Young expressed the opinion obiter that exclusivity provisions were *inter naturalia* of a lease and *did* bind singular successors. The decisions in both *Davie v Stark* and *Optical Express* were taken into consideration, though the issue was not discussed at great length.[2]

1 [2005] CSOH 142; this judgment was affirmed on appeal to the Inner House, but there the focus was entirely on the questions of construction – see 2007 GWD 06-94.
2 *Warren James (Jewellers) Ltd v Overgate GP Ltd* [2005] CSOH 142, at para 16 per Lord Drummond Young.

2.47   *Conclusion*   The authority would, therefore, appear to be conflicting, though perhaps moving in the direction of exclusivity provisions being *inter naturalia* of a lease. However, *Optical Express* remains the only modern case to have considered the issue in any great depth. The safest course for tenants is to assume that the opinion expressed in that case will prevail and to take whatever precautions they can to ensure transmission of the landlord's obligation.

2.48   This issue is important because it highlights a very common situation in shopping centre leases. As we will see later,[1] such a lease will often contain a use (or user) clause allowing the landlord to control the trade mix in the centre by confining the tenant to a particular type of business. In return, the landlord may promise the tenant a monopoly within the centre, which could be taken into account in arriving at the level of rent the tenant agrees to as well as influencing the tenant's decision whether or not to take on the lease in the first place.[2] It is therefore extremely important, from the tenant's point of view, that not only the original landlord, but the landlord's singular successors should be bound by any exclusivity agreement.

1 See para 11.6.
2 While a tenant may seek such an exclusivity undertaking in some retail environments, such as a shopping centre, the opposite may be the case in a city centre shopping area. Here it may be in the tenant's interest to seek an undertaking from the landlord that nearby units will *only* be let to tenants in the same line of business, thereby creating a specialist retail area from which all of the tenants will benefit. For an example of this, see *Ralph Lauren London Ltd v Trustee of the London Borough of Southwark Pension Fund* 2011 Hous LR 29, 2011 GWD 22-494. Despite the identity of the parties, this is a Scottish case that related to a shop in Glasgow city centre.

Possible solutions

2.49   The following may help deal with the problem faced by a tenant concerned about enforcing a lease term against his landlord's successors:

1. Any undertaking should be in the lease and not in a separate document. This may not be enough on its own, but is an essential precaution.
2. The tenant could get an express undertaking from the landlord, included as a term in the lease that, in any future disposal of the property, the landlord will bind the purchaser to the exclusivity agreement or option, as the case may be.[1]
3. It has been argued that, in certain very limited circumstances, the leasing of nearby premises to a tenant's business rival may amount to a derogation from the landlord's grant, though this could prove more problematic in Scotland than in England. This issue is dealt with in some depth in the next chapter.[2]
4   It has been suggested that a landlord could grant a standard security over its interest to secure performance of an option or other obligation by the landlord's successors.[3] This may be possible because standard securities can be used to secure an obligation *ad factum praestandum* (for the performance of an act) as well as a money obligation.[4] It is however likely to be very difficult to get a landlord to agree to this.

1 *The Advice Centre for Mortgages v McNicoll* 2006 SLT 591, at 605 per Lord Drummond Young, 2006 SCLR 602.
2 See para 3.19 et seq.
3 See Stewart Brymer 'Enforcing Commercial Lease Terms Against Successor Landlords' (2001) 50 Prop LB 3; *The Advice Centre for Mortgages v McNicoll* 2006 SLT 591, at 605 per Lord Drummond Young, 2006 SCLR 602.
4 Conveyancing and Feudal Reform (Scotland) Act 1970 s 9(8)(c).

LICENCES

Introduction

2.50   Having examined the essential requirements for the existence of a lease, we will now look at the situation where one or more of these requirements have not been met. Where there is no lease, there may nevertheless be a valid contract allowing a person to occupy or use another's land; such a contract may be known as a right of occupation or a licence. Alternatively, a person may occupy another's property without any contract or title at all, and we will also consider the legal consequences of that situation.

Licences[1]

Nature of licence

2.51   Although a licence falls short of being a lease, it may resemble one, and it is sometimes difficult to tell the difference between them. The concept of a licence is less developed in Scotland than in England, though even there determining the difference between licence and lease can still lead to litigation.[2]

A number of the early cases, which helped to develop the concept of a licence in Scotland, were rating appeals, several of which are cited below.[3]

1 Paton & Cameron pp 12-15; Fiona Rollo 'Licences to Occupy: Can Solicitors do More than Constitute in Writing What Could Amount to a Licence?' 2005 78 Prop LB 3. For a discussion of licences with particular reference to residential properties, see Robson para 3-02 et seq.
2 See, eg, *Monmouth Borough Council v Marlog* (1995) 27 HLR 30, [1994] 44 EG 240; the leading English authority on licenses is *Street v Mountford* [1985] AC 809, [1985] 2 All ER 289, HL.
3 References for more of these rating cases can be found in Paton and Cameron at pp 12–14.

Definition of licence

2.52   A licence is defined by Paton and Cameron as 'a contract, falling short of a lease, whereby not the heritage itself but a right to use a particular part of it or to put a particular part of it to some use is granted'[1] According to Paton and Cameron, the criteria for identifying a licence include:

(1) *The express terms of the agreement/the intention of the parties,*
eg whether the document calls itself a lease or a licence, or by the
customary relation set up by it, or both taken together.[2]

However, the fact that a document describes itself as a licence
does not prevent it from actually being a lease if all the necessary
requirements for the latter are present.[3] This is especially the case
if the attempt to create a licence is an obvious sham designed to
avoid the legal consequences of being a lease.[4]

(2) *Whether the occupant has exclusive possession.* The mere fact that
the area possessed is extremely small will not prevent the contract
being a lease.[5] The tenant need not have exclusive possession of
pertinents of the lease, for instance, where the tenant is given
rights to common parts of a development.[6]

If the landlord retains substantial possession rights, the contract
may be a licence.[7] We will see in the next chapter that one of the
obligations of a landlord at common law is to grant the tenant
exclusive possession.[8] However, more modern authority suggests
that the issue as to exclusive possession is not entirely clear-cut.[9]

(3) *Whether the contract lacks some other essential requirement of a
lease* for instance a rent,[10] or one of the other essential elements
for a lease at common law.[11]

1 Paton and Cameron p 12.
2 Paton and Cameron p 12; see also *Scottish Residential Estates Development Co v
Henderson* 1991 SLT 490.
3 *St Andrews Forest Lodges v Grieve* [2017] SC DUN 25, 2017 GWD 14-224.
4 *Brador Properties Ltd v British Telecommunications plc* 1992 SC 12, 1992 SLT 490;
see also para 2.55.
5 *A J Wilson & Co Ltd v Assessor for Kincardineshire* 1913 SC 704, 1913 1 SLT 29
(lease of ground for an advertisement hoarding).
6 *Gyle Shopping Centre General Partners Ltd v Marks and Spencer plc* [2014] CSOH 59,
GWD 18-352.
7 *Broomhill Motor Co v Assessor for Glasgow* 1927 SC 447, 1927 SLT 189 (lockup
garages where the owner kept keys, was allowed access for a number of purposes and
provided services – contracts were licences); *Chaplin v Assessor for Perth* 1947 SC 373,
1947 SLT 163 (lockup garages where the tenants not only had exclusive possession, but
no services were provided by the landlords and the whole of the rent in each case was
for occupation of the garage – contracts were leases); *Perth Burgh Council v Assessor
for Perth and Kinross* 1937 SC 549, 1937 SLT 383 (the use of an aerodrome landing
ground jointly along with a number of other parties – contract was a licence).
8 See paras 1.3 and 3.10.
9 See para 2.55.
10 *Mann v Houston* 1957 SLT 89; *Wallace v Simmers* 1960 SC 255, 1961 SLT 34;
Whillock v Henderson 2007 SLT 1222, 2007 GWD 38-663.
11 *Holloway Brothers (London) Ltd v Assessor for Edinburgh* 1948 SC 300, 1948 SLT 430
(no fixed subjects and no duration). See para 2.22 et seq.

2.53   In *Scottish Residential Estates Development Co v Henderson*[1] the occupant had exclusive possession of the property. However, not only did the terms of the agreement make it clear that the parties intended it to be a licence, but the licence was terminable at any time the owner might require to regain possession of the property. This meant that there was no duration. And while, as we saw above, a duration of one year may sometimes be implied,[2] in this case, the fact that there was no definite duration had been specifically agreed by the parties. The court found that there was no lease but a right of occupation.

1 1991 SLT 490.
2 See para 2.28.

Need for writing

2.54   A licence for more than a year must be in writing and otherwise conform to the Requirements of Writing (Scotland) Act 1995.[1]

1 Requirements of Writing (Scotland) Act 1995 s 1(2) and (7); *Caterleisure Ltd v Glasgow Prestwick International Airport Ltd* 2006 SC 602, 2005 SLT 1083; see also para 2.3 et seq.

How essential is exclusive possession?

2.55   *Brador Properties v British Telecom* The existence of exclusive possession as an absolute requirement for a lease has been questioned in several modern cases.

In *Brador Properties Ltd v British Telecommunications plc,*[1] the tenants of office premises were refused consent by their landlords (which was required by the lease terms) to sublet the property. Instead the tenants created a number of agreements with third parties which granted them possession of office rooms, but which were stated not to be leases. The tenants reserved a right of entry to the properties and also the right, on giving notice, to change the rooms allocated to any of the occupants.

The tenants therefore maintained that the contracts could not be leases, inter alia, because there was no exclusive possession nor were there definite subjects. It was held that the agreements were not licences but leases, and therefore unauthorised sublets. The occupants had been given sufficiently exclusive possession, and it did not matter that the identity of the subjects could change, provided that they were clearly identified and the mechanism for the change was agreed. Moreover, the court was required to scrutinise such agreements closely and was entitled to consider whether they were delusive devices to defeat the terms of the principal lease.

The court in *Brador* also rejected the English authority for the distinction between leases and licences and cast doubt on the Scottish authority quoted by Paton & Cameron regarding the need for exclusive possession. Since Rankine's definition of a lease included 'certain uses' as well as 'the entire control' of lands,[2] the Scottish concept of a lease was clearly wider than that in England, where exclusive possession was essential.[3]

1 1992 SC 12, 1992 SLT 490.
2 Rankine p 1.
3 *Street v Mountford* [1985] AC 809, [1985] 2 All ER 289, HL.

2.56 *Conway v Glasgow City Council* On the basis of this opinion in *Brador* it has been argued that exclusive possession is not in fact an essential requirement of a lease in Scotland.[1] However, in *Conway v Glasgow City Council*[2] it was held that a resident sharing a two-bed room in a hostel for homeless persons did not have a lease. The sheriff reserved his opinion on whether exclusive possession is necessary for a lease, but held that the degree of possession enjoyed by the tenant came nowhere near that required for a lease. However, he acknowledged that 'the law has come increasingly to talk of exclusive possession as a necessary condition of a lease'[3] and believed that this was consistent with the position in *Brador*.

In *St Andrews Forest Lodges v Grieve*[4] the sheriff, having considered the authorities on the issue, found that exclusive possession was the fifth 'cardinal element'[5] of a lease and an important feature in distinguishing a lease from a license.

1 Mike Dailly 'Lease or Licence in Scots Law' SCOLAG Journal Aug 1996, p 126.
2 1999 SCLR 248, 1999 Hous LR 20. This sheriff court decision was overturned by the sheriff principal (1999 SLT (Sh Ct) 102, 1999 SCLR 1058) but the sheriff's judgment was later reinstated on appeal to the Court of Session (2001 SLT 1472 (Note), 2001 SCLR 546). However, this was by agreement between the parties and the Inner House issued no opinions. In any case, the appeals did not relate to the distinction between a lease and a licence.
3 1999 SCLR 248 at 255.
4 [2017] SC DUN 25, 2017 GWD 14-224.
5 The four other cardinal elements being parties, subjects, duration and rent, see para 2.22 et seq.

2.57 *Reservations to landlord* It is well established, and indeed quite common, for a lease specifically to allow for certain rights to be reserved to the landlord, which strictly speaking encroach upon the tenant's right of exclusive possession, eg a right of access for repair, inspection etc. Also, the landlord of a furnished let may, within reason, provide that some of his or her effects may be kept in locked drawers, cupboards etc.[1] Any such encroachments, however, that are not sanctioned by the lease will be a breach of the landlord's common law obligation not to derogate from the grant.[2]

However, even when such reservations are contracted for, if they are excessive they may interfere with the tenant's exclusive possession to a sufficient extent to prevent the contract being regarded as a lease. It will be a matter of degree, to be determined according to the circumstances of each case, whether the possession is exclusive enough for the contract to qualify as a lease.

In *South Lanarkshire Council v Taylor*[3] a purported lease allowed the defender to occupy three areas at Lanark Racecourse for the grazing of horses. However, the contract contained a provision that the defender could be given 24 hours' notice to vacate any or all of these grazing areas in order to permit other events to take place. It was held that this provision was not necessarily inconsistent with the contract being a lease rather than a licence, and a proof before answer was allowed in order to determine the degree of encroachment involved.

1 *Miller v Wilson* 1919 1 SLT 223; see also para 3.10.
2 See para 3.11 and 3.14 et seq.
3 2005 1 SC 182, 2005 GWD 1-17.

2.58 *Conclusion* There therefore remains some controversy about the need for exclusive possession as a necessary element in a lease. Rankine's inclusion in his definition of a lease of 'certain uses of land' is consistent with the recognition of certain traditional types of lease (eg of sporting or mineral rights) where only certain uses of the land are granted.[1] It does not follow, however, that exclusive possession can be dispensed with in the case of leases (the vast majority) that fall outwith these special categories. Indeed, the authorities tend to suggest that exclusive possession is a requirement for a lease.

1 See para 1.16.

Season tickets

2.59 It has been held that a season ticket sold by a football club is merely a licence giving access to and egress from the allocated seat and a right to occupy that seat when matches are being played, and therefore does not confer a real right enforceable against the football club's administrators.[1]

1 *Joint Administrators of Rangers Football Club plc, Noters* 2012 SLT 599, 2012 GWD 13-261.

Lease or licence? Importance of distinction

2.60   The concept of a licence in Scots law therefore remains rather under-developed, and the borderline between leases and licences can be a little blurred. Nevertheless, many licences (or rights of occupation) do exist and are even recognised (though not defined) by statute.[1]

Determining whether a contract is a lease or a licence is important. For example a lease (though not a licence) will give a tenant a real right valid against the landlord's singular successors, requiring a new owner to recognise the lease if the property changes hands;[2] will entitle the landlord to traditional remedies, such as the right of hypothec for recovery of rent;[3] and (particularly in agricultural and residential tenancies) may give the tenant some measure of statutory protection.[4] In addition, tacit relocation[5] operates where there is a lease, but not a licence. The distinction also determines whether or not the occupant can be evicted without court action: where the occupant is a tenant under an expired lease court action is required; where the occupier had only a contractual right to occupy that did not amount to a lease he can be evicted without court action. [6]

1 See eg the Housing (Scotland) Act 2001 s 38(1)(a), the Requirements of Writing (Scotland) Act 1995 s 1(7) or the Land Tenure Reform (Scotland) Act s 8(4).
2 See para 2.30 et seq.
3 See para 6.1 et seq. It should be noted that the right of hypothec has been substantially weakened.
4 See parts 4 and 5.
5 See para 10.18 et seq.
6 *Ali v Serco Ltd* [2019] CSIH 54; 2019 SLT 1335.

Hostel residents

2.61   *Conway v Glasgow District Council*[1] highlighted the situation of the occupants of hostels for the homeless run by local authorities and other bodies. While the case law has so far denied such occupants the status of tenants, it is by no means inevitable that this will always be the case. One thing to emerge from the confusion surrounding the distinction between leases and licences is that in each individual case much will depend upon the terms of the agreement and the general circumstances of the case. If the pursuer in *Conway* had not shared her room, would the decision have been different? Hotel guests generally have an even more precarious tenure than licencees. And yet in England (where, according to *Brador* the definition of a lease is much narrower than in Scotland) the House of Lords has held that a long-term resident of a hotel had an assured tenancy.[2]

Section 7 of the Housing (Scotland) Act 2001 gives the Scottish Ministers power to pass regulations regarding hostel and other short term accommodation (including a right of residents not to be evicted without notice). When passed, these may clarify the legal status of such occupants. Significantly, however, while the section specifically precludes them from having Scottish secure or assured tenancies (including the short version of each) or a private residential tenancy[3] it contains nothing to exclude the possibility of a contract that would satisfy the requirements of a lease at common law. It is for the Scottish Ministers to provide further clarification.[4]

1 1999 SCLR 248, 1999 Hous LR 20; see also *Denovan v Blue Triangle (Glasgow) Housing Association Ltd* 1999 Hous LR 97.
2 *Uratemp Ventures Ltd v Collins* [2002] 1 AC 301, [2001] 3 WLR 806; for assured tenancies generally see Ch 17.
3 Housing (Scotland) Act 2001 s 7(2)(b).
4 As at the date of writing, regulations under this section have not yet been passed.

OCCUPATION WITHOUT TITLE

2.62   There is no lease involved in this situation, but we are once more in an anomalous area on the fringe of lease law. Where someone occupies another person's property without the benefit of a lease or on any other apparent legal basis, the onus is on that person to show that he or she is entitled to occupy gratuitously (in which case, as we saw above, there would be a licence). An occupant who is unable to demonstrate a right to gratuitous occupation, will be obliged to pay the owner a reasonable sum representing the annual worth of the property.[1]

Such a situation can come about in several ways: there may have been negotiations for a lease which have broken down,[2] the occupant may have had a lease and stayed on after its termination[3] or he or she may simply be occupying the property.[4]

1 Paton & Cameron pp 11–12.
2 *Shetland Islands Council v BP Petroleum Development Ltd* 1990 SLT 82, 1989 SCLR 48.
3 *Rochester Poster Services Ltd v AG Barr plc* 1994 SLT (Sh Ct) 2, although in such a situation violent profits may also be claimed – see para 10.38.
4 *GTW Holdings v Toet* 1994 SLT (Sh Ct) 16, although in such a situation violent profits may also be claimed – see para 10.38.

2.63   *Legal basis of obligation*   While the authorities are clear about the occupant's obligation to pay money, they are less so about the legal basis on which this happens. One suggestion is that it is a matter of implied contract, another that it derives from the principle of unjustified enrichment, giving rise to a claim of recompense.[1]

The legal basis of the obligation to pay may depend upon whether or not the owner ever agreed to the occupation, however informally. If there was such an agreement it may be a case of implied contract, if not, one of unjustified enrichment.[2]

1 See McBryde paras 5.62–5.67.
2 *See Shetland Islands Council v BP Petroleum Development* 1990 SLT 82 at 92 per Lord Cullen.

2.64   In *Renfrewshire Council v McGinlay*[1] the defender took over the occupancy of a shop from its tenant without the knowledge of the landlord. The landlord eventually discovered this and, after abortive negotiations to enter a lease with the occupant, terminated the occupancy and claimed arrears of rent based on recompense. The action failed because:

(1)   the pursuer's loss and the defender's gain did not arise from the same contract or transaction; and

(2)   recompense could not be claimed unless the pursuer had exhausted all other legal remedies, and in this case it could have claimed the rent from the actual tenants of the shop.

1 2001 SLT (Sh Ct) 79.

Chapter 3

Rights and obligations of the parties

INTRODUCTION

3.1   At common law, the landlord and tenant under a lease each owes the other a number of implied obligations.[1] All of these automatically apply unless the lease document specifically states otherwise. Some of them are commonly reinforced by inclusion in the lease, whereas others are often contracted out of.

The obligations of the tenant are:

(1)   to enter into possession, to occupy and use the subjects;
(2)   to use the property only for the purpose for which it was let;
(3)   to take reasonable care of the property;
(4)   to pay the rent when it becomes due; and
(5)   to plenish the subjects.

The obligations of the landlord are:

(1)   to place the tenant in full possession of the subjects let;
(2)   not to derogate from the grant;
(3)   to provide subjects that are reasonably fit for the purpose for which they are let; and
(4)   to carry out repairs.

The obligations of the tenant, of course, correspond to the rights of the landlord and vice versa.

1 Rankine chs 10 and 11; Paton and Cameron ch 9.

TENANT'S OBLIGATIONS

To enter into possession, to occupy and use the subjects

3.2   The tenant must take possession of the property on the date of entry; the date of entry will normally be stated in the lease, but if this has not been done, it will be the date of the lease.[1] Thereafter, the tenant must remain in possession for the remainder of the lease.

In *Graham and Black v Stevenson*[2] the tenant of an inn closed it down several months before the end of his lease in order to set up business elsewhere. Even although the rent had been paid until the end of the lease, the landlord and incoming tenant sued him for damages, and the incoming tenant was successful.[3] One might ask why a landlord would object to non-occupation, provided that the rent was still being paid. In the above case the reason was that the hotel was losing goodwill while it was closed and was likely to suffer damage by being left unheated during the winter.

In *Blair Trust Co v Gilbert*[4] the tenant of a farm was sent to prison for three years for culpable homicide. It was held that his resulting non-occupation of the property was a material breach of contract which entitled the landlord to rescind the contract. In that particular case, the obligation was actually written into the lease which, as we will see below, is quite common with this obligation.

We can see from the above cases that the tenant may be liable in damages for loss caused by the failure to occupy,[5] and that if there is a prolonged absence the landlord may be able to rescind the contract. However, it may be that the landlord does not want to end the lease, perhaps because it may prove difficult to find another tenant. At common law, the tenant can be compelled to occupy the property, but not to carry on business there.

In *Whitelaw v Fulton*[6] a tenant entered into the lease of a shop and then wanted to resile because he was unhappy with the condition of the property. It was held that he was not entitled to resile, but was obliged to continue in possession by furnishing the shop, in order to provide security for the rent.[7] He was also required to keep fires in it and air it, in order to prevent damage and deterioration. The court, however, could find no authority that would oblige the tenant to open the shop and carry on business there.

In modern times this has become an important issue in relation to the enforcement of so-called 'keep-open' obligations. This important topic will be considered in depth in the next chapter.[8]

---

1 Rankine p 338; Paton and Cameron p 135.
2 (1792) Hume 781.
3 The short report of the case does not make clear why the incoming tenant was able to sue given he was not a party to the lease.
4 1940 SLT 322, 1941 SN 2.
5 See also *Smith v Henderson* (1897) 24 R 1102, 5 SLT 96; *Mickel v M'Coard* 1913 SC 896, 1913 1 SLT 463.
6 (1871) 10 M 27, 9 SLR 25.
7 See para 3.9.
8 See para 4.7 et seq.

To use the property only for the purpose for which it was let

3.3   A tenant who uses the property for a purpose other than the purpose for which it was let is said to invert the possession. Rankine's explanation usefully sets the scene:

> 'Ordinary leases are granted with a view to a particular sort of possession, and to that only – the lease of a farm for agriculture or pasture; of a garden for horticulture; of a dwellinghouse for residence; of a mill for manufacture; of a shop for trading, and so forth. If the tenant trespasses beyond the limits thus generally, or by special covenant more particularly, laid down for his guidance, he is said to invert the possession.'[1]

The common law, therefore, confines the tenant within fairly broad categories of use – dwellinghouse, factory, shop etc -- but the lease contract may (and generally does) restrict the use more narrowly, sometimes to a particular type of business. This is done in a standard clause known as the use (or user) clause.[2]

If a tenant is in breach of this obligation, the landlord may raise an action of interdict to have the unauthorised use stopped. For example, in *Leck v Merryflats Patent Brick Co*[3] a tenant who had been leased a property for making bricks was stopped from using part of it as a private railway unconnected with the brickwork. And in *Bayley v Addison*,[4] the tenant of a meal mill was interdicted from using it as a mill for grinding sawdust. The reason why the change was considered sufficiently material to amount to inversion was that it had made the property uninsurable.

1 Rankine p 236.
2 See para 11.6.
3 (1868) 5 SLR 619.
4 (1901) 8 SLT 379; see also *Duke of Argyle v M'Arthur* (1861) 23 D 1236.

3.4   *Where there have been structural alterations*   Inversion is more serious if the change of use has been accompanied by structural alterations to the property, also without the landlord's consent, and in such a case the tenant can be compelled to reinstate the property.[1] In fact, even if there has been no change of use, a tenant is prohibited from making structural alterations without the landlord's consent, though only if the alterations are material,[2] and not trivial or temporary.[3] Modern leases generally contain an express provision prohibiting the tenant from carrying out alterations or additions to the leased property without the landlord's prior consent.[4]

1 *Leck v Fulton and Thomson* (1854) 17 D 408.

2 *Muir v Wilson* (1822) 1 S 444; *British Linen Co v Purdie* (1905) 7 F 923, 13 SLT 243.
3 *Morrison v Forsyth* 1909 SC 329, 16 SLT 343.
4 See para 11.10.

3.5 *Acquiescence* A landlord may be barred by acquiescence from objecting to the tenant's inversion of the possession. In *Moore v Munro*[1] the tenant was let a shop 'for carrying on the business of a grocer and provision merchant'. He divided the property, occupying part of it as a dwellinghouse, and the premises were entered in the Valuation Roll for three years running, under the description of 'House and Shop'. It was held that the landlord had acquiesced in the change of use and he failed in his action of interdict to have the residential use stopped.

1 (1896) 4 SLT 172; see also Rankine pp 238-9.

3.6 *Suicide* In *A and Another v B's Trustees*[1] it was held that a tenant of furnished lodgings in the west end of Glasgow had inverted the possession by committing suicide in the property.

1 (1906) 13 SLT 830.

To take reasonable care of the property

3.7 At common law a tenant has an obligation to take reasonable care of the subjects. If the tenant fails in this obligation, the landlord will not be liable for any resulting repairs and the tenant may be liable to the landlord in damages.[1]

In *Mickel v M'Coard*[2], where a tenant left a house empty during the winter without either turning off the water or giving notice to the landlord of her intentions, it was held that she was liable for damage caused by burst pipes.

If the tenant's negligent behaviour is of a continuing nature (for example by using the property in a way that creates a fire hazard) the landlord may obtain an interdict to have the offending practice stopped.[3]

The tenant's duty of care towards the property may not automatically end along with the lease. In *Fry's Metals Ltd v Durastic Ltd*,[4] factory and office premises were broken into and vandalised, after the lease had terminated but before the tenants had returned the keys to the landlords. It was held that the damage was caused by the tenants' negligence in having the alarm systems disconnected prematurely, and they were liable to the landlords in damages.

1 *Hardie v Black* (1760) M 13982; *Smith v Henderson* (1897) 24 R 1102; *Glebe Sugar Refining Co v Paterson* (1900) 2 F. 615; *Mickel v McCoard* 1913 SC 896, 1913 1 SLT 463.

2 1913 SC 896, 1913 1 SLT 463.
3 *Muir v Wilson* (1822) 1 S 406.
4 1991 SLT 689.

To pay the rent when it becomes due

3.8   Although implied, the obligation to pay the rent when it becomes due is also invariably written into the lease. If a rent is not stated, the onus will be on the tenant to prove that no payment of rent was intended, or alternatively be obliged to pay what the property is worth.[1]

Invariably the lease will also state the date when the rent is due; this is called the conventional term (ie the term of payment which the parties have agreed to). It is common for leases to state that rent will be payable in advance, either monthly or quarterly. In the rare event of no conventional term of payment being stipulated in the lease, a term of payment will be implied (the legal term). This varies according to the type of lease involved and the relevant common law rules are somewhat complex.[2]

1 *Glen v Roy* (1882) 10 R 239, 20 SLR 165; though where no rent is payable there is doubt as to whether a lease actually exists – see para 2.27–2.28 and 2.62 et seq.
2 See Rankine p 341 et seq; Paton and Cameron pp 139–141.

To plenish the subjects

3.9   The tenant is obliged to stock the subjects of let with sufficient moveable property to provide security for the rent.[1] This relates to the right of hypothec, which formerly gave the landlord the right to sell moveable property on the subjects of let in order to recover the rent.[2] The landlord could enforce this obligation by applying to the court for a plenishing order; this was a precautionary measure, which could be taken irrespective of whether or not the tenant was actually in rent arrears.

There is some authority for the principle that the obligation may only apply in situations where, in the ordinary state of things, the tenant would be expected to provide plenishing. In *Gardner v Andersons*[3] where premises had been let to be used for the business of auctioneers and valuators, and had already been fitted up by the landlords for that purpose, it was held that the tenants were not obliged to provide further plenishing.

It is believed that the obligation to plenish still exists, though there is now some doubt as to its exact scope as a result of legislation that has drastically restricted the landlord's right of hypothec.[4]

The common law obligation to plenish does not apply to agricultural or to residential subjects, as they are no longer subject to the right of hypothec.[5]

1 Rankine pp 399–401; Paton and Cameron pp 212–213.
2 See para 6.1 et seq.
3 (1889) 6 Sh Ct Rep 57.
4 See para 6.3 et seq.
5 Bankruptcy and Diligence etc (Scotland) Act 2007 s 208(3).

LANDLORD'S OBLIGATIONS

To place the tenant in full possession of the subject's let[1]

3.10   The tenant must not only be given possession of the leased property, but possession of all of the leased property. The landlord, therefore, will have no right to retain any part of the leased property, or any rights over it, unless this has been expressly provided for;[2] however, the landlord of a furnished house may, within reason, keep some personal effects in locked drawers, cupboards etc.[3]

Possession must also be given at the agreed date of entry and not later. If, therefore, there is someone else already in occupation, eg a prior tenant, it is up to the landlord to have the occupant removed in good time. If the landlord fails in this obligation to a material extent, the tenant may be able to rescind, or if not be entitled to damages or an abatement of rent.[4] Delays of 20 and 35 days in giving entry have been held to be sufficiently material to allow rescission by the tenant.[5]

1 Rankine p 200 et seq; Paton and Cameron pp 127–130.
2 *Baxter v Paterson* (1843) 5 D 1074.
3 *Miller v Wilson* 1919 1 SLT 223.
4 *Tennent's Trs v Maxwell* (1880) 17 SLR 463.
5 Rankine p 201.

Not to derogate from the grant

3.11   This is a corollary of (1). Once in the property, the tenant has the right to be maintained in possession, and the landlord must not do anything that would deprive, or partially deprive the tenant of possession. This is known as the landlord's obligation not to derogate from the grant.

This subject merits more extensive discussion than other obligations of the parties, and is dealt with in more detail below.[1]

1 See para 3.14 et seq.

To provide subjects that are reasonably fit for the purpose for which they are let[1]

3.12 This obligation and the obligation to carry out repairs should really be considered together, as the second is the corollary of the first. In relation to urban subjects, ie where the main subject of let is a building or buildings,[2] the landlord must provide subjects that are in a tenantable or habitable condition (or, to express it in another way, which are reasonably fit for the purpose of the let) .

This obligation and the obligation to carry out repairs are considered in some depth in a later section.[3] It should also be remembered that, in the case of agricultural and residential tenancies, there are a number of statutory provisions relating to repairs.[4]

1 Erskine *Principles of the Law of Scotland* (21st edn, ed Rankine), II, 17; see also Erskine An Institute of the Law of Scotland (8th edn ed Nicolson) II, 43, Bell Principles 1274, Rankine p 241 and Paton and Cameron p 130.
2 For the distinction between urban and rural leases, see para 1.12.
3 See para 3.26 et seq.
4 See Chs 15 and 19.

To carry out repairs

3.13 This important topic is also given a separate section below.[1]

1 See para 3.40 et seq.

DEROGATION FROM THE GRANT

Nature of obligation

3.14 As stated above,[1] this obligation follows on from the obligation to give the tenant full possession of the leased subjects. The landlord thereafter has an implied obligation not to encroach upon that possession.

Rankine defines the obligation as follows:[2]

'The general rule is that, possession once taken, the landlord shall do nothing, and, so far as in him lies, allow nothing to be done to oust the tenant from the subject let or any material part of it during the lease.'

This later came to be expressed as an obligation of the landlord not to derogate from the grant.[3] The tenant's legal remedies are damages in the form of an abatement in rent or, in extreme cases, rescission.[4]

1 See para 3.11.
2 Rankine p 213.
3 Although this passage from Rankine is the one most generally accepted as the source of the non-derogation principle as it affects leases (see, eg, Paton and Cameron p 128), the word 'derogation' is not actually used by Rankine here. The non-derogation principle applies within the law of contract generally, including leases, and is in fact much more complex – see Angus McAllister 'Leasing to a Tenant's Business Competitor: Is the Landlord in Derogation of his Grant' (2004) 2 Jur Rev 133.
4 Rankine p 217; see also para 4.29 et seq.

Huber v Ross

3.15   The issue has generally arisen in situations where the landlord has retained the ownership of property adjoining or near to the subjects let, and has done something with that property which affects the leased subjects.

In *Huber v Ross*[1] the top flat of a property was let to a tenant for the purposes of a photographic business. During the tenancy the landlord, who also owned the rest of the building, carried out alterations in the lower flats involving extensive building operations, which caused structural and other damage to the leased property and interference with and detriment to the tenant's business.

It was held that the landlord was not only bound to repair the structural damage caused to the leased property, but was also liable in damages for injury done to the tenant's furniture and materials, as well as to the tenant's business during the landlord's building operations and during the work of restoration. A useful formulation of the ratio was given in Lord Mackenzie's judgment:[2]

> 'The principle applicable is that, where a lease is granted for a special purpose which is known to the lessor, there is an implied obligation upon him not to do anything voluntarily to prevent the subject let from being used for the purpose for which it was let. This is the principle ... – that a granter cannot derogate from his grant. There is an implied warrandice to this effect in a lease in Scotland.'

1 1912 SC 898, 1912 1 SLT 399; see also *Lomond Roads Cycling Club v Dunbarton County Council* 1967 SLT (Sh Ct) 35 and *Golden Sea Produce Ltd v Scottish Nuclear plc* 1992 SLT 942; see also *Style Menswear Ltd, Petitioners* 2008 Hous LR 66, 2008 GWD 36-538, which applied *Huber*, although derogation from the grant was not actually plead.
2 *Huber v Ross* 1912 SC 898, at 918 per Lord Mackenzie.

3.16   Several important issues arise from this decision:

(a)   It was pointed out that the English principle that a landlord should not derogate from the grant is similar to that in Scotland, but that there are also important differences. One of these is an implied covenant of quiet enjoyment, owed by landlords in England but not in Scotland. The implied warrandice granted by Scottish landlords is analogous but not identical.

(b)   As a result, there does not appear to be a distinction in England between acts which the landlord does upon the property retained which have a physical effect upon the leased property and acts which have no such physical effect. In Scotland, however, the thing the landlord does must have some sort of physical effect upon the leased subjects.[1] Because of this the damages awarded in *Huber* in respect of injury to the tenant's business were confined to physical and tangible injury, such as from vibration and dust.

(c)   There was no evidence that the landlord had carried out the operations without due care and skill. Also, it was pointed out several times in the course of the judgment that there is a distinction between the situation where damage to property is caused by a neighbouring proprietor who is not the landlord and where it is caused by one who is. Although the point was not made explicitly, the distinction would appear to lie in the fact that for a landlord to be in derogation of the grant there is no need to prove negligence, since the action is based on an implied term of the contract.

1 *Huber v Ross* 1912 SC 898, at 910–911 per the Lord President. It has been argued that this distinction was based upon a misinterpretation of the English position and that the Scottish and English principles against derogation are in fact more similar – see Angus McAllister 'Leasing to a Tenant's Business Competitor: Is the Landlord in Derogation of his Grant' (2004) 2 Jur Rev 133. However, *Huber* remains the main authority on this issue and it has been followed in all subsequent cases.

Landlord's behaviour must be deliberate

3.17   On the other hand, even though it may not be necessary to prove that the landlord has been negligent, it has been held that only deliberate or voluntary behaviour by the landlord can amount to derogation. As a result, a landlord who has not been negligent will not be liable for omissions,[1] nor where the damage has been caused by the negligence of others outwith the landlord's control.[2]

1 *Golden Casket (Greenock) Ltd v BRS (Pickfords) Ltd* 1972 SLT 146 at 149 per Lord Dunpark.
2 *Chevron Petroleum (UK) Ltd v Post Office* 1986 SC 291, 1987 SLT 588.

Abatement of rent

3.18   The decisions in the cases cited above related to claims of damages and can be justified on the basis that, without either negligence or some kind of voluntary conduct by the landlord, there can be no claim for damages either under delict or breach of contract.[1]

There is authority for the view, however, that the tenant may nevertheless be entitled to an abatement of rent, not on the basis of delict or breach of contract, but on the basis of partial eviction, having been deprived of part of the subjects for which rent is being paid.[2] We will see later that total eviction from the leased subjects, caused either by damnum fatale or the actions of a third party, amounts to frustration of the lease and entitles the tenant to total relief from rent, as the contract has been brought to an end;[3] on this basis, partial eviction ought to entitle the tenant to partial relief. However, the authority for this view is sparse and not entirely consistent.[4]

1 Or, less obviously, a right by the tenant to retain rent, retention being a breach of contract remedy – see *Owlcastle Ltd v Karmik Ltd* 1993 GWD 33-2157; for the distinction between retention and abatement.
2 See eg *Deans v Abercromby* (1681) M 10122. Rankine takes a contrary view (see Rankine pp 221–222), one which, in turn, has been criticised as mistaken – see *Lusk v Todd* (1897) 13 Sh Ct Rep 265. The argument that the tenant may be entitled to an abatement is also consistent with the view that derogation and partial eviction (or encroachment), though they tend to be coupled together, are in fact separate principles – see Angus McAllister 'Leasing to a Tenant's Business Competitor: Is the Landlord in Derogation of his Grant' (2004) 2 Jur Rev 133.
3 See para 10.6 et seq.
4 See para 3.45 and also Angus McAllister 'The Landlord's Common Law Repairing Obligation' 2012 Jur Rev 263 at 274–76.

Lease to tenant in similar business: English authority[1]

3.19   We saw in the last chapter[2] that disputes often arise between landlord and tenant, particularly in shopping centres, if the landlord creates competition for a tenant by leasing nearby premises to someone in a similar line of business. There have been a number of attempts in England to establish that by such action a landlord is in derogation of the grant, though for many years it appeared to be settled authority that this is not the case.[3]

More recently, however, the English courts seem to have amended their position slightly. In *Oceanic Village Ltd v Shirayama Shokusan Co Ltd*[4] the tenants ran the gift shop at the London Aquarium. They brought an action against their landlords, who proposed to erect two kiosks on a walkway and sell items, including aquarium-related goods, which were usually found in gift shops.

The terms of the lease gave the tenants a gift-shop monopoly within the aquarium building. Unfortunately, the proposed kiosks did not fall within this express exclusivity because the walkway where they were to be situated was on the roof of the aquarium building and outwith the building as defined in the lease. However, the existence of the express provision contributed to circumstances which created an implied exclusivity that applied to the kiosks, though only in relation to aquarium-related goods. The landlords were therefore in derogation of their grant.

Deputy Judge Warren agreed, however, that there was no general principle forbidding a landlord from leasing to a tenant's rival, in particular that no term could be implied where there was only economic detriment to the tenant.

1 For a discussion in depth of this issue see Angus McAllister 'Leasing to a Tenant's Business Competitor: Is the Landlord in Derogation of His Grant' (2004) 2 Jur Rev 133; see also Joanna Sykes 'Taken for Granted' (2009) 159 NLJ 29 and Mark Pawlowski 'Question and Answer' (May/June) (2009) 13 L&T Review 111.

2 See para 2.43 et seq.

3 See eg *Port v Griffith* [1938] 1 All ER 295; *Romulus Trading Co Ltd v Comet Properties* [1996] 48 EG 157, [1996] NPC 52.

4 ([2001] L & TR 35, 7 EGCS 162; see also *Petra Investments Ltd v Jeffrey Rogers plc* [2000] L & TR 451, (2001) 81 P & CR 267 at 285 and 287 per Hart J, where it is suggested that the approach taken in *Port v Griffith* and *Romulus Trading* requires some qualification.

Scottish authority

3.20 The Scottish authority on this issue extends back over several centuries, and for most of the 19th century one old case was accepted as the main precedent.

In *Campbell v Watt*[1] the tenant, Mrs Watt, was granted a lease in terms of which she was to erect an inn that was to serve as a halfway house on the road between Glasgow and Greenock. The only local rival establishment selling liquor was a smithy, the lease of which was to be terminated, and Mrs Watt's lease contained a condition binding the landlord that 'in any set of a smithy to be erected by him, he shall take the tenant bound not to sell liquor of any kind to the prejudice of Mrs Watt.'[2] Several years later, the line of the Glasgow/Greenock road was altered, bypassing Mrs Watt's inn by about a mile, and Campbell, the landlord's singular successor, erected a rival inn at an appropriate part of the new road.

It was held that Mrs Watt might have obtained an interdict against the building of the new inn had she applied in time but, in any case, was entitled to an abatement of rent as it was considered to be 'in the *bona fides* of the transaction that the landlord should not set up a rival inn to the prejudice of his own tenant in the old one'.[3]

It should be noted that the lease in fact contained an express exclusivity provision, except that it only referred to a smithy that might sell alcohol and not to a rival inn.

1 (1795) Hume 788; see also para 2.44.
2 (1795) Hume 788 at 789.
3 (1795) Hume 788 at 790.

3.21   *Craig v Millar*   However, in *Craig v Millar*[1] a full court of 9 Inner House judges was assembled precisely in order to bypass the precedent set in *Campbell v Watt*; significantly, however, it did not actually overrule the earlier case, but merely distinguished it.

Premises in a densely populated part of Glasgow, which were used as a lodging house, were leased for a period of 7 years. (They consisted of 3 flats containing 300 beds!). Four years later, encouraged by the success of the tenant's business, the landlord converted nearby premises belonging to him, fitting them up with 512 beds, and leased them to a man named Robert Burns.

The tenant alleged that, as a result, his formerly profitable business was now making a substantial loss. He claimed that, by his violation of good faith, the landlord was in breach of an implied term of the contract. Derogation from the grant was not mentioned – the term was not commonly used in relation to leases at that time – but Rankine includes the case among those where the tenant has been partially deprived of possession.[2] And, as we saw above,[3] this is the principle that later came to be known as derogation from the grant.

It was held by a full court of the Inner House (with one dissension) that the landlord owed no implied obligation of the sort alleged, and that any undertaking of that kind would require to be expressly included in the contract:

> 'In my opinion, such a restriction on the use of property is not to be presumed or implied: restrictions on the use of property can only be imposed by law or paction. There is certainly no paction by which the alleged restriction on the pursuer's use of his property has been imposed. Nor is there any general rule of law which prevents a proprietor letting two different properties to different tenants for the same kind of business or occupation in the same town or the same street.'[4]

1 (1888) 15 R 1005, 25 SLR 715.
2 Rankine p 219.
3 See para 3.11.
4 *Craig v Millar* (1888) 15 R 1005 at 1028 per Lord Trayner.

3.22   *Miller v Clerical Medical*   In *Miller v Clerical Medical Investment Group Ltd*[1] the pursuer was the tenant of a shop in the Princes Square centre in Glasgow. In December 2000 the landlords granted a right of occupation of a kiosk in the entrance hallway for the sale of jewellery and other goods similar to those sold by the pursuer. It was held, applying *Craig v Millar,* that the landlords were not in derogation of their grant:

> 'It is clear from that decision that the granting of a lease to one tenant for the purposes of a particular business does not in itself restrain the landlord from letting his other remaining property to others for a business which may be in competition with that of the tenant. In order to advance the existence of such a restraint there must be found in the lease either an express undertaking by the landlord to that effect *or distinct provision from which it may clearly be implied that such an undertaking is given.*'[2]

1   2001 SCLR 990, 2001 GWD 25-973.
2   *Miller v Clerical Medical Investment Group Ltd* 2001 SCLR 990 at 995 per Lord Eassie (author's italics).

3.23   An implication of this kind was made in *Geoffrey (Tailor) Highland Crafts Ltd v GL Attractions Ltd.*[1] A small area within the leased premises was reserved to the landlords for use as an administrative office. An interdict was granted to prevent the landlords from using this office for the purpose of trading in competition with the tenants, such a restriction being implied from the terms of the reservation in the lease and from the surrounding facts.

1   2010 GWD 8-142.

Conclusion

3.24   A superficial reading of the authority would suggest that, in Scotland at least, and in the absence of an exclusivity agreement, there is no barrier preventing a commercial landlord from leasing nearby premises to a tenant's competitor or himself competing with the tenant. However, a closer examination suggests a more complex situation.

It should be noted that, despite being separated by more than two centuries and by the English border, there is a striking resemblance between the cases of *Campbell v Watt*[1] and *Oceanic Village Ltd v Shirayama Shokusan Co Ltd*:[2]

(a)   In both cases an express exclusivity in the lease was widened in scope by implication: in *Campbell* a prohibition against letting to a smithy for the sale of liquor was extended to other types of establishment and in *Oceanic Village* a monopoly within the aquarium was extended to cover kiosks just outside it. The decision in *Geoffrey (Tailor) Highland Crafts* is consistent with this; and

(b)   In both cases, business rivals were thin on the ground, in *Campbell* because the property was situated in a sparsely populated area and in *Oceanic Village* because the business in question was a comparatively rare one. This contrasts sharply with the situation, for example, in *Craig v Millar* which related to a very common type of business in the centre of a densely populated city, a distinction in fact noted by the court in that case.[3] Within the context of the law of contract generally, the courts are more inclined to look favourably upon restraints of trade in the former situation rather than the latter one.[4]

1   (1795) Hume 788.
2   [2001] L&TR 35, 7 EGCS 162.
3   See *Craig v Millar* (1888) 15 R 1005, at 1017 per the Lord Justice Clerk.
4   See eg *Stewart v Stewart* (1899) 1 F 1158, (1899) 7 SLT 52 (sparsity of population) and *Nordenfelt v Maxim Nordenfelt Guns and Ammunition Co Ltd* [1894] AC 535 (unusual business).

3.25   We can therefore move towards a more precise statement of the law in both Scotland and England:

(a)   There can be no generally implied prohibition against a commercial landlord leasing a nearby property to a tenant's business rival or to the landlord competing with the tenant. Each case must be decided according to its own circumstances; and

(b)   The courts are more likely to imply such a prohibition in circumstances where it is sought to extend the scope of an express exclusivity in the lease and/or business rivals of the tenant are thin on the ground.

This is consistent with most of the Scottish authority, including *Craig v Millar* and *Miller v Clerical Medical.*[1]

Unfortunately, however, as long as this principle is based on the landlord's obligation not to derogate from the grant (as opposed to some other principle, such as the *bona fides* of the transaction), and this seems to be the common approach in both countries, Scottish tenants are likely to be defeated by the decision in *Huber v Ross* restricting derogation to physical encroachment. *Huber v Ross* remains the leading authority on derogation, despite any suspicion that its reasoning may be flawed.[2]

It therefore remains advisable for Scottish tenants to seek an express exclusivity undertaking from the landlord. Unfortunately, as we saw in the last chapter, even if such a provision is contained in the lease document, it may be difficult to bind the landlord's singular successors.[3]

1 See the italicised passage in the quote from the latter judgment at para 3.22.
2 See para 3.16.
3 See para 2.43 et seq.

CONDITION OF THE PROPERTY: THE LANDLORD'S INITIAL OBLIGATION

Nature of obligation

3.26   We saw above that the landlord's initial obligation is to provide subjects that are reasonably fit for the purpose of the let, also expressed as an obligation to provide subjects that are in a tenantable or habitable condition.[1]

This does not mean that the property needs to be fit for a particular kind of business. For example, in *Glebe Sugar Refining Co v Paterson*[2] a warehouse was let to a sugar refining company which used it to store sugar. A month after they took entry the warehouse collapsed, and the tenants sued the landlords claiming that, because of insecure foundations, the building was unsuitable for the purpose of the let. It was held that, within the practice in their own trade, the tenants had overloaded the warehouse. They had therefore failed to ascertain for themselves the suitability of the subjects for their business, and *they* were held liable to the *landlords* in damages. It was in fact a case of the tenants failing in their implied obligation to take reasonable care of the property.[3]

1 See para 3.12. For a general discussion of both the initial and continuing obligations, as well as some related issues, see Angus McAllister 'The Landlord's Common Law Repairing Obligation' 2012 Jur Rev 263.
2 (1900) 2 F 615, 7 SLT 374.
3 See para 3.7.

3.27   *Remedies* If the condition of the property makes it substantially unsuitable, this will be a material breach of contract entitling the tenant to rescind. A rather graphic illustration of such a material breach is provided by *Kippen v Oppenheim*,[1] where a tenant was held to be entitled to refuse to take entry to a house and to rescind the lease on finding that it was:

'overrun and infested to a great extent, and in every part, with vermin, commonly called black beetles, clocks or cockroaches; that it was also infested with bugs; that there was also a nauseous and offensive smell in the house, and particularly in the dining-room, occasioned either by the presence of said vermin, or by some other occult cause, and that one of the bed-rooms was so damp that it could not be safely used to sleep in'.

A lesser breach may entitle the tenant to damages or to retain the rent.[2]

1 (1847) 10 D 242; see also *Brodie v Maclachlan* (1900) 8 SLT 145.
2 Rankine p 244.

3.28 *Rural leases* The landlord's initial obligation also applies to rural leases, but in practice it will only be of relevance where part of the subjects of let consists of buildings or other artificial structures.[1] Moreover, in *Paton v MacDonald*,[2] where land was leased for various motor sport activities, it was held that the landlord was only obliged to provide subjects for purposes that would be familiar to landlords in his position, and not necessarily for the specialist purposes of the tenant. This decision is consistent with the one in *Glebe Sugar Refining Co v Paterson*[3] considered above,[4] where it was held to be up to the tenants to satisfy themselves as to whether the subjects were suitable for a particular type of business.

In many rural leases, the repairing obligations of the parties will be governed by the legislation relating to agricultural leases.[5]

1 See Paton and Cameron p 130 and 134–135.
2 1973 SLT (Sh Ct) 85.
3 (1900) 2 F 615, 7 SLT 374.
4 See para 3.26.
5 See chs 15 and 16.

Meaning of 'tenantable or habitable'

3.29 This relates both to the landlord's initial obligation and also to the continuing obligation to carry out repairs which is discussed below. The expression 'tenantable or habitable' contains several distinct elements. The main ones are:

(1) The property should be wind and watertight;
(2) It should be free from damp;
(3) It should be in a safe condition.

To these there may be added freedom from vermin[1] and adequate drainage and water supply.[2] The case law on these latter two elements tends to be rather old, no doubt due to modern public health measures such as environmental health services and publicly maintained drainage, but they can sometimes be relevant.[3]

1 *Kippen v Oppenheim* (1847) 10 D 242 (see para 3.27); for decisions relating to the presence of rats, see *Anderson v Watson* (1894) 2 SLT 293; *Dunn v Stewart* (1896) 12 Sh Ct Rep 290; *Ward v Magistrates and Town Council of Glasgow* (1888) 4 Sh Ct Rep 19 & 292; *St. George Co-operative Society v Stewart* (1893) 9 Sh Ct Rep 86; and *Ovens v Hunter* (1917) 33 Sh. Ct. Rep. 213. The rather inconsistent line taken by these decisions suggests that the presence of rats was less conclusive proof of a house being uninhabitable than it might be today. Nowadays it is also likely to be considered a statutory nuisance – see para 19.44 para 19.41 et seq.

2 See eg *Tennent's Trustees v Maxwell* (1880) 17 SLR 463; *Brodie v MacLachlan* (1900) 8 SLT 145; *North British and Storage Transit Co v Steele's Trustees* 1920 SC 194; and more recently; *Royal Yacht Club v Granton Central Developments Ltd* 2020 SLT (Sh Ct) 77; some of the authority relating to illness caused by bad drainage will be considered below under safety.

3 As the recent decision of *Royal Yacht Club v Granton Central Developments Ltd* 2020 SLT (Sh Ct) 77 demonstrates.

3.30 *Wind and watertight* The landlord has a duty to keep the premises wind and water tight so as to be proof against the ordinary attacks of the elements.[1] However, this does not include liability for exceptional encroachments of water from other causes.

1 *Wolfson v Forrester* 1910 SC 675, 1910 1 SLT 318.

3.31 *Damp* It has long been established that the landlord's obligation can include the rectification of dampness,[1] despite at least one maverick decision to the contrary.[2] This can be either rising damp or (as in a number of modern cases) dampness due to condensation. In *Gunn v National Coal Board*,[3] where rising damp had caused dampness and mould in the house concerned, the tenant was held to be entitled to damages.

Moreover, the landlord's obligation will not be met if a house suffering from coldness and damp can only be rendered habitable by the application of excessive heating.[4] As Sheriff Kearney expressed it in *McCarthy v Glasgow District Council:*[5]

'[The] meaning of "habitable" must be related to the realities of life: for example a house that was uninhabitable by reason of being excessively cold or damp could not be said to be habitable simply because by applying a large amount of heat to the premises (and thereby incurring inordinate heating bills) it might be rendered habitable provided this unusual amount of heating were kept up. It has long been recognised ... that the landlord must take account of the realities of the situation ... '

If it can be proved that the building suffers from the type of defect that would be likely to cause such a problem, eg where it is inadequately insulated against the occurrence of condensation, there is a prima facie breach of the landlord's common law duty and the onus of proof will be upon the landlord to show that it was caused, or partly caused, by the tenant's failure to heat the property adequately.[6] This prima facie inference can be rebutted by 'evidence that the [tenant's] lifestyle was outside the spectrum of those which the [landlords] could reasonably have expected their tenants to follow'.[7]

In other words, if the level of heating applied by the tenant is so low that it is below what even the poorest tenant could afford, then a plea by the landlord of sole fault or contributory negligence may be possible, but otherwise the *prima facie* case against the landlord will be difficult to rebut. The test is an objective, not a subjective one. The fact that a particular tenant may be rich enough to afford excessive heating will not mean that the house is habitable.[8]

1 *Kippen v Oppenheim* (1847) 10 D 242; *McKimmie's Trs v Armour* (1899) 2F 156, (1899) 7 SLT 246.

2 *McGonigal v Pickard* 1954 SLT (Notes) 62.

3 1982 SLT 526; see also *McArdle v City of Glasgow District Council* 1989 SCLR 19.

4 See the stricter line taken on this issue in *Anderson v Dundee City Council* 2000 SLT (Sh Ct) 134; 1999 SCLR 518 and *Robb v Dundee City Council* 2001 SC 301; 2002 SLT 853 regarding statutory nuisance, discussed in para 19.45.

5 1996 Hous LR 81 at 86 per Sheriff Kearney (1988) SCOLAG 121; see also *Fyfe v Scottish Homes* 1995 SCLR 209; *Quinn v Monklands District Council* 1995 SCLR 393, 1996 Hous LR 86 and *Buchan v North Lanarkshire Council* 2000 Hous LR 98, 2000 GWD 21-835. The *Fyfe* case report includes a substantial commentary by Derek O'Carroll containing a review of the authority on this subject.

6 *Gunn v City of Glasgow District Council* 1992 SCLR 1018, 1997 Hous LR 3.

7 *Gunn v City of Glasgow District Council* 1992 SCLR 1018 at 1019 per Lord Morison applying an *obiter* statement by Lord Justice Dillon in the English case of *Quick v Taff-Ely Borough Council* [1985] 3 All E.R. 321 at 327; see also *McGuire v Monklands District Council* 1997 Hous LR 41 and *Buchan v North Lanarkshire Council* 2000 Hous LR 98.

8 *Quick v Taff-Ely Borough Council* [1985] 3 All ER 321 at 327.

3.32   *Safety* The landlord's common law duty includes a requirement to carry out the repairs necessary to rectify any danger that might cause the tenant injury or illness. There have been a number of cases, from Victorian times onwards, in which injuries were sustained as a result of such things as worn stairs, loose handrails on stairs or landings, or falling ceilings. A number of examples are given below;[1] they exhibit a common pattern of house tenants complaining to their landlords and receiving (generally unfulfilled) promises of action, the averments in *McKinlay v McClymont*[2] being perhaps typical:

'The said James McClymont, notwithstanding that he saw the condition of the ceiling and indicated that the matter would be attended to, walked out muttering that what he wanted was rent.'

In the 19th century there were also a large number of cases where the landlord was alleged to be in breach of the common law obligation because defective or inadequate drainage had led to the illness of the tenant or of the tenant's family.[3]

1 See paras 3.48–3.49.
2 (1905) 13 SLT 427, (1905) 43 SLR 9.
3 See eg *Scottish Heritable Security Co Ltd v Grainger* (1881) 8 R 459; *McNee v Brownlie's Trustees* (1889) 26 SLR 590; *Maitland v Allan* (1896) 4 SLT 121.

3.33 *Extent of liability* The House of Lords has held that a landlord is only liable for injury to the tenant and not to members of the tenant's family or other parties who enter the property.[1] However, although a claim under breach of contract may be restricted to the actual tenant, it is now thought that others will not be precluded from having a delictual claim, either under the general law of negligence or under the Occupier's Liability (Scotland) Act 1960. This is discussed in more depth later in relation to the landlord's repairing obligations in residential tenancies.[2]

1 *Cameron v Young* [1908] AC 176, 1908 SC(HL) 7.
2 See para 19.35 et seq.

Scope of initial obligation

3.34 We will see below that there is ample authority to the effect that the landlord's continuing obligation to carry out repairs is not a warranty and only arises when the landlord has been notified of the need for a repair.[1] However, it does not follow from this that the landlord's initial obligation *is* a warranty, nor is it clear what is meant by that term in the present context.[2] Rather than be diverted by discussions of terminology, it will be more useful to focus upon precisely what the authority on this issue tells us that the initial obligation commits the landlord to.[3]

1 See, for example, Rankine pp 241–242, quoting *Wolfson v Forrester* 1910 SC 675, 1910 1 SLT 318.
2 The initial obligation has been variously described as 'warrandice' (Bell *Principles* 1253; Rankine pp 240–241; Paton and Cameron p 130) 'a warranty' (*Brodie v Maclachlan* (1900) 8 SLT 145; *Mars Pension Trustees Ltd v County Properties & Developments Ltd* 1999 SC 267 at 268 and as an 'absolute obligation to warrant' (*McCarthy v Glasgow District Council* 1996 Hous LR 81 at 84). For an explanation of the distinction between 'warranties' and 'warrandice', which are not the same thing, see MacQueen and Thomson 4.60. Also, as Professor McBryde has pointed out, the word 'warranty', unlike the case in England, is not a term of art in Scotland – see McBryde 20-93.

3 Reference should also be made to *John Menzies v Ravenseft Properties Ltd* 1987 SLT 64 per Lord Wylie at 66 where it was suggested (arguably obiter) that neither the landlord's initial obligation nor the continuing obligations are warranties. It is submitted that this view was based upon a misinterpretation of the common law, particularly as laid down in *Wolfson v Forrester*. See the discussion of *Wolfson* in Angus McAllister 'The Landlord's Common Law Repairing Obligation' 2012 Jur Rev 263 at 266.

Duty of inspection

3.35   It is clearly established that a landlord has a duty, prior to entry, to inspect the subjects in order to ensure that they are in a tenantable or habitable condition.[1] This obligation is given statutory form in the case of residential leases.[2] Lack of notification by the tenant will not therefore absolve the landlord from liability for any defect which such an inspection ought to have revealed. A survey which is merely for the purpose of valuing the property may not be enough to satisfy this obligation.[3]

1 *Lamb v Glasgow District Council* 1978 SLT (Notes) 64; *Mearns v Glasgow City Council* 2002 SLT (Sh Ct) 49, 2001 Hous LR 130.
2 See para 19.20.
3 *Todd v Clapperton* 2009 SLT 837, 2009 Hous LR 48.

Latent defects

3.36   The situation is more problematic in relation to defects in the property, eg of design or construction, which were present at entry but only emerge later during the currency of the lease, and which could not reasonably have been revealed by the landlord's initial inspection. Once the landlord has been notified of such a defect (by which time, of course, it will no longer be latent) there is little doubt that under the continuing obligation the landlord will be obliged to repair the damage and will be responsible for any loss to the tenant caused by failing to do so timeously.[1]

However, there can be situations where the actual emergence of the defect causes the tenant loss or injury, eg where a ceiling falls without warning. Can the landlord be liable to the tenant in damages if a thorough inspection of the property was carried out before entry and failed to reveal the fault?

Rankine only mentions latent defects in passing, when discussing a landlord's liability for extraordinary repairs, and does not address the situation where no notification has occurred.[2] However, in several sheriff court cases in the late 19th and early 20th centuries it was held that a landlord was not automatically liable in damages to a tenant for a latent defect in such a situation.[3]

1 See para 3.41.
2 Rankine p 247, quoting an obiter comment of Lord Kinnear in *Turner's Trustees v Steel* (1900) 2 F 363 at 368, when also discussing extraordinary repairs.
3 *Harbison v Robb* (1878) 1 *Guthrie's Select Cases* 287, where the issue was discussed in some depth by Sheriff Guthrie drawing, in the absence of other authority, upon the Roman law of sale, the institutional writers and the law of sale of goods. This decision was followed, inter alia, in *McGlynn v Glasgow District Subway Company* (1901) 17 Sh Ct Rep 95 and *Craig v Hunter* (1918) 34 Sh Ct Rep 10.

3.37   *Mearns v Glasgow City Council*   However, a contrary opinion (also obiter and without reference to any of the authority quoted in the immediately preceding paragraph) was given by Sheriff Principal Bowen in *Mearns v Glasgow City Council*[1] where a defective plumbing repair carried out prior to the tenant's entry resulted in a burst pipe 15 years later. It was held that the landlord was liable under the initial obligation, as the defect should have been revealed by an inspection prior to entry. However, Sheriff Principal Bowen went on to say:

'Equally, if the defect falls to be regarded as latent I am not convinced that there is any more injustice in imposing responsibility for it on the landlord than there would be in making the tenant liable for the consequences.'[2]

1 2002 SLT (Sh Ct) 49, 2001 Hous LR 130.
2 *Mearns v Glasgow City Council* 2002 SLT (Sh Ct) 49, at 52 per Sheriff Principal Bowen.

3.38   *Todd v Clapperton*   This issue emerged again in *Todd v Clapperton*[1] where a tenant claimed damages for injuries to his hand caused by the breaking of a glass panel in an internal door which he was attempting to prevent from closing. The claim failed because the judge was not satisfied that the tenant had proved his version of the facts and that he had not, in fact, applied undue force.

However, Lord Bannatyne nevertheless took the view that the house was not in all respects reasonably fit for human habitation in terms of the Housing (Scotland) Act 1987[2] and that the tenant would have been entitled to damages had he proved his case. He went on to make the following obiter comments on the subject of latent defects:[3]

(1)   The issue should be construed on the same basis as the common law, of which the statutory provision is a re-statement.
(2)   The landlord's initial obligation is a warranty, which is a guarantee, ie an absolute obligation.
(3)   The landlord is therefore liable for latent defects, including any that would not have been discoverable by a reasonable inspection prior to entry.

(4)   Following the view expressed by Sheriff Principal Bowen in *Mearns*, it would be unjust if a landlord's obligation to provide a property that was reasonably fit for human habitation was not absolute.

1 2009 SLT 837, 2009 Hous LR 48; see also the thoughtful discussion of this case and related issues in Adrian Stalker 'Todd v Clapperton: The Evolving Law on Repairing Obligations and Claims against Landlords of Residential Property' 2010 SLT (News) 31.
2 The provision now contained in s 13 of the Housing (Scotland) Act 2006.
3 *Todd v Clapperton* 2009 SLT 837 at 849–50.

3.39   Although this Outer House decision is likely to be persuasive, and the arguments based upon equity are tempting, it is submitted that it should be regarded with some caution for several reasons:

(1)   The opinion on latent defects is obiter, as the tenant did not prove the facts alleged and the case was pleaded on the statutory, not the common law, obligation of the landlord.
(2)   None of the older authority on liability for latent defects was taken into account.
(3)   The designation of the landlord's initial obligation as a 'warranty' is less consistent in the earlier authorities than suggested and, in any case, is not necessarily the same as an absolute obligation.[1]

1 See the discussion of this issue in Angus McAllister 'The Landlord's Common Law Repairing Obligation' 2012 Jur Rev 263 at 270–274.

CONDITION OF THE PROPERTY: THE LANDLORD'S CONTINUING OBLIGATION

Repairing obligation

3.40   As already noted, the obligation to carry out repairs is really the corollary of the obligation to provide lease premises that are tenantable. Having moved into subjects that are reasonably fit for the purpose of the let, the tenant is entitled to stay on in subjects that remain so. The landlord's obligation in urban leases is to uphold the property in a tenantable or habitable condition during the currency of the lease.[1] In contrast to the situation with the initial obligation, there is no continuing obligation on the part of the landlord at common law to carry out repairs in the case of rural leases. These are the responsibility of the tenant, except perhaps in relation to extraordinary repairs.[2]

The property must be made habitable, even if this would require the sort of operation that would normally be considered an improvement rather than a repair.[3]

1 Erskine *Principles of the Law of Scotland* (21st edn, ed Rankine), II, 17; see also Erskine *An Institute of the Law of Scotland* (8th edn ed Nicolson) II, 43, Bell *Principles* 1274, Rankine p 241; Paton and Cameron p 131; for the definition of an urban lease, see para 1.12.
2 Paton and Cameron pp 134–135; *Little Cumbrae Estate Ltd v Island of Little Cumbrae Ltd* 2007 SC 525, 2007 SLT 631. For the distinction between urban and rural leases see para 1.12 and for repairing obligations in agricultural leases, see para 15.17.
3 *Marianski v Jackson* (1872) 9 SLR 80.

Need for notification

3.41 As already indicated, the landlord's continuing obligation to carry out repairs is not a warranty. This means, in effect, that the obligation does not arise until the tenant has drawn the need for the repair to the landlord's attention; there is therefore no breach of contract merely because the repair has become necessary, but only after the landlord has been notified and has failed to act.[1]

In *Hampton v Galloway & Sykes*[2] a landlord was not liable for damage caused to the leased premises by flooding from a blocked discharge pipe, even though the tenant had no access to the pipe and there was no way, prior to the flooding, that he could have known of the defect in order to notify the landlord. It was held that a landlord has no duty to periodically inspect the property to ascertain its condition when there is no reason to suspect that there is a problem.

However, once notified of a need for repairs, the landlord must carry them out within a reasonable time or the tenant will be entitled to rescind the lease.[3] The tenant may also, or alternatively, be entitled to damages.

There is no requirement that the notice should be in writing, and there has been a tendency in the case of residential tenancies for notification to be made orally. Not surprisingly, landlords have been known to deny that notice has been given, and cases have turned upon the competing credibility of the landlord's and the tenant's witnesses. Needless to say, written notice is recommended, in order to avoid such difficulties.

1 *Wolfson v Forrester* 1910 SC 675, (1910) 1 SLT 318.
2 (1899) 1 F 501.
3 *McKimmie's Trs v Armour* (1899) 2F 156; *Scottish Heritable Security Co Ltd v Granger* (1881) 8 R 459, 18 SLR 280.

Constructive notice

3.42   There is a supplementary issue in relation to constructive notice (ie where there has been no actual notification but there is good reason to believe that the landlord ought to have known about the need for repair). Can this also trigger the continuing obligation? In the case of residential tenancies, the statutory repairing obligation, which mirrors the common law obligation in many respects, may arise as a result of constructive notice.[1]

There is some authority that constructive notice is also possible at common law. In *Golden Casket (Greenock) Limited v BRS (Pickfords) Ltd*[2] Lord Dunpark quoted Gloag on *Contract*[3] to the effect that express notice was required, but went on to make the following obiter statement:

> 'Although this proposition is founded on high judicial authority, I think that it may be stated in too absolute terms. There may be cases in which a landlord would be liable for failure to repair a defect of which he had no actual knowledge but of which he ought reasonably to have known before it could have been discovered by the tenant.'[4]

This has been applied in subsequent sheriff court decisions where, for instance, it has been held that constructive notice had been given by the fact that the landlord's tradesmen had been sent out to the subjects on a number of occasions,[5] or where a landlord's attention has been drawn to one part of the house said to be in disrepair and the resulting inspection has failed to identify another.[6]

Needless to say, it is advisable in relation to all kinds of leases for the tenant to give the landlord express notice of any need for repairs and to give it in writing.

1 See the Housing (Scotland) Act 2001 Sch 4(3) and the Housing (Scotland) Act 2006 s 14(3); see also para 19.15.
2 1972 SLT 146.
3 Gloag, p 316.
4 *Golden Casket (Greenock) Limited v B.R.S.(Pickfords) Ltd* 1972 SLT 146 at 148 per Lord Dunpark.
5 *McGuire v Monklands District Council* 1997 Hous LR 41, applying the English Court of Appeal decision in *Sheldon v West Bromwich Corporation* [1973] 13 HLR 23, where it was held that a landlord was deemed to know that a tank, which had been examined by its plumber, was likely to burst.
6 *Galloway v Glasgow City Council* 2001 Hous L R 59 at 69 and 75. See also the discussion in Robson at 7.09.

EXCEPTIONS TO LANDLORD'S REPAIRING OBLIGATION

3.43   There are a number of situations where the landlord's common law repairing obligation does not apply:

Damnum fatale

3.44   It is long established at common law that the landlord is not liable to repair damage to the subjects caused by *damnum fatale*. This has been defined as, 'Loss arising from inevitable accident, which human means or prudence could not prevent.'[1] A more common description would be an act of God, a flood or a hurricane being obvious examples. The position is succinctly expressed in one of the earliest cases, *Lindsay v Home*,[2] which can be quoted in full:

> 'Lands being set in tack and thereafter being destroyed by overblowing with sand, will furnish action to the tenant to compel the setter either to grant diminution of the duty, according to the deterioration of the land and proportion thereof, or else to take back his own land, and free the tenant of payment of duty in all time coming.'

The tenant will therefore be entitled to an abatement of rent in proportion to the degree of damage, and where the damage is severe enough to amount to *rei interitus* or constructive total destruction, ie where the subjects of let have been totally destroyed or rendered unfit for the purpose of the let, the lease will be brought to an end.[3] In neither case is the landlord (or the tenant for that matter) obliged to repair the damage or to rebuild. The relevant principle is *res suo perit domino* which in this context means that 'as applied to accidents ... that all should bear the loss according to their interests.'[4]

It is, of course, implicit in the concept of *damnum fatale* that neither party is at fault, precluding a claim of damages by either. It is, however, consistent with the above principle that in cases of partial destruction, falling short of frustration, the tenant should be entitled to an abatement of rent, the tenant bearing the loss of the right to use part of the subjects and the landlord the loss of the rental income for that part.

1   *Trayner's Latin Maxims* (4th edn 1894) p 134.
2   (1612) M 10120; see also Rankine p 242. For a modern application of the rule, see *Little Cumbrae Estate Ltd v Island of Little Cumbrae Ltd* 2007 SC 525, 2007 SLT 631.
3   See para 10.6 et seq.
4   *Bayne v Walker* (1815) 3 Dow 233 at 238–239; see also *Little Cumbrae Estate Ltd v Island of Little Cumbrae Ltd* 2007 SC 525, 2007 SLT 631.

Actions of third parties

3.45   A landlord has no obligation to carry out repairs or liability to the tenant in damages where damage to the leased subjects has been caused by the actions of a third party or parties.[1] If the degree of damage is sufficiently severe as to render the subjects uninhabitable then, as in the case of *damnum fatale*, the lease will be terminated by frustration.

Whether or not the tenant may be entitled to an abatement of rent is less clear. In the case of frustration, there will of course be a total relief from rent as the lease will have ended. However, where there is partial destruction which does not amount to frustration, (ie partial eviction, including encroachment) the position is less clear. According to Rankine there is no entitlement to a rent abatement in such cases.[2]

However, this is inconsistent with the earliest authority. In the case of *Francis Hamilton* in 1667[3] the roof of the leased subjects was damaged when a neighbouring house fell on it. It was held that it 'was an accident without the pursuer's fault, and the tenant ought to pursue those whose tenement it was that fell.' However, the lords 'found it relevant to abate the duties in so far as he was damnified'. In *Allan v Roberton's Trustees*[4] the damage to the property, caused by the mining operations of third parties, was so severe that the lease was brought to an end by frustration. If the actions of third parties cause sufficient disrepair to bring about total eviction, and this entitles the tenant to total relief from rent, it would seem to follow that partial eviction for the same reason should entitle the tenant to partial relief.

If the situation is being equated with *damnum fatale*, presumably on the basis that neither the landlord nor the tenant is at fault, then one would expect the principle of *res suo perit domino* to apply here also.[5] Put more simply, if the landlord is not obliged to repair or rebuild, then the tenant is no longer receiving the benefit of the whole subjects, and should be entitled to an adjustment in the rent accordingly.[6]

1 Rankine pp 221-2 and 242; *Young v Colt's Trustees* (1832) 10 S 666; *Burrell v Gebbie* (1863) 6 SLR 187; *Allan v Roberton's Trustees* (1891) 18 R 932, 28 SLR 726; *North British Storage & Transit Co v Steele's Trs* 1920 SC 194, 1920 1 SLT 115.
2 Rankine pp 221–222.
3 (1667) M 10121; see also *Deans v Abercrombie* (1681) Mor 10122.
4 (1891) 18 R 932, 28 SLR 726; see also *North British Storage & Transit Co v Steele's Trs* 1920 SC 194, 1920 1 SLT 115.
5 See *Bayne v Walker* (1815) 3 Dow 233.
6 See also the discussion of this issue in Angus McAllister 'The Landlord's Common Law Repairing Obligation' 2012 Jur Rev 263 at 275–276.

Tenant's negligence

3.46 Where the damage has been caused by the tenant's own negligence, the tenant and not the landlord is liable. As we saw above, one of the tenant's common law duties is to take reasonable care of the property.[1]

1 See para 3.7 et seq.

Tenant's implied consent

3.47 A tenant who continues to occupy a property known to contain a danger (either of accident or illness) may be barred from holding the landlord liable for any injuries sustained as a result. There have been a large number of cases, dating from Victorian times until well into the 20th century, where landlords have used this as a defence in actions for damages by residential tenants (mainly of tenement properties) for injuries caused by disrepair.

Although these were cases of alleged breach of the lease contract, there has been a tendency to equate this defence with the delictual one of *volenti non fit* injuria.[1] The most straightforward examples of the defence succeeding were in situations where the danger was obvious from the beginning of the lease and the tenant had never, prior to the accident, notified the landlord of any need for repair;[2] as we saw above, lack of notification alone may be enough to relieve the landlord of liability as regards his ongoing repairing obligation.

1 This defence is discussed at para 19.38 et seq in relation to delictual claims under the Occupiers' Liability (Scotland) Act 1960.
2 *Russell v Macknight* (1896) 24 R 118; *Mechan v Watson* 1907 SC 25; (1906) 14 SLT 397; *Davidson v Sprengel* 1909 SC 566, (1909) 1 SLT 220.

3.48 *Webster v Brown* However, even where the landlord *has* been notified, but the tenant continues to occupy the property knowing of the danger, it may be held that the tenant has consented to it. In *Webster v Brown*[1] a tenant sued for damages in respect of injuries sustained when she slipped on a badly worn outside stair leading to the house. She averred that she had complained to the landlord's factor of the defect and that the landlord had subsequently announced his intention of putting in new steps.

However, the Inner House dismissed her action as irrelevant because she had thereafter continued to occupy the house and use the steps for a period of ten months prior to her accident. Her remedy, if the landlord failed to carry out the repair within a reasonable time, was to rescind the lease and leave the house, claiming damages for the expense of obtaining a new tenancy. If she continued to live there while knowing of the danger, she was held to have consented to it and remained at her own risk.

1 (1892) 19 R 765.

3.49   This decision seems a little harsh nowadays, but it has subsequently been accepted as good authority, most recently in 1961.[1] In a number of cases, however, the courts succeeded in distinguishing *Webster*, holding that a tenant who remained in occupation on the basis of assurances from the landlord that the repairs would be carried out,[2] or that there was in fact no danger should not be deemed to have accepted the risk.[3]

In *Mullen v Dunbarton County Council*,[4] where the tenant continued to occupy the property on the basis of assurances that a defective handrail would be repaired, there appeared to be some softening of the strict line taken in *Webster*. It was held that much depended upon the circumstances of the case, such as the character of the defect, the urgency of the repair or the urgency of the risk. It was also a matter of degree, as a danger may initially be trivial and only gradually become serious, which was the situation with the handrail in this case.

It was also observed, not long after the decision in *Webster*, that a tenant who was tempted to rescind was faced with a dilemma because, in any action raised by the landlord in order to recover the rent, the court might not agree that the landlord's breach was sufficiently material to justify rescission. As a result, many tenants remained 'pinned to the house by the dread of sequestration'.[5]

In spite of the above qualifications, almost 70 years after the decision in *Webster* it was still considered to be binding upon the Outer House.[6]

1 *McManus v Armour* (1901) 3 F 1079; *Proctor and Another v Cowlairs Co-operative Society Ltd* 1961 SLT 434.
2 *Shields v Dalziel* (1897) 24 R 849; *Grant v McClafferty* 1907 SC 201; *McKinlay v McClymont* (1905) 43 SLR 9; *Dickie v Amicable Property Investment Society* 1911 SC 1079.
3 *Caldwell v McCallum* (1901) 4F 371; see also the discussion of *volenti non fit injuria* as a defence to claims under the Occupiers' Liability (Scotland) Act 1960 at para 19.35 et seq.
4 1933 SC 380.
5 *Rice v Muirhead* (1896) 12 Sh Ct Rep 177 at 179 per Sheriff Lees.
6 *Proctor and Another v Cowlairs Co-operative Society Ltd* 1961 SLT 434.

Occupiers' Liability (Scotland) Act 1960

3.50   If a landlord escapes liability for breach of the lease contract because of the tenant's acceptance of danger, the tenant may still have a claim under the Occupiers' Liability (Scotland) Act 1960. Such a claim will only be possible in respect of leases where the landlord is responsible for repairs, which will rule out most commercial leases,[1] where the landlord's repairing obligation is generally contracted out of.[2] However, actions under the 1960 Act are relatively common in the case of residential leases and this subject is treated at some length in a later chapter.[3]

1 Although landlords tend to be responsible for keeping common parts in repair: see para 13.1.
2 See para 3.52
3 See para 19.25 et seq.

Landlord's obligation contracted out of

3.51 As with other common law obligations, it is possible for the lease terms to contract out of the landlord's repairing obligation, both in relation to the initial obligation and to the continuing obligation. This is virtually standard in commercial leases where the FRI lease (tenant's full repairing and insuring lease) is prevalent.

In such a case, it is essential that the lease should make the position absolutely clear, a principle reaffirmed in recent years:[1]

'[W]here the general common law imposes an obligation or liability upon one party to a contract, the contract will not be read as excluding that obligation or liability unless it makes it clear, at least by necessary implication, that that was the intention of the parties.'

From the landlord's point of view, therefore, the moral is quite obvious: if the parties have negotiated a full repairing lease, it is essential that the lease document properly reflects this intention. Otherwise, the common law may fill in the gap and make the landlord partially responsible for repairs.

Whether or not the repairing provisions in any particular lease fall short of this aim, leaving the landlord with a residual common law liability, will be a matter of interpretation of the lease in each case, making it difficult to generalise. However, some of the issues of construction that may arise, particularly in relation to extraordinary repairs, are considered in a later chapter.[2]

1 *Mars Pension Trustees v County Properties and Developments* 1999 SC 267, 1999 SCLR 117 at 121 per Lord Prosser; see also *Little Cumbrae Estate Ltd v Island of Little Cumbrae Ltd* 2007 SC 525, 2007 SLT 631.
2 See para 11.13 et seq.

3.52 Although landlord's repairing leases are rare in the commercial world, the landlord's common law obligation can still be important in relation to other types of lease. This is particularly the case with residential leases where, as we will see later, the landlord's common law liability has been reinforced by statute.[1] And, as we saw above, a number of modern cases have turned upon the common law element of the landlord's obligation.

1 See para 19.13 et seq.

Conclusion

3.53   It should be noted that, where a landlord escapes liability for repairs because of one of the above exceptions, it does not automatically mean that the tenant will be liable instead. In the case of *damnum fatale,* no-one is liable[1] and in the case of third party damage, the third party may be liable, either to the tenant or to the landlord, or to both. It is, of course, likely to be in the landlord's own interest to repair the property and to arrange for such eventualities to be covered by insurance. However, at common law the landlord is not legally obliged to do either of these. This illustrates how the common law may often be inadequate. It shows the need for a well-drawn lease agreement covering all foreseeable possibilities.

1 See *Little Cumbrae Estate Ltd v Island of Little Cumbrae Ltd* 2007 SC 525, 2007 SLT 631.

Chapter 4

Legal remedies of the parties 1: Standard breach of contract remedies

INTRODUCTION[1]

4.1 Since a lease is a contract, the standard legal remedies for breach of contract may be available to either the landlord or tenant if the other is in breach of the lease contract. In this chapter we will examine these remedies as they apply to leases. However, a landlord has, in addition, certain special remedies which we will examine in Chapters 5 and 6.

The standard breach of contract remedies, so far they apply to leases, are:

(1) specific implement and interdict, including the enforcement of 'keep-open' and repairing obligations;
(2) court action for debt;
(3) rescission;
(4) damages; and
(5) retention of rent.

Some of these have already been mentioned in Chapter 3, and we will refer to this chapter from time to time by way of illustration.

1 See Gloag Part IV, and the other law of contract texts referred to in the bibliography.

SPECIFIC IMPLEMENT AND INTERDICT: GENERAL[1]

Nature of remedy

4.2 A party faced with a breach of contract can seek a court decree that will force the other party to comply with the obligation that has been breached. There are two types of court decree that will achieve this, a positive one (specific implement) and a negative one (interdict).

The first applies where the offending party has failed in some positive obligation under the contract, (eg to carry out repairs).[2] This could therefore be available either to a landlord or a tenant, depending upon which of them was responsible for repairs. Specific implement is enforced by a decree *ad factum praestandum* (for the performance of an act).

Interdict applies where a party is carrying out some action prohibited under the contract. In chapter 3 examples were given of instances when the landlord used the remedy of interdict to stop the tenant from inverting the possession (ie using the property for a purpose other than that for which it was let).[3]

1 Gloag ch 36; see also other law of contract texts referred to in the bibliography.
2 This description, while sufficient for most purposes is, perhaps, an oversimplification: see N R Whitty, 'Positive and Negative Interdicts' (1990) 35 JLSS 453–456, 510–513; MacQueen and Macgregor, 'Specific Implement, Interdict and Contractual Performance' (1999) 3 Edin LR 239 at p 246; and L Macgregor 'Specific Implement in Scots Law' in J Smits, D Haas and G Helsen (eds), *Specific Performance in Contract Law: National and Other Perspectives* (Oxford; Intersentia, 2008), pp 80–82.
3 See para 3.3 et seq.

Consequences of breach

4.3   A party who fails to obey either of these types of court order is guilty of contempt of court and liable to a fine or imprisonment.[1] This is the only practical way of enforcing such a decree. In many cases there are better alternatives, which are faster and less expensive to invoke.

For example, in commercial leases, where the tenant is normally responsible for repairs, the landlord is generally given the power, if a tenant fails in a repairing obligation, to step in and do the repairs and charge them to the tenant.[2] It should be noted, however, that this right is not implied by law, but must be expressly reserved in the lease contract.

A tenant will also normally have a better remedy than specific implement. If the landlord fails to execute repairs, or carry out any other obligation, there may be no need for the tenant to go to the trouble and expense of raising a court action; it may be easier simply to retain the rent.[3]

There are also certain situations where specific implement is incompetent, and some of those which are particularly relevant to leases are considered below.[4]

1 For further discussion of this issue see para 4.20.
2 See para 11.23.
3 See para 4.39 et seq.
4 See para 4.5 et seq.

Interim orders[1]

4.4   At the outset of an action, if the court is satisfied on the balance of convenience that the pursuer has a prima facie case, the court may grant an interim interdict prohibiting the conduct complained of or interim specific implement[2] requiring the defender to do something until the case has been finally determined. Then the court may confirm the interdict or order for implement with a permanent one; however, if it declines to do so the pursuer may be liable in damages to the defender for any loss caused by the interim order.

By their nature interim orders tend to be more appropriate and more common in the case of interdict. However, interim orders of specific implement tend to be possible and can be obtained if the positive obligation the pursuer seeks to enforce is of a continuing nature; an obvious example is the obligation of a shop tenant to remain open and carry on business (a 'keep-open obligation') of the type discussed in the next section.[3]

1 Macphail *Sheriff Court Practice* (ed Welsh), 3rd edn (2006) 2.79 & 11.04; McBryde 23.23 & 23.08 et seq.
2 Courts Reform (Scotland) Act 2014 s 88(1)(b) for the Sheriff Court; Court of Session Act 1988 s47(2A) for the Court of Session.
3 See, eg, *Highland & Universal Properties Ltd v Safeway Properties Ltd* 1996 SLT 559.

Where specific implement incompetent

4.5   *Recovery of a liquid debt*   Specific implement cannot be used in order to recover a liquid debt. It is not therefore possible for a landlord to obtain a decree *ad factum praestandum* to recover rent. As we will see below, there is a separate type of court action designed for the recovery of debt.[1]

1 See para 4.26 et seq.

4.6   *Other cases*   Specific implement may not be competent to enforce a repairing obligation after the lease has ended.[1] This is discussed below.[2] It was also thought at one point that specific implement was incompetent to enforce so-called 'keep open' obligations. It is now settled that this is not the case, and this important topic will also be dealt with separately below. The court has a discretion to refuse to allow specific implement and will use that discretion where to order implement would cause undue hardship to the defender.[3] It may be difficult to show that *undue* hardship will arise as any hardship to the defender (eg the tenant in a keep-open action) must be measured against the benefit to the pursuer: the landlord having a unit that is open in his shopping centre with the benefits that brings to the centre and his other tenants.[4]

1 *Pik Facilities Ltd v Shell UK Ltd and Another* 2005 SCLR 958.
2 See para 4.25.
3 See the discussion of this issue in L Macgregor 'Specific Implement in Scots Law' in J Smits, D Haas and G Helsen (eds), *Specific Performance in Contract Law: National and Other Perspectives* (Oxford; Intersentia, 2008), pp 75–76.
4 See para 4.8 et seq.

'KEEP-OPEN' OBLIGATIONS

The traditional position

4.7   We saw in Chapter 3 that a tenant has a common law obligation to enter into possession and thereafter to occupy and use the leased subjects.[1] We also saw that this implied undertaking only obliges the tenant to occupy the property, but not to carry on business there.[2]

In commercial leases, however, this common law obligation is generally reinforced by an express undertaking on the tenant's part not only to occupy the property but also to carry on business there for the purpose or purposes specified in the use (or user) clause of the lease.[3] It is this provision that has come to be known as a 'keep-open' obligation.

There has never been any doubt that there are legal remedies open to the landlord for breach of such an obligation, either in its common law form or as expressed in the lease. Any loss may be recoverable as damages, and it is also a material breach of contract that would allow the landlord to rescind;[4] the latter remedy would be appropriate, for example, if a vacated property was falling into disrepair and the landlord could easily find a new tenant to replace the absentee one. The property could therefore be refurbished and relet, keeping the risk of a rental void to a minimum.

1 See para 3.2.
2 *Whitelaw v Fulton* (1871) 10 M 27, 9 SLR 25.
3 See para 11.6.
4 See paras 4.29 et seq and 4.37.

Enforcement by specific implement

4.8   In modern times, however, problems have arisen where it is not in the landlord's interest to terminate the lease, but instead to compel the tenant to continue to occupy and carry on business from the leased subjects. In periods of recession, the property may be difficult for the landlord to re-let, and the tenant could also find it difficult to find a new tenant to whom the lease could be assigned. A tenant which is trading badly, but which cannot get out of the lease, may decide to cut its losses by vacating the property while continuing to pay rent.

Landlords of shopping centres do not like this: at the very least it will create unwelcome blank frontage, and if the tenant in question is an anchor tenant, the viability of the centre may even be at stake. Landlords have, therefore, tried to enforce keep-open obligations by specific implement, by seeking a decree *ad factum praestandum.*

Grosvenor Developments v Argyll Stores

4.9   However, in *Grosvenor Developments (Scotland) plc v Argyll Stores Ltd*[1] (the first case where the present issue arose), it was doubted whether a general and continuing obligation to occupy property for the purposes stated in the use clause could be enforced by specific implement. In the words of Lord Kincraig:

'An order from the court must be precise and specific so that the defenders know throughout the period when the order is in force exactly what they are required to do and what they are prohibited from doing.'[2]

Although the above point was made obiter, it was initially followed in subsequent cases.[3]

1 1987 SLT 738.
2 *Grosvenor Developments (Scotland) plc v Argyll Stores Ltd* 1987 SLT 738 at 741 per Lord Kincraig.
3 Eg *Postel Properties v Miller and Santhouse plc* 1993 SLT 353, 1992 SCLR 799.

Retail Parks Investments v Royal Bank

4.10   The position changed in what is now the leading Scottish case on the subject, *Retail Parks Investments Ltd v Royal Bank of Scotland plc (No 2)*.[1] This related to premises occupied by the Royal Bank in the Sauchiehall Centre in Glasgow, which the tenants had occupied since 1977.

On learning that the tenants were planning to close the premises, the landlords successfully obtained an interim interdict against them vacating the premises and an interim order ordaining the tenants to use and occupy the property in terms of the lease. However, in the Outer House of the Court of Session, Lord Coulsfield (following *Grosvenor Developments*) refused to grant a permanent order of specific implement.

This was reversed on appeal to the Inner House. It was held that in principle specific implement was competent to enforce keep-open obligations. The court granted a decree of specific implement, requiring the tenants to use the premises as bank offices during all normal business hours. Effectively, this simply meant that the tenants should carry on using the property for the remaining seven years of the lease in the same way as they had done up until then.

1   1996 SC 227, 1996 SLT 669.

4.11   While recognising that each case had to be decided on its own merits, Lord McCluskey was able to formulate some general statements of the legal considerations to be kept in mind when assessing the competence of an action *ad factum praestandum*:[1]

(1)   The material wording of the contract must make it certain what the defender has to achieve in order to fulfil the obligation, though this will not by itself guarantee the granting of a decree of specific implement.

(2)   The grant of an interim order will not prevent the court, after full consideration of the case, from refusing to grant a permanent one. However, the history of the defenders' compliance with the order during the interim period may assist the court in reaching a view as to the sufficiency of its precision and specification.

(3)   An order of specific implement may require a number of distinct acts in order to secure compliance, and it may also remain effective over a period of years. However, the more numerous the required acts and the longer the period of time during which it is envisaged that the order will remain effective, the more necessary it will be to find terms for the order that will satisfy the need for adequate precision.

(4)   An order may specify the end to be achieved but leave open the precise means whereby that end is to be achieved, thereby allowing a degree of flexibility.

(5)   In considering the necessary degree of precision (bearing in mind that breach of the order could have serious, including penal, consequences) the court should consider the commercial realities which form the background to the undertaking of the parties' mutual obligations. In the present case, the defenders were a large commercial organisation that freely undertook the obligation with legal advice, and they had already occupied the subjects for the purpose stated in the lease for nearly 20 years without any apparent difficulty or misunderstanding as to what was required of them.

(6)   Even if the defenders experienced difficulties in knowing what was required of them, the matter would have to come before the court again before any penalty for breach could be imposed. The court would have to be satisfied that the breach was wilful and any imprecision in the wording of the order would be exposed; if satisfied that the breach was not wilful, the court could even give the defenders a further opportunity to comply before imposing a penalty. There should, therefore, be no insuperable difficulty in policing compliance with an order of the court pronounced in suitable terms.

1 *Retail Parks Investments Ltd v Royal Bank of Scotland plc (No 2)* (1996 SLT 669, at 678 per Lord McCluskey.

4.12   Furthermore, as both Lord Cullen and Lord Kirkwood pointed out, it did not matter if there were hypothetical situations where the effect of the order might be unclear, provided that it was generally clear what amounted to a breach:

'I do not accept that the correct test in deciding whether or not a court order ad factum praestandum is enforceable is to refer to potential difficulties which could arise in unspecified hypothetical borderline situations.'[1]

1 *Retail Parks Investments Ltd v Royal Bank of Scotland plc (No 2)* 1996 SLT 669, at 686 per Lord Kirkwood.

Importance of lease wording

4.13   Originally the landlords in *Retail Parks*[1] had sought an order requiring the bank to trade within specified hours and days, but later amended their motion to 'all normal business hours', which reflected the actual wording of the lease. This identifies another important point: a decree of specific implement may not be granted in terms that go beyond the lease wording.

Conversely, a decree of specific implement will not be granted in general terms 'to keep the premises in use and occupation' without reference to the permitted purposes in the use clause.[2] This is because the tenant's positive contractual obligation is defined by the lease terms, including the use clause, and because an order which omitted the purpose of the tenant's use and occupation would lack the necessary precision and clarity. This poses a lease drafting dilemma for landlords. It is likely to be easier to enforce a keep-open obligation with a fairly detailed use clause, However, an overly restrictive use clause can have the effect of depressing the level of rent that may be fixed at a rent review.[3]

1 *Retail Parks Investments Ltd v Royal Bank of Scotland plc (No 2)* 1996 SC 227, 1996 SLT 669.
2 *Co-operative Insurance Society Ltd v Halfords Ltd (No 1)* 1998 SLT 90, 1997 SCLR 719.
3 See para 12.91 et seq.

Subsequent cases

4.14   The *Retail Parks*[1] decision has been followed in subsequent cases. In *Co-operative Wholesale Society Ltd v Saxone Ltd*[2] a decree of specific implement was granted requiring the tenants to use the property as 'a high class shop' for the sale of 'footwear, hosiery, and handbags of all descriptions' as well as ancillary items. In the context, the phrase 'of all descriptions' did not mean that every description of footwear etc should be available, but only meant 'of any description whatsoever' thereby leaving the tenant free to sell any description of the three specified types of goods. It was therefore sufficiently precise.

In *Co-operative Insurance Society Ltd v Halfords Ltd (No 2)*[3] the court would have been prepared to grant specific implement; however, the lease made no mention of the business hours during which the tenants were to operate, or of the necessary reciprocal obligation on the landlords' part to keep the centre open during such hours, and the court did not feel able to import these obligations into the contract in order to make the lease workable. This highlights another important drafting point.

1 *Retail Parks Investments Ltd v Royal Bank of Scotland plc (No 2)* 1996 SC 227, 1996 SLT 669.
2 1997 SLT 1052; 1997 SCLR 835; see also *Oak Mall Greenock Ltd v McDonald's Restaurants Ltd* 2003 GWD 17-540.
3 1998 SC 212, 1999 SLT 685.

4.15   On the other hand, in *Highland and Universal Ltd v Safeway Properties Ltd (No 2)*[1] the Inner House were prepared to enforce an obligation to keep premises open 'throughout normal hours of business' for the purpose of 'the retail sale of all goods which may from time to time be sold in a high class retail store including the sale of wines, beers and spirits and the operation of part of the premises for cafe and restaurant purposes'. It was held that 'normal hours of business' could be interpreted as 'normal hours of business in the retail trade'.

This last case highlighted another important aspect of specific implement: that the court has a residual discretion to refuse an order *ad factum praestandum* on grounds of equity. However, this discretion will only be exercised in exceptional circumstances where, for example:

'... although the order would otherwise be competent, there exist very cogent reasons to refuse it and, in particular, where to grant it would be inconvenient and unjust, or cause exceptional hardship. The power has rarely, it seems, been used, and then only, it would appear, in cases where to enforce the obligation would be to impose a burden upon the defender grossly disproportionate to any advantage to the pursuer'.[2]

1 2000 SC 297, 2000 SLT 414.
2 *Highland and Universal Ltd v Safeway Properties Ltd (No 2)* 2000 SLT 414 at 424 per Lord Kingarth; see also *Oak Mall Greenock Ltd v McDonald's Restaurants Ltd* 2003 GWD 17-540.

Subtenancies

4.16   In *Britel Fund Trustees Ltd v Scottish and Southern Energy plc*[1] it was held that tenants were entitled to have a decree of specific implement, which had already been granted against them, amended to cover the future possibility of the property being sublet with the landlords' consent. In such an eventuality, the tenants' obligation would no longer be to keep open and trade from the premises but, during the period of the sublet, to ensure that the subtenant did so instead.

By consenting to a sublease a landlord signifies that the subtenant's occupation of the subjects will be acceptable as a vicarious performance of the keep-open provision in the head lease. However, in *Douglas Shelf Seven Ltd v Co-operative Wholesale Society Ltd*[2] it was held that this does not have the effect of qualifying the terms of the principal lease and of releasing the head tenant from the obligation to fulfil them.

1 2002 SLT 223, 2002 SCLR 54.
2 2007 GWD 9-167. For a useful analysis of this case, see Martin Hogg 'Damages for Breach of a Keep-open Clause: *Douglas Shelf Seven Ltd v Cooperative Wholesale Society Ltd* 2007 Edin LR 416; see also *Oak Mall Greenock Ltd v McDonald's Restaurants Ltd* 2003 GWD 17-540.

The English position

4.17   Whereas in Scotland specific implement is a legal right which will only rarely be refused on equitable grounds, in England the equivalent remedy of specific performance is a purely equitable remedy that will only exceptionally be granted.[1]

Although the English case law on keep-open clauses initially appeared to parallel that in Scotland, the traditional English position was re-asserted by the House of Lords in *Co-operative Insurance Society Ltd v Argyll*

Stores (Holdings) Ltd,[2] involving the closure of a Safeway supermarket. It was held that specific performance could not normally be used to enforce a keep-open obligation and that a landlord's only remedy was damages.

A distinction was made between court orders requiring the defendant to carry on an activity, such as running a business, and orders which require the defendant to achieve a result; the latter would allow, for example, the enforcement by specific performance of building contracts and repairing covenants. Much was made also about the difficulty in supervising an order for specific performance over a period of time, which would arise were an order granted compelling a tenant to keep open and trade from lease premises.

However, in *Highland and Universal Ltd v Safeway Ltd (No 2)*, it was pointed out that a number of decrees of specific implement had by now been granted in Scotland in relation to keep-open clauses without this having proved to be a problem.[3]

1 Gloag p 655; see also *Highland and Universal Ltd v Safeway Properties Ltd (No 2)* 2000 SLT 414 at 424 per Lord Kingarth; *Oak Mall Greenock Ltd v McDonald's Restaurants Ltd* 2003 GWD 17-540 and MacQueen and Macgregor 'Specific Implement, Interdict and Contractual Performance' 1999 3 Edin LR 239. See also para 4.15.
2 [1998] AC 1, [1997] 2 WLR 898. This leading case has subsequently been widely followed in England.
3 *Highland and Universal Ltd v Safeway Properties Ltd (No 2)* 2000 SLT 414, at 419 per Lord President Rodger and 425 per Lord Kingarth.

Interim remedies

4.18 If a tenant is unwise enough to tell the landlord in advance of its intention to vacate the property, it may be stopped from doing so by interdict.[1] Even a tenant that has already vacated can be ordered to re-occupy the property, prior to the granting of an interdict.[2] However, although an interim interdict may prevent the tenant from vacating the property, an interim order of specific implement will be required if the tenant is to be compelled to continue trading.

In *Co-operative Insurance Society Ltd v Halfords Ltd (No 1)*[3] at the interim stage a decree of specific implement requiring the tenants to carry on trading was refused because the order sought did not incorporate the wording of the use clause.[4] However, interim interdict was granted against vacating or removing from the premises and against displenishing the premises to the prejudice of the landlords' security for rent; the latter derived from the tenant's common law obligation to plenish the property in case the landlord had to exercise the right of hypothec.[5] As a result, the tenants were allowed to cease trading, but had to keep the shop fitted out, thereby reducing the landlords' problem of blank frontage.

1 *Church Commissioners for England v Nationwide Anglia Building Society* 1994 SLT 897.
2 *Church Commissioners for England v Abbey National plc* 1994 SC 651, 1994 SLT 959, at 965 per Lord President Hope; *Overgate Centre Ltd v William Low Supermarkets Ltd* 1995 SLT 1181.
3 1998 SLT 90.
4 See para 4.13.
5 See para 3.9 and para 6.1 et seq.

Damages[1]

4.19 Although specific implement is competent to enforce a keep-open provision, it is open to the landlord to submit a claim of damages instead. However, in this situation, the damages may be difficult to assess.[2]

The award of damages for breach of a keep-open provision does not preclude the landlord from later enforcing other provisions in the lease by specific implement (eg the obligation to maintain and repair the premises).[3] In other words, the landlord may have accepted damages as the price of allowing the subjects to remain closed, but will still be entitled to ensure that they are properly maintained.

1 For general consideration of damages as a remedy, see para 4.37 et seq.
2 For some of the issues relating to the assessment of damages for breach of a keep-open provision see *Douglas Shelf Seven Ltd v Co-operative Wholesale Society Ltd* 2007 GWD 9-167. For a useful analysis of this case, see Martin Hogg 'Damages for Breach of a Keep-open Clause: *Douglas Shelf Seven Ltd v Cooperative Wholesale Society Ltd* 2007 Edin LR 416.
3 *Douglas Shelf Seven Ltd v Co-operative Wholesale Society Ltd* 2009 GWD 3-56.

Penalties for breach of specific implement

4.20 It was stated at the beginning of the chapter that breach of an order of specific implement or interdict amounted to contempt of court, which could be punished by a fine or by imprisonment. In the past, there was some doubt as to whether a decree of specific implement could be enforced against a limited company or other corporate body and, because of that, whether it was competent at all in such cases.[1]

The reason was that, traditionally, the only penalty for breach of specific implement was imprisonment, and it was not practical to imprison all the members of a corporate body. This is of obvious importance in the present context, since the tenants in keep-open cases are invariably companies, few sole traders being likely to afford the expensive tactic of closing down a branch while continuing to pay rent.

Section 1 of the Law Reform (Miscellaneous Provisions) (Scotland) Act 1940 amended the law relating to specific implement by:

(1) restricting the maximum prison sentence for breach to six months;
(2) requiring that the breach should be wilful; and
(3) giving the court the discretion to make an alternative order to imprisonment.

This does not entirely remove the difficulty with regard to corporate bodies since, as Lord McCluskey pointed out in *Retail Parks*, the wording of the relevant section seems only to include natural persons.[2]

Nevertheless, *Retail Parks* and the other keep-open cases seem to have proceeded on the basis that a monetary penalty is possible. The rationale would appear to be that, at common law, the breach of any court order is contempt of court, punishable by a fine.[3]

1 Gloag p 659; *Lochgelly Iron and Coal Company Ltd v North British Railway Company* 1913 1 SLT 505 at 414 per Lord Kinnear.
2 *Retail Parks Investments v Royal Bank of Scotland (No 2)* 1996 SLT 669, at 677 per Lord McCluskey.
3 McBryde 23.26 and 23.27; see also *Postel Properties Ltd v Miller and Santhouse* 1993 SLT 353 at 356–357 per Lord Sutherland.

REPAIRING OBLIGATIONS

4.21 A court order *ad factum praestandum* is competent in order to enforce a repairing obligation. Whether or not it is raised by the landlord against the tenant or vice versa will of course depend upon which of them is responsible for repairs to the leased property. In the case of commercial leases, where the tenant's FRI lease is prevalent, the tenant will normally be the one responsible for repairs.[1] On the other hand, in the case of residential tenancies the landlord is likely to be responsible for repairs[2] and in the case of agricultural tenancies it may be either, depending upon the circumstances.[3]

1 See para 11.12 et seq.
2 See Ch 19.
3 See para 15.17.

Problems of specification

4.22 There are past examples of specific implement being successfully used in order to enforce a repairing obligation.[1] Such cases, however, are rare, and the few reported cases on the topic are more likely to be examples of failure. The main reason for this seems to have been the need for precision, the traditional rationale being that, since breach of such an order could bring about penal consequences, it is necessary for the defender to be absolutely clear about what has to be done in order to obey it. However, the measures that need to be specified in order to fulfil a repairing obligation are often lengthy, complex and may also involve technical detail. The result is that the court might consider the action incompetent due to lack of sufficient specification.[2]

1 *Marianski v Jackson* (1872) 9 SLR 80.
2 See, eg, *Renfrew District Council v McGourlick* 1987 SLT 538, 1988 SLT 127. (This was an attempt to enforce the repairing obligation of a local authority landlord by utilising the statutory provisions relating to statutory nuisance, but the problem relating to specification was the same.); *Gunn v Glasgow District Council* (1990) 1 SHLR. 213; *Nicol v Glasgow District Council* (1990) 1 SHLR 229. (The single volume of Scottish Housing Law Reports (SHLR) was published jointly in 1991 by Shelter (Scotland) and the Legal Services Agency). *Gunn* was successfully appealed to the Inner House, but only on the issue of damages – see para 3.31. In *Glasgow City Council v Anderson* 1997 Hous LR 102 an action of specific implement by landlords to enforce a tenant's stair cleaning obligation also failed. See also Michael Dailly 'The Law of Specific Implement' (1993) SCOLAG 102.

Relevance of 'keep-open' decisions

4.23 However, all of the authority referred to above predates the considerable developments in the law relating to specific implement described above in relation to the enforcement of 'keep open' clauses in commercial leases.[1] It will be seen that many of the objections regarding precision and the possibility of penal consequences have now been overcome. In the light of this, it may be worthwhile revisiting specific implement as a remedy in relation to repairing obligations. In particular, it should be borne in mind that the difficulties relating to the enforcement of 'keep-open' obligations related not only to their potential complexity but also the fact that the necessary actions had to be performed by the tenant over a number of years. Repairing obligations present only the first of these difficulties, but not the second, which ought to make the situation easier. Indeed, in *Cummings v Singh*[2] the Sheriff Appeal Court upheld a decision of the Sheriff to order specific implement against a tenant where an abatement order in relation to noise from the lease premises had been served on the landlord under section 80 of the Environmental Protection Act 1990. The lease obliged the tenant at its own expense to carry out all such work as may be required to the premises under any Act or by any local authority and to comply with all notices that may be served by public, local or statutory authority. The tenant defended the action on the basis that implement was only competent where what needed to be done was precise and clear. The court noted that the notice set out that something needed to be done to achieve an end. That end was clear. How it was to be achieved was left to the tenant. He was best placed to know how the noise was caused. How he abated the noise was a matter for the tenant.

1 See para 4.7 et seq, in particular the discussion of *Retail Parks Investments v Royal Bank of Scotland plc (No 2)* 1996 SLT 669 at para 4.10 et seq.
2 [2019] SAC (Civ) 11, 2019 Hous LR 41.

Repairing standard enforcement orders

4.24   Moreover, the repairing standard enforcement orders issued by the First Tier Tribunal, which were introduced by the Housing (Scotland) Act 2006, operate in a way that is very similar to specific implement.[1] In relation to private sector residential tenancies, therefore, this is probably the preferable remedy. However, in relation to those leases to which the 2006 Act does not apply (Scottish secure tenancies, commercial leases and agricultural leases) the experience of the Tribunal in granting repairing standard enforcement orders may give useful guidance on a more successful use of specific implement in order to enforce repairing obligations.[2]

1 See para 19.34.
2 For further discussion of this issue see A McAllister, 'Enforcing Repairing Obligations by Specific Implement' in F McCarthy, J Chalmers and S Bogle (eds), *Essays in Conveyancing and Property Law in Honour of Professor Robert Rennie* (Open Book Publishers; Cambridge, 2015) p 248.

Pik Facilities v Shell UK

4.25   In *Pik Facilities Ltd v Shell UK Ltd and Another*[1] the landlord sought to enforce certain repairing obligations after the lease had ended. It was held (applying the decision in *Sinclair v Caithness Flagstone Co Ltd*)[2] that specific implement was not competent in these circumstances, and that the appropriate remedy was damages. However, several points of particular interest should be noted:

(1)   The case did not fail because of lack of specification or precision. Lord Kingarth concluded (though without any great enthusiasm) that the pursuers' pleadings were adequate in this respect.[3]
This is significant as it is a potentially successful attempt to enforce a repairing obligation by specific implement which occurred after the 'keep-open' decisions heralded the possibility of a greater degree of flexibility in the application of this remedy. (This point

was made briefly by the pursuers' counsel at one point, though it was not picked up by Lord Kingarth in his judgment.)

(2)   To some extent the decision that specific implement was incompetent after the end of the lease was based upon the construction of the terms of that particular lease. The action failed because it was an attempt to implement an obligation that the tenant was obliged to carry out during the currency of the lease. There is some suggestion that, had the lease specifically provided for works to be carried out after the lease's expiry, this could have been enforced by specific implement;[4] and

(3)   The decision in this case does not offend against the general rule that, in Scots law, specific implement is to be regarded as a primary remedy.[5]

1   2005 SCLR 958. See also the earlier decision in *Pik Facilities Ltd v Shell UK Ltd* 2003 SLT 155, 2002 SCLR 832.
2   (1898) 25 R 703; (1898) 5 SLT 364.
3   *Pik Facilities Ltd v Shell UK Ltd and Another* 2005 SCLR 958 at 966 per Lord Kingarth.
4   See *Pik Facilities Ltd v Shell UK Ltd and Another* 2005 SCLR 958 at 968–969 per Lord Kingarth (including the reference to Gloag p 658).
5   *Pik Facilities Ltd v Shell UK Ltd and Another* 2005 SCLR 972 per Lord Kingarth. See also para 4.17.

COURT ACTION FOR DEBT[1]

Nature of action

4.26   A court action for debt is appropriate for a contractual obligation to pay a liquid sum of money and it is the standard remedy open to any creditor. Unlike specific implement and interdict, which can only be enforced by the indirect method of threatening the debtor with contempt of court, a court decree for debt can be enforced more directly by diligence (ie by the legal seizure of the debtor's property)[2] should they fail to pay following decree being granted.

The most relevant forms of diligence in the case of leases are attachments (which involve the seizure and eventual sale of the debtor's moveable property), arrestments (attachment of assets of the debtor which are held by a third party, such as money in a bank account) earnings arrestments (attachment of the debtor's wages or salary). Inhibiting the debtor (where any transfer of the debtor's heritable property in Scotland can be challenged by the inhibiting creditor) can also be a useful way to obtain payment from the debtor. This is because if the debtor wants to transfer his heritable property he will have to pay the creditor to have the inhibition discharged. So, while an inhibition does not directly result in payment by use of the debtor's assets in the same way as an attachment or arrestment, it can be a useful weapon for a creditor to use that results in payment.

Attachments can only be used against a debtor's domestic assets in exceptional circumstances, and a wide range of items is excluded.[3] For this reason, attachments are more appropriate for the recovery of rent in the case of commercial and agricultural rather than residential leases.

1 Walker 33.15–33.19; McQueen & Thomson 7.3–7.5.
2 For an overview of the law of diligence, see Gloag & Henderson ch 48; for a more detailed discussion see Macgregor at al *Commercial Law in Scotland* (Edinburgh, W Green (6th edn), 2020) ch 9; for summary diligence, see para 6.21 et seq.
3 See Macgregor et al, paras 9.8.1–9.8.1.2.

Rent arrears

4.27   In a landlord and tenant situation, the most obvious relevance of a court action for debt is for recovery of rent. If the lease contains a clause of consent to registration for execution, summary diligence is likely to be preferable[1] as it is faster and less expensive than raising a court action and then carrying out diligence if sums due remain unpaid. If the tenant becomes insolvent, the landlord's hypothec in its new restricted form may still give the landlord a preferential claim.[2]

1 See para 6.21 et seq.
2 See para 6.1 et seq.

Other debts

4.28   There can, of course, be debts other than rent which a tenant may owe to a landlord, or a landlord to a tenant, and for these a court action for debt would in all cases be the appropriate remedy. Examples include the one mentioned above where the lease document allows the landlord to do repairs and charge them to the tenant, or where the lease provides that the landlord may seek a sum of money from the tenant in lieu of bringing the lease premises into the condition required by the lease,[1] or the recovery of service charge.[2] If the service charge is included in the lease as part of the rent, rather than as a separate item, then the landlord's hypothec in its modified form may be available.[3]

1 See the discussion of this remedy in Garrity and Richardson, (2019), para 5.4.2.
2 See Ch 13.
3 See para 6.1 et seq.

RESCISSION[1]

Nature of remedy

4.29   Rescission is a self-help remedy which permits a party to terminate a contract. It is available only if the other party's action is sufficiently serious to constitute a material breach of the contract. Where the breach is not so serious, other remedies, such as damages[2] will be available.

Where there has been a total failure of performance by one of the parties the breach is clearly material;[3] in a landlord and tenant context, this would probably be the case where there was a total failure of a landlord to grant possession of the subjects or of the tenant to enter into possession, though not if there was merely a temporary delay in either of these occurrences.[4]

The situation is more difficult where there has only been a partial breach, eg where there has been a defective performance or a breach of only one of a number of stipulations contained in the contract. In such cases, what amounts to a material breach justifying rescission will be largely a matter of degree and much will depend upon the court's decision regarding the facts in any particular case. However, there are a number of precedents concerning certain types of breach in relation to leases.

In certain ultra-long leases, a provision that deems the tenant's failure to comply with any lease condition to be a material breach of contract is void.[5] Such a clause would effectively be a provision for conventional irritancy, which has been abolished in relation to ultra-long leases.[6]

It should be noted that there is a risk to the party purporting to rescind where it is unclear that the breach is material. If party A rescinds believing party B's breach is material and he is incorrect about that, the purported rescission by A will result in A being in material breach of contract, entitling B to rescind.[7]

1 Gloag p 602 et seq; see also the other law of contract references listed in the bibliography.
2 See para 4.37.
3 Gloag p 603.
4 See paras 3.2 and 3.10.
5 Leasehold Casualties (Scotland) Act 2001 s 5; as to long leases see Ch 8.
6 See para 5.6.
7 *Wade v Waldon* 1909 SC 571.

When breach material

4.30   In Chapter 3, we identified examples of material breaches in a landlord and tenant situation (eg the right of a landlord to rescind if the tenant does not remain in occupation of the property[1] or the right of a tenant to rescind if the landlord does not provide premises reasonably fit for the purpose of the let).[2] A tenant may be able to rescind because of the breach of a landlord's common law repairing obligation, provided that the landlord has been notified of the need for repair and has been given a reasonable time to respond.[3]

In *Davie v Stark*[4] a majority of the court was of the opinion that a landlord's breach of a term prohibiting him from leasing a shop adjoining that of the tenant to someone in the same trade was material and justified rescission.[5] And in *Scotmore Developments v Anderton*[6] the opinion was given, obiter, that breach of a term compelling a landlord to respond reasonably to a tenant's request for assignation would be material.

1 *Edmond v Reid* (1871) 9 M 782; *Blair Trust Co v Gilbert* 1940 SLT 322, 1941 SN 2; see para 3.2.
2 *Kippen v Oppenheim* (1847) 10 D 242; see paras 3.27 and 3.29.
3 *McKimmie's Trs v Armour* (1899) 2F 156.
4 (1876) 3 R 1114.
5 See also para 2.45.
6 1996 SLT 1304; as to consent to assignation see para 7.4 et seq.

When breach not material

4.31　　Mere non-payment of rent does not entitle a landlord to rescind,[1] though most leases will include this as a ground of termination by irritancy.[2]

In *Todd v Bowie*[3] the tenant of a 19-year farm lease was held not to be entitled to rescind at the end of the third year because of the landlord's failure of a lease obligation to put the fences into good tenantable repair. And in *Couper v McGuiness*[4] a tenant's failure to observe lease terms obliging him to keep the garden ground of the property in a clean and cultivated condition and to maintain a boundary fence was not considered material (though whether this was the ratio or was merely obiter is difficult to determine from the judgment).

In *Crieff Highland Gathering Ltd v Perth and Kinross Council*[5] it was held that the pursuers were not entitled to rescind a lease of a public park and recreation area. The failure of the defenders to carry out certain of their maintenance obligations was not sufficiently material to justify rescission, inter alia, because the lack of maintenance had not prevented the full and uninterrupted use of the subjects at all times, nor had there been a complete failure by the tenant to carry out maintenance and repair work, a significant amount of which had in fact been done. It was also observed that the courts have traditionally been reluctant to allow a rural lease without an irritancy clause to be brought to an end in circumstances where the tenant had made clear an intention to perform his or her obligations throughout the remaining period of the lease.[6]

In the opinion of Rankine, unauthorised assignation or subletting does not justify rescission, although the assignation or sublease may be reducible and damages may be claimed for any loss.[7]

1 Gloag p 618.
2 See para 5.5 and Ch 5 generally.
3 (1902) 4 F 435, (1902) 9 SLT 365.
4 (1948) 64 Sh Ct Rep 249.
5 2011 SLT 992, 2011 GWD 20-474.
6 *Crieff Highland Gathering Ltd v Perth and Kinross Council* 2011 SLT 992, at 1001-2 per Lord Pentland.
7 Rankine p 180.

Remediable breaches

4.32   A party intending to rescind will normally require to notify the other party of this intention, or else he may be held to have acquiesced in the breach. However, under the general law of contract there is no settled rule that where a breach is remediable the party in breach should be given an opportunity to remedy the situation before the other can rescind, though there has been judicial opinion to the effect that such a rule is desirable.[1]

In *Central Car Auctions Ltd v House of Sher (UK) Ltd*[2] the landlords allowed a mobile telephone company to install antennae and other telecommunications equipment on the roof of the leased subjects. The tenants alleged that this was a material breach of contract and attempted to rescind the lease.

It was held that this was a breach of a provision in the lease which entitled the tenants to peaceable possession of the subjects. However, whether or not the breach was material depended upon the facts of the particular case, and this breach was not material for several reasons:

(1)   The encroachment did not materially affect the ability of the tenants or of any subtenants to carry on their business. On the other hand, the breach might have been material if the equipment had been installed, not on the roof, but on the upper floor of the building, or if it had restricted the area in which the pursuers could park and work on vehicles;

(2)   The actings of the defenders that gave rise to the breach did not indicate any intention that the lease should end or that they were not prepared to fulfil their obligations under it;

(3)   The breach was remediable, as the equipment could have been removed very quickly. While this was not conclusive, it was an important matter to be taken into account when deciding whether or not the breach was material.

It should be noted that this appears to be a clear case of the landlord being in derogation of the grant, though the case seems to have been decided on the basis of a lease provision rather than that implied obligation. However, establishing derogation would not by itself have been enough to make the breach material.[3]

1 See McBryde 20.122 et seq.
2 [2006] CSOH 137, 2006 GWD 29-645.
3 See generally para 3.14 et seq.

4.33   However, there are situations where the possibility of the breach being remedied is more important. We have already seen that a tenant cannot rescind because of a breach of the landlord's common law repairing obligation unless the landlord has first been notified and has failed to act, the reason being that the obligation is not a warranty and only arises after notification.[1]

Importantly, under s 5 of the Law Reform (Miscellaneous Provisions) (Scotland) Act 1985, the court can only allow a lease to be rescinded by a landlord (or terminated by irritancy) for a non-monetary breach where it is satisfied that in all the circumstances a fair and reasonable landlord would do so. One of the circumstances the court should take into account is whether, where the breach is remediable within a reasonable time, the tenant has been given a reasonable time to remedy it.[2] This effectively means that the tenant must be given a chance to put right a remediable breach or the court may not consider that the landlord has the right to rescind. In the case of monetary breaches (eg non-payment of rent) the tenant must be given 14 days to pay.[3] It is only after that period with rent remaining unpaid that the landlord can terminate the lease (this will usually be by way of irritancy rather than rescission).

The above statutory provision only applies to rescission by *landlords* and not to rescission by a tenant.

1 See para 3.41.
2 See *Crieff Highland Gathering Ltd v Perth and Kinross Council* 2011 SLT 992, 2011 GWD 20-474.
3 Law Reform (Miscellaneous Provisions) (Scotland) Act 1985 s 4; see also para 5.23 et seq.

Rescission and irritancy

4.34   Mention has been made above of the landlord's remedy of irritancy, and this important topic is considered in detail in the next chapter.[1] Superficially the two remedies resemble each other, as each allows a landlord to terminate a lease prematurely as a result of the tenant's breach. Unlike rescission, however, irritancy is not available to a tenant but only to a landlord. And in its most common form (conventional irritancy) it can only be triggered by a breach specified in the lease, though there is no requirement at common law that such a breach needs to be material.

In modern times irritancy has been the preferred method of termination by landlords. The probable reason is that a landlord seeking to irritate will only have to satisfy the court that it has complied with the provisions of the Law Reform (Miscellaneous Provisions)(Scotland)Act 1985 and, in the case of non-monetary breaches, satisfy the court of the 'fair and reasonable landlord' test. In contrast, in the case of rescission it will also be necessary to satisfy the court that the breach is material.

On the other hand, rescission may be the landlord's only recourse in the rare cases where a lease does not contain an irritancy clause, or where there is a clause but it does not include the ground upon which the landlord seeks to terminate. And the fact that an irritancy clause may omit a particular ground will not preclude the court from considering that ground to be material and to justify rescission.[2]

1 See Ch 5.
2 *Blair Trust Co v Gilbert* 1940 SLT 322, at 324 per Lord Keith.

Future breaches

4.35   Another possible advantage of rescission is that it can apply to future (or anticipatory) breaches, whereas irritancy can only be triggered by past breaches.

In *Edmond v Reid*[1] a farm lease contained a clause requiring the tenant to reside there. The landlord raised an action for breach of the obligation and the tenant lodged a minute in court offering to keep a furnished house on the farm with a servant, and to reside there with her family for ten days in every two months.

Not only did the court hold that this failed to meet the residency requirement, but also that it amounted to an open declaration in court of the tenant's intention not to fulfil the obligation in the future. The residency obligation was not stated in the lease to be a ground of irritancy; in any case, that remedy would not have been competent, whereas rescission was:

> 'The case for Mrs Reid has been pleaded as if the summons were a declaration of irritancy expressed or implied in contravention of a condition; but that is not its nature. An irritancy is incurred by past breach of obligation; and on the contravention the irritancy, if there be one, takes effect, and the right is forfeited. But here the conclusions of the summons are entirely for the future, and relate solely to the effect of the refusal for the future to fulfil the conditions of the right. The tenant has judicially declared that she will not fulfil these conditions, and the question is, whether she can continue to maintain her possession on the provisions of a contract which she refuses to fulfil.
>
> I am of opinion that she is not entitled to do so ...'[2]

Conversely, if the tenant demonstrates a commitment to fulfilling the lease obligations in the future, this can be taken into account by the court in deciding that the breach was not sufficiently material to justify rescission.[3]

1 (1871) 9 M 282.
2 *Edmond v Reid* (1871) 9 M 282 at 784 per the Lord Justice Clerk.
3 *Crieff Highland Gathering Ltd v Perth and Kinross Council* 2011 SLT 992, 2011 GWD 20-474.

4.36 It has been argued that, conversely, rescission by a landlord is competent only in respect of future breaches and not for past ones. However, *Edmond v Reid* does not address this point and the subsequent authority for it is rather thin.[1] It may also be noted that this would result in the remedy of rescission operating on much narrower grounds than in other mutual contracts where a past material breach is sufficient to entitle rescission. There seems no reason why that should be the case. Nevertheless, it is probably true to say that in a contract of a continuing nature, such as a lease, rescission by either party will not normally be allowed for a one-off past breach, unless it is particularly serious.[2]

1 See 'To irritate or to rescind: two paths for the landlord?' by Martin A Hogg 1999 SLT (News) 1.
2 Walker para 33.43.

DAMAGES

4.37 Damages may be claimed in a court action as compensation for any loss resulting from a breach of contract. The measure of damages is the amount of the loss, so far as that can be quantified in monetary terms. The aim of a damages award is to put the party who has suffered a breach of contract, as far as money can do so, into the position he would have been in had there been no breach. Damages can be claimed in addition to any other breach of contract remedy, provided a loss has occurred as a result of the breach. The subject of damages is covered elsewhere[1] and here the discussion will be confined to some of the authority relating to leases.[2]

There are obviously cases where either a landlord or a tenant would be entitled to claim damages, some of which we saw in Chapter 3 (eg where a tenant's neglect caused the landlord to suffer a loss in the value of the property[3] or where breach of the landlord's repairing obligation caused dampness).[4]

Damages for breach of a keep-open provision has already been considered above.[5]

1 Gloag ch 38; see also the other references for law of contract listed in the bibliography.
2 For a discussion of damages as it relates to a breach of the repairing obligation in a commercial lease see Garrity and Richardson (2019), para 5.3.3 et seq.
3 *Mickel v M'Coard* 1913 SC 896, 1913 1 SLT 463; see para 3.7.
4 *Gunn v National Coal Board* 1982 SLT 526; see para 3.31.
5 See para 4.19.

Penalties

4.38   In any contract, the parties sometimes include a formula (known as liquidated damages) for calculating the damages payable in respect of a particular type of breach. If such a breach occurs, therefore, it will not be necessary for the court to assess the amount of damages but merely to apply the formula in the contract.

However, the liquidated damages provision must not impose on the party in breach a detriment out of all proportion to the innocent party's legitimate interest in performance of the contract[1] since the purpose of damages is to compensate the party who is not at fault and not to punish the party in breach. If the clause imposes a detriment out of all proportion to the legitimate interest in contractual performance, then no matter what the provision is called in the contract, it will be unenforceable and the court will instead assess damages in the normal way.

One such provision, which has routinely appeared in leases and other deeds from at least the early 19th century, has now been subjected to judicial scrutiny. In *Council of the Borough of Wirral v Currys Group plc*[2] the rent was payable in advance on the Scottish quarter days, 'with a fifth part more of each quarter's payment of liquidate penalty in case of failure in punctual payment and the interest of each quarter's payment at the rate of five per centum per annum from the time it falls due till paid'. It was held that this stipulation was a penalty and that the damages payable should be limited to the actual loss sustained. This would include the interest payment, the cost of diligence and perhaps some other expenses in addition.

In the case of agricultural leases, the common law in relation to penalties has been reinforced by statute.[3]

1 *Cavendish Square Holding BV v El Makdessi; ParkingEye Ltd v Beavis* (conjoined cases) [2015] UKSC 67; [2016] AC 1172.
2 1998 SLT 463, 1997 SCLR 805.
3 Agricultural Holdings (Scotland) Act 1991 s 48; Agricultural Holdings (Scotland) Act 2003 s 56.

RETENTION OF RENT[1]

4.39 Retention is a self-help remedy for breach of contract that allows a party to withhold performance of a contractual obligation (including the payment of money) where the other party is in breach. It arises from the principle of mutuality in contracts (ie that the obligations of the parties to a contract are reciprocal in nature).[2]

If a landlord is in breach of contract, therefore, the tenant has the right to withhold the rent and there is a long line of authority in support of this going back to the 19th century and earlier. On the other hand, it is an equitable remedy which the court may refuse in special circumstances.[3]

Retention can be a very useful remedy for a tenant: it may persuade the landlord to put right the breach without the need for court action, and in any action against the tenant for recovery of the rent the fact of the landlord's breach will be a relevant defence.[4]

For retention to be competent the breach must be more than trivial, though it need not be sufficiently serious to justify rescission;[5] nor does the tenant have to show that it would justify a claim of damages for an amount equal to the amount of rent retained.[6]

In *Sutherland v Barry*[7] tenants sought to retain rent and other sums due to their landlords because they had a damages claim against the landlords for fraudulent misrepresentation. It was held that retention was not valid because the damages claim arose from the law of delict, not the lease contract.

1 Rankine pp 326–335, Paton & Cameron pp 141–142; for a general account of the principle of retention, see the law of contract texts listed in the bibliography, particularly Gloag ch 35 and McBryde 20-62 et seq.
2 There is a statutory basis for retention of rent in agricultural tenancies: see para 15.26.

3 McBryde 20-77; L Richardson, 'The Scope and Limits of the Right to Retain Contractual Performance' 2018 Jur Rev (4), 209, p 218.
4 *Kilmarnock Gas-Light Co v Smith* (1872) 11 M 58; *John Haig & Co Ltd v Boswall-Preston* 1915 SC 339, 1915 1 SLT 26; *Fingland & Mitchell v Howie* 1926 SC 319, 1926 SLT 283.
5 Gloag p 623; *Inveresk plc v Tullis Russell Papermakers Ltd* [2010] UKSC 19; 2010 SC (UKSC) 106 per Lord Hope at para [43].
6 *M'Donald v Kydd* (1901) 3 F 923 at 928 per Lord Moncrieff, (1901) 9 SLT 114.
7 2002 SLT 418, 2002 Rep LR 13.

Contracting out etc

4.40 This common law right of a tenant to retain rent may be contracted out of by an express stipulation in the lease.[1] A tenant may also be barred from the right to retain the rent, for example by making no complaint during the currency of the lease and then, after its expiry, resisting a final rent demand with a claim of retention.[2]

However, during the currency of the lease the tenant will not be barred because of past payments from withholding rent for a breach that is still continuing. In *John Haig & Co Ltd v Boswall-Preston*[3] the landlord was bound under the lease to make repairs to the roof which were not done. The tenants were held entitled to retain their rent even though they had earlier made two rental payments without objection.

In residential leases contracting out of the tenant's right of retention could be considered to be an unfair term under The Consumer Rights Act 2015.[4]

1 *Skene v Cameron* 1942 SC 393, 1942 SLT 210; *Glasgow Corporation v Seniuk* 1968 SLT (Sh Ct) 47.
2 *Stewart v Campbell* (1889) 16 R 346; *British Railways Board v Roccio* 1970 SLT (Sh Ct) 11.
3 1915 SC 339, 1915 1 SLT 26.
4 Sections 62 and 63 and Sch 2 paras 2, 18 and 20; see para 21.11.

Functions of retention

4.41 Although a tenant's right of retention is long-established, some of the authority (particularly the older cases) can present difficulties and is not always easy to reconcile with the mutuality principle in contracts. It may help clarify things if we first of all note that retention can have two separate functions:

'The retention of rent seems to me to be warranted for one of two purposes – (1) to act as a compulsitor on the lessor in obtaining performance by him of his contractual obligation, such as to make

117

the house habitable; or (2) to satisfy *pro tanto* any counter-claim which the tenant is maintaining.'[1]

In other words, retention can be used by a tenant as a way of forcing implement by the landlord or for securing damages and it was the courts' earlier reluctance to recognise the second of these functions that caused some of the difficulty. It may therefore help if we consider each of these aspects separately, and later distinguish the right of retention from a tenant's right to an abatement of rent, with which it can become confused.[2]

1 *Fingland & Mitchell v Howie* 1926 SC 319, at 324 per Lord Anderson.
2 See para 4.47 and 6.18 et seq.

Retention to compel performance

4.42   Here the tenant is withholding rent in order to compel performance by the landlord (eg where the landlord has failed in an obligation to carry out repairs) and the rent will be paid over in full when the breach has been remedied. Retention is here being used as an alternative to an action of specific implement, and is obviously easier than that remedy for the tenant to employ.

This function has always been recognised by the courts.[1] In such cases, it was common for the tenant, pending the outcome of the action, to consign the full amount of the rental payment with the court, either by order of the court or voluntarily; this demonstrated that the tenant was in good faith and had not withheld the rent because of financial difficulty.

1 See eg *M'Donald v Kydd* (1901) 3 F 923, (1901) 9 SLT 114; *Earl of Galloway v McConnell* 1911 SC 846, (1911) 2 SLT 4; *John Haig & Co Ltd v Boswall-Preston* 1915 SC 339, 1915 1 SLT 26.

Retention to secure damages

4.43   A tenant who has suffered loss as a result of the landlord's breach may of course be entitled to damages, and may claim these by raising an action against the landlord. Alternatively, however, the tenant may simply withhold the rent and, if sued by the landlord, lodge a counterclaim for damages. If damages are awarded amounting to less than the rent owing, the tenant will have to pay over the balance retained.[1]

Though consistent with the principle of mutuality in contracts and the general law regarding retention,[2] this was originally thought incompetent in relation to retention of rent. However, it now appears to be accepted.[3]

1 *Christie v Wilson* 1915 SC 645, 1915 1 SLT 265.

2 See Gloag p 628; McBryde 20-72.
3 *Fingland & Mitchell v Howie* 1926 SC 319, 1926 SLT 283; *Euman's Trs v Warnock* 1931 SLT (Sh Ct) 25, (1930) 46 Sh Ct Rep 164; *Stobbs & Sons v Hislop* 1948 SC 216, 1948 SLT 248; *Renfrew District Council v Gray* 1987 SLT (Sh Ct) 70; *Pacitti v Manganiello* 1995 SCLR 557.

Residential tenancies

4.44   We will see in Chapters 17 and 18 that some residential tenants may enjoy a statutory right to security of tenure, which will allow the tenant to remain in occupation after the expiry of any notice to quit sent by the landlord. At that point the tenancy ceases to be a 'contractual tenancy' (in terms of the lease) and becomes a 'statutory tenancy'. Such a right is enjoyed by assured tenants and regulated tenants (who hold tenancies governed by regimes which still apply to tenancies entered before 1 December 2017 when the private residential tenancy was introduced). It is also enjoyed by social tenants with Scottish secure tenancies.

Under an even earlier system of controlled tenancies (now obsolete) a similar statutory protection was conferred. In 1948 the case of *Stobbs & Sons v Hislop*[1] was presented as a test case to determine whether a statutory controlled tenant, the contractual period of whose lease had ended, was entitled to retain his rent because of the landlord's failure to carry out repairs. It was held that he was not because:

(1)   retention was not an implied term of the contract (which the terms of the legislation would have extended to the statutory period of occupancy) but an equitable right; and

(2)   the common law right of retention was inconsistent with the statutory provision allowing for the suspension of rent increases in cases where the house was in need of repair, or even uninhabitable.

1 1948 SC 216, 1948 SLT 248.

4.45   However, there must be some doubt as to whether residential tenants under the tenures now current are similarly deprived of the right to retain rent. There are good reasons to believe that *Stobbs & Sons v Hislop* might not be followed today:

(a)   the rents under controlled tenancies were kept artificially low, rendering the tenancies uneconomic as far as most landlords were concerned. In the words of Lord Cooper:

'The old common law of retention of rent was built up at a time when there was a free market in heritable subjects, and it is neither logical nor just to apply it literally to the fundamentally altered situation created by the statutory tenancy.'[1]

It seems possible that a court might exercise its equitable power differently in the case of a residential tenancy where the landlord is allowed to charge a market rent.

(b)   The statutory provision allowing the suspension of a rent increase because of lack of repair has no equivalent in the current legislation.[2]

However, the situation remains uncertain.

1 *Stobbs & Sons v Hislop* 1948 SC 216 at 227 per Lord Cooper, 1948 SLT 248.
2 See Robson 4-17.

4.46   *Possible dangers* There are other reasons why a residential tenant (particularly in the private sector) should exercise caution before withholding rent:

(1)   As we saw above, it is possible to contract out of the common law right of retention .[1] Before trying to exercise the right, the tenant should carefully scrutinise the tenancy agreement to make sure that this has not been done, although as noted above such a provision may fall foul of the Consumer Rights Act 2015, and as such not bind the consumer.[2]

(2)   If the tenant has an assured tenancy, a short assured tenancy or a private residential tenancy from a private landlord, three month's rent arrears is a mandatory ground of eviction.[3] This means that if the rent retained amounts to three months or more, the sheriff may have no option but to grant possession if the landlord raises an action to evict the tenant; the tenant would have to be very careful to ensure that he lodged a defence (that the rent was being lawfully retained) within the correct timescales in the eviction action.

(3)   A tenant who has a short assured tenancy from a private landlord[4] will have no security of tenure beyond the contractual period of the lease, which can be as little as six months. If the tenant has caused trouble by retaining rent, this may influence the landlord's decision about whether or not to continue the tenancy beyond the initial period.

1 See para 4.40.
2 CRA 2015 s 62; see para 4.40.
3 See para 17.85.
4 See para 17.104 et seq.

Abatement and retention

4.47   Abatement can easily be confused with retention, since both are competent defences to an action by a landlord to recover rent withheld by a tenant. However, they derive from different principles, though the use of terminology in some of the cases does not always make this clear. Retention in its true sense is a breach of contract remedy and can only be available to a tenant when the landlord is in breach. Abatement, on the other hand, may be available whether or not the landlord is in breach: the principle is that the tenant is not at fault, and yet has been partially deprived of the subjects for which rent is being paid. Abatement of rent is considered in Chapter 6.

Chapter 5

Legal remedies of the parties 2: Irritancy

INTRODUCTION

5.1   Having examined those breach of contract remedies which apply to all contracts, we will now look at certain additional remedies which exist by virtue of the special nature of the lease contract. The most important (and controversial) of these is irritancy, which will be considered in this chapter. The following chapter will briefly examine three other remedies, the landlord's hypothec, abatement of rent and summary diligence.

NATURE OF IRRITANCY[1]

General

5.2   Irritancy means forfeiture and refers to a landlord's right to terminate a lease prematurely because of the tenant's breach of contract. The effect of irritancy is to bring to an end, not only the lease, but also all rights deriving from it such as those of a subtenant, whose tenure will also be ended,[2] or those of a heritable creditor with a right in security over the tenant's interest in a registered lease.[3]

Unlike rescission, irritancy can only be invoked in respect of a past and not a future breach.[4]

An irritancy can only be enforced by means of court action in order to obtain a decree of extraordinary removing, although some leases may be worded in a way that suggests otherwise, eg by a declaration 'that the lease shall *ipso facto* become null and the tenant obliges himself to remove without warning or process of removing'.[5]

There are two types of irritancy, legal (implied by law) and conventional (based upon a term in the lease contract). The former is virtually obsolete, but conventional irritancies are very much alive and have been the subject of some controversy. The law of irritancy is largely based on the common law, but there are statutory restrictions on its exercise which will be considered below.

The Human Rights Act 1998 may have some application to the law of irritancy, and this will be considered nearer the end of the chapter.[6]

1 Rankine p 532 et seq, Paton and Cameron ch 15.
2 Rankine p 198.
3 See para 8.19.
4 See para 4.35 et seq.
5 Paton and Cameron p 235; *Waugh v More Nisbett* (1882) 19 SLR 427.
6 See para 5.40 et seq.

Work of the Scottish Law Commission

5.3   The Scottish Law Commission considered the law of irritancy in 2003[1] and again in 2018.[2] In 2003 the Commission recommended a considerable strengthening of the current statutory controls on irritancy. However, these recommendations were not implemented. In 2018 the Commission sought views on whether the law of irritancy required to be reformed given market changes since the 2013 report, and, if so, which aspects of the law. At the time of writing the Commission has not yet published a report with recommendations on any change to the law now considered necessary.

Some of the main changes to irritancy, recommended in the Commission's 2013 Report, have been noted at appropriate points in the chapter.

1 Scottish Law Commission *Report on Irritancy in Leases of Land* (Scot Law Com No 191, 2003).
2 Scottish Law Commission Discussion Paper on Aspects of Leases: Termination (Scot Law Com No 165, 2018).

Legal irritancy

5.4   A legal irritancy is implied by law, and is therefore available to any landlord, whether or not there is any provision for irritancy in the lease document. At common law, the only ground of legal irritancy is non-payment of rent for two years.

If a legal irritancy has been incurred and the landlord has begun legal proceedings to evict the tenant, the tenant has the right to purge the irritancy by remedying the breach. The tenant may do this at any time before the landlord's irritancy action has been concluded and the landlord has obtained an extract decree from the court.

This means that, at any time before the landlord has reached the stage of being legally entitled to proceed with eviction, the tenant may pay off all the rent arrears; in such a case, the landlord will be forced to accept the money and the irritancy proceedings will be nullified.[1]

Common law legal irritancies are rarely encountered nowadays as very few landlords will be willing to allow rent arrears to accumulate for as long as two years, when there are other legal steps that could be taken at a much earlier date. There is another legal irritancy, imposed by statute, which allows certain agricultural tenants to be removed for six months rent arrears.[2]

The Scottish Law Commission recommended that both of these legal irritancies should be abolished, and replaced by an option to terminate the lease for non-payment of six months' rent which would be subject to the same statutory controls as conventional irritancies. The parties would be entitled to contract out of this termination option.[3]

1 Rankine pp 538–539, Paton and Cameron p 230.
2 Agricultural Holdings (Scotland) Act 1991 s 20. This provision only applies to 1991 Act tenancies and not to short limited duration or limited duration tenancies – see para 15.40.
3 Scottish Law Commission *Report on Irritancy in Leases of Land* (Scot Law Com No 191, 2003), paras 3.13 to 3.15.

Conventional irritancy

5.5   A conventional irritancy is so called because it exists by convention, or agreement. In other words, unlike a legal irritancy, it is not implied under the common law, but only exists if specifically provided for in the lease document. Virtually any breach of the lease, therefore, can be made a ground of conventional irritancy, and frequently is.

The grounds of conventional irritancy are those that have been included in the lease in question. This means that, as Rankine puts it, there is

'no limit to the number of conventional irritancies with which the caprice of a landlord and the necessities of a tenant may encumber a lease'.[1]

Common grounds of irritancy include bankruptcy, liquidation or receivership of the tenant or diligence being carried out against the tenant.[2]

Most importantly of all, arrears of sums due to the landlord eg rent is also a standard ground of conventional irritancy, though usually for a much shorter period of arrears than the two years implied by law. It is common for irritancy provisions in leases to permit the landlord to irritate if the tenant has failed to pay sums due within 14 or 21 days. This is usually described as the 'period of grace' within which the tenant may make a late payment without incurring an irritancy. Irritancy clauses have for many years been standard in commercial and agricultural leases.[3] They also often appear in residential leases, but in such cases their effect may be restricted by the statutory provisions regulating residential leases.[4]

It should be emphasised that irritancy is always a landlord's option. If a landlord is in breach of the lease, the tenant has only the normal remedies, eg rescission for a material breach, and the tenant cannot use irritancy as a pretext for ending a lease because of his or her own breach.[5]

1 Rankine p 532.
2 For a brief discussion of diligence most relevant to leases see para 4.26.
3 See para 15.41 et seq regarding irritancy in agricultural leases.
4 See para 17.72.
5 *Bidoulac v Sinclair's Tr* (1889) 17 R 144, 27 SLR 93.

Ultra-long leases

5.6   The Leasehold Casualties (Scotland) Act 2001 abolished irritancies in the case of ultra-long leases.[1] This is defined as a lease of not less than 175 years granted before 10 August 1914 with a ground rent or tack duty of not more than £150 per annum.[2] The abolition applies both to conventional irritancies (by making any irritancy provision in a lease void),[3] and also to legal irritancies.[4]

A potential loophole is plugged by also making void any provision that would deem any breach of the lease to be a material breach; such a clause operates in the same way as an irritancy provision.[5] This provision prevents a tenant from losing what is virtually a right of ownership in a practical sense because of failure to pay a very small amount of rent. It is not clear why only leases granted before 10 August 1914 are affected.

However, what is virtually a right of ownership from a practical perspective may be conferred by much shorter leases. The Royal Institution of Chartered Surveyors has estimated that in leases with an unexpired duration of 100 years or more the value of the landlord's interest is negligible,[6] and in shorter leases with a substantial unexpired duration the value of the tenant's interest may be substantially greater than that of the landlord. However, such leases are still subject to irritancy and there have been examples in recent years of long ground leases being prematurely terminated by this means.[7]

It might be thought that the provisions of the Long Leases (Scotland) Act 2012 for the conversion of the tenants' interests under ultra-long leases into ownership might alleviate this situation. However, the thresholds laid down in that Act exclude many leases with a lengthy unexpired term and a tenant's interest of substantial value.[8]

1 See Robert Rennie 'Leasehold Casualties' 2001 SLT (News) 235.
2 Leasehold Casualties (Scotland) Act 2001 s 5(1).
3 LC(S)A 2001 s 5(2).
4 LC(S)A 2001 s 6.
5 LC(S)A 2001 s 5(2); see also para 4.29 et seq.
6 See the Scottish Law Commission *Report on Conversion of Long Leases* (Scot Law Com No 204, 2006) at 2.17.
7 See paras 5.27 et seq & 5.36 et seq.
8 See para 8.38 et seq. It was not, of course, the function of the 2012 Act to reform the law of irritancy which, if thought necessary, could be done by other means.

COMMON LAW PRINCIPLES

Payment of rent after irritancy

5.7   After an irritancy has been incurred, if the tenant stays on in the property pending the outcome of the action of removing, the landlord is entitled to be paid a reasonable rent for the period of occupation.[1]

1 *HMV Fields Properties v Skirt 'n' Slack Centre of London Ltd* 1987 SLT 2; see also para 2.62 et seq.

Waiver of irritancy

5.8   Where the tenant continues to pay rent in circumstances such as those described in the immediately preceding paragraph, there should be no doubt about the basis on which it is being paid, because by continuing to accept rent without qualification or by acting in any other way that is inconsistent with the lease being terminated, the landlord may be held to have waived the right to enforce the irritancy. Whether the facts amount to waiver in any particular case will depend on the individual circumstances. It is therefore in the landlord's interest to make clear to the tenant the basis on which any rent payment tendered is accepted, ie as payment for occupation of the property, not as rent due under the lease.

In *HMV Fields Properties Ltd v Bracken Self Selection Fabrics Ltd*,[1] after a notice of irritancy had been given, several rental payments were made by the tenant by credit transfer into the landlord's bank account. Most of these were returned promptly, with the exception of one payment, made on 24 June 1985, which was not returned until December of the same year.

It was held that, although this was prima facie evidence of waiver, the surrounding circumstances were enough to establish that the landlord had not intended to give up its right to proceed with the irritancy. This was inferred from the history and mechanism of rental payments and the fact that the parties had gone to arbitration over the question of irritancy prior to the single payment being accepted.

1 1991 SLT 31, 1990 SCLR 677; see also *MacDonald's Trs v Cunningham* 1998 SLT (Sh Ct) 12, 1997 SCLR 986 and *Wolanski & Co Trustees Ltd v First Quench Retailing Ltd* 2004 Hous LR 110, 2004 GWD 33-678.

5.9 *Actings by tenant* Also, for waiver to be established, the tenant must be shown to have acted in some way in reliance upon the landlord's apparent abandonment of the right of irritancy, though there is no need to show that the tenant suffered prejudice as a result.[1] There is no direct authority as to what such actings might consist of; possible examples might include negotiations by the tenant with a potential assignee, or spending money on the property, eg on redecoration or improvement.

1 *MacDonald's Trs v Cunningham* 1998 SLT (Sh Ct) 12, 1997 SCLR 986; *Aubrey Investments v D S Crawford Ltd (in receivership)* 1998 SLT 628 at 633 per Lord Penrose.

5.10 *Previous late payment* Where non-payment of rent is a ground of irritancy, the lease normally gives the landlord the right to irritate in respect of any rental payment that is overdue for more than the stated period. This means that the option to irritate occurs separately each time a rental payment is sufficiently late, with the result that the landlord will not be held to have waived the right merely by failing to exercise this option in the past and having tolerated late payment.[1] Nor will a tenant be able to use the defence that the landlord is using the irritancy oppressively merely because of such past tolerence.[2]

1 *Lucas's Executors v Demarco* 1968 SLT 89 at 94 per Lord President Clyde.
2 *CIN Properties v Dollar Land (Cumbernauld)* 1992 SLT 211 at 214 per Lord Justice Clerk Ross, 1992 SCLR 44; see also para 5.27 et seq.

5.11 *Breach or delay by landlord* However, a landlord who is in material breach of the lease contract may be barred from enforcing an irritancy.[1] The landlord may also be barred if there has been a substantial delay since the tenant's breach.

In *Noble v Hart*[2] the lease of a restaurant allowed irritancy if the tenant, inter alia, failed to conduct the business properly or did anything else that might endanger the renewal of his licence. The landlord attempted to irritate the lease after the tenant had received a warning from the licensing court for being drunk and incapable while in charge of the business.

The action was dismissed because there was no averment that the incident was other than an isolated one, but it was also noted that the landlord did not raise the action until a year after the incident, by which time the tenant's licence had been renewed. Lord Moncrieff expressed the opinion that the landlord's action had to be taken at once, or at the term of Whitsunday or Martinmas following the alleged offence.[3] No legal principle was stated as the basis of this, but it is more likely to be an example of acquiescence rather than waiver.

1 *Macnab v Willison* 1960 SLT (Notes) 25.
2 (1896) 24 R 174.
3 *Noble v Hart* (1896) 24 R 174 at 177 per Lord Moncrieff.

Change of landlord

5.12   In *Life Association of Scotland Ltd v Blacks Leisure Group*[1] the lease required the landlords to serve a formal notice upon the tenants prior to exercising their right of irritancy.[2] After the service of the irritancy notice the property was sold, and it was held that the new landlords could not proceed with the irritancy without their predecessors having specifically assigned the notice to them.

Where a leased property has changed ownership, the new landlords cannot be held to have waived their right of irritancy on the basis of any conduct by their predecessors.[3] In *Ashford and Thistle Securities LLP v Kerr* [4] the tenant alleged that she had an arrangement with the original landlord to occupy the subjects rent free for the first few years of the lease in return for carrying out certain repairs and refurbishment. Before the expiry of this period, the landlords sold the property and the new landlords served an irritancy notice in respect of the rent that would have been due to their predecessors. It was held that the new landlords, as the original landlords' singular successors, could not be bound by their predecessors' agreement. However, the irritancy notice was invalid because it had not explained the basis upon which rent was now being demanded.

1 1989 SC 166, 1989 SLT 674.
2 As we will see, an irritancy warning notice is now required in most cases as a result of the Law Reform (Miscellaneous Provisions)(Scotland) Act 1985 ss 4 and 5; see para 5.21 et seq.
3 *What Every Woman Wants (1971) Ltd v Wholesale Paint and Wallpaper Co Ltd* 1984 SLT 133; see also para 5.8 et seq.
4 2007 SLT (Sh Ct) 60, 2006 SCLR 873.

Purging of conventional irritancies: the common law position

5.13   The most controversial aspect of conventional irritancies was that, prior to 1985, the tenant had no right to purge the irritancy unless the landlord agreed to it.[1]

In this way conventional irritancies differed from legal irritancies. Once the ground of irritancy had been incurred, the tenant might seek to remedy the breach, but the landlord was still entitled to proceed with eviction; for example, where the ground of irritancy was late payment of rent, the landlord, after beginning the irritancy proceedings, could accept payment of the arrears from the tenant but still enforce the irritancy.[2]

The only exception to this strict rule was that a conventional irritancy could be purged if its terms merely echoed the common law position in respect of legal irritancies, ie if the termination ground was two years rent arrears.[3] This is still the position,[4] but is of little practical importance, as few if any modern leases will contain such a generous irritancy provision.

1 Rankine pp 547–548; Paton and Cameron p 232; *Stewart v Watson* (1864) 2 M 1414; *McDouall's Trs v MacLeod* 1949 SC 593, 1949 SLT 449; *Lucas's Executors v Demarco* 1968 SLT 89. *McDouall's Trs* contains an extensive review of the prior authority, as far back as the 16th century.
2 Rankine pp 547–8; *McDouall's Trs v MacLeod* 1949 SC 593, 1949 SLT 449.
3 Rankine p 547; Paton and Cameron p 232; *McDouall's Trs v MacLeod* 1949 SC 593, 1949 SLT 449.
4 *British Rail Pension Trustee Co v Wilson* 1989 SLT 340.

5.14   *Dorchester Studios v Stone*   The above had been the law for a very long time (at least since the middle of the 19th century and perhaps earlier), but it is doubtful whether many tenants, when signing their leases, understood what draconian powers they were handing to their landlords. However, in 1975, they (or at least their agents) were given a sharp reminder.

In *Dorchester Studios (Glasgow) Ltd v Stone*[1] the tenants under a sublease incurred an irritancy by neglecting to pay their rent within the 21-day period of grace provided in the lease's irritancy clause. Eleven days after the expiry of this period, the landlords informed the tenants of their intention to evict them. The tenants immediately offered payment of the rent, but the landlords refused to accept it and raised an action in the sheriff court to enforce the irritancy. The court decided in the landlords' favour and the tenants appealed all the way to the House of Lords, who upheld the original decision, rejecting the tenants' defence that the irritancy had been used oppressively.[2]

After a pause for the implications of *Dorchester Studios* to sink in, a small outbreak of irritancy cases hit the casebooks, probably indicative of a much larger epidemic that did not reach the courts, or went unreported. All of them followed the decision in *Dorchester Studios*.[3]

1 1975 SC (HL) 56, 1975 SLT 153.
2 See para 5.15 et seq.
3 *HMV Fields Properties v Skirt 'n' Slack Centre of London Ltd* 1982 SLT 477; *HMV Fields Properties v Tandem Shoes Ltd* 1983 SLT 114; *What Every Woman Wants (1971) Ltd v Wholesale Paint & Wallpaper Co Ltd* 1984 SLT 133.

Oppression

5.15   A tenant's only traditional defence to an action of irritancy (which still applies, in theory at any rate) was that the landlord was misusing the power of irritancy by using it oppressively. The most often quoted definition of oppression in modern times is that of Lord Guthrie in *Lucas's Executors v Demarco*:[1]

> '"Oppression" infers that there has been impropriety of conduct on the part of the landlord. "Misuse of rights" or "abuse of irritancies" involves that the terms of the contract have been invoked by the landlord to procure an unfair consequence to the tenant. These terms "oppression", "misuse of rights" and "abuse of irritancies" are different expressions of the same idea.'

1 1968 SLT 89 at 96 per Lord Guthrie.

5.16   *Difficulties in establishing oppression*   There is a long line of judicial authority for the existence of this defence,[1] but while each of them explains why the circumstances in question did *not* amount to oppression, they are all much more reticent about giving concrete examples of what *would* qualify. In fact, there have been no cases since the 19th century where this defence has succeeded, those earlier cases in which it was successfully invoked were rather unusual circumstances[2] and the continuing trend has been to interpret the concept of oppression very narrowly.

Perhaps the best modern illustration of this is *HMV Fields Properties v Skirt 'n' Slack Centre of London Ltd*.[3] Here an irritancy clause was invoked by landlords who had only recently bought the property in question, a shop in Hamilton, subject to the sitting tenancy. Moreover, according to the tenants, the new landlords' directors were all directors of another company which was not only a trade competitor of the tenants throughout Scotland, but which also had a shop in Hamilton directly opposite the one leased to the tenants.

The tenants also alleged that the first notice they had been given of the change of landlords was two days before the rent was due, when an invoice was sent unobtrusively to the Hamilton shop in a plain brown envelope. By the time it had been forwarded to the tenants' head office in Dumfries and been paid, nearly a month had passed and the landlords proceeded to raise an action of irritancy because the rent had been paid outwith the 21-day period of grace in the lease.

All this led the tenants to suspect that the irritancy action might have been prompted by an ulterior motive. However, the court held that a defence of oppression will only succeed where there has been a clear abuse of rights or impropriety of conduct by the landlord, and that the landlord's motive is irrelevant. It was also suggested that oppression is not available as a defence where the tenant's failure to pay the rent is due to an oversight.

1 *Stewart v Watson* (1864) 2 M 1414; *McDouall's Trs v MacLeod* 1949 SC 593, 1949 SLT 449; *Lucas's Executors v Demarco* 1968 SLT 89; *Dorchester Studios (Glasgow) Ltd v Stone* 1975 SC (HL) 56, 1975 SLT 153; *HMV Fields Properties v Skirt 'n' Slack Centre of London Ltd* 1982 SLT 477; *HMV Fields Properties v Tandem Shoes Ltd* 1983 SLT 114; *CIN Properties v Dollar Land (Cumbernauld) Ltd* 1992 SLT 211, 1992 SCLR 44 (IH); *Aubrey Investments Ltd v D S Crawford Ltd (in receivership)* 1998 SLT 628 at 634 per Lord Penrose.
2 See Rankine p 548.
3 1982 SLT 477.

5.17   *Purpose of irritancy*   In *Dorchester Studios*, Lord Kilbrandon affirmed that the purpose of irritancy (unlike the English remedy of forfeiture) is not so much a remedy for rent arrears, but rather a means whereby a landlord can be rid of an unsatisfactory tenant who pays the rent late and may be financially unstable.[1]

One does not need to indulge in wild speculation to infer that in several of the modern cases (including *Dorchester Studios*) this was not the landlord's purpose, but rather that irritancy was being used as a device to obtain early vacant possession of the property for some purpose unconnected with the tenant.

This view is reinforced by the fact that, in two cases,[2] the landlords in each case raised an irritancy action in respect of the first rental payment due after they acquired the property. It is suggested that it would not be a misuse of ordinary language to describe such conduct as an abuse of the right of irritancy where 'the terms of the contract have been invoked by the landlord to procure an unfair consequence to the tenant'.[3]

1 *Dorchester Studios (Glasgow) Ltd v Stone* 1975 SC (HL) 56, 1975 SLT 153 at 156 per Lord Kilbrandon.

2 *HMV Fields Properties v Skirt 'n' Slack Centre of London Ltd* 1982 SLT 477 and
HMV Fields Properties v Tandem Shoes Ltd 1983 SLT 114.

3 See quote from *Lucas's Executors v Demarco* 1968 SLT 89 at para 5.15.

5.18   *Possible developments*   But, even if the landlord's motive was considered to be relevant (which the courts have repeatedly refused to entertain) there would still remain the problem of converting a reasonable suspicion into admissable evidence. A possible way forward may be found in an obiter statement by Lord Penrose in *Aubrey Investments v D S Crawford Ltd (in receivership)*[1] developing Lord Guthrie's test in *Lucas's Executors v* Demarco.[2] While acknowledging that a landlord's motive will not be enough on its own (which is not quite the same as saying that it is irrelevant) and that the landlord is entitled to have regard to his or her own interests, he also stated:

> 'Impropriety may be inherent in the act complained of, or inferred from surrounding facts and circumstances which colour an apparently regular exercise of contractual rights.'[3]

It is submitted that the circumstances in several of the earlier cases described above could well be considered as having satisfied this test, eg where a hitherto exemplary tenant is evicted for a single slip-up in paying the rent.

1 1998 SLT 628.
2 1968 SLT 89.
3 1998 SLT 628 at 634 per Lord Penrose.

5.19   Although it remains the case that the defence of oppression has never been successfully pleaded in modern times, in two more recent cases the respective judges have envisaged circumstances in which it feasibly might be. In *Whitbread Group plc v Goldenapple Ltd*[1] the irritancy action failed on other grounds. However, although the circumstances of the case did not satisfy the test for oppression, Lord Drummond Young (developing the opinion of Lord Penrose in *Aubrey Investments* that oppression may be implied from the surrounding facts and circumstances) went on to make the following obiter statement:

> 'Where there is a clear willingness to pay, and also some doubt as to the precise amount due, I consider that the use of an irritancy for non-payment of a trivial amount would amount to oppressive conduct.'[2]

However, none of these factors would be conclusive on its own, and a combination of them would be required.

In *Tawne Overseas Holdings v Firm of Newmains Farm*[3] the landlords claimed an additional rent, payable on default, and returned the tenants' cheque for the original rent. The court held that the additional rent was a penalty and therefore unenforceable,[4] and the action to enforce the irritancy failed. The principle underlying the decision was not made absolutely clear, but Lord Malcolm suggested that attempting to irritate on another ground after the penal rent had been declared unenforceable could amount to unfairness or oppression.

1   2005 SLT 281, 2005 SCLR 263.
2   *Whitbread Group plc v Goldenapple Ltd* 2005 SLT 281 at 300 per Lord Drummond Young, 2005 SCLR 263.
3   2008 Hous LR 18, 2008 GWD 6-116.
4   For penalties see para 4.38.

5.20   *Scottish Law Commission Recommendations*   The Scottish Law Commission recommended in 2003 that the common law defence of oppression, having little residual value, should be abolished.[1] This would be part of the package designed to strengthen the statutory controls.

Arguably, this abolition is not necessary. At the worst, the common law defence of oppression can do no harm; at best it may be of use in situations such as those described in *Whitbread* or *Tawne*, or in some other circumstances, as yet unforeseen.

1   Scottish Law Commission *Report on Irritancy in Leases of Land* (Scot Law Com No 191, 2003), paras 3.17 and 3.18.

STATUTORY CONTROL OF IRRITANCY

General

5.21   The main statutory restrictions on the use of irritancy are to be found in the Law Reform (Miscellaneous Provisions) (Scotland) Act 1985, which are considered in detail in the paragraphs immediately following. Brief notice will also be taken of further restrictions on irritancy which may apply in the case of insolvent companies.[1]

The possible application of the Human Rights Act 1998 to irritancy is considered in a separate section.[2]

1   See para 5.38.
2   See para 5.40 et seq.

The 1985 Act[1]

5.22   It was clear from *Dorchester Studios*[2] alone that the law was in need of reform. The situation was somewhat remedied by the Law

Reform (Miscellaneous Provisions) (Scotland) Act 1985, following earlier recommendations of the Scottish Law Commission.[3]

The 1985 Act applies equally to leases that were entered into before and after it came into force.[4] However, it applies only to commercial leases; residential leases (defined as 'land used wholly or mainly for residential purposes'), agricultural leases and leases of crofts and small landholdings are specifically excluded.[5]

This may be justified in the case of residential tenancies, since the statutory regulation of these tenancies severely restricts the use of irritancy.[6] However, conventional irritancy remains competent in relation to agricultural leases though, until fairly recently, the sparsity of modern case law suggested that it has given rise to fewer problems in this area.[7]

The Scottish Law Commission has recommended that the statutory protection against the effects of irritancy should apply to all types of lease.[8]

Contracting out of the Act is expressly forbidden.[9] However, the statutory provisions should be read in conjunction with any provisions in the lease that operate in the tenant's favour, and will not override the lease provisions if this would operate to the prejudice of the tenant.[10]

1 Law Reform (Miscellaneous Provisions) (Scotland) Act 1985. For the full text of the relevant sections see Appendix 1.
2 *Dorchester Studios (Glasgow) Ltd v Stone* 1975 SC (HL) 56, 1975 SLT 153.
3 Scottish Law Commission *Report on Irritancies in Leases* (Scot Law Com No 75,1983).
4 LR(MP)(S)A 1985 s 7(1).
5 LR(MP)(S)A 1985 s 7(1).
6 See para 17.44 et seq.
7 See, however, *Downie v Trustees of Earl of Stair's 1970 Trust* 2008 SC 41, 2007 SLT 827; *Tawne Overseas Holdings v Firm of Newmains Farm* 2008 Hous LR 18, 2008 GWD 6-116; *Mount Stuart Trust v McCulloch* 2010 SC 404, 2010 SLT 409.
8 Scottish Law Commission *Report on Irritancy in Leases of Land* (Scot Law Com No 191, 2003), paras 3.17 and 3.18.
9 LR(MP)(S)A 1985 s 6(1).
10 *Edinburgh Tours Ltd v Singh* 2012 Hous LR 15, 2012 GWD 4-75.

5.23 *Monetary breaches* The 1985 Act provides that, in the case of monetary irritancies, the landlord must, after the payment has become due, give the tenant at least 14 days written notice to pay the arrears; only on the lapse of that further period without payment may the irritancy be enforced.[1]

The 14-day period is mandatory and runs, not from the date of the notice, but from the date when it is served, if that is different.[2] The notice must make absolutely clear the date by which payment is to be made.[3] In *Scott v Muir* the Sheriff Principal of Lothian and Borders held that the notice also had to set out the periods over which the rent arrears arose as without this information it would be impossible to calculate the interest that was due to be paid. [4] Yet, in *Inverclyde Council v McCloskey*[5] the Sheriff Principal of North Strathclyde held that the periods over which the arrears had accrued were not needed for a valid notice. In may be that the differing opinions can be explained by the fact that in the former case the landlord demanded rent arrears together with interest on those arrears, while in the latter the landlord simply sought payment of the rent outstanding. A more relaxed approach to the requirements for a valid irritancy warning notice can be seen in *Shetland Leasing and Property Developments Ltd v Younger*[6] in which the defender argued that the notice did not contain an adequate specification of the rent said to be in arrears. The sum set out in the notice purported to be in relation to five months' non-payment of rent when the sum set out equated to more than four months' but not five months' rent. The sheriff noted that the tenant was a man of business and should be able to determine from his records the extent to which he was in arrears. It had been open to the tenant to respond to the notice by asserting that a lower sum was due to be paid but he had not done so. The notice issued by the landlord complied with s 4 of the 1985 Act and was valid.

If the irritancy clause, as it usually will, allows a period of grace for late payment, eg 21 days, the landlord may serve the notice before the end of this period; however, in such a case the tenant must be given the full period of grace: the period specified in the notice must be 14 days, or the expiry of the period of grace, whichever is the greater period.[7]

The landlord's notice has to be sent by recorded delivery. This means that the Royal Mail recorded delivery service must be used, and any other method of service, including service by sheriff officer, will not be valid.[8]

Where there has been a change of landlord, a notice may be served in relation to arrears due to the original landlord, but in such a case the terms of the notice must make clear the basis on which the rent is being demanded.[9]

It should be noted that s 4 applies not just to irritancies for non-payment of rent, but also to other monetary breaches, eg failure to pay a service charge or other sum owed by the tenant.

1 LR(MP)(S)A 1985 s 4. At the time of writing, s 8 and paras 6 and 7 of Sch 8 of the Coronavirus (Scotland) Act 2020 extend this period to 14 weeks. This change is in place until 31 March 2021 and may be extended further.
2 *Tawne Overseas Holdings v Firm of Newmains Farm* 2008 Hous LR 18, 2008 GWD 6-116. The case report, however, gives no explanation as to why the 1985 Act was thought to apply to a residential lease (see para 5.22), though the reason may be that the house was formerly used as a hotel.

3 *Wing v Henry Tse & Co Ltd* 2009 GWD 11-175; *Scott v Muir* 2012 SLT (Sh Ct) 179, 2012 Hous LR 20.

4 2012 SLT (Sh Ct) 179, 2012 Hous LR 20.

5 2015 SLT (Sh Ct) 57.

6 2014 Hous LR 9, Sh Ct.

7 LR(MP)(S)A 1985 s 4(3)(b).

8 *Kodak Processing Companies Ltd v Shoredale Ltd* 2010 SC 113, 2009 SLT 1151. For a discussion of this case see also Lynne Richmond 'Signed, sealed and … delivered?' 2010 SLT (News) 63. The writer suggests that, while the clear wording of the Act perhaps made this decision inevitable, the legislation should perhaps be amended to allow more flexibility in methods of service, inter alia, reflecting the fact that the Royal Mail no longer enjoys the monopoly it did in 1985. See also *Edinburgh Tours Ltd v Singh* 2012 Hous LR 15, 2012 GWD 4-75.

9 *Ashford and Thistle Securities LLP v Kerr* 2007 SLT (Sh Ct) 60, 2006 SCLR 873.

5.24 *Non-monetary breaches or events* In the case of non-monetary breaches (including change of circumstances such as liquidation or receivership which it is not strictly accurate to describe as breaches) the court may only enforce the irritancy in cases where *in all the circumstances* (author's italics) a fair and reasonable landlord would do so.[1]

Where there is a breach that is capable of being remedied within a reasonable time, eg a tenant's failure to carry out repairs, the court is to take into account, when making its decision, whether the tenant has been offered a reasonable opportunity to remedy the breach.[2]

1 LR(MP)(S)A 1985 s 5; see also *Blythswood Investments (Scotland) Ltd v Clydesdale Electrical Stores Ltd (in receivership)* 1995 SLT 150 (discussed at para 5.30).

2 See *Euro Properties Scotland Ltd v Alam* 2000 GWD 23-896 (discussed at para 5.34 et seq); *Cawdor (Countess) v Cawdor Castle (Tourism) Ltd* 2002 GWD 37-1232.

5.25 *Rescission* It should be noted that these provisions apply, not just to conventional irritancies, but to circumstances where a landlord is attempting to rescind a lease on the ground that there has been a material breach of contract.[1]

1 LR(MP)(S)A 1985, ss 4(1)(b), 5(1)(b); see also para 4.33.

5.26 Since the Act came into force there have been several court decisions which suggest that it has been only partially successful in remedying the problems it sought to address.

Monetary irritancies: CIN Properties v Dollar Land (Cumbernauld)

5.27 In *CIN Properties Ltd v Dollar Land (Cumbernauld) Ltd*,[1] the problems of conventional irritancies once more reached the

House of Lords, in circumstances even more spectacular than those in *Dorchester Studios*.[2] CIN were the head tenants under a 99-year ground lease of 6.73 acres, which comprised a substantial portion of Cumbernauld town centre. Dollar Land were in the unusual situation of being both the owners of the property and the subtenants, ie they were simultaneously the landlords and the tenants of CIN in respect of the same property. (This rather strange set-up was a legacy of the way the town centre development had originally been financed by Cumbernauld Development Corporation.)

As well as their continuing obligation to pay rent, Dollar Land had paid the development corporation (the original subtenants) a capital sum of £2.2 million for an assignation of the sub-lease to them. On the other hand, the rent which Dollar Land received, as head landlords, from CIN Properties was only a nominal rent of £1 a year. The value in this set up to Dollar Land was that the rent they had to pay to CIN as subtenants was approximately 77.5 per cent of the rents they received from the occupants of the premises under sub-under-leases, with the result that Dollar Land kept around 22.5 per cent of the rent received from the sub-under-lessees.

Dollar Land (the subtenants) were late and erratic in their quarterly rental payments to CIN during 1988 and failed to pay the rent due on 11 November 1988. On 15 December, in compliance with the 1985 Act, CIN Properties sent them a notice threatening irritancy if the rent was not paid by 4 January. Dollar Land failed to pay and, on 5 January, CIN began irritancy proceedings that eventually reached the House of Lords.

1 1992 SC(HL) 104, 1992 SLT 669.
2 *Dorchester Studios (Glasgow) Ltd v Stone* 1975 SC (HL) 56, 1975 SLT 153.

5.28 With considerable reluctance, their lordships enforced the irritancy. While recognising that in cases like the present one the penalty suffered by the subtenant (loss of a substantial investment) was out of proportion to the lapse that had engendered it, they nevertheless felt powerless to do anything about it. Parliament, in 1985, had already addressed the problem and enacted its own solution.

The inappropriateness of the traditional law to the modern long investment lease had already been recognised in *Dorchester Studios* when it had been noted that:

> 'The distinction between the feu contract and the lease has become unsubstantial since the former took to its death-bed. Moreover, the old view that the lease, unlike the feu contract, does not convey a right of property, wears today an air of unreality.'[1]

This view was further elaborated in *CIN Properties*:

> 'The basis of the distinction between a conventional irritancy in a
> feu contract, which is purgeable, and one in a lease, which is not
> purgeable, is said to be that a feu confers a right of property while
> a lease is merely a personal contract. But feus are in most instances
> granted with a view to a dwelling-house or some other building
> being erected on the land, and it must be of some materiality that
> irritancy after that had been done would result in the value of the
> building being lost to the feuar. For practical purposes it is not
> possible to see a distinction of any real significance between a feu
> and a building lease for 99 or 125 years.[2] While the rule excluding
> the opportunity of purgation may be entirely fair in cases where the
> payment of rent is the bare counterpart of the right of occupancy
> of, say, a farm, it is clearly capable of operating with extreme
> harshness in the case of a long building lease. In the *Dorchester
> Studios* case Lord Fraser of Tullybelton ... observed that if a tenant
> had agreed to a lease containing an irritancy it was not in principle
> unfair to hold him to his bargain. However, the tenant may not
> himself have negotiated the lease but may be an assignee, as in
> this case.'[3]

Lord Keith went on to point out that, in the event of the tenant going
bankrupt or into liquidation, the law could operate to the prejudice of
the tenant's creditors; they would forfeit the capital value of the tenant's
asset, which would instead accrue as an undeserved windfall to the
landlord. He also suggested that the courts could be given power to
attach conditions to a decree of irritancy, which could include an award
of compensation in respect of improvements carried out by the tenant,
eg by the erection of buildings.[4]

1 *Dorchester Studios (Glasgow) Ltd v Stone* 1975 SC(HL) 56 at 67 per Lord Kilbrandon.
2 The Royal Institution of Chartered Surveyors has estimated that in leases with an
  unexpired duration of 100 years or more the value of the landlord's interest is negligible
  – see para 5.6.
3 *CIN Properties Ltd v Dollar Land (Cumbernauld) Ltd* 1992 SLT 669 at 672 per Lord
  Keith of Kinkel.
4 *CIN Properties Ltd v Dollar Land (Cumbernauld) Ltd* 1992 SLT 669 at 672 per Lord
  Keith of Kinkel.

Unjustified enrichment

5.29   The above was not the end of the story and the dispute returned
to the House of Lords in *Dollar Land (Cumbernauld) v CIN Properties
Ltd*,[1] in which the former subtenants, under the equitable principle
of unjustified enrichment, claimed recompense for the benefit

CIN Properties had obtained at their expense. It was held that Dollar Land were required to establish three things:

(1)   that CIN had been enriched at their expense;
(2)   that there was no legal justification for the enrichment; and
(3)   that it would be equitable to compel CIN to redress the enrichment.

Dollar Land's claim failed under the second of these criteria: the benefit which they had lost in respect of their capital investment and rental revenue derived entirely from the sublease that had been terminated, and which had precisely spelled out the consequences of an irritancy. Effectively, any right of recompense had been contracted out of.

Although CIN Properties' enrichment was unusually extensive, it was pointed out that it was quite normal for irritancy to confer an advantage on a landlord at the tenant's expense, eg the right to retain a grassum paid when the lease was granted or buildings or other improvements made by the tenant, or to be able to relet the subjects in an improved market.[2]

1 1998 SC(HL) 90, 1998 SLT 992.
2 For another example of a ground lease being terminated by irritancy see the discussion of *Maris v Banchory Squash Racquets Club Ltd* 2007 SC 501, 2007 SLT 447 at para 5.36 et seq.

Non-monetary Irritancies: The 'Fair and Reasonable Landlord' test

5.30   For some time, before and after 1985, all the modern irritancy cases related to non-payment of rent. However, there are now several cases relating to the 'fair and reasonable landlord' test found in s 5 of the Law Reform (Miscellaneous Provisions)(Scotland) Act 1985. These, from the outset, took a rather unexpected direction.

In *Blythswood Investments (Scotland) Ltd v Clydesdale Electrical Stores Ltd (in receivership)*[1] the landlord sought to irritate two leases on the ground that the tenants had gone into receivership. The tenants' defence was that in all the circumstances of the case a fair and reasonable landlord would not irritate on this ground.[2] It was held that the phrase 'all the circumstances of the case' had the effect of making the provision much wider in its application than had probably been intended by the Scottish Law Commission, whose recommendations had been given effect in the 1985 Act. The criterion was not whether enforcement of the irritancy would operate in a penal fashion or what the court would regard as fair and reasonable. It was how a fair and reasonable landlord in the position of the actual landlord would act in all the circumstances of the case, circumstances which could include not only the interests of the tenant but also the interests of other tenants in the area and the fact that proceeding with the irritancy would confer considerable advantages on the landlord. Lord Cullen acknowledged that the criterion was so wide that it was likely to create practical difficulties in assessing the evidence. However, this case did not proceed to proof and it was left to subsequent cases to develop the theme.

In *Blythswood Investments* the leases in question contained a typical provision that the consent of the landlord to an assignation should not be unreasonably withheld or delayed in the case of a reputable and responsible assignee of sound financial standing. The tenants averred that, by securing an assignation to Scottish Power, they had met that requirement. It is submitted that such a situation may be a 'circumstance' that should be given some weight in determining whether or not a landlord is acting fairly and reasonably in proceeding with irritancy.

1 1995 SLT 150.
2 LR(MP)(S)A 1985 s 5; see also para 5.24.

Aubrey Investments v DSC (Realisations)

5.31   In *Aubrey Investments Ltd v DSC (Realisations) Ltd (in receivership)*[1] the landlord raised an irritancy action on the basis of the tenant's receivership. The landlord had initially agreed to give the receiver time to find a suitable assignee, but after several months became impatient with the lack of progress and began to negotiate directly with the proposed assignees with a view to directly granting them a new lease after the current one had been terminated. The receivers claimed inter alia that, in all the circumstances of the case, a fair and reasonable landlord would not proceed with the irritancy.

It was held that the landlord was entitled to proceed. Unlike *Blythswood Investments*,[2] this case did proceed to proof. The court accepted the basic reasoning of *Blythswood Investments* and provides the most thorough discussion to date of the 'fair and reasonable landlord' test.

1 1998 SLT 628 (sub nom *Aubrey Investments v D S Crawford Ltd (in receivership)* (procedure roll); 1999 SC 21, 2000 SLT 183 (final decision).
2 *Blythswood Investments (Scotland) Ltd v Clydesdale Electrical Stores Ltd (in receivership)* 1995 SLT 150.

5.32   Lord Macfadyen's judgment identified a number of criteria for the application of the principle:[1]

1.   When deciding whether or not to enforce the irritancy, the hypothetical fair and reasonable landlord should be assumed to

be in the same position as the actual landlord in the case at that time. The hypothetical landlord should generally be assumed to have the same state of knowledge as the actual landlord, with the qualification that he may be expected to have made enquiries that the actual landlord did not make. This develops Lord Cullen's observation in *Blythswood Investments*.[2]

2.   'All the circumstances of the case' may go beyond the landlord and tenant relationship defined in the lease to include the circumstances of a receiver who has not adopted the lease. However, the landlord can only take account of these circumstances to the extent that he can be taken to be aware of them, and is not obliged to give them much weight.

3.   The onus of proof that a fair and reasonable landlord would not irritate is on the tenant. This is inconsistent with the earlier Outer House decision in *Scottish Exhibition Centre Ltd v Mirestop Ltd (In Administration) (No 2)*[3] in which it was held that the onus of proof is on the landlord. It is submitted that it would be more appropriate for the onus to be upon the landlord, as the pursuer in the action. It would also help to redress the balance between the parties in an irritancy situation, which still appears to be weighted in favour of the landlord.

4.   The time when the 'fair and reasonable landlord' test falls to be applied is the time at which the landlord makes a formal attempt to rely on the irritancy, ie by serving a notice of irritancy. In *Euro Properties Scotland Ltd v Alam*[4] Lord Macfadyen modified his opinion to the effect that events occurring after service of the notice could also be taken into account, though this view has subsequently been doubted.[5]

5.   'Fairness' and 'reasonableness' are not separate criteria, but two overlapping expressions defining a single concept. Lord Macfadyen elaborated upon this in *Euro Properties v Alam*:

> '... I do not regard that as precluding examination of the separate elements of the criterion if different aspects of the circumstances of the case bring them into focus in different ways. In one case, a landlord may fail because what he seeks to do would be unfair. In another, he may fail because what he seeks to do would be unreasonable.'[6]

6.   The fact that some landlords might refrain from enforcing the irritancy in the same circumstances is not conclusive. Allowance must be made for the unusually lenient landlord, and for the landlord who has reasons of his own to choose not to irritate.

7.   The 'fair and reasonable landlord' test cannot be reduced to a balance of hardship, ie whether it would cause more hardship to the tenant

to be evicted than to the landlord if he were denied possession. There are other considerations to be taken into account and, in any case, the factors involved cannot be reduced to any common unit of measurement of their weight; in particular, the respective hardships cannot be reduced to cash terms. This seems a little strange since there is other legislation containing balance of hardship tests that have come before the courts on a number of occasions, eg in s 24(1) (d) of the Agricultural Holdings (Scotland) Act 1991[7] or s 1(3)(f) of the Tenancy of Shops (Scotland) Act 1949.[8]

8. Even a fair and reasonable landlord will eventually lose patience when there is delay, particularly in the uncertain situation when a receiver is in occupation.

9. A fair and reasonable landlord does not ignore his own commercial interests. He may find that he has to moderate the extent to which he pursues them, but the mere fact that a particular course of action brings with it a collateral benefit to the landlord does not taint it with unfairness or unreasonableness.

1 *Aubrey Investments Ltd v DSC (Realisations) Ltd (in receivership)* 1999 SC 21 at 42-50 per Lord Macfadyen.
2 *Blythswood Investments (Scotland) Ltd v Clydesdale Electrical Stores Ltd (in receivership)* 1995 SLT 150.
3 1994 GWD 15-917; there is a fuller report in 1996 SLT 8, but the relevant part of the judgment is omitted.
4 2000 GWD 23-896; the full judgment is on the Scottish Courts web site at www. scotcourts.co.uk; see paras 5.34 and 5.35.
5 See para 5.36.
6 At para 24.
7 See para 15.50.
8 See para 14.17 et seq.

5.33   Lord Macfadyen concluded by saying:

'The most difficult part of applying the fair and reasonable landlord test is to judge what weight should be attached to each of the multifarious considerations which such a landlord would take into account from all the circumstances of the case. All that can be done, after a critical examination of all the circumstances, is to take an overall view. In doing so, I remind myself that the fair and reasonable landlord is not the wholly altruistic landlord who subordinates his own interests to those of the tenant. He is, rather, the landlord who is prepared to exercise his right to irritate the lease, unless it would be unfair or unreasonable of him to do so.'[1]

He decided that the landlord had satisfied the test in s 5 and, as such, had terminated the lease.

1 *Aubrey Investments Ltd v DSC (Realisations) Ltd (in receivership)* 1999 SC 21 at 50 per Lord Macfadyen.

Euro Properties v Alam

5.34   In *Euro Properties Scotland Ltd v Alam*[1] the property in question was a Grade A listed building, its listing being largely due to the surviving elements of its 19th century use as a music hall. It was being used by the tenants as an amusement arcade. The tenants were responsible for repairs under the lease which, however, contained the usual provision entitling the landlord to carry out any necessary repairs and charge them to the tenants, if the tenants failed to do so after being given reasonable notice. The landlord received a listed building repair notice which it passed on to the tenants. After a long delay, during which some discussions took place but no repairs were carried out, the landlord sent the tenants a notice that it intended to irritate the lease unless inter alia the necessary work was begun within 21 days and completed within 60.

The court accepted the view of one of the expert witnesses that the whole repair process, involving as it did the participation of Glasgow council and Historic Scotland, would take between nine and 12 months, and that the deadline in the notice would have been impossible for the tenants to meet.

1 2000 GWD 23-896; the full judgment is on the Scottish Courts website at www. scotcourts.co.uk. See also the references to this judgment in the discussion of *Aubrey Investments* at para 5.32.

5.35   It was held:

(1)   that the tenants had not been afforded a reasonable opportunity to remedy the breach in terms of s 5(1) of the Law Reform (Miscellaneous Provisions) (Scotland) Act 1985;[1] and

(2)   that it was not prima facie fair and reasonable for the landlords to opt for irritancy when there was available an alternative remedy (by way of the landlord carrying out the repairs and charging them to the tenant) which would (a) not deprive the tenants of their interest in the lease but (b) nevertheless adequately protect the landlord's interest. As a result, Lord Macfadyen concluded that irritancy for failure to implement repair obligations was a course rarely adopted by fair and reasonable landlords. In any case, ending the lease would decrease the landlord's chances of recovering the repair costs from the tenants as well as depriving the landlord of the rental income; it might be different, however, if the rental void caused by irritancy was outweighed by the benefit of a more advantageous re-letting.

1 See para 5.24.

Maris v Banchory Squash Racquets Club

5.36   However, in *Maris v Banchory Squash Racquets Club Ltd*[1] the Inner House did, in fact, allow the landlord to irritate the lease for breach of a repairing obligation (though in this case the lease did not contain the standard provision allowing the landlord to carry out the repairs and charge them to the tenant).

The lease was a 99-year ground lease with an unexpired duration of 76 years. The rent was nominal. In accordance with the lease conditions, the tenant had constructed a squash court and associated buildings, binding itself to maintain and when necessary renew the subjects thereafter. After the subjects fell into considerable disrepair, the landlord issued an irritancy notice, giving the tenant a three-month deadline to carry out certain major repairs, failing which irritancy would proceed.

Within the period of the deadline, the tenant only succeeded in carrying out a few minor repairs, but between the expiry of the deadline and the court hearing the tenant obtained financial assistance and completed almost all of the required repairs.

However, the Inner House held that the relevant date for application of the fair and reasonable landlord test was the date when the irritancy was invoked, ie the expiry of the deadline in the notice, not the date when the irritancy action came to court. They doubted the soundness of Lord Macfadyen's view (given obiter in *Euro Properties v Alam*) that repairs carried out subsequently could sometimes be taken into account.[2] Since the repairs had barely started when the deadline expired, the court held that a fair and reasonable landlord could proceed with irritancy.

1 2007 SC 501, 2007 SLT 447.
2 See para 5.32.

5.37   Like *CIN Properties* this is an example of termination by irritancy of a ground lease with a long unexpired duration, where the tenant had paid for the development of the site, including the erection of buildings. The value of the tenant's interest which was forfeited is not mentioned, but presumably was substantial. The tenant had also incurred considerable expense carrying out the repairs, the value of which would now also accrue to the landlord. The comments of the House of Lords in *Dorchester Studios* and *CIN Properties* about the appropriateness of irritancy in such a situation would also seem to apply here.[1]

1 See para 5.28.

Protection of insolvent companies

5.38   If a company is subject to an administration order a landlord's right of irritancy is suspended in respect of any subjects leased to the company. The landlord cannot proceed with irritancy without the consent of the administrator or of the court.[1] Where a stand-alone moratorium (a process introduced by the Corporate Insolvency and Governance Act 2020) is in place a landlord cannot proceed with irritancy without the permission of the court.[2] This is part of a package of measures designed to assist the rescue of companies or, where that is not possible, prevent a particular creditor obtaining an unfair advantage. This purpose could otherwise be thwarted by certain hostile legal proceedings against the company, such as the use of irritancy.

Where a tenant company enters liquidation no action or proceeding can be taken against it without leave of the court.[3] As such, a landlord would require court consent to raise an action to evict the tenant should it refuse to vacate the premises following irritancy.

1 See the Insolvency Act 1986 Sch B1 para 43(5).
2 Insolvency Act 1986 s A21 (added by the Corporate Insolvency and Governance Act 2020).
3 Insolvency Act 1986 s 130(2).

Scottish Law Commission recommendations

5.39   In 2003 the Scottish Law Commission recommended that the minimum deadline for monetary breaches should be extended from 14 to 28 days, and that a similar deadline should be given in the case of remediable breaches (such as failure in a repairing obligation) to replace the fair and reasonable landlord test.[1] In the latter case, however, the tenant could apply to the court for an extension on the basis that the time allowed is unreasonably short, or that the work is substantially complete and more time is necessary to finish it.

In the case of non-remediable breaches other than insolvency, the fair and reasonable landlord test would be replaced by a power of the court to prevent or delay the exercise of irritancy where it considers that the termination of the lease would be a manifestly excessive response to the breach or other event.[2]

In cases of insolvency, the landlord would be required to serve a moratorium notice on the insolvency practitioner allowing a period of at least six months to allow the practitioner to assign the lease.[3] This was designed to complement the statutory restriction on irritancy that applies in the case of companies in administration.[4]

These recommendations, if implemented, would strengthen the statutory protection of tenants in many ways. However, it is arguable whether a strict 28-day deadline in the case of monetary breaches would go far enough to prevent the sort of situation in *CIN Properties*[5] where the premature termination of a valuable ground lease deprives the tenant of a substantial property right, resulting in a considerable loss to the tenant and a substantial windfall for the landlord. This is particularly the case since the Commission have made no recommendations for compensation being awarded to the tenant in such circumstances, as the House of Lords suggested in *CIN Properties*.

1 Scottish Law Commission *Report on Irritancy in Leases of Land* (Scot Law Com No 191, 2003), 3.31 and 3.41.
2 Scottish Law Commission *Report on Irritancy in Leases of Land* (Scot Law Com No 191, 2003), 3.63.
3 Scottish Law Commission *Report on Irritancy in Leases of Land* (Scot Law Com No 191, 2003), 3.48 et seq.
4 See para 5.38.
5 *CIN Properties Ltd v Dollar Land (Cumbernauld) Ltd* 1992 SC (HL) 104, 1992 SLT 66. See also *Maris v Banchory Squash Racquets Club Ltd* 2007 SC 501, 2007 SLT 447 and the discussion of these cases at paras 5.27 et seq and 5.36 et seq.

IRRITANCY AND HUMAN RIGHTS[1]

Vertical effect

5.40   The most obvious potential breach of a tenant's human rights as a result of irritancy is under Protocol 1, Article 1 of the European Convention on Human Rights, since the tenant has been deprived of a property right.[2] Where the landlord is a public authority (such as a local authority) there could be a direct breach of the convention, though the possibility of waiver could still arise.[3] Where the landlord is a private individual or body (and assuming that they are not carrying out functions of a public nature)[4] it seems clear that there can be no direct (or vertical) effect of the Convention.

In *Di Palma v United Kingdom*[5] the European Commission considered the forfeiture of an English lease, a remedy analogous to irritancy. The tenant had forfeited her interest (valued at £30,000) under a long residential lease because of failure to pay a service charge of £299.36. It was held that there was no violation of Protocol 1, Article 1. The lease, including the provisions for forfeiture, was a private contract between the parties for which the state had no responsibility. Its terms were 'neither directly prescribed or amended by legislation'.[6]

It should be noted right away that irritancy clauses *have* been amended by legislation in the Law Reform (Miscellaneous Provisions) (Scotland) Act 1985. Nevertheless, *Di Palma* might seem to dispose of the issue.

1 See para 1.27 et seq.
2 See para 1.36.
3 See para 5.42.
4 See para 1.29.
5 *Di Palma v United Kingdom* (1988) 10 EHRR CD149.
6 *Di Palma v United Kingdom* (1988) 10 EHRR CD149.

Horizontal effect

5.41   Section 6 of the Human Rights Act 1998 has added a new dimension by making it unlawful for public authorities, including the domestic courts, to act in a way that is incompatible with the Convention.[1] The provisions of Protocol 1, Article 1, therefore, could influence the development of the common law of irritancy, perhaps even making the defence of oppression more effective.[2]

Where legislation confers discretion upon a court, the court should, as far as possible, interpret the legislation and exercise their discretion compatibly with the convention. This could influence a court when applying the 'fair and reasonable landlord' test.[3]

1 HRA 1998 s 6(1) and (3)(a).
2 See para 5.15 et seq.
3 See para 5.24 and para 5.30 et seq.

Waiver of Convention rights[1]

5.42   It is established that at least some of the Convention rights may be waived by the alleged victim. This presents a serious difficulty for a tenant who has freely signed a lease containing an irritancy clause. Allied to this is the principle of freedom of contract, under which the tenant would be held to the terms of the lease. This was an important consideration in *Di Palma v United* Kingdom.[2]

The case for waiver is perhaps weaker where the rights of a subtenant or heritable creditor have been lost as a result of irritancy, since they did not sign the lease containing the irritancy clause.[3] However, they will arguably have accepted the irritancy provision when signing the sub-lease or granting the security.

1 See Reed & Murdoch *A Guide to Human Rights Law in Scotland* (4th edn 2017), paras 3.36–3.38.
2 *Di Palma v United Kingdom* (1988) 10 EHRR CD149.
3 See para 5.2.

Proportionality

5.43   Once human rights arguments have gained a horizontal foothold (perhaps in one of the ways suggested above) the principle of proportionality may follow.[1] Where a tenant is deprived of a £2.2 million investment because of failure to pay one quarter's rent (as in *CIN Properties v Dollar Land (Cumbernauld) Ltd*)[2] one can envisage a human rights argument to the effect that the remedy may be disproportionate to the breach.[3]

1 See para 1.39.
2 1992 SC(HL) 105, 1992 SLT 669.
3 See Kay Springham 'Property Law' in *A Practical Guide to Human Rights Law in Scotland* (ed Lord Reed) (2001), p 263.

5.44   To date there has been no case law on the application of the Human Rights Act to irritancy. The above discussion, therefore, is somewhat speculative.

CONCLUSION

5.45   After many years of unsuccessful pleas of oppression followed by the failure of the 1985 Act to provide sufficient protection for tenants, the law of irritancy still presents a considerable danger to commercial and agricultural tenants. The Scottish Law Commission proposed further statutory regulation which would afford further protection to tenants, but their report is nearly 20 years old and it is doubtful whether it will now be implemented.[1]

Meanwhile, when negotiating the terms of new leases, tenants' agents should continue to be vigilant regarding irritancy provisions and attempt, if possible, to have them modified in their clients' favour. However, it should also be remembered that irritancies are likely to operate most harshly in long ground leases and that there must be many of those still around that were granted before *Dorchester Studios (Glasgow) Ltd v Stone*[2] made irritancy a live issue in 1975. It is also, therefore, important for the agents of potential assignees to try to negotiate with landlords a modification of irritancy clauses where this seems necessary.

1 See para 5.3.
2 1975 SC(HL) 56, 1975 SLT 153.

Chapter 6

Legal remedies of the parties 3: Hypothec, abatement of rent and summary diligence

LANDLORD'S HYPOTHEC[1]

Nature of hypothec

6.1   The right of hypothec was formerly a very effective remedy for a landlord to ensure the payment of rent. Hypothec is a real right in security enjoyed by a landlord over moveable items kept by the tenant on the leased premises, known as the *invecta et illata* ('things brought in and carried in'). Traditionally, it covered not only moveable property actually owned by the tenant but could also include the property of third parties.[2] The hypothec was security for each year's rent successively, but not for arrears due for a previous year.[3]

The landlord's hypothec is a 'tacit' or 'legal' right, ie like a legal irritancy, it is implied by law and does not need to be specifically provided for in the lease. It is very old, originating in Scotland in the 17th century and deriving from Roman law.

1 Rankine pp 366–411; Paton and Cameron ch 13.
2 See eg *Dundee Corpn v Marr* 1971 SC 96, sub nom *Ditchburn Organisation (Sales) Ltd v Dundee Corp* 1971 SLT 218; *Scottish & Newcastle Breweries Ltd v City of Edinburgh District Council* 1979 SLT (Notes) 11. That is no longer the case: see paras 6.3 and 6.10.
3 Rankine, p 384.

Sequestration for rent

6.2   Traditionally, hypothec was enforced by a court action known as sequestration for rent, which led to the sale of enough of the tenant's moveable property to pay the rent. This was a very powerful remedy with several unique features. As well as the ability to sell property owned by third parties that was on the lease premises,[1] sequestration for rent was unaffected by the tenant's insolvency.[2] In addition, the moveables were attached at the beginning of the court action, at the time the court summons was served; this allowed the landlord to jump the queue in front of other creditors, who could generally not attach any moveable property until after their court decree had been granted.[3]

1 See eg *Dundee Corporation v Marr* 1971 SC 96, sub nom *Ditchburn Organisation (Sales) Ltd v Dundee Corp* 1971 SLT 218; *Scottish & Newcastle Breweries Ltd v Edinburgh District Council* 1979 SLT (Notes) 11.
2 The equalisation of diligences which affects arrrestments and attachments did not apply to sequestration for rent – see the Bankruptcy (Scotland) Act 1985 s 37(4) (now repealed; for the current provision see the Bankruptcy (Scotland) Act 2016 s 24(5)); Insolvency Act 1986 s 185.
3 Macphail *Sheriff Court Practice* (3rd edn ed Welsh, 2006) 23.18–23.20. Although it was possible to obtain arrestment on the dependence of a court action which would catch the tenant's moveable property that was in the hands of a third party. It is now possible to seek interim attachment pending the outcome of a court action: the Debt Arrangement and Attachment (Scotland) Act 2002 see s 9A–9S.

Sequestration for rent abolished: Bankruptcy and Diligence etc (Scotland) Act 2007

6.3   These unique privileges conferred upon landlords by the right of hypothec were almost entirely removed by section 208 of the Bankruptcy and Diligence etc (Scotland) Act 2007. The diligence of sequestration for rent was abolished[1] and the scope of the right of hypothec was restricted in several important ways:

(1)   It no longer applies to property kept in a dwellinghouse, on agricultural land or on a croft.[2] In fact, hypothec had already been abolished in relation to most agricultural tenancies more than a century earlier.[3]

(2)   It no longer applies to property which is owned by a person other than the tenant, or property acquired in good faith from the tenant by a third party.[4] Where property is owned in common by the tenant and a third party, the right of hypothec applies only to the extent of the tenant's interest in that property.[5]

(3)   It now only covers rent currently due and not future rent. The rationale for this is unclear and problematic.[6] On the other hand, it now covers *all* outstanding arrears and not just the current year's rent.[7] As noted above, hypothec traditionally covered only the current year's rent and not prior arrears.

1 Bankruptcy and Diligence etc (Scotland) Act 2007 s 208(1). Any sequestration for rent action raised before the Act came into force remained valid and had the same scope as before (except in relation to those aspects mentioned in point (2)) – see BADE(S) A 2007 s 208(10). This meant, for example, that the exclusion of the property of third parties was immediate and retrospective.
2 BADE(S)A 2007 s 208(3).

3 Hypothec Abolition (Scotland) Act 1880 s 1 (repealed by BADE(S)A 2007 s 226 and Sch 6 Pt 1).
4 BADE(S)A 2007 s 208(4) and (5).
5 BADE(S)A 2007 s 208(7).
6 BADE(S)A 2007 s 208 (8); see the discussion of this issue at paras 6.12 and 6.15.
7 BADE(S)A 2007 s 208 (8).

6.4   Despite the abolition of sequestration for rent as the principal means of enforcing the right of hypothec, it is specifically stated that it will continue as a right in security over corporeal property kept in or on the subjects of let.[1] In any insolvency proceedings (such as winding up or administration) or other process where there is ranking the landlord will have a preferential claim in respect of the items that are subject to the hypothec.[2] On the face of it, this appears to be straightforward enough, but the precise application of the right of hypothec during insolvency proceedings would appear to be proving problematic in practice.[3]

Any enactment or rule of law relating to the landlord's hypothec ceased to have effect to the extent that it is inconsistent with the above provisions. This means that the existing common law of hypothec, so far as it is consistent with the legislation, remains in force.

1 BADE(S)A 2007 s 208 (2)(a)
2 BADE(S)A 2007 s 208 (2)(b). 'Insolvency proceedings' is defined in subs (12).
3 See Alistair Burrow 'Unclear Security' 2010 55 JLSS 47; Sarah Skea and Andrew J M Steven 'The Landlord's Hypothec: Difficulties in Practice' 2010 SLT (News) 120.

General effect of the Act

6.5   The above provisions, particularly as a result of the abolition of sequestration for rent, have had a far-reaching effect on the landlord's right of hypothec. Virtually all that remains of this formerly powerful remedy, as a distinctive means of recovering rent arrears, is as a preferential claim if the tenant becomes insolvent.

The above provisions have been severely criticised by a number of commentators as ill-conceived and woefully under researched.[1] It is clear that they have been framed with little regard to the large body of existing common law rules relating to hypothec. As a result, determining which of these rules are consistent with the Act – and therefore still in force – and which are inconsistent – and therefore superseded – is not always easy. Some of the difficulties are considered below.

1 See eg Angus McAllister 'The Landlord's Hypothec: Down But Is It Out?' 2010 2 Jur Rev 65; Andrew J M Steven 'Goodbye to the Landlord's Hypothec?' 2002 SLT (News) 177 and 'Goodbye to Sequestration for Rent' 2006 SLT (News) 17; and Sarah Skea and Andrew J M Steven 'The Landlord's Hypothec: Difficulties in Practice' 2010 SLT (News) 120.

Hypothec as a real right

6.6   Although the continued existence of hypothec as a right in security, independently of any means of enforcing it, is confirmed by the Act,[1] nothing is said about the fact that the right of hypothec is a real right. As there is nothing to contradict this in the Act, presumably it still is. Hypothec confers a real right in security, quite independently of sequestration for rent or any other proceedings that may be used to enforce it.[2]

In other words, the right was not made real by the sequestration process; the effect of that process was to convert the real right of hypothec into a different kind of real right. The right of hypothec came into being automatically at the commencement of the lease and continued throughout it. It covered all moveable property that happened to be on the leased premises from time to time, but the tenant was free to do with that property as he or she wanted: any items acquired by the tenant automatically became subject to the landlord's hypothec, and any that the tenant disposed of automatically became free of it.

The process of sequestration converted this general real right into a real right of pledge, a fixed security that attached to the specific items that happened to be on the premises when the sequestration took place.[3] Obviously the abolition of sequestration for rent has removed the second right, but presumably not the first one.

There is a distinction, which the legislators seem to have overlooked, between a right in security, which exists whether or not the debtor is insolvent, and a preference, which only applies in the latter case when determining ranking among creditors.[4] One would therefore expect there to be some distinctive way by which to enforce the real right of hypothec apart from the ability to make a preferential claim in the event of the tenant's insolvency, a remedy which would be available whether or not the tenant was insolvent. Otherwise the existence of such a real right would be merely theoretical, and in practical terms meaningless. The suggestion by the Scottish Executive that hypothec may be enforced by an attachment does not fit the bill, as this is merely to say that a landlord has the same enforcement rights as any creditor.[5]

1 See para 6.4.
2 *Grampian Regional Council v Drill Stem (Inspection Services) Ltd (in receivership)* 1994 SCLR 36, a sheriff court decision founded upon a substantial weight of academic authority. See, in particular, GL Gretton 'Receivership and Sequestration for Rent' 1983 SLT (News) 277; see also WM Gloag and JM Irvine *Law of Rights in Security* (1897) p 424 and Angus McAllister 'The Landlord's Hypothec: Down But Is It Out?' 2010 2 Jur Rev 65.
3 Paton and Cameron p 199, quoting Bell *Commentaries* II, 27.

4 See Andrew J M Steven 'Goodbye to Sequestration for Rent' 2006 SLT (News) 17 at 18.
5 Such is the ambiguity created by the legislation that this may be an over simplification – see Sarah Skea and Andrew J M Steven 'The Landlord's Hypothec: Difficulties in Practice' 2010 SLT (News) 120.

6.7   Moreover, for a real right, the altered right of hypothec has some peculiar features. Previously there was a single right of hypothec which came into being along with the lease and remained in place, secured over the current year's rent at any one time. However, now that the right only applies to rent which is due and unpaid, there would appear to be a succession of rights of hypothec, each coming into being as soon as rent is owing and disappearing as soon as the rent is paid. This is the logical consequence of s 208(8) of the 2007 Act.[1]

1 BADE(S)A s 208(8); see also paras 6.12 and 6.14.

6.8   If the above seems over-theoretical, the moral is clear and practical. If the only practical significance of hypothec is to give the landlord a preferential claim in the tenant's insolvency, then there is little point in there being a right of hypothec at all. The landlord could simply be given a preference without it being dependent on whatever moveable property happens to be left on the leased premises at the time the tenant becomes insolvent. By that time there may be little of value left.

However, at common law, sequestration for rent was not the only enforcement measure relating to the landlord's hypothec: there were also certain precautionary measures which may still be valid. These will be discussed briefly below.[1]

1 See para 6.13 et seq.

Leases subject to hypothec

6.9   Now that the right of hypothec no longer applies to agricultural leases or property kept within dwellinghouses, its main application is to commercial leases.[1] However, the 2007 Act makes no mention of any other type of lease apart from these, with the result that the previous common law in relation to any such lease remains unchanged. Hypothec probably does not apply to sporting leases, at least in cases where the tenant does not have full possession of the subjects.[2] Presumably, however, it still applies to mineral leases.[3]

1 See para 6.3.
2 Rankine p 371.
3 *Liquidators of the Linlithgow Oil Co Ltd v Earl of Roseberry* (1903) 6 F 90.

Items covered by hypothec[1]

6.10   The items covered by the landlord's right of hypothec generally include all moveable items on the leased premises, eg stock-in-trade in the case of a shop lease, or machinery where the lease is of a factory, though no longer property belonging to a third party. At common law certain items were thought to be excluded, eg money, or the tenant's clothes.

1 Rankine pp 373–383; Paton and Cameron pp 202–206; BADE(S)A 2007 s 208(4).

6.11   *Property of subtenants*   It was formerly possible, where the property had been sublet, that the landlord could enforce the right of hypothec over the subtenant's effects in order to recover the rent due by the head tenant.[1] This will no longer be possible, under the general exclusion of property belonging to third parties. However, the head tenant (as the subtenant's immediate landlord) still has a right of hypothec over the subtenant's moveable property.

1 Rankine pp 397–399; Paton and Cameron pp 208–209.

Rent covered by hypothec[1]

6.12   The landlord's hypothec only covers rent but not other debts, eg service charges, that may be payable by a tenant to a landlord, unless, of course, such payments have been allowed for and included within the rental figure stated in the lease.[2]

Traditionally, it secured only the current year's rent and not prior arrears.[3] The current year of a lease normally runs from the anniversary of the date of entry.[4] However, hypothec now covers prior arrears also, though it is now stated to cover only rent that is due and unpaid.[5] This apparently straightforward change in fact creates a problem, both in theory and in practice, which will be examined further below.[6]

1 Rankine p 384; Paton and Cameron pp 206–208.
2 See para 13.13.
3 *Young v Welsh* (1833) 12 S 233.
4 *Donald v Leitch* (1886) 13 R 790; *Sawyers v Kinnair* (1897) 25 R 45.
5 BADE(S)A 2007 s 208(8).
6 See para 6.14.

Precautionary measures

6.13   At common law the now defunct sequestration for rent was not the only enforcement measure relating to the landlord's hypothec. It was the only one which operated as a mechanism for actual recovery of the arrears, but there were other actions which were designed to ensure that the leased subjects contained enough moveable property to secure the rent in the first place, and that this security would not be prejudiced by the later removal of that property. These remedies had largely fallen into disuse or, in the case of plenishing orders, were generally combined with a sequestration action, though theoretically separable. None of these measures are mentioned in s 208 of the 2007 Act and are presumably still competent. However, it also seems likely that those responsible for the legislation failed to take account of them at all, with the result that their precise application has now been thrown into some doubt.[1]

1 For an analysis of these rights in depth and an assessment of the current situation, see Angus McAllister 'The landlord's hypothec: Down but is it out?' 2010 2 Jur Rev 65.

6.14 *Plenishing order* We saw in Chapter 3 that a tenant traditionally had a duty to plenish the leased property, ie to keep moveable property on the premises of sufficient value to secure the rent.[1] If the tenant failed in this obligation, the landlord could apply to court for a plenishing order, requiring the tenant to restock the premises. In actions of sequestration for rent it was standard for the sequestration order to be combined with one that the tenant should replenish the property after the sale had been carried out.[2] Plenishing orders had otherwise fallen into disuse, but in theory can still be competent in a separate action.[3]

However, the scope of plenishing orders must now be in some doubt as a result of the provision that the right of hypothec applies to rent due and unpaid only. Previously a plenishing order could be sought whether or not the tenant was in arrears, as security for rent due in the current year. If this is no longer the case, which seems likely, it makes the right of hypothec a rather peculiar type of security.

1 See para 3.9.
2 Macphail *Sheriff Court Practice* (3rd edn ed Welsh, 2006) 23.18.
3 For modern authority that a tenant's obligation to plenish the subjects is still competent independently of a sequestration for rent action see *Co-operative Insurance Society Ltd v Halfords Ltd* (No 1) 1998 SLT 90 at 93–94 per Lord Hamilton, 1997 SCLR 719; see also para 4.18.

6.15 *Right of retention*[1] At common law, even when there was no rent owing, the landlord could nevertheless insist upon the entire *invecta et illata* remaining on the premises and could obtain an interdict to prevent the tenant from removing any of it, without first finding security. Since this right flowed naturally from the right of hypothec, it was not necessary for the landlord to show good cause, eg that the tenant is *vergens ad inopiam* (approaching insolvency).[2] When rent became due, the right of retention was confined to sufficient effects to cover one year's rent, though the reason for this was not absolutely clear.

This right would appear still to exist, as the right of the landlord to obtain an interdict to prevent the removal of moveable property is mentioned in passing in s 208 of the 2007 Act.[3] However, the scope of such an interdict must be in some doubt, now that hypothec is specifically stated to cover only rent which is due and unpaid. It seems unlikely that the right of retention will now cover the entire *invecta et illata* as this rule only applied in cases where no rent was owing; in other cases, however, whether it can still extend to security for one year's rent, when one year's rent may not be owing, is unclear.

1 Rankine pp 390–392; Paton and Cameron pp 213–214; *Preston v Gregor* (1845) 7 D 942; *Gray v Weir* (1891) 19 R 25, at 30 per Lord McLaren.

2 *Preston v Gregor* (1845) 7 D 942.

3 BADE(S)A 2007 s 208(5) and (6).

6.16 *Warrant to carry back*[1] Where items subject to hypothec have been removed, either by the tenant or by a third party, the landlord could apply to the court for a warrant to have them returned to the leased premises.[2] However, such a warrant was granted *periculo petentis* (at the pursuer's risk) and the landlord could be liable to the tenant in damages unless the tenant was formally notified and therefore able to attend the hearing.[3] However, such notice might not have been necessary where there were special circumstances, eg if the items had been removed clandestinely ('under cloud of night' or by a 'midnight flitting');[4] in such a case, giving the tenant notice might be an invitation to move the items again, into a place of hiding, before the sheriff officer's arrival.

In the past, where an interdict or a warrant to carry back was claimed it was normally as a prelude to an action of sequestration for rent.[5] In the case of a warrant to carry back it was likely to be after a warrant of sequestration for rent had been granted but not yet carried out because, for example, items subject to the hypothec had been removed. This was the situation in the only reported modern case on the subject,[6] where an interim interdict was also granted.

However, there seems to be no reason in theory why these remedies could not be used in other circumstances, for example to preserve the value of the landlord's preference when insolvency seems likely. Without them, the actions of other creditors may have left little of value by the time insolvency actually occurs.

1 Rankine pp 392–393; Paton and Cameron p 214.

2 *McLaughlan v Reilly* (1892) 20 R 41; *Novacold v Fridge Freight (Fyvie) Ltd (in receivership)* 1999 SCLR 409.

3 *Jack v Black* 1911 SC 691; see also *Johnston v Young* (1890) 18 R (JC) 6; *Gray v Weir* (1891) 20 R 25; *Shearer v Nicoll* 1935 SLT 313.
4 *McLaughlan v Reilly* (1892) 20 R 41; *Johnston v Young* (1890) 18 R (JC) 6; *Gray v Weir* (1891) 20 R 25.
5 J Graham Stewart *A Treatise on the Law of Diligence* (1898) p 475.
6 *Novacold v Fridge Freight (Fyvie) Ltd (in receivership)* 1999 SCLR 409.

Conclusion

6.17 Preserving the right of hypothec in its present mutilated form is pointless. Whether or not a landlord should have a preferential claim in respect of rent on tenant insolvency is a matter of policy. If it is decided that there should be such a preference, it can be conferred by a simple legislative measure, without being dependent upon a so-called right of hypothec which is a theoretical mess and of uncertain value in any particular case, since it depends on whatever items of moveable property happen to be left on the leased premises when the tenant becomes insolvent.

Given the restrictions on the right of hypothec it seems that it will only be of any real practical use to a landlord when the tenant is approaching insolvency or becomes insolvent. In those situations a landlord may be able to ensure, by way of court action (obtaining interdict or a warrant to carry back) or by discussion with the relevant insolvency practitioner appointed to the tenant, eg the liquidator or administrator, that there are moveables items left in the lease premises to give some worth to the landlord's right of hypothec.

Having considered a right available to the landlord at law, we now move on to consider a right available to the tenant.

ABATEMENT OF RENT

6.18 As noted in Chapter 4, abatement of rent is available where a tenant, through no fault of his own, is partially deprived of possession of the leased subjects. In *Muir v McIntyres*[1] a farm tenant was held entitled to an abatement where a number of farm buildings were accidentally destroyed by fire:

> '[I]t is quite settled in law that an abatement is to be allowed if a tenant loses the beneficial enjoyment of any part of the subject let to him either through the fault of the landlord or through some unforeseen calamity which the tenant was not able to prevent.'[2]

1 (1887) 14 R 470.
2 *Muir v McIntyres* (1887) 14 R 470 at 472 per the Lord President.

Other case law

6.19   In *Munro v McGeoghs*[1] the landlord was at fault, being in breach of a lease provision to give possession of certain farm buildings in tenantable condition. However, the basis of the decision was that the tenant had not got entire possession of the subjects let and was therefore entitled to an abatement of rent corresponding to the amount of the possession not delivered.

And in *Sharp v Thomson*[2] the partial destruction of a lade during a storm effectively meant that a farm, which had been partly arable and partly pastoral, ceased to be of any value as an arable farm. The tenant was held to be entitled to a rent abatement proportional to the lettable value of what had been destroyed. It was also observed 'that to warrant a claim for an abatement, [the damage] must be considerable, and that the consequent cost of making good the damage must be substantial'.[3]

The law in relation to abatement was given its most thorough consideration in modern times in *Renfrew District Council v* Gray,[4] in which a council house was in such a state of disrepair that for over a year it was effectively uninhabitable. The tenants were held to be entitled to an abatement of the rent in full for the relevant period, despite the fact that they remained in possession: they may not have had anywhere else to go, and could not be expected to have to pay rent for an uninhabitable house. Also, it was held that abatement did not need to be claimed in a separate action, or be the subject of a counter-claim, but could simply be submitted as a defence in an action by the landlord for the rent.

In the recent decision of *Fern Trustee 1 Ltd and Fern Trustee 2 Ltd v Scott Wilson Railways Ltd*[5] the Sheriff decided that abatement of rent was available to a tenant who had agreed to his right of occupation being infringed (by entering a remedial works agreement to allow defective cladding to the property of which the lease premises formed part to be repaired). For the Sheriff it was important that the landlord could have instructed the repair works without the tenant's consent.

A rent relief order, which may now be granted by the First-Tier Tribunal in residential leases from private landlords, is effectively a statutory form of abatement.[6]

1 (1888) 16 R 93.
2 1930 SC 1092, 1930 SLT 785.
3 *Sharp v Thomson* 1930 SC 1092 at 1097 per Lord Anderson.
4 1987 SLT (Sh Ct) 70.
5 [2020] GLA 45; [2020] 10 WLUK 472.
6 See para 19.34.

6.20   We saw in Chapter 4 that it was at one time thought incompetent for a tenant who had retained rent to counterclaim for damages in the landlord's action. In the earlier cases, therefore, abatement was possibly seen as a way of getting round this in cases where the landlord was in breach; in such cases nowadays, the tenant may have the choice either of retaining the rent and counterclaiming for damages; or abatement of the rent. In cases where the landlord is not at fault, a claim for abatement may be a tenant's only remedy.

It is tempting to leave the story there, but unfortunately one subsequent case succeeded in stirring the mud again. In *Pacitti v Manganiello*[1] the tenant of a shop withheld rent for the last part of his lease after his water supply had been inadvertently shut off as a result of plumbing works instructed by the landlord. The landlord was held entitled to the retained rent in full.

After considering the two functions of retention identified by Lord Anderson in *Fingland & Mitchell v Howie*,[2] the sheriff principal held that the first aspect (compelling performance by the landlord) was not relevant because the lease had ended and the tenant could not be awarded damages because he had not counter-claimed for them. Only a few of the relevant authorities were considered, and the possibility of abatement was not raised at all.

In light of *Renfrew District Council v Gray* and the earlier authority considered above, it seems possible that either a counterclaim of damages or a defence of abatement in *Pacitti* might have turned the decision in the tenant's favour.

1 1995 SCLR 557.
2 See para 4.41.

SUMMARY DILIGENCE[1]

Nature of remedy

6.21   We saw in Chapter 4 that when court action for debt is taken, the court decree can be enforced by diligence.[2] It is not usually possible to carry out diligence without court authority.

However, there is one situation where the court process can be bypassed and a creditor can proceed with diligence without first having to prove the debt, or otherwise obtain a court order. This is by a procedure known as summary diligence. The theory behind this rather surprising power is that, where it applies, the debtor concerned has consented in advance to the possibility of summary diligence being carried out. This is because he has signed a legal deed (in the present context a lease) which contains an acknowledgment of an obligation (in this case the undertaking to pay rent or other sums such as service charge to the landlord). The deed must also contain the debtor's consent to its being registered for execution, and this means that consent has been given to summary diligence.

1 Rankine pp 357–360; Paton and Cameron p 145; Gloag & Henderson 48.01; Writs Execution (Scotland) Act 1977 ss 1–3.
2 See para 4.26 et seq.

Registration for preservation and execution

6.22 Legal deeds, including leases, may be registered for preservation or for both preservation and execution in the Books of Council and Session, a public register maintained by the Keeper of the Registers of Scotland. This does not need to be done immediately after the deed has been signed, but can be done at any time thereafter. The deed is retained in the register for safe keeping, and in its place there is issued an extract (an official copy), which is legally equivalent to the original deed for most purposes.[1]

Often deeds are sent to the Books of Council and Session merely to ensure their preservation; however, if the deed contains a consent to registration for execution, this process can be carried out at the same time as registration for preservation. The Keeper keeps the deed in the usual way and issues an extract, but in this case adds to the extract a warrant for all necessary action to enforce payment of any sums payable in terms of the deed, ie to proceed with diligence. Such an extract for execution has the force and effect of a decree of the Court of Session,[2] which is why a court action is rendered unnecessary.

In respect of certain types of deed (including leases) registration for preservation and execution is also competent in the books of the appropriate sheriff court.

1 Writs Execution (Scotland) Act 1877 s 5.
2 WE(S)A 1877 ss 1 and 3.

Value of remedy

6.23 Summary diligence, therefore, can significantly speed up the debt-collection process and reduce the costs involved in obtaining payment. Obtaining a court decree takes time, particularly if the debtor lodges a defence to the action. But where a lease contains a consent to registration for execution, the landlord need only take the relatively short time necessary to obtain an extract from the Books of Council and Session if he does not already have one and then proceed with the appropriate form of diligence. The procedure will be the same as if a court decree had first been obtained.

Summary diligence and the Human Rights Act 1998[1]

6.24　The fact that summary diligence proceeds without a court hearing makes it vulnerable under Article 6 of the European Convention on Human Rights (right to a fair hearing), as well as Protocol 1, Article 1 (protection of property). This can be countered by the argument that the tenant has waived these rights by signing a lease containing a clause of consent to registration for execution.[2]

1 See para 1.27 et seq; see also Andrew J M Steven 'Property Law and Human Rights' 2001 4 Jur Rev 293.
2 For more on waiver of Convention rights, see paras 1.40 and 5.42.

Chapter 7

Assignation and subletting; Interposed leases

ASSIGNATION AND SUBLETTING: GENERAL[1]

7.1   An assignation is where a tenant's interest in a lease is transferred to another person (called the assignee), who thereafter takes the tenant's place under the original contract. The assignee becomes directly liable to the landlord for the rent and other obligations of the lease, and the original tenant (usually called the 'cedent') is relieved of all such liability for the future, having no further involvement with the lease.

In the case of a sublease, the tenant creates a second lease with the subtenant, but still has the same relationship with the landlord, remaining directly liable to the landlord for payment of the rent and performance of all other obligations under the original lease. There is no legal relationship between the landlord and the subtenant; the subtenant's landlord is the original tenant, usually in this context described as the principal (or head) tenant. A subtenant may in turn sublet all or part of the property (creating what is called sub-sub-leases or sub-under-leases) and, in theory, there is no limit to the number of times this may be done.

1 Rankine ch 9; Paton and Cameron ch 10.

7.2   Assignation is obviously the preferable choice for a tenant who wants rid of the property entirely, but there are many situations where it will be preferable to sublet instead. If the lease is a fairly long one, it may suit the tenant to sublet for a temporary period, while retaining the right to resume occupation at some future date before the term of the principal lease has expired. Or only part of the property may be sublet, the tenant remaining in occupation of the rest.

Most likely of all, the tenant will simply want to make a profit by charging the subtenant or subtenants a higher rent than that being paid to the landlord. Subletting is common in business leases where (for example) a landowner may lease land on a long ground lease to a

165

developer, who then builds an office block, shopping centre or industrial estate and sublets the individual units to different firms.

Unlawful discrimination

7.3 Under s 33 of the Equality Act 2010 it is prohibited for a person disposing of a property (including by assigning a lease or subletting)[1] to discriminate against a prospective tenant on the basis of one of the protected characteristics under the Act. The discrimination may consist of letting to the person concerned on less favourable terms, by refusing to let to the person, or by some other form of less favourable treatment. The protected characteristics are disability, gender re-assignment, pregnancy and maternity, race, religion or belief, sex, (ie gender) and sexual orientation.[2]

A person who has been subject to discrimination may bring a claim of damages in the sheriff court within six months.[3] An award of damages may include compensation for injured feelings.[4]

1 Equality Act 2010 s 38(3).
2 EA 2010 ss 4–12. This particular provision does not apply to the protected characteristics of age or marriage and civil partnership, which are protected characteristics in relation to other parts of the Act: EA 2010 s 32.
3 EA 2010 ss 114, 118 and 119.
4 EA 2010 s 119(4).

LANDLORD'S CONSENT: WHERE REQUIRED BY LEASE

7.4 It is a standard provision in leases of all kinds that the landlord's consent is required for any assignations or sublets.[1] Such a clause is enforceable. If in such a case a tenant assigns the lease without the landlord's consent, the assignation will be ineffective against the landlord.[2] The same is true of sublets.[3] If the prohibition against assignation and subletting is unqualified, the landlord's right is absolute and there is no obligation to give any reasons for a refusal of consent.[4]

Provided that the landlord's consent is necessary, minor variations in wording will not matter, eg it will make no difference if assignees and subtenants are allowed 'but only with the landlord's consent' or are prohibited 'except with the landlord's consent'.

'[A] variance in phrase will not affect the substance of the matter and --- in whatever form the thing is referred to the decision of the landlord, his approval is to be given or withheld according to his arbitrary wish.'[5]

In fact, even if the lease absolutely prohibits assignation or subletting, without any mention of the landlord's consent, the effect will be exactly the same, as the landlord may still choose to agree to an assignation or sublet.

1 See para 11.4; for the rules regarding assignation and subletting of agricultural tenacies see para 15.27 et seq,
2 *Marquis of Breadalbane v Whitehead & Sons* (1893) 21 R 138, (1893) 1 SLT 320.
3 Rankine p 198; Paton and Cameron p 168; see also para 7.36.
4 *Muir v Wilson* 20 Jan. 1820 FC 83; *Duke of Portland v Baird* (1865) 4 M 10; *Marquis of Breadalbane v Whitehead & Sons* (1893) 21 R 138, (1893) 1 SLT 320.
5 *Marquis of Breadalbane v Whitehead & Sons* (1893) 21 R 138 at 141 per the Lord President (1893) 1 SLT 320.

7.5   If both assignations and sublets are to be excluded, both have to be specifically mentioned: the prohibition of one of them only will not imply prohibition of the other.[1] However, in a case where a sublet had taken place with the landlord's consent it was held that a clause in the head lease requiring the landlord's consent for assignations and sublets implied a provision that it would also be required for a subsequent assignation of the subtenancy.[2]

Where a landlord's consent is required for an assignation and is granted, the consent only applies to that particular transaction, and further consents will be needed for any future assignations in each case.[3]

1 Rankine p 177.
2 *Sears Property Netherlands BV v Coal Pension Properties Ltd* 2001 SLT 761, 2000 SCLR 1002.
3 *Ramsay v Commercial Bank of Scotland* (1842) 4 D 405.

Attempts at evasion

7.6   The court will intervene to prevent any attempts to evade the requirement for the landlord's consent by disguising an assignation or sublet as some other kind or transaction.

In *Hatton v Clay & McLuckie*[1] the tenant of a shop removed all of his stock and granted possession to a person in a quite different line of business, who proceeded to stock the shop with her own goods. The tenant claimed that she was merely his shopkeeper, but the court held that the arrangement was a collusive device designed to get round a prohibition in the lease against assignation and subletting.

In *Brador Properties Ltd v British Telecommunications plc*[2] tenants of office premises attempted to evade a prohibition against subletting by granting what purported to be licences rather than leases, on the pretext that they reserved rights of entry and the right to change around the rooms allocated to the occupants. It was held that the contracts were a sham and were, in fact, unlawful sublets.[3]

1 (1865) 4M 263.
2 1992 SC 12, 1992 SLT 490.
3 See also para 2.55.

Unlawful discrimination

7.7 We saw above that under the Equality Act 2010 there is a prohibition of discrimination by landlords when letting a property or on tenants disposing of a property against persons possessing one of the protected characteristics under the Act.[1] There is a similar prohibition against such discrimination when a landlord or anyone else whose consent is required for an assignation or sublease, eg a head tenant, is asked for such consent.[2]

1 See para 7.3.
2 Equality Act 2010 s 34.

Consent 'not to be unreasonably withheld'[1]

7.8 A prohibition against assignation or subletting without the landlord's consent is frequently qualified by a statement that the consent 'will not be unreasonably withheld' or 'will not be unreasonably withheld or delayed'. This is particularly common in business leases, and will often have been inserted at the request of the tenant's agent.

Unfortunately, the addition of such a phrase adds an element of ambiguity. Who decides what is reasonable and what is unreasonable? The landlord and tenant will probably have different views, so the court (or possibly an arbitrator) will have to decide, and the door has thus been opened to litigation. However, it is a qualification that is difficult to escape from. It is in the tenant's interest to have some defence against the stranglehold of an unreasonable landlord and, as we will see in Chapter 12, too tight a control by a commercial landlord over assignations can limit the amount of rent that can be charged at rent review.[2]

There is a growing amount of authority regarding what is and is not reasonable in this context, and some useful principles have emerged.

1 See David Cabrelli 'When is refusal of consent by a landlord or tenant unreasonable?' 2002 SLPQ 117 and 'Landlord's refusal of a tenant's application for consent to

assignation of lease: An update' 2004 70 Prop LB 1. The first of Mr Cabrelli's articles
contains a survey of the authority in this area, including consideration of some of the
English authority.
2 See para 12.94.

General Principles: Burgerking v Rachel Charitable Trust

7.9   A comprehensive review of the relevant legal principles was
given by Lord Drummond Young in *Burgerking Ltd v Rachel Charitable
Trust.*[1] Tenants were proposing to sublet subjects in Paisley High Street
at the same rent as they paid under the head lease (£112,000 pa), but
subject to the deduction of a large reverse premium (a sum paid by
the tenant to the subtenant), which would effectively reduce the rent
payable by the subtenants to £12,000 pa. This had been a necessary
inducement in a very poor market in which only one suitable subtenant
had been found. The landlords refused consent to the sublease on the
grounds that:

(a)   The proposed subtenants did not meet a requirement of the lease
that they should be 'substantial and respectable ... of sound
financial standing and ...demonstrably capable of performing ...
the tenant's obligations under the proposed sublease'; and

(b)   The reverse premium to be paid to the subtenants as an inducement
was so great that the net amount payable by them would be well
below the market rent, which would reduce the market rent
obtainable for the property when it came to be re-let in three
years' time at the end of the lease. This would result in an erosion
in the value of the landlord's capital asset.

It was held that the landlords' first ground of refusal was unreasonable
because the proposed subtenants, although operating at the lower end
of the retail market, were a financially sound company and able to meet
the net rent payable by them after deduction of the premium. However,
the refusal was reasonable on the second ground, and this was sufficient
on its own for the tenant's application for an order that the landlord had
refused consent unreasonably to fail.

1 2006 SLT 224, 2006 GWD 6-112.

7.10   Lord Drummond Young reviewed the applicable law in some
detail:[1]

(1)   A landlord is not entitled to refuse consent to an assignation
or sublease on grounds that are collateral to the relationship of

landlord and tenant under the lease and have nothing to do with that relationship. In order to determine this it may be necessary to interpret the lease, and the landlord's decision will be vitiated if it has been based upon an erroneous interpretation.

(2)   The onus of establishing that consent has been unreasonably withheld is upon the tenant.

(3)   The landlord's decision should be upheld if his conclusions might have been reached by a reasonable man in the circumstances of the case; it is not necessary that the court should agree with the decision.

(4)   As a general rule the landlord need only consider his own interests in deciding whether or not to give consent. Where, however, there is a significant disproportion between the benefits to the landlord and the detriment to the tenant if consent is withheld it will be unreasonable for the landlord to refuse consent.

(5)   Only the reasons given by the landlord at the time of refusal and the landlord's state of mind at that time are relevant, and not any subsequent considerations.

(6)   Subject to the foregoing principles, the question of whether the landlord's consent has been withheld unreasonably is one of fact.

(7)   Where more than one reason for refusal has been given, the landlord's decision should normally be upheld if at least one of the stated reasons is valid. There are possible exceptions where the reasons are not independent of one another or the decision has been based upon an accumulation of reasons.

(8)   The decision as to whether the proposed subtenant or assignee is 'substantial and respectable' or 'of sound financial standing' should relate to the particular transaction and to the capacity of the person to carry on the business intended and to meet the expense of doing so in a regular way.

(9)   The reasonableness of any decision by a landlord must be considered in the particular circumstances of the case.

(10)   The test of reasonableness is an objective one.

(11)   The landlord must give reasons for the decision; otherwise it is impossible to know whether the requirement to act reasonably has been satisfied.[2] This contrasts with the situation where the lease gives the landlord an absolute right of refusal, in which case there is no need for reasons to be given.[3]

---

1 *Burgerking Ltd v Rachel Charitable Trust* 2006 SLT 224 at 228–229 per Lord Drummond Young. His lordship drew heavily upon the opinions of Balcombe LJ in *International Drilling Fluids Ltd v Louisville Investments (Uxbridge) Ltd* [1986] Ch at 519–521 and Lord Hamilton in *Legal and General Assurance Society Ltd v Tesco Stores Ltd* 2001 GWD 18-707 at paras 30–34, as well as the decision of the House of Lords in *Ashworth Frazer Ltd v Gloucester City Council* [2001] 1 WLR 2180; [2002] 1 All ER 377.

2 This followed the sheriff court decision in *Hutchison v Lodge St Michaels* Dec 5 1980 & Nov 19 1981 (reported in Paisley & Cusine *Unreported Property Cases from the Sheriff Courts* (2000) p 103).
3 See para 7.4.

7.11   Two of the above issues (the prohibition of collateral benefits and the suitability and financial standing of the proposed assignee or subtenant) merit further consideration in the light of other authority. To these can be added the additional issue arising when refusal has been based upon the intention of the proposed assignee or subtenant to put the subjects to a different use from that stated in the lease's use clause.

Collateral benefits

7.12   A landlord will be held to be unreasonable for seeking to obtain a collateral benefit in exchange for consent, ie some extra benefit not provided for in the lease.

In *Renfrew District Council v AB Leisure (Renfrew) Ltd (In Liquidation)*,[1] the clause in question provided that the landlord's consent to an assignation would not be unreasonably withheld, and in particular would not be withheld where the assignee's resources were adequate. As a condition of consenting to the assignation, the landlord wanted the arrears of rent to be paid. The court agreed that this was reasonable.

However, the landlord also wanted to make its consent conditional upon an immediate rent review taking place, a full repairing and insuring clause being added to the lease and rent reviews being reduced from five-yearly to three-yearly intervals. The court held that the landlord was not entitled to impose these three conditions, which effectively would have created a new lease in different terms.

On the other hand, in *Lousada & Co v JE Lesser (Properties) Ltd*[2] the landlord was held not to be acting unreasonably in making its consent conditional upon the conclusion of rent review negotiations; they were not (as in *Renfrew District Council*) seeking to obtain a collateral benefit in return for their consent, but only to secure their rights under the existing lease.

In *Forest Bio Products Ltd v Forever Fuels Ltd*[3] the need to pay rent arrears caused a dispute between the existing tenant and the prospective tenant. Forest's administrator entered into an asset sale agreement with Forever. Part of this agreement included the assignation of Forest's interest in a lease to Forever. The asset sale agreement provided that sums would be payable by Forever to Forest on the landlord's unconditional consent being given to the assignation. The landlord was prepared to consent to the assignation, provided Forest's arrears of rent under the lease were paid. Forest argued that as the condition related to something it was required to do, rather than the condition requiring Forever to do anything, the consent was unconditional and, as such, the sums under the asset sale agreement were payable. The Inner House held otherwise, finding that the landlord's unconditional consent meant consent with no conditions attached.

1 1988 SCLR 512, 1988 SLT 635.
2 1990 SC 178, 1990 SLT 823.
3 [2013] CSIH 103, 2014 GWD 1-7.

7.13   In *Scottish Tourist Board v Deanpark Ltd*[1] the landlord asked for a premium of £50,000 in return for granting its consent to a sublease. It was held that this was an attempt to obtain a collateral benefit and therefore unreasonable, being an attempt by the landlord to exploit the request for consent in order to obtain a sum of money that was not provided for in the lease. The landlord was accordingly in breach of contract by unreasonably withholding or delaying its consent.

It should be noted, however, that the demand for a premium was held to be unreasonable because the lease did not provide for such an arrangement; this implies that if the lease *had* so provided, the charging of a premium would have been allowed.

It has been argued that a landlord would not be refusing unreasonably in the converse of the above situation. This could occur if the tenant, instead of simply asking for an assignation of the lease as it stood, sought also to improve upon its terms; for example, the tenant might get a better price from the assignee if the landlord agreed to extend the term of the lease. In such a case the landlord would probably be justified in withholding consent.[2]

1 1998 SLT 1121, 1998 GWD 3-135.
2 See *Hutchison v Lodge St Michaels* Dec 5 1980 & Nov 19 1981 (reported in Paisley & Cusine *Unreported Property Cases from the Sheriff Courts* (2000) p 103, at 107 and editors' commentary at 109).

Suitability of assignee or subtenant

7.14   Where the lease provides that a proposed assignee or sub-tenant is to be respectable and responsible, respectability relates to reputation and responsibility to financial standing.[1] A landlord is entitled to require evidence of the proposed assignee or subtenant's ability to perform the tenant's obligations under the lease, particularly the tenant's ability to pay the rent.[2] It is not therefore unreasonable for a landlord to refuse to accept a new tenant who is unsuitable in this respect.[3]

On the other hand, as we saw above in *Burgerking*, the landlord may still be entitled to refuse consent in the case of a demonstrably suitable assignee or subtenant, if there is another good reason for the refusal.[4]

A less stringent financial test may be appropriate for proposed subtenants than for assignees, since in the former case the head tenant continues to have to pay the rent under the lease to the landlord. However, it has been noted that a landlord does have an indirect interest in the financial soundness of a proposed sub-tenant given the ability of the sub-tenant to meet its obligations under the lease may affect the ability of the tenant to comply with his obligations to the landlord.[5]

It may be reasonable for a landlord to turn down a proposed assignee and unreasonable to reject the same person as a subtenant. The validity of this argument was accepted by Lord Drummond Young in *Burgerking* (although not sufficiently to alter the final decision):

> 'The standards that apply to a subtenant need not … be as strict as those that apply to an assignee, who comes into a direct contractual relationship with the landlord.'[6]

1 *Burgerking Ltd v Castelbrook Holdings Ltd* [2014] CSOH 36, 2014 GWD 9-178.
2 The landlord need only consider the proposed assignee or sub-tenant's financial soundness and need not take into account the group of which the proposed assignee or sub-tenant forms part: *Burgerking Ltd v Castelbrook Holdings Ltd* [2014] CSOH 36, 2014 GWD 9-178.
3 *Continvest Ltd v Dean Property Partnership* 1993 GWD 40-2675; *Scottish Tourist Board v Deanpark Ltd* 1998 SLT 1121, 1998 GWD 3-135.
4 See para 7.9 et seq.
5 *Burgerking Ltd v Castelbrook Holdings Ltd* [2014] CSOH 36, 2014 GWD 9-178.
6 *Burgerking Ltd v Rachel Charitable Trust* 2006 SLT 224 at 235 per Lord Drummond Young.

Proposed change of use by assignee

7.15   In *Ashworth Frazer Ltd v Gloucester City Council*[1] the House of Lords held that there was no principle of law which stated that it was unreasonable for a landlord to withhold consent on the sole basis that the proposed assignee would breach a user covenant. Conversely, there was also no rule that it would always be reasonable to refuse consent on the same basis. Whether or not a landlord had acted unreasonably in refusing consent was a question of fact to be decided in each case and no particular case should be considered as laying down a binding precedent.

This English case was followed in Scotland in *Scottish Property Investment Ltd v Scottish Provident Ltd*,[2] in which a landlord refused consent to a sublease on the sole ground that the subtenants' proposed use of the subjects was different from that stated in the use clause of the head lease. The case went to proof before answer, but Lord Mackay of Drumadoon reached the preliminary view that the landlord was acting unreasonably.

Ultimately, the case turned on the construction of the lease, but it was a relevant factor that the lease was for 98 years, with no provision for breaks. Clearly, in a lease of that length, an assignation or sublet at some stage is much more likely, therefore it is less likely that it will be reasonable for the landlord to expect the original tenant's use to be preserved.[3]

1 [2001] 1 WLR 2180; [2002] 1 All ER 377.
2 2004 GWD 6-120. This case and that of *Ashworth Frazer* are analysed in some depth by David Cabrelli in 'Landlord's refusal of a tenant's application for consent to assignation of lease: An update' 2004 70 Prop LB 1.
3 Such inflexibility on the part of landlords can also rebound upon them by limiting the level of rent that can be charged at a rent review – see para 12.93.

7.16 Some of these issues had been anticipated in *Wooley and Another v Perth and Kinross District Council*[1] in which shop tenants whose business was the sale and maintenance of electrical appliances sought to assign the lease to a company which intended to use the premises as a pharmacy. In terms of the lease the local authority landlord was bound not to unreasonably withhold consent either to an assignation or to a change of use.

It was held that the landlord was not acting unreasonably in refusing consent because of its concern that the establishment of a new pharmacy in that particular location might prejudice the continued existence of other pharmacies in peripheral parts of the city, to the disadvantage of local residents. As the local authority, it had the right to consider the possible effects on the people whose interests it represented. Moreover it was entitled to reach this decision as landlord even though (in its capacity as planning authority) it had granted planning permission for the change.

In addition, Sheriff Wheatley gave no weight to the fact that the tenant had the bad luck to have a local authority as landlord, when other landlords might have been less motivated by the social aspects of their decision. It was his view that each decision had to be looked at from the standpoint of the particular landlord in the case.

This prompts speculation as to whether a proposed change of use by an assignee could be given by a landlord as a ground of refusal where there were no social issues involved. For example a landlord of retail premises might be motivated to prohibit a new use for purely commercial reasons.

A landlord of a shopping centre (whether local authority or private) might well be concerned to preserve the trade mix in the centre by stopping a new use that was already represented there. In the light of the principles now evolving, it seems likely that such a ground of refusal would be considered reasonable; as we saw above, landlords are generally entitled to consider only their own interests when reaching a decision.[2]

1 Jan 5 & 22 1986 (reported in Paisley & Cusine *Unreported Property Cases from the Sheriff Courts* (2000) p 110).
2 See para 7.10.

Tenant's remedies

7.17   Where a lease provides that the landlord's consent to an assignation or sublet will not be unreasonably withheld, the landlord's unreasonable refusal is a breach of contract that will entitle the tenant to damages.[1] It is also a material breach that would entitle the tenant to rescind.[2] However, often a tenant will raise an action for declarator that the landlord has unreasonably withheld its consent and seek an order requiring the landlord to consent to the assignation or subletting.[3]

1 *Renfrew District Council v AB Leisure (Renfrew) Ltd (in liquidation)* 1998 SCLR 512, 1998 SLT 635.
2 *Scotmore Developments v Anderton* 1996 SLT 1304; see also para 4.30.
3 For order of specific implement see para 4.2 et seq.

LANDLORD'S CONSENT: COMMON LAW POSITION

7.18   As we have already noted, the need for the landlord's consent to an assignation or sublet is a standard lease provision, which means that in almost all cases the legal position will be determined by the lease document. However, we should also consider the legal effect if such a provision is omitted; this may happen, for example, in a lease that has been constituted informally, or that has not been professionally drafted. In such a case the right of a tenant to assign or sublet will be determined by the common law, which requires the landlord's consent for certain categories of lease but not for others.

Delectus personae

7.19   Under the general law of contract, an executory contract, ie one where there is a continuing obligation or obligations requiring performance, cannot be assigned by one party without the other's consent if there is an element of *delectus personae* (choice of person).

This means that the person wanting to assign was chosen for the contract because of some personal quality or professional skill.[1] Often the position can be determined merely by the type of contract concerned: for example, partnerships and employment contracts are obvious examples of contracts where there will always be *delectus personae*.

Since a lease is an executory contract, the same principle will determine whether a landlord's consent is required for an assignation or sublet, and it has long been established that *delectus personae* is presumed to be present in some types of lease and to be absent in others. This presumption can be rebutted if the circumstances of the case clearly establish that there is *delectus personae* or that there is not.[2] However, whether or not the landlord's consent will be required will generally be determined by the category of lease in question.

The reasons why the tenant's identity was thought to be important to the landlord in some kinds of lease and not in others are now largely historical. According to Rankine, *delectus personae* is less likely to be present in urban than in rural leases because:

> 'there was not originally the same solidarity between the lessor and lessee of a house as between the landlord and tenant of a farm; and ... there may be more frequent and urgent calls to relinquish possession in the one case than in the other'.[3]

There is also less likely to be *delectus personae* in longer leases, whether urban or rural: a landlord's personal choice of tenant would require unusual longevity to survive a lease term of (say) 99 years. And although *delectus personae* is not limited to natural persons, it is less likely to be present in the case of a long lease to (for example) a corporation whose character is likely to change over time.[4]

1 See Gloag pp 416 et seq, McBryde 12–33 et seq, and the other law of contract references in the bibliography.
2 *The Scottish Ministers v Trustees of the Drummond Trust* 2001 SLT 665, at 668 per Lord Carloway, 2001 SCLR 495.
3 Rankine p 174.
4 *The Scottish Ministers v Trustees of the Drummond Trust* 2001 SLT 665, at 668 per Lord Carloway, 2001 SCLR 495.

Leases requiring consent

7.20   *Delectus personae* is presumed to be present in the following categories of lease, in respect of which the landlord's consent for assignations or sublets is required at common law. In relation to agricultural and residential leases, the matter is to a significant extent governed by legislation.[1]

(1) *Farm leases of ordinary duration* This means leases of up to 21 years.[2] This category does not extend to rural leases generally. In a 99-year lease granted for forestry purposes *delectus personae* was held not to be present.[3]

(2) *Furnished house lets* According to Rankine, the reason for this is that the contract is partly a lease and partly one for hire of the furniture, though he does not explain why this should make a difference.[4] A better explanation is that the landlord has a personal interest in the type of person who is using the furniture and other household belongings.[5] In any case, the point is largely academic, since the landlord's consent for assignations and sublets is a statutory requirement in respect of most residential tenancies, whether furnished or unfurnished, in both social and private sector tenancies.[6]

(3) *Sporting leases* This includes shooting leases and probably also leases of fishings as well as other sporting leases.[7]

(4) *Mineral leases* Here the landlord's consent is probably required, though in the only case to discuss the matter the court did not reach a definite conclusion.[8]

1 See para 15.27 et seq, Ch 17 and para 18.96 et seq.
2 Rankine p 173, Paton and Cameron pp 150–151.
3 *The Scottish Ministers v Trustees of the Drummond Trust* 2001 SLT 665, 2001 SCLR 495.
4 Rankine p 175.
5 Paton and Cameron p 150.
6 See paras 17.100 and 18.96 et seq.
7 *Earl of Fife v Wilson* (1864) 3M 323; *Mackintosh v May* (1895) 22R 345, 2 SLT 471.
8 *Duke of Portland v Baird* (1865) 4 M 10 at 16 per the Lord Justice Clerk; at 19 per Lord Cowan; and at 22 per Lord Neaves.

Leases not requiring consent

7.21 In the following categories of lease, *delectus personae* is presumed to be absent, and so the landlord's consent to assignations and sublets is normally not a common law requirement:

(1) *Farm leases of extraordinary duration* This probably applies to all leases over 21 years, and definitely to leases where the duration is 38 years or more.[1]

(2) *Unfurnished urban lets*[2] As we saw above, this is superseded in the case of residential lets where the landlord's consent is generally a statutory requirement. Most significantly of all, however, it still applies to virtually all commercial leases. The fact that these are freely assignable at common law emphasises the need, from the

landlord's point of view, for the lease to contain a provision that regulates the situation.

1 Rankine p 173, Paton and Cameron p 151; see also *The Scottish Ministers v Trustees of the Drummond Trust* 2001 SLT 665, 2001 SCLR 495.
2 Rankine p 174, Paton and Cameron p 151.

Implied consent or acquiescence[1]

7.22   Where a landlord's consent is required for an assignation or sublet but has not expressly been given, consent may nevertheless be implied from the landlord's conduct. This can only happen if the landlord knows of the assignation or sublet.[2] Beyond that, whether or not the landlord has impliedly consented or acquiesced in the assignation or subletting will depend upon the circumstances.

The fact that the landlord knew about the transaction and did not object to the assignee or subtenant having taken possession is relevant to establishing implied consent or acquiescence, but not conclusive if the landlord has otherwise made the lack of consent clear.[3] Acceptance of rent from an assignee is also relevant but not by itself conclusive.[4]

1 Rankine p 180; Paton and Cameron pp 155–156.
2 *Dalrymple's Trs v Brown* 1945 SC 190, 1945 SLT 220.
3 *Elphinstone v Monkland Iron and Coal Co Ltd* (1886) 13 R (HL) 98, at 102 per Lord Watson and 107 per the Lord Chancellor.
4 *Gray v Low* (1859) 21 D 293.

7.23   Two early cases, heard within a short time of each other, illustrate the principle being applied successfully.

In *Hay v McTier*[1] although the landlord gave no express consent to a sublet, he made enquiries about the subtenant's character and substance before he was given possession. Thereafter the subtenant was in possession for over 10 years, during which he paid rent to the landlord and was given receipts. After the head tenant absconded, the landlord obtained a decree of removing against him without disturbing the subtenant. It was held that his consent to the subtenancy was implied.

In *Maule v Robb*[2] the landlord's consent was also held to be implied although it had not been given expressly. After the subtenant had been in possession for several years, the landlord's factor wrote to him, asking for the rent to be paid directly to him in the future. The tenant did so for three years in a row, on each occasion receiving a receipt from the factor that acknowledged him as subtenant. The factor's initial letter, however, was considered to be the decisive circumstance.

1 (1806) Hume 836 (The judgment is contained within the report for *Maule v Robb* – see below).
2 (1807) Hume 835.

7.24 Actions by a landlord amounting to acquiescence only bar the person carrying them out and not that person's singular successors, except where the successor has notice of his predecessor's acquiescence.[1]

It has been said that landlord's consent to an assignation or subletting does not bind his singular successors.[2] Nevertheless it is suggested that, provided the assignation or sub-lease has been validly completed, the successor landlord acquires the property subject to the rights of the assignee or sub-tenant.

1 *Pickard v Reid* 1953 SLT (Sh Ct) 5, (1953) 69 Sh Ct Rep 63; Rankine, *The Law of Personal Bar and Estoppel* (1921), p 62; Reid and Blackie, *Personal Bar* (2006), para 10.36.
2 Gordon and Wortley, *Scottish Land Law,* (Vol I, 3rd edn, 2009), para 18.31.

COMPLETION OF ASSIGNATION

Need for writing

7.25 In terms of the Requirements of Writing (Scotland) Act 1995, an assignation of a lease transfers a real right in land, which means that it must be in writing if the lease is for a year or more.[1] The other provisions of that Act, so far as they apply to leases, apply to assignations also.[2] For assignations signed prior to 1 August 1995 (when the Act came into force), the law is the same as for leases signed before that date.[3]

We saw in Chapter 2 that the 1995 Act provides a form of statutory personal bar such that a party (A) will not be entitled to withdraw from a contract for want of form where the other party to the contract (B) has acted or refrained from acting on the basis of the contract, with A's knowledge and acquiescence; where B has been affected to a material extent and where, if A was able to withdraw from the contract, B would be adversely affected to a material extent.[4] We also saw that anomalies in the 1995 Act and the judgement in *The Advice Centre for Mortgages v McNicoll*[5] had cast significant doubt about the operation of the statutory form of personal bar as it applies to leases.[6] The observations made there apply equally in the case of assignations.

In *Morris v Eason*[7] the lease of a medical centre was still in the name of former partners in a GP practice, but the current partners occupied the centre and paid the rent, which was accepted by the landlord. It was held that the current partners had no right to the premises because a written assignation conforming to the Requirements of Writing (Scotland) Act 1995 had not been completed. However, the defenders unfortunately made no attempt to plead personal bar as a ground for occupancy.

As we saw above leases generally provide that landlord's consent to assignation is required. The easiest way to document this is to have the landlord sign or authenticate the deed noting their consent.

Needless to say, it is recommended that all assignations conform to the Requirements of Writing Act, in order to resolve any doubts about the matter. An assignation would therefore normally take the form of a deed (traditional or electronic) signed or authenticated by the tenant, and since the landlord's consent will usually be required, the easiest way to achieve this is to have the landlord sign or authenticate the deed also.

1 Requirements of Writing (Scotland) Act 1995 s 1.
2 See para 2.3 et seq.
3 See para 2.2.
4 See para 2.10 et seq.
5 2006 SLT 591, 2006 SCLR 602.
6 See para 2.16 et seq.
7 [2012] CSOH 125, [2012] GWD 27-564.

7.26 *Assignation of registered leases* Where the lease being assigned has been registered in the Land Register (or, in the case of older leases, in the Register of Sasines) the assignation itself must be registered and must conform to the provisions of the Requirements of Writing Act for registered deeds.[1]

1 ROW(S)A 1995, ss 6 and 9G; see also paras 2.5 et seq and 8.11 et seq.

Wording of assignation

7.27 No special form of words is required for the assignation of an unregistered lease, provided that the intention to assign is unequivocally expressed.[1] There are statutory forms of assignation for registered leases, which may be adapted for use in the case of unregistered leases also.[2]

1 Rankine pp 180–181; Paton and Cameron p 157.
2 See para 8.16.

Completion of assignee's title

7.28   In relation to the cedent, ie the tenant granting the assignation, the assignee's title is completed by the delivery of the assignation.[1] In relation to the landlord, it is completed by the landlord's consent or, where that is not required, by the assignation being intimated to the landlord by the assignee. Finally, the assignee will only obtain a real right valid against third parties by entering into possession of the subjects or (in appropriate cases) by registration of the assignation.

1 Rankine p 181, Paton and Cameron p 159.

7.29   *Intimation*   Where the landlord's consent is not required, the assignation must be intimated by the assignee to the landlord for it to be effective against the latter.[1] The landlord signing the assignation as a consenter is equivalent to intimation[2] and, in the case of a registered lease, so is registration of the assignation.[3]

In practice, one or both of the above is likely to occur, but in the rare cases where the lease does not require landlord's consent and it is not needed at common law, methods of formal intimation of assignations are specified in the Transmission of Moveable Property (Scotland) Act 1862.[4]

Intimation may be given by either:

(1)   a notary public delivering a certified copy of the assignation to the landlord; or

(2)   the holder of the assignation or that person's agent posting a certified copy to the landlord.

In the latter case, the landlord's written acknowledgement is sufficient evidence of intimation having been made. Providing a copy of the assignation to the landlord, together with written acknowledgement of receipt is valid intimation at common law.[5]

1 Rankine p 181, Paton and Cameron p 159.
2 *Smith v Place D'Or 101 Ltd* 1988 SLT (Sh Ct) 5.
3 Paton and Cameron p 159; *Edmond v Gordon* (1858) 20D (HL) 5 (though that case related to the assignation of a bond).
4 Transmission of Moveable Property (Scotland) Act 1862 s 2 (which does not seem to be confined to moveable property). These methods are not prescriptive, and other methods are possible – see Paton and Cameron p 159.
5 McBryde para 12.96

7.30   Although the assignation must be delivered to the assignee to complete the assignee's title in relation to the cedent, it is irrelevant in questions with the landlord, and intimation is all that is necessary for the assignation to be effective against him.

7.31 *Assignation and subletting; Interposed leases*

This can operate either in favour of or against the landlord. In *Smith v Place D'Or 101 Ltd*[1] the landlord irritated the lease on the ground of the assignee's bankruptcy and resumed possession from him. The original tenant claimed the right to possess the property because they had never delivered the assignation to the assignee, delivery having been postponed until the assignee had paid the final instalment of the price. The landlord was held to have the right to possession: after intimation they were entitled to regard the assignee as the tenant and to terminate the lease as a result of his breach.

1 1988 SLT (Sh Ct) 5.

7.31 *Possession*[1]   We saw in Chapter 2 that a tenant originally only obtained a real right valid against the landlord's singular successors by virtue of the Leases Act 1449 and that one of the pre-requisites for the operation of that Act was that the tenant must have entered into natural or civil possession of the property.[2]

Delivery and intimation of the assignation only confer personal rights upon the assignee, the first against the cedent and the second against the landlord. Like the original tenant, therefore, the assignee required to enter into possession to obtain a real right valid against the world in general, and in particular against the landlord's singular successors and the original tenant's creditors. This principle was affirmed in a number of cases in the early 19th century, in which assignations granted in security proved ineffective because the original tenant had remained in possession.[3]

The problem identified in these cases was addressed by the Registration of Leases (Scotland) Act 1857 under which registration in the Register of Sasines (nowadays registration in the Land Register) was deemed to be equivalent to possession by the tenant, and likewise equivalent to possession by an assignee after the assignation had been registered.[4] It will be recalled that leases of twenty years or more have to be registered for a real right to be obtained.[5] Where the tenant's interest in a registered lease is assigned the assignation must be registered for the assignee to obtain a real right.[6] Where a lease has not been registered, however, an assignee will still require to enter into possession to obtain a real right.

The above only applies in cases where the tenant who is assigning is in natural possession of the property. Where a lease is being assigned by the tenant of property that has been wholly sublet, it is sufficient for the assignation to be intimated to the landlord and for the assignee to take over collection of the rents. The assignee will automatically take over civil possession from the original tenant.[7]

1 Rankine pp 182–187; Paton and Cameron pp 160–162.

2 See para 2.37.
3 *Brock v Cabell* (1822) 2 S 52; *Kennedy v Forsyth* (1829) 7 S 435; *Inglis & Co v Paul* (1829) 7 S 469. See also *Clark v West Calder Oil Co* (1882) 9 R 1017. Nowadays the creditor of a tenant under a registered lease will obtain security by registration, not of an assignation, but of a standard security granted by the tenant.
4 See para 8.18.
5 See para 8.18.
6 Registration of Leases (Scotland) Act 1857 ss 1, 3 and 20B.
7 Rankine pp 182–183; Paton and Cameron p 160. For the difference between natural and civil possession see para 2.37.

Liability for rent

7.32   As we noted at the beginning of the chapter, after an assignation the assignee takes the place of the cedent (the previous tenant), relieving the cedent of all obligations under the lease. This was conclusively determined in *Skene v Greenhill*,[1] in which the court found that:

'After an assignation of a lease has been regularly executed, and duly intimated to and acquiesced in by the landlord, and the assignee admitted into possession, the obligation of the cedent for rents is limited to those due prior to the possession of the assignee.'

The court reserved its judgment regarding those cases where the landlord's consent is not necessary, though the position is probably the same; since an assignation will normally require the landlord's consent, it is not a point that will arise often.

The assignee therefore assumes sole liability for all rent from the date of taking possession, while the previous tenant remains liable for rent due prior to that date. The assignee, however, may also be liable for prior arrears, including a trustee in bankruptcy who adopts the lease.[2]

The previous tenant will normally be relieved of liability after the assignation, but can be made jointly liable with the assignee for future rental payments if there is an express provision in the lease to that effect.[3] Such a provision will have to be clearly made, and if it is at all ambiguous the presumption will be that only the current tenant is liable.[4] Needless to say, any attempt by a landlord to include such a provision should be resisted by the tenant, as it would burden the original tenant with a continuing liability.

Where the landlord's consent to an assignation is required but has not been obtained, the previous tenant continues to be liable to the landlord for the rent and all other obligations under the lease.[5]

1 (1825) 4 S 25.
2 Rankine pp 194–195; Paton and Cameron p 163; *Dundas v Morison* (1857) 20 D 225, at 228 per the Lord Justice Clerk and 229 per Lord Cowan.
3 *Burns v Martin* (1887) 14 R (HL) 20.

4 *Burns v Martin* (1887) 14 R (HL) 20, at 25 per Lord Watson.
5 *Gemmel v Low* (1823) 2 S 563; *Ramsay v Commercial Bank* (1842) 4 D 405.

SUBTENANCIES[1]

7.33   Rankine says:

'A sublease, being none the less a lease, though granted by a lessee, and not by a proprietor, is governed by the same rules as those which regulate the constitution and completion of all leases.'[2]

Thus the rules regarding the formation of a lease, in particular the provisions of the Requirements of Writing (Scotland) Act 1995 apply equally to subleases as they do to head leases.[3] A subtenant may acquire a real right valid against the head tenant's singular successors under the Leases Act 1449,[4] or by registering the sublease in the Land Register where its duration exceeds 20 years.[5]

A subtenant may also grant a sublease, and so on, and there is in theory no limit to the number of times this can happen. A head tenant naturally cannot grant greater rights to a subtenant than those conferred by the head lease, and so the sublease cannot give possession of more extensive subjects or a longer term than the head tenant has a right to; however, it is possible (and very common) for only part of the leased subjects to be sublet, and for the term of the sublet to be less than that of the head lease.

Unless the terms of the head lease have been incorporated into the sublease, they have no effect on the sublease. In *Robertson v Player*[6] the subtenant was unable to exercise an option of renewal which was contained in the head lease but not the sublease, and in *Fergusson v Brown*[7] the head lease contained restrictions on the sale of spirits, but no such provisions had been included in the sublease, which in fact made no mention of the head lease at all. It was held that the head tenant could not prevent the subtenant from obtaining a licence and selling wines and spirits on the property.

1 Rankine pp 190–193 and 195–199; Paton and Cameron pp 164–170.
2 Rankine p 190.
3 See para 2.1 et seq.
4 See para 2.30 et seq.
5 See para 8.11 et seq.
6 (1876) 4 R 218.
7 (1902) 9 SLT 341.

Limitations on subtenant's rights

7.34   Provided that a sublease has been lawfully constituted, the subtenant will normally have the right to possession of the subjects in questions both with the head tenant and with the landlord. However, in relation to the landlord, there are ways in which a subtenant remains vulnerable.

7.35 *Termination of head lease* If the head lease is terminated prematurely, eg by irritancy, any sublease will also come to an end, even if the subtenant was in no way at fault.[1] In such a case, however, the subtenant has a right to claim damages against the head tenant in respect of the right to occupy the subjects for the unexpired term of the sublease.[2]

Where a subtenancy only came about because of an interposed lease, it will *not* be ended by the termination of the interposed head tenancy.[3]

1 Rankine p 198; Paton and Cameron p 169. There is an exception in the case of residential leases which are assured, regulated or private residential tenancies from private landlords (see paras 17.41 and 17.75), but not in the case of Scottish secure tenancies from social landlords, as their subtenants have no protected status – see para 18.96.
2 *Middleton v Yorstoun* (1826) 5 S 162; *Middleton v Megget* (1828) 7 S 76; *Dick v Taylor's Trs* (1831) 10 S 19.
3 See para 7.42.

7.36 *Unlawful subleases* If the landlord's consent is required for subletting, any sublease granted without this consent can be reduced by the landlord.[1] The subtenant may also be liable to the landlord for violent profits, a form of penal damages that can be claimed from a possessor without title.[2]

1 Rankine p 198; Paton and Cameron p 168.
2 Rankine p 198; Paton and Cameron p 168; see also para 10.38.

TRANSFER OF TENANCY OF MATRIMONIAL HOME

7.37 It will be convenient to consider here a situation which is a kind of assignation, though not of the type considered above. It is not a voluntary assignation, but a compulsory one, which can be imposed by the court without the consent of either the landlord or the existing tenant.

The Matrimonial Homes (Family Protection) (Scotland) Act 1981 was passed to protect the interests of a spouse who might have no legal title to the matrimonial home either as joint owner or tenant. The Act gives the 'non-entitled' spouse (the one who is not the owner or tenant) occupancy rights to the home and also provides for the 'entitled spouse' to be excluded from the home in certain circumstances, eg where there is a history of domestic violence. Equivalent provisions are made in relation to civil partners in the Civil Partnership Act 2004.[1]

In the case of leased property the court also has the power, in appropriate circumstances, to transfer the tenancy from the entitled to the non-entitled spouse or civil partner.[2] This can happen either in the form of an order attached to a court decree for divorce or dissolution of a civil partnership or nullity of marriage or civil partnership, or as the result of a separate application to the court by the non-entitled spouse or civil partner.[3] Compensation may be payable by the non-entitled spouse or civil partner to the entitled spouse or civil partner in respect of the loss of the tenancy.[4]

The new tenant takes on all the liabilities of the tenancy, apart from any existing rent arrears, which remain the responsibility of the spouse or civil partner who was the original tenant.[5] If there is a joint tenancy, the court has the power to vest the tenancy in one party only.[6] The landlord must be notified and be given an opportunity to be heard.[7]

1 Civil Partnership Act 2004, ss 101–111.
2 Matrimonial Homes (Family Protection) (Scotland) Act 1981 s 13.
3 MH(FP)(S)A 1981 s 13(1) & (2); CPA 2004 s 112 (1) & (2).
4 MH(FP)(S)A 1981 s 13(1); CPA 2004 s 112(1).
5 MH(FP)(S)A 1981 s 13(5); CPA 2004 s 112(5).
6 MH(FP)(S)A 1981 s13(9); *G v G* 2001 Fam LR 99; CPA 2004 s112(9).
7 MH(FP)(S)A 1981 s 13(4); CPA 2004 s 112(4).

Excluded categories of lease

7.38   Certain types of lease are excluded from the provision, eg houses attached to agricultural holdings, crofts and other small landholdings or houses let in connection with the tenant's employment.[1]

Also excluded are leases for more than 20 years.[2] Since it has not been possible to create residential leases of this length since 1974,[3] this can only apply to leases entered before then. Presumably the reason for the exclusion is that a tenant's right under a lease with a long tenure is more akin to ownership, and the Acts make no provision for transfer of ownership from an entitled to a non-entitled spouse or civil partner. However, the latter will, of course, still have the benefit of the relevant Act's other provisions, including the right to occupy the matrimonial home[4] and (in certain circumstances) to obtain a court order to have the entitled spouse or civil partner excluded from the property.[5]

1 MH(FP)(S)A 1981 s 13(7); CPA 2004 s 112(7).
2 MH(FP)(S)A 1981 s 13(7); CPA 2004 s 112(7).
3 Land Tenure Reform (Scotland) Act 1974 s 8; see also para 8.28 et seq.
4 MH(FP)(S)A 1981 s 1; CPA 2004 s 101.
5 MH(FP)(S)A 1981 s 4; CPA 2004 s 104.

TRANSFER OF LANDLORD'S INTEREST[1]

7.39   Since leases are incidents of ownership, the landlord's interest in a lease transfers automatically with the transfer of ownership.[2] The tenant has no right of objection; furthermore, the new owner will only be bound to recognise the lease if the pre-requisites for the operation of the Leases Act 1449 have been fulfilled, or if the lease has been registered.[3]

We have already dealt with the transmission of lease conditions when there is a change of landlord.[4]

A landlord's interest is also transferred with the creation of an interposed lease. The final part of the chapter deals with this subject.

1 Paton and Cameron p 148.
2 Or, in the case of subtenancies, with the assignation of the head lease.
3 See paras 2.30 et seq and 8.11 et seq.
4 See para 2.40 et seq.

INTERPOSED LEASES

The 1974 Act

7.40   Where an interposed lease has been created, the tenant will end up with a new landlord, even though the original landlord has not sold the property.

This is a back to front method of creating a subtenancy. It occurs where a landlord under an existing lease grants a lease of the landlord's interest (the reversion) to a new tenant, the result being to interpose the new tenant between the landlord and the original tenant.[1] The latter, whose consent is not necessary, thereby becomes a subtenant, the newly created head tenant now being his landlord.

Interposed leases have always been valid in England; however, until 1974, they were thought to be illegal in Scotland.[2] The law of the two countries was brought into line by the Land Tenure Reform (Scotland) Act 1974, which made interposed leases legal, and extended this validity retrospectively to any interposed leases that had been created prior to the Act coming into force.[3]

An interposed lease can be longer or shorter or of the same duration as the original lease, and it may lease the whole subjects of the original lease or only part of them.[4]

1 But see, in this context, *Crewpace v French* 2012 SLT 126, 2011 SCLR 730, and the discussion of that case at para 2.25.

2 For a consideration of the law prior to 1974, see Paton and Cameron pp 170–171.
3 Land Tenure Reform (Scotland) Act 1974 s 17.
4 LTR(S)A 1974 s 17(1).

Registration of interposed lease

7.41   If an interposed lease is for more than 20 years it must be registered in the Land Register for the grantee of the interposed lease (the new head tenant) to obtain a real right valid against the landlord's singular successors.[1]

1 LTR(S)A 1974 s 17(1) and Registration of Leases (Scotland) Act 1857 ss 20B and 20C; see para 8.11 et seq.

Effects of interposed lease

7.42   The 1974 Act specifies several consequences flowing from the grant of an interposed lease:

(1)   The interposed head tenant will be deemed to have entered into possession.[1] Provided that the other criteria required for the application of the Leases Act 1449 have been fulfilled, this will ensure that the new head tenant will obtain a real right valid against the landlord's singular successors (except, as noted above, in those cases where this can only be done by registration in the Land Register).[2]

(2)   The interposed head tenant will be in the position of having received an assignation of the landlord's interest in the original lease.[3] The terms of the interposed lease will therefore be the same as the terms of the original lease, unless there has been an agreement to the contrary. This presumably means that the landlord and the new head tenant can agree to have different terms in the interposed lease, though the subtenant will have the same terms as before.

(3)   If the interposed lease comes to an end for any reason, the subtenant will revert to the original position of being a tenant directly under the original landlord.[4] This could occur either because the interposed lease was shorter than the original lease or because it had been terminated prematurely, eg by irritancy. This is an exception to the general rule that any sublease falls on the termination of the head lease.[5]

1 LTR(S)A 1974 s 17(1).
2 See para 7.41.
3 LTR(S)A 1974 s 17(2).
4 LTR(S)A 1974 s 17(2).
5 See para 7.35.

Relation to sale and leaseback transactions

7.43   A major reason for the change in the law was to facilitate sale
and leaseback transactions, a method of raising capital from property
which is sometimes preferable to a conventional loan transaction
(eg when interest rates are high). If part of the property has already
been leased, this will have the effect of demoting any existing tenants to
subtenants.

It was felt that this incidental and quite unintentional illegality was
perhaps discouraging the use in Scotland of a useful commercial
practice.[1]

1 For another example of a transaction that created interposed leases as a by-product, see
   The Conveyancing Opinions of J.M Halliday (ed Douglas J Cusine) (1992), Opinion 87.

Other advantages

7.44   In any case, quite apart from sale and leaseback situations,
the practice of interposing leases can be justified in its own right.
With commercial property it is convenient and very common to have
subtenancies, eg a landowner may lease land to a developer, who builds
(say) an office block and then sublets the individual offices.

There can also be situations where it will be convenient to create a
subtenancy by interposing a lease. A development company that has
completed a project (on land which they either own or hold on lease)
may, after leasing out the various units, want to retain the development
as an investment without having the trouble of day-to-day management.
They could achieve this by interposing a lease to a management company
between them and the tenants of the individual units. The legalising of
interposed leases, therefore, added an element of flexibility to Scottish
lease practice, which already existed in England.

Chapter 8

Long leases

GENERAL

8.1 There is no prescribed length of time that determines whether or not a lease should be regarded as a long lease, though, as we saw in the last chapter, there is at common law a rough division between leases of ordinary and those of unusual duration.[1] The statutory provisions considered below mainly apply to leases of more than 20 years.

However, much longer leases are common. Ground leases in particular often extend to 99 years or more, in some cases even to 999 years. Although many such leases, because of their extraordinary length, still exist today, new leases executed on or after 9 June 2000 are limited by statute to a maximum length of 175 years and the Long Leases (Scotland) Act 2012 introduced a scheme for the conversion of tenants' interests under ultra-long leases into ownership.[2]

1 See paras 7.20 et seq.
2 Abolition of Feudal Tenure etc (Scotland) Act 2000 s 67; see also paras 8.4 et seq and 8.38 et seq.

Leasehold interests and ownership

8.2 Perhaps the most notable characteristic of a long lease is that, the longer its term, the less it continues to resemble the basic concept of a contract conferring a temporary right of occupancy. We noted in chapter 1 that a lease of (say) 99 years confers upon the tenant something that is much more like a right of ownership.[1]

The rent may be relatively low, particularly in ground leases where the tenant has built or paid for the buildings. Also, a lease with a long unexpired term has a market value, and a tenant would normally be able to receive a capital sum (or grassum) in return for granting an assignation of the tenant's interest. If the unexpired term of the lease is long enough, the consideration may be comparable to the market price in an outright sale.

Even so, no lease, however long, will confer on the tenant a right that is *fully* equivalent to ownership. Sooner or later the termination date will arrive and the property will revert to the landlord, in some cases even although it may include a building or buildings that have been built or paid for by the tenant.[2] Also, we saw in Chapter 5 that even the tenant of a long lease remains vulnerable to its being terminated by irritancy.[3]

The difference between an absolute and a leasehold title, no matter how tenuous it may seem in some cases, is still recognised by the courts. In *McConnell v Chassels*[4] the purchaser of a shop was held entitled to resile from the contract when it transpired that the seller was not the absolute owner of the property, but a tenant under a 999-year lease.

1 See para 1.7 et seq; see also judicial opinions in *Dorchester Studios v Stone* 1975 SC (HL) 56 and *CIN Properties v Dollar Land (Cumbernauld) Ltd* 1992 SLT 669, quoted in para 5.28.
2 See para 10.39 et seq.
3 See para 5.27 et seq.
4 (1903) 10 SLT 790; see also *Fleming v Boswell* 1948 CLY 4378.

Incidence of long leases

8.3   Long leases of commercial subjects are more common than outright sales of such property. This is partly due to the influence of the English business lease on its Scottish counterpart. Also, when disposing of land for commercial development, there is more incentive for the landowner to grant a long lease which, in addition to any capital sum which the parties agree to, will also provide a periodic return in the form of rent. In the past, Scottish landlords might instead have feued the land and imposed a periodic feuduty, but this has not been possible since 1974.[1]

As we will see below, long leases of residential property are prohibited.[2]

There are a number of statutory provisions relating to long leases, which will be our main concern in this chapter.

1 Land Tenure Reform (Scotland) Act 1974 s 1 (now repealed by Sch 13 Pt 1 of the Abolition of Feudal Tenure etc (Scotland) Act 2000, which made it redundant).
2 See para 8.28 et seq.

MAXIMUM LENGTH OF LEASES

Reasons for limit

8.4   Section 67 of the Abolition of Feudal Tenure etc (Scotland) Act 2000 restricts all new leases to a maximum length of 175 years. Otherwise, if the length of leases had remained unrestricted the feudal system might have been perpetuated under another name by a system of leasehold tenure similar to that in England; for example, a landowner could have granted a lease of (say) 999 years, imposing conditions and charging a periodic rent. For very similar reasons a 20-year restriction had already been imposed on residential leases.[1]

In the case of non-residential leases a much higher limit was thought appropriate because of the widespread use of long commercial leases both north and south of the border.

1 See para 8.28 et seq.

175-year maximum

8.5   If a lease executed on or after 9 June 2000 is granted for a period of more than 175 years, it will automatically take effect as a lease for 175 years exactly.[1]

If the lease contains an option requiring either the landlord or the tenant to renew it, then the duration of the renewed lease will be added to that of the original lease for the purpose of calculating the latter's length;[2] for example, if a lease is granted for 150 years with an option to renew it for a further 150, this will be treated as a lease for 300 years and will end after 175 years, 25 years into the period of renewal. Otherwise, the use of such options could have been used to circumvent the statutory restriction.

1 AFT(S) A 2000 s 67(1).
2 AFT(S)A 2000 s 67(2).

Tacit relocation

8.6   The statutory rule does not prevent a lease from being continued beyond the 175-year limit by tacit relocation.[1]

1 AFT(S)A 2000 s 67(3)(a). For an explanation of tacit relocation, see para 10.18 et seq.

Statutory extensions

8.7   It is also stated that the statutory restriction will not prevent 'the duration of any lease being extended by, under or by virtue of any enactment'.[1] This is presumably intended to preserve any security of tenure given to tenants by statute.

At the moment such security of tenure is enjoyed by certain agricultural tenants,[2] certain tenants of dwellinghouses,[3] and also (though to a limited extent) by the tenants of shops.[4] However, the main relevance of this provision will of course be to any statutory security of tenure that may exist in the future, when the lease is finally due to end.

1 AFT(S)A 2000 s 67(3)(b).
2 See Chs 15 and 16.
3 Security of tenure may carry a lease of a dwellinghouse beyond the statutory maximum length of 20 years for such leases: see para 8.28 et seq. Residential leases are dealt with in Chs 17 and 18.
4 See Ch 14.

Transitional provisions

8.8 *Obligations to renew* A new lease of more than 175 years was allowed if it was in implement of an obligation entered into before 9 June 2000, eg where there was an earlier lease containing an option to renew it for a period of more than 175 years.[1]

1 AFT(S)A 2000 s 67(4)(a).

8.9 *Second renewals* If a lease of more than 175 years was entered after 9 June 2000 in terms of the above exemption, eg because an earlier lease contained an option to renew, a second such renewal is allowed if the new lease contains a similar option.[1] However, no further renewals are allowed. This provision was designed to preserve the *status quo* regarding existing long leases until the legislation (now contained in the Long Leases (Scotland) Act 2012) regarding the conversion of these tenancies into ownership came into force.[2]

At first sight this provision for a second renewal seems odd, since one renewal for more than 175 years might seem a sufficient transitional period. However, a second renewal is required to protect the interests of certain tenants, such as those under the so-called Blairgowrie leases, pre-2000 leases for 99 years which are perpetually renewable by the tenants for further periods of 99 years at a time.

Tenants under such leases, since their tenure is effectively perpetual, will now qualify to have their interest converted into ownership under the 2012 Act, even if they appear to fall below the threshold for conversion.[3]

1 AFT(S)A 2000 s 67(4)(b).
2 See para 8.38 et seq.
3 See para 8.39 et seq.

8.10 *Subleases*[1] The 175-year restriction applies to subleases as well as to leases. However, in the case of a lease of more than 175 years granted before 9 June 2000 (or, in terms of paragraphs 8.8 and 8.9 above granted after that in implementation of an earlier obligation) the tenant could grant a sublease in excess of 175 years *after* that date.

Any such sublease, of course, could not exceed the term of the head lease. However, if a lease for 200 years, for example, had been granted on 31 January 2000 (shortly before the restriction came into force) a sublease (say) of up to 190 years could still have been granted ten years later. The subtenant's interest in any such lease will now qualify for conversion into ownership under the Long Leases (Scotland) Act 2012.[2]

1 AFT(S)A 2000 s 67(4)(c) and (5).
2 See para 8.39.

REGISTERED LEASES

8.11   We saw in Chapter 2 that, although writing is normally required for the creation of leases, they can be relatively informal, and any defects may be able to be cured by the actings of the parties.[1]

However, it is desirable for longer leases that have a capital value to be completed with greater formality. If a tenancy is a marketable asset, it is all the more important for there to be a proper document of title. This is particularly so if the tenant wants to borrow money on the security of the tenant's interest; the creditor requires something of legal substance on which to attach the right of security. It is for these reasons that a lease can be registered.

1 See para 2.9 et seq.

Requirements for registration

8.12   *Basic requirements*   A lease may be registered if:

(a)   it is valid[1]
(a)   it is self-proving where it is a traditional document;[2] and
(b)   its duration exceeds 20 years.[3]

A lease for an initial period of less than 20 years may be registered if it contains an obligation on the part of the landlord to renew it for a fixed period or periods that would extend its duration beyond 20 years.[4]

At the time of writing only leases that are traditional documents can be registered. A lease that is an electronic document can be authenticated and may be self-proving[5] but is not yet accepted for registration by the Keeper.[6]

Certain other conditions for registration need to be met for a lease to be registered. These conditions depend on whether the lease relates to registered or unregistered land.[7] It may be noted that when an application is made to register a lease and the land in respect of which the lease is granted has not been registered in the Land Register this will induce automatic plot registration of the land. In other words, the owner's interest in the land, as well as the lease will be registered.[8]

1 See s 25(1) and 26(1) Land Registration (Scotland) Act 2012; as to validities of a lease see para 2.22 et seq.
2 See para 2.5 et seq.
3 Registration of Leases (Scotland) Act 1857 s 1 (as amended).
4 ROL(S)A 1857 s 17.
5 Requirements of Writing (Scotland) Act 1995 s 9B and 9C and Electronic Documents (Scotland) Regulations 2014 (SSI No 83); see para 2.6.
6 See reg 2 of the Land Register of Scotland (Automated Registration) etc Regulations 2014 (2014 SSI No 347) which authorises certain types of deeds, including an assignation of a lease where it relates to the whole of a registered plot, to be registered as digital registration documents. While digital registration of such documents is authorised, it is not, at the time of writing, taking place except in relation to discharges of standard securities. It may be noted that in terms of reg 2(3) of the 2014 Regulations and rule 7 of the Land Register Rules etc (Scotland) Regulations 2014 (SSI No 150), the Keeper may make provision for other types of deed to be registered in electronic form.
7 The law of land registration is outwith the scope of this work. See ss 22, 24–26 of the Land Registration etc (Scotland) Act 2012; KCG Reid and GL Gretton, *Land Registration* (2017) ch 8.
8 See KCG Reid and GL Gretton, *Land Registration* (2017) para 7.9; Registers of Scotland, *Leases and Automatic Plot Registration* (https://kb.ros.gov.uk/land-and-property-registration/leases-and-the-land-register/leases-and-automatic-plot-registration) (2018).

8.13 *Fishing leases* A lease of over 20 years granting the right to fish for freshwater fish in inland waters can be registered.[1] Such a lease for an initial period of less than 20 years may be registered if it contains an obligation on the part of the landlord to renew it for a fixed period or periods that would extend its duration beyond 20 years.[2]

1 ROL(S)A 1857 s 20D(a) (inserted by LR(S)A 2012 Sch 2 para 16).
2 ROL(S)A 1857 s 20D(b).

8.14 *Time of registration* A lease can be registered at any time after execution, either before or after the date of entry.

8.15 *Other registrable documents* Any documents that affect the tenant's interest under a registered lease may (and should) also be registered: these include any assignation of a registered lease,[1] any renunciation of such a lease,[2] any extract decree of reduction of the lease,[3] any other deed terminating the lease, extending its duration or otherwise altering its terms,[4] and any standard security (or assignation or discharge thereof) granted over the tenant's interest.[5]

Such documents (apart from the extract decree) are also generally subject to the provisions of the Requirements of Writing (Scotland) Act 1995, which applies not only to the creation, but also to the transfer, variation or extinction of a real right in land.[6] At the time of writing, discharges of standard securities can take the form of electronic as well as traditional documents provided they relate to the whole of a registered plot of land.[7]

1 ROL(S)A 1857 s 3.
2 ROL(S)A 1857 s 13.
3 ROL(S)A 1857 s 14.
4 ROL(S)A 1857 s 20A (inserted by LR(S)A 2012 s 52(2)).
5 Conveyancing and Feudal Reform (Scotland) Act 1970, ss 9(2), 14 and 17.
6 See para 2.3.
7 See para 8.12.

8.16 *Forms* The Registration of Leases (Scotland) Act 1857 does not prescribe any form for a registrable lease, but does provide forms, inter alia, for assignations and renunciations.[1] These forms are illustrative only and need not be rigidly adhered to.[2]

1 ROL(S)A 1857 Schs A and G. See also Schs ZA and ZG (inserted by LR(S)A 2012 Sch 2 paras 17 and 22) which contain forms specifically designed for the Land Register.
2 *Crawford v Campbell* 1937 SC 596, 1937 SLT 449.

8.17 *Registration of extract* If a lease has already been registered for preservation in the Books of Council and Session or elsewhere, an extract may be used instead of the original for the purpose of registration in the Land Register.[1] If the original of the lease has been lost, a copy containing a suitable declaration by the current landlord and tenant may be registered instead.[2]

1 ROL(S)A 1857 s 19.
2 Long Leases (Scotland) Act 1954 s 26.

Registration equivalent to possession

8.18 Registration of a lease in the Register of Sasines was equivalent to possession of the property by the tenant, and also rendered unnecessary the other criteria for the operation of the Leases Act 1449.[1] One of the effects of registration, therefore, is to create a real right valid against the landlord's singular successors.

In the case of long leases registered in the Land Register, this principle has been taken a stage further: the Leases Act 1449 has been superseded and registration is now the only way of obtaining such a real right.[2] This effectively makes the registration of long leases obligatory, as registration will be required if the tenant is to obtain a real right.

1 ROL(S)A 1857 s 16(1) (as amended); see also para 2.39.
2 ROL(S)A 1857 ss 20B and 20C (inserted by LR(S)A 2012 s 52 and Sch 2 para 16). See also para 2.39.

Lease as security for a loan

8.19 Registration of a lease helps to make it a marketable commodity, which may be used as security for a loan. This may be achieved if the tenant grants a standard security in favour of the creditor (the same type of deed that is used to create a security over an ownership interest).[1] However, since a standard security only becomes effective by registration, it can only be granted over a tenant's interest that itself is registered.

1 See Conveyancing and Feudal Reform (Scotland) Act 1970 s 9.

CREATION AND VARIATION OF LEASE OBLIGATIONS

Transmission of obligations

8.20 We saw in Chapter 2 that the effect of the Leases Act 1449 was to create a real right valid against the landlord's singular successors, and we have just seen above that a similar result is obtained by registration of a lease. A further consequence is that the lease obligations, so far as they are not of a personal nature, can be enforced against the tenant by the landlord's singular successors.[1]

Furthermore, when the tenant's interest in a lease is assigned, the new tenant automatically takes over all the original tenant's obligations under the lease.[2] This effectively means that the obligations in a lease run with the land, ie they are effective not only against the original parties to the contract, but also to the successors in title of both landlord and tenant.

When we also consider the fact that there are many leases with very long terms, and that long leases can be registered, then lease conditions begin to acquire very similar characteristics to the real burdens and conditions that appear in owners' titles.

1 See paras 2.40 et seq.
2 See paras 7.1 and 7.32.

Creation of obligations

8.21   *General position*   While conditions enforceable by a landlord can, of course, be contained in the lease, at common law there was no authority to suggest that it was competent for a tenant to grant an assignation incorporating new conditions that would be valid, not only against the assignee, but also against the assignee's singular successors. Moreover, it was extremely doubtful whether a tenant, even under a registered lease, was entitled to grant a deed of conditions.

8.22   *1985 Act*   The Law Reform (Miscellaneous Provisions) (Scotland) Act 1985 made it possible for the granter of an assignation of a registered lease (the cedent) to impose conditions which, when the assignation is registered, will be effectual against the assignee's singular successors.[1] This provision applies retrospectively. It also became possible for a deed of conditions to be granted in relation to leasehold property and for its terms to be incorporated by reference into an assignation.

An obligation in an assignation cannot be created for the periodical payment of a sum of money unless it is:

(a)   rent or an apportionment of rent;
(b)   a continuing expense, eg a service charge; or
(c)   is imposed under a heritable security.

1 ROL(S)A 1857 s 3(2)–(4) (added by the Law Reform (Miscellaneous Provisions) (Scotland) Act 1985 s 3 and subsequently amended).

8.23   This facility adds a general flexibility into lease practice which can be useful. For example, it can be employed in commercial leases as an alternative to subletting, if a proliferation of subleases is thought undesirable.

In such cases, of course, subletting may be used, not just to impose new obligations on the various subtenants, but also to earn a profit by subletting at a higher total rent than that paid by the head tenant to the head tenant's landlord. For this reason, therefore, subletting may remain the preferred method in many cases.

Variation or discharge of lease obligations

8.24   *Voluntary variation*   The parties of course have the right to vary lease conditions by agreement. Such an agreement should conform to the Requirements of Writing (Scotland) Act 1995.[1]

1 See para 2.3 et seq.

8.25 *Variation by Lands Tribunal*[1] Since 1970 it has been possible for title conditions to be varied or discharged by the Lands Tribunal for Scotland.[2] The definition of title condition includes not only the conditions contained in the titles of owners but also the tenant's obligations in registrable leases where the obligation relates to the land.[3] If a landlord refuses to vary or discharge a lease obligation (or only agrees to do so at a price) the tenant may have the alternative of applying to the Lands Tribunal.

1 See Gordon and Wortley (Vol II, 3rd edn, 2020), ch 26.
2 Conveyancing and Feudal Reform (Scotland) Act 1970, Pt I, now repealed and replaced by Pt 9 of the Title Conditions (Scotland) Act 2003.
3 TC(S)A 2003 s 122(1).

8.26 *Excluded categories* The Lands Tribunal's powers do not extend to all types of title condition. The following are the main exclusions relevant to leases:

(1) Where the lease or other deed creating the condition prohibits a Lands Tribunal application within a specified period, which must not exceed five years.[1] Otherwise there is no such restriction (although, as we will see below) the Lands Tribunal is entitled to refuse an application for variation or discharge of a condition that has been created very recently.[2]

(2) An obligation to pay rent, or an obligation of relief relating to any such payment.[3]

(3) An obligation relating to the right to work minerals or to any ancillary right in relation to minerals.[4] This effectively excludes the obligations in mineral leases.

(4) Obligations in leases of agricultural holdings, small landholdings and crofts.[5]

(5) A condition that relates to the tenant rather than the land. In *George T Fraser Ltd v Aberdeen Harbour Board*,[6] the Court of Session upheld the Lands Tribunal's refusal to amend the alienation clause in a lease by adding a qualification that the landlord's consent to any assignation would not be unreasonably withheld. In addition to the fact that the alienation provision did not relate to the land, the variation sought would have enlarged or expanded upon the tenant's rights, which is normally outwith the powers of the Lands Tribunal.

(6) An irritancy provision, since it is not a title condition, but a condition relating to the enforcement of a condition.[7] The case quoted relates to an irritancy provision in a feu charter (and these no longer exist), but there seems to be no reason why the same principle should not apply to irritancy provisions in leases.

1 TC(S)A 2003 s 92.
2 See para 8.27.
3 TC(S)A 2003 s 122(1).

4 TC(S)A 2003, Sch 11 para 1; ancillary rights are as defined in s 2 of the Mines (Working Facilities and Support) Act 1966.
5 TC(S)A 2003, Sch 11 para 3; see also Chs 15 and 16.
6 1985 SC 127, 1985 SLT 384. See also *Propinvest Paisley LP v Co-operative Group Ltd (sub nom Co-operative Group Ltd v Propinvest Paisley Ltd)* 2012 SC 51, 2011 SLT 987.
7 *Highland Regional Council v Macdonald-Buchanan* 1977 SLT (Lands Tr) 37.

8.27   *Lands Tribunal decision*   The Lands Tribunal may only grant an application where they are satisfied that it is reasonable to do so.[1] The 2003 Act sets out ten factors which the Tribunal may have regard to; these include the practicability or cost of compliance, the time that has elapsed since the condition was created, the purpose of the condition, and whether it prevents a use for which there is planning permission or other consent.[2]

The Lands Tribunal has the power to award compensation to the landlord or to other owners whose land would have benefited from the continuance of the condition, eg neighbouring landowners.[3]

1 TC(S)A 2003 s 98. The automatic granting of unopposed applications in relation to some real burdens does not apply in the case of other title conditions, including the conditions in registered leases.
2 For the full list see TC(S)A 2003 s 100. It includes the Lands Tribunal's original criteria under s 1 of the Conveyancing (Scotland) Act 1970.
3 TC(S)A 2003 s 90(6) and (7).

PROHIBITION OF LONG RESIDENTIAL LEASES

The 1974 Act

8.28   As already mentioned, long leases of residential property are a special case. The Land Tenure Reform (Scotland) Act 1974 prohibits the creation of long leases of dwellinghouses for a period in excess of 20 years.[1] There are now a number of exceptions to this rule, discussed in the paragraphs below.

The position in Scotland is in marked contrast to that in England, where long leases of residential property are a common alternative to freehold ownership.

1 LTR(S)A 1974 s 8 (as amended). For further discussion of the Green Paper which preceded the Act see the 4th edition of this work.

Reasons for the prohibition

8.29   This ban on long residential leases was designed to plug a potential loophole in the 1974 Act, the main purpose of which was to prohibit the creation of new feuduties and set up machinery for the redemption of existing ones; this was an earlier stage in the reform of the feudal system of land holding in Scotland, now completed by the Abolition of Feudal Tenure etc (Scotland) Act 2000. It was feared that landowners, being now unable to impose a continuing feuduty payment when selling land outright, might instead copy the English system and grant long leases instead. This would effectively have perpetuated feuduties under another name, with the added disadvantage that the property would eventually revert to the landlord.[1]

As we saw above, a limit of 175 years has now been placed for similar reasons on non-residential leases, along with the final abolition of feudal tenure.[2]

1 See Green Paper *Land Tenure Reform in Scotland* (1972) para 63.
2 AFT(S)A 2000 s 67; see also para 8.4 et seq.

Leases affected

8.30   The provisions apply to every lease for more than 20 years executed after 1 September 1974. It is made an implied condition of every such lease that no part of the property shall be used as, or as part of, a private dwelling-house,[1] though breach of this will not by itself render the lease void or unenforceable.[2] This provision applies to subleases as well as to leases.[3] Attempts at evasion by putting the grantee on some other legal basis are prevented by extending the definition of prohibited leases to include liferents and other rights of occupancy (such as licences) where they would involve payment of money.[4]

Even if a lease does not have an express duration of more than 20 years, it will still count as such if it could extend beyond that length without the consent (express or implied) of one of the parties. This could happen, for example, if it was granted for the duration of the tenant's life, or if either party could hold the other to a renewal option.[5]

In the latter case, it is not necessary that the party who does not want to renew should be legally obliged to, provided that failing to agree to an extension could make that party liable for a monetary payment or some other sanction. However, option provisions in leases granted before 1 September 1974 can still be enforced, even if the effect is to extend the lease beyond 20 years.[6]

The provisions do not apply to a lease of under 20 years that is extended beyond that period by the process of tacit relocation, as this involves the implied consent of *both* parties. [7]

1 LTR(S)A 1974 s 8(1).
2 LTR(S)A 1974 s 9(1).

3 LTR(S)A 1974 s 10(1).
4 LTR(S)A 1974 s 8(4) ; for licences, see para 2.51 et seq.
5 LTR(S)A 1974 s 8(4).
6 LTR(S)A 1974 s 8(4).
7 For tacit relocation, see para 10.18 et seq.

Exceptions

8.31   The prohibition does not apply in the following cases:

(1)   Leases of caravan sites.[1]

(2)   Leases where the residential use is ancillary to a non-residential one, and it would be detrimental to the efficient exercise of the non-residential use if the residential one was not allowed.[2] Possible examples could include a caretaker's flat in an office block or a manager's flat in a hotel. The situation would be less clear cut where a shop and house are leased together or where a person runs a business from home; in such cases it would depend upon whether the commercial or the residential use was the dominant one.

(3)   Leases of agricultural holdings, small landholdings and crofts.[3]

(4)   Leases executed after March 1 2011 where the *lessee* is a social landlord, a body connected to a social landlord or a rural housing body.[4] A social landlord for this purpose is defined as 'a registered social landlord, local authority landlord or a local authority which provides housing services'.[5] A body is connected to a social landlord if either of them is a subsidiary of the other (or they are both subsidiaries of the same parent body), or either of them has the power to control the other's affairs.[6] A rural housing body is a body prescribed by order under s 43(5) of the Title Conditions (Scotland) Act 2003.[7]

(5)   Leases executed after March 1 2011 where the *lessee* is a body prescribed, or of a type prescribed, by the Scottish Ministers by statutory instrument.[8]

(6)   From 1 December 2017 leases which are private residential tenancies in terms of the Private Housing (Tenancies)(Scotland) Act 2016.[9] A lease is a private residential tenancy where the tenancy is one under which the property is let to an individual as a separate dwellinghouse[10] and the tenant occupies the property or any part of it as his only or principal home.[11] Schedule 1 of the 2016 Act lists tenancies which cannot be private residential tenancies. Private residential tenancies do not have a fixed duration but continue until terminated by the parties in accordance with the 2016 Act. These tenancies are discussed in detail in Chapter 17.

1 LTR(S)A 1974 s 8(2).
2 LTR(S)A 1974 s 8(3).

3 LTR(S)A 1974 s 8(5); see also Chs 15 and 16.
4 LTR(S)A 1974 s 8(3A) (inserted by the Housing (Scotland) Act 2010 s 138).
5 Housing (Scotland) Act 2010 s 165.
6 H(S)A 2010 s 164.
7 TC(S)A 2003 s 122(1).
8 LTR(S)A 1974 s 8(3A)(d) (inserted by the Private Rented Housing (Scotland) Act 2011 s 36).
9 LTR(S)A 1974 s 8(3ZA) (inserted by the Private Housing (Tenancies)(Scotland) Act 2016 Sch 4).
10 It should be noted that the effect of PH(T)(S)A 2016 s 2(4) is that a tenancy can be a private residential tenancy where it lacks certain essential facilities to be regarded as a separate dwelling but the tenant has access to associated shared facilities. As such, a tenant who had exclusive use of a bedroom but a shared kitchen and bathroom would have a private residential tenancy.
11 PH(T)(S)A 2016 s 1.

8.32 Exception (4) was introduced to facilitate the availability of social housing by allowing social landlords to obtain funding by methods which the 20-year rule might have prohibited on a technicality. For example, if the social landlord obtained funding by a sale and leaseback arrangement and the lease *to* the social landlord was for more than 20 years, this would breach the rule by virtue of the fact that the ultimate occupant or occupants would be residential tenants. This would be the case even if the residential subtenants themselves (as would generally be the case) were on much shorter leases which were well under 20 years. This situation would of course be quite unrelated to the mischief which the 20-year rule was designed to address.

Exception (5) is designed to extend the same funding flexibility to the private sector. In order to prevent abuse of this concession, a number of safeguards are put in place. The landlord will have to be a particular corporate body or type of body, ie not a private individual, that has been prescribed by statutory instrument, under which the Scottish Ministers have the power to impose conditions and restrictions, eg as to the type of leases to be exempted and the consequences of breach of the conditions. The latter should include a provision for the protection of the interests of tenants or occupiers of any dwellinghouses on the leased subjects.[1]

Exception (6) was needed to take account of the creation of a new form of tenancy, the private residential tenancy, created by the Private Housing (Tenancies)(Scotland) Act 2016.[2] This new type of tenancy was designed to replace short assured tenancies and assured tenancies,[3] with the aim of providing tenants with increased security of tenure. Such tenancies are open-ended and can only be brought to an end on notice by the tenant; agreement between the landlord and tenant; or by a decision of the First-Tier Tribunal on an application

by the landlord that a ground for eviction specified in Schedule 3 of
the Act exists.

1 LTR(S)A 1974 s 8(3B) to (3D) (inserted by Private Rented Housing (Scotland) Act
2011 s 36). For further discussion of this provision, see Robert Rennie 'The 20 year
rules and the McLetchie amendment' 2012 Edin LR 114.
2 For details of this type of tenancy see Ch 17.
3 Such tenancies entered into before the coming into force of the PH(T)(S)A 2016 on
1 December 2017 remain in place but no new assured or short assured tenancies could
be entered into from that date.

Consequences of breach

8.33   *Termination of lease*   If a property, or part of it, subject to a
lease of over 20 years, is used as a dwellinghouse without the landlord's
consent, the landlord may give the tenant 28 days' notice to stop the
residential use, failing which the lease may be terminated.[1] It is a
defence to any action of removing by the landlord that the residential
use has ceased[2] and the tenant is further protected by the court having
power to postpone implementation of its decree, or even to rescind it,
should it emerge that there was in fact a valid defence to the action.[3]

If only part of the leased property is used residentially, the lease is only
terminable in relation to that part. In such a case, the court decree should
make any necessary adjustment to the rent or other lease conditions in
relation to the remaining part.[4] It should also contain a conveyancing
description of the part terminated,[5] which will allow the extract decree
to be registered in the Land Register.

1 LTR(S)A 1974 s 9.
2 LTR(S)A 1974 s 9(3).
3 LTR(S)A 1974 s 9(6).
4 LTR(S)A 1974 s 9(5).
5 LTR(S)A 1974 s 9(5).

8.34   *Where landlord has consented*   The above provisions
presuppose a situation where the property has been granted on a long
lease for non-residential purposes, and the tenant has begun to use it, or
part of it, as a dwellinghouse without the landlord's consent.

If a building has been leased, the landlord will, of course, normally
know what kind of use it has been designed for; however, conversions
or other adaptations could be made by tenants, or a landlord might
have granted a ground lease, unaware of the type of building the tenant
intended to erect. However, if it is proved that the landlord has approved
the residential use, either expressly or by acquiescence, the tenant may
not be removed, but the remaining duration of the lease will be restricted

to a period of 20 years after the year in which the notice of breach of the prohibition on residential use was given.[1]

This defence is only open to a person actually in occupation of the property, and so would not be available to a head tenant where the property has been sublet.[2] However, it *would* be open to a subtenant, not only in an action of removing by the head tenant, but also where the landlord is seeking to terminate the head lease;[3] termination of the latter, of course, would also terminate the subtenant's right. This will apply even if the sublease is not a long lease, ie if it is for 20 years or less.[4]

1 LTR(S)A 1974 s 9(4).
2 LTR(S)A 1975 s 10(3).
3 LTR(S)A 1975 s 10(4).
4 LTR(S)A 1975 s 10(5).

8.35 *Intimation to heritable creditors and subtenants* A landlord who has raised an action to terminate a lease in accordance with the above provisions must give intimation of the action to any heritable creditors or subtenants whose interest is revealed by a 20-year search of the Register of Sasines, the Land Register or the Valuation Roll or otherwise, the last being in order to reveal any subtenants whose interest is not registered.[1] In view of the fact that residential property no longer appears in the Valuation Roll, any search for subtenants without a registered interest will have to be in some other publication, eg the Electoral Roll.

1 LTR(S)A 1974 s 10(2); LR(S)A 1979 s 29(2).

Interaction with housing legislation

8.36 *Statutory regulation of residential tenancies* We will see in due course[1] that there is much statutory regulation of residential tenancies. The most common categories of housing lease are the Scottish secure tenancy under the Housing (Scotland) Act 2001 (lets from councils and other social landlords) and the private residential tenancy under the Private Housing (Tenancies)(Scotland) Act 2016 (lets from private landlords). There are still a number of assured tenancies under the Housing (Scotland) Act 1988 (the system which preceded the private residential tenancy) and some regulated tenancies under the Rent (Scotland) Act 1984, the system which preceded the assured tenancy, still survive.

It is a common feature of all these systems that the tenant may have security of tenure.

1 See Pt 5.

8.37 *Types of tenancy* Section 8(7) of the Land Tenure Reform (Scotland) Act 1974 provides as follows:

'Nothing in this Part of this Act shall prevent a tenancy from being or becoming a protected or statutory tenancy [ie a regulated tenancy] within the meaning of the Rent (Scotland) Act 1984 or a Scottish secure tenancy within the meaning of the Housing (Scotland) Act 2001 (asp 10), but nothing in either of those Acts restricting the power of a court to make an order for possession of a dwelling-house shall prevent the granting of a decree of removing under s 9(1) of this Act.'

This means that a long lease of a property used residentially may still be terminated even if it qualifies as a regulated or Scottish secure tenancy. However, the omission (presumably accidental) of any reference to the Housing (Scotland) Act 1988 leaves the position of assured tenants uncertain. This problem is somewhat mitigated by the fact that the vast majority of assured tenancies are short assured tenancies where there is no security of tenure. The omission of the 1988 Act from s 8(7) of the Land Tenure Reform (Scotland) Act is perhaps now less of a concern given that from 1 December 2017 no new assured tenancies could be created, with the introduction of private residential tenancies under the Private Housing (Tenancies) (Scotland) Act 2016. It will be remembered that private residential tenancies are exempted from the prohibition on residential leases in excess of 20 years.

CONVERSION INTO OWNERSHIP

Introduction

8.38 It was noted earlier that when a lease is long enough the tenant's interest is very similar to ownership, and if the lease has a very long unexpired term it can have a market value equivalent to that of ownership.[1] However, such a tenant does not have the security of an ownership title, and in due course the tenant's interest will revert to the landlord. Even prior to that, the tenancy can be vulnerable to drastic landlords' remedies such as irritancy.

Also, historically long leases were often granted as a substitute for feudal grants where there was a title restriction forbidding the latter. It therefore makes sense to have a scheme equivalent to that for the abolition of feudal tenure, under which the tenants' interests of very long leases can be converted into ownership.

An earlier scheme for the conversion of long residential leases was introduced for a limited period (5 years) by Part I of the Long Leases (Scotland) Act 1954, during which time the incidence of such leases was substantially reduced. The Long Leases (Scotland) Act 2012 introduced a new scheme to continue this process in relation to all types of long lease where the lease qualifies on the basis of length and certain other criteria. The Act largely implements the recommendations of the Scottish Law Commission.[2]

Under the 2012 Act the rights of tenants under qualifying leases converted to ownership on the appointed day: 28 November 2015.[3] Prior to the 2012 Act coming into force it was estimated by the Scottish Executive, based on evidence from a study by the Scottish Law Commission, that there were in the region of 9,000 ultra-long leases eligible for conversion.[4]

There is not the space here to consider these complex provisions in great depth, and what follows is an overview.

1 See paras 1.7 et seq and 8.2.
2 *Report on Conversion of Long Leases,* Scot Law Com No 204, December 2006.
3 Long Leases (Scotland) Act 2012 s 70 which came into force on 28 November 2013.
4 See Sarah Harvie-Clark *Long Leases (Scotland) Bill* SPICe Briefing, 2 February 2012, available at: www.parliament.scot/researchbriefingsandfactsheets/s4/sb_12-11.pdf.

Qualifying leases[1]

8.39   A lease is a qualifying lease if, immediately before the appointed day:

(1)   it is registered;
(2)   it was granted for a period of more than 175 years;
(3)   it has an unexpired term of more than 100 years (in the case of residential leases) or of more than 175 years (in any other case). A residential lease in this context means that the subjects of the lease wholly or mainly comprise a private dwelling house.

A lease will *not* qualify if:

(a)   the annual rent payable under the lease is over £100;
(b)   the subjects of the lease include a harbour (either wholly or partly) in relation to which there is a harbour authority;
(c)   the lease is granted for the sole purpose of allowing the tenant to install and maintain pipes or cables; or
(d)   it is a mineral lease, or it includes minerals for the exploitation of which a royalty is payable.

Where a lease has been divided, eg by a partial assignation, each part is treated as a separate lease.

A lease that would otherwise be a qualifying lease is exempt if it was not registered by 28 November 2014, that notwithstanding the fact that it was not registered it constituted a real right in land and the lease is subsequently registered.[2]

Where the subjects have been sublet, the lease of the subtenant who actually occupies the subjects is the one that may qualify. Where it is only partially sublet, the head tenant's lease can be a qualifying lease in relation to the part that has not been sublet.[3] In other words, where there is a hierarchy of sublets, only the person actually occupying the subjects has the right to become an owner.

1 LL(S)A 2012 s 1.
2 LL(S)A 2012 s 65.
3 LL(S)A 2012 s 3.

8.40 *Determination of rent* The level of rent to be taken into account when determining whether or not a lease is a qualifying lease is decided by reference to the lease, to a registered assignation of the lease, or to a registered minute of variation or agreement in relation to the lease.[1] Any element of rent expressed in non-monetary terms should be disregarded,[2] as should any element of rent that is variable from year to year, eg where a turnover rent is payable.[3] There are special provisions where a *cumulo* rent is payable in respect of two or more leases.[4]

1 LL(S)A 2012 s 2(1)–(3).
2 LL(S)A 2012 s 2(5).
3 LL(S)A 2012 s 2(6).
4 See LL(S)A 2012 s 2(4) and Pt 3.

8.41 *Determination of lease duration*[1] In determining the duration of a qualifying lease, the following rules apply:

(1) Any break provision allowing the lease to be terminated prior to the ish should be disregarded.[2]

(2) Where the lease includes a provision requiring the landlord to renew the lease, the duration of the renewed lease should be added to the duration of the first lease. The combined duration is also the operative duration in terms of the Act in the case of consecutive leases, ie where, during the currency of a lease, a new lease is granted which will take effect from the expiry of the first lease.[3]

Special provisions are also included to cover the rare cases where the duration has been expressed wholly or partly by reference to the lifetime of a person.

1 LL(S)A 2012 s 71.
2 For breaks, see para 10.2.
3 See also para 8.9.

Conversion into ownership

8.42   On 28 November 2015, the tenants' interests in qualifying leases converted into ownership. The rights of the landlord and of any head tenants were extinguished.[1]

The tenant of a qualifying lease was able to opt out of conversion by registering an exemption notice at least two months before 28 November 2015.[2] The tenant was able to change his mind by registering a recall notice. When this is done the tenant's interest in the lease converted to ownership on the first Whitsunday or Martinmas falling six months after the notice is registered.[3]

It was also possible to opt out of conversion by the landlord and tenant coming to an agreement that the annual rent immediately before 28 November 2015 or at any point in the five-year period ending on 7 August 2012 was more than £100, and that agreement being registered two months before 28 November 2015.[4] Finally, and in the absence of an agreement regarding rent between landlord and tenant, the landlord could make an application to the Lands Tribunal for an order confirming that the rent was more than £100 in the periods set out in the preceding sentence. This application had to be made before 22 February 2015 and the order registered two months before 28 November 2015.[5]

1 LL(S)A 2012 s 4.
2 LL(S)A 2012 s 63. Four such notices were registered: see KCG Reid and GL Gretton, *Conveyancing 2015* (2016), p 105.
3 LL(S)A 2012 s 67. For the meaning of Whitsunday and Martinmas see para 1.22 et seq.
4 LL(S)A 2012 s 64. One such agreement was registered: see KCG Reid and GL Gretton, *Conveyancing 2015* (2016), p 105.
5 LL(S)A 2012 ss 64 and 69.

Consequences of conversion

8.43   All rights and obligations arising expressly or by implication from a qualifying lease and any superior lease, apart from a personal right that does not run with the land, were extinguished on the appointed day.[1] Any subordinate real rights to which the tenant's interest was subject attached to the new owner's interest after conversion, eg a heritable security over the tenant's interest became a security over the new ownership interest.[2] However, a heritable security or proper liferent over the former landlord's interest was extinguished.[3]

If the qualifying lease, or any superior lease or partial assignation of a lease, had previously resulted in the land being divided, conversion created any servitudes, eg a right of way that would have been created if this prior division had come about as the result of a conveyance.[4]

Prior to 28 November 2015 , the landlord could lay claim to any sporting rights of game or of fishing which were reserved from a superior or qualifying lease by registering a notice to that effect.[5]

1 LL(S)A 2012 s 5.
2 LL(S)A 2012 s 6.
3 LL(S)A 2012 s 6(4).
4 LL(S)A 2012 s 7.
5 LL(S)A 2012 ss 8 and 9. No such notices were registered: see KCG Reid and GL Gretton, *Conveyancing 2015* (2016), p 105.

Real burdens

8.44 Part 2 of the Long Leases (Scotland) Act 2012 sets out at considerable length the process whereby certain lease conditions[1] convert to real burdens to which the former tenant's new ownership title will be subject. Any real burden so created must conform to s 3 of the Title Conditions (Scotland) Act 2003.[2]

An entitled person[3] (usually the landlord of the qualifying lease but sometimes a third party, such as a neighbouring owner) was able to convert a qualifying condition into a real burden by registering a notice to that effect prior to 28 November 2015.[4] Section 14 sets out certain conditions, at least one of which must be met, before a burden will be created. These include that the benefited property has on it a permanent building used wholly or mainly as a place of human habitation or resort which sits within 100 metres of the burdened property (forming all or part of the land held under the qualifying lease), or that the qualifying condition comprises a right of pre-emption or redemption.[5] The need to satisfy one of these conditions may be dispensed with by agreement of the parties,[6] failing which by order of the Lands Tribunal.[7]

The Act also makes provision for certain leasehold conditions which were enforceable by a public body to be converted to personal real burdens, eg conservation burdens, by registration of a notice before 28 November 2015.[8]

Certain conditions automatically converted into real burdens on 28 November 2015. For instance, conditions which regulated the maintenance, management, reinstatement or use of property which constituted a facility of benefit to other land (such as a common part of a tenement or a common area for recreation) automatically converted to facility burdens.[9] Likewise, where a condition related to the provision of a service (such as the supply of electricity) this automatically converted to a service burden.[10] Where conditions were imposed on a group of properties under a common scheme these automatically converted to community burdens.[11]

1 LL(S)A 2012 s 10.
2 LL(S)A 2012 s 11.
3 LL(S)A 2012 s 13.
4 LL(S)A 2012 s 14. Three such notices were registered: KCG Reid and GL Gretton, Conveyancing 2015 (2016), p 105.
5 For rights of pre-emption and redemption see also LL(S)A s 23. Two notices were registered under s 23: KCG Reid and GL Gretton, Conveyancing 2015 (2016), p 105.
6 LL(S)A 2012 ss 17–20.
7 LL(S)A 2012 ss 21–22.
8 LL(S)A 2012 ss 24–27. No such notices were registered: KCG Reid and GL Gretton, Conveyancing 2015 (2016), p 105.
9 LL(S)A 2012 s 29.
10 LL(S)A 2012 s 29(2).
11 LL(S)A 2012 s 31.

Compensation

8.45   The former landlord was able to claim compensation from the former tenant by serving a notice on the tenant in prescribed form by 28 November 2017.[1] The amount of the compensation payable was based upon a formula derived from the annual rent, similar to the approach taken in the Abolition of Feudal Tenure etc (Scotland) Act 2000 in relation to the compensation of former feudal superiors, ie with reference to 2.5% Consolidated Stock.[2]

1 LL(S)A 2012 s 45.
2 LL(S)A 2012 ss 47–49.

8.46   *Additional payments*   Additional payments could be claimed by former landlords in respect of certain other rights that were lost on conversion,[1] eg where there was a right to review the rent from time to time; where the rent was variable, eg where it was based on the tenant's turnover;[2] where there were reversionary rights or landlords' break provisions;[3] or where there was development value, eg where a lease condition prohibited a particular kind of development, such as commercial development. The latter was only payable where the lease condition did not convert to a real burden.

The amount of any additional payment was based on what the right in question was worth as at 28 November 2015.[4] The former landlord had to serve notice in the prescribed form on the tenant by 28 November 2017 setting out the amount claimed.[5] Where the former landlord and tenant were unable to agree on the amount to be paid, a referral could be made to the Lands Tribunal.[6]

Where either the basic compensation or any additional payment was more than £50 the former tenant had the right to pay the compensation by instalments.[7]

1 LL(S)A 2012 ss 50–55.
2 See para 12.137 et seq.
3 See para 10.2.
4 LL(S)A 2012 s 52.
5 LL(S)A 2012 s 50.
6 LL(S)A 2012 ss 55.
7 LL(S)A 2012 ss 45(5), 50(5) and 57.

RENEWAL OF LONG LEASES

8.47   A long lease sometimes contains an obligation upon the landlord to grant a renewal of the lease at its expiry. However, the situation may arise (particularly in the case of very long leases) where the landlord fails to grant a renewal because the identity of the current landlord is unknown. Where the lease is probative and exceeds 20 years[1] the tenant may apply to the sheriff, who has the power to make an order directing the sheriff clerk to execute a renewal of the lease in the landlord's place.[2]

A landlord whose identity is known must have been given notice of the tenant's desire for a renewal before an application to the sheriff can be made;[3] the period of notice is three months, unless the lease specifies a longer period.[4] Where the landlord is unknown or cannot be found the sheriff may order that the landlord be regarded as having failed to renew or may dispense with the need for notice.[5]

1 See para 8.11 et seq.
2 Land Registration (Scotland) Act 1979 s 22A. Despite the repeal of s 28(1) of the 1979 Act by the Land Registration (Scotland) Act 2012 Sch 5 para 19(5) the definition of long lease in s 28(1) continues to apply for the purpose of s 22A: see s 120(2) of the LR(S)A 2012.
3 LR(S)A 1979 s 22A(4).
4 LR(S)A 1979 s 22A(5).
5 LR(S)A 1979 s 22A(7).

Extinction of leasehold casualties[1]

Nature of casualties

8.48   Casualties were additional payments that were once payable from time to time by feudal vassals to their superiors and, until much more recently, also by the tenants of long leases to their landlords. They could arise either at stated intervals during the currency of the lease, or on the occurrence of a particular event, such as on the assignation of the lease or on the death of the current tenant.[2]

1 See the detailed commentary by David A Brand on the Leasehold Casualties (Scotland) Act 2001 contained in Current Law Statutes; and Robert Rennie 'Leasehold Casualties' 2001 SLT (News) 235; for a lively account of the mischief addressed by the Act, see also John Sinclair 'Casualties: Suitable Cases for Treatment' 1996 SLPQ 125.
2 For the definition of a leasehold casualty see the Leasehold Casualties (Scotland) Act 2001 s 10.

8.49 *Leasehold casualties* Leasehold casualties appeared frequently in long leases, eg for 999 years, granted in the 19th century and earlier as an alternative to feuing, for example in situations where feuing was prohibited. Feudal casualties were abolished by the Feudal Casualties (Scotland) Act 1914, but leasehold casualties survived. Section 16 of the Land Tenure Reform (Scotland) Act 1974 prohibited the creation of new casualties after 1 September 1974,[1] but casualty provisions in leases entered before that date remained in force.

1 The right to include rent review provisions in leases was specifically excluded from the prohibition; it will be left to the reader, after reaching the end of Chapter 12, to decide whether or not this is a mixed blessing.

8.50 *Modern problems* Leasehold casualties seem largely to have been forgotten about until the 1990s, when the activities of parties known as the 'title raiders' brought them to public attention. The title raiders were so called from their practice of exploiting the archaic residues of the feudal system in order to extract money from owners and tenants, one of their procedures being to purchase the landlords' interests under long leases and immediately re-introduce demands for casualty payments.

In many cases these payments could be substantial (sums of £5,000, £10,000 and even £18,000 were known of) because not only could they include arrears of payments that had not been demanded for many years, but also in many cases they were based on the current rental value; this would not only take account of the considerable inflation during the course of the 20th century, but also reflect the value of the buildings which might originally have been provided or bought by the tenant.

Extinction of leasehold casualties

8.51 *2001 Act* Under the Leasehold Casualties (Scotland) Act 2001, provisions for casualty payments in leases and subleases of 175 years or more which were granted before 1 September 1974, ie before the prohibition of new casualties, are now void.[1] This means that casualty payments were no longer due after the 'relevant day' (10 May 2000).[2]

When calculating the duration of the lease, any break provisions should be disregarded; however, where there is an option to renew the duration of the renewal will be added to the duration of the original lease.[3]

The reason for the 175-year threshold is that virtually all casualty provisions are in leases longer than this, and setting a lower threshold could inadvertently have affected provisions in modern commercial leases.[4]

As already noted, irritancy rights in relation to such leases were also abolished.[5]

1 LC(S)A 2001 ss 1(1) and 10(1).
2 LC(S)A 2001 s 10(1). This provision is retrospective, in order to prevent attempts by landlords to extract last minute payments.
3 LC(S)A 2001 s 10(2).
4 See the Scottish Law Commission *Report on Leasehold Casualties* Scot Law Com No 165, March 1998, para 8.2.
5 LC(S)A 2001 s 5; see also para 5.6.

8.52 *Liability for arrears* Tenants were liable for arrears of casualty payments due before 10 May 2000, but only where these were payable during their own period of occupancy; they were no longer liable for casualty payments due by previous tenants.[1]

1 LC(S)A 2001 s 7.

8.53 *Compensation* Landlords had a right to claim compensation from the tenant for the extinction of any casualty by serving notice on the tenant within one year of the Act coming into force, ie by 12 April 2002.[1] A tenant's obligation to pay compensation prescribed five years after the landlord's notice of a claim.[2]

1 LC(S)A 2001 ss 2 and 3.
2 Prescription and Limitation (Scotland) Act 1973 Sch 1 para (1)(aa) (inserted by LC(S)A 2001 s 4).

Chapter 9

Succession to leases[1]

DEATH OF TENANT

9.1   The death of the tenant may bring a lease to an end, but not necessarily so. The general position regarding the succession to leases is regulated by the Succession (Scotland) Act 1964, which will be considered in this chapter. The special statutory provisions relating to agricultural and residential tenancies are considered later;[2] in relation to these types of lease, reference should be made to later sections of this work.

The Succession (Scotland) Act 1964 abolished the former rule under which a deceased person's heritable property was inherited by a single heir. Its provisions in relation to leases were designed to ensure that a tenancy could be transferred to a single successor even where the estate fell to be divided between two or more people. Unfortunately, these provisions are a little complex, and some of the distinctions they create are unlikely to have much application in practice.

On the tenant's death, a lease will initially vest in the tenant's executor (except in the case of a private residential tenancy or a Scottish secure tenancy),[3] who will have the duty to dispose of it in accordance with the law.[4] In order for this to occur, the executor must have obtained confirmation.[5] Who, if anyone will thereafter succeed to the tenancy will partly depend upon whether or not the tenant has made a bequest of the lease in his will. Where there is a bequest, the legatee may not want to take on the lease, and so the situation will also depend upon whether he or she accepts the bequest.

1 See generally Paton and Cameron ch 11; 9 *Stair Memorial Encyclopaedia* (Reissue, 2011) paras 302–326; Hiram *The Scots Law of Succession* (2nd edn, 2007) 2.42–2.49; Gordon & Wortley (3rd edn 2009) paras 18-40–18-54.
2 See paras 15.72 et seq, 16.10, 17.144 et seq and 18.81 et seq.
3 In these types of tenancy the lease does not vest in the executor but passes to the successor automatically see the terms of the Private Housing (Tenancies) (Scotland) Act 2016 ss 67–69 and Housing (Scotland) Act 2001 s 22; succession to these types of tenancy are discussed in paras 17.148 et seq and 18.81 et seq respectively.
4 Succession (Scotland) Act 1964 s 14(1) & s 36(2); *Cormack v McIldowie's Executors* 1975 SC 161, 1975 SLT 214.
5 *Cormack v McIldowie's Executors* 1975 SC 161, 1975 SLT 214; see also *Rotherwick's Trustees v Hope* 1975 SLT 187 at 189 per Lord Robertson.

9.2   *Succession to leases*

9.2   *Bequest of lease*   In principle, a tenant may bequeath the lease
to anyone, and such a bequest will be effective if the landlord agrees to
the transfer after the tenant's death.[1] However, if the landlord objects to
the bequest, its effectiveness will depend upon whether the lease can be
assigned without the landlord's consent, since a bequest is considered to
be a form of assignation.[2]

1 *Kennedy v Johnstone* 1956 SC 39 at 47 per Lord Sorn, 1956 SLT 73.
2 *Reid's Trustees v Macpherson* 1975 SLT 101. For the rules relating to assignation,
  see ch7.

9.3   *Assignation allowed*   If the lease expressly or by implication
allows assignation, a bequest will be effective without the landlord's
consent. However, this situation will not arise very often; although there
is a common law right to assign in many cases, it is invariably contracted
out of by a lease provision prohibiting assignation without the landlord's
consent.[1] If the landlord's consent is *not* required, the change of tenant
(as with assignations) should be intimated to the landlord.[2]

1 See para 7.4 et seq.
2 *Grant's Trustees v Arrol* 1954 SC 306, 1954 SLT 250; see also para 7.29.

9.4   *Implied prohibition*   Where there is no express prohibition of
assignation, but there is an implied condition to that effect, the position
is governed by s 29(1) of the Succession (Scotland) Act 1964. There
could be an implied prohibition, for example, where a lease did not
contain a clause prohibiting or restricting alienation,[1] but assignation
was prohibited at common law because there was *delectus personae*.[2]

The tenant has a right to bequeath the lease 'to any one of the persons who,
if the tenant had died intestate, would be, *or would in any circumstances
have been* (author's italics) entitled to succeed to his intestate estate'.
This would appear to allow the beneficiary to be selected from any of
the classes of person listed in ss 2–5 of the Act, and not just from those
first in line of succession.

Thus, for example, a tenant could bequeath to a brother, sister, nephew,
or niece, even where he or she is survived by children. However, as we
saw above, most leases *do* contain an express prohibition of assignation,
and so these provisions are unlikely to be invoked very often.

1 See para 11.4.
2 See para 7.19 et seq.

9.5   *Express prohibition*   Where the lease contains an express
prohibition against assignation (the normal situation) any bequest
will only be effective with the landlord's consent. If this provision
contains the common qualification that the landlord's consent will not

be unreasonably withheld, then any refusal may be subject to legal challenge.[1] However, even where the landlord does successfully object to the bequest, the lease will not necessarily come to an end. Instead, it will be disposed of in the same way as if the tenant had died intestate, in accordance with the rules set out in the next paragraph.

1 See para 7.8 et seq.

Where no bequest

9.6　　Under this heading we will consider the situation where the lease has not been the subject of a valid bequest either because:

(a)　　the tenant has died intestate;
(b)　　the tenant left a will that does not dispose of the lease;
(c)　　there was a bequest which was not accepted; or
(d)　　there was a bequest which the landlord successfully objected to.

In such cases, even where the lease contains an express prohibition of assignation, the executor may transfer the lease, without the landlord's consent, to any one of the persons entitled to succeed to the deceased's intestate estate, or to claim legal rights or the prior rights of a surviving spouse or civil partner out of the estate, in or towards satisfaction of that person's entitlement or claim. However, a transfer to anyone else would require the landlord's consent except in the case of an agricultural lease which is a 1991 Act tenancy or a lease of a croft.[1] The landlord has a right to object to the successor in the case of a 1991 Act tenancy, in which case the matter may have to be determined by the Land Court.[2]

If the lease is of the family dwellinghouse and the tenant has died intestate, the executor may be required to transfer the tenancy to the tenant's spouse or civil partner,[3] but otherwise would appear to have some discretion in the choice. If the executor is one of those entitled to succeed to the intestate estate, but not the only one, a conflict of interest could arise; in such a case, by transferring the tenancy to himself or herself, the executor could be liable to the other beneficiary or beneficiaries under the principle of *auctor in rem suam* (one who acts for his own behoof).[4]

1 S(S)A 1964 s 16(2) and (2A). This is subject to s 16(4A) which deals with the transfer of a short limited duration tenancy, a limited duration tenancy, a modern limited duration tenancy and a repairing tenancy where the lease can be transferred to the same individuals as noted above or to any other person. The transfer will only be made where it is in the best interests of the deceased's estate: see s 16(4E). These tenancies are discussed in Ch 15.
2 See para 15.78.
3 S(S)A 1964 s 8(1); see also para 17.144 et seq and 18.81 et seq.
4 *Inglis v Inglis* 1983 SC 8, 1983 SLT 437.

Termination of lease

9.7   Where the tenancy is not transferred by the executor, the lease will come to an end. If:

(a)   at any time the executor is satisfied that the tenant's interest cannot be disposed of according to law and so informs the landlord;[1] or

(b)   the tenant's interest is not so disposed of within one year of the tenant's death either the landlord or the executor may serve a notice on the other, terminating the lease.[2] The period of notice is six months.[3] The six-month period is stated as being without prejudice to any enactment prescribing a shorter period of notice; presumably this may refer to the period of notice laid down in the Sheriff Courts (Scotland) Act 1907 for non-agricultural leases (normally 40 days) or the minimum 28-day period prescribed by the Rent (Scotland) Act 1984 in respect of residential tenancies.[4]

The above relates to leases other than agricultural leases. In the case of agricultural leases, the position is slightly different and a little more complex.[5]

The one year period may be extended by agreement between the landlord and the executor or, failing agreement, by the sheriff on an application by the executor.[6] However, if the executor allows the year or such extended period to elapse without having transferred the tenancy, then the landlord has an absolute right to terminate the tenancy.[7]

1 S(S)A 1964 s 16(3). This is subject to s 16(4C) in the case of a short limited duration tenancy, a limited duration tenancy, a modern limited duration tenancy or a repairing tenancy where the termination will only occur where it is in the best interests of the deceased's estate; see s 16(4E). These tenancies are discussed in Ch 15.

2 S(S)A 1964 s 16(3).

3 S(S)A 1964 s 16(4).

4 See para 10.30.

5 See para 15.80 et seq.

6 S(S)A 1964 s 16(3)(b) and (8A).

7 *Rotherwick's Trustees v Hope* 1975 SLT 187 at 189 per Lord Robertson; *Gifford v Buchanan* 1983 SLT 613 at 616 per Lord Robertson and Lord Grieve; *Sproat v South West Services (Galloway) Ltd* 2000 GWD 37-1416 (the full judgment can be found at www.scotcourts.gov.uk).

9.8   *Damages* Where the executor terminates the lease, the landlord may have a claim of damages in respect of its premature termination; however, such a claim is enforceable only against the estate of the deceased and not against the executor personally.[1]

1 S(S)A 1964 s 16(5); see also Paton and Cameron pp 187–189; 9 *Stair Memorial Encyclopaedia*, para 320.

9.9 *Breach by executor* If a landlord brings an action of removing against an executor in respect of a breach of a condition of the lease, the court may not grant decree in the action unless it is satisfied that the condition is one which it is reasonable to expect the executor to have observed, having regard to the fact that the tenant's interest is vested in him or her in the capacity of executor.[1]

1 S(S)A 1964 s 16(7).

Special destinations[1]

9.10 The law stated above in relation to bequests and intestate succession may be overridden by a special destination in a lease, or in an assignation of a lease. A special destination is a provision in a document of title that effectively contracts out of the law of succession by nominating the person or persons entitled to succeed.

The most common example (in leases and elsewhere) is where title is taken in the name of two persons and the survivor of them; on the death of one of them, his or her share will accrue to the survivor, whether or not that person would have inherited under the law of succession. The lease will initially vest in the executor, but only for the purpose of conveying it to the person entitled to it under the destination.[2]

The above is merely a brief overview of a subject that is complex and controversial.[3]

1 Paton and Cameron pp 173–175; 9 *Stair Memorial Encyclopaedia*, para 307.
2 S(S)A 1964 s 18(2).
3 For an appreciation of some of the underlying complexities, see GL Gretton 'Destinations and Leases' 1982 SLT (News) 213; *Cormack v McIldowie's Executors* 1975 SC 161, 1975 SLT 214; John M Halliday 'What Makes a Destination Special' (1977) 22 JLSS 16; and Scottish Law Commission *Report on Succession* (Scot Law Com No 215, 2009) paras 6.61–6.66.

Liferent leases

9.11 If a lease states that it will come to an end on the tenant's death (a so-called 'liferent lease'), it will not form part of the tenant's estate and so will not pass to the tenant's executor.[1] Instead, the lease will automatically come to an end when the tenant dies. It is not believed that liferent leases are very common.[2]

1 S(S)A 1964 s 36(2).
2 But see *Special Case presented by Mountain's Trustees* [2012] CSIH 73, 2012 GWD 33-663. See also para 15.8.

9.12 *Exclusion of successors* A liferent lease should be distinguished from one which has a definite ish but the destination purports to exclude the tenant's successors or executors. If effective, this would contract out of the Succession (Scotland) Act 1964 to prevent the lease from vesting in the executor and it would end on the tenant's death even although its stated duration had not yet expired. However, it is doubtful whether such a provision would, in fact, be effective in preventing the lease from vesting in the executor.[1]

1 See AGM Duncan 'Agricultural Tenancies: the Exclusion of Successors' (1988) 33 JLSS 384.

Partnerships

9.13 Section 33(1) of the Partnership Act 1890 provides:

'Subject to any agreement between the partners, every partnership is dissolved as regards all the partners by the death or bankruptcy of any partner.'

A partnership will therefore come to an end with the death of one of the partners unless they have agreed otherwise. Such an agreement would normally be in the partnership contract and may either be express or implied from the general terms of the contract.[1]

However, in the case of a lease to a partnership, whether the death of a partner will bring the *lease* to an end is a quite separate issue. The general rule, formulated by the House of Lords in *Inland Revenue v Graham's Trustees*,[2] is that the dissolution of the partnership will terminate the lease. This is because the firm is a separate legal person from its partners, and this person will end with the dissolution of the partnership.[3]

However, this general statement is subject to several qualifications. Where the partnership is dissolved, by death or otherwise, the lease may nevertheless continue if it is assignable. And even where the parties have contracted for the partnership to survive the death of a partner, the position may depend upon whether the lease was granted to the partnership as originally constituted or to the 'house'.

1 *Gordon v Thomson Partnership* 1985 SLT 122.
2 1971 SC(HL) 1, 1971 SLT 46.
3 Partnership Act 1890 s 4(2). This is not the position in English law where the partnership does not have separate legal personality from the partners.

9.14 *Assignable leases* In *Lujo Properties Ltd v Green*[1] a firm of solicitors was dissolved, not by death, but by one of the partners giving notice to that effect.[2] The landlord of the office premises leased to the firm sought to hold the former partners liable for the tenants' pecuniary obligations for the remainder of the lease term.

In theory the dissolution of the partnership had brought the lease to an end, as in *Graham's Trustees*; however, since the lease was assignable, it was an asset of the dissolved firm that could be realised by assignation to a new tenant. It was held that, in the event of such an assignation, the lease would revive.

We have already seen that modern leases, even if freely assignable at common law, normally make the landlord's consent an express requirement.[3] A lease which totally prohibits assignation, or prohibits it without the landlord's consent, will therefore not be assignable in the above sense. However, the test of assignability in *Lujo* is 'where the tenant can procure an effective assignation without the concurrence of the landlord'.[4]

A lease is therefore assignable in cases where (as in *Lujo*) it contains the very common provision that the landlord's consent to an assignation will not be unreasonably withheld.[5] In such a case, the tenant can assign without the landlord's consent if the court considers that the landlord's refusal is unreasonable.

It was also held in *Lujo* that, under s 38 of the Partnership Act 1890, the former partners remained liable in respect of any transactions left uncompleted at the time of dissolution. This meant that, in the absence of an assignation, they remained liable to the landlord for the tenants' pecuniary obligations under the lease (including a sum equivalent to rent) for the duration of its unexpired term.

1 1997 SLT 225; see also *Primary Health Care Centres (Broadford) Ltd v Ravangave* 2008 Hous LR 24 at 27 per Lord Glennie, 2008 GWD 7-136.
2 See PA 1890 s 32.
3 See paras 7.4 et seq and 11.4.
4 *Lujo Properties Ltd v Green* 1997 SLT 225 at 237 per Lord Penrose.
5 See para 7.8 et seq.

9.15   *Leases granted to the 'house'*   The death of a partner will not bring a lease to a partnership to an end if the lease has been granted to the 'house'. This means that the tenant is the business itself, ie the partners of the firm from time to time, as opposed to the partnership as constituted when the lease was entered into.

A lease will be to the house if that appears from its wording to be the intention of the parties.[1] A lease to the partners as trustees for the firm and their successors in office as such trustees is a lease to the house,[2] but not where the reference to successors is absent.[3] A reference in the destination to 'partners present and future' is an indication that the parties intend the lease to be to the house;[4] on the other hand, in the absence of this or other such indication, the exclusion of assignees will normally imply that the lease is *not* to the house.[5]

1 *Inland Revenue v Graham's Trustees*, 1971 SC (HL) 1, 1971 SLT 46 at 47 per Lord Reid and 49–50 per Lord Guest.
2 *Lujo Properties Ltd v Green* 1997 SLT 225 at 228 per Lord Penrose.
3 *Moray Estates Development Co v Butler* 1999 SLT 1338, 1999 SCLR 447.
4 *Moray Estates* supra at 1344 per Lord Hamilton.
5 *Jardine-Paterson v Fraser* 1974 SLT 93 at 98 per Lord Maxwell.

9.16 *Leases not granted to the house* There remains to be considered the situation where the lease is not to the house, but, under the terms of the partnership contract, the firm will not be dissolved by the death of a partner. In such a case will the death of a partner end the lease?

On one view the lease will continue since a partnership is a separate legal person from its partners,[1] and so the identity of the tenant will not have changed. Alternatively, it could be argued that the lease should end because the landlord was not a party to the partnership agreement; if it was intended that the lease should survive the death of a partner, the lease document, to which the landlord *was* a party, could have provided that the lease was granted to the house.

The latter view was taken by the Outer House of the Court of Session in *Jardine-Paterson v Fraser*,[2] but that decision is inconsistent with the later Inner House judgement in *Gordon v Thomson Partnership*.[3] However, *Jardine-Paterson* was not referred to in that case, and the parties had agreed that the decision would hinge solely upon the interpretation of the partnership agreement.

The position would therefore appear to be somewhat uncertain. If it is intended that a lease to a partnership should survive the death of a partner, it is therefore advisable for its terms to make clear that it is being granted to the house.

1 PA 1890 s 4(2).
2 1974 SLT 93.
3 1985 SLT 122.

Chapter 10

Termination of leases

PREMATURE TERMINATION

10.1　There are a number of ways in which a lease may come to an end. As well as termination at the contracted expiry date (the ish) there are many situations where it may end prematurely, at some point prior to the ish. In some cases, the termination occurs in accordance with the lease terms, in others it comes about quite independently of them.

The following are the main causes of premature termination:[1]

(1)　break;
(2)　renunciation;
(3)　irritancy;
(4)　rescission;
(5)　frustration;
(6)　tenant's insolvency (which may end the lease); and
(7)　death of tenant (which may end the lease).

1 See also the disussion of confusio at para 2.24.

Break[1]

10.2　A break can occur when there is an appropriate break clause in the lease. Break clauses may be broadly divided into three types:

(a)　landlord-only breaks;
(b)　tenant-only breaks; and
(c)　mutual breaks.

A landlord-only break is where the lease allows the landlord, by notice to the tenant, to terminate the lease at some intermediate point prior to its expiry date, but where there is no corresponding right given to the tenant. A tenant-only break is where only the tenant has an option to terminate and a mutual break is where either party may exercise such an option. The lease may state one or more dates for the occurrence of a break, eg halfway through its duration, or every five years.

In *Ben Cleuch Estates Ltd v Scottish Enterprise*[2] a tenant's notice purporting to exercise a break provision was held to be invalid because it had erroneously been sent to the landlord's parent company instead of the actual landlord. However, because the parent company had been misleadingly represented as being the landlord, particularly by the issue of rent notices stating that this was the case, the landlord was personally barred from disputing the validity of the break notice.

In *Prudential Assurance Co Ltd v Excel UK Ltd*[3] it was held that a notice purporting to exercise a break on behalf of only one of two joint tenants was invalid.

The decision of the Inner House in *Hoe International Ltd v Andersen*[4] suggests that notices may not need to be sent precisely as provided by the lease. For the court an important consideration was whether the recipient of a notice is prejudiced by it not being issued in line with the contractual provisions. It should, however, be noted that this case did not relate to a notice exercising a break. Given the drastic effect of such a notice, in terminating a lease before its ish, it is suggested that the party issuing a notice, and those advising him, ensure that the notice is issued in accordance with the requirements of the lease.

In *Allied Dunbar Assurance plc v Superglass Sections Ltd (No 1)*[5] it was held that tenants were not precluded from exercising a tenant's break because they were (according to the landlords) in material breach of their repairing obligations under the lease. However, in *Arlington Business Parks GP Ltd v Scottish & Newcastle Ltd,*[6] where the lease provided that the break option would be ineffective if the tenant was in breach of any of its obligations, the break was held not to have been validly exercised where the tenant was in breach of its repairing obligations at the time of service of the notice.

In *Marks and Spencer plc v BNP Paribas Securities Services Trust Co (Jersey) Ltd*[7] the tenant served a break notice in July 2011 which would have the effect of bringing the lease to end in January 2012. The break option was conditional on there being no arrears of rent. In December 2011 the tenant paid the quarter's rent in compliance with its obligations under the lease. Rent was payable in advance so in paying a quarter's rent in December the rent was paid until March 2012. The tenant sought to recover rent for the period following the end of the lease in January. It was unsuccessful. The Supreme Court held that there was no express obligation in the lease requiring the landlord to repay rent for this period to the tenant. The Court was not willing to imply such a term into the lease. The case serves as a cautionary tale for those drafting leases containing break options.[8]

---

1 For calculation of the period of break notices, see para 10.30. For the rule regarding postal notices see para 10.33. For rules regarding the validity of notices in the context of rent reviews, see para 12.43 et seq.

2 2008 SC 252, 2008 GWD 7-135. See also *Batt Cables plc v Spencer Business Parks Ltd* 2010 SLT 860 and *AWD Chase De Vere Wealth Management Ltd v Melville Street Properties Ltd* 2010 SCLR 521, 2009 GWD 38-652, but also *Hexstone Holdings Ltd v AHC Westlink Ltd* [2010] L & TR 22, 32 EG 62.
3 [2010] 1 P&CR 7, [2010] L&TR 7.
4 [2017] CSIH 9; 2017 SC 313.
5 2003 SLT 1420, 2003 GWD 36-1013. See also *RPS RE II A LLP v CBS Outdoor Ltd* [2013] CSOH 7, 2013 GWD 4-121.
6 [2014] CSOH 77, 2014 GWD 14-261.
7 [2015] UKSC 72, [2015] 3 WLR 1843.
8 In 2018 the Scottish Law Commission sought views on whether the Apportionment Act 1870 should be amended to deal with the situation: Scottish Law Commission *Discussion Paper on Apects of the Law of Leases: Termination*, Scot Law Com 165, 2018. No recommendations have yet been made.

Renunciation

10.3   Since the purpose of all contracts, including leases, is to legally bind the parties, neither party to a lease may renounce it unilaterally, unless of course there is some legal ground of termination.

In *Salaried Staff London Loan Co Ltd v Swears and Wells Ltd*,[1] where a tenant repudiated a lease without the landlords' consent, it was held that the landlords were not limited to a claim of damages for the breach of contract; they were entitled to enforce all of the tenants' obligations, including the continued payment of the rent.

However, there is no reason why both parties, if they want, cannot agree to a premature termination. Where there is no express agreement to that effect, renunciation of a lease can be implied from the actings of the parties. However, since renunciation requires mutual consent, it requires actings by *both* parties and cannot be implied from the actings of one party alone.

Renunciation will be implied, for example, if the parties enter a new lease of the property on different terms, or if the tenant purchases the landlord's interest;[2] in the latter case, should the landlord, for any reason, fail to give the tenant a good title, the lease may revive.[3]

In *Kingston Communications plc v Stargas Nominees*[4] it was held that the landlord had not impliedly agreed to a renunciation of the lease merely because it knew that the tenant's receivers had sold the tenant's business to a third party, which was now occupying the leased subjects, and moreover had accepted some rental payments forwarded by the receivers on the new occupant's behalf.

1 1985 SC 189, 1985 SLT 326. The Scottish Law Commission has identified this case as an example of one party to a contract unreasonably proceeding with an unwanted performance. Under its 1999 recommendations for a change in the law, a landlord in this position could not require the tenant to continue paying the rent indefinitely if the property

could easily be re-let, or if it was otherwise unreasonable for the landlord to require the lease to continue. The landlord's right to claim damages would be unaffected (Scottish Law Commission *Report on Remedies for Breach of Contract*, Scot Law Com 174, 1999, paras 2.1 to 2.10). However, in 2018 the Commission did not repeat that recommendation for reform, considering that it is best that the law be developed through judicial activity (Scottish Law Commission, *Report on Review of Contract Law: Formation, Interpretation, Remedies for Breach and Penalty Clauses,* Scot Law Com 252, 2018, para 12.45).

2 *BG Hamilton Ltd v Ready Mixed Concrete (Scotland) Ltd* 1999 SLT 524, particularly at 527 per Lord Hamilton, 1998 GWD 35-1819; see also *Knapdale (Nominees) Ltd v Donald* 2001 SLT 617, 2000 SCLR 1013 and para 2.24.

3 *BG Hamilton Ltd v Ready Mixed Concrete (Scotland) Ltd* 1999 SLT 524, 1998 GWD 35-1819.

4 2005 1 SC 139, 2005 SLT 413.

Irritancy

10.4   Irritancy has been considered fully in Chapter 5.

Rescission

10.5   Either party may rescind a lease contract if the other is guilty of a material breach of contract.[1]

1 See para 4.29 et seq.

Frustration

10.6   *Supervening impossibility* Any contract of a continuing nature may end prematurely if its purpose is frustrated.[1] One of the ways this can happen is by supervening impossibility, ie where the contract becomes impossible to perform because of something that occurs after it has been entered into.

Performance may be rendered impossible by *rei interitus* (total destruction of the contract's subject matter) or by constructive total destruction, ie damage falling short of total destruction, but nevertheless so severe that the subject matter is no longer fit for the purpose of the contract. Provided that the cause of the damage is accidental and not the fault of one of the parties, the effect is to bring future performance of the lease to an end.

Thus a lease may be terminated prior to its expiry date if the leased property is accidentally destroyed or severely damaged (most commonly as a result of fire).[2]

1 Gloag ch 19, esp pp 347–349; Walker paras 31.49–31.57; McBryde ch 21.

2 *Duff v Fleming* (1870) 8 M 769, 7 SLR 480; *Cantors Properties (Scotland) Ltd v Swears & Wells Ltd* 1978 SC 310, 1980 SLT 165, affirming 1977 SLT (Notes) 30.

10.7 *Constructive total destruction* In the case of leased property, it will be rare for the subjects to be completely destroyed, and so the question will invariably arise as to whether the damage is sufficiently severe to amount to frustration. Some useful guidance can be obtained from the judgements in *Duff v Fleming*.[1]

It is a question of degree in each case, but there will be constructive total destruction if the tenant's beneficial use and enjoyment of the property has entirely ceased. This would not be the case, for example, if the tenant had temporarily lost the use of a room, but there *would* be frustration (in the case of a dwellinghouse, for example) if the subjects had been rendered completely uninhabitable.

Destruction of a building will amount to frustration when it is the main subject of let, but not where it is merely an accessory, as in the case of a farmhouse in an agricultural let.

'The true test of the effect of the injury is, whether, without rebuilding, the subject was in any respect fitted for the purpose for which it was let.'[2]

1 (1870) 8 M 769, 7 SLR 480.
2 *Duff v Fleming* (1870) 8 M 769, at 771 per the Lord Justice Clerk.

10.8 *Duff* was distinguished in *Allan v Markland*[1] where the tenant purported to abandon the lease of a shop after it had been damaged by fire. The fire was relatively minor and almost entirely confined to the back shop, the front shop being only slightly affected. It was held that the damage was insufficiently severe to frustrate the lease. It would have been perfectly feasible for the tenant, though subject to considerable inconvenience, to have continued with his business from the front shop for the short time necessary for the landlord to carry out the repairs. In the words of Lord Shand:

'[A] case of destruction is not made out by showing that the premises have been made uncomfortable and, I would add, unsuitable for the purpose of the lease for a short time ... [W]hen such a calamity as a fire, affecting both parties, has accidentally occurred, a tenant may reasonably be called on to submit to considerable inconvenience as the natural and often necessary consequence; and if the injury to the premises be short of destruction, and the damage may be repaired within such a time that the term 'considerable inconvenience' would fairly describe all that the tenant has to undergo, he is not entitled to throw up his lease, but is in my opinion bound to give his landlord an opportunity of having the damage repaired, insisting, as he is no doubt entitled to do, that no time shall be lost in having the premises restored to their former condition.'[2]

However, Lord Shand confirmed the decision in *Duff*, that it was always a matter of degree depending upon the circumstances of the individual case.

The point does not seem to have been raised in *Allan v Markland*, but in such cases of partial destruction, falling short of frustration, the tenant should be entitled to an abatement of rent while the repairs are being carried out. This is because of the encroachment upon the tenant's possession during this period.[3] A provision to this effect would normally be included in the lease.[4]

1 (1882) 10 R 383.
2 *Allan v Markland* (1882) 10 R 383, at 389–90 per Lord Shand.
3 See para 3.45.
4 See para 11.8.

10.9 Frustration can also occur in circumstances where there is no actual physical damage to the property but something else happens that makes it impossible for the lease to continue. In *Mackeson v Boyd*,[1] a 19-year tenancy of a furnished mansion house was interrupted during the Second World War, when the property was requisitioned by the military authorities and the tenant was ejected. The court held that it had become impossible for the tenancy to continue and that the tenant was entitled to abandon the lease.

1 1942 SC 56, 1942 SLT 106; see also *Tay Salmon Fisheries Co Ltd v Speedie* 1929 SC 593, 1929 SLT 484.

10.10 *Supervening illegality* A contract may also be terminated by frustration if performing it becomes illegal because of a subsequent change in the law.

In *Robert Purvis Plant Hire Ltd v Brewster*[1] the tenants alleged that their lease had been frustrated by supervening illegality because the planning authority had issued an enforcement notice preventing their use of the subjects for the purpose of the let. It was held that the illegality was created, not by the enforcement notice, but by the tenants' failure to obtain planning permission for their proposed use. This requirement predated the commencement of the lease and was not a supervening event, with the result that there was no frustration.

1 2009 Hous LR 34, 2009 GWD 12-181.

10.11 *English position* The doctrine of frustration is common to the law of contract in both Scotland and England. In theory, therefore, it should be possible for an English lease to be terminated by frustration; however, the English courts have not applied the doctrine to leases in the way that the Scottish courts have done, and the circumstances where an English lease may be terminated by frustration are rare.[1]

1 *National Carriers Ltd v Panalpina (Northern) Ltd* [1981] AC 675; [1981] 1 All ER 161.

10.12 It is common for commercial leases to contain a provision contracting out of the operation of frustration.[1]

1 See para 11.8.

Tenant's insolvency[1]

10.13 *Bankruptcy* At common law the bankruptcy of the tenant does not automatically bring a lease to an end. Instead the tenancy passes to the tenant's trustee in bankruptcy,[2] who has the option whether or not to adopt the lease. If the lease is adopted, the trustee becomes liable for all future rent and past arrears, which might prove to be a disincentive.[3] Also, it is common to find a provision in leases prohibiting the transmission of a lease to a trustee in bankruptcy, and most leases include bankruptcy as a ground of irritancy.

In practice, therefore, the tenant's bankruptcy may bring the lease to an end. It may, however, continue if the trustee assigns the lease to a new tenant, which may be worthwhile if the unexpired term of the lease is sufficiently long for it to have a capital value. An assignation, of course, would normally require the consent of the landlord, who may prefer to terminate the lease if the property is one that can easily be re-let.[4]

If a trustee chooses not to adopt a lease, and the tenant is no longer in possession, the landlord may claim damages for any loss, though not if the lease has been terminated by irritancy, this being at the landlord's own option.[5]

Certain residential tenancies will not vest automatically in the trustee, but only if the trustee serves a notice to that effect on the tenant. This applies to assured tenancies under the Housing (Scotland) Act 1988, protected tenancies under the Rent (Scotland) Act 1984, Scottish secure tenancies under the Housing (Scotland) Act 2001 and private residential tenancies under the Private Housing (Tenancies)(Scotland) Act 2016.[6] This gives the bankrupt tenant a measure of protection against the loss of his or her home.

1 Rankine p 693 et seq; Paton and Cameron ch 12.
2 Bankruptcy (Scotland) Act 2016 s 78.
3 *Dundas v Morison* (1857) 20D 225.
4 Although if the lease provides that the landlord's consent is not to be unreasonably withheld the landlord may have to consent to the trustee in bankruptcy's proposed assignation: see para 7.8 et seq.

10.14 *Partnerships* If the lease is to a partnership, the bankruptcy of one of the partners will dissolve the partnership, unless the partners have agreed otherwise.[1] If the partnership does end, this may terminate the lease;[2] however, in certain circumstances the former partners may have the right to assign it, failing which they could have a potential liability to the landlord in respect of the lease's unexpired term.[3]

1 Partnership Act 1890 s 33(1).
2 *Inland Revenue Commissioners v Graham's Trustees* 1971 SC(HL) 1, 1971 SLT 46; see also para 9.13 et seq.
3 *Lujo Properties v Green* 1997 SLT 225; see also para 9.14.

10.15 *Liquidation or receivership* If the tenant is a limited company, the lease will automatically come to an end when the company is wound up, as the tenant will then no longer be in existence. However, the lease will probably prohibit the transmission of the tenancy to a liquidator or receiver, and receivership or liquidation, or other insolvency events, are standard grounds of conventional irritancy. The lease will probably, therefore, be terminable by the landlord at an earlier stage. As with bankruptcy (and for similar reasons) the lease may continue if the landlord agrees to an assignation.

10.16 *Dissolution of a company – Crown disclaimer* When a company is struck from the Register of Companies it ceases to exist. Any assets, including an interest as tenant under a lease pass to the Crown.[1] The Crown, via the Queen's and Lord Treasurer's Rembrancer, can disclaim the property.[2] Where that occurs, the property is deemed never to have vested in the Crown[3] and the lease will come to an end.[4] But what happens if the company is restored to the Register of Companies? When it revives what happens to its interest in the lease given the Companies Act provides that on restoration the company is deemed never to have ceased to exist?[5] The Inner House has held that when a company is restored it does not regain its interest in the lease that has been disclaimed by the Crown.[6]

1 Companies Act 2006 s 1012.
2 CA 2006 s 1013.
3 CA 2006 s 1014.
4 CA 2006 s 1020.
5 CA 2006 s 1032.
6 *ELB Securities Ltd v Love* [2015] CSIH 67, 2015 SLT 721. It should be noted that a different view has been taken in England see *Re Fivestar Properties Ltd* [2015] EWHC 2782 (Ch); [2016] 1 WLR 1104.

Death of tenant[1]

10.17   We saw in the last chapter that the death of the tenant does not automatically terminate a lease, but that, instead, it will normally vest in the tenant's executor who may transfer it to a successor. Nevertheless, the lease may come to an end in the following circumstances:

(1)   If it states that it will come to an end on the tenant's death (a so-called 'liferent lease');[2]
(2)   Where the executor terminates the lease because the tenant's interest cannot be disposed of according to law;[3]
(3)   Where it is terminated because the executor has failed to transfer it timeously (normally within one year) to a successor of the tenant;[4] or
(4)   In some cases on the death of a partner, where the lease is to a partnership.[5]

1 See Ch 9.
2 See para 9.11.
3 See para 9.7.
4 See para 9.7.
5 See para 9.13 et seq.

TERMINATION AT ISH: TACIT RELOCATION[1]

Nature of tacit relocation

10.18   Having considered the various ways in which a lease may end prematurely, we must now look at the procedure for bringing it to an end at the contracted termination date (the ish).

Despite the fact that the ish is a mutually agreed term of the contract, a lease does not automatically come to an end at that time. This will only happen if either the landlord or the tenant chooses to end the lease by sending the other a notice to quit. If neither sends such a notice, the law presumes that both want the lease to continue and it is automatically extended for a further period by the principle of *tacit relocation* (silent renewal).

If the original lease duration was less than a year, the extension will be for the same period, eg a six-month lease will be extended for a further six months, a three-month lease for another three months etc. If the original lease duration was a year or more, the period of extension will be one year.

If neither party sends a timeous notice to quit prior to the expiry of the extended period, a further extension of the same length will take place. Furthermore, until such time as either party issues a notice to quit to end the lease at the current termination date, it will continue to be extended indefinitely in the manner just described. Notices to quit are discussed below.[2]

The Scottish Law Commission fairly recently sought views on whether tacit relocation should be dis-applied in relation to commercial leases given its operation does not accord with the expectations of laymen, who expect the lease to end on the date stipulated in the lease without any action having to be taken. No recommendations have yet been made.[3]

1 See Rankine ch 22; Paton and Cameron ch 14; Gordon and Wortley Vol 1, 18.25–18.27. For a thorough modern examination of the law on this subject see Simon Halliday 'Tacit Relocation' 2002 Jur Rev 201; what follows owes much to this article. For the position in relation to agricultural tenancies see para 15.34 et seq.
2 See para 10.29 et seq.
3 Scottish Law Commission's Discussion Paper on Aspects of Leases: Termination (Scot Law Com, 2018, 165), ch 2.

Terms of extension

10.19 With a few exceptions that are noted below, a lease on tacit relocation continues on exactly the same terms and conditions as the original lease contract. The main exception to this rule is the duration: as we saw above, a lease for more than a year will be extended for one year only. Nor will the extended lease incorporate any terms that are inconsistent with a lease from year to year.

In *Commercial Union Assurance Co v Watt & Cumine*,[1] the leases in question contained options to renew on the same terms, but the expiry date passed without the tenant exercising the options, or either party taking steps to terminate the leases. It was held that the leases had continued for a year on tacit relocation, but that the option rights were no longer enforceable.

1 1964 SC 84, 1964 SLT 62; see also *Sea Breeze Properties Ltd v Bio-Medical Systems Ltd* 1998 SLT 319, 1997 GWD 8-341.

10.20 It should be noted that the effect of tacit relocation is to continue or extend the existing lease for a further period.[1] It is therefore not strictly correct (despite the literal meaning of the term) to talk of a lease being renewed by tacit relocation, as this might suggest that a new lease had been created.

1 *Douglas v Cassillis & Culzean Estates* 1944 SC 355, 1945 SLT 258.

Exceptions

10.21 There are certain categories of lease to which it is thought that the principle of tacit relocation may not apply because, for example, their nature indicates that the intention of the parties was to enter a contract for a fixed term, as this would rebut the presumption that the parties have silently agreed to the continuation of the lease:[1]

(1) Seasonal lets of grazing lands, and shooting and fishing leases, which normally only exist during a particular part of the year.[2]

(2) On the same principle, the letting of holiday accommodation, and leases of student residences by educational institutions.

(3) Agricultural leases that are short limited duration, limited duration tenancies or modern limited duration tenancies. These are fixed-term leases, and the common law of tacit relocation is effectively superseded by statutory provisions that spell out the procedures for termination and continuation of such leases.[3] The terms of the Sheriff Courts (Scotland) Act 1907 relating to notices to quit have been specifically disapplied in the case of short limited duration tenancies, limited duration tenancies, modern limited duration tenancies and repairing tenancies.[4]

(4) Certain residential tenancies. In the case of assured, regulated and Scottish secure tenancies, tacit relocation may operate in the normal way until such time as a notice to quit has been sent. After that, the contractual tenancy will convert to a statutory tenancy, and tacit relocation will no longer be necessary.[5] Given their open-ended nature tacit relocation does not apply to private residential tenancies.[6]

(5) Express relocation. There may be an express provision in the lease for the occurrence of periodical renewals after the stated termination date. For example, residential leases often contained a provision that the lease will initially last for one year and thereafter continue on a monthly basis. The continuation of a lease on this basis cannot be considered to be 'tacit' relocation as it is based, not upon an implied presumption, but upon an express term of the lease. A provision of this kind is valid and will be given effect to.[7]

(6) Where tacit relocation has been contracted out of.[8]

1 Simon Halliday 'Tacit Relocation' 2002 Jur Rev 201 at 204–206.
2 See paras 1.16 and 15.14. See also Rankine p 599.
3 Agricultural Holdings (Scotland) Act 2003, ss 4, 8 and 8A–8E. See also para 15.34 et seq. However, this is *not* the case with 1991 Act tenancies – see para 10.23.
4 Sheriff Courts (Scotland) Act 1907 s 37A (inserted by AH(S)A 2003 Sch 1 para 1).
5 See paras 17.69, 17.71 and 18.43. There is some doubt regarding the position of short Scottish secure tenancies – see Simon Halliday 'Tacit Relocation' 2002 Jur Rev 201 at 205–206 and P Robson and S Halliday 'Annotations to the Housing (Scotland) Act 2001, s 36' in *Current Law Statutes*, 2001.
6 See para 17.28.

7 *Cavriani v Robinson* 2002 Hous LR 67. In that case, the monthly continuation was held to be 'tacit relocation'. However, it is submitted that the above interpretation, proposed by Professor Halliday in his article, is the correct one. In either event, the practical result is the same.
8 See para 10.23.

Joint tenants

10.22 If only one of joint tenants gives notice to quit, this will be enough to terminate the lease and prevent it from being continued by tacit relocation.[1] Even although the other joint tenant or tenants may not have wanted the lease to end, the presumption that all of the parties have silently agreed to the lease's continuation will have been rebutted.

It should follow that the same principle would apply where there are common landlords, but not all of them have given notice. There is no direct authority for this, but the weight of academic authority would appear to support this view.[2]

1 *Smith v Grayton Estates Ltd & Anr* 1960 SC 349, 1961 SLT 38.
2 See Paton and Cameron p 226 and Simon Halliday 'Tacit Relocation' 2002 Jur Rev 201 at 213–214. For a contrary opinion see AGM Duncan *Actions of Ejection and Removing* Scot Law Com Research Paper, 1984, para 4.5.

Contracting out

10.23 In theory, as the principle of tacit relocation is based on the implied consent of the parties, it should be possible for the parties expressly to agree something different in the lease contract.

Despite there being some doubt about the matter in various commentaries,[1] there is clear authority that parties can contract out of the operation of tacit relocation. In *MacDougall v Guidi*[2] the lease of a shop contained a provision that the lease 'shall not be capable of renewal or continuation by tacit relocation'. It was held that this provision was effective in terminating the lease at the ish and that the landlord was entitled to remove the tenant, even though less than 40 days' notice had been given.

In the case of 1991 Act agricultural tenancies, contracting out of tacit relocation is expressly forbidden by statute and any lease term purporting to do so will be ineffective.[3] The position is different in the case of short limited duration, limited duration and modern limited duration tenancies, where the statutory provisions relating to termination effectively supersede the common law of tacit relocation.[4]

It would appear that contracting out is possible with other types of lease.[5] The Scottish Law Commission fairly recently sought views on whether the law should be clarified (seemingly by legislation) that parties to commercial leases should have the right to contract out. No recommendations have yet been made.[6]

1 See the discussion in the Scottish Law Commission's *Discussion Paper on Aspects of Leases: Termination* (Scot Law Com, 2018, 165), para 2.13 et seq.
2 1992 SCLR 167.
3 Agricultural Holdings (Scotland) Act 1991 s 3; see also para 15.46.
4 See para 10.21.
5 It has been argued that the position is slightly more complex than this – see Simon Halliday 'Tacit Relocation' 2002 Jur Rev 201, at 206 et seq.
6 Scottish Law Commission's *Discussion Paper on Aspects of Leases: Termination* (Scot Law Com, 2018, 165), ch 2.

Implied exclusion

10.24 Even where it has not been contracted out of (and a timeous notice to quit has not been sent) tacit relocation may be excluded by circumstances that are inconsistent with a continuation of the existing lease by implied consent, eg where a new lease has been agreed by the parties.[1]

However, in the absence of an agreement between the parties, some kind of notice will be required. In *Signet Group plc v C & J Clark Retail Properties Ltd*,[2] where the tenants closed down their business at the premises and removed from them before the date when notice was due, it was held that this unilateral act, which the landlords were not known to be aware of, was not enough to prevent the onset of tacit relocation.

1 Paton and Cameron p 226; *McFarlane v Mitchell* (1900) 2 F 901, (1900) 8 SLT 35.
2 1996 SC 444, 1996 SLT 1325.

Effect of delay

10.25 If the tenant continues to occupy the subjects after expiry of a notice to quit and continues to pay rent which is accepted by the landlord, the effect of the notice will be nullified and tacit relocation will revive. However, mere delay, either by the landlord in enforcing an order for recovery of possession,[1] or by the tenant in vacating the subjects[2] will not be enough for the lease to continue.

If tacit relocation has been contracted out of, or otherwise excluded[3] it cannot revive as it was never a possibility in the first place. However, it

is possible that a new lease may be created informally by the actings of
the parties, though not necessarily on the same terms.[4]

1 *Taylor v Earl of Moray* (1892) 19 R 399.
2 *Tod v Fraser* (1889) 17 R 226.
3 See para 10.21 et seq.
4 Simon Halliday 'Tacit Relocation' 2002 Jur Rev 201, at 209–10. See also para 2.9 et seq.

Notice to quit part of the subjects

10.26   In order to defeat the presumption of tacit relocation, a notice
to quit must be sent in respect of the whole subjects of let and notice to
quit part of the subjects only will not suffice. However, following the
decision in *Regent Quay Development Co Ltd v Tyco Fire & Integrated
Solutions (UK) Ltd*[1] it is likely that a notice to quit that erroneously
omits to mention part of the premises in the notice but otherwise makes
clear that the entire lease is coming to an end would, on the basis of the
reasonable recipient test,[2] be sufficient to bring the lease to an end.

In *Gates v Blair*[3] a dwelling house and shop were let together for a
cumulo rent. It was held that a notice to quit which applied only to the
shop was not sufficient to prevent the operation of tacit relocation in
relation to the whole subjects.

1 [2016] CSIH 73; 2016 GWD 31-555.
2 As to which see *Mannai Investment Co Ltd v Eagle Star Life Assurance Co Ltd*
   [1997] AC 749.
3 1923 SC 430, 1923 SLT 257.

Subtenancies[1]

10.27   In all cases it will be necessary for a notice to quit to be
served on the head tenant in order to prevent tacit relocation of the head
lease. This will also have the effect of preventing tacit relocation of the
sublease, as all rights in it derive from the head lease. If the subtenancy
is unlawful, the landlord can thereafter proceed to evict the subtenant.

However, the situation is more problematic in relation to a lawful
subtenant whose occupation is legitimate. Although the sublease will
have been terminated, and tacit relocation avoided, by the service of a
notice to quit on the head tenant, it has been held that the subtenant will
also require to receive notice in order to be removed.[2]

It has been suggested that this could cause difficulty if the landlord
was unaware of the existence of the subtenancy.[3] However, although at

common law there are many categories of lease where lawful sublets can occur without the landlord's consent, in practice this will normally be forbidden by the alienation clause in the lease and the landlord's consent will be required.[4] The landlord, therefore, is likely to know of the existence of any lawful subtenancies.

The Scottish Law Commission has recommended that a copy of any notice to quit served on the head tenant should be served, either by the landlord or the head tenant, upon any subtenant in possession of the subjects.[5] Until such time as these recommendations have been implemented, it is suggested that it would be good practice for landlords to do this in any case.

1 Rankine pp 599–600, Paton and Cameron p 224, Simon Halliday 'Tacit Relocation' 2002 Jur Rev 201, at 215–216.
2 *Robb v Brearton* (1895) 22 R 885.
3 *Johnson Brothers (Dyers) Ltd v Feggans* (1931) 47 Sh Ct Rep 200 at 202.
4 See paras 7.4 et seq and 11.4.
5 *Report on Recovery of Possession of Heritable Property* Scot Law Com No 118, 1989, para 4.22.

Practical importance of tacit relocation

10.28   We saw above that when a lease continues by tacit relocation, it does so on the same terms and conditions as the original lease. One of these conditions will be the amount of rent payable, and this is why it is so important for landlords or their agents to be aware of the law here.

When a tenant's lease is due to end, the landlord may be happy for it to continue, but may want to increase the rent. This can be done by terminating the existing lease and negotiating a new one at a revised rent. If the landlord fails to send a notice to quit, or sends it late, the tenant will be able to insist that the lease continues for a further year at the old rent, and since this might by now be several years behind the current market rental, the landlord's negligence could result in a substantial loss, particularly at the rent levels charged for commercial properties.

TERMINATION AT ISH: NOTICE TO QUIT

Introduction

10.29   In respect of notices to quit (and the related topic of removings) not only is the common law somewhat unclear, but the effect of statutory intervention (particularly the Sheriff Courts (Scotland) Act 1907) has been to increase the muddle, with the result that the law is both unnecessarily complex and confusing. This has been recognised by the Scottish Law Commission which commissioned research on the matter and followed it with recommendations for simplifying the law.[1] However, no legislation resulted from those recommendations. The issue has again been looked at by the Commission[2] although no recommendations have yet been made. It is hoped that legislative change is implemented following any recommendations that are made on this occasion given the difficulties the current state of the law creates in practice.

1 A G M Duncan Actions of Ejection and Removing Scot Law Com Research Paper 1984; Report on Recovery of Possession of Heritable Property (Scot Law Com No 118, 1989).
2 Scottish Law Commission's Discussion Paper on Aspects of Leases: Termination (Scot Law Com, 2018, 165), chs 3 and 4.

Period of notice

10.30 In the case of 1991 Act agricultural tenancies, the period of notice must be not less than one year and not more than two years prior to the date of expiry.[1] In the case of short limited, limited and modern limited duration tenancies and repairing tenancies, there are special provisions regarding termination that are described elsewhere.[2]

Crofts are also subject to strict statutory control, which restricts the power of landlords to terminate a crofter's lease except in particular circumstances laid down by the legislation.[3] However, a crofter may terminate his or her lease by giving the landlord one year's notice to terminate the tenancy as at any term of Whitsunday or Martinmas.[4]

Where the landlord wishes to use the procedure of summary removing provided by section 34 of the Sheriff Courts (Scotland) Act 1907 Act[5] (ie to be able to eject the tenant without raising an action of removing) and the lease is of land exceeding two acres, is for three years or more and is not subject to the legislation relating to agricultural leases or crofts, the period of notice is not less than one year or more than two years. Where the landlord wishes to use summary removing, the lease is of land exceeding two acres and is for less than three years, the minimum period of notice is six months.[6]

Where the landlord in a lease of land exceeding two acres does not wish to use the summary removing process the period of notice is 40 days. Where the tenant gives notice in respect of a lease of land exceeding two acres the period of notice is 40 days.[7]

For all leases other than those mentioned above 40 days' notice is needed for a lease of more than four months. For all leases of four months or less, the period of notice is one-third of the duration of the let.

In the case of dwelling-houses, these provisions are subject to a statutory minimum of four weeks.[8] This rule will generally be superseded by the statutory provisions for terminating the various forms of residential tenancy.[9]

1 Agricultural Holdings (Scotland) Act 1991 s 21; see also para 15.46.
2 See paras 10.21 and 15.34 et seq.
3 See generally Ch 16.
4 Crofters (Scotland) Act 1993 s 7. For Whitsunday or Martinmas, see para 1.22 et seq.
5 *M7 Real Estate Investments Partners Vi Industrial Propco Ltd v Amazon UK Services Ltd* [2019] CSOH 73, 2019 SLT 1263 made clear that the notice periods set out in s 34 of the 1907 Act only apply where the procedure for removing provided by that section is to be used. The notice periods are not otherwise of general application.
6 Sheriff Courts (Scotland) Act 1907 s 34.
7 *Lormor Ltd v Glasgow City Council* [2014] CSIH 80, 2014 SLT 1055.
8 Rent (Scotland) Act 1984 s 112.
9 The relevant legislation is discsused in Ch 17.

10.31   It is assumed that a lease requiring 40 days' notice will expire either at Whitsunday or Martinmas[1] (now redefined as 28 May and 28 November respectively).[2] However, in cases where the lease provides for a termination date other than one of those terms, it is generally assumed that the period of notice will be calculated in relation to that other date;[3] for example, if a lease requiring 40 days' notice expires on 31 March, 40 days' notice should be given prior to that date.

In calculating the period of notice, both the date of service and the termination date should be excluded – 40 clear days' notice must be given. In a case where 40 days' notice prior to 15 May was required, it was held that the notice had to be served no later than 4 April, and one served on 5 April was insufficient to prevent the lease from being continued by tacit relocation.[4]

Where the lease actually specifies the period of notice, and states that it should be 'not less than' a particular period, the same principle will apply; this rule applies not only to notices to quit but also to other types of notice, eg a break notice.[5]

1 Removal Terms (Scotland) Act 1886 s 4.
2 Term and Quarter Days (Scotland) Act 1990; see also para 1.22 et seq.
3 Rankine p 573; Paton and Cameron p 270.
4 *Signet Group plc v C & J Clark Retail Properties Ltd* 1996 SC 444; 1996 SLT 1325.
5 *Esson Properties Ltd v Dresser UK Ltd* 1997 SC 304;1997 SLT 949.

1886 Act

10.32   Under the Removal Terms (Scotland) Act 1886, where a lease is due to end at Whitsunday or Martinmas and 40 days' notice is required, the notice to quit must be given at least 40 days prior to 15 May or 11 November respectively; however, a tenant who has to be removed, unless the lease expressly stipulates otherwise, need not do so until noon on the 28th day of the month concerned.[1]

Although the 1886 Act, on the face of it, applies only to houses, a house is defined very widely as a 'dwelling-house, shop or other building and their appurtenances', as well as houses let with agricultural land.[2] Commercial and at least some agricultural leases, therefore, would appear to fall within its scope.

The provisions of this Act sit rather uneasily with those of the Term and Quarter Days (Scotland) Act 1990, which has redefined Whitsunday and Martinmas as 28 May and 28 November respectively 'for the purposes of any enactment or rule of law'.[3]

Nevertheless, in cases where the Removal Terms (Scotland) Act 1885 applies, it may still be necessary to serve 40 days' notice prior to 15 May or 11 November; to do otherwise would be to shorten the periods of notice prescribed by the Act. It is unclear if the wording of the Term and Quarter Days (Scotland) Act would warrant such an interpretation.

1 Removal Terms (Scotland) Act 1886 s 4.
2 RT(S)A 1886 s 3.
3 Term and Quarter Days (Scotland) Act 1990 s 1(1) and (2)(a); see also para 1.22 et seq.

Postal notices

10.33 Where it can be proved that a notice has been sent by post, there is a presumption that it has been delivered, which can be rebutted by evidence to the contrary.[1] This applies to all types of notice and not merely to notices to quit.

1 *Chaplin v Caledonian Land Properties Ltd* 1997 SLT 384.

Requirement of writing

10.34 In the case of urban leases[1] there is no requirement at common law for written notice and an oral intimation by either party is thought to be sufficient.[2] Needless to say, this is not advisable. In the case of 1991 Act agricultural tenancies, limited duration tenancies and modern limited duration tenancies, as well as in the case of dwellinghouses, written notice is required by statute.[3]

Finally, ss 34 to 37 of the Sheriff Courts (Scotland) Act 1907 require notices to be in writing, and forms of notice are also prescribed by the

Act. However, there has long been some doubt as to whether these provisions are applicable generally, but the weight of authority strongly favours the interpretation that they only apply where the removing procedures introduced by the 1907 Act are to be used.[4]

1 For the definition of urban leases, see para 1.12.
2 Paton and Cameron pp 272–273; *Craighall Cast-Stone Company Ltd v Wood Brothers* 1931 SC 66, 1931 SLT 67. In *Brucefield Estate Trustees Ltd v Computacentre (UK) Ltd* [2017] SC 38, 2017 Hous LR 66 the tenant argued, unsuccessfully, that the landlord had given notice by their actings when their agent enquired about the covenant strength of the existing subtenant.
3 Agricultural Holdings (Scotland) Act 1991 s 21(3); Agricultural Holdings (Scotland) Act 2003 ss 8 and 8B; Rent (Scotland) Act 1984 s 112.
4 Paton and Cameron p 273; *Craighall Cast-Stone Company Ltd v Wood Brothers* 1931 SC 66, 1931 SLT 67; *MacDougall v Guidi* 1992 SCLR 167; *Lormor Ltd v Glasgow City Council* [2014] CSIH 80, 2014 SLT 1055; *M7 Real Estate Investments Partners Vi Inductrial Propco Ltd v Amazon UK Services Ltd* [2019] CSOH 73, 2019 SLT 1263.

Contracting out

10.35   In the case of agricultural leases that are 1991 Act tenancies, the statutory minimum period of notice of one year cannot be contracted out of and any provision in the lease document for a shorter period will not be effective.[1]

In relation to other types of lease, it should follow that if tacit relocation can be contracted out of, then the lease can substitute a shorter period of notice, or dispense with the requirement for notice altogether.[2] In such a case, however, it will not be possible to use the eviction procedure introduced by the Sheriff Courts (Scotland) Act 1907.[3]

1 Agricultural Holdings (Scotland) Act 1991 s 21; see also para 15.46.
2 See para 10.23
3 *MacDougall v Guidi* 1992 SCLR 167 at 171–172; see also para 10.30.

Practical considerations

10.36   It will be seen that the state of the law in this area is unsatisfactory. The only safe advice to give practitioners is to play it safe at every stage. In particular, the following points should be noted:

(1)   Given recent Inner House authority[1] it is clear that the time limits set out in s 34 of the Sheriff Courts (Scotland) Act 1907 are not of general application and need only be adhered to when the landlord wishes to utilise the removing procedure created by that Act.[2] While the weight of authority is that the 1907 Act is purely procedural and did not alter the substantive law of tacit

relocation it would be prudent for notice to be given in writing (as required under the 1907 Act) and the forms set out in the Act to be used. In addition, in the cases of 1991 Act agricultural tenancies, limited duration tenancies, modern limited duration tenancies and residential tenancies, the respective provisions of s 21 of the Agricultural Holdings (Scotland) Act 1991, ss 8 and 8B of the Agricultural Holdings (Scotland) Act 2003 and s 112 of the Rent (Scotland) Act 1984 should be complied with.[3]

(2)   If the lease is one to which the Removal Terms (Scotland) Act 1886 applies, 40 days' notice should be given prior to 15 May or 11 November. This is against the spirit of the Term and Quarter Days (Scotland) Act 1990, but the relationship of the two Acts to each other does not seem to have been thought through, and the above seems the only safe course. However the 1886 Act only applies in cases where the lease states the ish to be either Whitsunday or Martinmas and requires that 40 days' notice should be given. Such provisions are more likely to appear in commercial than residential leases.

(3)   Any provision in a lease substituting a shorter period for any of the statutory periods of notice may be effective (except in the case of 1991 Act agricultural tenancies). However, if the tenant requires to be evicted, the procedure introduced by the Sheriff Courts (Scotland) Act 1907 cannot be used unless the provisions of that Act regarding notice have been complied with.

1 *Lormor Ltd v Glasgow City Council* [2014] CSOH 80, 2014 SLT 1055.
2 See para 10.30.
3 See para 10.30.

REMOVINGS

10.37   The physical removal of the tenant from the leased subjects is a separate issue from the legal termination of the lease. Where the landlord requires vacant possession, eg because the parties have failed to agree to a renewal, the tenant may nevertheless fail to move out of the subjects, despite the fact that the lease has been legally brought to an end. This may be the case where the lease has been prematurely terminated in one of the ways described above,[1] (an 'extraordinary removing') or where the ish has arrived after due notice to quit has been given (an 'ordinary removing').[2]

In either case the landlord can only evict the tenant by means of a court action. In the case of lets of dwelling-houses, this principle is reinforced by statute.[3] However, the necessity for court action to evict a tenant whose lease has ended is also a common law principle that applies to all leases except where the landlord wishes to use the procedure provided for by s 34 of the Sheriff Courts (Scotland) Act 1907.[4] The tenant's position is in contrast to the position of anyone otherwise occupying property without right or title, who may be removed without a court order.[5]

A landlord who attempts to evict a tenant without a court action may be liable to the tenant in damages.[6] Furthermore, in the case of residential tenancies, the common law has been considerably reinforced by statute: any coercion or harassment of a residential occupier by the landlord, or anyone else, may make the person responsible not only liable in damages, but also subject to criminal proceedings.[7]

1 See para 10.1 et seq.
2 See Paton and Cameron p 245.
3 See Ch 17 in relation to private rented accomodation and para 18.52 et seq for social tenancies. It is possible for the landlord of a Scottish secure tenancy to recover possession of the premises where they have been abandoned (see para 18.77).
4 Rankine p 578, Paton and Cameron p 248. See the discussion of this issue in *Reid v Redfern* [2019] SC (Dum) 34 at paras 45–50. Section 34 of the 1907 Act is discussed at para 10.29 *et seq*.
5 *Ali v Serco Ltd* [2019] CSIH 54, 2019 SLT 1335.
6 Rankine p 592; Paton and Cameron p 249.
7 See para 17.152 et seq.

Violent profits[1]

10.38   At common law, a payment known as violent profits may be due to an owner of heritable property from anyone (not just a former tenant) who occupies the property illegally. Violent profits are a form of penal damages designed to act as a deterrent against illegal occupancy and to compensate the owner for being deprived of the benefits of possession.

They may, therefore, be payable by a tenant who continues to occupy a property after the lease has been legally terminated.[2] However, they may not be payable by a tenant who remains on in the property with the landlord's consent while negotiating a new lease, even if the negotiations fall through, though a sum in lieu of rent may be payable on a different legal basis.[3]

The measure of violent profits derives from very old authority and custom, and varies according to the area concerned. In burghs it is estimated at double the rent. Elsewhere, it is based on the greatest profit that the landlord could have made, either by personally possessing the property or by letting it to others, together with compensation for any damage caused to it by the illegal possessor. If a tenant lodges a defence to an action of removing, the sheriff has discretion to demand caution (security) for violent profits.[4] In an extraordinary removing, such as irritancy, caution for violent profits may be refused on the ground that the tenant cannot be branded as a violent possessor until the irritancy or other termination ground has been proved.[5]

The Scottish Law Commission has recommended that violent profits should be abolished and that a landlord's claim should be based on a common law claim of damages in respect of any loss resulting from the occupant's failure to remove and wrongful retention of possession. It also recommended that the court should still have the discretion to require the defender to find caution for such a claim.[6]

1 Rankine pp 580–586; Paton and Cameron pp 279–283.
2 *Jute Industries Ltd v Wilson & Graham Ltd* 1955 SLT (Sh Ct) 46, (1955) 71 Sh Ct Rep 158.
3 See para 2.62 et seq.
4 Macphail *Sheriff Court Practice* (3rd edn 2006, ed Welsh) para 23.16 and 31.289.
5 *Simpson v Goswami* 1976 SLT (Sh Ct) 94, *Imperial Hotel (Glasgow) Ltd v Brown* 1990 SCLR 86, *Ashford & Thistle Securities LLP v Kerr* 2006 SLT (Sh Ct) 37.
6 *Report on the Recovery of Possession of Heritable Property* Scot Law Com No 118, 1989, paras 10.11 and 10.17.

TENANT'S FIXTURES AND IMPROVEMENTS[1]

10.39 It may be that, during the currency of the lease, the tenant will make some additions to the property which may have the effect of improving the property and increasing its value. This will naturally raise questions about the position regarding such items when the lease comes to an end. Can they be taken away by the tenant, or must they be left on the property? In the latter case, can the tenant claim any compensation from the landlord?

We will see later that the tenant under an agricultural lease may be entitled to compensation for any improvements made to the land.[2] Alternatively, a 1991 Act agricultural tenant may remove fixtures at the end of the lease, after first giving the landlord an opportunity to purchase them.[3]

In a dwellinghouse leased from a social landlord (eg a local authority or housing association), a tenant may be reimbursed at the end of the lease for improvements made with the landlord's consent.[4] In other leases, the position regarding additions by the tenant will often be regulated by the lease document.[5] Here we will consider the position at common law which will apply where the lease is silent on the matter.

1 For a discussion of fixtures see Garrity and Richardson, para 2.5 et seq.
2 See para 15.55 et seq.

3 See para 15.21.
4 See para 19.51 et seq.
5 See para 11.10.

Accession

10.40 If an item added to a property is sufficiently attached to it, eg a building or something attached to a building, it will become part of the property, as a heritable fixture.[1] Since the heritable property that is being leased belongs to the landlord this means that any fixture added to that property will also belong to the landlord, even though the fixture might have been added or paid for by the tenant.[2] However, there are two exceptions to this rule which have long been recognised at common law.

1 See KGC Reid *The Law of Property in Scotland* (1996) para 578 et seq.
2 For the application of this in relation to rent reviews, see paras 12.70 et seq.

Trade fixtures

10.41 Trade fixtures added by the tenant may be removed by the tenant provided they can be removed without any substantial damage to the property. A trade fixture is something that has been attached to the property for the purpose of the tenant's trade or business, eg heavy factory machinery that may be bolted to the floor. In *Syme v Harvey*[1] the tenants of a nursery garden were held entitled, at the end of their lease, to remove greenhouses, forcing pits and hotbed frames added by them for the purpose of their trade.

Although it is normally at the end of a lease that questions relating to trade fixtures arise, the right of the tenant to remove trade fixtures is an incident of the landlord and tenant relationship which can be exercised during the currency of the lease also.[2]

1 (1861) 24 D 202.
2 *David Boswell Ltd v William Cook Engineering Ltd* 1989 SLT (Sh Ct) 61 (sub nom *Lloyds Bowmaker Ltd v William Cook Engineering (Evanton) Ltd* 1988 SCLR 676).

Ornamental fixtures

10.42 A similar rule applies to ornamental fixtures, which are things that have been attached for the better enjoyment of the articles themselves, rather than with the purpose of improving the property. In the English case of *Spyer v Phillipson*,[1] the tenant of a flat installed valuable antique panelling, ornamental chimney pieces and 'period' fireplaces, the last two requiring a small amount of structural alteration. After the tenant's death, his executor was held entitled to remove the additions: they had been installed, not in order to benefit the property, but for the enjoyment of the articles themselves. The executor could remove the items notwithstanding the fact that their removal would cause some damage to the property.

1 [1931] 2 Ch 183; [1930] All ER 457, CA.

PART 3
COMMERCIAL LEASES

Chapter 11

Commercial lease terms

INTRODUCTION: COMMERCIAL LEASES IN GENERAL

11.1   As we have already noted,[1] commercial leases are leases of
shops, offices, factories and other business premises. We also saw that,
at common law, the minimum requirements for any lease are a landlord,
a tenant, subjects of let, a rent and a duration.[2] However, the sort of lease
normally encountered nowadays usually goes far beyond these basics,
and this is particularly true of the modern commercial lease, which can
be a very lengthy, complex and forbidding document. The purpose of
this book is to give a general account of the law of leases, and so it is
outwith our scope to provide styles of documents,[3] or to give detailed
advice on all of the many practical considerations practitioners involved
in the drafting or revisal of such documents need to keep in mind.[4]

1 See Chapter 1.
2 See para 2.22 et seq.
3 For commercial lease styles, see *Greens Practice Styles: Commercial Leases* (2011);
   and the Property Standardisation Group's style lease documents, available at www.
   psglegal.co.uk/leases.php.
4 Such specialist advice can be found in Ross & McKichan *Drafting and Negotiating
   Commercial Leases in Scotland*, David Cockburn and Robin Mitchell *Commercial
   Leases* and Kenneth S Gerber *Commercial Leases in Scotland: A Practitioner's Guide*.

11.2   However, so much of the common law of landlord and tenant
is normally contracted out of in commercial leases that to look at the
law in isolation would give a misleading impression of what actually
happens in practice. The purpose of the present chapter, therefore, is
to draw attention to some of the more important provisions that are
commonly found in commercial leases, although many of these clauses
can be found in other types of lease as well.

It should also be kept in mind that, for many decades now, Scottish
commercial lease practice, and commercial lease styles, have been
heavily influenced by English lease practice. However, the underlying
common law of and statute pertaining to the two countries, particularly
in this area, remains quite distinct. This difference can lay a number
of traps for the unwary practitioner, who should therefore regard this
pervasive English influence with some degree of caution.[1]

This account is not intended to be comprehensive but may enable the reader to establish some basic landmarks in a complex modern commercial lease. Provisions relating to rent reviews and service charges are considered sufficiently important for each to need a chapter on its own; the subject of rent reviews in particular has accumulated a huge body of case law, much of it highly complex, and has therefore been considered in some depth in the next chapter.

Some other common clauses are discussed more briefly below, with the important topic of repairs and improvements being given its own separate section at the end.

1 See, for example, the position regarding frustration of leases (see para 10.11), or the English Landlord and Tenant Act 1954, which has no equivalent in Scotland.

STANDARD LEASE TERMS

Duration

11.3   The typical duration of commercial leases has tended to vary over the years as a result of market demands. For many years, the standard institutional lease, ie a lease granted for the purpose of property investment by a financial institution such as a bank, insurance company or pension fund was 25 years. This was designed to give landlords an assured return on their investment over a substantial period of time. Trends have changed significantly in the last decade. For instance, in the first half of 2019 the average length of new leases entered into across the UK was 6.3 years.[1] The reasons for this and some of the implications are discussed in the next chapter in the context of rent reviews.[2]

1 MSCI and BNP Paribas, *UK Lease Events Review 2019*, available to download at:www. realestate.bnpparibas.co.uk/2019/nov/2019-uk-lease-events-review-what-are-latest-trends.
2 See para 12.2.

Alienation

11.4   The alienation clause will almost invariably include the standard provision prohibiting the tenant from assigning or subletting the lease without the landlord's consent.[1] These provisions are important since they enable the landlord to retain control over the choice of tenant who occupies the property. As we saw above, the omission of this clause would allow the tenant of a commercial lease to assign or sublet without the landlord's consent, that being the position at common law.[2]

A tenant would normally want the clause modified by the addition of a qualification that the landlord's consent 'will not be unreasonably withheld or delayed'. The implications of this have already been considered.[3]

1 See para 7.4 et seq.
2 See para 7.18 et seq, particularly para 7.21.
3 See para 7.8 et seq.

Payment of rent

11.5   The dates when the rent is payable will depend upon what is stated in the lease. The most common provision in commercial leases is for it to be paid quarterly in advance at the four Scottish quarter days, ie Candlemas (28 February), Whitsunday (28 May), Lammas (28 August) and Martinmas (28 November).[1]

There will usually also be a provision for interest to be paid to the landlord in the event of late payment of rent or of any other sum of money due under the lease. Since this provision could be invoked at any time over the period of the lease, during which time interest rates will fluctuate, it is normal not to state a specific rate in the lease, but to provide a formula related to a current bank rate. The landlord should be careful not to state a rate that is too high, otherwise a court might find it to be a penalty, ie an attempt to punish the tenant rather than a sum representing the landlord's legitimate interest in the rent (or other sum due) being paid on time; if this happened, the clause would be unenforceable.[2]

1 See para 1.22 et seq.
2 See para 4.38.

Use of premises

11.6   The clause dealing with the use of the premises is generally referred to as the 'use clause' or 'user clause'. It reinforces the common law provision that the tenant may only use the property for the purpose for which it was let, not only by stating the general category of the subjects, eg shop, office, factory or dwellinghouse, but also, in the case of commercial leases, laying down the type of business that has to be carried on. The latter is particularly important in shop leases, where the landlord may want to control the trade mix and ensure that there are not too many shops of the same type in one area; it may also be possible to charge a shop tenant a higher rent, if the tenant can be assured of a monopoly or partial monopoly in the locality.

However, as we will see in Chapter 12, keeping this degree of control, while it may be advantageous in terms of estate management, could rebound upon the landlord financially, by limiting the amount of rent that can be charged at rent review.[1] It is therefore not in the landlord's interest to tie the tenant down too tightly to a particular use of the premises.

One possibility is to allow a qualification that the landlord's consent to a change of use 'will not be unreasonably withheld'. In leases of properties other than shops, eg offices or factories, it may be worth considering whether it is necessary to limit the tenant to a specific type of business at all, as the considerations of trade mix that apply with retail premises are less relevant with other types of property. Another solution is to limit the tenant to a use within a particular class of the Town and Country Planning (Use Classes) (Scotland) Order 1997.[2] This could have the effect of limiting a property to a general category of use, without specifically stating a particular kind of business; on the other hand, it could create practical problems if the order is later amended or replaced during the currency of the lease.[3]

It is common in use clauses for there also to be a prohibition against any uses of the property that would cause a nuisance to neighbouring tenants or otherwise affect the amenity of the area.

1 See para 12.91 et seq.
2 SI 1997/3061.
3 See *Brewers' Company v Viewplan plc* [1989] 45 EG 153, [1989] EGCS 78.

Insurance

11.7   The most common type of commercial lease today is the tenant's full repairing and insuring lease (the FRI lease), in which the tenant is made entirely responsible for all repairs and for payment of the insurance premiums. The landlord, however, will normally be the one to effect the insurance in the first instance. If the lease subjects are part of a shopping centre, office block or industrial estate the landlord may recover the cost of the premiums from the tenant by way of the service charge.[1]

1 See ch 13. See also *Barras v Hamilton* 1994 SC 544, 1994 SLT 949.

11.8   *Frustration* It is common in insurance clauses for the landlord to contract out of the common law doctrine of *rei interitus*. We saw in Chapter 10 that a lease may be terminated prematurely by supervening impossibility if the premises are totally or almost totally destroyed by fire or otherwise.[1] In order to ensure that a tenant is held for the full term of the lease (and that the landlord's investment will be maximised), the lease is likely to provide that, in the event of such damage or destruction, it will not end but will carry on in full force and effect. The tenant, however, would normally be given the right to an abatement of rent for the period during which the property was being rebuilt and a right to terminate the lease should it not be rebuilt within a specified period of time.

1 See para 10.6 et seq.

11.9   *Extent of cover*   Unless the insurance policy specifically provides otherwise, the insurance cover will not provide indemnity for any more than the actual loss suffered, even if the insured amount is greater.[1] This would normally be the market value of the property but, exceptionally, may be the reinstatement cost if the property is one for which there is no market.[2] A tenant whose obligation is merely to maintain the property, and not to replace it in the event of accidental destruction or damage, has no insurable interest to recover its value, merely as a result of having paid the premiums.[3]

1 *Castellain v Preston* (1883) 11 QBD 380; *Leppard v Excess Insurance* [1979] 1 WLR 512, [1979] 2 All ER 668.
2 *Carrick Furniture House Ltd v General Accident Fire and Life Insurance Corporation Ltd* 1977 SC 308, 1978 SLT 65.
3 *Fehilly v General Accident Fire and Life Assurance Corpn Ltd* 1982 SC 163, 1983 SLT 141.

Alterations and additions

11.10   We have already seen that, at common law, a tenant is prohibited from making major alterations to the property and may be required to reinstate it.[1] We have also noted that any additions made by the tenant to the leased property may be heritable fixtures and become the property of the landlord, subject to the tenant's right to remove trade or ornamental fixtures.[2] However, these common law provisions will normally be regulated, and possibly reinforced, by the lease terms.

It is normal for leases to provide that the tenant may not make any alterations or additions to the premises without the landlord's consent. Also, where alterations have been made, with or without consent, the landlord will hold the tenant bound, if so required, to remove any alterations or additions at the end of the lease.

The landlord in this situation is not trying to prevent the tenant from making alterations, but trying only to keep control of the situation. It is important to ensure that any alterations are of a sufficiently high standard and are not damaging the property in any way. Also, the landlord will not want the property changed too much to suit the tenant's specialist business, as this might reduce its market value in the event of a relet to another tenant.

If any additions by the tenant have the effect of substantially adding to the value of the property, there is a danger that the tenant could end up paying for these improvements a second time if their value is reflected in the new rent payable after a review. We will see later that rent review clauses normally allow for this by providing that the value of tenant's improvements should be disregarded when the reviewed rent is fixed.[3]

1 See para 3.4.
2 See para 10.41 et seq.
3 See para 12.70 et seq.

Irritancy

11.11 An irritancy clause is a standard provision that allows the landlord to terminate the lease if any one of a number of specified breaches by the tenant should occur. This controversial subject has already been fully dealt with in Chapter 5. Despite the modification in the law by legislation, a wise tenant will not accept an irritancy clause in unqualified form, but will want to reserve the right, within a reasonable period, to remedy any breach that might give rise to irritancy.

REPAIR AND MAINTENANCE

General

11.12 We saw in Chapter 3 that, at common law, the landlord is obliged to keep the property in a tenantable or habitable condition.[1] We also noted earlier that the most common type of commercial lease today is the tenant's full repairing and insuring lease (the FRI lease), in which the tenant is made entirely responsible for all repairs and for payment of the insurance premiums.[2]

In such leases, therefore, it is necessary to contract out of the landlord's common law obligation by specifically making the tenant responsible for all repairs.[3] In order best to ensure that the value of the property is maintained, the landlord will usually also reserve the right, in the event of the tenant failing in these maintenance obligations, to carry out any necessary repairs and to charge them to the tenant. These will normally be set out in a Schedule of Dilapidations served upon the tenant,[4] particularly towards the end of the lease, when the landlord has to prepare the property for reletting to a new tenant. The landlord will probably also reserve a right of access to the property to inspect its condition.

In lease subjects where there is multiple occupancy, eg office blocks or shopping centres, the landlord will normally be the one to undertake any repairs and maintenance to parts of the building that are not let to tenants and will recoup a proportion of the cost from each tenant by way of a service charge.[5]

It is also common for a landlord to contract out of the common law obligation to provide subjects that are reasonably fit for the purpose of the let.[6] This is done by inserting a clause that the tenant accepts the property as being in good condition and repair and fit for the purpose of the let.

The combined effect of these standard provisions goes to the heart of the concept of the FRI lease. The investment landlord wants a 'clear lease', ie one where the return on the investment is maximised by passing as many overheads as possible on to the tenant. This is fine for the landlord, but we must also look at things from the tenant's point of view, and it is clear that an overenthusiastic application of this principle may not only involve the latter in additional expense, but also put the tenant in some danger.

1 See para 3.40 et seq.
2 See para 11.7.
3 Regarding the standard of clarity required to properly exclude the landlord's obligation, see *Mars Pension Trustees Ltd v County Properties and Developments Ltd* 1999 SC 267, 2000 SLT 581. See also para 3.51 et seq.
4 See para 11.23.
5 See Ch 13.
6 See para 3.26 et seq.

Inherent (latent) defects[1]

11.13 The most obvious manifestation of the above is seen in the vexed question of inherent (or latent) defects. The meaning of the term 'inherent defect' will depend upon how it is defined in the lease in question. However, it usually arises either in construction of the property, or when significant works are carried out to the property and there is some fault of construction or design that was not apparent at the beginning of the lease. At a future date the defect may emerge, requiring expensive repair work, or even substantial rebuilding. It seems unfair that this should be the responsibility of the tenant. The question arising here is: do the normal terms of an FRI lease make it so?

In England it has been held that a fairly standard tenant's repairing obligation made the tenant responsible for the rectification of inherent defects, provided that it fell short of having to reconstruct substantially the whole of the premises.[2]

It is doubtful whether a simple repairing obligation could have that effect in Scotland,[3] unless it also completely contracted out of the landlord's common law obligations, not only of continuing maintenance, but also the initial obligation to provide tenantable or habitable subjects at entry. Also, in extreme cases, the defect may cause sufficient damage to amount to frustration by constructive total destruction, thus relieving the tenant of responsibility. However, as we have already seen, these common law provisions can be, and often are, contracted out of in commercial leases. The difference between the two countries boils down in practice to one of lease wording: provided that the lease provisions are sufficiently comprehensive in their scope, a Scottish tenant may also be made liable for damage caused by inherent defects.[4]

It is therefore in the tenant's interest to insist that the repairing obligation be modified to free the tenant of such responsibility. A landlord will be inclined to resist this, of course, and the outcome will depend on the respective negotiating strengths of the parties, depending upon the state of the market at the time the lease is entered into.

It should be pointed out, however, that the landlord has other directions in which to look for reimbursement. It may be possible to insure against the defects, or the landlord may have a claim against the contractor responsible, provided that the latter's errors have not been sufficiently prevalent to induce bankruptcy.[5]

1 For a discussion of the common law relating to inherent (also known as latent) defects see para 3.36 et seq.
2 *Ravenseft Properties Ltd v Davstone (Holdings) Ltd* [1980] QB 12, [1979] 1 All ER 929.
3 See para 11.15.
4 *Thorn EMI Ltd v Taylor Woodrow Industrial Estates Ltd* (1982) Court of Session (Outer House), 29 October (unreported).
5 For further discussion of the subject of inherent defects (as well as repairing obligations generally) see Garrity and Richardson, *Dilapidations and Service Charge* ch 4; Ross & McKichan *Drafting and Negotiating Commercial Leases in Scotland* ch 8; David Cockburn and Robin Mitchell *Commercial Leases* ch 5 and Kenneth S Gerber *Commercial Leases in Scotland: A Practitioner's Guide*, ch 13.

Extraordinary repairs

11.14   Allied to this is the question of whether it is fair to make the tenant liable for extraordinary as well as ordinary repairs.[1] It would appear to be possible for the lease terms to impose a liability for extraordinary repairs, though such an imposition will have to be clearly stated.[2]

In *House of Fraser plc v Prudential Assurance Co Ltd*[3] it was held that the lease wording was sufficiently comprehensive to make the tenants liable for the cost of such a repair, in that case to a defective retaining wall. (It was also alleged by the tenants, to no avail, that the defect in the retaining wall was an inherent one.) However, it was pointed out in that case that there was no magic formula for distinguishing between ordinary and extraordinary repairs, and that the no man's land between them could be very broad:

> '[T]he common law ... does not give any very precise method of distinguishing between ordinary and extraordinary repairs ...No clear, universally applicable principle or talisman for distinguishing between the two emerges.'[4]

1 See *Lord Advocate v Shipbreaking Industries Ltd (No 2)* 1993 SLT 995.
2 For authority on this and discussion of the distinction between ordinary and extraordinary repairs, see *Napier v Ferrier* (1847) 9D 1354; *Turner's Trustees v Steel* (1900) 2 F 363, *sub nom Steel v Findlay and Others* (1900) 7 SLT 301; *Sharp v Thomson* 1930 SC 1092, 1930 SLT 785; *McCall's Entertainments (Ayr) Ltd v South Ayrshire Council (No 2)* 1998 SLT 1421; and Garrity and Richardson, *Dilapidations and Service Charge* para 3.4.
3 1994 SLT 416.
4 *House of Fraser plc v Prudential Assurance Co Ltd* 1994 SLT 416 at 419–420 per Lord McCluskey.

11.15   However, in *Co-operative Insurance Society Ltd v Fife Council*[1] Lord Glennie undertook an extremely thorough review of the leading case law on this distinction, from early in the 19th century onwards, from which he concluded that there were three main considerations that should normally be taken into account in order to distinguish between ordinary and extraordinary repairs:

(1)   the origin of the damage, eg whether or not it was caused by a fortuitous event, unanticipated and outwith the control of either party;
(2)   the extent or seriousness of the damage and the likely cost of repairs; and (allied to this)
(3)   the nature of the damage and whether it would require total reconstruction or something short of that.[2]

On this basis, it was held that the obligation upon the tenant in the instant case to keep the subjects 'in good and substantial repair and maintained, renewed and cleansed in every respect' did not have the effect, merely by the use of the word 'renewed', of making the tenant liable for extraordinary repairs.

In many commercial leases a tenant will be under an obligation to repair and renew the lease subjects irrespective of their age or state of dilapidation, or the cause or extent of the damage or destruction, whether by a defect latent, inherent or patent. Such clauses seek to ensure that the tenant is liable for extraordinary as well as ordinary repairs.

1 [2011] CSOH 76, 2011 GWD 19-458.
2 *Co-operative Insurance Society Ltd v Fife Council* [2011] CSOH 76 at para 19 per Lord Glennie.

The standard of repair

11.16   A tenant under a commercial lease will often accept the lease premises as being in good and tenantable condition and suitable for the purpose let, oblige itself to keep the premises in that condition and return them to the landlord in that condition at the end of the lease. This obligation is an important one for the landlord's investment, ensuring that the condition of the premises do not deteriorate during the life of the lease.[1]

Where the premises are not in good condition at lease commencement a tenant will want to reflect that to ensure that it is not obliged to improve the subjects, but rather to return them to the landlord in the same condition as they are at the beginning of the lease. In such a case the lease should refer to a schedule of condition agreed between the parties, drawn up at the beginning of the lease setting out its present condition, though the absence of such a schedule will not be fatal if there is otherwise sufficient evidence of the building's initial condition.[2]

1 See paras 11.17–11.21 and 11.23. For a detailed discussion of what such a repairing obligation entails see Garrity and Richardson, *Dilapidations and Service Charge* ch 4.
2 *McCall's Entertainments (Ayr) Ltd v South Ayrshire Council (No 2)* 1998 SLT 1421.

The passage of time

11.17   Even in cases where a building was new when a lease was granted, it is obvious that it will no longer be so at the end (for example) of a 25-year term (which was the traditional length of investment leases by financial institutions)[1] and, of course, some leases may be even longer than that. While keeping in mind that the full extent of the tenant's obligation will always depend upon the particular terms of the lease in question, it can be stated that a standard repairing obligation will not normally require the tenant to reverse the ageing process so as to provide a building that is as good as new:

'Time must be taken into account; an old article is not to be made new; but so far as repair can make good, or protect against the ravages of time and the elements, it must be undertaken.'[2]

1 In more recent years it has become common to have much shorter commercial leases (see paras 11.3 and 12.2) but, needless to say, many longer leases are likely to be around for some time.

2 *Anstruther-Gough-Calthorpe v McOscar* [1924] KB 716, per Atkin J at 734.

11.18 It was held in *West Castle Properties Ltd v The Scottish Ministers*[1] that an obligation to maintain the property 'in good and tenantable condition and repair' does not require the tenants to reverse the natural ageing process. They were not required to keep the premises in as new a condition as they had been at the commencement of the lease, but in fulfilling their obligations were entitled to take account of the increasing age of the building.

1 2004 SCLR 899, 2004 GWD 20-444; see also *Proudfoot v Hart* [1890] 25 QBD 42 and *Anstruther-Gough-Calthorpe v McOscar* [1924] KB 716.

11.19 *Westbury Estates v Royal Bank* In *Westbury Estates Ltd v The Royal Bank of Scotland PLC*[1] a 25-year lease of office property contained a comprehensive repairing provision, including an obligation to maintain the property in good and substantial repair and condition, which 'was designed to cover what the older Scottish cases would have treated as extraordinary repairs'.[2] The landlord sought to make the tenant liable at the end of the lease for the replacement of certain electrical and mechanical items, including the lifts, the fire alarm, the electrical wiring, the boiler and the convector heaters. Although these items were in working order, the landlord maintained that they had reached the end of their economic life and would not be acceptable to an incoming tenant.

Lord Reed held that the lease, like any other contract, ought to be interpreted by reference to the circumstances when it was entered, ie in 1979, not 25 years later. This could not include the guidelines laid down by the Chartered Institute of Building Service Engineers (CIBSE), which were not in existence when the lease began. The requirements of a hypothetical new tenant might be relevant, but were concerned:

'not with what a tenant would expect or accept (something which might depend on market conditions, rent and the other terms of the lease), but with what would make the premises reasonably fit for occupation. Even if it were proved, for example, that commercial landlords would normally replace a boiler which was 15 years old (and that incoming tenants would normally expect such a boiler to have been replaced), that would not entail that subjects with a 15-year old boiler, which remained in perfect working order and continued to perform satisfactorily, were not in "good and substantial repair and condition".'[3]

1 2006 SLT 1144, [2006] CSOH 177.
2 *Westbury Estates Ltd v The Royal Bank of Scotland plc* 2006 SLT 1144 at 1146 per Lord Reed.
3 *Westbury Estates Ltd v The Royal Bank of Scotland plc* 2006 SLT 1144 at 1151 per Lord Reed.

11.20   In *Co-operative Insurance Society Ltd v Fife Council*,[1] Lord Glennie, in the course of his review of the case law on extraordinary repairs, suggested that the decisions in *West Castle Properties* and *Westbury Estates* had extended the debate beyond the common law distinction between ordinary and extraordinary repairs. Even when the tenant's obligations go beyond the scope of ordinary repairs, so as to include extraordinary repairs, there might nevertheless be limits on that obligation to renew.[2]

1 [2011] CSOH 76, 2011 GWD 19-458.
2 *Co-operative Insurance Society Ltd v Fife Council*, [2011] CSOH 76, 2011 GWD 19-458 at para 24.

Landlord's satisfaction

11.21   If a lease provides that repairs will be carried out 'to the satisfaction of the landlord' the landlord must be reasonable in deciding what standard of repair will meet this criterion.[1]

1 *Taylor Woodrow Property Co v Strathclyde Regional Council* 1996 GWD 7-397; *Lowe v Quayle Munro Ltd* 1997 SC 346, 1997 SLT 1168.

Landlord's repairing obligations

11.22   These are not common in commercial leases, though more so in other types of lease.[1] We saw earlier that at common law the landlord had an initial obligation to provide tenantable or habitable subjects, but that thereafter the continuing obligation to carry out repairs is not a warranty, ie the obligation does not arise until the defect has been drawn to the landlord's attention.[2] However, where there is an obligation to maintain a part of the subjects that is within the landlord's control, eg the exterior of a building, no notice is required for the obligation to arise.[3]

1 For example, in residential leases – see Ch 19.
2 See para 3.41 et seq.
3 *Taylor Woodrow Property Co v Strathclyde Regional Council* 1996 GWD 7-397.

Dilapidations[1]

11.23 This term refers to the process whereby necessary repairs are identified in order to establish the work required to fulfil the repairing obligation under a lease. In the case of commercial leases, of course, this obligation will generally be the tenant's, as the lease will be on FRI terms.

The landlord will normally notify the tenant of required repairs by serving a Schedule of Dilapidations. This may be done either during the currency of the lease, in order to establish what needs to be done to fulfil the tenant's continuing obligation,[2] or at the end of the lease, so as to determine the work required to restore the property to the condition required by the lease. As noted above, the lease will normally allow the landlord to carry out the repairs and charge the tenant with their cost.[3] At the end of the lease the tenant may agree to pay the landlord the cost of dilapidations rather than be the one to carry out the repairs. It may be that the lease contains a provision entitling the landlord to demand from the tenant a sum of money in lieu of requiring the tenant to bring the premises into the condition required by the lease.[4]

In the event of the tenant failing to carry out required repairs the landlord would have recourse to the appropriate legal remedy, eg an action of damages or an action for payment.[5]

The subject of dilapidations is an important one in commercial lease practice, on which detailed practical advice can be obtained from the texts referred to above.[6] These were all written by practitioners, who were able to draw upon their experience in commercial lease practice. The underlying law, which is the primary concern of this book, can be found in other chapters.[7]

1 See Garrity and Richardson *Dilapidations and Service Charge* chs 4 and 5 , David Cockburn and Robin Mitchell *Commercial Leases*, 5.21–5.26, and Kenneth S Gerber *Commercial Leases in Scotland: A Practitioner's Guide* ch 14.
2 It has been held that a notice is not required to trigger the tenant's obligation to keep the premises in repair during the term of the lease: *L Batley Pet Products Ltd v North Lanarkshire Council* [2014] UKSC 21, [2014] 3 All ER 64; *PDPF GP Ltd v Santander Ltd* [2015] CSOH 40, 2015 Hous LR 45.
3 See para 11.12.
4 See para 4.28.
5 For landlord's remedies generally see Chs 4–6.
6 See footnote 1.
7 See, in particular, Ch 3, from para 3.26 onwards.

Chapter 12

Rent reviews

GENERAL[1]

Historical background

12.1   The subject of rent reviews is undoubtedly one of the most complex and important areas of modern lease law. In relation to commercial leases, where the rent levels can be extremely high, the amount of money at stake in a dispute may be considerable.

Since the Second World War, financial institutions, such as banks, insurance companies and pension funds, have widely invested in commercial property. At the same time, there has been an increasing trend for companies and firms to rent the property they occupy rather than tie up their capital by buying it. And because the years since 1945 have also seen many periods of high inflation, particularly in the 1970s, it has become normal for rents to be periodically reviewed to keep up with rising rental values. Many leases of 25 years' duration make provision for rent review every five years.

For several decades there was a deluge of rent review case law, though there have been far fewer new cases in more recent years. Undoubtedly one of the reasons for this trend is the current demand for much shorter leases, which will avoid the need for a rent review clause in many cases. However, one also hopes that the drafters of leases have learned from the many hard lessons taught by the rent review case law, so as to avoid the many traps and pitfalls that lie in wait in this area.

Most of the case law is English, but the main topics have also come before the Scottish courts. As a result, we can be fairly confident that rent review law in the two countries is substantially the same, though there are certain important differences that we will note later.

1 For further consideration of rent reviews from the Scottish viewpoint, see Ross and McKichan *Drafting and Negotiating Commercial Leases in Scotland* ch 6; David W Cockburn and Robin Mitchell *Commercial Leases* ch 8; and Kenneth S Gerber *Commercial Leases in Scotland: A Practitioner's Guide* chs 10 and 11.

Length of commercial leases

12.2   If we have a lease of comparatively short duration (say five years), reviewing the rent is typically not a problem. There is unlikely to be provision for rent review in the lease. As we have already seen, the landlord will simply serve a notice to quit prior to the end of the term, preventing the onset of tacit relocation and allowing the tenant to be removed if necessary.[1] The landlord may then invite the tenant to stay on, under a new lease at a new rent. As long as the notice to quit is sent in time, the matter is comparatively simple.

However, both landlords and tenants may want leases of a longer duration. A financial institution will want its rental yield to be secure and not subject to periodic uncertainty by the need to find a new tenant: the onus will be upon a tenant who wants out of the lease to find someone to assign to. Tenants, on the other hand, may want the legal right to stay on in the premises for a reasonably extended period. This is particularly true in Scotland, where there is no equivalent of the (English) Landlord and Tenant Act 1954, allowing tenants of business premises to apply for a renewal of their lease when it is due to end.[2]

The demand for longer leases is of course subject to market conditions, and in recent years there has been a widespread movement towards shorter leases. This has mainly been tenant-driven, as the property recession in the late 1980s put tenants in a stronger negotiating position and in less need of security of tenure in a market where properties were more readily available. As a result, the length of the standard institutional lease, once apparently fixed at 25 years, has now fallen dramatically. In 2000 it was estimated that commercial lease lengths had reduced to 15–20 years,[3] but as at 2019, the average length for new commercial leases entered into in the UK was 6.3 years.[4]

1   See generally Ch 10, from para 10.18 et seq.
2   There is a very limited right available under the Tenancy of Shops (Scotland) Act 1949, discussed in Chapter 14.
3   See Stewart Brymer 'Length of Leases' 44 Prop LB, March 2000.
4   MSCI and BNP Paribas, *UK Lease Events Review 2019*, available to download at www. realestate.bnpparibas.co.uk/2019/nov/2019-uk-lease-events-review-what-are-latest-trends.

Need for a review clause

12.3   Nevertheless, reviews will still be required for many leases. And, of course, many leases from the days of longer lease terms are still extant. Also, the situation is quite different in the case of ground leases,[1] where a tenant who has built or paid for the buildings will naturally want a lengthy period of tenure, over the course of which the landlord will want to review the ground rent from time to time. Not only is there likely to be a continuing demand for new ground leases, but there is also a substantial backlog of older leases, the earliest of them containing rent review clauses drafted before the many hard lessons taught by the case law had been learned.

In short, the complex law explored in this chapter is likely to remain pertinent for some time yet.

A rent review clause becomes necessary when each party wants a binding contract over a lengthy period. The landlord will not agree to this unless there is some mechanism for changing one of the main contractual terms, ie the level of rent, at more frequent intervals.

1 See para 1.18.

Drafting problems

12.4   This may seem straightforward enough, but if we gain nothing else from the rent review case law, we will learn the folly of such a naïve outlook, as we see past clauses, again and again, being minutely scrutinised by the courts and found wanting; as drafting pitfalls, which the most able lawyer could have been forgiven for overlooking, have proved fatally expensive for either landlord or tenant. Knowledge of the law in this area is therefore essential for the lawyer who wants to avoid such mistakes in future leases.

Problems of generalisation

12.5   A major difficulty with rent review case law is that the issues are normally matters of construction, ie interpreting the wording of a particular lease. And although similar provisions appear in different leases, there can be an infinite number of variations in the wording of individual documents. The result is that any attempt to build a structure of principle from the case law is liable to rest on a foundation of shifting sands. The nature of the problem has been recognised by the courts, notably by the English Court of Appeal in 1992:

> 'However, if I may say so, to try to apply one authority given in relation to a different rent review clause in different circumstances to another situation is always a dangerous course to adopt, and in the normal event it is more appropriate for issues of this sort to be determined by looking at the facts of the particular case and applying those facts to the particular rent review clause which is under consideration.'[1]

1 *Patel v Earlspring Properties* [1991] 46 EG 153 at 154 per Woolf LJ.

12.6   Judge Colyer (in considering the validity of a rent review notice) later elaborated upon this theme:

> 'The task of the court is to construe a document – that is the lease – and then, in the light of that decision on the construction of the document, to conclude whether in the facts of a particular case the communication made by that particular tenant does or does not satisfy the requirements of the instrument which has just been construed. It is quite wrong, therefore, in my view, slavishly to take decided cases and to say: "Well, here was a letter written in identical terms in relation to an identical clause. Without more ado that is conclusive; the court must come to the same conclusion in this case as it came to in the other case." In this manner a seductive jurisprudence is being constructed about the phraseology of rent review clauses, and even that of letters given in response to them. I have to say that I think this is entirely misguided. We must bear in mind that unless they are landmark decisions which lay down principles of law ... all such decisions will be either pure construction of documents or pure decisions on facts of particular cases, or a combination of both. So "precedent" is not wholly compelling or conclusive, although it may provide illustration or inspiration for arguments as to the instruction and effect of leases.'[1]

1 *Prudential Property Services Ltd v Capital Land Holdings Ltd* (sub nom *Woolwich Property Services Ltd v Capital Land Holdings Ltd*) [1993] 15 EG 147 at 151, (1993) 66 P&CR 378.

12.7   The incidence of rent review clauses that are essentially similar but different in points of detail has also added to the complexity of the law by encouraging judges to draw fine and often artificial distinctions in reaching their decisions. Fortunately, the courts have attempted to counter this tendency, notably in their development of the 'presumption of reality', a principle of construction that favours the commercial purpose of the rent review clause.[1]

1 See para 12.79 et seq.

Topics to be considered

12.8   Although rent review cases are likely to turn upon points of construction, there are still quite a number of landmark decisions and other useful illustrations from which recurring themes emerge to allow for a certain amount of generalisation. The main topics to be discussed are:

(1)   the mechanism for initiating a review, including the consequences of late notice;

(2)   the basis on which the new rent will be calculated; and

(3)   the methods of settling disputes, by an arbitrator or expert.

There remain innumerable decisions that turn upon unique points of interpretation, from which it is impossible to generalise, but we will look at one or two examples, to illustrate the sort of disaster that can result from careless draftsmanship.

Finally, we will briefly look at two alternative methods of calculating a new rent level, by index- linked or turnover rents.

THE REVIEW MECHANISM

Whether time is of the essence

12.9   Some of the most serious problems to have arisen concern the procedure when a rent review date arrives. These difficulties may best be understood by initially asking a number of hypothetical questions.

What happens if a landlord lets a rent review date pass without asking for a review? Is the right to review the rent lost until the next review date in the lease, which may be four or five years in the future? Or can the rent be reviewed late? If it is the latter, can the landlord charge the increase retrospectively to the missed review date, or only from the later date when the process began?

Many leases in the past have tried to clarify matters by laying down a strict timetable for initiating a review. For example, a lease may specify a minimum period (say six months) prior to the review date for the landlord to send the tenant a 'trigger' notice, stating the proposed new rent. The tenant may be given a fixed period (often as little as 21 days) within which to challenge the landlord's proposal. There may also be a time limit for referring the matter to a third party in the event of a dispute.

Such timetables may superficially seem to be a good idea, but it eventually became clear that they create more problems than they solve. Will a landlord who is late in sending a trigger notice or referring a dispute to arbitration be stuck with charging the old rent for another five years? Or will a tenant who fails to send a counter-notice within the prescribed period have to pay the landlord's proposed new rent until the next review date?

Bearing in mind that the figure in the landlord's trigger notice, being the first salvo in the negotiating battle, may well be unrealistically high, the consequences to the tenant of such a slip could be financially disastrous.[1] On the other hand, if such consequences are not to follow a failure to observe the time limits, what is the point of having a timetable at all?

1 See eg *Fox & Widley v Guram* [1998] 03 EG 142, [1998] 1 EGLR 91 – figure in landlord's trigger notice: £14,000; independent estimate of the market rent: £3,500; see also para 12.43 et seq.

12.10 *The United Scientific principle* The key to answering these questions is found in the leading cases of *United Scientific Holdings Ltd v Burnley Borough Council* and *Cheapside Land Development Co Ltd v Messels Service Co.*[1] These two cases, which raised basically the same principles, were heard together in the House of Lords.

In each case there had been a failure on the part of the landlords to adhere to the rent review timetable and in each case the Court of Appeal upheld the tenants' view that the landlords had lost their right to review the rent until the next review date. However, the House of Lords reversed that judgment and found for the landlords in each case. The ratio of the decision is found in Lord Diplock's often-quoted dictum:

> 'So upon the question of principle which these two appeals were brought to settle, I would hold that in the absence of any contra-indications in the express words of the lease or in the inter-relation of the rent review clause itself and other clauses or in the surrounding circumstances the presumption is that the time-table specified in a rent review clause for completion of the various steps for determining the rent payable in respect of the period following the review date is not of the essence of the contract.'[2]

In other words, there is a presumption that time is not of the essence in relation to the review timetable. This means that, unless there are circumstances to rebut the presumption, neither party will be penalised merely for failing to adhere strictly to the timetable.[3] And a landlord who reviews late will be entitled to backdate the increase to the original review date. This last point had been decided in the earlier case of *CH Bailey Ltd v Memorial Enterprises Ltd,*[4] and was quoted with approval in the *United Scientific* and *Cheapside* cases.

1 [1978] AC 904, [1977] 2 All ER 62.
2 *United Scientific Holdings Ltd v Burnley Borough Council and Cheapside Land Development Co Ltd v Messels Service Co* [1978] AC 904 at 930. Although this principle has gained wide acceptance and is now firmly established as an authoritative statement of the law in both England and Scotland, it does nevertheless have its critics – see the discussion in *Lancecrest Ltd v Asiwaju* [2005] EWCA Civ 117, [2005] L&TR 22, per Neuberger LJ at para 14 et seq.

3 Other examples include *McDonald's Property Co Ltd v HSBC Bank plc* [2001] 36 EG 181, [2002] 1 P&CR 25; and *Iceland Foods plc v Dangoor and others* [2002] 21 EG 146, [2002] 2 EGLR 5.
4 [1974] 1 All ER 1003, [1974] 1 WLR 728.

12.11 The decision in these cases reversed what had been thought to be the position in English law. At the core of the court's reasoning was the point that delay in fixing a new rent does not cause any serious detriment to a tenant. Instead, it may be to the tenant's advantage to have the use of the money representing the difference between the old and new rents for a longer period before having to pay it to the landlord.

This contrasts with the considerable detriment to a landlord who is unable to increase the rent until the next review period (ten years in the *United Scientific* case). Moreover, a tenant who wants to know what the new rent is going to be can get a fair idea of the current market level by consulting a surveyor.

Alternatively, if a landlord fails to send a trigger notice in time, it is open to the tenant to send a notice specifying a period within which the landlord is required to notify the tenant if the rent review is going ahead. Such a notice, if sent by the tenant, would make time of the essence in relation to the landlord's reply.[1]

1 See para 12.18.

12.12 *Application to Scotland* The *United Scientific* principle applies in Scotland, though subject to some qualifications. This will be discussed in detail below.[1]

1 See para 12.32 et seq.

Retrospective reviews

12.13 After the decisions in *United Scientific* and *Cheapside*, a number of landlords woke up to the idea that this apparent change in the law offered them the chance to put right past blunders that they had thought irreparable.

Before long there began to appear a number of English cases in which the landlords were held entitled to review the rent retrospectively. In many of these the time that had elapsed since the review date was considerable, eg 18 months,[1] 22 months,[2] 24 months,[3] and even 27 months.[4] In one case[5] six years was held to be an unreasonable delay, but that case was later overruled by the Court of Appeal in *Amherst v James Walker Goldsmith & Silversmith Ltd.*[6]

1   *H West & Son v Brecht* (1982) 261 EG 156.

2   *Printing House Properties Ltd v J Winston & Co Ltd* (1982) 263 EG 725.

3   *Vince v Alps Hotel Ltd* (1980) 258 EG 330.

4   *London and Manchester Assurance Co Ltd v GA Dunn & Co* (1983) 265 EG 39, 265 EG 131, CA. While most of these cases occurred in the years immediately following the *United Scientific* decision, more recent examples of late reviews can also be found – see, eg *Lancecrest Ltd v Asiwaju* [2005] L&TR 22, 16 EG 146; *Idealview Ltd v Bello* [2010] 1 EGLR 39, 4 EG 118 (a delay of 13 years).

5   *Telegraph Properties (Securities) Ltd v Courtaulds Ltd* (1981) 257 EG 1153.

6   [1983] Ch 305, [1983] 2 All ER 1067, CA.

12.14   It is perhaps worth looking at that last case a little more closely, as it was a particularly extreme application of the United Scientific doctrine. In *Amherst* the landlord's notice, in terms of the lease, should have been served by 25 December 1974. They were a month late in serving it and the tenant refused to accept the notice as valid, the tenant's claim being upheld in court.

However, in 1980, the landlord, encouraged by the *United Scientific* decision, served a fresh notice on the tenant. It was held that time was not of the essence and the landlord was entitled to review the rent retrospectively despite the fact that it had served the new notice five years after the review date. In the course of his judgment, Oliver LJ said:

> 'I know of no authority for the proposition that the effect of construing a time stipulation as not being of the essence is to substitute a fresh implied term that the contract shall be performed within a reasonable time ... I would in fact go further and suggest that, despite what Lord Salmon said in the United Scientific case, even delay plus hardship to the tenant would not disentitle the landlord to exercise the right which he has, on the true construction of the contract, unless the combination amounted to an estoppel ...
>
> In particular, I cannot, speaking for myself, see how the right can be lost by "abandonment". So far as I am aware, this is not a term of art but I take it to mean the unilateral signification of an intention not to exercise the contractual right in question. If that is right I cannot see how it could bind the landlord save as a promise (promissory estoppel) or as a representation followed by reliance (equitable estoppel) or as a consensual variation of the agreement or as a repudiation accepted by the other party.'[1]

1   [1983] Ch 305 at 315–316.

12.15 *The Scottish position* This case is incompatible with the Scottish authority, under which the landlord may be held to have waived the right to a review by having continued to accept rental payments at the old rate. The result of this has been to limit the effect of the *United Scientific* principle in Scotland, making retrospective reviews less likely.[1] It is not entirely clear, despite the *Amherst* judgment, why the principle of waiver has not been similarly applied in England.

1 See para 12.37 et seq.

Rebuttal of presumption

12.16 Although there is a general presumption in relation to rent review timetables that time is not of the essence, there are a number of situations where it has been established that this presumption has been rebutted and time *is* considered to be of the essence:

Where the lease expressly states that time is of the essence in relation to the review timetable or any part of it[1]

12.17 This is the most straightforward situation. Problems have mainly arisen where the lease is ambiguous about which provision or provisions are subject to the declaration that time is of the essence.

For example, in *London and Manchester Assurance Co Ltd v GA Dunn & Co*[2] it was held that a declaration that time was of the essence applied only to the tenant's counter-notice and not to the landlord's trigger notice. The landlord was allowed to review two years late; moreover, in accordance with the lease terms the rent was assessed, not as at the original review date, but at the postponed date, when levels were higher.

1 See Ross and McKichan para 6.9.
2 [1983] 265 EG 39.

Where the tenant serves a notice on the landlord making time of the essence

12.18 This is known as an 'ultimatum procedure'. It is clear from Lord Diplock's judgment in *United Scientific* that the tenant has this option. There are no reported instances of a landlord who has forgotten to ask for a review being given such a reminder by a tenant. This is perhaps unsurprising, though if the lease allowed for a downwards as well as an upwards valuation, it might be to a tenant's advantage to serve such a notice at a time when rents were falling.

Also, there are other contexts when a tenant might use the ultimatum procedure. In *Visionhire Ltd v Britel Fund Trustees Ltd*[1] a lease provision entitled the tenants, if the landlords had not referred the dispute to arbitration by the review date, to send a notice requiring them to do so within three months. It was held that sending such a notice made time of the essence, and that it was unnecessary for the tenants to serve a further notice in order to achieve this.

On the other hand, a tenant may only be entitled to send such a notice if no other remedy is available. In *Factory Holdings Group v Leboff International,*[2] the tenant sent a notice to the landlord requiring the landlord to refer the dispute to arbitration within 28 days and purporting to make time of the essence. In terms of the lease it was equally open to the landlord and the tenant to apply for the appointment of an arbitrator. It was held that the tenant was not entitled to serve a notice making time of the essence because, in the particular circumstances of the case, there was no need for that remedy.

1   1991 SLT 883, 1992 SCLR 236. See also *Banks v Kokkinos* [1999] 3 EGLR 133, [1998] NPC 171; and *Barclays Bank plc v Savile Estates Ltd* [2003] 2 P&CR 28, [2002] 24 EG 152. See also para 12.32.
2   [1987] 1 EGLR 135, 282 EG 1005.

Where there is an inter-relationship between the rent review clause and a tenant's break provision[1]

12.19   This is the one contra-indication specifically mentioned in *United Scientific* as implying that time is of the essence and rebutting the presumption. The reason is clear.

If the tenant is given the option of terminating the lease prematurely, and is required to give notice of this intention at some point after the landlord's last date for sending a rent review trigger notice, the presumption is that the purpose of the break provision is to allow the tenant to get out of the lease if the new rent is too high. Time is of the essence in relation to the tenant's notice exercising the break, because the landlord needs to know whether or not it will be necessary to look for another tenant.[2] It would therefore be unfair on a tenant who let its opportunity to terminate the lease pass only to receive a late trigger notice from the landlord demanding an unacceptably high rent.

Subsequent to the *United Scientific* decision, there have been a number of English cases where an inter-related rent review and break clause have been held to make time of the essence.[3]

However, there have also been cases where the presence of a break clause has not had that effect. *In Edwin Woodhouse Trustee Co v Sheffield Brick Co*,[4] the tenant had a right to break at the rent review date. The tenant had to give six months' notice in order to exercise the break, but there was no corresponding provision for a landlord's trigger notice. It was held that time could not be of the essence in relation to a date that was not specified in the lease.

1 For tenant's breaks see para 10.2.
2 *United Scientific Holdings Ltd v Burnley Borough Council, Cheapside Land Development Co Ltd v Messels Service Co* [1978] AC 904 at 929 per Lord Diplock, [1977] 2 All ER 62.
3 *Al-Saloom v Shirley James Travel Service Ltd* (1981) 42 P&CR 181, (1981) 259 EG 420, CA; *Legal and General Assurance (Pension Management) Ltd v Cheshire County Council* (1983) 46 P&CR 160, (1983) 265 EG 781; *Coventry City Council v J Hepworth & Sons Ltd* (1983) P&CR 170, 265 EG 608, CA; *William Hill (Southern) Ltd v Govier & Govier* (1984) 269 EG 1168.
4 (1983) 270 EG 548.

12.20   In *Metrolands Investments Ltd v JH Dewhurst Ltd*,[1] the rent review and break timetables, on the surface, seemed closely integrated. However, one of the events in the landlord's timetable was the actual obtaining of the arbitrator's decision (as opposed to a referral to arbitration or applying for an arbitrator to be appointed). As this was outwith the landlord's control, it was held that time could not be of the essence in relation to the rent review timetable.

The fact that the tenant would want to know the new rent before deciding whether or not to exercise the option to break was countered by the fact that, under the terms of the lease, the tenant also had the right to begin the arbitration process if a delay seemed likely. Slade LJ said:

'For these reasons there can, in our judgment, be no doubt that the potential detriment to which the lessor under this particular lease would have exposed itself by agreeing that time should be of the essence as regards the stipulated date for the obtaining of the arbitrator's decision would have far outweighed any potential detriment to which the lessee would have exposed itself by agreeing that it should not be.'[2]

This is fine as far as the landlord is concerned but it is not really satisfactory from the tenant's point of view. The tenant might very well have had the right to initiate arbitration proceedings, but had no more control than the landlord over when the arbitrator would reach a decision, and might still have lost the right to exercise the option to break by the time the new rent was known. It is difficult to see how that particular lease could have been interpreted in a way that was entirely fair to both parties.

1   [1986] 3 All ER 659, (1986) 52 P&CR 232, CA.
2   *Metrolands Investments Ltd v J H Dewhurst Ltd* [1986] 3 All ER 659, CA at 670–671, (1986) 52 P&CR 232.

12.21   These and other familiar arguments cropped up in the Scottish case of *Scottish Development Agency v Morrisons Holdings Ltd.*[1] There a tenant's break clause and the rent review clause were held not sufficiently inter-related to make time of the essence because:

(1)   there was no provision for a landlord's trigger notice, whereas notice by the tenant was required to exercise the break;
(2)   the lease required the rent to be assessed by the Valuation Department for Scotland, and the landlord had no control over the timing of that (it took two years!);
(3)   the lease required the valuation to be made as at the rent review date and the valuation could not be known for certain in advance of that date; and
(4)   it was open to the tenant to make its own enquiries about the likely rent level (presumably the same option was open to the tenant in *Metrolands*, though the point was not made in that case).

1   1986 SLT 59.

12.22   Time *was* held to be of the essence in *Central Estates Ltd v Secretary of State for the* Environment.[1] A 42-year lease had four rent review dates, which in each case could be activated by the landlords serving a trigger notice 12 months before the relevant date. In respect of the second review date only, which was midway through the lease, there was a mutual break provision which could be exercised by six months' notice from either party. This was considered to be a sufficient interrelation to rebut the presumption.

While acknowledging the reasons for the distinction in *Metrolands* and other cases, where time had been held not to be of the essence, the Court of Appeal felt that the weight of authority favoured the view that interrelated rent review and break provisions generally did make time of the essence. In particular, the following points were made:

(a)   It did not matter that the lease contained four review dates but that only the one in dispute coincided with a break provision. This led to the odd possibility that time could be of the essence in relation to one rent review date but not the others. (One judge favoured this view, another concluded that if time was of the essence in relation to one review date the same must be true of the others, and the third reserved his opinion.)

(b)   It did not matter that the break was a mutual one and not tenant-only. Since the lease provided for an upwards or downwards valuation then, just as too high an increase might cause the tenant to want out of the lease, so the landlord might want to do the same if there was a prospect of the rent falling; and

(c)   Even if the break provision might have been included for a purpose unconnected with the rent review, it is enough to make time of the essence if the result of the review would have some impact on the tenant's decision whether to operate the break clause.

1   (1996) 72 P&CR 482, [1995] NPC 106.

Where the lease contains other contra-indications making time of the essence

12.23   In other words, although time is not made expressly of the essence, somewhere in the lease there is wording to indicate that this was the parties' intention. Here it is difficult to draw general principles because so much has depended on the individual wording of particular leases, and considerable financial consequences to both landlords and tenants have hung upon minor differences in what seem to be substantially similar clauses.

In *Drebbond Ltd v Horsham District Council*,[1] a notice by the landlord requiring arbitration had to be served within three months 'but not otherwise'. It was held that these last three words made time of the essence, as did the words (in a much later case) 'but not at any other time'.[2] In *Mammoth Greeting Cards Ltd v Agra Ltd*[3] the same was true in relation to the tenants' counter-notice, where failure to respond within two months meant that the rent 'shall be conclusively fixed at the amount stated in the lessor's notice'.

On the other hand, in *Touche Ross & Co v Secretary of State for the Environment,*[4] a notice had to be given 'as soon as practicable and in any event not later than' a particular period. It was held that time was not of the essence. (Admittedly, that case also hinged on the fact that part of the timetable – the appointment of a surveyor by the President of the Royal Institution of Chartered Surveyors – was outwith the control of the parties, the same reason given in the 'break' cases.)

In *Lewis v Barnett*,[5] the penalty laid down in the lease for the landlord failing to apply in time for the appointment of a surveyor was that the landlord's trigger notice would 'be void and of no effect'. Time was held to be of the essence. And a provision that timeous service of the landlord's trigger notice was to be a 'condition precedent' of the review taking place was held in one case[6] not to make time of the essence, whereas in another[7] it was held that it did.

While the above cases indicate some uncertainty regarding the circumstances in which the *United Scientific* presumption may be rebutted, the law regarding one type of contra-indication has now been sufficiently clarified for it to be considered under a separate heading. This is where the rent review clause contains a so-called 'deeming provision'.

1 (1979) 37 P&CR 237, (1978) 246 EG 1013, DC.
2 *First Property Growth Partnership LP v Royal & Sun Alliance Property Services Ltd* [2003] 1 All ER 533, 2 P&CR 20.
3 [1990] 29 EG 45.
4 (1983) 46 P&CR 187, 265 EG 982, CA.
5 (1982) 264 EG 1079, CA.
6 *North Hertfordshire District Council v Hitchin Industrial Estate Ltd* [1992] 37 EG 133.
7 *Chelsea Building Society v R & A Millet (Shops) Ltd* (1994) 67 P&CR 319, [1994] 09 EG 182.

Where the lease contains a deeming provision

12.24 Unlike the other contra-indications listed above, this is not specifically mentioned in *United Scientific*. It merits separate consideration because of the number of cases on the subject and because the conflict between them (which at one point indicated a possible divergence between English and Scots law) has now been resolved.

A 'deeming' (or 'default') provision is one that clearly spells out the consequences that are to follow if a deadline in the review timetable is missed. After many years of uncertainty, it would now appear to be settled that such a provision makes time of the essence.

The difficulties arose as a result of two English Court of Appeal cases, heard within a short time of each other, which were in apparent conflict. The uncertainty was not alleviated by differing views in subsequent cases as to whether the two judgments could be reconciled.

12.25 *Henry Smith's Charity v AWADA* In *Trustees of Henry Smith's Charity v AWADA Trading and Promotion Services Ltd*,[1] the first of these cases, the lease contained an elaborate timetable, in which the consequences of failing to meet any of the various deadlines were clearly spelled out. In particular, if the tenant failed to send a counter-notice within one month of the landlords' trigger notice, the amount in the trigger notice was deemed to be the market rent. Conversely, if a counter-notice was sent and the landlord failed to apply for the appointment of a surveyor within two months, the figure in the counter-notice was so deemed. The landlords served their trigger notice in time but were late in referring the matter to arbitration.

It was held that if the parties had agreed to confine their movements so tightly, they must be presumed to have meant it, and time was held to be of the essence. The landlords had wanted the rent raised to £29,000 per annum but were held to the existing rent of £8,000 per annum for another five years.

1 (1984) 47 P&CR 607, 269 EG 729, CA.

12.26   *Mecca v Renown Investments*   In the second case, *Mecca Leisure v Renown Investments (Holdings) Ltd*[1] the tenants failed to send a counter-notice within 28 days which, in terms of the lease, meant that they were deemed to have accepted the figure in the landlords' trigger notice; if this had been enforced, the rent would have been increased to £46,250 from the rent of £12,400 fixed at the previous review five years earlier.

The majority of the court held that the mere presence of a deeming provision was not conclusive in rebutting the presumption, that on a proper construction of the relevant clause it had not been rebutted, and that accordingly time was not of the essence.

However, in a prophetic dissenting judgment, Browne-Wilkinson LJ felt unable to distinguish the instant case from *Henry Stewart's Charity*, the need for certainty in commercial and property law being paramount. And his view was that a deeming provision is virtually decisive in displacing the *United Scientific* presumption:

'To hold that time was not of the essence of the tenants' counter-notice would involve not simply extending the time-limits within which the parties' bargain could be performed but an alteration of the parties' bargain itself.'[2]

Nevertheless, the majority opinion prevailed, leaving the lower courts in some subsequent cases with the task of reconciling two binding precedents that were in apparent conflict, and having to make some very fine distinctions in the process.[3]

1 (1985) 49 P&CR 12, (1984) 271 EG 989, CA.

2 (1985) 49 P&CR 12 at 24 per Browne-Wilkinson LJ.

3 See eg *Taylor Woodrow Property Co Ltd v Lonrho Textiles Ltd* (1986) 52 P&CR 28, (1985) 275 EG 632.

12.27 *Bickenhall Engineering v Grandmet* In *Bickenhall Engineering Co Ltd v Grandmet Restaurants Ltd,*[1] the issue before the Court of Appeal was once again whether the tenants by their delay were deemed to have accepted the rent in the landlords' trigger notice. This time the tenants were saved because the provisions relating to their counter-notice were spread over two clauses, creating an ambiguity and allowing the presumption against time being of the essence to operate.

For the presumption to be displaced, said Neil LJ, 'the contra-indications must be clear and explicit'. Brown LJ agreed, but in an obiter statement indicated his approval of the dissenting opinion in *Mecca*. In the process he offered a useful analysis, subsequently approved by the same court, of the situations in which the *United Scientific* principle might operate:

'There are, as it seems to me, three ends to which it may be argued that the *United Scientific* presumption can be put:

1.　In the absence of any express terms specifying what is to happen in default of the exercise of the rights given to the respective parties within the permitted periods of time (ie in the absence of a deeming provision), the presumption applies: time is not of the essence unless and until it is made so, and in the result a time stipulation cannot be strictly enforced against whoever fails to observe it ...

2.　In the event of dispute whether or not there is such an express deeming provision, the presumption applies as a rule of construction to assist the resolution of that dispute.

3.　Even if there *is* such an express deeming provision the presumption can nevertheless still apply to defeat both it and the strict enforcement of the separate time stipulation.

In my judgement, the presumption applies in situations 1 and 2, but not in 3. Situation 1 was that arising in *United Scientific* itself. Situation 2 I believe to be the present case ...[2]

1 [1995] 10 EG 123, [1994] NPC 118.

2 *Bickenhall Engineering Co Ltd v Grandmet Restaurants Ltd* [1995] 10 EG 123 at 129 per Brown LJ; for later examples of the first situation, see *McDonald's Property Co Ltd v HSBC Bank plc* [2001] 36 EG 181, [2002] 1 P&CR 25; and *Iceland Foods plc v Dangoor and others* [2002] 21 EG 146, [2002] 2 EGLR 5; for another example of the second situation (where the facts were similar to those in *Bickenhall*) see *Wilderbrook Ltd v Olowu* 2006 2 P&CR 4, [2005] NPC 133. See also para 12.53.

12.28 *Starmark Enterprises v CPL Distribution Ltd* The uncertainty was resolved by the Court of Appeal in *Starmark Enterprises Ltd v CPL Distribution Ltd*.[1] The issue was once again whether failure to serve a counter-notice in time meant that the tenant was deemed to have accepted the figure in the landlord's trigger notice (£84,800 as opposed to the tenant's proposal of £52,725).

Despite the fact that the relevant lease provision was virtually identical to the one in *Mecca*, the court declined to follow that case and unanimously held that the deeming provision made time of the essence, with the result that the tenant was held to the landlord's figure.

After approving the analysis by Brown LJ in *Bickenhall*, Kay LJ concluded that the instant case fell into the third of his categories, and went on to say:

'Whilst in a lease with no deeming provision attached to the rent review clause (as was the case in each of the appeals in *United Scientific*) the provisions as to time can properly be described as laying down "the administrative procedure or machinery", the same approach cannot be taken to that part of a clause which contains an express deeming provision. To read such a provision as mere administrative procedure is to rewrite the contract by which the parties agreed to be bound. That, as observed by Slade LJ in *AWADA*, is something that the court cannot do. Nowhere in *United Scientific* is there anything that would permit the court to rewrite a contract.'[2]

And as Gibson LJ observed:

'To give proper effect to the parties' intentions, the applicable principle which in my view governs this and other like cases is that where the parties have clearly stipulated the consequences of no proper notice being served within the specified period, that is a contraindication rebutting the presumption that time is not of the essence.'[3]

Since the tenant's application for leave to appeal to the House of Lords was refused, the matter would appear to be settled. A clear and unambiguous deeming provision, in England at any rate, makes time of the essence.

1 [2002] Ch 306, [2002] 2 WLR 1009.
2 *Starmark Enterprises Ltd v CPL Distribution Ltd* [2002] Ch 306 at 319 per Kay LJ.
3 *Starmark Enterprises Ltd v CPL Distribution Ltd* [2002] Ch 316 at 331 per Gibson LJ.

12.29 In *Secretary of State for Communities and Local Government v Standard Securities Ltd*[1] a lease provided that, in the event of the landlords failing to appoint an independent surveyor in time, the rent would remain the same. It was held that there was no difference in principle between a deeming provision triggered by the failure to serve a notice in time and one which was triggered by a failure to apply for the appointment of a third party in time, and no difference between a provision deeming one party to have agreed to pay a particular amount and one that operated by providing that the rent for the next review period would be the same as the existing rent. *Starmark* was applied and time was held to be of the essence.

1 [2008] 1 P&CR 23.

12.30 The authoritative line of precedent in England is therefore *Henry Smith's Charity v AWADA*, the dissenting opinion in *Mecca*, the obiter analysis in *Bickenhall,* and finally, *Starmark*.

12.31 *Scottish position* It should be said that the uncertainty on this point did not last quite so long in Scotland, where the courts had already endorsed the dissenting judgment in *Mecca*.[1] In fact in *Starmark* Kay LJ took some comfort from the fact that the court's judgment had been anticipated in Scotland, Australia and New Zealand (described by the judge at first instance as 'powerful foreign decisions').[2]

The *Starmark* decision has therefore confirmed that the laws of Scotland and England are in line on this issue and has cleared up what was threatening to be a divergence between the two countries.[3]

It should also be said that certainty has been bought at the cost of some danger, particularly to tenants whose leases contain deeming provisions in relation to the service of a counter-notice. More about this will be said later.

1 *Visionhire Ltd v Britel Fund Trustees Ltd*, 1991 SLT 883, 1992 SCLR 236; *Charterhouse Square Finance Co Ltd v A & J Menswear* 1998 SLT 720.
2 *Starmark Enterprises Ltd v CPL Distribution Ltd* [2000] 46 EG 196 at 201 per Neuberger J.
3 See para 12.33.

The United Scientific principle in Scotland

12.32 *Visionhire v Britel Fund Trustees* The *United Scientific* principle was first accepted in Scotland in a series of Outer House decisions without the underlying theory being considered in any great depth.[1] The principle was subjected to its first close scrutiny from the Scottish viewpoint in *Visionhire Ltd v Britel Fund Trustees Ltd*,[2] in which the landlord, after initiating the review process, allowed the review date to pass without submitting the matter to arbitration. In such a situation the lease allowed the tenant to send the landlord a notice containing its own rental proposal, which would prevail if the landlord then failed to submit to arbitration within three months. The tenant sent a notice proposing the existing rent and the landlord failed to make the application within the three-month deadline. The landlord was therefore about to lose its right to review unless it could establish that time was not of the essence.

The Lord Ordinary decided that the presumption against time being of the essence was a purely English principle which did not apply in Scots law, and this caused some agitation among the legal and surveying professions in Scotland who saw themselves (unlike their English colleagues) being deprived of a safety net – albeit, as we have seen, a net full of large holes.

However, an appeal to the Inner House reversed this aspect of the Lord Ordinary's decision:

'It seems to me therefore that there is no essential difference between the positions adopted in the two countries and that the rules which according to English law are stated as presumptions are really to be seen as rules of construction which take their place along with various other rules in order to ascertain what the intention of the parties truly was in order that the contract which they have made should be enforced.'[3]

Unfortunately for the landlord, in the particular circumstances of this case, ie the service of a notice by the tenant, the presumption was rebutted, time was of the essence and the landlord lost its right to review. The affirmation of the general principle, however, confirms that the English authority is relevant and clears up some of the complications in the Scottish position; unfortunately, as we will see shortly, it does not clear up all of them.[4]

1 *Scottish Development Agency v Morrisons Holdings Ltd* 1986 SLT 59; *Yates, Petitioner* 1987 SLT 86; *Leeds Permanent Pension Scheme Trustees Ltd v William Timpson Ltd* 1987 SCLR 571; *Legal and Commercial Properties Ltd v Lothian Regional Council* 1988 SLT 463, 1988 SCLR 201.
2 1991 SLT 883, 1992 SCLR 236.
3 1991 SLT 833 at 888 per Lord President Hope.
4 See para 12.37 et seq.

12.33 *Deeming provisions* Although it did not relate to a deeming provision, *Visionhire* signalled the more strict line that Scots law should take in relation to the development of the presumption in general and to deeming provisions in particular. Prior to that there had been some conflict, one Outer House decision having anticipated the Inner House's line (*Yates, Petitioner*),[1] and another having taken a more liberal approach, allowing the *United Scientific* rule to override a deeming provision in relation to a tenant's counter notice (*Legal and Commercial Properties Ltd v Lothian Regional Council*).[2]

In *Visionhire* Lord President Hope approved *Henry Smith's Charity* and the dissenting judgment in *Mecca* and favoured an interpretation of the *United Scientific* principle that anticipated the view of the English courts in *Bickenhall* and *Starmark*:[3]

> 'The function of the rule is to fill the gap where there is an absence of provision or a lack of clarity on the point, not to override express provisions in the contract which show either expressly or by necessary implication that the parties intended that the time limit was to be strictly applied.'[4]

1 1987 SLT 86.
2 1988 SLT 463.
3 *Bickenhall Engineering Co Ltd v Grandmet Restaurants Ltd* [1995] 10 EG 123, [1994] NPC 118; *Starmark Enterprises Ltd v CPL Distribution Ltd* [2002] Ch 306, [2002] 2 WLR 1009; see para 12.25 et seq.
4 *Visionhire Ltd v Britel Fund Trustees Ltd*, 1991 SLT 883 at 889 per Lord President Hope.

12.34 In *Charterhouse Square Finance Co Ltd v A & J Menswear*[1] the above approach was applied to a deeming provision. The lease provided for the landlord to send a trigger notice containing the proposed new rent. Unless the tenant challenged this by sending a counter-notice within 21 days, the rent would be fixed at the landlord's figure. The landlord served a trigger notice on 3 May 1996, proposing a new rent of £85,000 (the existing rent is not mentioned in the case report). On 28 May the tenant intimated by letter to the landlord that they had passed the matter to their surveyors, who sent a formal counter-notice on 31 May, a week after the expiry of the 21-day deadline.

It was held that the default provision displaced the presumption against time being of the essence, and the tenant was held to the landlord's figure. In the words of Lord Macfadyen:

> 'In my opinion the existence of what has been variously called a deeming or default provision, ie a provision providing for the consequences of failure to adhere to the agreed time limit, will in general demonstrate that the parties intended the time limit to be strictly enforced ... I have difficulty ... in envisaging circumstances in which a default provision could take effect without time being held to be of the essence ... If the parties have agreed on [the] consequences, it is not for the court to moderate the effect of the clause by reference to fairness, or by weighing the prejudice which the defenders will

suffer. It seems to me that to give effect to the defenders' submission would be to alter materially the parties' contract.'[2]

1 1998 SLT 720.
2 1998 SLT 720 at 725–726 per Lord Macfadyen.

12.35 *Scottish Life Assurance v Agfa-Gevaert* This reluctance of the Scottish courts to interfere with the clear terms of the contract was also demonstrated in a slightly different context in *Scottish Life Assurance Co v Agfa-Gevaert Ltd.*[1] In that case the tenant was held to the figure in the landlord's trigger notice, not because the tenant failed to send its own notice in time, but because it did not contain a counter-proposal in respect of the reviewed rent. This was required by the lease, in wording which the court held made it mandatory.

On the face of it the requirement for the tenant to specify a figure did not seem to serve any particularly useful purpose, but as Lord Caplan put it:

'It is a well-established principle that the court will not generally interfere with the terms that parties have agreed for their contracts. It is not the function of the court to adjust an explicit contractual term to moderate the effect on parties... [It] cannot readily be assumed that commercial interests do not know what they are doing and that there are not perfectly sensible reasons for demanding in the contractual terms formal notice of a party's negotiating position. It would certainly be most ill-advised, even if it were relevant, for the court to conclude that the provisions of clause 7 have no sensible commercial basis.'[2]

As for the consequences suffered by the tenant:

'The result which follows is somewhat harsh on the [tenants], who in all probability have simply made a mistake. It may even be that the [landlord] was taking advantage of such misunderstanding on their part. However, this is simply a consequence of parties having the privilege of fixing their own contractual terms. If they accept contractual terms, they are bound by them irrespective of any disadvantage that may ensue from a failure to observe them through misjudgement.'[3]

1 1998 SC 171, 1998 SLT 481. See also para 12.45.
2 *Scottish Life Assurance Co v Agfa-Gevaert Ltd* 1998 SC 171 at 175 per Lord Caplan.
3 *Scottish Life Assurance Co v Agfa-Gevaert Ltd* 1998 SC 171 at 176 per Lord Caplan.

12.36 In *Prow v Argyll and Bute Council*[1] it was a mandatory requirement in the review timetable that the tenant should send a counter-notice within three months if it required the review to be referred to arbitration. It was held that this was equivalent to a deeming provision, time was of the essence, and the tenant was held to the figure in the landlord's trigger notice.

1 [2013] CSIH 23, 2013 GWD 21-438.

Waiver of right to review

12.37 *Banks v Mecca Bookmakers* In relation to rent review machinery, this is the one area where there remains a substantial difference between Scots and English law.

In *Banks v Mecca Bookmakers (Scotland) Ltd*,[1] the landlord had several leases with the tenant, whom the landlord notified in April 1978 of its wish to review the rents. This was nearly a year after the rent review date in some of the leases, and nearly two years after it in others. It was held that the acceptance by the landlord of rent at the old rate after the review dates, without qualification or any explanation, implied abandonment of the landlord's right to seek a review until the next review dates.

Pointing out that the concept of waiver was not raised in *CH Bailey Ltd v Memorial Enterprises Ltd*[2] or in the *United Scientific* and *Cheapside* cases, Lord Grieve went on to say:

'As I understand the law of Scotland the question of "waiver" is concerned with whether or not a right under a contract has been abandoned. It is a question of fact, and, as such, the question whether or not a person has abandoned a right cannot be affected one way or the other by prejudice suffered by the person who alleges that the right has been abandoned. Accordingly in cases such as this where the issue is concerned with the alleged abandonment of a right, prejudice need not be averred, and indeed would be irrelevant if it was.'[3]

1 1982 SC 7, 1982 SLT 150.
2 [1974] 1 All ER 1003, [1974] 1 WLR 728.
3 1982 SLT 150 at 153. While prejudice need not be averred it is necessary that the party pleading waiver has conducted his affairs on the basis of the right having been abandoned: see *Evans v Argus Healthcare (Glenesk) Ltd* 2001 SLCR 117, approved in *City Inn v Shepherd Construction* [2010] CSIH 68; 2011 SC 127; see also para 12.39.

12.38 Neither the concept of waiver nor the *Banks* case were referred to in *Amherst v James Walker Goldsmith & Silversmith Ltd*,[1] even though it was heard a year after the Scottish case had been reported.

It is clear that the two cases are incompatible, one rejecting and the other recognising the concept of abandonment, one giving a landlord the right to backdate even where the tenant has suffered hardship, the other depriving the landlord of the right to review even without hardship. What is not clear is whether the discrepancy reflects an underlying difference in the law of the two countries or merely a different interpretation of common principles (though there has been some indication in the English authority that waiver may be possible south of the border in exceptional circumstances).[2]

1 [1983] Ch 305, [1983] 2 All ER 1067, CA; see para 12.14.
2 See eg *Lancecrest Ltd v Asiwaju* [2005] EWCA Civ 117, [2005] L&TR 22, per Neuberger LJ at para 14 et seq; but see also *Idealview Ltd v Bello* [2010] 1 EGLR 39, 4 EG 118 (where a retrospective review was allowed after 13 years).

12.39 *Later authority* For a number of years *Banks* remained the sole Scottish authority on this point. However, in *Falkirk District Council v Falkirk Taverns Ltd*[1] a plea of waiver was again attempted, this time unsuccessfully. Once again the landlord had accepted rent at the old rate after the review date but, unlike the situation in *Banks*, had initiated the review process in time and (according to the landlord's averments) had continued to assert in correspondence its intention to review the rent (the delay having been caused by a misunderstanding of the legal position). The Lord Ordinary did not criticise *Banks*, or even discuss its merits at all, but held that the above facts, alleged by the landlord, were grounds for distinguishing it.

A more direct affirmation was given in *Waydale Ltd v MRM Engineering*.[2] In circumstances very similar to *Banks* the landlord tried to impose a retrospective review and a plea of waiver was again accepted.

Banks and Waydale were subjected to criticism in *AWG Group Ltd v HCP II Properties 101 GP Ltd*,[3] principally on the need for reliance by the party claiming that the right to review had been abandoned. Lord Doherty was of the view that the party claiming waiver needs to show that he conducted his affairs on the basis that the right had been abandoned.[4] In *AWG* the court found that the landlord had not waived the right to review the rent in 2014 despite a delay of over two years, during which the current passing rent was paid and accepted. Initially invoices for the rent had contained a statement that they were 'without prejudice to review on 26/02/14' but this statement did not appear on later invoices. A brochure for the sale of the landlord's interest in the premises in 2015 stated that the next review date was in 2019. The court found that these factors, neither separately nor cumulatively, were enough to infer that the landlord had waived the right to review. The case was distinguished from *Banks* and *Waydale* given that the lease in *AWG* contained a clause providing that no demand or acceptance of rent at a rate other than that to which the landlord may be entitled following a review was to be deemed a waiver by the landlord of the right to review the rent. This case highlights the benefit to landlords of including such a provision in their lease.

1 1993 SLT 1097.
2 1996 SLT (Sh Ct) 6.
3 [2017] CSOH 69, 2017 Hous LR 30.
4 [2017] CSOH 69, 2017 Hous LR 30, para [31].

12.40 *Amount of delay required* In *Banks* the period of delay since the review dates was just under one year in respect of some of the leases and just under two years in the case of the others. In *Waydale* it was 16-and-a-half months. Where the period is shorter, it is less clear how much of a delay will be required to constitute waiver. In *Banks*, Lord Grieve suggested that it need not be very much:

'In my opinion there is only one inference that can reasonably be drawn from [the facts], and that is that the pursuer abandoned his right to institute a review of the rents on acceptance of the tendered rents at Whitsunday 1976 and Whitsunday 1977, [the review dates] or at latest on acceptance of the same rents tendered the following quarter.'[1]

In *Waydale*, Sheriff Principal Risk hinted that a slightly longer period might be required:

'I reject the argument that to find waiver established in the circumstances of this case is tantamount to holding that time was of the essence in seeking rent review. The time which must elapse and the number of rent payments which must be accepted before waiver can be inferred are questions of fact and degree. It is simply not the case that to uphold the defenders' argument here leads logically to the proposition that waiver could be established after one month's delay and acceptance of one instalment of rent.'[2]

What amounts to waiver, therefore, is a matter of fact and degree to be established in each case. There must be some doubt, however, as to whether a single payment at the old rate, which was due in advance on the rent review date itself, would be sufficient.

What is clear is that the substantial retrospective reviews that have been allowed in England could not occur in Scotland unless it had been made plain (as in *Falkirk Taverns* and *AWG Group*) that the landlord was not abandoning the right to a review. This could be done, for example, by provision in the lease to that effect (as in *AWG Group*), or making a clear qualification when accepting payments at the old rate (as occurred in *Falkirk Taverns*).

1 *Banks v Mecca Bookmakers (Scotland) Ltd* 1982 SLT 150 at 154.
2 *Waydale Ltd v MRM Engineering* 1996 SLT (Sh Ct) 6 at 9.

12.41 *Prescription* In the English case of *Idealview Ltd v Bello*[1] it was held that a retrospective review after 13 years was not time-barred under section 19 of the Limitation Act 1980, because the obligation to pay the backdated rent increase did not actually arise until after the review had taken place. It is suggested that the same principle is likely to apply in relation to section 6 of the Prescription and Limitation (Scotland) Act 1973.

1 [2010] 1 EGLR 39, 4 EG 118.

12.42 *The United Scientific principle and waiver* It should be emphasised that the presumption against time being of the essence and waiver of the right to review are quite separate principles. The former *does* apply in Scotland but its effect may be limited in some of its more extreme applications if waiver can be established.

It may help to distinguish between two separate types of case. The first is where the landlord has in fact initiated the rent review process prior to the review date, but either the landlord or the tenant has not strictly conformed to the review timetable laid down in the lease, eg where there has been late service of a landlord's trigger notice or of a tenant's counter-notice. Here it is clear that Scots and English law are in line and that the *United Scientific* principle applies in both countries: this is confirmed by *Visionhire* and the other Scottish authority and the threatened divergence in relation to deeming provisions has now been resolved.

The second situation is where the landlord has let the review date pass entirely and has continued to accept rent at the old rate without qualification before deciding (or remembering) to ask for a review. It is plain that this makes no difference in England, from the number of late reviews that were allowed there after the decision in *United Scientific*.[1] But in Scotland the landlord may be held to have waived the right to a review, and be prevented from increasing the rent until the next review date.

1 See para 12.13 et seq.

Validity of notices

12.43 We have seen that, where time is of the essence, disaster can strike either landlord or tenant: a late trigger notice or reference to arbitration can cost a landlord the right to review, or a tenant serving a late counter-notice may be stuck with the landlord's optimistic first proposal.

Unfortunately the dangers do not end there. Even if a landlord indicates the intention to review in time, or the tenant expresses disagreement with the proposed rent within the required period, such a communication may be ineffective if it does not amount to a valid notice in terms of the lease.

Where time is not of the essence this need not matter, as a replacement notice which does meet the necessary requirements can be sent late.[1] But when time is of the essence, this luxury is not available, and a timeous notice worded with insufficient care may have the same unfortunate consequences as no notice at all.

Once again it is difficult to generalise, as the requirements for a valid notice will vary according to the lease terms. However, the case law reveals a number of lessons that should be of help to the drafters of notices.

1 *RM Prow (Motors) Ltd Directors Pension Fund Trustees v Argyll and Bute Council* [2013] CSIH, 2013 GWD 12-260.

12.44 *Wording of notice* If its wording is too informal, or contains extraneous material, a notice may be invalid. In *Yates, Petitioner*[1] this was the result when a trigger notice was couched in informal terms, included social pleasantries, and seemed more like an invitation to negotiate than a formal notice.

Also, there have been many cases in England where tenants indicated in time that they were unhappy with the landlord's proposed new rent, but the wording of their communication rendered it ineffective as a counter-notice. Examples include:

'We would hardly need add that we do not accept your revised figure';[2]

'Our client contends ... that the open market rental value ... is at this time less than the present rental value';[3]

'We cannot agree with your rent increase';[4]

'Will you please accept this letter as counter-notice to the effect that we consider that the rent of £50,000 is excessive and will appreciate it if you will kindly forward to us the comparables on which you have based this figure';[5]

and

'I am writing to inform you that the Board does not accept your proposed increase of £6,500'.[6]

Subsequently, the courts seem to have taken a slightly more liberal view and the following have been held to be valid counter-notices:

'Please accept this letter as formal objection and counter-notice. We would suggest an early meeting to discuss the matter in detail';[7] and

'I note that your assessment of rental is £190,000 per annum which I consider to be excessive'.[8]

However, much will still depend upon the requirements of the particular lease. Recourse may be available to the reasonable recipient test in terms of which the content of the notice is considered according to what a reasonable recipient, taking into account the context in which the notice was served, would understand the notice to mean.[9]

Care must also be taken to ensure that the notice is addressed to the correct person. In *West Dunbartonshire Council v William Thompson and Son (Dumbarton)* Ltd,[10] the Inner House found that a notice designing the tenant as 'Wm Thompson & Sons Ltd' instead of its correct designation, 'William Thompson and Son (Dumbarton) Ltd' was invalid.

More recently the Inner House, in the context of a notice served under a share purchase agreement, indicated a less strict approach. In *Hoe International Ltd v Andersen*,[11] the court was of the view that despite the notice not being addressed to the party required by the contract it was nonetheless valid. The court considered the important question was whether the recipient had suffered any prejudice by service not complying with the contract. If not, then the court should be slow to hold that the notice was invalid.

1 1987 SLT 86; see also *Dunedin Property Investment Co Ltd v Wesleyan & General Assurance Society* 1992 SCLR 159 as another Scottish example.
2 *Bellinger v South London Stationers Ltd* (1979) 252 EG 699.
3 *Oldschool v Johns* (1980) 256 EG 381.
4 *Amalgamated Estates Ltd v Joystretch Manufacturing Ltd* (1980) 257 EG 489.
5 *Edlingham Ltd v MFI Furniture Centres* (1981) 259 EG 421.
6 *Horserace Totalisator Board v Reliance Mutual Assurance Society* (1982) 266 EG 218.
7 *Glofield Properties Ltd v Morley* [1988] 02 EG 62.
8 *Barrett Estate Services Ltd v David Greig (Retail) Ltd* [1991] 36 EG 155; see also *Patel v Earlspring Properties* [1991] 46 EG 153.
9 *Mannai Investment Co Ltd v Eagle Star Life Assurance Co Ltd* [1997] AC 749.
10 [2015] CSIH 93, 2016 SLT 125.
11 [2017] CSIH 9; 2017 SC 313.

12.45   *Amount of rent*   If a lease requires the landlord's trigger notice not only to intimate the intention to review, but also to state the proposed rent, then the omission of a rental figure may invalidate the notice.[1]

Where a notice inadvertently stated one amount in words followed by another in figures, this was not held to be fatal;[2] needless to say, this is not recommended practice.

It may not be necessary for the tenant's notice to state a counter-proposal,[3] but this will depend on the lease provisions.

In *Scottish Life Assurance Co v Agfa-Gevaert Ltd*[4] the lease required the subtenants to propose an alternative figure in their counter-notice, and this had not been done. It was held that the lease wording made the inclusion of a rental figure mandatory, and the subtenants were held to the principal tenants' proposal of £90,000 (which represented an increase of £15,000).

Unless the lease specifically requires it, the landlord is normally under no obligation to state a rent in the trigger notice that is a genuine pre-estimate of the market rent. In *Fox & Widley v Guram*[5] the tenants failed to serve a counter-notice and were held to the landlord's figure of £14,000, even though an independent surveyor had estimated the market rent to be £3,500.

1 *Commission for the New Towns v R Levy & Co Ltd* [1990] 28 EG 119.
2 *Durham City Estates Ltd v Felicetti* [1990] 03 EG 71.
3 *Patel v Earlspring Properties* [1991] 46 EG 153.
4 1998 SC 171, 1998 SLT 481; see also para 12.35.
5 [1998] 03 EG 142.

12.46   *'Subject to contract' and 'without prejudice'*   The attachment of either or both of these phrases to a piece of correspondence will normally reserve the legal position of the party using the phrase.

Although they originate in other areas of law, they may have some function in rent reviews while the parties are merely in negotiation; on the other hand, their use may also allow one party to change their mind after agreement was thought to have been reached.[1]

The main problems arise when one of these phrases is added, either by a landlord or a tenant, to a notice which the lease makes a formal requirement. If the sender is lucky the words 'subject to contract' or 'without prejudice' may in a particular context be considered merely to be 'meaningless estate agent's verbiage' and have no effect;[2] at the worst, an otherwise satisfactory notice may be rendered legally ineffective.[3]

The phrase 'subject to contract', unlike the situation in England, has no recognised technical meaning in Scotland, but is open to construction in the particular circumstances and may have the effect of preventing a contractual agreement being concluded.[4]

1 *Henderson Group plc v Superabbey Ltd* [1988] 39 EG 82.
2 *Royal Life Insurance v Phillips* (1991) 61 P&CR 182, [1990] 43 EG 70 (also useful for a review of the case law on this topic).
3 *Shirlcar Properties Ltd v Heinitz* (1983) 268 EG 362.
4 *Stobo v Morrisons (Gowns) Ltd* 1949 SC 184, 1949 SLT 193.

12.47 *Purpose of notice* When considering the requirements of the lease in question, the purpose which the notice is designed to achieve should always be kept in mind.

For example, if the purpose of a tenant's counter-notice is merely to challenge the figure in the landlord's trigger notice, then a clear written indication of disagreement may be enough.[1] In *Lancecrest Ltd v Asiwaju*[2] the stated purpose of the tenant's counter notice was to challenge the landlords' right to review the rent at all, on the basis that the trigger notice had been sent out of time. However, although this challenge failed because time was held not to be of the essence, it was also held that the notice sufficiently indicated the tenant's objection to a review and was therefore a valid counter notice.

On the other hand, there have been a number of rent-review clauses where the purpose of a counter-notice is also an election by the tenant to have the rent determined by a third party, and here more will be required. In *Prudential Property Services Ltd v Capital Land Holdings Ltd*[3] Colyer J (after a useful review of the earlier authority) confirmed that such a notice, to be valid, must make it clear that the tenant is exercising the relevant election either by (a) indicating that the letter is a counter-notice under the relevant clause or (b) spelling out the consequences which it is intended to achieve.

The notice in that case was held to be valid despite containing a reference to the wrong clause of the lease; it would, in any case, have been rather unfair to penalise the tenant for this as the wrong reference had been repeated from the landlord's trigger notice!

1 *Barrett Estate Services v David Greig (Retail)* [1991] 36 EG 155.
2 [2005] L&TR 22, 16 EG 146.
3 (*sub nom Woolwich Property Services Ltd v Capital Land Holdings Ltd*) (1993) 66 P&CR 378, [1993] 15 EG 147.

12.48 It was held in one Scottish decision that for an error to invalidate a notice there has to be something that might mislead the other party.[1] In *Fox & Widley v Guram*[2] where the landlord's trigger notice stated the rent review date to be 25 May instead of 23 May, it was held that the mistake was not fatal as nobody could have been misled.

1 *Prudential Assurance Co v Smiths Foods* 1995 SLT 369.
2 [1998] 03 EG 142; see also *Durham City Estates Ltd v Felicetti* [1990] 03 EG 71.

12.49 *Postal notices* Where it can be proved that a notice has been sent by post, there is a presumption that it has been delivered, which can be rebutted by evidence to the contrary.[1]

In the English case of *WX Investments Ltd v Begg*[2] a tenant's counter-notice, which had been sent by recorded delivery post within the 14-day deadline, was only delivered out of time because of the repeated inability of the landlord to accept delivery. It was held that the notice was presumed to have been delivered on the first occasion on which the postal service attempted to deliver it, which was within the deadline.[3]

1 *Chaplin v Caledonian Land Properties Ltd* 1997 SLT 384; this case related to a break notice, but the principle is of general application.
2 [2002] 1 WLR 2849, [2002] L&TR 39.
3 This case was an application of s 196 of the purely English Law of Property Act 1925 and therefore needs to be treated with extreme caution in Scotland. However, it has been suggested that the English legislation regarding postal delivery is merely a restatement of the common law both north and south of the border – see *Chaplin v Caledonian Land Properties Ltd* 1997 SLT 384 at 387 per Lord Rodger.

12.50 *Notice transmitted electronically* Where a lease required notices to be sent in writing, a notice sent by facsimile transmission has been held to be sufficient.[1] The same would apply to a notice sent as an email attachment.[2] An email itself can constitute a valid notice in writing.[3]

It is, of course, always possible that the particular requirements of the lease in question may preclude any of the above methods. The terms of the lease should therefore always be carefully checked.

1 *EAE (RT) Ltd v EAE Property Ltd* 1994 SLT 627.
2 The Legal Writing (Counterparts and Delivery)(Scotland) Act 2015 s 4 permits delivery of a traditional document by electronic means.
3 *Our Generation Ltd v Aberdeen City Council* [2019] CSIH 42; 2019 SLT 1164.

12.51 Since a notice that may have the effect of altering the rent is arguably constituting a contract that will vary a real right in land section 1 of the Requirements of Writing (Scotland) Act 1995 should be complied with. [1]

1 See para 2.3 et seq.

Practical considerations

12.52 *Drafting of lease* The law regarding review machinery may be difficult, but the lessons to be learned from it are easier to formulate:

(1) When drafting a rent review clause in a new lease, do not include a strict timetable. The tenant has signed a lease containing rent review dates and should not have to be reminded when they are due to arrive. The landlord will probably, as a matter of practice, write informally to the tenant well in advance of the date, proposing a new rent and starting off negotiations, but there is no need for a formal requirement to send a trigger notice.

If the tenant is worried about the possibility of the review date being missed and a retrospective increase being imposed perhaps years later, the solution is simple. A provision can be inserted in the lease allowing the landlord to review late, but at some later anniversary of the review date rather than retrospectively.

On the other hand, landlords may want to include a provision expressly allowing them to review retrospectively and backdate the increase, and whichever prevails will depend on the relative negotiating strengths of the parties. In either case it is in the tenant's interest to make sure that the date of valuation is still the original review date. Otherwise the landlord might, at a time of rental stagnation, be tempted to deliberately postpone the review until rent levels have risen again.

(2) A landlord would be advised to include a disclaimer to the effect that accepting rent at the old level after the rent review date will not amount to a waiver of the right to review.[1]

(3) In addition to the general inadvisability of having a strict timetable, it is in the interests of both parties to avoid including 'deeming' provisions, since it is now established that this makes time of the essence.

A tenant in particular should resist a provision deeming acceptance of the landlord's rental figure if a counter-notice is not sent on time. If the tenant loses the right to challenge the landlord's figure, the consequences could be financial disaster; we have seen above several examples of the degree of optimism shown by landlords in their trigger notices, eg in *Mecca Leisure v Renown Investments (Holdings) Ltd*,[2] where the landlord sought to raise the rent from £12,400 to £46,250).

---

1 See the discussion of *AWG Group Ltd v HCP II Properties 101 GP Ltd* [2017] CSOH 69; 2017 Hous LR 30 at para 12.39 above.

2 (1985) 49 P&CR 12, (1984) 271 EG 989, CA.

12.53 *Review clauses in existing leases* There remains the problem of older leases which predated much of the case law, before the lessons from it could be learned. The incidence of such leases will have lessened by the passage of time, however, some such leases, eg long ground leases, will still be extant and have rent reviews still to come. Some practical considerations:

(1) In order to minimise the possibility of missing a review date, the landlord's agent should have a proper administrative system for providing a reminder when the rents in the various leases in the landlord's portfolio are due for review, and when any necessary notices have to be sent.

(2) The landlord's agent should check the rent review terms of *each individual lease* where a review is due, and make sure that all time limits are strictly observed, whether or not time is stated to be of the essence. No matter how standard the terms of the lease, an individual check is still necessary: when the lease was drafted, many years before, the standard style might have been different, or the tenant's agent might have negotiated changes, now forgotten.

(3) The tenant's agent should also check the lease and make sure that all time limits incumbent upon the tenant are observed, particularly if it is necessary to send a counter-notice to the landlord's trigger notice.

(4) The agents of both landlords and tenants should emphasise to their clients the necessity of immediately passing on any notices they receive. In *Charterhouse Square Finance Co Ltd v A & J Menswear*[1] the tenants only contacted their agents after the time limit for serving their counter-notice had expired, and as a result were held to the figure in the landlord's trigger notice.

(5) As well as meeting all deadlines laid down, both landlord and tenant should observe any requirements of the lease regarding the form of the notices involved. If no requirements are laid down, the notice should be made as formal as possible, stating the sender's intentions clearly and unambiguously. In particular, if the lease requires the tenant's counter-notice to include a rental figure, it is essential in order to ensure the notice's validity that this be done.[2]

1 1998 SLT 720.
2 *Scottish Life Assurance Co v Agfa-Gevaert Ltd* 1998 SC 171, 1998 SLT 481; see also generally para 12.43 et seq.

VALUATION CRITERIA

12.54 Once they have safely passed through the minefield of the review timetable and a review has been initiated, the parties to a lease will require to fix the amount of the new rent. Apart from the fact that an arbitrator or other third party might be required to resolve any disagreement, it might be thought that the process from now on would be relatively straightforward.

Unfortunately it is not so and the danger of severe financial loss to either party remains just as real. The following cautionary tale will illustrate the point.

In *Goh Eng Wah v Yap Phooi Yin*,[1] an appeal to the Privy Council from the Federal Court of Malaysia, the tenant under a 30-year ground lease erected a cinema at its own expense. At a subsequent rent review, it was held that the level of rent should be based on the value of both the land and the building, even although the tenant had paid for the latter itself.

Effectively, therefore, the tenant was paying for the cinema twice: once when it erected it, then again in the form of an inflated rent. Lord Templeman said:

'[If] the parties intended that the rent fixed by an arbitrator should ignore the buildings on the land, they should and would have given express instructions to the arbitrator for that purpose'.[2]

In other words, the job of an arbitrator or other independent party is to value the property on the ground, subject to any instructions in the lease. Unless the lease says otherwise, therefore, the valuation must include the effect of any additions or improvements provided by the tenant, even if these consist of a complete building.

1 [1988] 32 EG 55.
2 *Goh Eng Wah v Yap Phooi Yin* [1988] 32 EG 55 at 55.

The hypothetical letting

12.55 We will return to this subject shortly when discussing the disregard of tenant's improvements. The above story, however, should be enough to illustrate that a rent review clause, to be fair to both parties, will have to contain valuation criteria a little more subtle than a simple request to fix a market rent.

The way this is normally achieved is by means of a fiction called the hypothetical letting. After all, if it is a market rent that is to be fixed at the review date, we must ask ourselves how that is normally determined.

The answer is that it is usually fixed in quite different circumstances from those a landlord and tenant are in at a rent review date. A market rent is what a tenant will be willing to pay and a landlord willing to accept for premises that are vacant and available for let. Usually there will be other premises which the tenant could choose instead. Likewise, the landlord will possibly have other tenants to choose from. Neither party, therefore, is under any legal or other compulsion. Moreover, the premises are as provided by the landlord, not yet altered in any way by the tenant. Nor has the property acquired any value in the way of goodwill brought about by the tenant having occupied the property over a period of time.

This is in contrast to the real situation of the parties at a rent review date. The premises are not vacant, the property is not actually on the market. It is occupied by the tenant. Without the landlord's agreement, the tenant is not at liberty to go elsewhere, nor is the landlord free to take another tenant. They are both bound by the contract of lease. It may be that one of them wants out but is being held to the bargain by the other.

Moreover, the tenant, by having occupied the property over a period of time, may be committed to it in other ways, by having made improvements, or by having established goodwill in that particular location. Even in the absence of these, it would probably be easier not to have to move. Unlike the fictional tenant on the lookout for suitable premises, our tenant may well have a vested interest in staying put.

The hypothetical letting, therefore, is a simulation of a real market situation, created for the purpose of a rent review. It is a construction to be made by the valuer in accordance with the instructions in the rent review clause.

The way this is usually achieved is by stating a number of factors that should be taken into account and others that should be left out when making the rental valuation, ie the normal assumptions and disregards.

The normal assumptions

12.56   It is, of course, up to the parties to decide what these should be when drawing up the lease, but common assumptions to be found are:

(1)   that there is a willing lessor and a willing lessee;
(2)   that the premises are vacant;
(3)   that no premium is payable by either party;
(4)   as to the length of the term of the lease yet to run;
(5)   that the tenant's obligations under the lease have been fulfilled; and
(6)   that the hypothetical let is on the same terms as the actual lease.

As we will see, numbers (1), (2), (5) and (6) of these may be implied without being expressly stated in the lease, but it is probably safer to include them. These are not all of the assumptions that are sometimes made, but are some of the more common and important ones.[1]

1 For a more detailed consideration of valuation assumptions, see Ross and McKichan paras 6.19–6.30.

The assumption of a willing lessor and a willing lessee

12.57   The best analysis of these fictional characters was made by Donaldson J in *FR Evans (Leeds) Ltd v English Electric Co Ltd*.[1] Neither of them is the actual landlord or tenant but 'is a complete abstraction, and, like the mule, has neither pride of ancestry nor hope of posterity':

> '[The willing lessor] is a hypothetical person with the right to dispose of the premises on an 18-year lease. As such, he is not afflicted by personal ills such as a cash-flow crisis or importunate mortgagees. Nor is he in the happy position of someone to whom it is largely a matter of indifference whether he lets in October 1976 or waits for the market to improve. He is, in short, a willing lessor. He wants to let the premises at a rent which is appropriate to all the factors which affect the marketability of these premises as industrial premises – for example, geographical location, the extent of the local labour market, the level of local rates and the market rent of competitive premises, that is to say, premises which are directly comparable or which, if not directly comparable, would be considered as viable alternatives by a potential tenant.

> Similarly, in my judgment, the willing lessee is an abstraction – a hypothetical person actively seeking premises to fulfil needs which these premises could fulfil. He will take account of similar factors, but he too will be unaffected by liquidity problems, governmental or other pressures to boost or maintain employment in the area and so on.'[2]

These parties may resemble the actual landlord and tenant, but they need not do so. They are a necessary invention for our market simulation.

In *Dennis & Robinson v Kiossos Establishment*[3] the rent at review was to be a 'full yearly market rent', defined, inter alia, as being that 'at which the property might reasonably be expected to be let on the open market …' It was held that these words implied the assumptions of a willing lessor and lessee (as well as the fact that there would be a letting of the property and a market in which that letting was agreed), even though these assumptions were not expressly stated in the lease.

1 (1978) 36 P&CR 185, (1977) 245 EG 657.
2 *FR Evans (Leeds) Ltd v English Electric Co Ltd* (1978) 36 P&CR 185 at 189-190, 191, (1977) 245 EG 657.
3 (1987) 54 P&CR 282, (1987) 282 EG 857, CA.

The assumption that the premises are vacant

12.58   In the real world, as opposed to the hypothetical let, the tenant may have sublet the property and, if this was taken into account, it might affect the rental value at review. It could have the effect of either increasing or decreasing the rental value depending on the terms of the sublease and the amount of rent payable under it, and thus could either favour the landlord or the tenant.

It is generally thought fairer to both parties to assume vacant possession so that any distortion by subletting will not be taken into account. The assumption of vacant possession will also mean that the tenant's fixtures and fittings, which might have added to the rental value, will also be disregarded.

If no assumption of vacant possession is made, the other terms of the lease may imply it[1] though not if actual sublets were in existence or contemplated at the beginning of the lease.[2]

If vacant possession is assumed, this could imply that any preliminary works necessary to fit out the property for the purpose of the tenant's business had yet to be carried out, and that a reduction in rent was due in order to take account of the fact. But at the time of a rent review the property is already fitted out, and so such an assumption is not in accordance with reality.

The assumption of vacant possession, therefore, is often qualified by a further assumption that the premises are fit for immediate occupation and use.[3]

1 *Avon County Council v Alliance Property Co Ltd* (1981) 258 EG 1181.
2 *Forte & Co Ltd v General Accident Life Assurance Ltd* (1987) 54 P&CR 9, (1986) 279 EG 1227; *Laura Investment Co Ltd v Havering London Borough Council (No 2)* [1993] 08 EG 120, [1992] NPC 117.
3 See also para 12.97 et seq.

The assumption that no premium is payable by either party

12.59   If a tenant pays a capital sum (or premium) at the beginning of the lease, then presumably the rent agreed may be at a lower level than it would have been without such an additional payment. Alternatively, in times of recession a reverse premium may be paid by the landlord (possibly in the form of a rent-free period) as an inducement to the tenant to agree to a rent that may be above the true market level.[1]

In order to determine the true market rent at a rent review, therefore, it should be assumed that no such premium is payable by either party.

1 See also para 12.97 et seq. For an extreme example of a situation where a substantial reverse premium was proposed, see the discussion of *Burgerking v Rachel Charitable Trust* 2006 SLT 224, 2006 GWD 6-112 at para 7.9 et seq.

The term of the lease still to run

12.60   Different assumptions may be made here. Two possible alternatives are that, either the full term of the lease should be taken into account, or only the unexpired residue.

For example, let us suppose that we are at year 20 of a 25-year lease with five-yearly rent reviews. Depending on which assumption is made, this can be valued either as a 25- year lease or a five-year lease.

Each of these assumptions could favour either the landlord or the tenant, depending upon the market conditions prevailing. At one time the assumption that the full term of the lease was left to run would have been thought to favour the landlord, as a tenant would generally have been willing to pay more for a longer period of security of tenure.[1] In recent years, however, when there has been an increasing demand from tenants for shorter leases, this can no longer be assumed to be the case.

Moreover, if the unexpired term of an FRI lease is particularly long, it may be the landlord and not the tenant who will prefer a shorter hypothetical term for rent review purposes. This is because an unusually long FRI lease might involve the tenant in rebuilding works at some stage, thereby making the lease terms more onerous; this, as we will see later, may depress the level of rent that will be fixed at review.[2]

1 *Lynnthorpe Enterprises Ltd v Sidney Smith (Chelsea) Ltd* [1990] 40 EG 130.
2 See *Norwich Union Life Insurance Society v British Railways Board* (1987) 283 EG 846 and para 12.96; see also *Brown v Council of the City of Gloucester* [1998] 16 EG 137, [1997] NPC 154; and *Westside Nominees Ltd v Bolton MBC* (2001) 81 P&CR 11, [2000] L&TR 533.

12.61   Whichever party it might favour in a given market, the reality of the situation is that only the unexpired term of the lease will remain at the review date. It is therefore in accordance with the presumption of reality[1] to assume this and the court, in the absence of express words to the contrary, will not normally assumes that there is a lease for the full original term dating from the review date.[2]

In *Lynnthorpe Enterprises Ltd v Sidney Smith (Chelsea) Ltd*[3] the lease provided that the hypothetical tenancy was to be for a term of years equivalent to the term of the lease. The landlord argued that the full term of the lease should be assumed to remain as at the review date; the court, however, held that the hypothetical term should run from the beginning of the lease, effectively the same as saying that, as at the review date, only the unexpired term would remain.

Likewise, in *St Martins Property Investments Ltd v CIB Properties Ltd*[4] the hypothetical let was stated to be 'for a term equal in duration to the original term thereby granted'. It was held that the original term ran from the beginning of the lease and that the unexpired period should be assumed.

1 See para 12.79 et seq.
2 *Lynnthorpe Enterprises Ltd v Sidney Smith (Chelsea) Ltd* [1990] 40 EG 130; *British Gas plc v Dollar Land Holdings plc* [1992] 12 EG 141; *Ritz Hotel (London) Ltd v Ritz Casino Ltd* [1989] 46 EG 95. See also *Prudential Assurance Co Ltd v Salisbury Handbags Ltd* [1992] 23 EG 117, (1993) 65 P&CR 129 and para 12.83.
3 [1990] 40 EG 130; see also *Chancebutton Ltd v Compass Services UK & Ireland Ltd* [2005] 1 P&CR 8, [2004] 31 EG 94.
4 [1999] L&TR 1.

12.62   There is a possible exception to the above rule if the circumstances are such that to assume the hypothetical term to be the lease's unexpired duration would come into conflict with the presumption of reality.[1]

In *Brown v Council of the City of Gloucester*[2] the lease in question was a 125-year ground lease. Although it was contemplated that the tenant would develop the site, there was no obligation to do so and at the time of the first review the land was still unbuilt upon. The lease provided that the reviewed rent should be 10% of the rent of notional buildings assumed to be constructed and sublet. The lease did not state what the term of these hypothetical sublets should be, and the tenant argued that the unexpired residue of the ground lease should be assumed, ie 120 years. However, the court disagreed.

As we will see later, such a long lease of a building, if it was on FRI terms, would be sufficiently onerous for the tenant to be able to claim a reduced rent.[3] In the real world, although a ground lease might typically be for 125 years, any subleases of buildings, once the land was developed, would invariably be for much shorter terms. The subject matter of the actual let (undeveloped land) was different from that of the hypothetical let (land and buildings) and so it could not be assumed that the term of the one would be appropriate for the other.

The court therefore substituted an assumption that the notional buildings were let on the open market for such term as a landlord might reasonably be expected to grant and a tenant might reasonably be expected to take in all the circumstances available at the review date.

1 For an explanation of the presumption of reality, see para 12.79 et seq.

2 [1998] 16 EG 137, [1997] NPC 154; see also *Westside Nominees Ltd v Bolton MBC* (2001) 81 P&CR 11, [2000] L&TR 533.

3 See para 12.96.

12.63   However, despite the above, the full term of the lease will be assumed if the lease clearly provides that it should, and the presumption of reality will not be applied mechanistically in order to displace the natural wording of the lease.[1]

1 *Canary Wharf Investments (Three) v Telegraph Group Ltd* [2004] 2 P&CR 24, [2003] 46 EG 132.

12.64   In England the situation is further complicated by the fact that a tenant may have a right to renew the lease under the Landlord and Tenant Act 1954 and this may mitigate any effect on the rental value towards the end of a lease.[1] As this act does not apply in Scotland, no such considerations need be taken into account here.

1 *Pivot Properties Ltd v Secretary of State for the Environment* (1981) 41 P&CR 248, (1980) 256 EG 1176, CA.

The assumption that the tenant's obligations under the lease have been fulfilled

12.65   If, for example, necessary repairs have not been carried out, this will probably have the effect of lowering the value of the property. If the lease is a full repairing one then the tenant could potentially benefit, by way of a lower rent, from having failed in a lease obligation. This would obviously be unfair to the landlord, and so an assumption in the above terms is usually made. If not included, it may be implied.[1]

Another application of this principle (which may be stated as a separate assumption) is the assumption that any destruction of or damage to the property has either not occurred or that the property has been reinstated. This will, of course, generally reflect the reality of the situation: even if the property is not yet reinstated at the date of the review, under the lease conditions it generally will be, from the insurance proceeds.

The tenant may want a qualification that the reinstatement assumed should only cover works that fall within the tenant's repairing obligation or are covered by insurance; otherwise (for example) the reviewed rent might include the value of works that had not been carried out and which were the responsibility of the landlord.

1 *Harmsworth Pension Fund Trustees v Charringtons Industrial Holdings* (1985) 49 P&CR 297, 274 EG 588.

The assumption that the hypothetical let is on the same terms as the original lease

12.66 There are many terms in a lease that may affect the rental value of the property. For example, a landlord who undertakes to repair or to insure the property will be able to charge a higher rent than if these were the tenant's responsibility.

This assumption is therefore fair as it reflects the actual position of the parties. If the terms of the lease do not indicate otherwise, this is another assumption that will normally be implied, ie that the hypothetical lease is on the same terms as the actual lease (other than as to the amount of rent).[1]

However, so much can hang on minute differences of wording in individual leases, that once more it is best to include this assumption and to make it clear and explicit; we will see below that infelicitous wording of this assumption can sometimes have unexpected and unwanted consequences.[2]

If a lease provides that the hypothetical let is to be on the same terms as the actual lease, this will include any subsequent variations to those terms that may be agreed by the parties, though not any conditions that are personal in nature and do not bind the parties' successors in title.[3]

In the present context, though not necessarily in other contexts, the expression 'terms of the lease' includes the lease's duration.[4]

1 *Basingstoke and Deane Borough Council v Host Group Ltd* [1988] 1 WLR 348, 1 All ER 824, CA.
2 See para 12.80.
3 *Lynnthorpe Enterprises Ltd v Sidney Smith (Chelsea) Ltd* [1990] 40 EG 130; *Commercial Union Life Assurance Co Ltd v Woolworths* [1996] 1 EGLR 237.
4 *Brown v Council of the City of Gloucester* [1998] 16 EG 137, [1997] NPC 154; *Westside Nominees Ltd v Bolton MBC* (2001) 81 P&CR 11, [2000] L&TR 533; see also para 12.60 et seq.

The usual disregards

12.67 Unlike the assumptions, these have a statutory origin and derive from section 34 of the Landlord and Tenant Act 1954 (which does not apply to Scotland). Under that Act a tenant of business premises in England may apply for a renewal of the lease when it is due to come to an end. If the court grants a renewal, the rent is fixed subject to the disregards set out in section 34.

Their statutory application is therefore when leases are due to end, rather than to rent reviews in mid-term, but the same disregards are generally incorporated into rent review clauses by the terms of the lease, both in Scotland and England. They are:

(1) any effect on rent of the tenant being in occupation;
(2) tenant's goodwill;
(3) tenant's improvements; and
(4) the effect of any licence.

It is of course open to the parties to include disregards different from or additional to those in the Act, but those set out above are the most commonly encountered.

Effect of the tenant being in occupation

12.68 As we have already seen, the hypothetical tenant, who is willing to pay the market rent for the desired property, is a free agent, not yet in occupation of a property and not committed to any one property. Any attempt by the landlord to charge more than the market rent is liable to make such a tenant go elsewhere.

The actual tenant at rent review is less fortunate, in all probability being committed to the property actually occupied, because of goodwill built up there, because of improvements made to that property, or simply because it would be inconvenient to go to the trouble and expense of moving. In the real world such a tenant might be prepared to pay over the odds to stay put. It is generally felt that this is not a factor that the landlord should be entitled to take account of, hence the disregard.

Incidentally, at the end of a lease, as opposed to a mid-term rent review, there seems to be nothing to prevent a Scottish landlord from charging extra rent because the tenant does not want to move. This may be prevented in England by the operation of the Landlord and Tenant Act 1954.

Effect of the tenant's goodwill

12.69 A tenant who has been in business for a period of time, and has been operating well, is likely to have enhanced the value of that business by the build-up of goodwill.

This value is mainly personal to the tenant, rather than something that attaches to the property. However, it is possible that some of it will rub off on the property, particularly in the case of shops, if a business of a particular kind has been carried on in the same location for a long time. A new tenant, who wanted to operate the same type of business, might well be prepared to pay extra in rent to secure that particular property.

This is therefore a feasible component of the market rent, but it would be unfair at rent review to charge extra to the tenant who had been the one to generate that goodwill in the first place.

Even if not expressly stated, this disregard may be implied from the previous one (the disregard of the effect of the tenant being in occupation).[1]

1 *Prudential Assurance Co Ltd v Grand Metropolitan Estate Ltd* [1993] 32 EG 74.

Tenant's improvements

12.70 *Need for disregard* We saw at the beginning of the section, as illustrated in the case of *Goh Eng Wah v Yap Phooi Yin*,[1] why it was right to disregard the effect of tenant's improvements (especially if, as in that case, the improvement involved erecting an entire building): it is unfair that a tenant should be charged for improvements twice, once when paying the capital cost of them, and then again in the form of a higher rent.

Section 34 of the Landlord and Tenant Act 1954 addresses this by requiring the value of improvements carried out under a lease obligation to the landlord to be disregarded, and this exception is usually also included in rent review clauses.

Goh Eng Wah is not an isolated case. In the leading case of *Ponsford v HMS Aerosols Ltd*[2] a factory was leased for 21 years with rent reviews at seven-year intervals. A year after the lease began, the premises burned down and were rebuilt by the landlord from the insurance money. However the tenant, with the landlord's permission, decided to take the opportunity afforded by the rebuilding process to incorporate substantial improvements in the building, which the tenant paid for at a cost of £31,780. When the rent came to be reviewed, the tenant argued that any value it had added to the premises should not be taken into account in assessing the new rent. But nothing was said about this in the lease. It merely said that the tenant should pay a 'reasonable' rent for the relevant period. The House of Lords confirmed, by a majority of three to two, that this did not mean the improvements should be disregarded in assessing the rent.

In *Ravenseft Properties Ltd v Park*[3] the tenant in question erected a supermarket, half on its own land, half on land leased from someone else. It was held that the rent of the leased portion should include the value of the part of the building erected there. There are other cases of tenants suffering a similar fate.[4]

1 [1988] 32 EG 55. See para 12.54.
2 [1979] AC 63, [1978] 2 All ER 837.

3 [1988] 50 EG 52.
4 *Sheerness Steel Co plc v Medway Ports Authority* [1992] 12 EG 138; *Laura Investments v Havering* [1992] 24 EG 136, [1992] NPC 44.

12.71 *Other contra-indications* Where there is no specific disregard, the tenant may nevertheless be saved by other provisions in the lease; for example, if a lease consistently distinguishes between the land and the buildings erected on it, this may be enough to establish that rent should be payable only in respect of the land,[1] and in a case where the rent was described in the lease as a 'ground rent' the result was the same.[2]

Such indications may be enough to displace the *prima facie* assumption that the land should be valued together with all buildings erected upon it.

However, the distinctions between those cases where the lease wording has saved the tenant from disaster and those where it has not have tended to be rather fine, and there is no substitute for a clearly-stated disregard of the tenant's improvements.

This is arguably the most important of all the valuation criteria and should always be expressly included in a rent review clause as an essential component of the hypothetical letting.

1 *Ipswich Town Football Club Co Ltd v Ipswich Borough Council* [1988] 32 EG 49; *British Airways PLC v Heathrow Airport* [1992] 1 EGLR 141, 19 EG 157; *Braid v Walsall Metropolitan Borough Council* (1999) 78 P&CR 94, [1998] NPC 35; *Coors Holdings Ltd v Dow Properties Ltd* [2007] 2 P&CR 22, [2007] NPC 37.
2 *Guildford Borough Council v Cobb* [1994] 16 EG 147, 1 EGLR 156.

12.72 *Scottish position* Although all of the case law referred to above is English, there is no doubt that the same principles apply in Scotland. We have already seen that any buildings or other heritable fixtures added to the leased subjects would normally become the property of the landlord,[1] and it would seem to follow that, in the absence of agreement to the contrary, they should be included in any rental valuation of the property.

This interpretation is implicit in *Pik Facilities Ltd v Lord Advocate*[2] and the matter was discussed at some length in *Ashtead Plant Hire Co Ltd v Granton Central Developments Ltd.*[3]

1 See para 10.39 et seq.
2 1997 SCLR 855.
3 [2020] CSIH 2; 2020 SC 244. See the discussion of this case at para 12.89.

12.73 *Trade fixtures* Unless the lease clearly states otherwise, trade fixtures will *not* normally be included in the rental valuation at a rent review.[1] Trade fixtures are those added for the purposes of the tenant's business, and which the tenant is entitled to remove.[2]

1 *New Zealand Government Property Corp v HM & S Ltd* [1982] QB 1145, (1982) 44 P&CR 329; *Ocean Accident & Guarantee Corporation v Next plc* [1996] 33 EG 91, [1995] NPC 185.
2 See para 10.41.

12.74 *New lease with same landlord* If a tenant enters a new lease with the same landlord, it should be made clear in the new lease that the value of improvements made during the currency of the earlier lease or leases should also be disregarded.

In *Brett v Brett Essex Golf Club Ltd*,[1] the tenant golf club laid out the land as a golf course and built a clubhouse. Later they entered into a new lease of the property with the same landlord. As the course and clubhouse were already incorporated in the property when the new lease was entered, it was held that their considerable value could not be disregarded as a tenant's improvement when the rent came up for review.

1 (1986) 52 P&CR 330, 278 EG 1476, CA; see also *Panther Shop Investments Ltd v Keith Pople Ltd* (1987) 282 EG 594.

12.75 *Landlord's consent* It is a usual provision in leases that tenants must obtain their landlord's permission before carrying out any alterations or improvements. Also, in rent review clauses it is common to qualify the disregard of improvements to the effect that they will only be disregarded where the landlord's permission has been obtained for them.

Such a provision was included in the lease in *Hamish Cathie Travel England Ltd v Insight International Tours Ltd*.[1] The tenant failed to get the landlord's consent to alterations he made and it was held that their value could not be disregarded at the rent review.

1 [1986] 1 EGLR 244.

12.76 *Standard of improvements* In *Orchid Lodge (UK) Ltd v Extel Computing Ltd*,[1] the tenant carried out alterations of a very high standard (described by the landlord's lawyer as a 'Rolls-Royce job'). It was agreed that the standard disregard of tenant's improvements (incorporated from the Landlord and Tenant Act 1954) meant that the full value of these could not be taken into account.

However, since it was also to be assumed that the premises were fit for use and occupation, the landlord argued that the rent should include the value of whatever hypothetical improvements (of a lower standard than those actually carried out) would have been necessary to make the premises fit for occupation for the tenant's use.

The Court of Appeal held that all improvements, actual or hypothetical, had to be discounted; to do anything else would have involved the surveyor valuing a 'hypothetical building in a dreamland of his own'.[2]

1 [1991] 32 EG 57, [1991] 2 EGLR 116; see also *Iceland Frozen Foods plc v Starlight Investments Ltd* [1992] 07 EG 117, 1 EGLR 126
2 [1991] 32 EG 57 at 59 per Dillon LJ.

12.77 *Alterations that lower the property's value* It should be noted that the improvements disregard does not always work in the tenant's favour: it can be in the landlord's interest also to have it included.

The reason is that alterations made to the property may not always add to its value. They may be to a poor standard. Or they may have the effect of adapting the premises for the specialised business of the tenant, which could lower their market value to other tenants with different types of business. It would obviously be unfair to the landlord if this had the effect of lowering the rent that could be charged at review.

In light of this, it would perhaps be more accurate to refer in the disregard to 'alterations' or 'alterations and improvements' rather than merely 'improvements' carried out by the tenant. This ensures a situation that is fair to both parties.

Another way of dealing with this point is to include an assumption that no work has been carried out by the tenant that has diminished the rental value of the premises.[1]

1 See Ross and McKichan para 6.25.

Effect of a licence

12.78 This may refer to a betting or gaming licence, or a licence to sell alcohol. The theory is that any effect on rent caused by the fact that the tenant holds such a licence should be disregarded, presumably because this value is personal to the tenant and not an attribute of the property.

This can be important, as it is a field where a lot of money may be involved. In *Cornwall Coast Country Club v Cardrange Ltd,*[1] which related to a casino in Mayfair, the case turned on, inter alia, the precise effect of a lease provision for the disregard of the tenant's gaming licence. The tenant's estimate of the market rent was £180,000, whereas the landlord thought it should have been £3,000,000. Obviously this is an area where the stakes can be high.

1 [1987] 1 EGLR 146, (1987) 282 EG 1664; see also *Daejan Investments v Cornwall Coast Country Club* (1985) 50 P&CR 157, (1985) 273 EG 1122; and *Ritz Hotel (London) Ltd v Ritz Casino Ltd* [1989] 46 EG 95.

Presumption of reality

12.79   Just as the presumption against time being of the essence has operated to modify some of the harsher consequences of rent review timetables, another presumption, the presumption of reality, has developed that may mitigate the more wayward effects of the valuation criteria in some leases.

The presumption may be rebutted by the clear intention of the parties as expressed in the lease wording; however, where different interpretations are possible, the court will choose the one that conforms to the commercial reality of the situation.

An early manifestation of the principle was its application to clauses that had conferred undeserved windfalls upon landlords by excluding the effect of future reviews.

12.80   *Excluding the effect of future reviews*   We saw earlier that there is generally included an assumption that the hypothetical let will be on the same terms as the original let.[1] In many clauses there was added a qualification that the terms will be the same 'other than those relating to rent'. The obvious reason for this is that the valuer should be free to depart from the original rent stated in the lease when fixing a new rent at review.

However, there have been cases where it has been held that a qualification in these terms also excludes the rent review terms.[2] This can confer an unexpected (and undeserved) windfall upon the landlord. It means, for example, that a lease with rent reviews will be valued as if there were no reviews at all, and the landlord will be able to charge a premium (as much as 20 per cent in some cases) on the untrue assumption that there will be no further opportunity to raise the rent before the end of the lease.

1 See para 12.66.
2 See eg *National Westminster Bank v Arthur Young McLelland Moores & Co (No 1)* [1985] 1 WLR 1123, 2 All ER 817.

12.81   *The British Gas rules*   In *British Gas Corporation v Universities Superannuation Scheme Ltd*[1] the then Vice-Chancellor, Sir

Nicholas Browne-Wilkinson, made an admirable attempt to steer such interpretations back into the realm of reality.

Pointing out that the logical conclusion of excluding all provisions relating to rent would be an absurd situation in which the valuer had to ignore the tenant's obligation to pay the rent and the landlord's remedies for non-payment, he went on to produce rules of thumb to assist interpretation in such cases:

'(a) words in a rent exclusion provision which require all provisions as to rent to be disregarded produce a result so manifestly contrary to commercial common sense that they cannot be given literal effect;

(b) other clear words which require the rent review provision (as opposed to all provisions of the lease) to be disregarded ... must be given effect to, however wayward the result, and

(c) subject to (b), in the absence of special circumstances it is proper to give effect to the underlying commercial purpose of a rent review clause and to construe the words so as to give effect to that purpose by requiring future rent reviews to be taken into account in fixing the open market rental under the hypothetical letting.'[2]

1 [1986] 1 All ER 978, 1 WLR 398.
2 *British Gas Corporation v Universities Superannuation Scheme Ltd* [1986] 1 All ER 978 at 984.

12.82   In *Equity & Law Life Assurance plc v Bodfield Ltd*[1] the Court of Appeal approved the guidelines but emphasised that they were not mechanistic rules of construction to be applied rigidly in every case. Priority had always to be given to the actual wording of the individual lease, and in that particular case and in some others subsequent to the *British Gas* decision, the wording was nevertheless held to be sufficiently clear to exclude the effect of future reviews.[2]

There are other cases, however, where the guidelines have been successfully applied.[3]

1 [1987] 1 EGLR 124, (1987) 54 P&CR 290.
2 *General Accident Fire & Life Assurance Corpn plc v Electronic Data Processing Co plc* (1987) 53 P&CR 189, 281 EG 65; *Prudential Assurance Co Ltd v Salisbury Handbags Ltd*, [1992] 23 EG 117, (1993) 65 P&CR 129.
3 *British Home Stores plc v Ranbrook Properties Ltd* (1988) 16 EG 80; *Prudential Assurance Co Ltd v 99 Bishopsgate Ltd* [1992] 03 EG 120, 1 EGLR 119.

12.83   Even where the effect of future reviews has been clearly excluded, the presumption of reality may operate in some other respect to steer the hypothetical let away from absurdity and back to common sense and commercial reality.

In *Prudential Assurance Co Ltd v Salisburys Handbags Ltd*[1] the effect of the exclusion was potentially very serious for the tenant since, following the first review in 1982, the unexpired term of the lease was 85 years. Thus the tenant faced the possibility that, at seven-yearly intervals throughout the currency of the lease, the rent would be determined on the preposterous assumption that there would be no reviews for almost a century. It was held that such a lease was 'so far outside the experience and expertise of an ordinary valuer as to be properly regarded as extinct'.[2]

There was no express provision that the term of the hypothetical let should be the actual unexpired term of the lease; in such circumstances it was held inappropriate to assume this, and instead it was held preferable to assume a much shorter term, which might vary at each review at the discretion of the valuer, depending upon the prevailing market conditions. This would presumably have the effect of the tenant paying a more realistic rent, both at the current review and those in the future.[3]

1 [1992] 23 EG 117, (1993) 65 P&CR 129.
2 *Prudential Assurance Co Ltd v Salisburys Handbags Ltd* [1992] 23 EG 117 at 119 per Mr Justice Chadwick.
3 See also *Brown v Council of the City of Gloucester* [1998] 16 EG 137, [1997] NPC 154; and para 12.62.

12.84   *Headline rents*   The phrase 'presumption of reality' has been expressly used and the principle applied to prevent landlords from charging inflated (or 'headline') rents in another situation where well-intended review provisions have yielded bizarre interpretations. This topic is considered in depth below.[1]

1 See para 12.97 et seq.

12.85   *Other applications of the principle*   In recent years there have been a number of other cases where the courts have interpreted valuation criteria in favour of commercial common sense and fairness to the parties. Not all have expressly used the phrase 'presumption of reality', but the principle applied has effectively been the same.

In *Historic House Hotels Ltd v Cadogan Estates*[1] the landlord granted various licences authorising alterations to be made by the tenant. The tenant in turn agreed that, when the works were completed, the lease conditions would apply to the altered premises as if they had originally been included in the lease.

In relation to the lease conditions generally this was an obvious common sense provision. However, the landlord argued that the provision had the effect of excluding the alterations from the disregard of tenant's improvements in the lease; in other words, that they were deemed to have been part of the original premises provided by the landlord and not a tenant's improvement at all.[2] In rejecting this interpretation, Dillon LJ said:

> 'Regarding this as a commercial bargain between the parties I would expect something very much clearer if it was to be established that a disregard normally regarded as fair and reasonable is to be inapplicable ... I would not expect a matter so unexpected as overriding the disregard to be dealt with in such an oblique manner as this.'[3]

1 [1995] 11 EG 140, [1994] NPC 119.
2 See para 12.70 et seq.
3 *Historic House Hotels Ltd v Cadogan Estates* [1995] 11 EG 140 at 141.

12.86 In *Ashworth Frazer Ltd v Gloucester City Council*[1] the council granted a lease of an area of land for development. The lease contained a formula whereby the reviewed rent was to be based either on the existing rent or on a proportion of the rents 'receivable' from sublets.

The tenants disposed of the developed site by partial assignments (assignations) rather than by subletting, and one of their assignees argued that, there being no sublets, the formula was unworkable and the existing rent should remain payable; this was £702, an apportionment of the original ground rent, which of course was a mere fraction of the rental value of the developed property.

The court held that 'receivable' did not mean rents which the tenant was entitled to receive from existing subtenants (of which there were none), but those capable of being received from hypothetical subtenants. The word 'receivable' could bear either interpretation and the latter accorded 'with the clear commercial purpose of the rent review provisions'.

1 [1997] 26 EG 150, [1997] NPC 2.

12.87 In *Dukeminster (Ebbgate House One) Ltd v Somerfield Property Co Ltd*[1] the review clause in the lease of a warehouse allowed the rent to be fixed at the level paid for notional premises, which were, somewhat vaguely, defined as similar warehouse properties within a 35-mile radius of the leased property in Ross-on-Wye.

Since there was a wide variation among the rents of the qualifying properties, the landlord wanted to select the highest of these. The court, however, favoured an amendment to the formula, restricting its application to similar warehouses actually in Ross-on-Wye or in a comparable location. This was the commercial solution:

'[I]n the absence of clear words, notional premises cannot be taken to be such as to produce a valuation, whether it be too high or too low, which cannot reasonably have been intended to apply to the actual premises.'[2]

Deciding what were comparable locations, the court believed, was an exercise within the expertise of experienced valuers.

However, in *Beegas Nominees Ltd v Decco Ltd*,[3] where a very similar provision was expressed in clear and unambiguous terms and there was no reason to suppose that an error had crept into the drafting of the lease, it was held that the terms of the lease should be applied, even although it meant departing from normal valuation practice.

1   (1998) 75 P&CR 154, [1997] 40 EG 157.
2   (1998) 75 P&CR 154 at 158 per Nourse LJ.
3   [2003] 43 EG 138, 153 NLJ 1271.

12.88   In *Brown v Council of the City of Gloucester*[1] the court refused to apply the unexpired term of 120 years in a ground lease to notional sublets of buildings that had yet to be built, since in the real world leases of developed sites were in practice never granted for such extended terms and, if they had been, would have been at a much reduced rent.

1   [1998] 16 EG 137, [1997] NPC 154; see also paras 12.62 and 12.83.

12.89   In *Ashtead Plant Hire Co Ltd v Granton Central Developments Ltd*[1] the Inner House held that a disregard of 'the value of any buildings or other constructions erected on and any improvements carried out to the lease subjects' was limited to buildings and improvements carried out by either the landlord or tenant after the lease had been entered into. As such, buildings which were already erected at lease commencement should not be disregarded. The court was clear that commercial common sense was of importance in interpreting the lease and that disregarding the buildings standing at lease commencement would have resulted in a windfall gain for the tenant at review, and a disproportionate burden on the landlord.

1   [2020] CSIH 2; 2020 SC 244.

12.90   The presumption of reality, therefore, can steer the valuation criteria in some leases in the direction of commercial good sense; in other cases, however, where the lease wording is sufficiently clear, wayward valuations may still be the result.

Effect of lease restrictions

12.91   If the provisions of a lease are particularly onerous, it can have the effect of depressing the level of rent that may be fixed at a rent review.

This is because a restrictive lease is a less marketable commodity than one which is not. In a real market situation there will be fewer potential tenants willing to take it on. The same will therefore be true of the hypothetical letting, provided that it is on the same terms as the actual lease; and, as we saw above, this is normally assumed to be the case.[1] Problems in this area have generally related to restrictive use (or user) clauses or restrictive provisions regarding alienation (assignation or subletting), but other onerous restrictions can have a similar effect.

This means that, when a lease is being drafted, a landlord may have to balance two conflicting priorities. From the point of view of estate management, it will be desirable to have lease conditions that maximise the landlord's control of the situation, particularly regarding how the property may be used and to whom the lease may be assigned. However, if this control is too tight, this policy may rebound upon the landlord financially when the rent comes to be reviewed.

1 See para 12.66.

12.92   *Use clause*   In *Plinth Property Investments v Mott, Hay & Anderson*[1] a lease provided that the property could only be used as an office for the purpose of the tenant's business of consulting civil engineers. The court held that, at rent review, the arbitrator was justified in fixing a rent considerably lower than the full market rental (£89,000 instead of £130,455). This was because the lease was theoretically only assignable to other civil engineers and therefore had a lower market value than if the use had not been thus restricted.

The landlord argued that if the tenant ever wanted to assign, it would be willing to waive the restriction, but this was held to be irrelevant; the tenant was entitled to assume that the landlord would insist upon its legal rights. Alternatively, if the landlord agreed to a change it might insist on the tenant paying some financial consideration in return.

A landlord cannot get round this difficulty by unilaterally imposing a wider range of uses on the tenant purely to justify a rent increase at rent review. In *C & A Pensions Trustees Ltd v British Vita Investments Ltd*[2] it was held that the landlord was not entitled to impose upon the tenant an additional number of authorised uses which the tenant had neither requested nor wanted.

1 (1979) 38 P&CR 361, (1978) 249 EG 1167.
2 (1984) 272 EG 63.

12.93   On the other hand, if the landlord goes even further and restricts the use, not just to a narrow category, but to one named person, ie the actual tenant, it will not have the effect of depressing the rent payable at review. This would create a hypothetical lease with only one possible tenant, which is incompatible with an open market situation, and the court will be forced to amend the lease to make the rent review provisions workable.

In *Law Land Co Ltd v Consumers Association Ltd*[1] the Court of Appeal held in these circumstances that the hypothetical lease should have a use clause in which the tenant's name had been deleted, thereby opening up the hypothetical market by freeing it of any use restrictions at all.

However, any use restriction which is less total, and is compatible with some kind of hypothetical market, however restricted, will have a similar effect to that in *Plinth*.[2]

1 (1980) 255 EG 617, 2 EGLR 109, CA; see also *Orchid Lodge (UK) Ltd v Extel Computing Ltd* [1991] 32 EG 57, 2 EGLR 116; and *Post Office Counters Ltd v Harlow District Council* (1992) 63 P&CR 46, [1991] 36 EG 151.
2 *James v British Crafts Centre* (1988) 55 P&CR 56, (1987) 282 EG 1251; *SI Pension Trustees Ltd v Ministerio de Marina de la Republica Peruana* [1988] 13 EG 48; *Homebase Ltd v Scottish Provident Institution* 2004 SLT 296, 2004 SCLR 44.

12.94   *Alienation*   A restrictive alienation clause, eg an absolute prohibition against assignation without the landlord's consent, will have a similar effect as a restrictive use clause in depressing the rent level at a review.[1] Such a clause also restricts the number of potential tenants in the hypothetical market.

1 *Post Office Counters Ltd v Harlow District Council* (1992) 63 P&CR 46, [1991] 36 EG 151 (a reduction of 7.5%); see also *Fiveways Properties Ltd v Secretary of State for the Environment* [1990] 31 EG 50 (a reduction of 5.5%).

12.95   *Avoiding the effects of restrictions on use and/or alienation*   There are several methods by which a landlord may seek to avoid the above difficulty:

(1)   By a provision that the landlord's consent to an assignation or subletting or (as the case may be) to a change of use 'will not unreasonably be withheld'. This will probably open up the restriction sufficiently to allow the full market rent to be charged.[1]
(2)   By widening the category of permitted uses. While a landlord of a shopping centre (for example) may want to limit each tenant to a particular business in order to control the trade mix, it is arguable whether this is equally necessary for other types of commercial property.
One way to achieve a broader control is to limit the tenant to a use within a particular class of the use classes order.[2] This could (for

example) prevent a change from shop to office use, or from light to heavy industry, without restricting the hypothetical market in a way that would depress the rent.[3]

(3) By keeping restrictions in the use clause or alienation clause of the actual lease, but assuming more liberal provisions in the hypothetical lease for the purpose of a rent review. Such an arrangement may be enforceable.[4] However, the lease wording will have to make the situation absolutely clear in order to overcome the presumption that the terms of the hypothetical lease will be the same as those of the actual lease.[5]

However, if such an assumption were to apply, the valuer would be entitled to take into account the fact that, in the hypothetical world created for the purpose of rent review, the tenant would be free to apply for planning permission for an alternative use, even although the actual terms of the lease might prohibit this in the real world.[6] This could also therefore counter the depressive effect of the lease restriction upon the rent.

1 *Tea Trade Properties Ltd v CIN Properties Ltd* [1990] 22 EG 67.
2 Currently the Town and Country Planning (Use Classes) (Scotland) Order 1997 (SI 3061).
3 For examples of this method and some associated problems see *Wolff v Enfield London Borough Council* (1988) 55 P&CR 78, (1987) 281 EG 1320 and *Brewers' Company v Viewplan* [1989] 45 EG 153.
4 *Bovis Group Pension Fund Ltd v GC Flooring & Furnishing Ltd* (1984) 269 EG 1252; *Sheerness Steel Co plc v Medway Ports Authority* [1992] 12 EG 138, 1 EGLR 133; *McDonalds Real Estate LLP v Arundel Corporation* [2008] 2 EGLR 53, 30 EG 84.
5 *Basingstoke & Deane Borough Council v the Host Group Ltd* [1988] 1 WLR 348, (1987) 284 EG 1587; *Postel Properties Ltd v Greenwell* [1992] 47 EG 106
6 *McDonalds Real Estate LLP v Arundel Corporation* [2008] 2 EGLR 53, 30 EG 84.

12.96 *Other lease restrictions* Onerous provisions other than those relating to use or alienation, eg the tenant's obligation to carry out repairs, can also have the effect of narrowing the hypothetical market. In *Norwich Union Life Insurance Society v British Railways Board*[1] the tenant's repairing obligation included an obligation to 'rebuild, reconstruct or replace' the property when necessary. As the lease was for 150 years, it was held that such rebuilding by the tenants might well prove necessary and this was considered sufficiently onerous to justify a rent reduction of 27.5%.

1 (1987) 283 EG 846; see also para 12.62.

Effect of rent-free periods and inducements

12.97 *Period for fitting out etc* It has for a long time been common for landlords, at the beginning of a lease, to allow a tenant a period free of rent. Traditionally this would be for at least three months, or even longer, and it acknowledged the fact that there would be an initial period when the tenant would not be earning money from the property and might be incurring some expense.

A tenant who was intending to occupy the property personally would need to spend some time and money fitting it out for that purpose; in the case of a larger property, the tenant might intend to sublet part or all of it and would need time to find subtenants.

12.98 As we have seen, the purpose of the hypothetical letting is to simulate a market situation, ie apply the valuation criteria for a new let to a mid-term rent review. It could be argued from this (and some tenants did) that, following a review, a tenant would be entitled to the same rent-free period as the one at the beginning of a lease, perhaps not a gap in the rental payments, but the equivalent benefit in the form of a rent reduction.

There is some logic in this, but it does not accord with reality, as a tenant, after a rent review, would not in fact normally have to fit out the property or find subtenants.

Nevertheless, in *99 Bishopsgate v Prudential Assurance Co Ltd*,[1] it was held by the Court of Appeal that the standard assumption of vacant possession[2] had precisely this effect:

> 'On the review of the rent of a 30-storey office building in the City, the arbitrator found that the most likely tenant would have wanted only part of the building for his own use and would have sublet the rest. He would have bargained for a rent-free period to cover the time needed to find subtenants and the rent-free period he would have to allow them to fit out their premises. Having regard to the size of the building in relation to the general supply of similar office space in the City, he would have been able to secure a 16-month rent-free period on a 14-year letting. The arbitrator therefore found that if one had to assume that the building was empty one would have to discount the rent which would have been paid by a tenant whose activities were already up and running.'[3]

The judge at first instance and the Court of Appeal both agreed that this necessarily followed from the assumption of a letting with vacant possession.

1 (1985) 273 EG 984.
2 See para 12.58.
3 *99 Bishopsgate Ltd v Prudential Assurance Co Ltd*, as paraphrased by Hoffman LJ in *Co-operative Wholesale Society Ltd v National Westminster Bank plc* [1995] 01 EG 111 at 112, [1994] NPC 147.

12.99 *'Fit for immediate occupation and use'* Landlords sought to get round the above problem by including an assumption that the property was 'fit for immediate occupation and use', or some such phraseology.

Then some of them tried to argue that this assumption not only had the intended effect of denying a tenant a deduction in lieu of a rent-free period, but also allowed the landlord to charge more than the market rate. After all, a hypothetical tenant in the hypothetical open market who was entering premises that were already fitted out should perhaps be prepared to pay more as a result.

However, the courts have not been prepared to go along with this, and have held that the effect of the assumption is (as originally intended) to deprive the tenant of the right to a discount, without giving the landlord an undeserved bonus.[1] This is obviously fair and reflects the reality of the situation.

1 *London & Leeds Estates Ltd v Paribas Ltd* (1993) 66 P&CR 218, [1993] 30 EG 89; see also *Iceland Frozen Foods plc v Starlight Investments Ltd* [1992] 07 EG 117, 1 EGLR 126 and *Pontsarn Investments v Kansallis-Osake-Pankki* [1992] 22 EG 103, [1992] NPC 56.

12.100 *Inducements and headline rents* Landlords have sought other ways of getting round the above problem, eg by including an assumption 'that any rent-free period or concessionary rent or any other inducement ... which may be offered in the case of a new letting in the open market at the relevant date of review shall have expired or been given immediately before the relevant date of review'.[2] In due course, however, such assumptions also proved to have an unintended effect, in this case to the advantage of landlords.

The leases that came before the courts for scrutiny in this connection were mainly entered into before the property market went into recession towards the end of the 1980s. When they were drafted, rent-free periods were generally only granted for the reasons given above, ie to allow tenants time for fitting out and/or to find subtenants, and it was right that this should not allow them to claim equivalent concessions at rent review.

However, with the recession the practice grew up of landlords granting extended rent-free periods for a quite different reason. In order to maintain rent levels at a time when market forces might have caused them to fall, landlords often persuaded tenants of new lets to pay 'headline' rents, above the real market level, in return for which tenants would be granted substantial rent-free periods. The length of these would vary according to the state of the market or the length of the lease, but were frequently for a period of years.

The question then arising was this: could a clause designed to deny a tenant a discount at review in respect of a rent-free period for fitting-out etc, also deprive the tenant of a discount for the other type of rent-free period? If it did, a tenant at a rent review could be saddled with a headline rent, substantially above the market level, and the landlord would receive an undeserved windfall. The reviewed rent would be fixed in comparison with those agreed for new lets, but without the benefit of any inducement that might have persuaded a new tenant to pay over the odds.

1 *Co-operative Wholesale Society Ltd v National Westminster Bank plc* [1995] 01 EG 111, [1994] NPC 147.

12.101   As usual, individual cases differed according to the wording of the particular leases, but it soon became clear that tenants could, in some circumstances, end up paying headline rents. Several cases where this happened were taken to the Court of Appeal, which gave a joint judgment in respect of four of them.[1] In only one of these, where the wording allowed no other conclusion, was the tenant left paying a headline rent.[2]

In its construction of the clauses, the court applied the 'presumption of reality'[3] ie that courts should favour the construction most likely to give effect to the commercial purpose of the lease:

> 'So, in the case of rent-free periods, it is easy to see why the parties should not wish to allow the tenant a reduction simply because the fiction of vacant possession entails that the incoming tenant would have the expense of moving in and fitting out. A clause which excludes the assumption that he would have this expense is more in accordance with the presumption of reality than one which does not. On the other hand, a clause which deems the market rent to be the headline rent obtainable after a rent-free period granted simply to disguise the fall in the rental value of the property is not in accordance with the basic purpose of a rent review clause. It enables a landlord to obtain an increase in rent without any rise in property values or fall in the value of money, but simply by reason of changes in the way the market is choosing to structure the financial packaging of the deal.

> It therefore seems to me that, in the absence of unambiguous language, a court should not be ready to construe a rent review clause as having this effect.'[4]

However, if the terms of a lease clearly oblige a tenant to pay a headline rent, this will be enforced.

1 *Co-operative Wholesale Society Ltd v National Westminster Bank plc*; *Scottish Amicable Life Assurance Society v Middleton Potts & Co*; *Broadgate Square plc v*

Lehman Brothers Ltd; and *Prudential Nominees Ltd v Greenham Trading Ltd* [1995] 01 EG 111, [1994] NPC 147.

2 *Broadgate Square plc v Lehman Brothers Ltd* ibid.

3 See para 12.79 et seq.

4 *Co-operative Wholesale Society Ltd v National Westminster Bank plc* [1995] 01 EG 111 at 113 per Hoffmann LJ.

12.102 *Scottish authority* In *Church Commissioners for England and another v Etam*[1] the approach of the English courts was followed and the above extract from *Co-operative Wholesale Society v National Westminster Bank* was quoted with approval. As a result, the landlord was held *not* to be entitled to charge a headline rent.

The rent review clause in this case does not make easy reading, and it illustrates the point that attempts by landlords to protect their positions with unduly complex wording may be self-defeating. Once the court has steered its way through the double negatives and apparent contradictions, it may arrive at an interpretation that is the opposite of the one intended; at best, enough ambiguity may be created for it to apply the presumption of reality.

1 1997 SC 116, 1997 SLT 38; see also Ian Doran 'Rent Review: Headline Rents and Open Market Rents' (1995) 40 JLSS 349.

12.103 *Effect of onerous lease provisions*[1] We saw above that unduly onerous or restrictive lease provisions will have the effect of depressing the level of rent that may be fixed at review. It has been argued that a rent review provision that unambiguously allows the imposition of a headline rent is an onerous provision that will have such an effect.[2] In other words, a clear mandate to fix a headline rent may prevent a headline rent being fixed.

1 See para 12.91 et seq.

2 Ian Doran 'Rent Review: Headline Rents and Open Market Rents' (1995) 40 JLSS 349; see also Richard Porter and Michael Langdon 'Headline Rents – the Current Problems' [1995] 02 EG 130.

Upward or downward reviews

12.104 One important valuation criterion remains to be considered. In the past it has been normal for rent review clauses to provide that any review should be upward only. At one time this would not worry tenants: in the mid-1970s, for example, when inflation was high, the prospect of rents falling would not seem very likely.

Since then, however, there have been periods of recession in the property market when rental values have fallen; in such a market, a tenant whose lease contains an upwards-only provision may emerge from a rent review with a rent that is higher than the current market value.

12.105   There are three main forms that the relevant provision is likely to take:

(1)   *Upward only (or 'ratchet') provision*   This states that the reviewed rent will be the existing rent, or the market rent, whichever is the higher. If rents have fallen, therefore, the rent will stay the same, but can never go down.

(2)   *'Floor' or 'threshold' provision*   This allows reviews to be either upward or downward, subject to the proviso that the rent may not drop below a stated level. Usually this will be the original rent fixed at the beginning of the lease. In such a case, therefore, the first review will necessarily be upward only.

In subsequent reviews, however, a downward review may be allowed if the market rent is now lower than the one fixed at the previous review. It is not clear how many of these clauses were intended to operate in this way; at least some of them seem to be failed attempts at ratchet provisions, drafted at a time when falling rents were not anticipated.

(3)   *Upward or downward provision*   This allows the rent to be fixed at the current market level, whether or not it would involve an increase or decrease, and without being subject to any threshold or floor. The review may be initiated either by the landlord or the tenant.

12.106   *New leases*   In new leases it is obviously in the interest of tenants to negotiate a review provision of the third type. The right of the tenant, as well as the landlord, to initiate a review is a necessary corollary: otherwise, when rents are falling, the landlord may conveniently neglect to send a trigger notice, and the mere presence in the lease of an upward or downward review does not automatically give the tenant the right to initiate a review unless this has also specifically been provided for.[1] As a result, a rent review provision that allows for downward reviews but without giving the tenant this power, will in practice be no different from an upward-only clause since, at a time of falling rents, the landlord will be able to prevent a review taking place at all.

Landlords, of course, may well resist the inclusion of such provisions and, as usual, the result may depend upon the relative negotiating strengths of the parties.

1   *Hemingway Realty Ltd v Clothworkers Co* [2005] L&TR 21, 19 EG 176.

12.107 *Older leases* In the case of leases drafted before the possibility of falling rents seemed likely, problems of construction have arisen where the lease failed to make it absolutely clear whether or not a ratchet provision was intended, or whether a landlord had the right to prevent a downward review by failing to initiate the review process.

A number of such leases came before the courts in the mid-1990s, when their rents came to be reviewed for the first time since the previous recession. Not surprisingly, they tended to turn upon individual points of construction from which it is difficult to generalise.

12.108 A ratchet provision has been assumed in several cases where the lease wording implied that this was intended.[1] Where it is clear from the lease that only the landlord can trigger a review this is an indication (though it is not conclusive) that a ratchet provision is intended,

'as the parties would not have contemplated that the landlord would seek a review in circumstances where it was likely that the rent would not be increased'.[2]

1 *Brimican Investments Ltd v Blue Circle Heating Ltd* [1995] EGCS 18, [1995] NPC 18; *Secretary of State for the Environment v Associated Newspapers Holdings Ltd* (1996) 72 P&CR 395, [1995] NPC 161; *Melanesian Mission Trust Board v Australian Mutual Provident Society* (1997) 74 P&CR 297, 41 EG 153; *Standard Life Assurance v Unipath Ltd* [1997] 38 EG 152, (1998) 75 P&CR 473; in *Associated Newspapers* the decision that the rent review clause contained a ratchet and not a 'floor' provision resulted in the rent being fixed at £1,575,000 instead of £530,000.
2 *Standard Life Assurance v Unipath Ltd* [1997] 38 EG 152 at 154 per Aldous LJ.

12.109 Even if there is not a clear upward-only provision, the landlord may nevertheless prevent a downward review if the lease makes it plain that only the landlord has the right to initiate the process.[1]

On the other hand, if the lease terms appear to make the occurrence of a review mandatory, the landlord's sole right to initiate the process may be considered merely to be machinery which cannot be utilised to prevent a review from taking place.[2]

1 *Harben Style Ltd v Rhodes Trust* [1995] 17 EG 125, [1994] NPC 99; *Sunflower Services Ltd v Unisys New Zealand Ltd* (1997) 74 P&CR 112, [1997] NPC 21.
2 *Royal Bank of Scotland v Jennings* (1998) 75 P&CR 458, [1997] 19 EG 152; *Addin v Secretary of State for the Environment* [1997] 14 EG 132, [1997] 1 EGLR 99.

12.110 *Presumption of reality* We saw earlier that problems of construction can be resolved in favour of the interpretation that most favours the commercial purpose of a rent review provision.[1] However, the presumption may be of limited value in deciding whether a rent review provision is a ratchet or upward/downward one, as both are consistent with commercial practice. In *Secretary of State for the*

Environment v Associated Newspapers Holdings Ltd[2] it was held that ratchet provisions, being common in commercial leases, could not be considered as conferring a windfall upon the landlord.

On the other hand, in *Norwich Union Life Insurance Society v Attorney General*[3] it was held that evidence that only a small minority of commercial leases negotiated in the open market lacked a ratchet provision was also consistent with an upwards/downwards provision having been negotiated on commercial terms: the possibility of a downward review might have been compensated for by other lease provisions that favoured the landlord.

It has also been decided that a provision allowing an upward or downward review is not inherently unfair: whereas a ratchet provision may operate against a tenant's interest, an upward/downward provision, being designed to produce a market rent in all cases, is fair to both parties.[4]

In *Addin v Secretary of State for the Environment*[5] the underlying commercial purpose of the lease was instrumental in preventing the landlord from frustrating a downward review by failing to send a trigger notice.

1 See para 12.79 et seq.
2 (1996) 72 P&CR 395 at 400 and 401 per Gibson LJ.
3 [1995] EGCS 85, [1995] NPC 86.
4 *Forbouys v Newport Borough Council* [1994] 24 EG 156; this case related to the renewal of an English lease under the Landlord and Tenant Act 1954.
5 [1997] 14 EG 132, [1997] 1 EGLR 99.

SETTLING OF DISPUTES: ARBITRATOR OR EXPERT

Need for independent determination

12.111   Arguably, the machinery for independent determination of the rent is the most important element in a rent review clause. If the review mechanism or the valuation criteria are wrong, the result will be flawed, but there will still be a result; however, without some formula for deciding between the parties in the event of a disagreement, a rent review clause may well be unenforceable.

12.112   Unlikely as it seems, there have been cases where clauses provided for a rent to be 'agreed between the parties' and left it at that. The outcome has varied, depending upon the seriousness of the defect and the construction of the lease as a whole. Sometimes such a provision has been held void from uncertainty,[1] sometimes a workable formula has been written into the contract by the court,[2] and sometimes the rent has been left as it was.[3]

1 *King's Motors (Oxford) Ltd v Lax* [1969] 3 All ER 665, [1970] 1 WLR 426.
2 *Brown v Gould* [1972] Ch 53, [1971] 3 WLR 334; *Beer v Bowden* [1981] 1 WLR 522, [1981] 1 All ER 1070; *Thomas Bates & Son Ltd v Wyndham's (Lingerie) Ltd* [1981] 1 WLR 505, [1981] 1 All ER 1077.
3 *King v King* (1981) 41 P&CR 311, 255 EG 1205.

12.113 In the Scottish case of *Crawford v Bruce*[1] a 10-year lease provided that the rent should be £3,250 'with a review of the rent on the expiry of each three year period'. After reviewing the English authority, the court decided that it could only imply a term into the contract on the ground of necessity if that was required in order to give it efficacy.[2] Here, although the rent review provision was void from uncertainty, there was no hiatus or gap that had to be filled by the court in order to make the contract workable. It was consistent with the terms of the lease that the initial rent, if unaltered by a review, should remain payable for the full term of the lease.

1 1992 SLT 524, 1992 SCLR 565.
2 For implication of terms in fact see *Mark and Spencer plc v BNP Paribas Securities Services Trust Co (Jersey) Ltd* [2015] UKSC 72; [2016] AC 742.

12.114 In *City of Aberdeen Council v Clark*[1] the rent review clause in a 99-year ground lease contained no valuation criteria apart from a provision that the rent should be in respect of the ground exclusive of buildings. There was also provision for a landlord's trigger notice and, failing agreement on the rent, a reference to arbitration in normal terms. The tenant argued that the review provision was void from uncertainty and, following *Crawford v Bruce*, that the rent should remain the same for the duration of the lease.

However, the court distinguished *Crawford* on the grounds that the lease was for 99 years rather than 10 – it would have been extraordinary if the parties had not intended rent reviews over such a period – that it had contained a separate review clause, that there was a provision for triggering the review and that there was a procedure for reference to arbitration:

'Thus in this case not only were there express provisions aimed at enabling parties to bind themselves to the initiation of a rent review but they had specifically invoked these procedures. They had thus passed to a stage (not available in *Crawford*) where they were contractually bound to proceed with the review. If at that stage, anything at all was lacking, it would be the specification of an effective machinery for ascertaining the quantification of the reviewed rent—'[2]

It was therefore held that the review clause was enforceable. The court instructed that the rent should be fixed on the basis of the provisions of the existing lease for its unexpired term at the date of the review, and that it should be fixed on a reasonable basis, but otherwise was prepared to leave the details of the valuation to the skill and experience of the arbiter.

1 1999 SLT 613.
2 *City of Aberdeen Council v Clark* 1999 SLT 613 at 618.

12.115 The moral of the above cases is plain: it is absolutely essential to have some means of fixing the rent independently of the parties themselves. Beyond that, as the *City of Aberdeen* case demonstrates, minimal provision regarding that may be adequate such that the review clause is not void from uncertainty. However, some additional valuation criteria are desirable.

Arbitrator or expert

12.116 In the context of a hypothetical letting, the provision for independent determination of the rent is usually achieved by providing for disputes to be referred either to an arbitrator[1] or an expert.[2] The difference between the two is not the type of individual involved – each is likely to be a chartered surveyor – but the role that the third party is called upon to play.

Generally, the lease will provide that the arbitrator or expert, as the case may be, will be chosen by the parties. In either case, if they fail to agree, the selection will be made by the Chairman for the time being of the Scottish Branch of the Royal Institution of Chartered Surveyors.

In Scotland, the law of arbitration was formerly governed largely by the common law, although certain areas were covered by statute. It is now comprehensively governed by the Arbitration (Scotland) Act 2010.

1 Formerly known in Scotland as an 'arbiter'.
2 For a detailed comparison of the roles of arbiter (or 'arbitrator') and expert, see Alan McMillan and Shona Wilson 'Experts and Arbiters: Ne'er the Twain Shall Meet?' 2008 Jur Rev 273.

12.117 The difference between the role of an arbitrator and that of an expert is that an arbitrator performs a quasi-judicial function, hearing submissions and expert testimony put forward by both parties. An expert, on the other hand, is simply asked to carry out the professional task of making a valuation. Using an expert has the advantage of comparative speed and cheapness. However, there is a danger of choosing what has come to be called an 'eccentric expert', who may reach a valuation far removed from what either the landlord or the tenant contemplated.

Right of challenge: arbitrator

12.118   In Scotland, an arbitrator's award is normally final and binding upon the parties.[1] However, it may be challenged by an appeal to the Outer House of the Court of Session on one of the following grounds:

(1)   that the tribunal (the arbitrator or arbitrators) did not have jurisdiction to make the award;[2]

(2)   serious irregularity;[3] or

(3)   that the tribunal erred on a point of Scots law;[4]

Grounds (1) and (2) are mandatory, but ground (3) may be contracted out of in the lease.[5] Provisions contracting out of the stated case procedure under section 3 of the Administration of Justice (Scotland) Act 1972 contained in leases that predate the 2010 Act will have the effect of contracting out of ground (3) above (which had no equivalent in the old law).[6]

1   Arbitration (Scotland) Act 2010 s 11.
2   A(S)A 2010, Sch 1 rule 67.
3   A(S)A 2010, Sch 1 rule 68.
4   A(S)A 2010, Sch 1 rule 69. See *Arbitration Application No 2 of 2011* 2011 Hous LR 72, 2011 GWD 38-785.
5   A(S)A 2010 s 9 and Sch 1 rule 69.
6   A(S)A 2010 s 36(8).

12.119   *Referral on a point of law*   The Arbitration (Scotland) Act 2010 also provides a procedure for a referral on a point of law to be made to the Outer House at an earlier stage.[1] This replaces the stated case procedure under section 3 of the Administration of Justice (Scotland) Act 1972 (now repealed) and, as with that former procedure, the right to make such a reference may be contracted out of in the lease. Provisions contracting out of the 1972 Act contained in leases that predate the 2010 Act apply to the new procedure.[2]

In *Grahame House Investments Ltd v Secretary of State for the Environment*[3] a surveyor agreed to act as an arbiter in a rent review dispute having, on the same day, accepted an appointment to act as an independent expert in relation to other premises owned by the same landlord in the same office building. In a stated case, the tenant challenged the arbiter's impartiality, given that he had already issued his decision as expert for the other premises and, the tenant argued, he would not be able to consider the issue in the arbitration with an open mind. It was held that he was not disqualified from acting as arbiter.

1   A(S)A 2010 Sch 1 rules 41 and 42.
2   A(S)A 2010 s 36(8).
3   1985 SC 201, 1985 SLT 502.

Right of challenge: expert

12.120   The jurisdiction of an expert is a matter of contract between the parties and so, if the lease provides that the expert's decision will be final and binding upon them (as it usually will) then it will not normally be open to challenge.[1] The position is the same whether the expert's decision is a 'non-speaking valuation' (in which the expert gives no explanation of the decision) or a 'speaking valuation' (in which an explanation is given).[2]

Exceptionally, an expert's certificate may be challenged on grounds of fraud or collusion 'as fraud or collusion unravels everything',[3] or on the ground of mistake if it is clear that the expert has departed from the evidence in a material respect:[4] since the conclusive nature of the decision is a matter of contract, it follows that the parties will not be bound where the expert has failed to abide by the contract's terms.

1   *Campbell v Edwards* [1976] 1 WLR 403, 1 All ER 785; *Baber v Kenwood Manufacturing Co Ltd* [1978] 1 Lloyds LR 175, (1977) 121 SJ 606; *Jones v Sherwood Computer Services* [1992] 2 All ER 170, [1992] 1 WLR 277.
2   *Jones v Sherwood Computer Services* [1992] 2 All ER 170 at 177 per Dillon LJ, [1992] 1 WLR 277; *Pontsarn Investments Ltd v Kansallis-Osake-Pankki* [1992] 22 EG 103, [1992] NPC 56. Although it may be noted that in *Cine-UK Ltd v Union Square Developments Ltd* [2019] CSOH 3, 2019 SCLR 635 the court considered it significant, albeit not determinative, in deciding that the expert's decision was final and binding on matters of fact and law that the expert was not required to give reasons for her decision.
3   *Campbell v Edwards* [1976] 1 WLR 403 at 407 per Lord Denning.
4   *Jones v Sherwood Computer Services* [1992] 2 All ER 170, [1992] 1 WLR 277.

12.121   Provided that the lease makes the position clear, the expert's decision will also be final on questions of law, such as construction of the lease.[1] In *Ashtead Plant Hire Co Ltd v Granton Central Developments Ltd*,[2] the court opined that to oust the jurisdiction of the court on the interpretation of the lease the wording would have to be very clear indeed. Where the position is clear that the expert's decision is final and binding on matters of law, it may nonetheless be possible, prior to his decision, for a court ruling to be obtained regarding the basis on which the expert is to proceed; however, this will require the consent of both parties, and the court has no jurisdiction to hear such an application if it is presented unilaterally by only one party.[3]

The court may, however, review an expert's decision if the lease fails to make it sufficiently clear that it was intended to be final and binding.[4]

1   *Jones v Sherwood Computer Services* [1992] 2 All ER 170, [1992] 1 WLR 277 at 179 per Dillon LJ; *Nikko Hotels (UK) Ltd v MEPC* [1991] 28 EG 86, 2 EGLR 103; *Pontsarn Investments v Kansallis-Osaki-Pankki* [1992] 22 EG 103, [1992] NPC 56; *Cine-UK Ltd v Union Park Developments Ltd* [2019] CSOH 3, 2019 SCLR 635.
2   [2018] CSOH 107, 2018 GWD 39-477.

3 *Norwich Union Life Insurance Society v P & O Property Holdings Ltd* [1993] 13 EG 108, [1993] NPC 1, CA. This appears to be inconsistent with *Postel Properties & Daichi Lire (London) v Greenwell* (1993) 65 P&CR 239, [1992] 47 EG 106; however, the former, being a Court of Appeal decision, is the more authoritative.

4 *National Grid Co plc v M25 Group Ltd (No 1)* [1999] 08 EG 169, 1 EGLR 65; *Franborough Properties Ltd v Scottish Enterprise* 1996 GWD 27-1619 (otherwise unreported).

Professional negligence

12.122 Arbitrators, since they perform a quasi-judicial role, enjoy the same immunity from actions of negligence as judges and others involved in the court process.[1]

On the other hand, an expert *can* be liable for negligence. This applies not only to surveyors carrying out a rent review valuation, but also generally to cases where parties have agreed to entrust a valuation or other decision to a professional person.[2] It also applies where a surveyor is used to fix the amount of a service charge.[3]

In *Zubaida v Hargreaves* (a rent review valuation) the Court of Appeal gave guidance on the standard of care required by an expert valuer:

'In an action for negligence against an expert, it is not enough to show that another expert would have given a different answer. Valuation is not an exact science; it involves questions of judgment on which experts may differ without forfeiting their claim to professional competence. The fact that a judge may think one approach better than another is therefore irrelevant ... The issue is not whether the expert's valuation was right, in the sense of being the figure which a judge after hearing the evidence would determine. It is whether he has acted in accordance with practices which are regarded as acceptable by a respectable body of opinion in his profession ...'[4]

1 Arbitration (Scotland) Act 2010, Sch 1 rule 73; *Sutcliffe v Thackrah* [1974] AC 727, 2 WLR 295.
2 *Sutcliffe v Thackrah* [1974] AC 727, 2 WLR 295 (architect's certificate); *Arenson v Casson Beckman Rutley & Co* [1977] AC 405, 3 WLR 815 (valuation of company shares by an accountant); *Campbell v Edwards* [1976] 1 WLR 403 at 407 per Lord Denning (valuation by surveyor of a lease's surrender value).
3 See para 13.14 et seq.
4 [1995] 09 EG 320 at 320–321 per Hoffmann LJ.

Expert's terms of reference

12.123 We saw above that the basic distinction between an arbitrator and an expert is that the arbitrator performs a quasi-judicial role, hearing submissions and expert testimony put forward by both parties, whereas an expert is simply asked to carry out the professional task of making a valuation.[1]

However, a professional valuer is unlikely to reach a decision without some research or other investigation, and the form this investigation takes can sometimes make the expert's procedure resemble that of an arbitrator, with the result that the distinction between the two may become less clear.

This has sometimes led, both in England and Scotland, to experts' valuations being challenged as invalid, on the basis that the expert has exceeded his or her authority by having performed a quasi-judicial role, even where the expert has appeared to conform to the terms of the lease, and even kept within the guidelines laid down by the Royal Institution of Chartered Surveyors. In Scotland, where, prior to the Arbitration (Scotland) Act 2010, arbitration was largely governed by the common law, it was even suggested by some commentators that, in rent review clauses in Scottish leases, a reference to a decision by an expert will result *de facto* in an arbitration, unless the expert's role is limited absolutely to that of valuer, without any power to decide between conflicting sets of facts or on points of law.[2]

Leaving the expert's decision open to challenge might not be the only consequence of this. If the expert was in fact acting as an arbitrator, the result could arguably be to confer on him or her the immunity from actions for professional negligence enjoyed by arbitrators, but not normally by experts.

1 See para 12.117.
2 See ED Buchanan, 'Rent Review Clauses in Commercial Leases', *Journal of the Law Society of Scotland (Workshop Section)* p 369 (July 1983); Ross and McKichan para 6.46.

12.124 However, the English authority suggests that an expert may properly have a wider function than mere valuation, and the Scottish authority has more recently followed suit.

12.125 *AGE Ltd v Kwik Save Stores* In *AGE Ltd v Kwik Save Stores Ltd*[1] a rent review had been determined by an independent expert, as prescribed in the lease. The landlord sought judicial review of the expert's decision on the ground that, in seeking written submissions and in providing reasons for his decision, the expert had acted as an arbiter.

1 2001 SC 144, 2001 SLT 841. For an earlier indication of the Scottish position, see *Franborough Properties Ltd v Scottish Enterprise* 1996 GWD 27-1619 (otherwise unreported).

12.126 In deciding the issue, Lord Hardie adopted guidelines laid down by Lord Wheatley in the House of Lords in *Arenson v Casson Beckman Rutley & Co* for deciding when a professional person is acting in an arbitral role:[1]

> '(a) there is a dispute or difference between the parties that has been formulated in some way or other; (b) the dispute or difference has been remitted by the parties to the person to resolve in such a manner that he is called upon to exercise a judicial function; (c) where appropriate, the parties must have been provided with an opportunity to present evidence and/or submissions in support of their respective claims in the dispute; and (d) the parties have agreed to accept his decision.'

1 [1977] AC 405 at 428 per Lord Wheatley.

12.127 In *AGE Limited v Kwik Save Stores Ltd*, Lord Hardie held that the surveyor was not acting as an arbiter but as an expert. Quite apart from the fact that this was how he was designated in the lease, failure to agree to the amount of the market rent was not enough by itself to constitute a dispute or difference between the parties to the lease,[1] nor did referring the decision to a third party amount to the formulation of a difference or dispute. It followed that the surveyor could not have been acting in a judicial fashion.

Moreover, Lord Hardie considered that Lord Wheatley must have intended that, in an arbitration, the formulation of any difference or dispute would be by the parties and would occur prior to the reference to the arbiter being made:

> 'Any alternative meaning would result in experts being able to transform informal references to them into arbitrations by their formulating the dispute after the reference to them has occurred. In my opinion this should not be permitted without the unequivocal agreement of the parties. If an expert were able to transform informal references into arbitrations without the consent of the parties, the effect would be that the expert could alter the terms of a lease to which he was not a party. Moreover he would be clothing himself with immunity from claims by either or both of the parties arising from his negligence. In the present case I do not consider that the [surveyor] intended such a result.'[2]

The court considered that the expert was entitled, as part of his or her investigations, to ask for written submissions, but, unlike an arbiter, was not confined to consideration of them only:

> 'I have also concluded, and I understood it to be conceded by counsel, that if the second respondent were truly an expert, he was entitled

to rely upon his expertise in determining a market rental value. In particular, unlike an arbiter, he could rely upon his own experience and was not confined to the submissions of parties. Moreover, in the event of the second respondent acting negligently he would be liable in damages to either or both parties whereas an arbiter would enjoy immunity from such claims. Accordingly I am of the opinion that the second respondent, as an expert, was under an obligation to undertake such investigation as he considered necessary to inform his opinion. The views which I have reached relating to the practical differences between arbiters and experts are consistent with the guidance given to members of the Royal Institution of Chartered Surveyors both at the time that the lease was entered into and at the time of the appointment of the second respondent.'[3]

1   It has been pointed out that the failure of two parties to agree on a rental figure would amount to a 'difference' between them in the ordinary sense of the word – see Alan McMillan and Shona Wilson 'Experts and Arbiters: Ne'er the Twain Shall Meet?' 2008 Jur Rev 273 at 282.
2   *AGE Ltd v Kwik Save Stores Ltd* 2001 SLT 841 at 845 per Lord Hardie.
3   *AGE Ltd v Kwik Save Stores Ltd* 2001 SLT 841 at 846 per Lord Hardie.

12.128   *Holland House v Crabbe and Edmont*   A very similar situation to that in *AGE v Kwik Save Stores* was considered by the Inner House in *Holland House Property Investments Ltd v Crabbe and Edmont*.[1] The tenant challenged the validity of an expert surveyor's determination of a rental figure on the basis that the surveyor had exercised a judicial or quasi-judicial function by requiring the presentation of evidence, the exclusion of privileged material, allowing the possibility of expert evidence being obtained, and allowing each party to comment upon the other's submissions. As a result, it was claimed that he had breached the rules of natural justice and that his determination should be set aside.

It was held that it was an essential requirement that a formulated dispute be in existence prior to the appointment of the surveyor for him to be acting as an arbiter (or arbitrator) in exercising his functions. The expert had therefore not exceeded his authority and his determination was valid. The Inner House approved the decision in *AGE Ltd v Kwik Save Stores*.

In deciding whether the expert was acting as such and had conformed to his or her terms of reference, particular regard should be paid to the terms of the lease and how the third party was described there:

'The essence of the matter, in our judgment, is that in the present case, the parties were not inviting the surveyor, at the time the matter was referred to him, to adjudicate as between their rival contentions and to decide which side he preferred, having regard solely to the material which parties chose to put before him, which characteristics define the nature of adversarial judicial and arbitral procedures in our system. Rather they were inviting him, using his expertise and experience, to fix the consideration which was appropriate, at the relevant time, under their agreement, the lease.

Although clearly each case falls to be decided, having regard to its own particular circumstances and according to what was contracted for by the parties, the wording of clause FOURTH is the kind of language which is frequently adopted in rent review clauses in commercial leases. We agree with counsel for the respondents that by using wording of that sort the parties, absent other material pointing to what their agreement was, are aiming to arrive at the appropriate level of rent by a relatively speedy and informal means, when they themselves are unable to agree upon the matter. It would be regrettable if that commercial purpose could be put at risk by arguments emerging, after the conclusion of the parties' agreement on the matter, to the effect that by virtue of some procedure adopted by the valuer himself he had become an arbiter. Provided the language of the provisions in the lease is clear then only a subsequent agreement between the parties themselves can convert his role from that of an independent expert into a quasi-judicial role.'[2]

1 2008 SC 619, 2008 SLT 777.
2 *Holland House Property Investments Ltd v Crabbe and Edmont* 2008 SC 619 at 635 and 636 per Lord Clarke.

12.129 *Arbitration (Scotland) Act 2010* The above cases were of course decided before the Scottish law of arbitration was profoundly changed by the passing of the Arbitration (Scotland) Act 2010, substituting a comprehensive statutory regime for the previous one that rested largely upon the common law.

However, it has been suggested that the principles decided in the above cases have not been affected by the passing of that Act, since no attempt has been made there to formulate a statutory definition of the concept of arbitration or, more particularly, to distinguish between arbitration and valuation. As a result, this will continue to be something that falls to be determined by the courts.[1]

1 Arbitration (Scotland) Act 2010 s 2; Davidson, Dundas & Bartos *Arbitration (Scotland) Act 2010* (2014) p 19.

12.130 *Conclusion* It would therefore appear to be settled law that the expert's role can extend substantially beyond that of making a simple valuation. The terms of the lease will go a long way in deciding the exact terms of reference. However, an expert will not be exercising a quasi-judicial role unless the parties have already formulated a dispute, beyond a mere disagreement on the amount of the rent, which they have asked the third party to adjudicate upon. Nor can the expert unilaterally alter his or her status to arbitrator without the consent of the parties.

On the other hand, an expert, unlike an arbitrator, will be entitled to go beyond the evidence and submissions of the parties and make further investigations. This is particularly important, as he or she will continue to have no immunity from claims on the ground of professional negligence.

PROBLEMS OF CONSTRUCTION

12.131   In the introduction to this chapter, we noted that it is difficult to generalise about rent review case law because every case is in essence concerned with interpreting the wording of an individual lease.[1] And so, while we have rightly concentrated so far on those areas where some general principles can be drawn, there remains a large number of rent review cases which turned upon unique points of construction.[2]

Since, by their nature, such cases have limited value as precedents, little would be gained by cataloguing them at length. However, before moving on we will briefly look at a couple of examples, if only to illustrate how devoting insufficient care to the wording of a rent review clause can have bizarre and sometimes disastrous consequences.

1 See para 12.5 et seq.
2 For consideration of the principles of contractual interpretation, which is outwith the scope of this book, see MacQueen and Thomson, para 4.25 et seq; Garrity and Richardson para 4.2 et seq; for a consideration of some issues of construction in relation to a rent review provision in a Scottish lease, see *The Howgate Shopping Centre Ltd v Catercraft Services Ltd* 2004 SLT 231, 2004 SCLR 739.

12.132   In *Holicater Ltd v Grandred Ltd*[1] the rent review clause provided, inter alia:

'Unless the landlord and tenant shall agree by not later than three months prior to the review date the market rent payable from a review date such market rent shall be determined ... by a person acting as an Expert ... on the application of either the Landlord or the Tenant made at any time before the said next review date or the expiration of the term as the case may be (time being of the essence).'

The tenant contended that the landlord had lost its right to review because it failed to refer the dispute to an expert by the review date. While this was probably in accordance with the lease draftsman's intention, the Court of Appeal held that, in relation to the phrase 'the said next review date', the word 'said' had to be rejected as meaningless, and so the landlord had until the next review date to refer to the expert, ie another five years.

The above result was not exactly disastrous for either party, though there is certainly something odd about time being declared to be of the essence in relation to a five-year deadline.

1 [1993] 23 EG 129, [1993] NPC 224.

12.133 More serious consequences followed from the decision in *Stedman v Midland Bank plc*,[1] where the lease was for a period of 71 years and the disputed part of the rent review clause read as follows:

> 'PAYING therefor during the first year of the said term the yearly rent of eight hundred pounds rising by annual increases of Ten pounds each to eight hundred and forty pounds in the fifth year and thereafter at a rent to be agreed or in default of agreement to be fixed by an Arbitrator to be appointed by the parties hereto.'

The landlord claimed that, after the first five years, for which the increases had already been determined, there were to be annual reviews throughout the lease. Once again, this was probably what the drafter had intended. However, the Court of Appeal decided that the actual words used could only mean that there would be a once-and-for-all review at year five, after which the rent would stay the same for the remaining 66 years of the lease.

1 [1990] 03 EG 76.

ALTERNATIVE METHODS OF RENT REVIEW

12.134 Having now seen the potential for unforeseen complication and financial peril inherent in the rent review procedures we have examined so far, it is tempting to look for some other method that may avoid such hazards. However, although alternatives do exist, they too have drawbacks. We will briefly consider two of these alternatives.

Index linked rents

12.135 This is a method by which the rent is varied simply by reference to a published index, such as the Retail Price Index. It is therefore jacked up automatically in line with inflation, avoiding (in theory) all of the potential difficulties with which this chapter has so far been concerned.

Unfortunately, if we substitute for a system involving fallible human judgment one in which there is no human judgment involved at all, the result is not necessarily better. First of all, rent increases may not always be in line with the general level of inflation: sometimes rents lag behind other prices, at other times they shoot ahead. But there is no government index that measures only property values. There are several privately produced indexes that do this, but even they are not sufficiently sophisticated to take into account, except in very broad terms, all the regional variations and other local factors that could affect the market value of a particular property. The result, therefore, may be easy to calculate, but it may not be the market rent. For example, during the property recession in the late 1980s, a rent based on an index of prices would have produced increases at a time when open market rents were falling.

Moreover, to frame a clause that works properly involves some sophistication of drafting; index linking, therefore, does not offer immunity from litigation over the meaning of clauses.[1] If there are few reported cases, it is probably because such clauses are still fairly rare in the UK.

1   For a brief review of some of the decided cases, see HW Wilkinson 'Rents and the Retail Price Index', New Law Journal March 27 1987, p 288; see also *Wyndham Investments Ltd v Motorway Tyres & Accessories Ltd* [1991] 30 EG 65, 2 EGLR 114.

12.136   *Other fixed formulae*   A similar effect to index linking is sometimes achieved by including in the lease some other fixed formula for the calculation of the rent. However, this approach can also lead to problems of interpretation that lead to litigation.[1]

1   See eg *Unilodge Services Ltd v University of Dundee* 2001 SCLR 1008 (where a lease of student accommodation linked rent increases to the average percentage increase in rents by the other universities in Scotland for student accommodation) and *City Wall Properties (Scotland) Ltd v Pearl Assurance* [2007] NPC 114, 2008 GWD 5-93 (where the rent of a car park was linked to the increase in car parking rates at other public car parks in the area).

Turnover rents

12.137   This is a method by which the rent is linked to a percentage of the gross turnover in the tenant's business.[1] The landlord's 'cut' therefore varies according to whether the tenant is doing well or badly.

Turnover rents are common in America and are often used in Britain too, mainly in relation to retail properties.

1   In *Debenhams Retail plc v Sun Alliance & London Assurance Co Ltd* [2006] 1 P&CR 8, [2005] 38 EG 142 a lease defined turnover as 'the gross amount of the total sales' and

it was held that, for the purpose of calculating turnover rent, VAT should be included. For a discussion of some of the following issues and other considerations relating to turnover rents see David Smith, 'Turnover Rent Leases: Are They The Way Forward? (1996) SJ 978; and Karen Mason and Amanda Gray 'Fashion Trend de Nos Jours' *Estates Gazette* July 2009, p 80. For a fairly recent Scottish example of a turnover rent see *Manchester Associated Mills Ltd v Mitchells & Butler Retail Ltd* [2013] CSOH 2, [2013] 4 EG 107 (CS).

12.138   *Advantages and disadvantages*   This method can be criticised for not necessarily achieving a market rent. It could result, for example, in an anomalous situation where there were two adjoining identical shops with quite different rents, simply because one tenant was trading more successfully than the other. The one paying more might well feel unfairly penalised for being successful.

On the other hand, even the most competently run business can hit bad times, and a turnover rent can cushion the effect of a difficult period by easing the rent burden when takings are down; as a result, turnover rents tend to be more popular during periods of recession, as they provide an element of flexibility that may protect the tenant from insolvency.

Nor is it necessarily correct to think of the landlord's percentage as unearned income. Having a stake in their tenants' success provides landlords with an incentive to provide better services and generally be more interested in looking after their tenants' interests.

Another problem with turnover rents is the difficulty of obtaining an accurate estimate of a tenant's turnover: apart from procedural problems (what to do about returned goods, for example) the tenant has an obvious motive to falsify the figures. This problem has been resolved in some modern shopping centres, where the presence of all the tenants within one building allows their tills to be linked to a common computer, monitored by the landlord.

It has also been observed that the use of turnover rents in America has led to the rather ruthless practice of linking the level of turnover to the landlord's right to terminate a lease prematurely: in other words, a tenant whose performance is not satisfactory can be replaced by one who provides the landlord with a bigger cut.

12.139   *Other issues*   Where the lease provides for the payment of a turnover rent, it is particularly important to the landlord that it should include a 'keep open' provision, as the rent level will obviously be adversely affected should the tenant cease trading.[1]

Also, turnover rents are personal to a particular tenant, so leases including turnover rents will generally have a restriction on alienation, so that they will revert to an open-market rent in the event of an assignation or sublet.

Finally, we should note that it is not the normal practice for rents to be calculated *entirely* by reference to turnover. Usually there is a base rent which will be topped up by a percentage of the tenant's turnover. Since the base rent will probably be subject to review by the normal method, this means that turnover rents are not really an alternative method of calculation, but merely a supplementary one. They may have their attractions, but they are not going to avoid the incidence of disputes and the need to resort to arbitration or litigation.

1 For the law relating to 'keep open' clauses see para 4.7 et seq.

Chapter 13

Service charges

GENERAL

Nature of service charges

13.1   Service charges typically arise in properties where a number of tenants share common areas, facilities or parts of a building, and the landlord provides common services for them. The kinds of service that can be involved are extensive, but typically include things like cleaning of common parts, gardening, heating and air conditioning, security, fire prevention, refuse disposal, maintenance and provision of car parks, toilet facilities and administration and management.[1] Most of these are what one might expect from the meaning of the word 'service'. However, items normally included in service charges extend some way beyond this usual meaning.

We have seen that the most common type of commercial lease nowadays is the tenant's FRI (full repairing and insuring) lease. Where the property is self-contained, this can be achieved simply by making the tenant responsible for repairs, insurance and any other outgoings.[2] In the case of properties in multiple occupation, however, it would be quite impractical for the tenants to be responsible for maintaining the fabric of the property in a piecemeal fashion.

It therefore makes sense for the landlord, not only to provide common services of the type mentioned in the first paragraph, but also to undertake the maintenance and repair of the common parts of the property. Thereafter the landlord will recover a proportion of the cost of these services and repairs from each tenant. We are not therefore dealing with a negligible item in a tenant's expenditure, and it is necessary to include a properly drafted provision in the lease to regulate the situation.

It should be noted that the expression 'the common parts' (unlike, for example, 'common property') has no defined meaning either under statute or at common law and it is up to the parties when drafting the lease to clearly identify what the term includes.[3] Otherwise there may be some uncertainty regarding which outlays the landlord can recover as

339

service charge. For instance, in *Blackwell v Farmfoods (Aberdeen) Ltd*[4] it was held that the lease wording did not make the tenant liable to pay for a repair to the common parts of the building, so this liability reverted to the landlord without recourse to the tenant for the cost.

1 For a more detailed consideration of service charge see Garrity and Richardson, *Dilapidations and Service Charge*, ch 6; Ross and McKichan ch 11; Cockburn and Mitchell ch 6; and Gerber ch 29; for a useful consideration of drafting issues in relation to service charge clauses, see also Paul Clark 'Service Charges in Commercial Leases' 2009 L&T Review 156.
2 In such properties, however, the landlord is still likely to take the precaution of being the one to insure the property, thereafter recovering this outlay from the tenant – see para 11.7.
3 *Marfield Properties v Secretary of State for the Environment* 1996 SC 362, 1996 SLT 1244.
4 1991 GWD 4-219.

13.2 *RICS statement* The Royal Institution of Chartered Surveyors has produced a Professional Statement in relation to service charges in commercial property,[1] which sets out mandatory requirements for those regulated by the RICS. The Professional Statement came into effect on 1 April 2019 and superseded the RICS Code of Practice.[2]

1 *Service Charges in Commercial Property* (2018).
2 *Service charges in commercial property* (3rd edn 2014).

Properties subject to service charges

13.3 Service charges can arise in different types of property. In England they occur regularly in residential property; in Scotland there is little tradition of long leases of residential property.[1] We may nevertheless find service charges in Scotland in residential lets of shorter duration.

They also occur regularly in industrial estates and in office blocks, where services undertaken by the landlord help to provide a pleasant working environment for the tenants and their staff.

However, service charges are probably most important in shopping centres. There the services are being provided, not just for the tenants and their workers, but predominantly for members of the public visiting a centre. A high standard of service is therefore required to attract the public into a centre, with the result that service charges for tenants in shopping centres tend to be relatively high.

A number of important issues need to be dealt with in drafting a service charge clause. These include the tenant's obligation to pay service charge (including the method of apportionment between tenants and the method of collection), the landlord's obligation to provide services and repair to the common parts and, finally, whether a reserve or sinking fund should be set up.

1 See para 8.28 et seq.

THE TENANT'S OBLIGATION

To pay the service charge

13.4   The lease will oblige the tenant to pay the service charge and will set out how this will be calculated. The lease will also set out the services the landlord will provide and its obligations in relation to repair and maintenance of the common parts.

There is a correlation between the amount and extent of services provided by the landlord and the cost of the service charge to the tenant. It is in the landlord's interests to ensure that the common parts of the property are kept in good order and repair. The tenant also has an interest in the building in which the lease subjects are located being sufficiently maintained and adequate services provided. However, the tenant will want to seek to ensure that the works the landlord can carry out and charge back to the tenant via the service charge are kept under control. This will be done by setting out in the lease what work and services the landlord is able to include within the service charge. However, it will not be possible for all work and services that may be required to be set out in the lease. This is especially true in the case of longer leases where, for instance, services not yet available are developed and considered necessary or desirable for the property.

13.5   *Sweeper clauses*   A lease may therefore include a sweeper or 'catch all' clause to deal with work or services that have been omitted or future developments during the life of the lease. Such a clause may provide, for example, 'any other services provided by the landlord from time to time'. The tenant would be advised, however, to make sure that the sweeper clause is not too general in nature and is suitably qualified so as not to give the landlord unlimited discretion in extending the scope of work and services and, as such, the amount of the service charge. For example, the sweeper clause could be limited to the work and services that are 'reasonably necessary' or 'in keeping with the principles of good estate management'.

If the sweeper clause comes at the end of a list of services that belong to a particular category, the *eiusdem generis* rule may operate to

341

exclude services of a different type. For example, in *Lloyd's Bank plc v Bowker Orford*[1] the services chargeable to the tenants were listed as lift maintenance, provision of a caretaker, cleaning of common parts, provision of hot water and 'any other beneficial services which may properly be provided by the lessors'. It was held that the latter did not extend, inter alia, to external and internal repairs.

In *Douglas Shelf Seven Ltd v Co-operative Wholesale Society Limited*[2] the lease contained specific obligations on the part of the tenant to pay a proportion of repairs to and insurance of the common parts, and went on also to oblige the tenant to pay 'the professional charges of the Landlords' surveyors' in connection with these outlays 'and in general in connection with the management and administration of the whole subjects and the said shopping development'.

The landlord argued that 'charges' had a wider meaning than 'fees' and that this last part was a sweeper provision entitling it to recover the cost of providing security guards and other security services within the shopping centre. It was held that, whether one called the item 'fees' or 'charges', it referred only to the cost of the surveyors' professional activities, not to any outlay they may have made on the landlord's behalf. The landlord was therefore not entitled to reclaim the cost of security services.

1 [1992] 31 EG 68, 2 EGLR 44.
2 [2009] CSOH 3, 2009 GWD 3-56.

Other considerations

13.6   What a landlord is able to recover via the service charge will naturally vary in accordance with the terms of the particular lease and how it is construed.

In the past, courts were inclined to interpret service charge provisions *contra proferentem* and to exclude doubtful items unless the lease contained a clear and unequivocal provision allowing them, the justification being that tenants should be fully aware of what was required of them.[1] This is no longer the position. Recent Supreme Court authority[2] shows that service charge provisions are subject to the general rules of contractual interpretation.[3] As such, the court should give effect to the natural and ordinary meaning of the words in the lease and should not look for ambiguity in the terms to rewrite the parties' bargain. That was so even when the clear words of the lease produced an absurd result.[4]

In *Boots UK Ltd v Trafford Centre Ltd*[5] a lease provided that the landlord should meet half the cost of service charges that amounted to promotion, which was defined as 'advertising and other forms of promotion of the centre intended to bring additional custom to the centre'. It was held that this did not include Christmas decorations, entertainment, a Santa's grotto, and a large television screen displaying information about the centre. Although all these items would benefit the centre, they did not fall within the ordinary meaning of the word 'promotion'. As a result, the landlord was not obliged to share the cost of these services.

In *Boldmark Ltd v Cohen*,[6] where the landlord borrowed money in order to finance the provision of services, it was held that it was not entitled to recover interest payments on this borrowing from the tenant without a clear mandate from the lease. The onus was upon the landlord to show that the tenant had contracted to pay interest.

In *Plantation Wharf Management Co Ltd v Jackson*,[7] the lease stated that the service charge included the fees, charges and expenses of professional advisers engaged in the enforcement of any individual tenant's obligations 'in the interests of good estate management'. It was held that legal fees incurred in recovering service charges from tenants who were unwilling to pay were included within this and were recoverable.

On the other hand, in *Twenty Two Clifton Gardens Ltd v Thayer Investments SA*,[8] where the lease allowed the landlord to recover the cost of services 'deemed necessary for the better use and enjoyment of the property by the lessees and other occupiers' the landlord could not include its legal costs and surveyor's fees incurred in proceedings against tenants.

1 See eg *Gilje v Charlgrove Securities Ltd* [2002] L&TR 33, 1 EGLR 41 (in which a service charge provision allowing the landlord to recover the wage of a resident caretaker could not include a notional rent for the flat which he occupied rent-free) or *St Mary's Mansions Ltd v Limegate Investment Co Ltd* [2003] HLR 24, 1 EGLR 41 (where a provision allowing the recovery of the fees of auditors and the landlord's managing agents could not extend to the legal costs of collecting rent and service charges.)
2 *Arnold v Britton* [2015] UKSC 36, [2015] AC 1619.
3 For a discussion of those principles see Garrity and Richardson, *Dilapidations and Service Charge*, para 4.2.
4 *Arnold v Britton* [2015] UKSC 36, [2015] AC 1619.
5 [2008] EWHC 3372.
6 (1987) 19 HLR 135, (1985) 277 EG 745.
7 [2012] L&TR 18.
8 [2012] 2 EGLR 56, [2013] 26 EG 101.

Implication of reasonableness

13.7   In *Finchbourne Ltd v Rodrigues*,[1] the court implied a term into the lease that the service charge recoverable from the tenant should be fair and reasonable.

'In my opinion the parties cannot have intended that the landlords should have an unfettered discretion to adopt the highest conceivable standard and to charge the tenant with it.'[2]

In Scotland, a similar decision was reached following a separate line of Scottish authority in *Lowe v Quayle Munro Ltd*,[3] where it was held to be implied that the repair costs chargeable to the tenants should be reasonably incurred, and that a lease provision that they should be 'properly incurred' meant the same thing.

An item may be disallowed as excessive even in cases where it appears, in part at least, to have been sanctioned by the lease. For example, in *Veena SA v Cheong*[4] the landlord of a small block of seven luxury flats was allowed under the leases to pass the cost of a porter's services on to the tenants. It was held that this could not extend to the cost of a full-time porter. This was unreasonable, as a part-time porter would have been sufficient for a block of that size.

1   [1976] 3 All ER 581, CA; see also *Morgan v Stainer* [1993] 33 EG 87, 25 HLR 467.
2   [1976] 3 All ER 581, CA at 587 per Cairns LJ.
3   1997 SC 346, 1997 SLT 1168, following *Rockliffe Estates plc v Co-operative Wholesale Society Ltd* 1994 SLT 592 and *Taylor Woodrow Property Co Ltd v Strathclyde Regional Council* 1996 GWD 7-397 (otherwise unreported).
4   [2003] 1 EGLR 175. Note, however, that in England, though not in Scotland, there is a statutory requirement under the Landlord and Tenant Act 1985 for service charges in residential properties to be reasonable.

13.8   However, while *Finchbourne* has been considered to be good general authority, it has been distinguished in several cases, particularly in relation to the right of landlords to recover insurance premiums.

In the Scottish case of *Victor Harris (Gentswear) Ltd v the Wool Warehouse (Perth) Ltd*,[1] where the lease gave the landlords complete control over fixing the insurance, there was held to be no implication that the amount recoverable from the tenants should be reasonable; insurance was considered to be in a quite different category from the situation where it might be necessary to restrict the landlord's right to improve the property at the tenant's expense.

The English Court of Appeal reached a similar conclusion in *Berrycroft Management Co Ltd v Sinclair Gardens Investments (Kensington) Ltd*[2] where it was held to be irrelevant that the landlords could have obtained a cheaper rate elsewhere.

1   1995 SCLR 577.
2   (1997) 29 HLR 444, [1997] 22 EG 141; see also *Sepes Establishment Ltd v KSK Enterprises Ltd* [1993] 2 IR 225, affirmed by the Irish Supreme Court 21 May 1996, (unreported).

13.9 In another Scottish case, *WW Promotions (Scotland) Ltd v De Marco*,[1] where the certificate of the landlord's surveyor was declared in the lease to be final, it was held that it was therefore up to the surveyor to decide on reasonableness, and that his certificate could not thereafter be challenged by the tenant on the ground that the charges were unreasonable.

1 1988 SLT (Sh Ct) 43, 1988 SCLR 299; see also para 13.17.

13.10 While the common law may provide some defence, therefore, it is safer for the tenant to revise the lease to build in protection from unreasonable charges.

Apportionment of service charges[1]

13.11 *Methods of apportionment* A problematic area can be the method of apportioning the service charges among the various tenants in the property. One common method is to base it on the floor area occupied by each tenant, and another is to tie it to the rateable values of the various units.

The former has the disadvantage that it could lead to complaints from tenants of larger units that the extra amount they pay is disproportionate to the extra benefits they receive from the provision of the services. The rateable value system caters for this in that larger units are valued proportionately less.

However, a system of apportionment based upon rateable value has other drawbacks. In a new development, the rateable values will not be known at the outset and may have to be estimated. Also, they would be subject to individual appeals by tenants, which could lead to uncertainty and confusion.

A third method, which combines the virtues and avoids some of the difficulties of the above, is to apportion according to 'weighted' floor area. This involves basing the apportionment on floor area, but incorporating a formula whereby larger areas are given a 'discount' and thereby pay proportionately less.

In *Bradford & Bingley Building Society v Thorntons plc*[2] the landlord had the option of basing the apportionment either on floor area or rateable value. (The lease actually referred to the obsolete expression 'gross annual value', but this mistake was considered to be rectifiable.) The landlord chose the latter method, which resulted in the tenants being liable for a disproportionately high amount. However, the lease also provided that the tenant should pay an 'equitable share' and the court held that this implied that the landlord should show some restraint in selecting the method of apportionment.[3]

1 For a fuller discussion of this issue see M Noor and M Pitt 'A Discussion of UK Commercial Property Service Charges' (2009) 8 Journal of Retail & Leisure Property 119.
2 1998 GWD 40-2071; the full judgment can be obtained from the Scottish Courts website at www.scotcourts.gov.uk
3 See para 13.7 et seq.

13.12 *Fixed percentage*   Instead of including a formula in the lease for working out the apportionment, the landlord may want to avoid uncertainty by stating a fixed percentage of total services for which the tenant is liable.

This may have been worked out on the basis of floor area or rateable value or otherwise, but the tenant will have agreed to the percentage when signing the lease and so (theoretically) there should be no grounds for dispute. However, the inflexibility of this may itself lead to problems, eg if the landlord should later want to add to the property.

In *Pole Properties Ltd v Feinberg*,[1] the defendant, a tenant in a block of flats was due, according to his lease, to pay two-sevenths of any increase in the cost of central heating fuel. The landlord later extended the property by building a new block of flats on an adjoining site and making the central heating system common to both blocks.

A new proportion therefore had to be worked out for the tenant's share, which he contested because it took no account of the fact that the new flats were more intensively heated, with radiators in more of their rooms. The court held that the situation had so radically altered that the terms of the lease no longer applied. The tenant would have to pay what was fair and reasonable in the circumstances, ie according to the heating facilities provided for him.

Incidentally, this pinpoints a criticism that could be made of all the apportionment methods mentioned above: that they do not necessarily reflect the amount of the services which the respective tenants actually use or enjoy.

1 (1982) 43 P&CR 121, (1981) 259 EG 417, CA.

Methods of collection

13.13   The lease will also require the method of collection to be specified. This can either be done by the landlord charging a higher rent, to include the provision of services, or by providing that the cost of services will be recovered as a separate charge.

The former method has the attraction of simplicity and is used widely in England, as it makes it easier to enforce the English remedy of forfeiture for non-payment of rent. This does not apply in Scotland but including service charge as part of rent would (in theory at least) make the landlord's hypothec available for its recovery.[1]

However, for accounting and tax purposes, it may be better from the landlord's point of view to have the service charge shown as a separate item.

1 This point is much less relevant since the considerable weakening of the landlord's right of hypothec as a result of s 208 of the Bankruptcy and Diligence etc (Scotland) Act 2007; see para 6.1 et seq.

Certificate by surveyor or managing agent

13.14 It is common for landlords to specify in the clause relating to service charge that the amount of the charge will be as certified by the landlord's surveyor or other agent. It is also common for it to be stated that the certificate of such an agent will be final and binding upon the parties, and also that the agent will be acting as an expert and not an arbitrator.

13.15 *Independence of agent* Since any dispute may fall to be resolved by a person who has been employed by the landlord, this may give rise to questions regarding the agent's impartiality and fitness to perform such a role.

In *Finchbourne Ltd v Rodrigues*,[1] the lease provided that the amount of the tenant's service charge contribution should be 'ascertained and certified by the Lessors' Managing Agents'. It was held that this required the landlord and the managing agents to be separate persons. The managing agents were a firm that was wholly owned by the landlord and the certificate was therefore invalid.

1 [1976] 3 All ER 581, CA.

13.16 However, apart from the basic principle that the landlord and managing agent should not be the same person, the courts have not insisted upon complete independence on the part of the person granting the certificate.

In *Concorde Graphics Ltd v Andromeda Investments Ltd*[1] it was held that there was nothing wrong in principle with a landlord's surveyor certifying the service charge; however, in that particular case they were precluded from doing so since they had also taken legal action on the landlord's behalf to recover the charge and this had created a conflict of interest.

In *New Pinehurst Residents Association (Cambridge) Ltd v Silow*[2] the landlord of three blocks of flats were a limited company whose shareholders were the tenants of the flats. The managing agents, whose duties included certification of the service charge, were a committee comprising six of the tenant/shareholders. It was held that they were competent to act as managing agents since they were separate legal persons and it did not matter that they were also tenants.

And in *Skilleter v Charles*[3] the managing agents were a limited company, formed by the landlord and his wife, which managed properties other than the one that was the subject of the dispute. It was held that, since the company was not a complete sham, the landlord was entitled to employ it to manage the properties, including the certification of service charges.

1 (1983) 265 EG 386.
2 [1988] 1 EGLR 227, CA.
3 (1992) 24 HLR 421, [1992] 13 EG 113.

13.17 *Finality of certificate*[1] Where the lease provides that the decision of the landlord's surveyor is to be final, the parties are not normally entitled to look beyond the terms of the certificate on the grounds that the surveyor has made a mistake or that the service charge is unreasonable.[2]

However, in the absence of such a provision, a service charge certificate may be open to challenge by either party.

In *Scottish Mutual Assurance plc v Jardine Public Relations Ltd*[3] the lease provided that the service charge payable by the tenants should be 'a fair proportion fairly and reasonably determined by the Landlord's Surveyors' and that they should be 'reasonably and properly incurred.' Immediately prior to the end of the tenant's three-year lease, the landlord sought payment of more than £27,500 towards the cost of long-term repairs to the roof. It was held that it was unreasonable to charge the tenant with such a large proportion of the cost. Although the certificate of the landlord's surveyors was declared to be final on the question of service charge, there was declared to be an exception 'in the case of manifest error' and charging the tenant such an amount in these circumstances was held to be such an error.

In *Universities Superannuation Scheme Ltd v Marks & Spencer plc*[4] where the landlord's agents had undercharged the tenants by a substantial amount, the landlord was held entitled to recover the balance retrospectively, based upon the tenant's service charge obligation as stated in the lease. The certificate was not, in terms of the lease, final, binding or conclusive.

1 See also para 13.19.
2 *W W Promotions (Scotland) Ltd v De Marco* 1988 SLT (Sh Ct) 43, 1988 SCLR 299, discussed in para 13.9.
3 1999 EGCS 43 (otherwise unreported).
4 [1999] L&TR 237, [1999] 04 EG 158.

13.18 *Expertise of agent* Where the lease provides that the agent making the certification is to act as an expert, it is not necessary (unless the lease requires it) for the agent to be professionally qualified, provided that he or she has a sufficient degree of expertise.[1]

However, in *St Modwen Developments (Edmonton) Ltd v Tesco Stores Ltd*,[2] a local authority granted a 99-year lease of a supermarket, under which the amount of the service charge was to be ascertained and certified by the local authority's borough treasurer. After the lease had been assigned to a private landlord, the service charge was certified by the landlord company's finance director.

It was held that there was a considerable difference between what might be expected of a public officer such as a local authority's borough treasurer and the finance director of a company, and that it could not be assumed that the original parties to the lease had intended to confer the same power to whoever might happen to have a financial role in the organisation of some future assignee. As a result, the certificates issued by the finance director had no contractual force.

1 *New Pinehurst Residents Association (Cambridge) Ltd v Silow* [1988] 1 EGLR 227, CA.
2 [2007] 1 EGLR 63, 6 EG 166.

13.19 *Questions of law* It was once thought to be the case that the landlord's surveyor or other agent, when acting as an expert and not an arbitrator, was precluded from deciding disputes that involved interpretation of the lease or other questions of law.[1]

However, it now seems to be accepted that an expert can decide such questions, provided that the lease makes it sufficiently clear that the necessary authority has been given by the parties. In *Franborough Properties Ltd v Scottish Enterprise*,[2] the lease provided that the landlord's surveyor's certificate would be final and conclusive except in the case of manifest arithmetical error. The court found that the certificate was final and conclusive as to the quantification of costs but was not conclusive as to whether an item was properly a common part or a service, and as such, whether it could be included within the service charge.[3]

1 *Re Davstone Estates Ltd's Leases* [1969] 2 Ch 378, [1969] 2 All ER 849; see also *WW Promotions (Scotland) Ltd v De Marco* 1988 SLT (Sh Ct) 43, at 45 per Sheriff Principal Caplan.

2 See also para 12.120 et seq and the authority quoted there, particularly *Nikko Hotels (UK) Ltd v MEPC* [1991] 28 EG 86, at 100 per Knox, J, [1991] 2 EGLR 103.
3 *Franborough Properties Ltd v Scottish Enterprise* 1996 GWD 27-1619 (otherwise unreported).

13.20 *Conclusion* It should be noted that all of the above cases turn on questions of the construction of the lease. Even *Finchbourne* does not imply that service charges can never be fixed by the actual landlord: only that, where the lease entrusts this to the landlord's agent, the very concept of agency requires that the agent should be a separate legal person from the principal.

And so, while it is very common for landlords' agents to be given the power to conclusively fix the amount of service charge, it is open to tenants, when entering leases, to negotiate for a more independent method of determination. However, while the latter is the norm for other issues (such as rent reviews), it is arguably less appropriate for periodic charges that may occur several times in one year. There is also likely to be a benefit in the party dealing with certification of the service charge being familiar with the property, rather than an independent third party.

The system of certification by the landlord's agent has the practical merit of avoiding a proliferation of disputes, and also entrusts the matter in the hands of a party who should have some familiarity with the relevant property. In such a case, if the service charge is to be recoverable, the landlord should comply with the procedure for collection agreed by the parties and laid down by the lease. Failure to do so could prove fatal to the landlord's ability to recover the service charge.[1]

On the other hand, in cases where the amounts involved are likely to be sizeable, tenants may consider it preferable for the lease to give them some right of challenge.

1 *Leonora Investment Co v Mott Macdonald Ltd* [2008] ECWA Civ 857, 2 P&CR DG15 but see also *Univeristies Superannuation Scheme Ltd v Marks & Spencer plc* [1999] L&TR 237 where the terms of the lease meant that the landlord could enforce payment of the servce charge notwithstanding problems with the surveyor's certificate.

THE LANDLORD'S OBLIGATION

Provision of services

13.21 The tenant's agent should ensure that the lease, as well as obliging the tenant to pay for the service charge, actually contains an undertaking by the landlord to provide the services and carry out works to the common parts.

One would have thought that this would be implied – it does not make much sense to charge the tenant for services that may not have been received – but this is not necessarily the case. In *Duke of Westminster v Guild*,[1] the lease obliged the tenant to contribute to the maintenance of a drain, but there was no corresponding obligation on the part of the landlord actually to do the maintenance, and the court refused to imply a condition to this effect into the lease.

1 [1985] QB 688, [1984] 3 All ER 144, CA.

Unfair Contract Terms Act

13.22 It is also worth noting that the Unfair Contract Terms Act 1977 applies to the provision of services by landlords. The Act does not apply to leases in general but does specifically apply to services relating to the use of land.[1]

This means that if the landlord purports in the lease to exclude or restrict its liability for breach of an obligation in the provision of services or works to the common parts, such a disclaimer may be ineffective.

If the exclusion or restriction relates to death or personal injury, the exemption clause will be void; in other cases, the court will only enforce it if it considers the exclusion or limitation to have been fair and reasonable when the contract was entered into.[2]

1 Unfair Contract Terms Act 1977 s 15.
2 UCTA 1977 s 16.

13.23 *English position* It has been held that the equivalent provisions in the English part of the Unfair Contract Terms Act do not apply to service charges.[1]

However, the English provisions are substantially different from those in the Scottish part of the Act (for example, they make no mention of services relating to the use of land) and it seems unlikely that a similar decision would be reached in Scotland.

1 *Unchained Growth III plc v Granby Village (Manchester) Management Co Ltd* [2000] 1 WLR 739, [2000] L&TR 186.

RESERVE OR SINKING FUNDS

Nature and purpose of funds

13.24 Some leases provide for the establishment of a reserve or sinking fund, ie a common fund to which all tenants contribute and from which service charges are paid. This can be advantageous to tenants in that it will spread the load of charges evenly over a number of years. A reserve fund is used to deal with spending on regularly occurring items which do not arise every year (such as an obligation to redecorate the common parts once every three years). A sinking fund is used to deal with infrequently occurring expenditure (such as replacing lifts or an air conditioning system).

A lease may effectively create a reserve or sinking fund whether or not that terminology has been used. Whatever name is given to the fund, the nature of the arrangement will depend upon what the lease provides, particularly in relation to the disposal of any surplus payments which the landlord may have accumulated. In other words, the lease must make it clear whether such payments have to be returned to the tenant at the end of the lease or whether the landlord may hold on to them to meet future expenditure.

13.25 In *Secretary of State for the Environment v Possfund (North West) Ltd and others*[1] the tenants, during the currency of their lease, made payments to a fund, of which a sum exceeding £600,000 was earmarked for the replacement of the air conditioning plant in the property.

At the end of their lease the tenants sought repayment of this sum, as the air conditioning plant had not yet been replaced and the money had not been spent. It was held that the money in the fund belonged to the landlord and did not have to be repaid.

Although that decision turned on the judge's construction of the lease terms, he was influenced in his interpretation by the commercial reality underlying the situation: during the currency of the lease the tenant had enjoyed the benefit of the air conditioning system, a depreciating asset which the landlord would eventually have to replace. It was irrelevant that the replacement had not been necessary during the term of the tenant's lease.

1 [1997] 39 EG 179, [1996] NPC 151.

13.26 However, in *Brown's Operating System Services Ltd v Southwark Roman Catholic Diocesan Corp*,[1] the lease (described by the court as being badly drawn) did make some provision for the landlord to retain excess service charge payments in advance of future works. The Court of Appeal held that *Possfund* had not laid down general principles but had been decided upon its own facts. In the present case, the lease, properly construed, fell short of creating a reserve or sinking fund. As a result, the tenant was entitled to have unpaid service charges met from the surplus and to be given the balance at the end of the lease. According to Smith LJ:

> 'The real question in issue, as it seems to me, is whether the money held by the landlord (whether held in reserve or retained as excess) was held to its own account or to the account of the tenant.'[2]

In other words, if the landlord is to be entitled to retain any surplus funds at the end of the tenant's tenancy, the lease must make this absolutely clear.

1 [2008] 1 P&CR 7, [2007] L&TR 25.
2 *Brown's Operating System Services Ltd v Southwark Roman Catholic Diocesan Corp* [2008] 1 P&CR 7, at para 30 per Smith LJ.

Disadvantages of funds

13.27   Reserve or sinking funds also have disadvantages for a landlord. There may be liability for income tax or corporation tax on the fund payments. This can be partially avoided by setting up a trust fund, but even then, any income on the trust may be taxable.

As a result of these tax complications, sinking funds have not been widely used in relation to commercial properties.[1]

1 For a more detailed discussion of sinking funds and their tax implications, see Ross & McKichan paras 11-24–11-32.

Chapter 14

Tenancy of shops

INTRODUCTION

14.1   A major difference between the law of Scotland and England is the lack of statutory control of business leases in Scotland. There is, however, a minor exception to this in the form of the Tenancy of Shops (Scotland) Act 1949 which gives limited security of tenure rights to shop tenants.[1]

The Act was originally passed as a temporary measure to protect the rights of shopkeepers, but after a number of yearly extensions was made permanent in 1964.[2]

This modest protection is in contrast to the situation in England where, under the Landlord and Tenant Act 1954, up to 15 years additional security of tenure can be granted in the case of all types of business tenancy.[3] In Scotland the maximum extension is one year and the legislation only applies to shops.[4]

The full text of the Tenancy of Shops (Scotland) Act 1949 is contained in Appendix 2.

The Scottish Law Commission has recently considered the Act and sought views on whether it should be repealed. The feeling seems to be that the Act is little used and is an anomaly to the commercial leasing market in which there is no other statutory regulation.[5] No recommendations have yet been made.[6]

1 Tenancy of Shops (Scotland) Act 1949; for concise overviews of the 1949 Act see also Richard Turnbull 'The Tenancy of Shops (Scotland) Act 1949 – Time for renewal?' (2005) 79 Prop LB 3 and Gordon Junor '"Can we keep the shop?" – Invoking the Tenancy of Shops (Scotland) Act 1949' (2009) 98 Prop LB 5.
2 This was done by the Tenancy of Shops (Scotland) Act 1964, which repealed s 3(3) of the 1949 Act, the section that originally limited the latter Act's duration to one year. It has been suggested that the subsequent repeal of the 1964 Act by the Statute Law Repeals Act 1974 may have accidentally repealed the 1949 Act by retrospectively restoring s 3(3) and the Act's temporary status. However, this possibility was anticipated and prevented by s 11(1) of the Interpretation Act 1889 (now replaced, with retrospective effect, by s 15 of the Interpretation Act 1978).
3 The maximum length was extended from 14 to 15 years by the Regulatory Reform (Business Tenancies) (England and Wales) Order 2003 (SI 2003/3096) reg 26.

4 See, however, the Reserve and Auxiliary Forces (Protection of Civil Interests) Act 1951 ss 38 to 40, under which a similar protection can in certain circumstances be extended to other types of business premises where the tenant is a member of the reserve or auxiliary forces.
5 Although there is the Law Reform (Miscellaneous Provisions)(Scotland) Act 1985 ss 4–7 making provision on irritancy: see para 5.22 et seq.
6 Scottish Law Commission *Discussion Paper on Aspects of Leases: Termination* (Scot Law Com No 165, 2018) ch 6.

Definition of shop

14.2   A shop is defined for the purposes of the Act as including, 'Any premises where any retail trade or business is carried on.'[1] Crown property is included.[2]

Retail trade or business is stated to include the business of a barber or hairdresser, the sale of refreshments or intoxicating liquors, the business of lending books or periodicals when carried on for purposes of gain, and retail sales by auction. It does not include the sale of programmes and catalogues and other similar sales at theatres and places of amusement.[3] The Act therefore applies to hairdressers and barbers, cafés, pubs, profit-making libraries and auction salerooms, but not to theatres or other places of activity where retail sales are incidental.

1 Shops Act 1950 s 74(1) (replacing the definition in the Shops Acts 1912 to 1936). The Shops Act 1950 has now also been repealed, but no replacement definition appears to have been passed.
2 TOS(S)A 1949 s 2.
3 Shops Act 1950 s 74(1). This assumes that the definition of shop in the now repealed 1950 Act is still the accepted one – see footnote 1.

14.3   *Included within definition* The above definition has been further clarified by a number of court decisions. The principle emerging seems to be that premises that are not exclusively retail may still come within the definition of a shop as long as the retail element is substantial.

Properties held to come within the definition include a sub post office,[1] opticians' premises,[2] premises used for the repair of boots and shoes where a minor but substantial part of the tenant's income came from articles for sale,[3] and garage premises where the tenant's profits derived equally from retail activities and repair work, even though a larger area was used for repairs.[4]

1 *King v Cross Fisher Properties Ltd* 1956 SLT (Sh Ct) 79, (1956) 72 Sh Ct Rep 203.
2 *Craig v Saunders & Connor Ltd* 1962 SLT (Sh Ct) 85, (1962) 78 Sh Ct Rep 154.
3 *Oakes v Knowles* 1966 SLT (Sh Ct) 33.
4 *Thom v British Transport Commission* (1952) 68 Sh Ct Rep 290, 1954 SLT (Sh Ct) 21; see also *Grosvenor Garages (Glasgow) Ltd v St Mungo Property Co Ltd* (1955) 71 Sh Ct Rep 155.

14.4 *Excluded from definition* Among those properties excluded from the definition of a shop, and hence from the application of the Act, are a blacksmith's premises,[1] a travel agent's,[2] and a dry cleaner's.[3] Also held to be excluded from the definition was a builder's yard because not only was the retail element subsidiary, but the property was mainly open space which was not, in the court's opinion, the type of property the Act was intended to protect.[4]

1 *Golder v Thomas Johnston's (Bakers) Ltd* 1950 SLT (Sh Ct) 50.
2 *Wright v St Mungo Property Co Ltd* (1955) 71 Sh Ct Rep 152; but see also *Swarbrick v Glover* 1954 CLY 1823, an application under the English Leasehold Property (Temporary Provisions) Act 1951.
3 *Boyd v A Bell & Sons Ltd* 1970 JC 1, 1969 SLT 156.
4 *Green v M'Glughan* 1949 SLT (Sh Ct) 59, (1949) 65 Sh Ct Rep 155.

APPLICATIONS FOR RENEWAL[1]

Procedure

14.5 The Act can be invoked when a shop lease is due to expire and the landlord has sent the tenant a notice to quit. The tenant, if unable to obtain a renewal on satisfactory terms may, within 21 days, apply to the Sheriff Court for a renewal of the lease. It has been noted that the Act indicates that something must be done by the tenant to negotiate or seek renewal before coming to court, although given the 21-day timescale and where the notice to quit is wholly unexpected, the tenant need do no more than start the process of negotiation and be met with something other than a favourable reaction before making an application.[2]

The tenant is not excluded from making an application if the landlord has, in fact, offered to renew the tenancy, but the proposed renewal is on terms which the tenant considers to be unsatisfactory. This means that the threat of invoking the Act can be used by a tenant as a bargaining tool to negotiate better terms.[3]

In order to avoid disputes about whether an application was made timeously, tenants should avoid leaving it to the last minute. This is demonstrated in *Superdrug Stores Ltd v Network Rail Infrastructure Ltd*[4] in which it was held that the time when a valid application occurs is with 'the presentation of a procedurally valid summons accompanied by the appropriate fee to the sheriff clerk, together with a request, implicit or explicit, that the summons should be processed'. As a result, it was eventually held that the application in question had been made timeously, but only by a narrow majority after two appeals.

The sheriff may renew the lease for a period not exceeding one year on such conditions as in all the circumstances he or she thinks reasonable.[5] The word 'may' is used in its normal sense, ie the sheriff's power is discretionary.[6] The conditions imposed may include a rent increase.[7]

The parties will thereafter be considered to have entered a new lease for that period.[8] In order to remove the tenant at the end of the extended period, the landlord will be required to send a fresh notice to quit.[9]

1 TOS(S)A 1949,s 1(1) & (2).
2 *Select Service Partner Ltd v Network Rail* 2015 SLT (Sh Ct) 116 at paras 33–34.
3 See Richard Turnbull 'The Tenancy of Shops (Scotland) Act 1949 – Time for Renewal?' (2005) 79 Prop LB 3.
4 2006 SC 365 , 2006 SLT 146.
5 TOS(S)A 1949 s 1(2),
6 *Robertson v Bass Holdings* 1993 SLT (Sh Ct) 55.
7 TOS(S)A 1949 s1(2); *McDowall v Thomson* (1950) 66 Sh Ct Rep 101; *Craig v Saunders & Connor Ltd* 1962 SLT (Sh Ct) 85, (1962) 78 Sh Ct Rep 154.
8 TOS(S)A 1949 s1(2).
9 *White v Paton* (1953) 69 Sh Ct Rep 176; *Pow v Fraser & Carmichael* 1953 SLT (Sh Ct) 20; *Scottish Gas Board v Kerr's Trs* 1956 SLT (Sh Ct) 69, (1956) 72 Sh Ct Rep 139; but see also *Hill v McCaskill's Trustees* 1951 SLT (Sh Ct) 41, (1951) 67 Sh Ct Rep 128 and 'The Law Society of Scotland Newsletter' 1953 SLT (News) 155.

14.6 In *Temperance Permanent Building Society v Kominek*[1] the landlord served a notice to quit upon the tenant, but subsequently entered negotiations with the tenant for the grant of a new 10-year lease. However, negotiations broke down before agreement had been reached and the landlord proceeded with eviction. It was held that the landlord was not personally barred from doing so because the tenant, on the strength of these abortive negotiations, had refrained from making a timeous application for renewal under the 1949 Act.

The sheriff has the discretion to correct a procedural error in a tenant's application in a case where the landlord has suffered no prejudice as a result.[2]

Although no case seems to have turned on the point,[3] it has been the practice for renewals to be granted from the date of expiry of the notice to quit, ie the lease's ish, rather than from the date of the sheriff's decision; if it were otherwise, a year's renewal from the latter date would effectively result in an extension beyond the one-year maximum which the Act permits.

Proceedings under the Act are judicial, not administrative, so an award of expenses is competent.[4]

1 1951 SLT (Sh Ct) 58, (1951) 67 Sh Ct Rep 154.
2 *Borthwick v Bank of Scotland* 1985 SLT (Sh Ct) 49.
3 See, however, *Hill v McCaskill's Trustees* 1951 SLT (Sh Ct) 41, (1951) 67 Sh Ct Rep 128.
4 *Lennon v Craig* 1949 SLT (Sh Ct) 56, (1949) 65 Sh Ct Rep 144; *Hunter v Bruce* 1949 SLT (Sh Ct) 57, (1949) 65 Sh Ct Rep 146; *Kerr v Totten* 1965 SLT (Sh Ct 21).

Parties to whom the Act applies

14.7 The Act has been interpreted quite strictly regarding the parties to whom its provisions apply.

In *Cuthbertson v Orr's Trustees*[1] where the landlord, after serving a notice to quit, concluded missives for the sale of the shop, it was held that the purchaser had no title to oppose the tenant's application for renewal. Not only was the case heard prior to the purchaser's date of entry, but the purchaser was not entitled to take advantage of the notice to quit served by its predecessor. (Presumably the position would have been different if the purchaser had served the notice to quit and had already become the owner at that time; however, the judgment in *Cuthbertson* is not entirely clear on this point.)

In *Ashley Wallpaper Co Ltd v Morrisons Associated Companies Ltd*[2] it was held that a subtenant had no right to apply for an extension from the head tenant, since a subtenant is not a tenant within the meaning of the Act.

In *James Craig (Glasgow) Ltd v Wood & Selby Ltd*[3] the landlord of a shop was itself a tenant under a 99-year lease. The sheriff, quoting *Ashley* with approval, applied a similarly restrictive meaning to the term 'landlord', holding that it only applied to the owner of the subjects. In fact, however, this led to a decision that seems incompatible with *Ashley*: on the authority of that case the occupier of the shop, as subtenant, should have had no right to make an application at all. Instead it was granted an extension on the basis that its immediate landlord had no title to oppose the application. (Admittedly the owner of the property, as head landlord, was cited as a co-defender; however, if a subtenant does not qualify as a tenant under the Act, this should have made no difference.)

1 (1954) 70 Sh Ct Rep 273.
2 1952 SLT (Sh Ct) 25, (1952) 68 Sh Ct Rep 94.
3 (1953) 69 Sh Ct Rep 164.

Interim order

14.8 The sheriff, if satisfied that it will not be possible to dispose finally of the application before the notice to quit takes effect, may make an interim order authorising the tenant to continue in occupation for a period of up to three months, at such rent and on such other terms as he or she may think fit.[1] However, even if the tenant fails to ask the sheriff for an interim order and the lease has expired by the time of the sheriff's decision, a renewal may still be granted.[2]

1 TOS(S)A 1949 s 1(5).
2 *McMahon v Associated Rentals Ltd* 1987 SLT (Sh Ct) 94.

Further applications

14.9   A further application may be made by the tenant at the end of the renewed term, and at the end of any future period of renewal that may be granted. Such an application will only be competent if the landlord has sent a fresh notice to quit to which the tenant can respond;[1] however, if the landlord does *not* serve a fresh notice, a new application to the court will not be necessary, as the lease will continue by tacit relocation.[2] Each application should be regarded on its own merits, without the court being influenced by any arguments that might have been put forward at earlier applications.[3]

1 *White v Paton* (1953) 69 Sh Ct Rep 176.
2 *White v Paton ibid; Pow v Fraser & Carmichael* 1953 SLT (Sh Ct) 20; *Scottish Gas Board v Kerr's Trs* 1956 SLT (Sh Ct) 69, (1956) 72 Sh Ct Rep 139; for an account of ·tacit relocation see para 10.18 et seq.
3 *Wallace v Bute Gift Co Ltd* 1954 SLT (Sh Ct) 55.

Appeals

14.10   The unsuccessful party has the appeal rights available in a summary cause.[1]

1 TOS(S)A 1949 s 1(7); Sheriff Courts (Scotland) Act 1971 s 38; see also *McMahon v Associated Rentals Ltd* 1987 SLT (Sh Ct) 94; *Jalota v Salvation Army Trustee Co* 1994 GWD 12-770.

GROUNDS FOR REFUSAL[1]

14.11   The sheriff may dismiss the tenant's application for renewal if satisfied that one of the following grounds applies:[1]

1 TOS(S)A 1949 s 1(3).

Breach of lease

14.12   The tenant is in breach of a material tenancy condition. Where a lease provided that the shop should be used exclusively as a newsagents and stationers, the tenant was held to be in material breach of a tenancy provision for selling cigarettes and tobacco.[1]

1 *McCallum v Glasgow Corpn* (1955) 71 Sh Ct Rep 178.

Bankruptcy

14.13   The tenant is bankrupt or (in the case of a limited company) unable to pay its debts.

Landlord's offer to sell

14.14   The landlord has offered to sell the tenant the premises at a price, failing agreement, to be fixed by arbitration.[1]

1 See *J Bartholomew & Son v Robertson* (1960) 76 Sh Ct Rep 64; see also *Hunter v Bruce* 1949 SLT (Sh Ct) 57, (1949) 65 Sh Ct Rep 146.

Alternative premises

14.15   The landlord has offered to afford the tenant on reasonable terms alternative premises that are suitable for the purpose of the tenant's business. The Act does not specify whether such premises have to be offered on lease or whether an offer to sell the tenant another suitable property could meet this criterion; however, even if only an offer of lease is intended, an offer to sell alternative premises may be a relevant consideration for the sheriff when deciding whether it is reasonable to dismiss the application.[1]

Premises where the tenant would have suffered a loss in passing trade have been held unsuitable.[2] And in *Robertson v Bass Holdings*[3] the tenant occupied licensed premises in a pleasant suburban area of Edinburgh where its service of food was a main attraction. Two alternative lets offered by the landlord were held to be unsuitable. One of the properties was situated some distance away and its food trade was incidental, while the other was a town centre pub with a history of violence, particularly from rival football supporters. Furthermore, both properties had a turnover significantly lower than that of the leased premises.

1 See para 14.22.
2 *Hurry v M'Lauchlan* (1953) 69 Sh Ct Rep 305.
3 1993 SLT (Sh Ct) 55.

Tenant's notice to quit

14.16   The tenant has given notice to quit and, as a result of receiving the notice, the landlord has contracted to sell or let the premises or has taken other steps that would cause the landlord to be seriously prejudiced if denied possession.[1]

1 See *McDowall v Thomson* (1950) 66 Sh Ct Rep 101.

Hardship

14.17   Greater hardship would be caused by renewing the lease than by refusing the application.

14.18 *Tenancy of shops*

There have been a number of cases on this ground, though much has depended upon the facts of the individual case and upon the sheriff's discretion. 'Hardship' is to be understood in its generally accepted sense and mere inconvenience to either landlord or tenant is not enough to qualify under this ground.[1] It was suggested in one case that 'where the relative hardships appear equally balanced, the application should normally be decided in favour of the tenant'.[2]

1 *Hamilton Central Co-operative Society Ltd v Simpson* (1952) 68 Sh Ct Rep 148.
2 *Loudon v St Paul's Parish Church* 1949 SLT (Sh Ct) 54 at 55 per Sheriff Prain.

14.18 *Tenant's hardship* Tenancies have been renewed on the ground of the tenant's greater hardship where termination would result in the loss of the tenant's sole means of livelihood[1] or where the tenant's savings have been invested in the business carried out in the shop.[2]

In cases where a lease is renewed because of the tenant's greater hardship, the court may decide to mitigate any hardship to the landlord by increasing the rent.[3]

1 *McDowall v Thomson* (1950) 66 Sh Ct Rep 101; *Thom v British Transport Commission* 1954 SLT (Sh Ct) 21, (1952) 58 Sh Ct Rep 290; *MacLeod v MacTavish* 1952 SLT (Sh Ct) 20, (1952) 68 Sh Ct Rep 62; *King v Cross Fisher Properties Ltd* 1956 SLT (Sh Ct) 79, (1956) 72 Sh Ct Rep 203.
2 *Skelton v Paterson* (1954) 70 Sh Ct Rep 287.
3 *McDowall v Thomson* (1950) 66 Sh Ct Rep 101; *Craig v Saunders & Connor Ltd* 1962 SLT (Sh Ct) 85, (1962) 78 Sh Ct Rep 154.

14.19 *Landlord's hardship* The tenancy may may not be renewed on the ground of the landlord's hardship if renewal would prevent the use of the property for the landlord's own business,[1] or would result in the landlord continuing to be saddled with an uneconomic investment.[2]

It has been suggested in more than one case, though none seem to have been decided directly on this point, that the imposition of several successive yearly renewals could eventually amount to greater hardship for a landlord.[3] The fact that the landlord may want to sell the property will not normally amount to hardship since, as we saw above, the application of the Act can be avoided by an offer to sell the shop to the tenant;[4] however, there may be an exception to this in special circumstances, eg where the landlord also owns adjoining properties which are only saleable in conjunction with the shop.[5]

1 *Shelleys v Saxone Shoe Company Ltd* (1950) 66 Sh Ct Rep 31; *Anderson v National Bank of Scotland Ltd,* (1957) 73 Sh Ct Rep 10; *Jalota v Salvation Army Trustee Co* 1994 GWD 12-770.
2 *Loudon v St Paul's Parish Church* 1949 SLT (Sh Ct) 54, (1949) 65 Sh Ct Rep 138; *St George Co-operative Society Ltd v Burnett's Trustee* (1953) 69 Sh Ct Rep 325.
3 *Wallace v Bute Gift Co Ltd* 1954 SLT (Sh Ct) 55; *White v Paisley Co-operative Manufacturing Society Ltd* 1956 SLT (Sh Ct) 95, (1956) 72 Sh Ct Rep 289.

4 *Cunningham v Watt's Trustees* (1954) 70 Sh Ct Rep 224; see also para 14.14.
5 *Cunningham ibid; St George Co-operative Society Ltd v Burnett's Trustee* (1953) 69 Sh
   Ct Rep 325.

14.20 *Hardship of corporate bodies* A limited company or other corporate body may suffer hardship in terms of the Act.[1] It has been held that the relevant test includes such matters as undue disruption of legitimate transactions and business.[2] Financial hardship may also be relevant.[3]

1 *St George Co-operative Society Ltd v Burnett's Trustee* (1953) 69 Sh Ct Rep 325;
   Anderson v National Bank of Scotland Ltd, (1957) 73 Sh Ct Rep 10; *White v Paisley Co-
   operative Manufacturing Society Ltd* 1956 SLT (Sh Ct) 95, (1956) 72 Sh Ct Rep 289.
2 *Loudon v St Paul's Parish Church* 1949 SLT (Sh Ct) 54, (1949) 65 Sh Ct Rep 138;
   Jalota v Salvation Army Trustee Co 1994 GWD 12-770.
3 *St George Co-operative Society Ltd v Burnett's Trustee* (1953) 69 Sh Ct Rep 325.

14.21 *Hardship of third parties* Normally only hardship suffered by the landlord or tenant may be taken into account; hardship suffered by a third party[1] or by the public in general[2] is irrelevant.

However, there may be an exception to this where there is sufficient proximity between the interests of the third party or parties and that of the landlord or the tenant, eg where a majority of the third party's shareholders were also shareholders of the landlord company.[3] And in *Jalota v Salvation Army Trustee Co*[4] it was held that there was sufficient proximity, when considering hardship, between the defender and the people who were in receipt of the Salvation Army's services.

1 *Hurry v M'Lauchlan* (1953) 69 Sh Ct Rep 305.
2 *King v Cross Fisher Properties Ltd* 1956 SLT (Sh Ct) 79, (1956) 72 Sh Ct Rep 203.
3 *Mowat v Cockburn Hotel (Edinburgh) Company Ltd* 1954 SLT (Sh Ct) 76, (1954) 70 Sh
   Ct Rep 289.
4 1994 GWD 12-770.

Reasonableness[1]

14.22 Whether or not one of the grounds of dismissal has been established, the sheriff has an overriding discretion to dismiss a tenant's application 'if in all the circumstances he thinks it reasonable to do so'. In *Edinburgh Woollen Mill v Singh* the sheriff, having spent some time considering the background to and policy of the Act,[2] opined that the court's role was 'to avoid injustice in the historic context of widespread economic oppression of small scale shop traders'[3] thus suggesting a narrowing of the discretion granted to the court in determining an application. This approach to the court's discretion was doubted in *Select Service Partner Ltd v Network Rail,* where the sheriff found that the Act gives the sheriff the widest discretion to refuse an application where that is reasonable in all the circumstances.[4] The sheriff noted that, 'there is nothing in the Act to suggest that the protection given to tenants is exceptional or that any discretion is to be used only sparingly'.[5]

Case discussion on the sheriff's discretion tends to overlap with consideration of the 'greater hardship' ground. For example, the imposition of several successive yearly renewals, as well as increasing the hardship suffered by a landlord, may also eventually make it reasonable to dismiss a tenant's application.[6] On the other hand, it may be unreasonable to refuse a temporary extension, if only because the tenant may need time to relocate elsewhere.[7]

Where a tenant was unable to pay an economic rent, it was considered reasonable to dismiss his application, since the purpose of the Act is to protect tenants from eviction, not to subsidise them economically.[8] And in deciding if it is reasonable to refuse a tenant's application, it may be relevant for the sheriff to take into account the fact that the landlord has offered to sell (as opposed to lease) suitable alternative premises to the tenant, or has offered to pay the tenant compensation.[9]

1 TOS(S)A 1949 s 1(3).
2 This approach has been criticised on the basis that reference to material extraneous to the Act is only permissible when the wording of the statute is ambiguous, obscure or could lead to absurdity: see *Select Service Partner Ltd v Network Rail* 2015 SLT (Sh Ct) 116.
3 2013 SLT (Sh Ct) 141 at para 29.
4 2015 SLT (Sh Ct) 116 at para 19.
5 2015 SLT (Sh Ct) 116 at para 18.
6 *Wallace v Bute Gift Co Ltd* 1954 SLT (Sh Ct) 55.
7 *Stenhouse v East Kilbride Development Corporation* 1962 SLT (Sh Ct) 35, (1961) 77 Sh Ct Rep 157; *Robertson v Bass Holdings* 1993 SLT (Sh Ct) 55.
8 *Stenhouse v East Kilbride Development Corporation* 1962 SLT (Sh Ct) 35, (1961) 77 Sh Ct Rep 157; *Hamilton Central Co-operative Society Ltd v Simpson* (1952) 68 Sh Ct Rep 148.
9 *Robertson v Bass Holdings* 1993 SLT (Sh Ct) 55; in that case, however, it was held that the alternative accommodation was unsuitable and the amount of compensation offered inadequate.

PART 4
AGRICULTURAL LEASES

Chapter 15

Agricultural leases

INTRODUCTION

Historical background

15.1   Since the late 19th century, leases of agricultural land have been subject to statutory control by a series of enactments generally known as the Agricultural Holdings Acts. The broad object of this legislation was to encourage tenants to farm well and to make any necessary improvements to the land, while at the same time ensuring that the landlords received a proper economic rent. Under the common law, of course, fixtures and other improvements added by the tenant would accrue to the landlord at the end of the lease.[1] The legislation, which continued to develop over the course of the 20th century until the most recent consolidating Act in 1991, addressed this problem by giving tenants indefinite security of tenure and, in certain cases where this was denied and leases were terminated, by paying the tenant compensation, including compensation for improvements. The legislation also regulated the landlord and tenant relationship in a number of other ways.

However, in more recent years it became apparent that the system needed to be reformed. The security of tenure provisions, coupled with the right of tenants in many cases to inherit leases, meant that landlords could be denied vacant possession over many decades. They responded by an almost universal practice of granting new leases, not to individuals, but to limited partnerships which included the landlord. This is basically an artificial device which allows landlords to circumvent the security of tenure provisions.[2]

1 See para 10.39 et seq.
2 For a description of how limited partnerships operate in this context see *MacFarlane v Falfield Investments Ltd* 1998 SC 14, 1998 SLT 145.

Fixed-term leases

15.2   As a result, far-reaching changes were introduced by the Agricultural Holdings (Scotland) Act 2003. Two new types of fixed-term tenancy were introduced where the tenant has no right to security of tenure beyond the contractual term of the lease:

(1)   Short Limited Duration Tenancies (SLDTs) with a *maximum* length of five years; and

(2)   Limited Duration Tenancies (LDTs) with a *minimum* length of 10 years.[1]

Fixed term leases between five and 10 years cannot normally be created.

The old law (revised in a number of ways but preserving the security of tenure right) continues to apply to leases entered into before 27 November 2003 ('1991 Act tenancies'). New 1991 Act tenancies can still be created, but only by agreement of the parties.[2]

The 2003 Act also introduced measures to curb the use of limited partnerships,[3] as well as other innovations, including the right of tenants to diversify, and a right of pre-emption for tenants with 1991 Act tenancies.[4]

Further changes were made by the Land Reform (Scotland) Act 2016, which amended the 2003 Act by introducing two new forms of agricultural tenancy:

•   Modern Limited Duration Tenancies (MLDTs), an updated version of LDTs; and

•   Repairing tenancies.

1 The original minimum length was 15 years – see para 15.11.
2 See para 15.9.
3 See the Agricultural Holdings (Scotland) Act 2003 ss 70–74. In *Salvesen v Riddell* [2013] UKSC 22, 2013 GWD 14-304 the Supreme Court held that s 72(10) (a transitional measure) was incompatible with a landlord's property rights under Protocol 1 Article 1 of the European Convention on Human Rights. (See para 1.36). For the sequel to *Salvesen*, see *McMaster v Scottish Ministers* [2018] CSIH 40, 2018 SC 546.
4 See para 15.32 et seq.

Current legislation

15.3   The current law, therefore, is contained in two main statutes:

(1)   The Agricultural Holdings (Scotland) Act 1991 (the most recent consolidating act), which has been substantially amended and added to by the 2003 Act; and

(2)   The Agricultural Holdings (Scotland) Act 2003.

Subsequent amendments have been made by The Public Services Reform (Agricultural Holdings) (Scotland) Order 2011,[1] by the Agricultural Holdings (Amendment) (Scotland) Act 2012 and by the Land Reform (Scotland) Act 2016. The 2016 Act followed a wide-ranging review of agricultural holdings legislation by an expert group appointed by the Scottish Government.[2]

This chapter only attempts to give a broad overview of the legislation relating to agricultural leases, with a selective reference to relevant cases.[3]

1 SSI 2011/232.
2 Scottish Government, *Review of Agricultural Holdings Legislation: Final Report* (Edinburgh 2015), available at www2.gov.scot/Resource/0046/00468852.pdf.
3 For a more detailed account that is sufficiently recent to take on board the provisions of the 2016 Act see Lord Gill, *Law of Agricultural Tenancies in Scotland* 4th edn (2016).

The Tenant Farming Commissioner

15.4   Part 2 of the Land Reform (Scotland) Act 2016 established the Scottish Land Commission, with various functions centred around the promotion of best practice in the use of land in Scotland. One of the Commissioners is a Tenant Farming Commissioner (TFC).[1]

The TFC has a number of specific functions:[2]

(a)   To prepare codes of practice on agricultural holdings.[3]
(b)   To promote the codes of practice.[4]
(c)   To inquire into alleged breaches of the codes of practice.[5] This is without prejudice to any time limit for proceedings in the Land Court under any enactment.[6] The TFC is entitled to require a response from anyone with an interest in the relevant tenancy[7] and require any person 'to provide such information as the Commissioner considers appropriate for the purposes of the inquiry',[8] and may impose a penalty of up to £1,000 for non-compliance.[9] The Commissioner does not, however, have any power to penalise breaches of the codes of practice.
(d)   To prepare a report on the operation of agents of landlords and tenants within 12 months of the day that the relevant provisions came into force, i.e. by 1 April 2018.[10]
(e)   To prepare recommendations for a modern list of improvements to agricultural holdings.[11]
(f)   To refer for the opinion of the Land Court any question of law relating to agricultural holdings.
(g)   To collaborate with the Land Commissioners in the exercise of their functions to the extent that those functions relate to agriculture and agricultural holdings.
(h)   To exercise any other functions conferred on the Commissioner by any enactment.

It will readily be seen that the TFC can be expected to have a significant impact on agricultural tenants and landlords, and these functions are to be exercised with a view to encouraging good relations between landlords and tenants.[12]

In April 2020, the Scottish Government published a review of the functions of the Tenant Farming Commissioner.[13] The review found strong support for the TFC retaining all existing functions, though with a feeling also that it was too early to reach a settled view on the matter. There was some support both for an expansion of the TFC's role in dispute resolution and for powers to impose penalties for breaches of codes of practice. The latter was among the recommendations in the review.[14]

1 LR(S)A 2016 s 4.
2 LR(S)A 2016 s 24(1).
3 See LR(S)A 2016 s 27 for a non-exhaustive list of matters these codes of practice may cover. The codes of practice that have been issued by the TFC are available at: https://landcommission.gov.scot/our-work/tenant-farming/codes-of-practice.
4 This is to be done in accordance with LR(S)A 2016 s 28.
5 Detailed provisions are found in LR(S)A 2016 ss 29–34.
6 LR(S)A 2016 s 29(6).
7 LR(S)A 2016 s 30(4)(c).
8 LR(S)A 2016 s 31(1).
9 LR(S)A 2016 s 31(2)–(3).
10 LR(S)A 2016 s 36(1)(b). The report and related documents are available at: https://landcommission.gov.scot/our-work/tenant-farming/reviews.
11 This is to be done in accordance with LR(S)A 2016 s 37.
12 LR(S)A 2016 s 24(2).
13 Scottish Government, A review of the functions of the Tenant Farming Commissioner (2020), available at: www.gov.scot/binaries/content/documents/govscot/publications/research-and-analysis/2020/04/review-functions-tenant-farming-commissioner/documents/review-functions-tenant-farming-commissioner/review-functions-tenant-farming-commissioner/govscot%3Adocument/review-functions-tenant-farming-commissioner.pdf. This was issued in compliance with LR(S)A 2016 s 24(3)–(5), which required the Scottish Ministers to undertake such a review and publish its findings within three years of the relevant provisions coming into force, ie by 1 April 2020. Section 24 permits the Scottish Ministers to amend the functions of the Tenant Farming Commissioner by regulations, following this review.
14 Scottish Government, Tenant Farming Commissioner Review p. 16.

Contracting out

15.5   Contracting out of the legislation is not universally prohibited but is expressly forbidden in many instances, which the 2003 Act has significantly added to. These cases will be noted as we go along.

In some other cases, although there has been no express prohibition, the courts have held that the mandatory wording of the provision has precluded contracting out. It was suggested by the House of Lords in *Johnson v Moreton*[1] that, in the latter cases, the underlying distinction is between those provisions that affect only the private contractual interests of the parties (where contracting out is allowed), and those that involve the public interest, including the welfare of the tenant and the proper farming of the land (where contracting out is forbidden). Contracting out is prohibited, for example, in respect of the provisions for a written notice to quit,[2] entitlement to compensation,[3] and, most importantly of all, security of tenure.[4]

1 [1980] AC 37, [1978] 3 All ER 37, HL.
2 AH(S)A 1991 s 21(1).
3 AH(S)A 1991 s 53.
4 *Johnson v Moreton* [1980] AC 37, [1978] 3 All ER 37, HL.

Structure of chapter

15.6   The remainder of the chapter, therefore, will be divided into the following topics:

(1)   Types of agricultural tenancy;[1]
(2)   General provisions regarding lease terms;[2]
(3)   Security of tenure (1991 Act tenancies only);[3]
(4)   Tenants' compensation rights;[4]
(5)   Succession to agricultural leases;[5]
(6)   Dispute resolution.[6]

1 See para 15.7 et seq.
2 See para 15.15 et seq.
3 See para 15.43 et seq.
4 See para 15.56 et seq.
5 See para 15.74 et seq.
6 See para 15.84 et seq.

TYPES OF AGRICULTURAL TENANCY

15.7   The following are now the main types of agricultural tenancy:

(1)   1991 Act tenancies
(2)   Short Limited Duration Tenancies (SLDTs);
(3)   Limited Duration Tenancies 'LDTs);
(4)   Modern Limited Duration Tenancies (MLDTs);
(5)   Repairing tenancies;
(6)   Leases for grazing or mowing; and
(7)   Crofts and small landholdings.

Crofts and other small landholdings are regulated by their own separate legislation. These provisions are rather complex, but an overview of them is given in the next chapter.[1]

The provision in the 1991 Act which allowed leases for less than a year to be entered into with the consent of the Scottish Ministers has been repealed.[2] This provision was rendered unnecessary by the introduction of short limited duration tenancies.

1 See Ch 16.
2 AH(S)A 1991 s 2, repealed by the AH(S)A 2003 s 1(3).

15.8 *Definition of 'agricultural lease'* The types of lease to which the 1991 Act applies were known as agricultural holdings, and an agricultural holding is defined in that Act as 'a lease of agricultural land', which in turn is defined as 'land used for agriculture for the purposes of a trade or business'.[1] 'Agriculture' is given a very comprehensive definition, but generally includes all arable, pastoral and livestock-raising activity.[2] In *O'Donnell v McDonald*[3] it was held that the lease of a riding school which incidentally involved the grazing of horses was not a lease of land used for agriculture. As a result, the lease was a commercial lease which could be terminated at the ish and not a 1991 Act tenancy in respect of which the tenant enjoyed security of tenure.[4] In addition, as the definition indicates, the agricultural use must be 'for the purposes of a trade or business'. It has been held that the occasional sale of surplus produce, from land primarily occupied to serve the occupier's needs, does not constitute such use.[5]

The 1991 Act defines 'lease' as 'a letting of land for a term of years, or for lives, or for lives and years, or from year to year.[6] As with other types of lease, agricultural leases can be created informally.[7] However, in *Bell v Inkersall Investments Ltd*[8] it was held that the existence of an agricultural lease of an estate could not be implied by the fact that the tenant had enjoyed a series of temporary grazing lets of part of the land, as these were quite different types of contract.

The same definitions would appear to apply to the new types of tenancy introduced by the 2003 Act.[9]

In all cases the tenant cannot be an employee of the landlord.[10]

A lease of agricultural land that does not fall within the definitions of any of the tenancies regulated by the 1991 and 2003 Acts is not necessarily invalid.[11]

1 AH(S)A 1991 s 1.
2 AH(S)A 1991 s 85(1).
3 2008 SC 189, 2007 SLT 1227.
4 See para 15.43 et seq.
5 *Gunn v Luyken* 2019 GWD 6-77, Land Court.
6 AH(S)A 1991 s 85(1). A liferent lease, contingent upon the 'life' of a single individual is excluded from this definition – see *Special Case presented by Mountain's Trustees* [2012] CSIH 73, 2012 GWD 33-663.

7 See para 2.9 et seq. See also *Morrison-Low v Paterson (No 1)* 1985 SC (HL) 49, 1985 SLT 255.
8 2006 SC 507, 2006 SLT 626.
9 This is implied by the wording of s 1 of the 2003 Act; see also AH(S)A 2003 s 93.
10 AH(S)A 1991 s 1(1), AH(S)A 2003 ss 4(1), 5(1) (repealed subject to saving provision contained in the Land Reform (Scotland) Act 2016 (Commencement No 6, Transitory and Saving Provisions) Regulations 2017 SSI/299 reg 4), 5A(1) and 5C(1)).
11 *Special Case presented by Mountain's Trustees* [2012] CSIH 73, 2012 GWD 33-663 (a liferent lease). See also para 9.11.

1991 Act tenancies[1]

15.9   This mainly refers to leases of agricultural holdings entered into prior to 27 November 2003 when the relevant provisions of the 2003 Act came into force. New 1991 Act tenancies can also be entered into after that date, but only if both parties agree to this in writing prior to the commencement of the tenancy.[2] There is no obvious reason why landlords would normally agree to this.

The statutory rights of 1991 Act tenants under the old law have largely been preserved and will be considered at the relevant points throughout the chapter.

The 1991 Act did not allow agricultural leases for a term of less than a year.[3] If an agricultural lease was entered into purporting to be for less than a year prior to 27 November 2003, and it is one to which the 1991 Act would otherwise apply, it will have taken effect as a lease from year to year, bringing it within the ambit of the 1991 Act. Any such leases that still exist will therefore be 1991 Act tenancies.

A 1991 Act tenancy may be converted into a modern limited duration tenancy of the same land for not less than 25 years by agreement between the parties.[4] The tenant has certain compensation rights as a result of the conversion.[5]

1 AH(S)A 1991; AH(S)A 2003 3 s 1.
2 AH(S)A 2003 s 1(2).
3 AH(S)A 1991 s 2 (repealed by AH(S)A 2003 s 1(3)).
4 AH(S)A 2003 s 2A. But see *Edinburgh City Council v Little* 2008 SLCR 18 in which the tenant lost the right to demand a limited duration tenancy because he had earlier entered into an agreement to renounce his 1991 Act tenancy.
5 AH(S)A 2003 s 2A(4).

Short Limited Duration Tenancies (SLDTs)[1]

15.10   A short limited duration tenancy is a lease of agricultural land for a term of not more than five years. It is a lease entered into after

27 November 2003 (or which otherwise does not qualify as a 1991 Act tenancy).

Where an SLDT for less than five years expires and the tenant remains in occupation of the land with the landlord's consent, the lease will take effect as if it were a lease for five years, or such lesser period as the parties agree.[2]

There are anti-avoidance provisions to deal with a situation where an SLDT is allowed to run over the five-year limit. In such a case, the lease, by default, will become a modern limited duration tenancy of 10 years commencing at the start of the term of the short limited duration tenancy, ie the term will be extended by five years.[3] The same will happen if, before the term of the SLDT expires, the parties agree in writing to convert the lease to a modern limited duration tenancy.[4]

This can also happen if an SLDT has been terminated but the parties enter a new lease of the same land within a year. The term of the first lease will be added to that of the second, and if the combined term exceeds five years, the tenancy will be a modern limited duration tenancy.[5]

1 AH(S)A 2003 s 4.
2 AH(S) A 2003 s 4(3).
3 AH(S)A 2003 s 5(2) (substituted by The Public Services Reform (Agricultural Holdings) (Scotland) Order 2011, SSI 232, art 8). This amendment, which results from the reduction of the minimum length of LDTs from 15 to 10 years, is not retrospective, so any such conversions that occurred before 22 March 2011 will have resulted in an LDT of 15 years commencing *after the expiry of* the SLDT. (The Public Services Reform (Agricultural Holdings) (Scotland) Order 2011, SSI 232, art 10(5).) See para 15.11.
4 AH(S)A 2003 s 5A(2)(a).
5 AH(S)A 2003 s 4 (4) and (5) and s 5A (3) (as amended by The Public Services Reform (Agricultural Holdings) (Scotland) Order 2011, SSI 232, art 7).

Limited Duration Tenancies ('LDTs')[1]

15.11   A limited duration tenancy was a lease of agricultural land for a term of not less than 10 years. It is no longer competent to create a limited duration tenancy. Any new lease of agricultural land for a term of at least 10 years (unless it is a 1991 Act tenancy) will be instead a Modern Limited Duration Tenancy.

1 AH(S)A 2003 s 5 (repealed subject to savings).

Modern Limited Duration Tenancies ('MLDTs')

15.12   Modern limited duration tenancies were introduced by the Land Reform (Scotland) Act 2016, which amended the 2003 Act. With effect from 30 November 2017, it is no longer competent to create a limited duration tenancy. Existing LDTs are unaffected, unless the parties agree to convert the lease to an MLDT.[1]

As was the case with LDTs, an MLDT must have a term of at least 10 years. There is no provision for the creation of a fixed-term lease with a term between five and 10 years. Any lease purporting to have such a term will take effect as a lease of 10 years and will be a modern limited duration tenancy.[2] In addition, as noted above, a short limited duration tenancy of five years or less which is allowed to run on with the landlord's consent will also become a modern limited duration tenancy. There are certain differences between LDTs and MLDTs:

- Where the tenant is a 'new entrant', the parties may agree a break clause at five years.[3]
- While, as with an LDT, the landlord has to provide fixed equipment, the landlord is permitted to contract out of the obligation to renew or replace it.[4]
- The termination procedure is the same. However, if the lease continues beyond the ish, the period for which it automatically renews is different.[5]

1 AH(S)A 2003 s 2B.
2 AH(S)A 2003 s 5A(4).
3 See para 15.38.
4 See para 15.17.
5 See para 15.37.

Repairing tenancies

15.13   Repairing tenancies are a new form of agricultural lease, for which the relevant provisions have not yet been brought into force.

The idea behind repairing tenancies is that the tenant takes on the full responsibility for provision of fixed equipment and for its maintenance, renewal and replacement.[1] In exchange, the tenant benefits from a longer term of at least 35 years.[2] The lease must provide for a 'repairing period' of at least five years. The repairing period may be extended by agreement, or by the Land Court on application by either party.[3] To qualify as a repairing tenancy, the lease must expressly identify itself as such[4] and must require the tenant, during the repairing period, 'to improve the land comprised in the lease in order to bring it into a state capable of being farmed, after the expiry of the repairing period, in accordance with the rules of good husbandry'.[5] It is clearly anticipated that repairing tenancies will only be used where that is required, though it is not formally a requirement that that be the case.

A repairing tenancy is essentially a modified form of the modern limited duration tenancy. There are, though, a number of important differences:

- During the repairing period, the tenant cannot be held liable for not farming the land in accordance with the rules of good husbandry.[6]
- Special provision is made for a break clause to be exercised during the repairing period.[7]
- Unless otherwise agreed, the whole obligation to provide, maintain, renew and replace fixed equipment falls on the tenant.[8]
- Resumption of land by the landlord is not permitted until five years have elapsed from the expiry of the repairing period.[9]

Other differences will be noted as we proceed.

1 Scottish Government, *Review of Agricultural Holdings Legislation: Final Report* (2015) recommendation 25.
2 AH(S)A 2003 s 5C(1)(a).
3 AH(S)A 2003 s 5C(2)–(4).
4 AH(S)A 2003 s 5C(1)(e).
5 AH(S)A 2003 s 5C(1)(d).
6 AH(S)A 2003 ss 5D and 18B(2). See para 15.16.
7 AH(S)A 2003 ss 5C(5) and 8G. See para 15.39.
8 AH(S)A 2003 s 16B(5). See para 15.17.
9 AH(S)A 2003 s 17A. See para 15.31.

Leases for grazing or mowing[1]

15.14 This special category applies to a lease under which agricultural land is let for the purpose of its being used only for grazing or mowing during some specified period of the year. This need not be expressly provided in the lease, ie presumably it can also be implied from the circumstances, for example if the land is actually used for one of these purposes.

The maximum period allowed is 364 days, though typically it will be for a particular season of the year. At least one day must elapse after the expiry of the lease before it can be relet to the same tenant for the same purpose.

If such a tenancy is allowed to run on past the termination date with the landlord's consent it will, by default, become a short limited duration tenancy. This will be for five years unless the parties agree to a shorter term.[2]

1 AH(S)A 2003 s 3.
2 AH(S)A 2003 s 4(2).

GENERAL PROVISIONS REGARDING LEASE TERMS

Written leases[1]

15.15 These provisions apply equally to 1991 Act tenancies, short limited duration tenancies, limited duration tenancies, modern limited duration tenancies and repairing tenancies (the relevant provisions in the 2003 Act having largely repeated or incorporated those in the 1991 Act).

Where there is no written lease embodying the terms of a tenancy, either party may require the other to enter into a written agreement for this purpose. This should include the basic terms included in Schedule 1 to the Agricultural Holdings (Scotland) Act 1991, as well as the provisions regarding maintenance of fixed equipment.[2] If there is a written lease, but it does not incorporate these terms, either party may likewise require the other to enter into an amended lease that does. Six months' written notice should be given by the party requiring the lease, or the amendment, failing which the terms of the lease will be referred to the Land Court.

1 AH(S)A 1991 s 4 (as amended) and sch 1; AH(S)A 2003 s 13.
2 See para 15.17.

15.16 *Lease terms* The basic lease terms laid down by Schedule 1 are as follows:

(1) The names of the parties.
(2) Particulars of the land, with sufficient description to identify its extent by reference to a map or plan of the fields and other parcels of land.
(3) The duration of the let, or durations if different for different parts of the land.
(4) The rent and the dates on which it is payable.
(5) An undertaking by the landlord to reinstate or replace any building damaged by fire, if this is required by the rules of good estate management. The landlord is also required to insure all such buildings for their full value. The insurance requirement does not apply to government departments or other landlords who, with the approval of the Scottish Ministers, have made provision for defraying the cost of such reinstatement; the reason for this is that landlords, such as the government, who own a large amount of property, may find that bearing the cost of any fire damage themselves is cheaper than paying the necessary insurance premiums.
(6) An undertaking by the tenant, so far as required by the rules of good husbandry, to return the full equivalent manurial value of any harvested crops destroyed by fire, which were grown on the land for consumption there. The tenant is also required to insure all such harvested crops, as well as dead stock, though there is a similar exemption as in (5) where the tenant is a government department or the permission of the Scottish Ministers has been given.

The first four of these conditions, of course, are basically the essential provisions that any lease must have at common law.[1] They would therefore have been legally necessary, even if the Act had not specifically included them.

1 See para 2.22 et seq.

Maintenance of fixed equipment[1]

15.17 The 1991 Act provides for certain maintenance provisions to be included in every 1991 Act tenancy, and there are parallel, though not quite identical, provisions in the 2003 Act in relation to short limited duration, limited duration and modern limited duration tenancies.

The landlord is bound to provide such fixed equipment as is necessary in a thorough state of repair. In the case of 1991 Act tenancies this must be done at the commencement of the lease or as soon as reasonably practicable thereafter. This was also the situation in the case of short limited and limited duration tenancies entered into before 22 March 2011, but since that date the rule is that it must be done within 6 months of the tenancy's commencement, or as soon as reasonably practicable thereafter if other statutory obligations of the landlord prevent it.

Broadly speaking, 'fixed equipment' means all permanent buildings or structures necessary for the holding, including farm buildings, fences, hedges and dykes, gates, ditches, drains, service roads and electrical equipment, among others.[2] Both landlord and tenant have maintenance obligations in relation to the fixed equipment. The landlord is bound to make such replacement or renewal of the fixed equipment as is made necessary by natural decay or fair wear and tear. Otherwise, the maintenance obligation falls upon the tenant, ie to keep it in a good state of repair, fair wear and tear excepted.

In the case of modern limited duration tenancies, the parties are permitted to contract out of the landlord's obligation to renew or replace fixed equipment.[3] This is a change from the position with limited duration tenancies.

In a repairing tenancy, the whole obligation to provide, maintain, renew and replace fixed equipment falls on the tenant, unless otherwise agreed.[4]

1 AH(S)A 1991 s 5 (as amended); AH(S) A 2003 s 16 (as amended).
2 AH(S) A 1991 s 85(1); AH(S) A 2003 s 93.
3 AH(S)A 2003 s 16A(5).
4 AH(S)A 2003 s 16B(5).

15.18 *Post-lease agreements* It was formerly the case in relation to 1991 Act tenancies that either party could agree to be responsible for the other's obligations regarding the fixed equipment.[1] However, any agreement by the parties in a short limited duration, limited duration, modern limited duration or repairing tenancy requiring the tenant to bear the expense of any work required to fulfil the landlord's obligations is of no effect.[2]

The same applies to 1991 Act tenancies where such an agreement has been made after the 2003 Act came into force; furthermore, if any agreement was made prior to that for the tenant to carry out or pay for any of the landlord's obligations, there is a procedure whereby the tenant can have the agreement nullified.[3]

Presumably it is still possible (if rather unlikely) for the landlord to agree to relieve the tenant of some of the tenant's obligations in relation to fixed equipment.

In the case of all of these types of tenancy, any agreement requiring the tenant to pay the whole or part of a fire insurance premium in respect of the fixed equipment will be null and void.[4] This also applies to modern limited duration tenancies and repairing tenancies, despite the general power to contract for the tenant to be responsible for replacement or renewal of fixed equipment.[5]

1 AH(S)A 1991 s 5 (3) (now repealed).
2 AH(S)A 2003 ss 16(6), 16A(7) and 16B(8).
3 AH(S)A 1991 s 5 (4A) to 4(D) (added by the AH(S) A 2003 s 60(b), as amended by The Public Services Reform (Agricultural Holdings) (Scotland) Order 2011, SSI 232, art 4). See *Telfer v Buccleuch Estates Ltd* [2012] CSIH 47, 2013 GWD 20-403. Note that the amended procedure introduced by the 2011 Order only applies in cases where the notice by the landlord or the tenant was given on or after 22 March 2011.
4 AH(S)A 1991 s 5(4); AH(S) A 2003 s 16(7).
5 AH(S)A 2003 ss 16A(8) and 16B(9).

15.19 *Schedule of fixed equipment*[1] In the case of short limited duration, limited duration, modern limited duration and repairing tenancies entered into on or after 22 March 2011, the parties must agree to a schedule specifying the fixed equipment and its condition, which will be deemed to be part of the lease. Both parties may agree to vary or substitute this schedule at a later date during the currency of the lease. Unless otherwise agreed, the cost should be borne equally by the parties. In the case of SLDTs and LDTs entered into before 22 March 2011, the only equivalent obligation was to have specified the fixed equipment in the lease.

Although these provisions relate only to SLDT, LDTs, MLDTs and repairing tenancies, a similar function is fulfilled in the case of 1991 Act tenancies by the obligation to make a record of the fixed equipment.[2]

1 AH(S)A 2003 ss 16(2), (3) and (5); 16A(2), (3), (4) and (6); 16B(1)-(4).
2 See para 15.20.

Record of holding[1]

15.20 Since disputes may arise, either during a tenancy or at its termination – regarding, for example, who provided certain fixtures, or whether neglect of a holding was inherited by or caused by the tenant – it is useful to have some independent evidence by which to establish the facts. In relation to 1991 Act tenancies, the 1991 Act therefore provides for written records of certain aspects of a holding to be made, some of them compulsory, some optional. Such a record is to be made by a person appointed by agreement between the parties, failing which by the Scottish Ministers. The following are the types of record that may be made:

(a) A record of the condition of the fixed equipment. This *must* be made at the beginning of the tenancy and is deemed to form part of the lease.

(b) A record of the condition of cultivation of the holding and of the condition of the fixed equipment. This may be made at any time during the currency of the lease but is not compulsory unless either the landlord or the tenant demands it.

(c) Any improvements made by the tenant, or fixtures or buildings which the tenant is entitled to remove.[2] This only needs to be made if the tenant demands it.

In relation to (b) and (c), the parties may agree to make a record of only part of the holding, or of the fixed equipment only.

The cost of making a record, unless the parties have agreed otherwise, is borne in equal shares. Any dispute may be referred by either party to the Land Court.

These provisions apply only to 1991 Act tenancies and not to short limited duration, limited duration, modern limited duration or repairing tenancies. However, it is now necessary for a schedule of fixed equipment to be made in the case of these forms of tenancy,[3] and there is nothing to prevent the parties creating any other kind of record on a voluntary basis.

1 AH(S)A 1991 s 5(1) and s 8 (as amended).
2 See para 15.21.
3 See para 15.19.

Tenant's right to remove fixtures[1]

15.21 We saw above that the necessary buildings and other basic equipment necessary to run the farm have to be provided by the landlord as fixed equipment.[2] However, in the case of 1991 Act tenancies, there is a further statutory provision to cover the situation where additional fixtures may have been added by the tenant. These may be removed either during the tenancy or within six months after the lease has ended. A fixture is defined as 'any engine, machinery, fencing or other fixture'. The same right applies to buildings erected by the tenant, other than ones where there is an entitlement to compensation for improvements.

A fixture or building may only be removed if the tenant is up to date with the rent and has performed all other obligations of the lease. Also, the tenant must give the landlord one month's written notice of the intention to exercise this right, which will give the landlord the option of buying the fixture at its value to an incoming tenant. If the fixture is in fact removed, the tenant must make good all damage caused by its removal.

The 2003 Act appears to contain no equivalent provision in relation to other forms of tenancy. However, the common law in relation to a tenant's right to remove trade fixtures would presumably apply in such cases, subject to any contrary provision in the lease.[3]

1 AH(S)A 1991 s 18.
2 See para 15.17.
3 See para 10.41.

Rent reviews[1]

15.22 As with any other kind of lease, if its contractual duration is of any length, the landlord will have included provision for rent reviews at regular intervals. In general terms, the parties are free to agree their own provisions for rent review. In addition, in the case of 1991 Act tenancies, limited duration tenancies, modern limited duration tenancies and repairing tenancies, there are supplementary provisions for rent review laid down by statute.[2] (There is no such provision in the case of short limited duration tenancies, presumably because this is thought unnecessary in the case of leases with a maximum length of five years.)

1 AH(S)A 1991 ss 13–15 (as amended); AH(S)A 2003 ss 9–11.
2 AH(S)A 2003 s 9(A1) (inserted by Agricultural Holdings (Amendment) (Scotland) Act 2012 s 2, amended by LR(S)A 2016 Sch 2 para 8(a)).

15.23 In the case of 1991 Act tenancies, statutory rent reviews can only take place after the date when the contractual term of the lease could have been brought to an end by notice to quit, which would normally be at a break in the lease or during any extended security of tenure that may have been granted by the Land Court;[1] apart from that, any provision for rent review will be dependent upon the terms of the lease. In *AC Stoddart & Sons v Coltstoun Trust Trustees* [2] it was held that either party could initiate a rent review (in this case the tenant) at a break in the lease, even though that break could only be exercised by one party (in this case the landlord).

1 See para 15.43 et seq.
2 (Sub nom *AC Stoddart & Sons, Coltsoun (1995) v Balfour Thomson* CA) 2007 SC 655, 2007 SLT 593.

15.24   In the case of limited duration and modern limited duration tenancies the statutory rent review procedure can be initiated in mid-term in cases where there is no provision for rent review in the lease. Where there is such a provision, but it is limited to upward-only reviews, or the review may only be initiated by the landlord, such a provision will be void and the statutory procedure will apply by default.[1] This proviso only applies to MLDTs or to LDTs entered into on or after 12 September 2012.[2]

A repairing tenancy may not validly make provision for rent review at all. Rent review in a repairing tenancy will always be subject to the statutory procedure.[3]

1 AH(S)A 2003 s 9(A1) (inserted by Agricultural Holdings (Amendment) (Scotland) Act 2012 s 2, amended by LR(S)A 2016 Sch 2 para 8(a)).
2 AH(A)(S) A 2012 s 4(2).
3 AH(S)A 2013 s 9(1A), prospectively inserted by LR(S)A 2016 s 102(2)(c).

15.25   In the case of 1991 Act tenancies, repairing tenancies, LDTs and MLDTs, the review can be initiated by one of the parties serving prior written notice on the other of not less than one year or more than two years,[1] and the minimum period between reviews is three years. The onus of proof as to when a notice has been served will normally be upon the party who serves it.[2]

The new rent is determined by the Land Court according to the valuation criteria prescribed by the legislation.[3]

Apart from the above provisions, the rent may also be varied in certain circumstances:

(a)   when questions relating to lease terms, fixed equipment or insurance premiums have been referred to the Land Court;[4]
(b)   when improvements to the holding have been made by the landlord;[5] and
(c)   where the tenant has been removed from part of the holding.[6]

1 This is clear in the case of LDTs, MLDTs and repairing tenancies, though the wording of s 13(1) of the 1991 Act which relates to 1991 Act tenancies is somewhat ambiguous.
2 *Donald v Cordale Investments Ltd* 1996 SLCR 1.

3 AH(S)A 1991 s 13 (3) to (7A) (as amended); AH(S)A 2003 ss 13(3)–(8) and 9A– 9C. The whole procedure for 1991 Act tenancies is prospectively replaced by LR(S)A 2016 s 101 which, when it comes into force, will insert a new Sch 1A into the 1991 Act.
4 AH(S)A 1991 s 14 (substituted by the AH(S) A 2003 Sch, para 16); AH(S)A 2003 s 11.
5 AH(S)A 1991 ss 14A–15; AH(S)A 2003 ss 10–10F.
6 AH(S)A 1991 s 31; AH(S)A 2003 ss 17(4) and 17A(2); see para 15.31. Section 17(4) of the 2003 Act also applies to short limited duration tenancies.

Right of tenant to withhold rent[1]

15.26 The following provisions apply to the 1991 Act, short limited duration, limited duration, modern limited duration and repairing tenancies. Where the Land Court has made an order under section 84 of the 2003 Act in relation to the landlord's failure to fulfil any obligation towards the tenant in respect of fixed equipment and the landlord has failed to comply with such an order in a material regard, the tenant may apply to the Land Court for a further order:

(a) authorising the tenant to carry out the necessary work; and/or
(b) authorising the tenant to withhold payment of the rent, on condition that the tenant consigns the amount of rent payable with the Land Court.

The tenant may recover any reasonable costs of carrying out the work by applying to the Land Court.

If the work has been carried out and the costs met, the landlord may subsequently apply for the order to be lifted and any remaining sum consigned to be released to the landlord.

In these circumstances the landlord is not entitled to irritate the lease or otherwise terminate it on the ground that the rent has not been paid.

Any provision of the lease attempting to contract out of the above rights will be of no effect.

These provisions are, of course, a statutory development of the tenant's common law right to retain the rent.[2]

1 AH(S)A 1991 s 15A (added by AH(S)A 2003 s 64); AH(S)A 2003 s 12.
2 See para 4.39 et seq.

Assignation and subletting

15.27 *1991 Act tenancies*[1] Whether or not a 1991 Act tenant had the right to assign or sublet was originally governed either by the common law or by the terms of the lease. At common law it was not possible for a tenant to assign or sublet without the landlord's consent where the lease was of ordinary duration, ie for up to 21 years, possibly more.[2] In many cases, however, assignation and subletting would be under the control of the landlord by virtue of the lease's alienation clause.[3] This is still the general rule in relation to most assignations or sublets of 1991 Act tenancies.

However, the 2003 Act introduced a statutory right of 1991 Act tenants to assign the lease to any of the persons who would, in any circumstances, be entitled to succeed to the tenant's estate on intestacy by virtue of the Succession (Scotland) Act 1964. The Land Reform (Scotland) Act 2016 further expanded the category of statutorily permitted assignees. The list is now as follows:[4]

(a) any person who would 'in any circumstances'[5] have been entitled to succeed to the tenant's estate on intestacy, ie any spouse, civil partner or blood relative of the tenant;
(b) a spouse or civil partner of a child of the tenant;
(c) a spouse or civil partner of a grandchild of the tenant;
(d) a spouse or civil partner of a sibling of the tenant;
(e) a sibling of the tenant's spouse or civil partner;
(f) a spouse or civil partner of such a sibling;
(g) a child (including a step-child) of such a sibling;
(h) a grandchild (including a step-grandchild) of such a sibling;
(i) a step-child of the tenant;
(j) a spouse or civil partner of such a step-child;
(k) a descendant of such a step-child;
(l) a step-brother or step-sister of the tenant;
(m) a spouse or civil partner of such a step-brother or step-sister;
(n) a descendant of such a step-brother or step-sister.

The tenant must give the landlord written notice of the intention to assign, and the landlord may withhold consent if there are proper grounds for doing so. The grounds on which the landlord may withhold consent depend on whether the proposed assignee is a 'near relative'. A person is a near relative if he or she falls into one of the following categories:[6]

(a) parent of the tenant;
(b) spouse or civil partner of the tenant;
(c) child of the tenant;
(d) spouse or civil partner of such a child;
(e) grandchild of the tenant;
(f) sibling of the tenant;
(g) spouse or civil partner of such a sibling;
(h) child of a sibling of the tenant;

(i) grandchild of a sibling of the tenant;
(j) sibling of the tenant's spouse or civil partner;
(k) spouse or civil partner of such a sibling;
(l) child of such a brother or sister; or
(m) grandchild of such a brother or sister.

Where the proposed assignee is a near relative, the landlord may object to that person acquiring only on the following grounds:[7]

(a) that the person is not of good character;
(b) that the person does not have sufficient resources to farm the holding with reasonable efficiency; or
(c) that the person does not have sufficient training or experience to be able to farm the holding with reasonable efficiency.

The last of these grounds does not apply if the person is undertaking a course of relevant training in agriculture, or begins one within six months of the date of the tenant's notice, which is expected to be completed within four years.

In other cases, the landlord may only withhold consent if it is reasonable to do so.[8] In particular, the landlord may withhold consent if not satisfied that the proposed assignee would have the ability to pay either the rent or the cost of adequate maintenance of the land, or that the proposed assignee has the skills or experience that would be required properly to manage and maintain the land in accordance with the rules of good husbandry.

The landlord must give the tenant written notice of any such withholding of consent within 30 days, and if no such intimation is made, the landlord will be deemed to have consented to the proposed assignation.[9]

Any lease term or other agreement between the landlord and tenant purporting to prohibit assignation in the above circumstances will be null and void.[10]

Where the tenant has diversified, the tenant may, despite any prohibition, sublet for a purpose that is ancillary to the non-agricultural use. Otherwise subletting will presumably be governed by the terms of the lease, failing which by the common law.[11]

1 AH(S)A 1991 s 10A (added by AH(S)A 2003 s 66).
2 See para 7.20.
3 See para 7.4 et seq.
4 AH(S)A 1991 s 10A(1A). This limitation of potential assignees can, however, be avoided by converting the lease to a modern limited duration tenancy (which does not have this limitation) in terms of AH(S)A 2003 s 2A.
5 Thus the assignee can be anyone potentially succeeding on intestacy, not necessarily someone who would so succeed in the actual circumstances of the tenant's death.
6 AH(S)A 1991 s 10A(6).

7 AH(S)A 1991 s 10A(3A), (3B).
8 AH(S)A 1991 s 10A(3).
9 AH(S)A 1991 s 10A(4).
10 AH(S)A 1991 s 10A(5).
11 See para 7.18 et seq.

15.28 *Short limited duration tenancies*[1] Assignation or subletting of short limited duration tenancies is completely prohibited by the 2003 Act.

1 AH(S)A 2003 s 6.

15.29 *Limited duration, modern limited duration and repairing tenancies*[1] Under the 2003 Act, the tenant of a limited duration or modern limited duration tenancy may assign the lease with the landlord's consent. In this case there is no limitation of potential assignees to those falling within a fixed list of family members, with the result that, in relation to assignations, the Act has superseded both the common law and any alienation provisions in the lease. Otherwise the provisions regarding the requirement to give the landlord notice, the landlord's grounds of refusal and the possibility of deemed consent are exactly the same as in the case of 1991 Act tenancies.

However, in the case of limited duration tenancies (but not modern limited duration tenancies) there is an additional provision giving the landlord the right, on receiving notice of the tenant's intention to assign, to acquire the tenant's interest under the lease. The landlord must give the tenant written notice of this within 30 days of the tenant giving notice, and the terms upon which the landlord acquires the tenant's interest must be no less favourable to the tenant than any reasonable terms upon which the proposed assignation was to have been made.

Unlike the situation with 1991 Act tenancies, it is stated that the tenant under a limited duration tenancy may sublet, but only on such basis as the lease expressly permits.

In the case of a repairing tenancy, the position depends on whether the repairing period has expired. During the repairing period, the tenant may not sublet or assign without the landlord's consent, and the landlord may only refuse consent in the case of an assignation if it is reasonable to do so. After the repairing period, the same rules apply as with a modern limited duration tenancy.

1 AH(S)A 2003 ss 7 (LDTs), 7A and 7B (MLDTs), 7C and 7D (repairing tenancies).

15.30 *Grazing or mowing lets* There is no reference to assignation or subletting of grazing or mowing lets in the legislation, which means that this will be governed either by the common law or by the alienation provisions in the lease. In other words, assignation or subletting will normally be prohibited without the landlord's consent.[1]

1 See paras 7.4 et seq and 7.18 et seq.

Resumption of land by landlord[1]

15.31 A lease of agricultural subjects may often contain a clause entitling the landlord to resume part of the land in certain circumstances. In the case of 1991 Act tenancies this is largely governed by the terms of the lease, apart from provisions governing the tenant's entitlement to compensation, and it will not be possible for the landlord to resume unless express provision is made in the lease.[1] It should normally also be done for non-agricultural purposes,[2] and be done in good faith.[3] The tenant must be given sufficient notice (at least two months) to allow him or her to make any compensation claims arising on the resumption.[4]

The 2003 Act goes much further in relation to short limited duration, limited duration and modern limited duration tenancies by allowing resumption by the landlord in all cases, unless the lease specifically prohibits it.[5] The resumption must be for a non-agricultural purpose for which planning permission is required and has been obtained. In the case of SLDTs (but not LDTs or MLDTs) it may be the tenant who has obtained that permission.

The landlord must give the tenant a minimum of one year's written notice of the intention to resume and the tenant, within 28 days, may respond by serving a notice terminating the tenancy.

Where part of the land is resumed, the tenant is entitled to a proportionate reduction in rent.

If land has been resumed for mineral exploitation and later becomes available and suitable for agricultural use again, it is to be restored to the tenancy, provided that any compensation paid to the tenant in relation to the resumption was calculated taking this into account.

In the case of a repairing tenancy, there may be no resumption of land by the landlord until five years have elapsed from the expiry of the repairing period. Thereafter, the same rules apply as with MLDTs.[6]

1 See, though, AH(S)A 1991 s 29, which allows what is in effect a statutory resumption in certain limited circumstances.
2 The reason for this is that, in terms of AH(S)A 1991 s 21(7), only such resumptions are excluded from the notice to quit procedure.
3 See eg *Fothringham v Fotheringham* 1987 SLT (Land Ct) 10 and, for discussion, R Rennie et al, *Leases* (W Green 2015) para 31-27
4 *Palmers Exrs v Shaw* 2004 SC 408.

Tenant's right to diversify

15.32 Part 3 of the Agricultural Holdings (Scotland) Act 2003 gives agricultural tenants the right to diversify by using the land for a non-agricultural purpose.[1] This right applies to 1991 Act, limited duration, modern limited duration and repairing tenancies, but not to short limited duration tenancies.[2] The right cannot be contracted out of in the lease.[3] The landlord must be notified and has the right to object to the diversification or to impose conditions.[4] Any dispute will be resolved by the Land Court, which has the option of allowing the diversification subject to conditions of its own.[5] If the landlord fails to object or seek to impose conditions, the diversification will be allowed by default.

A detailed timetable for the giving of notice by the tenant and for the landlord's response is set out in sections 40 and 40A of the 2003 Act.

When the lease terminates either the tenant or landlord may have a claim of compensation from the other, depending upon whether the diversification has either decreased or increased the value of the land.[6]

1 This does not, however, allow the tenant to abandon farming altogether. We are concerned here with diversification rather than an outright change of use, and an entire or almost entire abandonment of farming will result in the lease no longer being an agricultural one at all: see eg *Fyffe v Esslemont* 2018 SLCR 5.
2 AH(S)A 2003 s 39.
3 AH(S)A 2003 s 39(2).
4 AH(S)A 2003 s 40.
5 AH(S)A 2003 s 41.
6 See paras 15.67 and 15.71.

Tenant's pre-emptive right to buy[1]

15.33 Part 2 of the Agricultural Holdings (Scotland) Act 2003 gives 1991 Act tenants (but not short limited or limited duration tenants) a right to buy the land from the owner of the land. This effectively means the landlord, since the right to buy is not given to subtenants.[2]

The right to buy cannot be exercised at any time, but only when the owner plans to dispose of the land, ie it is a right of pre-emption. In addition, the right can only be exercised if the tenant has earlier registered an interest in acquiring the land in the Register of Community Interests in Land.[3] Thereafter, if the owner plans to dispose of the land, the tenant must be notified and may submit an offer to purchase it.[4] This must be accepted by the owner provided that the requisite procedure (set out in section 32 of the 2003 Act) has been complied with.

The need to register is prospectively removed by amendments that have not yet come into force.[5] At the time of writing, it is not known when these amendments will come into force

The price is to be agreed by the parties, or fixed by a valuer. If they cannot agree on the choice of valuer, one can be appointed by the Land Court or a person nominated by them.[6] Detailed instructions for the valuer are set out in sections 34 to 36 of the 2003 Act. Either the seller or the tenant may appeal against the valuation to the Lands Tribunal.[7]

There are a number of situations where the right to buy cannot be exercised. These include where the owner is disposing of the land otherwise than for value, where the land is being compulsorily acquired, and where the sale is in implementation of the community right to buy under Part 2 of the Land Reform (Scotland) Act 2003.[8] However, any scheme that is designed to avoid the exercise of the tenant's right will not be exempt.[9]

1 For discussion of some issues arising from the tenant's pre-emptive right to buy, see Craig Anderson, 'Agricultural tenants and the right to buy: Some Thoughts on Part 2 of the Agricultural Holdings (Scotland) Act 2003' 2006 SLT (News) 241.
2 AH(S)A 2003 s 25(2).
3 AH(S)A 2003 s 25.
4 AH(S)A 2003 ss 28 and 29.
5 Land Reform (Scotland) Act 2016, s 99.
6 AH(S)A 2003 s 33.
7 AH(S)A 2003 s 37.
8 AH(S)A 2003 s 27(1).
9 AH(S)A 2003 s 27(2).

Termination and continuation

15.34 *1991 Act tenancies* This will be covered in some detail later in the chapter.[1] The 1991 Act specifies a period of notice (between one and two years), and failure by either party to send a timeous notice to quit will result in the lease being extended by tacit relocation in accordance with the common law.[2] Where the landlord does serve a timeous notice to quit, the lease may nevertheless, in certain circumstances, be extended indefinitely under the statutory provisions governing security of tenure.

A 1991 Act tenancy may also be terminated by conversion to a modern limited duration tenancy in accordance with section 2A of the 2003 Act,[3]

or in certain circumstances where the tenant is a limited partnership that has been dissolved.[4]

1 See para 15.43 et seq.
2 See para 10.18 et seq.
3 See para 15.9.
4 AH(S)A 2003 ss 72 and 73.

15.35 *Short limited duration tenancies* The 2003 Act provides that an SLDT may be terminated by agreement between the parties.[1] As already noted, it also provides for the situation where the tenant continues in occupation after the ish with the landlord's consent: in such a case the lease will either convert (where the term of the lease was less than five years) to an SLDT of five years, or a lesser period by agreement, or (where the term of the lease was for five years) to a modern limited duration tenancy of 10 years.[2]

Rather oddly, the Act does not cover the situation where the parties are not agreed, ie where either the landlord or the tenant wants to terminate an SLDT at the ish but the other wants the lease to continue. Moreover, the statutory periods of notice applied to agricultural leases under the Sheriff Courts (Scotland) Act 1907 have been specifically disapplied in relation to short limited duration and limited duration tenancies.[3] It has been suggested that an SLDT will therefore automatically terminate at its ish without notice.[4] The better view, though, now seems to be that the statutory notice periods contained in the 1907 Act are concerned only with the procedure for removing the tenant, and need not be adhered to unless the landlord seeks to use the removing procedure contained in that Act.[5] Needless to say, a reasonable period of notice is recommended, whatever the position.

1 AH(S)A 2003 s 6(2).
2 See para 15.10.
3 AH(S)A 2003 Sch para 1.
4 See Somerled M Notley *Scottish Agricultural Law Handbook* (2009) p 157.
5 See para 10.36.

15.36 *Limited duration, modern limited duration and repairing tenancies*[1] Any of these tenancies may be terminated by agreement between the landlord and tenant, provided that the agreement is made in writing, is entered into after the commencement of the tenancy, and makes provision for the payment of compensation payable by the landlord or tenant to the other. It may also be extended by agreement between the parties.

Failing such agreement, the termination and, in certain cases, the continuation of LDTs is governed by a complex statutory procedure, including what is effectively a statutory form of tacit relocation, although the terms under which this takes effect differ from the common law which it supersedes. (Note, however, that the procedure applies only to termination by the *landlord* and that termination by the tenant is much more straightforward.) The position is somewhat simpler with MLDTs (and with repairing tenancies, to which the same rules are applied, subject to any break clause in terms of section 5C).

1 AH(S)A 2003 ss 8 (LDTs), 8A (MLDTs) and 8F (repairing tenancies).

15.37 At the expiry of the term of a limited or modern limited duration tenancy, the landlord may terminate the tenancy, but two different types of written notice must be served on the tenant. The landlord must first of all serve a preliminary notice of the intention to terminate the lease not less than two years or more than three years prior to the ish. This must be followed by a notice to quit not less than one year or more than two years prior the ish and at least 90 days must have elapsed since service of the preliminary notice.

If the tenancy is not terminated in this manner it continues automatically. In the case of an MLDT, the lease is extended for successive periods of seven years.[1]

In the case of an LDT, the lease continues on a cycle of continuations, ie a first short continuation of three years then (failing termination at the end of that period) by a second short continuation of three years and (failing termination of that) by a long continuation of 10 years.[2] This cycle may be repeated indefinitely.

The first short continuation in an LDT may be terminated at its expiry in the same way as the main term of the lease, ie by a double notice procedure of a preliminary notice followed by a notice to quit, within the same timetable.

The second short continuation in an LDT only requires a single notice, ie a notice to quit. However, the tenant must be given at least two years' notice. In order to terminate the lease at the end of the continuation period, therefore, the notice must be served within the first year of the continuation. If served later than this, then the continuation period will be extended by the amount required in order to give the tenant the full two years' notice.

If no notice has been served by the end of the second short continuation, a long continuation will take effect, ie the lease will be further extended for a period of 10 years. At the end of that period it may be terminated by the same double notice procedure described above, failing which a further series of continuations will begin.

15.38 *Agricultural leases*

In the case of both an MLDT and an LDT, termination by the tenant is much simpler. The tenant may terminate a limited duration or modern limited duration tenancy at the end of the term by serving written notice on the landlord of not less than one year or more than two years.

1 AH(S)A 2003 s 8E(1), inserted by LR(S)A 2016 s 87.

2 The reduction of the continuation period from 15 to 10 years was not retrospective in effect. This means that, in the case of LDTs entered before 22 March 2011, the length of a long continuation is still 15 years (The Public Services Reform (Agricultural Holdings)(Scotland) Order 2011 (SSI No 232) arts 7 & 10(4)).

15.38 *Break clauses in modern limited duration tenancies* Special provisions apply in an MLDT where the tenant is a 'new entrant'. As this term is defined,[1] it essentially requires that the tenant has not been a tenant or owner of agricultural land within the previous five years.

Where the tenant is a new entrant, it is competent for the lease to contain a break clause which, if exercised, will bring the lease to an end after five years.[2] The break is exercised by giving in writing at least one year's notice, and not more than two year's notice.[3] The tenant may exercise the break clause without restriction. The landlord, however, may only exercise it if (a) the tenant is not using the land in accordance with the rules of good husbandry, or (b) is otherwise failing to comply with any other provision of the lease.[4]

1 Agricultural Holdings (Modern Limited Duration Tenancies and Consequential etc Provisions) (Scotland) Regulations 2017 SSI No 300 reg 3.

2 AH(S)A 2003 ss 5B, 8D(2), (4).

3 AH(S)A 2003 s 8D(3), (5).

4 AH(S)A 2003 s 8D(6).

15.39 *Break clauses in repairing tenancies*[1] In a repairing tenancy, the lease may contain a break clause. This may be exercised by the tenant at any time until the expiry of the repairing period[2] by giving not less than one year and not more than two years of a date that is not later than the end of the repairing period. The landlord may exercise the break at the end of the repairing period, giving written notice of at least one year and not more than two years before the end of the repairing period. The tenant need give no reasons for exercising the break. The landlord, by contrast, must state reasons in the notice. The landlord is only permitted to exercise the break clause if the tenant has breached a provision of the lease, with the exception that it is not permitted to do this on the grounds that the tenant is not farming the land in accordance with the rules of good husbandry.

1 AH(S)A 2003 ss 5C(5) and 8G.

2 See para 15.13

Irritancy

15.40 *Legal Irritancy* As with other types of lease, an agricultural lease can be terminated prematurely on the ground of legal irritancy where there are two years arrears of rent though, as already observed, this remedy is rarely used for any type of lease.[1] In the case of 1991 Act tenancies there has been added a statutory legal irritancy, which can apply either during the contractual term of the lease or after the security of tenure provisions have been invoked.[2] Where six months' rent is due and unpaid the landlord can raise an action in the Land Court for the tenant's removal at the next term of Whitsunday or Martinmas (28 May or 28 November).[3]

The court will grant decree against the tenant unless the tenant can either pay the rent due or find sufficient security, to the court's satisfaction, for the rent due and an additional one year's rent. A lease terminated in this way will be treated as if it had expired naturally at that term. The tenant will therefore be entitled to the usual waygoing rights such as compensation for improvements, but not compensation for disturbance.

As noted earlier, this provision cannot be enforced where the tenant has a statutory right to withhold rent.[4]

There is no equivalent provision in the 2003 Act relating to short limited duration, limited duration tenancies, modern limited duration tenancies or repairing tenancies.

The Scottish Law Commission has recommended that both of the above legal irritancies should be abolished, and replaced by an option to terminate the lease for non-payment of six months' rent which would be subject to the same statutory controls as conventional irritancies. The parties would be entitled to contract out of this termination option.[5]

1 See para 5.4.
2 AH(S)A 1991 s 20 (as amended by AH(S)A 2003 Sch para 19).
3 Term and Quarter Days (Scotland) Act 1990 s 1; see also para 1.22 et seq. See also para 10.33 in relation to the requirement to serve written notice.
4 See para 15.24.
5 Scottish Law Commission *Report on Irritancy in Leases of Land* (Scot Law Com No 191, 2003), paras 3.13–3.15. The recommendations in this report have not been implemented, but see now Scottish Law Commission, *Discussion Paper on Aspects of Leases: Termination* (Scot Law Com DP No 165, 2018) chapter 7.

15.41 *Conventional irritancy*[1] The common law in relation to conventional irritancies applies to agricultural tenancies in the same way as it does to any other type of lease.[2] However, the protection given to tenants of commercial leases under the Law Reform (Miscellaneous Provisions) (Scotland) Act 1985 does not apply to agricultural tenancies.

This means that, once the irritancy has been incurred, the tenant has no right to purge the irritancy by payment of rent or by putting right a remediable breach unless the lease contains a provision to that effect.[3]

In relation to short limited duration, limited duration and modern limited duration tenancies, it is in general for the landlord and tenant to provide in the lease the grounds of conventional irritancy.[4]

In relation to all of the different types of agricultural lease, certain exceptions apply, considered in the next paragraph.

1 AH(S)A 2003 ss 18–19.
2 See para 5.5.
3 See paras 5.13 et seq and 5.21 et seq. The Scottish Law Commission has recommended that this protection should be extended to all types of lease, including agricultural tenancies – see Scottish Law Commission *Report on Irritancy in Leases of Land* (Scot Law Com No 191, 2003), paras 3.17 and 3.18.
4 AH(S)A 2003 ss 18(1) (SLDTs and LDTs), 18A(1) (MLDTs) and 18B(1) (repairing tenancies).

15.42 *Exceptions* There are certain statutory exceptions where irritancy is excluded:

(1) In the case of all types of agricultural tenancy, it is provided that any term allowing the lease to be irritated solely on the ground that the tenant is not or has not been resident on the land will be of no effect. In relation to 1991 Act tenancies (but not the other forms of tenancy) there is implied in its place an undertaking by the tenant, if not resident on the holding, to ensure that a person who has the skills and experience necessary to farm the holding in accordance with the rules of good husbandry resides there instead.[1]

(2) In the case of all types of agricultural tenancy, conservation activities or diversification by the tenant will not normally give the landlord the right to irritate the lease on the ground that the tenant is not using the land in accordance with the rules of good husbandry.[2]

(3) As noted earlier, the landlord may not irritate where the tenant has a statutory right to withhold rent.[3]

(4) In the case of modern limited, limited and short limited duration tenancies and repairing tenancies, the landlord may not enforce any right to remove the tenant on grounds of irritancy unless the tenant has been given not less than two months' written notice before the removal date to this effect.[4] There is no equivalent provision applying to 1991 Act tenancies, although where the tenant has a right to waygoing claims, the landlord must give the tenant sufficient notice (normally at least two months) in order to make such claims timeously.[5]

(5)　In the case of arrears of rent in a limited duration or short limited duration tenancy (but not a modern limited duration tenancy), before this two months' notice can be given, the tenant must first have been given a written demand for payment followed by two months to make that payment.[6]

(6)　In a modern limited duration tenancy or repairing tenancy, this two months' notice cannot be given until the tenant has been given at least 12 months to remedy the breach of the lease.[7]

(7)　In a repairing tenancy, there may be no irritancy on the basis of the tenant's failure to use the land in accordance with the rules of good husbandry.[8]

In all cases, of course, it is possible that a provision for the giving of notice may be contained in the lease.

1　AH(S)A 1991 s 16A (inserted by AH(S)A 2003 s 65); AH(S)A 2003 ss 18(2), 18A(2) and 18C(1).
2　AH(S)A 1991 s 85 (2A) and (2B) (inserted by the AH(S)A 2003 s 69(2)); AH(S)A 2003 ss 18 (3) to (5), 18A(3) to (5) and 18B(1).
3　See para 15.26.
4　AH(S)A 2003 ss 18 (6) and (7), 18A(8), 18B(1).
5　*Palmer's Executors v Shaw* 2004 SC 408, 2004 SLT 261. However, in that particular case it was held that the fact that the tenant was more than three months in arrears with his rent meant that he had been given sufficient notice, as he was deemed to have known that this made him vulnerable to irritancy under the terms of the lease. See also *Downie v Trustees of Earl of Stair's 1970 Trust* 2008 SC 41, 2007 SLT 827.
6　AH(S)A 2003 s 18(2A) (inserted by LR(S)A 2016 s 123(2)).
7　AH(S)A 2003 ss 18A(6), 18B(1). Section 18A(7)(b) allows the Land Court to extend this period on the application of the tenant.
8　AH(S)A 2003 s 18B(2).

1991 ACT TENANCIES: SECURITY OF TENURE

15.43　As mentioned above, one of the main purposes of the agricultural holdings legislation was to provide greater security of tenure for farm tenants. Like the tenant in any other kind of lease, an agricultural tenant has the contractual right to stay on in the property until the expiry date of the lease and can only be removed before then in extraordinary circumstances, for example if there has been a breach justifying irritancy. When the lease is due to end, the tenant may be able to stay on if the landlord agrees to a new lease, or (in the case of 1991 Act tenancies) if the old one is allowed to be renewed automatically by tacit relocation.[1]

1　For tacit relocation, see para 10.18 et seq. In the case of limited duration and modern limited duration tenancies, which are fixed-term tenancies, the operation of tacit relocation has been replaced by the statutory provisions – see para 15.35 et seq.

15.44   On the other hand, in the case of 1991 Act tenancies, a landlord who wants to remove a tenant at the end of the lease may be legally prevented from doing so. In certain cases, the tenant will have the right to stay on in the property indefinitely, long after the contractual term of the lease has expired.

This extended security of tenure is not automatic. In some exceptional cases the landlord will have an absolute right to remove the tenant, provided that the correct statutory procedure has been followed. In all other cases the Land Court has the power to decide whether the tenant should be granted security of tenure. There are certain statutory criteria to which they should have regard when reaching their decision, but they are not bound by them and have a wide discretion in each individual case.

15.45   *Prohibition of contracting out*   The Act does not contain a specific prohibition against contracting out of the security of tenure provisions, but in *Johnson v Moreton*[1] the House of Lords held that the mandatory wording of the equivalent English provisions precluded this.

1 [1980] AC 37, [1978] 3 WLR 538, HL.

Notice to quit

15.46   As in other types of lease, the tenant cannot be removed at all unless either party serves a notice to quit for the requisite period before the end of the lease. A landlord's notice should be as prescribed either by the Removal Terms (Scotland) Act 1886 or by the Sheriff Courts (Scotland) Act 1907.[1] In the case of 1991 Act tenancies the statutory period of notice is not more than two years or less than one year before the date of expiry.[2] This provision cannot be contracted out of, ie any clause in the lease substituting a longer or shorter period of notice would not be enforceable.[3]

If notice is not served, or is not served in time, the lease will continue from year to year by tacit relocation until proper notice is served; this is, of course, the common law rule for all leases, but here it has been given statutory reinforcement.[4] The operation of tacit relocation cannot be contracted out of.[5]

1 AH(S)A 1991 s 21(5); *Rae & Cooper v Davidson* 1954 SC 361,1955 SLT 25. See also
   Gemmell v Andrew 1975 SLT (Land Ct) 5 and *Taylor v Brick* 1982 SLT 25; see also
   para 10.29 et seq.
2 AH(S)A 1991 s 21(3).
3 AH(S)A 1991 s 21(1).
4 AH(S)A 1991 s 3.
5 AH(S)A 1991 s 3; see also para 10.23.

Exceptions to security of tenure[1]

15.47 If any of the grounds of removal specified in section 22(2) applies, the landlord has an absolute right to remove the tenant. The notice to quit must expressly state which of the six grounds of removal applies. The tenant may refer any question relating to the notice, eg regarding its validity, to the Land Court within one month after its service, but otherwise has no right to challenge the removal.[2]

1 AH(S)A 1991 s 22(2) (as amended).
2 AH(S)A 1991 s 23(2) (as amended).

15.48 *Section 22 grounds*[1] The six grounds of removal are as follows:

(a) The landlord has let permanent pasture to the tenant for a definite and limited period to use as arable land on condition that the tenant sows grass again at the end of the let.

(b) The land is required for a use other than agriculture for which planning permission requires to be obtained and has been obtained. Outline planning permission is sufficient for this purpose.[2]

(c) Within the period of nine months immediately prior to service of the notice to quit, an application has been made to the Land Court and the court has granted a certificate that the tenant's responsibilities to farm in accordance with the rules of good husbandry were not being fulfilled.[3] Such an application may be made under section 26 of the 1991 Act.

(d) At the time the notice to quit was served, the tenant was in arrears with rent or was in breach of another term of the lease which is remediable. The landlord cannot recover possession on this ground if the tenant has justifiably retained the rent because of the landlord's breach of contract.[4] This includes situations where the Land Court has authorised the withholding or rent by the tenant because of the landlord's failure to fulfil an obligation in relation to fixed equipment.[5] The landlord must have given the tenant two months' notice to pay the rent arrears or a reasonable period of notice to remedy the breach.[6]

(e) At the time the notice to quit was served, the landlord's interest had been materially prejudiced by the tenant's breach of a term of the lease which could not be remedied in reasonable time and at economic cost.

(f) At the time the notice to quit was served, the tenant was bankrupt, ie apparently insolvent in terms of section 16 of the Bankruptcy (Scotland) Act 2016.[7]

1 AH(S)A 1991 s 22 (2)(a)–(g) (as amended).

2 *North Berwick Trust v James B Miller & Company* 2009 SC 305, 2009 SLT 402.
3 *Luss Estates Co v Firkin Farm Co* 1985 SLT (Land Ct) 17, 1984 SLCR 1; *Cambusmore Estate Trustees v Little* 1991 SLT (Land Ct) 33.
4 *Alexander v The Royal Hotel (Caithness) Ltd* 2001 SLT 17, [2001] 1 EGLR 6; for retention of rent, see para 4.39 et seq.
5 AH(S)A 1991 s 15A (added by the AH(S)A 2003 s 64). See para 15.26.
6 *Macnabb v A & J Anderson* 1955 SC 38, 1955 SLT 73.
7 See *Trustees of the West Errol Trust v Lawrie* 2000 SLT 911, 1998 GWD 22-1104.

15.49   In all of the above cases except (b), ie where the land is required for a use other than agriculture, the tenant loses the right to compensation for disturbance, but not the other waygoing rights, such as the right to compensation for improvements.[1]

1 AH(S)A 1991 s 43(2).

15.50   Where a planning application is being made in respect of land subject to an agricultural tenancy or tenancies, there is a statutory requirement for the applicant to serve notice of the application on all agricultural tenants on the land.[1] And so, even though it is too late for the tenant to challenge the landlord after planning permission has been obtained, there will have been an opportunity at an earlier stage to lodge objections.

1 Town and Country Planning (Scotland) Act 1997 s 35.

Security of tenure

15.51   In all cases other than (a)-(f) listed above the tenant may, within one month from the service of a notice to quit, serve a counter-notice on the landlord invoking the right to security of tenure.[1] Thereafter the landlord will only be able to remove the tenant by applying to the Land Court and establishing that one of five removal grounds applies. The relevant ground must be specified in the landlord's application to the court.[2] Ideally, this should be done by stating the relevant ground or specifically referring to it, but the Act does not say that and the proper test is whether the tenant has been given fair notice of the case the landlord intends to present to the court.[3]

1 AH(S)A 1991 s 22(1); see also *Kildrummy (Jersey) v Calder(No 1)* 1994 SLT 888.
2 *O'Donnell v Heath* 1995 SLT (Land Court) 15.
3 *Mining (Scotland) Ltd v Fyfe* 1999 SLT (Land Court) 6; 1999 SLCR 22.

Section 24 grounds[1]

15.52

(a)   The carrying out of the purpose for which the landlord seeks to terminate the tenancy is desirable in the interests of good husbandry.[2] This is in relation to the leased subjects regarded as a separate unit, the management of the landlord's estate as a whole being covered by (b) below.

(b) The carrying out is desirable in the interests of sound management of the estate of which the land consists or forms part.[3]

(c) The carrying out is desirable for the purposes of agricultural research, experiment, education etc.

(d) Greater hardship would be caused by withholding than by giving consent to the operation of the notice,[4] or

(e) The landlord's purpose is to employ the land for a use other than agriculture for which planning permission (whether required or not) has not been obtained.[5]

1 AH(S)A 1991 s 24(1)(a)–(e) (as amended).
2 *Prior v J & A Henderson Ltd* 1984 SLT (Land Ct) 51, 1983 SLCR 34.
3 *Altyre Estate Trs v McLay* 1975 SLT (Land Ct) 12; *Prior v J & A Henderson Ltd* 1984 SLT (Land Ct) 51, 1983 SLCR 34; *North Berwick Trust v James B Miller & Company* 2009 SC 305, 2009 SLT 402.
4 *Somerville v Watson* 1980 SLT (Land Ct) 14; see also *Hutchison v Buchanan* 1980 SLT (Land Ct) 17; *Prior v J & A Henderson Ltd* 1984 SLT (Land Ct) 51, 1983 SLCR 34; *Lindsay-MacDougall v Peterson* 1987 SLCR 59; and *Lowie v Davidson* 1988 SLCR 13.
5 This appears to be the plain import of s 24(1)(e) which actually reads, 'that the landlord proposes to terminate the tenancy for the purpose of the land being used for a use, other than agriculture, not falling within s 22(2)(b) of this Act' (see para 15.43). However, in *North Berwick Trust v James B Miller & Company* 2009 SC 305 at 309–310 per Lord Gill, the Inner House of the Court of Session expressed obiter the view that this would *not* entitle the Land Court to agree to the termination of a lease in cases where planning permission *was* required, which could include cases where the grant of planning permission was extremely unlikely. This makes sense but is not, it is submitted, what the Act actually says.

15.53 The onus of proof is on the landlord to establish that one or more of the above grounds exists.[1] And even where the landlord succeeds in discharging that onus, the Land Court still have the discretion to refuse the landlord's application if it appears to them that:

(a) a fair and reasonable landlord would not insist on possession; or

(b) where the notice is to quit the whole of the holding, that use of the land for the purpose for which the landlord proposes to terminate the tenancy would not create greater economic and social benefits to the community than would exist were the tenancy not terminated.[2]

1 *McLaren v Lawrie* 1964 SLT (Land Ct) 10.
2 AH(S)A 1991 s 24(2) (as amended); see also *Altyre Estate Trs v McLay* 1975 SLT (Land Ct) 12.

Notice to quit part of the holding

15.54 In some cases, the landlord may not want all of the leased area back and may therefore serve on the tenant a notice to quit part of the subjects at the lease's termination date.[1] However, this may not suit the tenant, who may prefer to move out entirely, rather than farm a reduced area. Furthermore, the smaller area may not be economically viable. Since the contractual period of the tenant's lease will be about to end, the tenant will of course be entitled to leave the entire subjects, provided that the landlord has been given a minimum of one year's notice to quit.

However, if the landlord were to serve notice a bare year before the end of the lease, the tenant could be held for a further year by tacit relocation to only part of the subjects. Furthermore, we will see below that a tenant who is denied security of tenure generally has a right to compensation for disturbance of up to two years' rent.[2] If the reduced area is unviable, it might be considered unfair for the tenant to get disturbance only for the part that the landlord wanted back.

1 For the situations in which such a notice would be valid see AH(S)A 1991 s 29.
2 See para 15.63 et seq.

15.55 Accordingly, where the landlord serves a notice to quit for part of the holding the tenant, within 28 days, may serve a counter-notice making the landlord's notice take effect for the full holding.[1] This allows the tenant to claim the compensation payable on removal from the whole farm as an alternative to continuing in occupation of the reduced area. However, if the part claimed back by the landlord is less than one-fourth of the subjects either in area or rental value and the diminished area is reasonably capable of being farmed as a separate unit, compensation for disturbance will be restricted to the part included in the landlord's notice to quit.[2]

This means that the tenant will always be entitled to leave the whole subjects, but only if a significant part is being reclaimed by the landlord will a disturbance payment be payable for all of the land leased rather than just the part that the landlord wants back.

Alternatively, the tenant will generally have the right to refer the matter to the Land Court which may grant security of tenure for the whole subjects, despite the landlord's notice.

1 AH(S)A 1991 s 30.
2 AH(S)A 1991 s 43(7).

TENANT'S COMPENSATION RIGHTS

15.56 Under the Agricultural Holdings (Scotland) Act 1991 there are a number of compensation rights that a tenant may be entitled to claim from the landlord, generally at the end of the lease. There are also some situations where the landlord may claim compensation from the tenant. The oldest and most fundamental statutory right of the agricultural tenant, dating back from the very first Act in 1883, is to receive compensation for any improvements that the tenant has made to the holding, to which there have been added a number of other compensation rights. In many cases the Agricultural Holdings (Scotland) Act 2003 has extended these rights to all the main categories of agricultural tenancy, to include short limited duration, limited duration and modern limited duration tenancies as well as 1991 Act tenancies. In addition, the Scottish Ministers are empowered to make regulations providing for the application of these rules to repairing tenancies.[1]

The following categories of compensation are discussed below:

(1) Improvements;
(2) Disturbance;
(3) Reorganisation (1991 Act tenancies only);
(4) Diversification and cropping of trees;
(5) Other compensation rights.

In nearly all cases these involve a compensation claim by the tenant from the landlord, but there are also some situations where the landlord may claim compensation from the tenant. With a few limited exceptions, none of these compensation rights can be contracted out of.[2]

1 AH(S)A 2003 s 59A (inserted by LR(S)A 2016 s 98(2)).
2 AH(S)A 1991 s 53; AH(S)A 2003 s 59.

Compensation for improvements

15.57 An agricultural tenant is entitled at the termination of the lease to obtain from the landlord a sum which fairly represents the value of certain improvements made by the tenant to the property.[1] These rights apply to 1991 Act tenancies, short limited duration tenancies, limited duration and modern limited duration tenancies.

In some cases it will be a condition of the payment of compensation that the tenant has served notice on the landlord of the intention to carry out an improvement, and in other cases the landlord's written consent will be required before it can be carried out. If the tenant fails to comply with these requirements in the cases where they are necessary, the right to compensation will be lost.[2] This right of compensation can arise even if it is the tenant who gives the notice to quit, or if the termination has come about as a result of the tenant's breach of the lease. This is because, whatever the circumstances of the lease's termination, the tenant has still added to the value of the holding.

The amount of compensation payable will be calculated on the basis of the value of the improvement to an incoming tenant as agreed between the parties, subject to certain adjustments.[3] Failing agreement, the compensation will be fixed by the Land Court.[4]

Where an outgoing tenant is due compensation for improvements, the landlord is not entitled to pass that liability on to an incoming tenant or, where the compensation has already been paid, recover the money from the incoming tenant. Any agreement to this effect will be void.[5]

The provisions described here relate to improvements begun on or after 1 November 1948.[6]

Temporary provision (called an 'amnesty') was made by the Land Reform (Scotland) Act 2016 to allow tenant farmers to establish their right to compensation for improvements even where evidence to support the claim might be deficient.[7] The 2016 Act allowed tenants a period of three years and six months from 13 June 2017 to serve a notice on the landlord asserting the right to compensation come the termination of the lease,[8] with a right on the part of the landlord to object to the notice and provision for disputes to be resolved, ultimately, by the Land Court. This applied to 1991 Act tenancies and also to short limited, limited and modern limited duration tenancies.[9]

1 AH(S)A 1991 s 34; AH(S)A 2003 s 45.
2 AH(S)A 1991 ss 37 and 38; AH(S)A 2003 ss 48 and 49.
3 AH(S)A 1991 s 36 (as amended); AH(S)A 2003 s 47.
4 AH(S)A 1991 s 60 (substituted by the AH(S)A 2003 s 75); AH(S)A 2003 s 77.
5 AH(S)A 1991 s 35; AH(S)A 2003 s 46.
6 Broadly similar provisions apply to old improvements made prior to that date, but they are governed by earlier legislation and are not considered here – see Somerled M Notley *Scottish Agricultural Law Handbook*, 2009, 2.4.1.
7 LR(S)A 2016 ss 112–118.
8 The original period of three years was extended by the Land Reform (Scotland) Act 2016 (Supplementary Provisions) (Coronavirus) Regulations 2020 SSI No 174.
9 AH(S)A 1991 s 34A, AH(S)A 2003 s 45A (inserted by LR(S)A 2016 s 113).

15.58 *Write down agreements* It was formerly possible for the parties to enter into an agreement regarding the amount of compensation payable, substituting a different amount from that laid down by the legislation. The 2003 Act has prohibited all such agreements.[1] In addition, any agreements entered before the relevant section of the 2003 Act came into force have been retrospectively rendered void in relation to improvements that should have been the landlord's statutory responsibility at the beginning of the lease.[2]

1 AH(S)A 2003 s 59.
2 AH(S)A 1991 s 33A (added by AH(S)A 2003 s 43).

15.59 *Categories of improvement* There are three categories of improvement that may qualify for compensation. The following is a brief selection of some of the types under each category; for the full list, the reader is referred to Schedule 5 to the 1991 Act.[1]

1 This applies to 1991 Act tenancies and also, under s 45(2) of the 2003 Act, to short limited duration, limited duration and modern limited duration tenancies.

15.60 *Improvements requiring consent*[1] To be entitled to compensation, the tenant must have obtained the landlord's written consent before carrying out the improvements.[2] This category includes laying down permanent pasture, making water meadows or works of irrigation and the planting of orchards or fruit bushes.

1 AH(S)A 1991 Sch 5 Part I.
2 AH(S)A 1991 s 37; AH(S)A 2003 s 48.

15.61 *Improvements requiring notice*[1] The tenant will not be due compensation unless the landlord has been given prior written notice of the tenant's intention to carry out the improvements, not less than three months before they are begun.[2] Included in this category are land drainage, making or improvement of farm access or service roads, making or removal of permanent fences (including hedges, stone dykes and gates), erection, alteration or enlargement of buildings and repairs to fixed equipment. If the landlord objects to the improvement, there is provision for the matter being determined by the Land Court.[3]

1 AH(S)A 1991 Sch 5, Part II.
2 AH(S)A 1991 s 38; AH(S) A 2003 s 49.
3 AH(S)A 1991 s 39, AH(S)A 2003 s 49(2); *Renwick v Rodger* 1988 SLT (Land Ct) 23; *Whiteford v Trustees for Cowhill Trust* 2009 SLCR 188.

15.62 *Other improvements*[1] Improvements in this category require neither the consent of nor notice to, the landlord. They include protecting fruit trees against animals, eradication of bracken, whins or broom, application to the land of purchased manure and fertiliser and laying down temporary pasture.

1 AH(S)A 1991 Sch 5 Pt III.

Compensation for disturbance[1]

15.63 *1991 Act tenancies* Subject to certain exceptions noted below, compensation for disturbance is paid in the case of 1991 Act tenancies where the lease has been terminated, or partially terminated, in the following circumstances:

(1)   The landlord has given the tenant notice to quit. If the tenant has given the landlord notice, there will be no entitlement to compensation for disturbance.

(2)   The landlord has given the tenant notice to quit part of the subjects. As we saw above,[2] in such a case the tenant is entitled to serve a counter notice making the notice to quit take effect for the whole subjects. If the part remaining is unviable, ie less than a quarter either of the area or in rental value, the tenant will be entitled to the full amount of compensation. In other circumstances (where the part remaining is viable or the tenant has not served a counter notice) the tenant will be entitled to reduced compensation, proportionate to the area which the landlord has reclaimed.[3]

1   AH(S)A 1991 s 43 (as amended).
2   See para 15.54 et seq.
3   AH(S)A 1991 s 43 (7).

15.64   *Where not payable*   A 1991 Act tenant's right to compensation for disturbance is excluded in all the cases (with one exception) where the landlord has an absolute right to remove the tenant at the ish.[1] These are mostly cases where the tenant could be said to be at fault in some way, eg because the tenant is in breach of contract or is bankrupt. The exception (where disturbance *is* payable) is where the land is required for a use other than agriculture for which planning permission requires to be obtained and has been obtained.

1   See para 15.44 et seq.

15.65   *Short limited duration, limited duration and modern limited duration tenancies*[1]   As SLDTs, MLDTs and LDTs are, by their nature, fixed-term contracts, there is normally no right to compensation for disturbance when the lease comes to an end at the ish. However, in cases where, in accordance with section 17 of the 2003 Act,[2] the landlord has resumed part of the land, or the entire land, before the lease is due to end, compensation for disturbance will be payable to the tenant. Where part of the land is resumed, the same rules will apply as in the case of 1991 Act tenancies, ie the full amount of compensation will only be paid if the remaining land is unviable on its own.

1   AH(S)A 2003 s 52.
2   See para 15.31.

15.66   *Amount of compensation*[1]   In respect of all four types of tenancy, the minimum amount of compensation payable is one year's rent at the rate payable immediately before the termination of the tenancy. If the tenant can prove additional loss directly attributable to the removal, additional compensation can be claimed.

1 AH(S)A 1991 s 43(3) and (4); AH(S)A 2003 s 52(2).

Sum for reorganisation of tenant's affairs[1]

15.67   *1991 Act tenancies*   Where (and only where) compensation for disturbance is payable to a 1991 Act tenant, the landlord may also have to pay, in certain circumstances, a sum to assist in the reorganisation of the tenant's affairs. The amount of this sum is four times the annual rent of the holding at the rate payable immediately prior to the termination of the tenancy. Where compensation for disturbance is only payable in respect of part of the holding, the sum is four times the appropriate portion of the annual rent.

In *Copeland v McQuaker*[2] it was held that the sum for reorganisation was payable even although additional loss could not be proved; it was not compensation as such, but a fixed sum which, if it was applicable, was paid regardless of loss.

The provisions which govern when the sum for reorganisation is payable are rather complex. However, broadly speaking, it appears that the sum need only be paid where the landlord wants the land for some use other than agriculture. In all other cases payment can be avoided, provided that the landlord states in the notice to quit the reason for recovery of possession. The reasons that may be given roughly correspond to the Land Court's four other criteria for removal, ie interests of good husbandry, interests of sound estate management, required for agricultural research etc, hardship to the landlord.[3]

There is, therefore, an onus on the landlord to ensure that the notice to quit is worded correctly if an unnecessary payment is to be avoided. Even so, if the matter has gone to the Land Court, the landlord may still be required to pay the sum if the Court is satisfied that the land is required for a use other than agriculture, even though the landlord stated another ground as the basis of the right to terminate.[4]

Where the lease can be terminated without the tenant being able to claim security of tenure,[5] the sum for reorganisation will likewise only be payable when the land is required for a use other than agriculture.

Contracting out of the above provisions is not allowed.

1 AH(S)A 1991 ss 54 and 55.
2 1973 SLT 186.
3 See para 15.50; see also *Barns-Graham v Lamont* 1971 SC 170, 1971 SLT 341 and *Copeland v McQuaker* 1973 SLT 186.

4 AH(S)A 1991 s 55(2)(b).
5 See para 15.43 et seq.

15.68 *Short limited duration, limited duration and modern limited duration tenancies* It was noted above that in the case of short limited duration and limited duration tenancies compensation for disturbance is only payable in very limited circumstances.[1] The sum for reorganisation of the tenant's affairs is not payable at all in the case of these types of tenancy.

1 See para 15.63.

Compensation for diversification and for cropping of trees[1]

15.69 This relates to the provisions governing diversification by the tenant.[2] Compensation may be payable where the tenant has diversified by using the land for a purpose other than agriculture and also where the tenant has planted trees. The compensation may be payable either by the tenant to the landlord or by the landlord to the tenant, depending upon whether the rental value of the land has been decreased or increased as a result. The provisions governing the amount of compensation are rather complex, but broadly speaking the amount is based upon the extent to which the value of the holding has either been increased or reduced, as the case may be.

This compensation right applies to 1991 Act tenancies and to limited duration and modern limited duration tenancies, but not to short limited duration tenancies.

1 AH(S)A 1991 s 45A (added by AH(S)A 2003 s 51); AH(S)A 2003 s 53(2).
2 See para 15.32.

Compensation for vacant possession[1]

15.70 In the case of 1991 Act, limited duration and modern limited duration tenancies (but not short limited duration tenancies) the landlord and the tenant may enter into an agreement for the tenant to quit the holding and give the landlord vacant possession at some point prior to the end of the lease. This may arise either at the instance of the landlord, if the landlord wants to sell the land with vacant possession, or at the instance of the tenant,[2] should the tenant want to quit.

In either case, the tenant will be entitled to compensation representing half the difference between the sale value of the land with vacant possession and its sale value with the tenant still in occupation. In the first of these two situations, ie where the landlord wants to sell with vacant possession, the value with vacant possession will be determined by the actual price received; otherwise the relevant value will be fixed by a valuer. The cost of any valuation or valuations will be deducted from the compensation paid.

Any such agreements are entirely voluntary. However, the fact that the tenant will share in any resulting increase in value provides an incentive for cooperation.

1 AH(S)A 2003 s 55.
2 For the case where the tenant offers to relinquish the lease, new provision is prospectively made by LR(S)A 2016 ss 110–111, in relation to 1991 Act tenancies only. These provisions are not yet in force at the time of writing.

Other compensation rights

15.71 *At end of lease* Other waygoing rights to which a tenant may sometimes be entitled at the end of the lease include compensation for continuous adoption of a special standard of farming ('high farming')[1] and, in certain circumstances, additional payments where the holding has been compulsorily acquired.[2] These both apply to 1991 Act tenancies, short limited duration tenancies, limited duration tenancies and modern limited duration tenancies.

1 AH(S)A 1991 s 44; AH(S)A 2003 s 53(1).
2 AH(S)A 1991 ss 56 and 57; AH(S)A 2003 s 54.

15.72 *Damage by game* In relation to all four types of tenancy, a tenant may, in certain circumstances, claim compensation for damage caused to crops by game. This is not a waygoing claim but can arise at any time during the currency of the lease.[1]

1 AH(S)A 1991 s 52 (as amended); AH(S) A 2003 s 53(3).

15.73 *Landlord's compensation* In certain circumstances, in addition to those already mentioned,[1] the landlord may be due compensation from a 1991 Act tenant, notably where the tenant has been responsible for a deterioration in the holding.[2] There appears to be nothing in the 2003 Act expressly extending this provision to short limited duration, limited duration, modern limited duration and repairing tenancies so, in these cases, it is probably advisable for landlords to seek to provide for this contingency in the lease contract.

1 See para 15.69.
2 AH(S)A 1991 s 45.

SUCCESSION TO AGRICULTURAL LEASES[1]

Introduction

15.74   We saw in Chapter 9 that a lease may be inherited either under testate or intestate succession. We also saw that, in some cases, the landlord could object to the succession and prevent the transmission to the new tenant. The same is broadly true of succession to agricultural leases; however, here the position is further regulated by the Agricultural Holdings (Scotland) Acts 1991 and 2003 and is a little more complex.

1 See also Ch 9.

Bequest of lease (testate succession)[1]

15.75   The position is the same in the case of 1991 Act tenancies, short limited duration tenancies, limited duration tenancies, modern limited duration tenancies and repairing tenancies. The tenant under any of these types of lease is entitled to bequeath the lease by will to any one of a list of family members. Since a bequest is virtually a form of assignation, this therefore forms an exception to the common law rule that agricultural leases, other than those of unusual duration, cannot be assigned without the landlord's consent.[2]

1 AH(S)A 1991 s 11; AH(S)A 2003 s 21; see also para 9.2 et seq.
2 See para 7.19 et seq.

15.76   *Contracting out*   There is no express prohibition against contracting out, and in *Kennedy v Johnstone*[1] it was held that a provision in an agricultural lease expressly excluding the tenant's legatee was valid. It follows that a prohibition of assignation will have the same effect. As such a provision is standard, bequests will be precluded without the landlord's consent, unless there is a qualification that the landlord's consent to an assignation will not unreasonably be withheld, thereby opening refusal by the landlord to legal challenge.[2] However, even if such a challenge is successful, the landlord will still have a statutory right to object, as noted below.[3]

1 1956 SC 39, 1956 SLT 73.
2 See paras 7.8 et seq.
3 See para 15.78.

15.77   *Categories of legatee*   The 1991 and 2003 Acts do not give a tenant the right to bequeath the lease to anyone at all, but only to a person selected from a limited class of individuals. It must be bequeathed to any of the following:[1]

(a) any person who would 'in any circumstances'[2] have been entitled to succeed to the tenant's estate on intestacy, ie any spouse, civil partner or blood relative of the tenant;

(b) a spouse or civil partner of a child of the tenant;

(c) a spouse or civil partner of a grandchild of the tenant;

(d) a spouse or civil partner of a sibling of the tenant;

(e) a sibling of the tenant's spouse or civil partner;

(f) a spouse or civil partner of such a sibling;

(g) a child (including a step-child) of such a sibling;

(h) a grandchild (including a step-grandchild) of such a sibling;

(i) a step-child of the tenant;

(j) a spouse or civil partner of such a step-child;

(k) a descendant of such a step-child;

(l) a step-brother or step-sister of the tenant;

(m) a spouse or civil partner of such a step-brother or step-sister;

(n) a descendant of such a step-brother or step-sister.

(o) Anyone falling within one of these categories may be chosen as legatee. It is thus possible to bypass a nearer relative in favour of a more remote one.

1 AH(S)A 1991 s 11(1A), AH(S)A 2003 s 21(1A) (both amended by Land Reform (Scotland) Act 2016 ss 107–108).

2 Thus the legatee can be anyone potentially succeeding on intestacy, not necessarily someone who would so succeed in the actual circumstances of the tenant's death.

Procedure

15.78 A legatee who wants the tenancy must notify the landlord of this within 21 days of the former tenant's death, unless prevented from doing so by some unavoidable cause.[1] In *Coats v Logan,*[2] the legatee failed to notify the landlord in time and was prevented from acquiring the tenancy; moreover, since he had actually accepted the bequest and this fact had been recorded in the confirmation, the tenant's executors were unable to dispose of the tenancy as intestate estate. As a result, the landlords were able to terminate the tenancy.

However, in *Morrison-Low v Paterson, No 1*[3] the tenant's two sons carried on in occupation of the holding for six years after their father's death, continuing to pay rent and otherwise interacting with the landlord. It was held that a tenancy had been constituted by the actings of the parties.

The landlord may object to the bequest by sending, within one month of the legatee's notice, a counter-notice objecting to the legatee as tenant. The landlord may thereafter refer the matter to the Land Court within one month of the date on which the counter-notice is given.[4]

The grounds of objection vary depending on whether the legatee is a 'near relative' of the tenant. This term has the same meaning as it does in relation to assignation of agricultural leases.[5] In the case of a near relative, the landlord may object to that person acquiring on the following grounds:[6]

(a) that the person is not of good character;
(b) that the person does not have sufficient resources to farm the holding with reasonable efficiency; or
(c) that the person does not have sufficient training or experience to be able to farm the holding with reasonable efficiency.

The last of these grounds does not apply if the person is undertaking a course of relevant training in agriculture, or begins one within six months of the date of the legatee's notice, which is expected to be completed within four years.

In the case of a legacy to someone other than a near relative, there are no specific grounds. If the legatee challenges the counter-notice, it is enough for him or her to show 'any reasonable ground ... for not declaring the bequest to be null and void'.[7]

If a legatee does not accept a bequest, or the bequest is nullified by the Land Court, the lease will be treated as part of the deceased tenant's intestate estate.

1 AH(S)A 1991 s 11(2); AH(S)A 2003 s 21(2).
2 1985 SLT 221.
3 1985 SC(HL) 49, 1985 SLT 255 (HL).
4 AH(S)A 1991 ss 12A (near relatives), 12B (acquirers other than near relatives) (inserted by Land Reform (Scotland) Act 2006 s 109); AH(S)A 2003 s 21(2).
5 See para 15.27.
6 AH(S)A 1991 s 12A(3), (4).
7 AH(S)A 1991 s 12B.

Intestate succession

15.79 In cases of intestacy, as with other types of lease, the lease will initially pass to the executor, who has the power to transfer it to a new tenant.[1] In most cases this can be done without the landlord's consent, even in cases where the lease contains an express or implied prohibition against assignation. This is the position in the case of limited duration and short limited duration tenancies, in respect of which the executor's power to transfer the tenancy is unrestricted, provided that the transfer is in the best interests of the deceased's estate.[2]

In the case of 1991 Act tenancies, the landlord's consent is equally unnecessary.[3] However, in this case the executor's right to assign is subject to the landlord's right to object to the new tenant.

1 Succession (Scotland) Act 1964 s 16 (as amended); see para 9.6 et seq.
2 S(S)A 1964 s 16 (4A)–(4E) (inserted by AH(S)A 2003 s 20).
3 S(S)A 1964 s 16(2) and (2A) (the latter inserted by the Crofting Reform etc Act 2007 s 15(3)).

15.80 *Objection by landlord* The landlord has a right to object to the new tenant, along similar lines to those in the case of a bequest. Within 21 days of acquiring the lease, the new tenant must notify the landlord of the fact, and the landlord may within one month send a counter-notice objecting to the tenant.[1] The grounds of objection are the same as with testate succession. The Land Court has the power, similar to that which it has with bequests, to either confirm the succession or terminate the tenancy. In the case of an acquirer who is a near relative, termination will take effect from such Whitsunday or Martinmas as the court specifies.[2] Where the acquirer is not a near relative, the landlord is to specify a term of Whitsunday or Martinmas at least one year and no more than two years from the date of the counter-notice.[3]

As with testate succession, in the case of intestate succession the onus is upon the landlord, within one month of serving a counter notice, to apply to the Land Court to have the lease terminated.[4] If the lease is thus terminated, the would-be successor may be entitled to compensation for improvements, but not for disturbance.[5]

1 AH(S)A 1991 s 12; AH(S)A 2003 s 22.
2 AH(S)A 1991 s 12(2); AH(S)A 2003 s 22(2).
3 AH(S)A 1991 s 12A(6)(b).
4 AH(S)A 1991 s 12B(2)(b).
5 AH(S)A 1991 s 12(5).

15.81 *Acquisition by landlord* In the case of short limited duration, limited duration, modern limited duration and repairing tenancies (but not 1991 Act tenancies), the landlord has another option. We saw above that the landlord can respond to the acquirer's notice by objecting to the new tenant, but that the matter may end up in the Land Court, which may or may not terminate the tenancy. Alternatively, on receiving the new tenant's notice, the landlord is entitled to acquire the tenant's interest. Within 30 days of receiving the acquirer's notice, instead of objecting to the new tenant, the landlord may instead send a written notice that he or she intends to acquire the tenant's interest. The terms upon which the landlord acquires that interest must be no less favourable to the person than any reasonable terms upon which the lease was transferred to the person.[1]

Effectively this means that the tenancy can be terminated, but that in this case it will be for value. For a landlord wanting to regain possession of the land, therefore, this may be a safer option than taking the risk of an adverse Land Court decision.[2]

1 AH(S)A 2003 s 22(3).
2 It will be noted that the statutory deadlines will not allow two bites at the cherry, as the Land Court's decision will come too late for the landlord to take advantage of the acquisition procedure.

15.82 *Executor's failure to transfer tenancy* As with other types of lease, the lease may terminate if the executor fails to transfer the tenancy.[1] If (a) at any time the executor is satisfied that the tenant's interest cannot be disposed of according to law and so informs the landlord or (b) the tenant's interest is not so disposed of within one year of the tenant's death (or within one year of the Land Court's determination), the lease may terminate.[2]

In the case of short limited duration and limited duration tenancies, this happens automatically,[3] but in the case of 1991 Act tenancies either the executor or the landlord must give the other party notice. The period of notice is either such period as the parties may agree, or, failing agreement, a period of not less than one year or more than two years ending at a term of Whitsunday or Martinmas.[4]

In the case of short limited duration, limited duration, modern limited duration and repairing tenancies there is a proviso that terminating the lease must be in the best interests of the deceased's estate.[5]

1 See para 9.7 et seq.
2 Succession (S) Act 1964 s 16(3) (as amended).
3 S(S)A 1964 s 16(4C)–(4D) (inserted by AH(S)A 2003 s 20).
4 S(S)A 1964 s 16(4).
5 S(S)A 1964 s 16(4E) (inserted by AH(S)A 2003 s 20).

Security of tenure (1991 Act tenancies)[1]

15.83 The earlier part of this section related to situations where the tenant died before the contractual term of the lease ended. What the successor inherited, therefore, whether by bequest or through intestacy, was the unexpired portion of the lease. In the case of 1991 Act tenancies there is a remaining issue as to whether the successor will enjoy the same right as the original tenant would have had to claim extended security of tenure when the lease comes to an end.[2]

Formerly, the broad position (under the former section 25 of the Agricultural Holdings (Scotland) Act 1991) was that a successor who was not a near relative had no right to security of tenure, with the result that the landlord was entitled to terminate the lease at the ish. These provisions have now been repealed,[3] replaced by the procedures outlined above for objecting to successors to the original tenant. As a result, henceforth anyone who has succeeded to a 1991 Act tenancy will have the same security of tenure as the original tenant. A detailed account of the previous position may be found in earlier editions of this book.

1 AH(S)A 1991 s 25.
2 See para 15.43 et seq.
3 By the Land Reform (Scotland) Act 2016 s 109(5).

DISPUTE RESOLUTION

Introduction

15.84   The Agricultural Holdings (Scotland) Act 2003 fundamentally changed the procedure for the resolution of disputes relating to agricultural tenancies. It was formerly the case that almost all disputes had to be determined by arbitration, a complex and expensive process. Now the emphasis has shifted in favour of disputes being resolved by the Land Court, although arbitration is still possible. At the same time, arbitration procedure was greatly simplified, and other methods of dispute resolution (such as mediation) were made possible.

Although the 1991 Act still contains separate provisions for dispute resolution, these have been greatly modified by the 2003 Act, with the result that the provisions relating to 1991 Act tenancies are largely similar to those for other types of agricultural tenancy. Further changes have been made by the Land Reform (Scotland) Act 2016.

Land Court jurisdiction[1]

15.85   The Land Court's wide jurisdiction includes determination of the following:

(1)   Whether a particular type of tenancy, eg 1991 Act, limited duration etc, exists or has terminated;
(2)   Any question or difference between the landlord and tenant regarding the tenancy, whether arising during its currency or after its termination;
(3)   Claims by one of the parties against the other arising out of the termination (or partial termination) of the tenancy; and

(4)   Any other issue of fact or law relating to the tenancy or to a matter of agriculture, which the landlord or tenant reasonably require to have resolved.[2]

(5)   Disputes relating to the tenant's pre-emptive right to buy[3] and to assignation of the lease are specifically included. Others are specifically excluded, in particular certain matters relating to the succession to agricultural tenancies, namely:

(a)   Who is entitled to succeed a deceased tenant on intestacy;

(b)   The validity of any bequest or transfer of an interest under the lease; or

(c)   Whether any transfer is in the best interests of the deceased's estate.[4]

Applications for a determination by the Land Court may be made by either party or by the parties jointly.

Any lease term or other agreement purporting to contract out of the Land Court's jurisdiction will be void.[5]

1 AH(S)A 1991 s 60 (substituted by AH(S)A 2003 s 75); AH(S)A 2003 s 77.
2 For the definition of 'agriculture' see para 15.8.
3 See para 15.33.
4 See para 15.72 et seq.
5 AH(S)A 1991 s 61B (inserted by AH(S)A 2003 s 76); AH(S)A 2003 s 81.

Arbitration

15.86   Subject to a number of notable exceptions, the parties may agree to submit a dispute to arbitration instead of to the Land Court.[1] They may also have resort to an alternative form of dispute resolution such as mediation. However, this can only be done after the dispute has arisen since, as noted above, any lease term purporting to exclude the Land Court's jurisdiction will be void.[2]

The exceptional cases, where the Land Court has exclusive jurisdiction,[3] include certain questions relating to succession to a tenancy[4] and certain questions relating to notices to quit 1991 Act tenancies.[5]

The arbitration procedure is set out in section 61A of the 1991 Act[6] and in section 79 of the 2003 Act.

1 AH(S)A 1991 s 61 (substituted by the AH(S)A 2003 s 76); AH(S)A 2003 s 78.
2 See para 15.83.
3 See AH(S)A 1991 s 61(2) (substituted by AH(S)A 2003 s 76); AH(S)A 2003 s 78(2).
4 See para 15.72 et seq.
5 See paras 15.34 and 15.46.
6 AH(S)A 1991 s 61(A) (inserted by the AH(S)A 2003 s 76).

Appeals

15.87   Appeals against Land Court decisions on points of law may be made to the Court of Session, unless the Land Court determination was itself an appeal, eg from an arbitration.[1] It is also possible for the Land Court to remit a case to the Court of Session in the course of a hearing, either at their own instance or following a request from a person with an interest in the dispute.[2]

Any party to an arbitration may appeal to the Land Court against an arbiter's award on a point of law.[3]

1 AH(S)A 2003 s 88.
2 AH(S)A 2003 s 85.
3 AH(S)A 1991 s 61A(6); AH(S)A 2003 s 79.

Chapter 16

Crofts and small landholdings

CROFTS

16.1   Crofts are small agricultural holdings situated mainly in the
Highlands and Islands of Scotland. A croft will generally consist of a
small area of land exclusive to the landholder (known as 'inbye land'),
plus a share in a larger area of common grazing. The inbye land may or
may not contain a house. There are almost 18,000 crofts in Scotland and
approximately 33,000 people living there.[1]

Crofting tenure was traditionally confined to the seven crofting counties,
namely Argyll, Caithness, Inverness, Ross and Cromarty, Sutherland,
Orkney and Shetland. However, the Crofting Reform etc Act 2007[2] gave
the Scottish Ministers the power to extend crofting tenure to other areas
of Scotland. This has now been done, with effect from 4 February 2010,
in relation to Arran, Bute, Greater and Little Cumbrae, Moray and those
parts of the local government area of Highland outwith the crofting
counties.[3]

The statutory regulation of crofting has a long and complex history and
there is much case law. It is a specialist area on its own, and all that has
been attempted here is an overview, which may enable the reader to
establish some basic landmarks.[4]

1 See www.crofting.scotland.gov.uk/faq
2 Crofters (Scotland) Act 1993 s 3A (inserted by the Crofting Reform etc Act 2007 s 6).
3 The Crofting (Designation of Areas) (Scotland) Order 2010, SSI No 29.
4 For the most up-to-date general account see D Flyn and K Graham, *Crofting Law*
   (Edinburgh University Press 2017); because of the considerable extent and complexity
   of the legislative changes made in the last 15 years, earlier specialist texts should be
   treated with some caution.

Crofting legislation

16.2   The current legislation is mainly consolidated in the Crofters
(Scotland) Act 1993, though this has been substantially amended by
the Crofting Reform etc Act 2007 and the Crofting Reform (Scotland)
Act 2010.[1] In addition, the Transfer of Crofting Estates (Scotland) Act

1997 enabled government-owned crofting estates to be sold to bodies representing local crofting communities, and Part 3 of the Land Reform (Scotland) Act 2003 introduced a crofting community right to buy.[2] However, prior to this there is a long history of legislation relating to crofts and small landholdings, some of which remains wholly or partly in force.

In 2017, the Scottish Government published a consultation document on various aspects of crofting legislation.[3] No legislation has as yet resulted from this process.

1 For a useful overview of developments in crofting law, see Eilidh IM Ross 'A Time to Take Stock – Crofting Law in 2012' (2012) 120 Prop LB 5; Eilidh Ross MacLellan, 'Crofting Law Update for 2015' (2015) 136 Prop LB 1.
2 See para 16.15.
3 Scottish Government, *Crofting Consultation 2017: A consultation on the future of crofting law* (2017), available at: https://consult.gov.scot/agriculture-and-rural-communities/crofting-consultation-2017/user_uploads/00523679-2.pdf.

History of the legislation

16.3   The first Act was the Crofters Holdings (Scotland) Act 1886, which had as its purpose the alleviation of hardship suffered by crofters in the highlands and islands of Scotland and applied only to the seven crofting counties. It conferred on crofters a statutory right to a fair rent, security of tenure, compensation for improvements at the end the lease and the right to bequeath the tenancy to a family member. These rights remain central within the current law. The Crofters Commission (now renamed the Crofting Commission) was set up to implement the Act.

The Small Landholders (Scotland) Act 1911 extended this statutory protection beyond the crofting counties to the whole of Scotland. A distinction was made between a small landholder and a statutory small tenant, the former enjoying more legal privileges because the tenant (or the tenant's predecessors) had provided most of the buildings and permanent improvements on the holding. Also, the Crofters Commission was replaced by the newly set up Scottish Land Court.

Finally, the special needs of the crofting counties were recognised again when they were given separate legal status by the Crofters (Scotland) Act 1955. Among other things, this abolished, in the crofting counties, the distinction between small landholders and statutory small tenants. However, this distinction remained in the rest of Scotland.

Small landholdings other than crofts

16.4 The legislation relating to small landholders and statutory small tenants remains in force, conferring on tenants parallel rights to those enjoyed by crofters, notably the right to a fair rent, security of tenure, compensation for improvements, and the right to bequeath the tenancy.[1] It is not known how many of these small landholdings remain in existence, but the dearth of case law since they went their separate ways in 1955 (in contrast to the continuous flood of crofting decisions) suggests that the number is very small. This may decrease further with the extension of crofting tenure into other areas of Scotland.[2]

In March 2017, the Scottish Government issued a report reviewing legislation governing small landholdings.[3] This concluded that further work was necessary before any major reforms could be proposed.

1 The main statutes relating to small landholders and statutory small tenants, which remain partly in force, are the Crofters Holdings (Scotland) Act 1886, the Small Landholders (Scotland) Act 1911, the Land Settlement (Scotland) Act 1919 and the Small Landholders and Agricultural Holdings (Scotland) Act 1931.

2 See para 16.1. At least some of the occasional modern decisions relating to small landholdings relate to areas to which crofting tenure is now being extended – see eg *Arran Properties Ltd v Currie* 1983 SLCR 92.

3 Scottish Government, Review of Legislation Governing Small Landholdings in Scotland (2017), available at: www.gov.scot/publications/review-legislation-governing-small-landholdings-scotland/. This was done in accordance with the Land Reform (Scotland) Act 2016 s 124.

Definition of croft

16.5 The definition of a croft and of a crofter is contained in section 3 of the Crofters (Scotland) Act 1993. This much-amended section is somewhat complex but, broadly speaking, the main types of holding which qualify as crofts are:

(a) All holdings in the crofting counties which were small landholdings or statutory small tenancies immediately prior to 1 October 1955;

(b) New crofts created between 1955 and 1961 by order of the Land Court, followed by registration under the Crofters (Scotland) Act 1955;

(c) Crofts created by direction of the Secretary of State under the Crofters (Scotland) Act 1961; and

(d) New crofts created in accordance with section 3A of the 1993 Act,[1] and the new crofts thus created can be situated either in the crofting counties, or in one of the new areas to which crofting tenure has now been extended;[2] this can result from an application by the owner of the land or (in the case of the new areas only) from an application either by the owner or by the tenant. The landowner and the crofter may apply to the Crofting Commission for the croft to be enlarged by the addition of non-crofting land, provided that the total area does not substantially exceed thirty hectares.[3]

A property that falls within the definition will be a croft, even if it does not currently have a tenant.[4]

'Crofter' is defined in the 1993 Act as the tenant of a croft.[5] An 'owner-occupier crofter' is the former tenant of a croft (or the successor of a former tenant) who exercised his or her acquisition right.[6]

1 Crofters (Scotland) Act 1993 (added by the Crofting Reform etc Act 2007 s 6).
2 See para 16.1.
3 C(S)A 1993 s 4 (as amended).
4 *Innes v Crofting Commission* 2017 SLCR 144. Indeed, in that case, the land was considered to be a croft even though it had been registered in error. See also para 16.16, on decrofting.
5 C(S)A 1993 s 3(3).
6 C(S)A 1993 s 19B (inserted by the Crofting Reform (Scotland) Act 2010 s 34). See para 16.12. Thus the term 'owner-occupier crofter' is narrower than the literal words would suggest. A person who owns the croft he or she occupies is not necessarily an 'owner-occupier crofter'.

The Crofting Commission

16.6   The Crofting Commission (formerly known as the 'Crofters Commission') is the body responsible for the administration and regulation of crofting tenure.[1] The name change was introduced by the Crofting Reform (Scotland) Act 2010, which also considerably extended the Commission's functions (including some that were previously within the jurisdiction of the Scottish Land Court) and sought to make it more democratic and accountable by including elected members.[2]

The Crofting Commission, which came into being on 1 April 2012,[3] is a Non-Departmental Public Body (NDPB), which operates independently of the government, but for which the Scottish Ministers are ultimately responsible.

1 Further information about the Crofting Commission can be obtained at www.crofting.scotland.gov.uk
2 See the Crofting Reform (Scotland) Act 2010, Part 1.
3 The Crofting Reform (Scotland) Act 2010 (Commencement No 2, Transitory, Transitional and Saving Provisions) Order 2011, SSI No 334.

The Crofting Register

16.7   It was formerly the responsibility of the then Crofters Commission to compile and maintain a register of crofts, containing some basic information about crofts and their occupants.¹ Under Part 2 of the Crofting Reform (Scotland) Act 2010 a new and more comprehensive register has been set up by the Keeper of the Registers of Scotland, which is map-based and operates in a similar way to the Land Register of Scotland.

Registration is required for all new crofts, but is voluntary in the case of existing crofts, unless one of a number of specified trigger events occurs. First registration is induced by the occurrence of certain transactions relating to the croft, including sale or a change in tenancy.²

1 Originally under s 15 of the Crofters (Scotland) Act 1955 and latterly under s 41 of the Crofters (Scotland) Act 1993.
2 See the CR(S)A 2010 s 4.

Conditions of tenure

16.8 *The statutory conditions* The Crofters (Scotland) Act 1993 sets out a number of statutory conditions of tenure for crofts.¹ These can normally only be contracted out of with the consent of the Crofting Commission, though in certain cases the only requirement is that the party wanting to change the condition intimates this to the Commission.

The statutory conditions relate inter alia to the payment of rent, assignation and subletting, the provision of fixed equipment, prohibiting the dilapidation of buildings or deterioration of the soil, division of the croft, erection of buildings, reasonable access by the landlord, and the sale of alcohol. The conditions where intimation only is sufficient for contracting out are those relating to assignation, acquisition of the croft² and the crofter's right to share in the value of land resumed by the landlord or compulsorily acquired.³

1 C(S)A 1993 s 5 and Sch 2. Note that the sections of the 1993 Act referred to in this and the immediately following paragraphs have been substantially amended, mainly by the Crofting Reform etc Act 2007 and the Crofting Reform (Scotland) Act 2010.
2 See para 16.12.
3 C(S)A 1993 s 5(3)(b).

16.9 *Requirement for residency etc* The Crofting Reform (Scotland) Act 2010 requires crofters to be ordinarily resident on or within 32 kilometres of the croft, and also imposes duties to cultivate and maintain the croft land and not to misuse or neglect it.¹ Similar duties are placed on the owner-occupiers of crofts.² These provisions are enforced by the Crofting Commission,³ which may also grant permission for a crofter to be absent from the croft.⁴

1 C(S)A 1993 ss 5AA, 5B and 5C (inserted by CR(S)A 2010 s 33).

2 C(S)A 1993 s 19C (inserted by CR(S)A 2010 s 34).
3 C(S)A 1993 s 26A et seq (inserted by CR(S)A 2010 s 37).
4 C(S)A 1993 s 21B et seq (inserted by CR(S)A 2010 s 35).

16.10   *Crofter's rights*   Crofters have the right to a fair rent,[1] compensation for improvements,[2] security of tenure,[3] and the right to bequeath the lease.[4]

1 C(S)A 1993 s 6.
2 C(S)A 1993 ss 30–35.
3 C(S)A 1993 s 5(2).
4 C(S)A 1993 s 10.

Common grazings

16.11   Crofters who share common grazings may appoint a grazings committee,[1] whose duties include maintaining and improving the grazings,[2] and making regulations with regard to them.[3] Trees may be planted on common grazings with the consent of the Crofting Commission and the landlord.[4]

1 C(S)A 1993 s 47.
2 C(S)A 1993 s 48.
3 C(S)A 1993 s 49.
4 C(S)A 1993 s 50.

Acquisition right[1]

16.12   A crofter has the right (first introduced in 1976) to buy the croft from the landowner. If terms cannot be agreed with the owner, the matter will be dealt with by the Land Court. The right to buy the house and any garden ground is absolute, but whether the crofter can acquire the rest of the land is at the discretion of the Land Court.

1 C(S)A 1993 ss 12–19.

16.13   *Clawback on resale*   An owner-occupier who sells the croft, or any part of it, within 10 years of the date of purchase from the landlord is required to pay to the landlord a sum amounting to one half of the difference between the market value of the land and the consideration paid. The clawback period was increased from five to 10 years by the Crofting Reform (Scotland) Act 2010, as part of an effort to reduce speculation on croft land.[1]

1 C(S)A 1993 s 14(3) (as amended).

Transfer of crofting estates

16.14 This relates to the large number of crofting estates owned by the government. The Transfer of Crofting Estates (Scotland) Act 1997 gives the Scottish Ministers power to dispose of these estates to crofting trusts or other bodies representative of the local crofting community.[1] The Scottish Ministers have a discretionary power to give financial assistance in the establishment of suitable bodies for the receipt of such transfers.[2]

1 Transfer of Crofting Estates (Scotland) Act 1997 ss 1 and 2.
2 TCE(S)A 1997 s 3.

Community right to buy

16.15 Part 3 of the Land Reform (Scotland) Act 2003 introduced a crofting community right to buy. Land eligible for such purchase includes tenanted crofts (including statutory small tenancies outwith the crofting counties),[1] common grazings or pasture, land held runrig (a form of common ownership),[2] salmon fishings in inland waters and mineral rights (other than oil, coal, gas, gold or silver).[3]

It does not include crofts that are owner-occupied, eg where the crofter has already exercised the right to buy on an individual basis.[4] Additional land which is not croft land may also be purchased if it is contiguous to and in the same ownership as the eligible croft land; this may include sporting rights (such as shooting or fishing leases), but not salmon fishings.[5]

The purchaser must be a company limited by guarantee, a Scottish charitable incorporated association or a community benefit society, and must be controlled by members of the local community.[6] Effectively, this is a right of compulsory purchase from the landowner that may be exercised at any time. However, an application to buy must be approved by the Scottish Ministers, after public consultation and a local ballot. The Ministers are only able to give consent if a range of criteria have been satisfied, eg that the land is eligible land, any proposed development is compatible with sustainable development and that the right to buy is in the public interest.[7] The price is the market value as assessed by an independent valuer.[8]

The owner has a right to appeal to the sheriff against the purchase[9] and to the Land Court against the valuation.[10]

The Crofting Commission is required to keep a public register of crofting community rights to buy, containing information about all purchase applications.[11]

1 See para 16.4.
2 See WM Gordon and Scott Wortley *Scottish Land Law* (3rd edn 2009) 15-181 and 15-182.
3 Land Reform (Scotland) Act 2003 s 68.

4 LR(S)A 2003 s 68(3); see paras 16.10 and 16.11.
5 LR(S)A 2003 s 70.
6 LR(S)A 2003 ss 71–73, as amended by the Community Empowerment (Scotland) Act 2015 s 62. LR(S)A 2003 s 71(A1)(b) allows further permitted types of body to be prescribed by regulations.
7 LR(S)A 2003 ss 74 and 75.
8 LR(S)A 2003 ss 88–89.
9 LR(S)A 2003 s 91.
10 LR(S)A 2003 s 92.
11 LR(S)A 2003 s 94, prospectively amended by the Community Empowerment (Scotland) Act 2015 s 72.

Decrofting

16.16   Decrofting refers to the process whereby the Crofting Commission may issue a direction releasing untenanted croft land from crofting control. An application for such a direction can be made by the landlord of the croft in question, but a hold was put on similar applications from owner-occupier crofters because of a legal technicality. This difficulty has been addressed by the Crofting (Amendment) (Scotland) Act 2013 which allows owner-occupier crofters to apply to the Crofting Commission for a decrofting direction.[1]

1 Crofters (Scotland) Act 1993 s 24A (inserted by the Crofting (Amendment) (Scotland) Act 2013 s 1). This provision is effective retrospectively. For an account of the background to the 2013 Act and an explanation of the legal difficulties that made it necessary see Tom Edwards *Crofting (Amendment) (Scotland) Bill* SPICe Briefing (2013) available at www.parliament.scot/ResearchbriefingsAnd Factsheets/S4/SB-13-25pdf.

COTTARS

16.17   A cottar enjoys a special kind of tenure which occurs only in the crofting counties.[1] A cottar is someone who occupies a house, with or without garden ground (but without arable or pasture land), either rent free, or under a yearly tenancy at a rent of not more than £6 per year.[2] A cottar occupying rent free is distinguished from a squatter by the fact that the former has the landowner's permission to occupy the property.[3] A cottar who is removed from the property is entitled to compensation for permanent improvements.[4] Since 1976, a cottar has had the same right as a crofter to buy the house he or she occupies from the landowner.[5]

1 See the definition of 'cottar' in the Crofters (Scotland) Act 1992 s 12(5), which specifies that the land must be within the crofting counties.
2 C(S)A 1993 s 12(5).
3 *Duke of Argyll's Trs v MacNeill* 1983 SLT (Land Ct) 35, 1982 SLCR 67.
4 C(S)A 1993 s 36.
5 C(S)A 1993 s 12.

PART 5
RESIDENTIAL LEASES

Chapter 17

The private sector: Assured, regulated and private residential tenancies

INTRODUCTION

Historical background

17.1   Leases of dwelling-houses from private landlords have been subject to statutory regulation since the early years of the 20th century. This began in 1915 with the first in a series of Acts (known as the Rent Acts, or Rent Restriction Acts), which were designed to protect tenants from exploitation because of housing shortages. This was done by restricting the amount of rent that landlords could charge and giving tenants security of tenure.

In the years that followed, the Rent Acts developed into perhaps the most notoriously complex legislation in legal history; more significantly, the standard rent that was imposed became uneconomic as a result of inflation, and this probably hastened the decline of many properties into slum condition.

After a brief period of decontrol, a new system of regulated tenancies was introduced in 1965. These were subject to fair rents, an attempt to strike a balance between the needs of landlords and tenants: this was done by allowing landlords periodic rent reviews and a return on their capital, but without being able to benefit from any additional inflationary effect caused by housing shortages. However, these changes were not enough to bring private investment back into the market for privately rented housing. In 1989, a new system of assured tenancies was introduced, which allowed market rents to be charged. This approach is broadly retained in the current system of private residential tenancies, though provision now exists for areas to be designated as 'rent pressure zones', in which rent rises are restricted.[1]

When rent control was first introduced, a large proportion of the British population rented their homes from private landlords. Over the course of the 20th century, this proportion greatly diminished, along with the rise in owner-occupation and socially rented housing from local authorities and, more recently, housing associations. Social tenancies are also regulated by statute and will be examined in the next chapter.

1 See below, para 17.40.

STATUTORY REGULATION OF THE PRIVATE SECTOR

Statutory regulation of the private sector can be divided into four main phases:

17.2   *Controlled tenancies*   This was the main system from the onset of rent control until the introduction of regulated tenancies. However, the two systems continued in parallel until controlled tenancies were finally abolished in 1980.

17.3   *Regulated tenancies*[1]   Regulated tenancies were introduced by the Rent Act 1965. As with controlled tenancies, tenants of dwelling-houses once again enjoyed security of tenure and freedom from eviction. In place of the old standard rent there was introduced a system of fair rents, to be fixed in individual cases by the local rent officer. Rent officers are independent government officials appointed and paid by the Scottish Ministers.[2] One or more rent officers will normally serve for each registration area, which are the areas served by local authorities.[3]

There are still some regulated tenancies in existence, mainly tenancies that were entered into prior to 1989. It will therefore be necessary to include some coverage of the law regarding them, but only after consideration of private residential tenancies, which are now the dominant tenure.

1 Also referred to as 'protected tenancies' or 'statutory tenancies', depending upon whether the security of tenure provisions have been invoked.
2 Rent officers' functions may now be contracted out to rent registration service providers, who are not government employees (Rent (Scotland) Act 1984 ss 43A, 43B and 43C (inserted by the Deregulation and Contracting Out Act 1994 Sch 16 paras 6 and 7)).
3 Rent (Scotland) Act 1984 s 43 (as amended).

17.4   *Assured tenancies*   From 2 January 1989 (when the appropriate part of the Housing (Scotland) Act 1988 came into force), there could, apart from a few limited exceptions to cover transitional cases, be no new regulated tenancies. Instead, new tenancies of dwellinghouses were subject to a system of assured tenancies, although existing regulated tenancies continue to be subject to the old system. Assured tenants are not subject to the fair rent system operating in the case of regulated tenancies and the parties are free to negotiate a market rent.

There are two types of assured tenancy, the 'normal' assured tenancy and the short assured tenancy. 'Normal' assured tenants enjoy security of tenure similar to that of regulated tenants (and are often referred to as 'statutory assured tenancies' once these security of tenure provisions have been invoked). However, it has been estimated that this first category accounted for no more than 6% of private sector tenancies.[1] By far the most prevalent form of these types of assured tenancy was the short assured tenancy, in respect of which the tenant had no security of tenure at all, beyond a statutory minimum lease length of six months. It is not difficult to work out why landlords were inclined to prefer this type of tenancy.

It is no longer competent to create a new assured or short assured tenancy.[2] Existing tenancies of these kinds continue, however, so it is still necessary to consider them. There is a right to convert an existing assured or short assured tenancy to a private residential tenancy by agreement.[3] However, as the law on private residential tenancies is generally much more in favour of tenants than that on short assured tenancies (which formed the great majority of private sector tenancies), it is unlikely that many landlords will agree to this.

1 The Scottish Government *Review of the Private Rented Sector* (2009) para 4.56.
2 PH(T)(S)A 2016 s 75, Sch 5 paras 1 and 2, amending the Housing (Scotland) Act 1988.
3 H(S)A 1988 s 46A, inserted by PH(T)(S)A 2016 Sch 5 para 3.

17.5 *Private residential tenancies* Unless it falls into an excluded category,[1] a tenancy of residential property that is created after 1 December 2017 will be a private residential tenancy.

1 See paras 17.15 et seq.

17.6 *Common law tenancies* As already noted, certain categories of occupancy agreement are excluded from becoming private residential tenancies. In such cases, the common law of leases will apply to the agreement, except insofar as any particular provision applies to residential tenancies generally.[1]

1 See, eg, the protection of residential occupiers from unlawful eviction at paras 17.152 et seq.

17.7 The original Rent Acts were United Kingdom statutes. In more recent years, Scotland has had its own separate legislation, although significant similarities have remained in the two countries, and the decisions of English courts in this field remain highly persuasive. The present Scottish law is mainly contained in the Rent (Scotland) Act 1984 (regulated tenancies), the Housing (Scotland) Act 1988 (assured tenancies), the Housing (Scotland) Act 2006 (which applies to both assured and regulated tenancies) and the Private Housing (Tenancies) (Scotland) Act 2016 (which governs private residential tenancies).

Human Rights Act 1998[1]

17.8 Chapter 1 introduced this subject in general terms, and in the next chapter we will examine in some depth the human rights dimension as it applies to residential lets by social landlords. In particular, there has been much activity in relation to alleged infringements of article 8 (the right to respect for private and family life) in eviction cases. In the area of social housing the Human Rights Act has a direct (or vertical) effect because local authorities (and, when exercising their housing function, many other social landlords also) qualify as public authorities, and so are directly prohibited from acting in contravention of the European Convention on Human Rights.

1 See paras 1.27 et seq above. See also paras 18.7 et seq, 18.57 and 19.4 et seq.

17.9 Private landlords, not being public authorities, do not have any direct liability, and so tenants cannot raise proceedings against them solely because of the breach of a Convention right or rights. However, because the courts themselves are classed as public authorities,[1] the Human Rights Act may have an indirect (or horizontal) effect. In particular, the duty of the courts to interpret legislation, as far as possible, in a way that is compatible with the Convention, means that human rights concerns have the potential to influence court decisions, eg in eviction cases where the court has the discretion to decide whether eviction would be reasonable. (Whether the eviction would be 'proportionate' is fast becoming an important element in such a decision.)[2] It should not be forgotten, of course, that the tenant is not the only person whose human rights would need to be considered, if the Convention was held to have horizontal effect in private tenancy cases. The landlord's human rights and, in particular, the property protection contained in article 1 of protocol 1 to the Convention, would also need to be considered. In addition, where neighbours have allegedly been affected by the tenant's conduct, their human rights may also be engaged.

It should also be kept in mind that much of the legislation applicable to the private sector is similar, sometimes identical, to that which applies to social tenancies (eg eviction for rent arrears, criminal activity, anti-social behaviour etc), so decisions in that area may well influence those in private sector cases.

1 See paras 1.29 and 1.31.
2 See para 1.39 et seq and para 18.12 et seq. At the same time, the fact that these eviction grounds already include a requirement to consider reasonableness may reduce the urgency of human rights arguments.

17.10 The application of the Convention to tenancy proceedings was considered in the Supreme Court decision in *Manchester City Council* *v Pinnock*,[1] which is examined in depth in the next chapter.[2] The most basic principle to emerge, both in *Pinnock* and in a number of European decisions, is that the loss of one's home is the most extreme form of interference with the right to respect for private and family life, and should therefore be taken into account in eviction cases. However, in *Pinnock*, the Supreme Court also made it clear that its judgment only applied to possession proceedings brought by social landlords, and it specifically reserved its position in relation to evictions by private landlords.[3] However, it equally did not rule out a private sector application and Convention-based arguments have been put forward in a number of cases on private sector tenancies.[4] Such arguments were, though, rejected by the Inner House of the Court of Session in *Ali v Serco Ltd*,[5] even though, in that case, the accommodation provider was carrying out delegated public functions (the housing of asylum seekers.) As things currently stand, there seems to be very limited scope for human rights arguments in relation to private sector tenancies. The situation, though, is a developing one.

1 [2010] 3 WLR 1441, [2011] 1 All ER 285.
2 See para 18.12 et seq.
3 *Manchester City Council v Pinnock* [2010] 3 WLR 1441, at 1456 per Lord Neuberger of Abbotsbury.
4 See eg *Ford v Alexander* [2012] EWHC 266 (Ch), [2012] BPIR 528 or *Telchadder v Wickland (Holdings) Ltd* [2012] ECWA Civ 635, [2012] HLR 35 (reversed *sub nom Wickland (Holdings) Ltd v Telchadder* [2014] UKSC 57, [2014] 1 WLR 4004, on non-human rights grounds), both private sector eviction cases (though not involving leases) in which Article 8 was unsuccessfully pleaded.
5 [2019] CSIH 54, 2020 SC 182. For developments in England, see eg S Nield, 'Shutting the Door on Horizontal Effect: McDonald v McDonald [2016] UKSC 28; [2016] 3 WLR 45' 2017 Conv 60; S Pascoe, 'The End of the Road for Human Rights in Private Landowners' Disputes?' 2017 Conv 269.

PRIVATE RESIDENTIAL TENANCIES

Definition

17.11   As we saw earlier, new tenancies that would formerly have been assured tenancies will now be classified as private residential tenancies if they were created after 1 December 2017, when the Private Housing (Tenancies) (Scotland) Act 2016 came into force.[1]

The Private Housing (Tenancies) (Scotland) Act 2016 ('PH(T)(S) A 2016') provides that a tenancy is a private residential tenancy where three requirements are met:[2]

(a)   the property is let to an individual as a separate dwelling;[3]
(b)   the tenant occupies the property as his or her 'only or principal home';[4] and

(c)   the tenancy does not fall into a category excluded from being a private residential tenancy.[5]

The tenancy does not cease to be a private residential tenancy simply because paragraph (b) ceases to be satisfied.[6]

It is also important to note that paragraph (b) does not require that the property be *let* for the purpose of the tenant occupying it as his or her only or principal home. Rather, it is a question of whether the tenant does, in fact, occupy the property in this way. As a result, a tenancy that is not initially a private residential tenancy may subsequently become one. Indeed, strictly speaking it is incorrect to talk of the landlord granting, or the parties creating, a private residential tenancy. Rather, the parties create a tenancy or a contract for occupation of the property, which then becomes a private residential tenancy when the tenant comes to occupy the property as his or her only or principal home.

1 Private Housing (Tenancies) (Scotland) Act 2016 (Commencement No 3, Amendment, Saving Provision and Revocation) Regulations 2017 (SSI No 346). For an overview of the 2016 Act, see P Robson, 'Reviving Tenants' Rights? The Private Housing (Tenancies) (Scotland) Act 2016' 2018 Jur Rev 108.
2 PH(T)(S)A 2016 s 1(1).
3 See para 17.1.
4 See para 17.15.
5 See pras 17.16-17.27.
6 PH(T)(S)A 2016 s 1(2).

17.12   *Separate dwelling*   The general qualification for a private residential tenancy is that a house is let as a separate dwelling.[1] The definition of 'separate dwelling' includes flats as well as self-contained dwellinghouses.[2] It may also include part of a house, possibly no more than a single room, if it is let as a separate dwelling.[3] On the other hand, where the house which is the subject of let contains a number of units of habitation (which may be sublet by the tenant), then the leased property is not a separate dwelling but a number of dwellings.[4]

It does not matter if some of the accommodation is shared with other tenants as long as there is a part that is occupied exclusively by the tenant.[5] It may even be enough that the tenant has sole occupation of a bedroom within a shared flat.[6]

In *Uratemp Ventures Ltd v Collins*[7] the meaning of 'dwelling' in this context was considered in detail by the House of Lords. It was held that a room in a hotel occupied by a long-term resident qualified as a dwelling, and whether the room had cooking facilities was not conclusive: the purpose of the legislation was 'to protect people in the occupation of their homes, not to encourage them to cook their own meals'.[8]

This does not mean that hotel guests will normally enjoy private residential tenancies: as well as the need for the subjects to be a separate dwelling, it is also necessary that they should be 'let', ie that the contract is a lease. This was the case in *Uratemp* because (among other things) the tenant had exclusive possession; more typically a hotel guest will, at the most.[9] On the same principle, a houseboat may qualify as a separate dwelling, but may be precluded from being a private residential tenancy if (as is likely to be the case) it is considered to be moveable rather than heritable property and is thus unable to be the subject of a lease.[10]

Unlike the tenant in *Uratemp*, a hotel guest will be excluded in most cases because the hotel room is not his only or principal home.[11]

Where land is let along with the house (other than agricultural land of more than two acres), the land will be included within the private residential tenancy provided that the main purpose of the letting is the provision of a home for the tenant.[12]

1 Private Housing (Tenancies) (Scotland) Act 2016 s 1.
2 Such at least is the implication of PH(T)(S)A 2016 s 9.
3 *Langford Property Co Ltd v Goldrich* [1949] 1 KB 511, [1949] 1 All ER 402, CA.
4 *Cole v Harris* [1945] KB 474, [1945] 2 All ER 146, CA.
5 *Horford Investments Ltd v Lambert* [1976] Ch 39, [1974] 1 All ER 131, CA; *St Catherine's College (Oxford) v Dorling* [1979] 3 All ER 250, [1980] 1 WLR 66, CA.
6 *Affleck v Bronsdon* [2020] UT 44.
7 [2001] 3 WLR 806, [2002 1 All ER 46.
8 *Uratemp Ventures Ltd v Collins* [2001] 3 WLR 806 at 823 per Lord Millet.
9 See *Brillouet v Landless* (1996) 28 HLR 836; for licences, see paras 2.50 et seq. The requirement of exclusive possession in order to constitute a lease has been argued to be less essential in Scotland than in England – see paras 1.3 and 2.55 et seq.
10 *Chelsea Yacht and Boat Co Ltd v Pope* [2000] 1 WLR 1941, [2001] 2 All ER 409; for Scottish authority see *Assessor for Glasgow v RNVR Club (Scotland)* 1974 SC 67, 1974 SLT 291.
11 See para 17.13.
12 PH(T)(S)A 2016 s 2(3).

17.13 *Only or principal home* It is also a requirement for a private residential tenancy that the tenant (or at least one of them if there are joint tenants) must occupy the house as his or her only or principal home.[1]

In relation to regulated tenancies, it has been held that a tenant may qualify in this respect even when only residing in the house part of the time, though in the case of a prolonged absence the onus is on the tenant to establish an intention to return, and the court will look with particular care at two-home cases.[2] A tenant who sublets the property in its entirety,[3] or who lives elsewhere while allowing another person, eg a mistress, to occupy the property instead,[4] will not normally be considered to be in occupation.[5]

However, a tenant who sublets part of the property, while remaining in occupation of the rest, will not lose the right to security of tenure, provided that he or she intends at some future date to reoccupy the part sublet.[6] Nor will a tenant who was forced to move out because a breach of the landlord's repairing obligation rendered the house uninhabitable.[7] A corollary to the requirement that the tenant must occupy the property as his or her only or principal home is that, for there to be a private residential tenancy, the tenant (or, in the case of joint tenants, at least one of them) must be a human being (and not, for example, a limited company).

1 PH(T)(S)A 2016 s. 1(1)(b). See also paras 18.23 and 18.64.
2 *Brickfield Properties Ltd v Hughes* (1988) 20 HLR 108, (1988) 24 EG 95, CA; see also *Notting Hill Housing Trust v Etoria* [1989] CLY 1912; *City of Edinburgh Council v Baillie* 2004 Hous LR 15; *East Lothian Council v Skeldon* 2004 Hous LR 123.
3 *Menzies v Mackay* 1938 SC 74, 1938 SLT 135.
4 *Colin Smith Music Ltd v Ridge* [1975] 1 All ER 290, [1975] 1 WLR 463, CA.
5 However, see also *Ujima Housing Association v Ansah* (1998) 30 HLR 831, [1997] NPC 144 and *Fanning v Waltham Forest Community Based Housing Association* [2001] L&TR 41.
6 *Regalian Securities Ltd v Ramsden* [1981] 2 All ER 65, [1981] 1 WLR 611, HL.
7 *Viking Property Co Ltd v Rawlinson* County Court, 11 June 1999 (unreported); digested in 1999 CLY 3714.

17.14   *Business use*   If a house is partly used by the tenant to carry on a business, it is thought that there may nevertheless be a private residential (or an assured or a regulated) tenancy, provided that the residential use is not negligible.[1] However, there cannot be such a tenancy if the business element comprises premises licensed for the sale of alcohol for consumption on the premises, or if it is a shop to which the Tenancy of Shops (Scotland) Act 1949 applies.[2]

1 See AGM Duncan & JAD Hope *The Rent (Scotland) Act 1984* (1986) 58-23. The authors applied this principle to regulated tenancies from case law relating to controlled tenancies, and there seems no reason why it should not be extended to assured tenancies and private residential tenancies also: see *Cargill v Phillips* 1951 SC 67, 1951 SLT 110 and *Cowan and Sons v Acton* 1952 SC 73, 1952 SLT 122.
2 See paras 17.17 and 17.18.

Excepted categories

17.15   There are various categories of agreement that do not qualify as private residential tenancies. These are all identical, or substantially similar, to tenancies that were excluded from regulation under the Housing (Scotland) Act 1988 and the Rent (Scotland) Act 1984,[1] so many of the cases on regulated and assured tenancies are likely to be highly persuasive. The exclusions are contained in Schedule 1 to the Private Housing (Tenancies) (Scotland) Act 2016. The Scottish Ministers may make regulations modifying the list of exclusions.[2] Before doing so, they must 'consult such persons representing the interests of tenants and landlords under private residential tenancies as they think fit'.[3]

1 See paras 17.68 and 17.111.
2 PH(T)(S)A 2016 s 6(1).
3 PH(T)(S)A 2016 s 6(2).

17.16 (1) *Tenancies at a low rent* These are tenancies where the rent is less than £6 a week (or its equivalent, if the payment period is different), unless the tenancy has previously had the status of assured tenancy or private residential tenancy[1] In determining the appropriate level, sums payable by the tenant in respect of services, repairs, maintenance or insurance are to be disregarded.

1 PH(T)(S)A 2016 Sch 1 para 1.For the law applying to assured tenancies, see Assured Tenancies (Tenancies at a Low Rent) (Scotland) Order 1988, SI 1988/2069. See also para 2.35 on leases at nominal rent.

17.17 (2) *A tenancy to which the Tenancy of Shops (Scotland) Act 1949 is capable of applying*[1] In the case of regulated tenancies, a sublet of a residential element of a shop tenancy could be protected.[2] That proviso does not apply in the case of private residential tenancies (or assured tenancies).

1 PH(T)(S)A 2016 Sch 1 para 2. See Ch 13 above for the Tenancy of Shops (Scotland) Act 1949. The Housing (Scotland) Act 1988 had slightly different wording, referring simply to tenancies to which the 1949 Act applies. This would not seem to make any difference to the intended interpretation.
2 Rent (Scotland) Act 1984 s 10(2).

17.18 (3) *Licensed premises*[1] This refers to premises that are licensed for the sale of alcoholic liquor on the premises (not to those licensed for off-sales only). The lease of a public house may include a dwellinghouse for the use of the person or persons operating the pub (an arrangement perhaps more common in England than it is in Scotland). This will not be a private residential (or, previously, an assured) tenancy, presumably because the dwellinghouse element is an adjunct of a commercial let.

1 PH(T)(S)A 2016 Sch 1 para 3.

17.19 (4) *Tenancies of agricultural land*[1] This refers to cases where the house is let under an agricultural lease (either a 1991 Act tenancy or a short limited duration, limited duration, modern limited duration or repairing tenancy)[2] and it is occupied by the person responsible for farming the land; the latter may be either the tenant or the tenant's servant or agent. This exception also includes any tenancy including agricultural land two acres or more in extent, which does not already qualify as an agricultural lease.

1 PH(T)(S)A 2016 Sch 1 para 4. The previous law, applying to assured tenancies, was in substance much the same, but made a distinction between tenancies of agricultural holdings and other tenancies of agricultural land (H(S)A 1988 Sch 4 para 6).
2 See Ch 15.

17.20   (5) *Student lets*   This exception applies where the landlord is the student's educational institution.[1] It also applies where the landlord is an 'institutional provider of student accommodation', letting property that has been given planning permission for this use 'on the basis that the let property would be used predominantly for housing students'.[2] The landlord is an institutional provider of student accommodation if the property is part of a building or complex containing at least 30 properties with the same landlord, and which are let or intended to be let to students.[3] The exception allows landlords of student property to remove ex-students from their properties in order to make way for new students.

A student who leases directly from any other category of landlord has the same rights as anyone else. The tenancy does not fall within this exception simply by virtue of the fact that the tenant is a student. Nor, it is assumed, is a student prevented from occupying a property as his or her only or principal home solely by virtue of the fact that he or she has another residence elsewhere.[4]

Even though these lets are in general terms regulated by the common law, temporary provision under the Coronavirus (Scotland) (No 2) Act 2020 is in force at the time of writing, allowing tenants in student lets to terminate the let early on giving at least 28 days' notice in writing (seven days' notice if the tenant took occupation under the let before 27 May 2020).[5]

1 A detailed definition of the kinds of institution that qualify for this exception is included in PH(T)(S)A 2016 Sch 1 para 5(2). However, in simple terms, it covers universities and other institutions of higher and further education. It also includes the Royal College of Surgeons of Edinburgh. Previously a list of relevant educational establishments was contained in separate regulations, the Assured Tenancies (Exceptions) (Scotland) Regulations 1988 SI 1988/2068.
2 PH(T)(S)A 2016 Sch 1 para 5(3).
3 PH(T)(S)A 2016 Sch 1 para 5(4).
4 See, in a different context, *Fox v Stirk* [1970] 2 QB 463.
5 Coronavirus (Scotland) (No 2) Act 2020 Sch 1 paras 2–3.

17.21   (6) *Holiday lets*[1]   Obviously someone who takes a lease of a holiday cottage for two weeks or a month should not have the right to claim extended security of tenure. However, the word 'holiday' is not defined in the relevant legislation, and the concept of a holiday let has been extended by the courts to cover some rather unlikely holiday situations.

The way in which the parties' agreement describes their relationship will be persuasive. In *McHale v Daneham*,[2] the tenants of premises in Maida Vale were foreign visitors working in London and the tenancy had endured for over six months before the landlord attempted to recover possession. The tenancy agreement stated that a holiday let was intended. The court held that the legislation envisaged the possibility of a 'working holiday', and that this was a holiday let. The tenants were denied protection as regulated tenants. Nevertheless, the court will not necessarily confirm a let to be a holiday let merely because the lease says so, if there is other evidence to show that this is a sham designed by the landlord to evade the effects of the legislation. It may be that this exclusion is best read alongside the requirement for the property to be the tenant's 'only or principal home'.[3] If the property is, in fact, the tenant's only or principal home, it is hard to see how on any view it can be considered to be occupied for a holiday. Equally, if it is not the tenant's only or principal home, the tenancy is not a private residential tenancy even without the exclusion for holiday lets.

1 PH(T)(S)A 2016 Sch 1 para 6. Such agreements are likely to fall within the category of short-term lets, on which see paras 20.31–20.34.
2 (1979) 249 EG 969; see also *Barns-Graham v Ballance* 2000 Hous LR 11, *R v Rent Officer for the London Borough of Camden* (1983) 7 HLR 15.
3 See para 17.15

17.22 (7) *Where the landlord is resident* The wording of this provision is somewhat lengthy and complex, but basically it means that security of tenure is denied where the landlord and tenant occupy the same house or flat. A similar exception has existed in the case of assured and regulated tenancies for some time, but the definition of resident landlord has been amended several times to exclude unintended interpretations.

The wording of the provision relating to private residential tenancies is therefore designed to make it clear that a landlord is not regarded as resident where the landlord and the tenant occupy entirely separate flats within a single building. This is done by including a condition that either (i) the tenant is entitled to use facilities in common with the landlord,[1] or else (ii) at the time of the creation of the tenancy the landlord has some means of access through the tenant's house or vice versa.[2]

In the latter of these cases, the property must have been the landlord's only or main residence when the tenancy was granted and the landlord must have continued to be resident thereafter. This exception will continue to apply where there has been a change of landlord, provided that the new landlord is also resident, and there are limited exceptions to the need for continuous residence to cover any transitional period.[3] Where the tenancy is granted by joint landlords, only one needs to be resident to fall within this exception.[4]

1 PH(T)(S)A 2016 Sch 1 para 8.
2 PH(T)(S)A 2016 Sch 1 para 9.
3 PH(T)(S)A 2016 Sch 1 para 9(4).
4 PH(T)(S)A 2016 Sch 1 para 11; *Cooper v Tait* (1984) 271 EG 105, (1984) 48 P&CR 460, CA.

17.23 (8) *Police and Ministry of Defence tenancies.* There is no private residential tenancy where the landlord is the Scottish Police Authority[1] or the Secretary of State for Defence.[2]

1 PH(T)(S)A 2016 Sch 1 para 12. H(S)A 1988 Sch 4 para 10 had a more general exclusion for Crown tenancies.
2 PH(T)(S)A 2016 Sch 1 para 13.

17.24 (9) *Local authority and other* tenancies[1] Under this heading there are excluded lettings where the landlord is one of the following:

(a) A local authority landlord within the definition given in section 11 of the Housing (Scotland) Act 2001. Such a landlord is either 'a local authority, a joint board or joint committee of two or more local authorities, or the common good of such a council or any trust under the control of a local authority'.[2]

(b) A registered social landlord within the definition given in section 165 of the Housing (Scotland) Act 2010.

(c) A co-operative housing association within the definition given in section 1 of the Housing Associations Act 1985.

(d) Scottish Water.

The reason for these exceptions is that such tenancies would normally qualify as Scottish secure tenancies, which afford tenants more substantial rights than private residential tenancies.[3]

1 PH(T)(S)A 2016 Sch 1 paras 14–15.
2 H(S)A 2001 s 11(3).
3 See Ch 18. PH(T)(S)A 2016 Sch 1 para 15 and Housing (Scotland) Act 2001 s 32(7) make it clear that, where a Scottish secure tenancy is assigned or sublet, no private residential tenancy is created.

17.25 (10) There are various further exceptions. Lets by local authorities in fulfilment of their statutory duties to homeless persons[1] and ex-offenders[2] are not private residential tenancies. Arrangements made by or on behalf of the Secretary of State for the accommodation of asylum seekers and displaced persons also do not create private residential tenancies.[3] Likewise excluded are lets by charities providing accommodation to veterans or care leavers.[4]

1 PH(T)(S)A 2016 Sch 1 para 16.
2 PH(T)(S)A 2016 Sch 1 para 17.
3 PH(T)(S)A 2016 Sch 1 paras 18 and 19. *Ali v Serco Ltd* [2019] CSIH 54, 2020 SC 182.
4 PH(T)(S)A 2016 Sch 1 para 22.

17.26 (11) *Shared ownership agreements*[1]   This refers to a situation where a tenant has an 'equity share' in the property, ie as well as paying a periodic rent the tenant has paid a capital sum and remains entitled to a percentage of the house's value. In effect, therefore, he or she is part tenant, part owner, though, strictly speaking, such an arrangement does not constitute a lease.[2] For people who cannot yet afford to take the full plunge into owner-occupation this arrangement provides a useful halfway stage between tenancy and ownership.

The statutory definition[3] also includes agreements whereby basically the same arrangement is managed by trustees in respect of a group of houses, as well as any other agreement approved by the Scottish Ministers whereby a person acquires a *pro indiviso* right while having exclusive occupancy of a house.

Such agreements will not be private residential tenancies, though presumably the tenant's equity share (if not the terms of the agreement) will provide a measure of security, as the arrangement could not be terminated without the tenant being paid his or her share of the property's value.[4]

1 PH(T)(S)A 2016 Sch 1 para 20.
2 *Clydesdale Bank plc v Davidson* 1998 SC (HL) 51, 1998 SLT 522. See para 2.24.
3 Housing (Scotland) Act 2001 s 83(3).
4 For the general issues arising here, see W M Gordon & S Wortley, *Scottish Land Law* 3rd edn (Vol 1, SULI/W Green 2009) para 15-29 et seq.

17.27 (12) *Transitional cases*   These are (a) protected tenancies under the Rent (Scotland) Act 1984; (b) housing association tenancies to which Part VI of that Act applies; (c) contracts under Part VII of that Act; and (d) assured tenancies.[1] Private sector lets entered into before 1 December 2017 are still governed by the law in force at the time of their creation.

There is some doubt about the status of tenancies, purporting to be assured or short assured tenancies, which were entered into shortly before 1 December 2017, but which were intended to begin after that date. Unfortunately, PH(T)(S)A 2016 makes no provision for this situation. In *Butler v Ormidale Properties*,[2] the First-Tier Tribunal held that, in such a case, the tenancy was a private residential tenancy. The basis for this, said the Tribunal, was that it 'clearly was the Scottish Parliament's intention that new domestic tenancies formed after 1 December 2017 between private individuals would be constituted as Private Residential tenancies'.[3] The counter-argument would be that a contract is formed, not when performance is to take place, but when the parties agree to form it. A tenancy is a contract. The tenancy is therefore formed when it is agreed by the parties, not when the tenant takes entry. It was not possible to create a private residential tenancy before 1 December 2017, as no such thing existed at that time, so in the absence of any contrary provision, a tenancy agreed before that date cannot be a private residential tenancy. Accordingly, the Tribunal's view may not convince as stated. It gains more support from the wording of PH(T)(S)A 2016 s 1(1)(b), however, which provides, *inter alia*, that a tenancy is a private residential tenancy where 'the tenant occupies the property... as the tenant's only or principal home'. This wording (as opposed to, say, 'the tenant is intended to occupy...') suggests an interpretation to the effect that, although a tenancy is created when agreement is reached, this only becomes a private residential tenancy when the tenant actually moves in.

1 PH(T)(S)A 2016 Sch 1 para 21.
2 First-Tier Tribunal, 25 March 2019.
3 Para 29.

PRIVATE RESIDENTIAL TENANCIES: CREATION AND TERMS

Creation

17.28   Strictly speaking, it is probably not quite accurate to describe a private residential tenancy as a lease.[1] As we have seen,[2] any agreement that meets the requirements laid down by PH(T)(S)A 2016 will become a private residential tenancy on the tenant taking up occupation in the required way, regardless of whether it meets the general requirements for being a lease. This having been done, the agreement will be regulated by that Act, rather than by the general law of leases. Nonetheless, the usage is convenient, and it is expressly provided that references in legislation to the terms 'tenancy' or 'lease' are to be construed as including private residential tenancies, unless a contrary intention appears. References to landlords, tenants and property being let are also to be interpreted accordingly.[3] There are important similarities between private residential tenancies and leases. For example, as with any lease that has become a real right, the landlord's interest in the private residential tenancy transfers to any new owner of the property.[4] There are, though, certain important differences here from the general law on leases, and these should not be lost sight of.

First, a private residential tenancy does not require writing for its constitution, as long as it otherwise satisfies the requirements for a private residential tenancy.[5] Where the agreement is not made in writing, the private residential tenancy is constituted when the tenant begins to occupy the property, in accordance with the agreement, as his or her only or principal home. This differs from the general law of leases, in that a lease with a duration of more than a year normally requires writing.[6] No such requirement applies to private residential tenancies, however long they last.

Second, unlike other forms of lease,[7] a private residential tenancy does not require an ish.[8] Even if the tenancy agreement specifies an anticipated end date, the provisions on termination of private residential tenancies will render such an end date unenforceable.[9] Likewise, it is not competent for the tenant to give notice terminating the tenancy before the tenancy has begun.[10] Accordingly, any attempt to circumvent the termination provisions by having the tenant sign a purported notice terminating the tenancy on an identified future date will be ineffective.

Third, although a private residential tenancy requires an agreed rent just as much as does any other kind of lease,[11] the private residential tenancy will not cease to be such even if the rent obligation is subsequently removed or ceases to have effect.[12]

Fourth, unlike other forms of lease, private residential tenancies are not normally subject to the jurisdiction of the normal courts. The normal forum for civil proceedings arising from a private residential tenancy is the First-Tier Tribunal, which has the jurisdiction that a sheriff would otherwise have.[13] The jurisdiction of the Sheriff Court (though not of the Court of Session) is excluded.

1 See V Wahle, 'Private residential tenancies – a new form of lease?' (2018) 152 Prop LB 4.
2 See para 17.13
3 PH(T)(S)A 2016 s 5.
4 PH(T)(S)A 2016 s 45.
5 PH(T)(S)A 2016 s 1(1).
6 See para 2.3 et seq.
7 See para 2.36.
8 PH(T)(S)A 2016 s 4(a).
9 See paras 17.42 et seq.
10 PH(T)(S)A 2016 s 49(1)(a)(ii).
11 See para 2.27.
12 PH(T)(S)A 2016 s 4(b).
13 PH(T)(S)A 2016 s 71.

Terms

17.29 To a great extent, the parties are free to agree the terms of the tenancy. However, PH(T)(S)A 2016 permits the Scottish Ministers to prescribe statutory terms for private residential tenancies.[1] The regulations by which the statutory terms are prescribed may provide that, in some circumstances, a statutory term is not a term of a private residential tenancy.[2] They may also provide that, in some or all circumstances, the parties may modify a statutory term.[3] Except to the extent that regulations permit the parties to omit or vary a statutory term, all of the statutory terms are included in the tenancy agreement regardless of any express agreement to the contrary. PH(T)(S)A 2016 provides for certain terms that must be included in the regulations.[4]

The following are the statutory terms.[5] In practice, a tenancy agreement is likely to be considerably more extensive. The Scottish Government has produced a Model Private Residential Tenancy Agreement, which the parties may use as it stands or adapt to their needs, subject to the statutory terms.[6]

1 PH(T)(S)A 2016 s 7(1). Provision for such terms has been made in the Private Residential Tenancies (Statutory Terms) (Scotland) Regulations 2017 SSI 2017 No 408.
2 PH(T)(S)A 2016 s 7(3)(a).
3 PH(T)(S)A 2016 s 7(3)(b).
4 PH(T)(S)A 2016 s 8 Sch 2.
5 This account follows the numbering in the Private Residential Tenancies (Statutory Terms) (Scotland) Regulations 2017 SI 2017 No 408, rather than in PH(T)(S)A 2016 Sch 2, which has slightly different numbering. The statutory terms are found in the Schedule to the 2017 Regulations.
6 This may be found at www.gov.scot/publications/scottish-government-model-private-residential-tenancy-agreement/pages/1/#:~:text=The%20Private%20Residential%20 Tenancies%20%28Information%20for%20Tenants%29%20%28Scotland%29,the%20 Private%20Residential%20Tenancy%20Statutory%20Terms%20Supporting%20Notes.

17.30 *Rent payments in cash.* Where a rent payment is made in cash, the landlord must provide a written receipt stating the date of payment, the amount paid and either the amount remaining outstanding or confirmation that no further amount remains outstanding. This term is not capable of being varied in the tenancy agreement.

17.31 *Rent increases.* The rent may only be increased in accordance with the provisions of PH(T)(S)A 2016 Pt 4 ch 2.[1] The parties may not contract out of these provisions.

1 See below, paras 17.38 et seq.

17.32 *Subletting etc.* The tenant may not sublet the property, take in a lodger, assign the tenancy or 'otherwise part with, or give up to another person, possession of the let property (or any part of it).' Presumably 'possession' here means natural possession, and it is not enough for the tenant to retain civil possession through someone else occupying in the tenant's absence. Equally, it may be assumed that a temporary absence will not amount to the tenant parting with possession.[1] The parties may not contract out of this term.

1 See paras 17.13 and 17.55.

17.33   *Occupancy by over-16s other than the tenant.* The tenant must inform the landlord of the name of any person aged 16 or over (who is not a joint tenant) who occupies the property as his or her only or principal home[1] and of that person's relationship to the tenant. The tenant must also inform the landlord if any such person ceases to have the property as his or her only or principal home. The parties are free to modify this term[2] except where the person concerned is in a 'qualifying relationship' with the tenant,[3] is a member of the tenant's family,[4] or is a resident carer.[5] These categories of person have potential rights to succeed to the tenancy on the tenant's death.[6]

1 On the definition of 'only or principal home', see para 17.13.
2 Private Residential Tenancies (Statutory Terms) (Scotland) Regulations 2017 SSI 2017 No 408 reg 3.
3 As defined in PH(T)(S)A 2016 s 70(1)(a). A qualifying relationship is one in which the parties are married or in a civil partnership with each other or are living together as though married.
4 As defined in PH(T)(S)A 2016 s 70(1)(b), read with s 70(2), (3). In simple terms, a family member for these purposes is someone who is a parent, grandparent, child, grandchild, brother or sister of the tenant or of anyone in a qualifying relationship with the tenant, or anyone who is in a qualifying relationship with a parent, grandparent, child, grandchild or sibling of the tenant.
5 As defined in PH(T)(S)A 2016 s 69(5).
6 See paras 17.148–17.151.

17.34   *Access for repairs etc.* The tenant is to allow access for repairs and inspections. The tenant is entitled to at least 48 hours' notice, except in cases where access is required urgently. Access may only be taken under this head to carry out work that the landlord is entitled or obliged to carry out, to inspect the property to determine if work of that kind needs to be carried out, in pursuance of any entitlement or obligation to carry out an inspection, or for the purpose of valuing the property. The tenant is to allow 'reasonable use of facilities within the let property' in connection with the purpose for which access has been taken. The parties may not contract out of this term.

17.35   *Termination of tenancy.* The tenancy may only be brought to an end in accordance with the provisions of PH(T)(S)A 2016 Pt 5.[1] The parties may not contract out of this term, though they may agree to vary the relevant notice period after the tenancy has begun.[2]

1 See below, para 17.42 et seq.
2 See para 17.43.

Tenancy information

17.36   As we have seen,[1] a private residential tenancy does not require writing for its constitution. However, where the terms are not set out in full in writing, the landlord is required to provide the tenant with a document which sets out all of the terms of the tenancy.[2] Regulations[3] have been made providing that this may be done using either the Model Private Residential Tenancy or 'a tenancy agreement drafted by the landlord'.[4] It is not clear how the terms of the Model Private Residential Tenancy can be said to set out the terms of the tenancy (which is, after all, first and foremost a contract between the parties) where the parties have not agreed to use the Model Private Residential Tenancy. Presumably we are to read the regulations as authorising the landlord to impose those terms on the tenant, except to the extent that contrary terms have been agreed. Again, in the case where a 'tenancy agreement drafted by the landlord' is used, it is hard to see that as an 'agreement' unless it accurately reflects what the parties actually agreed. Presumably, therefore, a purported agreement that does not accurately reflect what was actually agreed will be ineffective and will not satisfy the obligation to provide written terms. The landlord may not use these provisions to impose terms not actually agreed to by the tenant and which are not statutory terms.

This duty must be complied with by the day on which the tenancy commences or, where the tenancy only subsequently becomes a private residential tenancy, within 28 days of the date it becomes a private residential tenancy.[5] Any change in terms must also be reduced to writing within 28 days.[6]

Whether or not the tenancy was originally constituted in writing, further information must also be provided.[7] Where the written terms of the tenancy are in the form of the Model Private Residential Tenancy, the landlord must provide the Easy Read Notes for this.[8] Where the written terms of the tenancy are in the form of a tenancy agreement drafted by the landlord, the landlord must provide the Private Residential Tenancy Statutory Terms Supporting Notes.[9] Probably, though not certainly, the latter situation is intended to include those cases where the parties use some set of written terms obtained from a third party.[10] Oddly, no provision is made for the situation, less common but hardly impossible, where the tenancy agreement is drafted by the tenant or jointly by tenant and landlord.

The tenancy terms and notes may be given either on paper or electronically.[11] No charge may be required for their provision.[12]

In addition, from time to time legislation may impose further information requirements on landlords, whether in relation to private residential tenancies or more generally. Such requirements include the following:

- to carry out regular inspections of gas appliances and of the electricity supply and electrical fixtures, and provide the tenant with records of these inspections;[13]
- to provide the tenant with an energy performance certificate;[14] and
- to provide the tenant with written information about the landlord's repair obligations.[15]

Further requirements of landlords are found in Chapter 20.

1 See para 17.28.
2 PH(T)(S)A 2016 s 10(1).
3 Made under PH(T)(S)A 2016 s 12.
4 Private Residential Tenancies (Information for Tenants) (Scotland) Regulations 2017 SSI 2017 No 407 reg 2(2).
5 PH(T)(S)A 2016 s 10(2).
6 PH(T)(S)A 2016 s 10(3).
7 PH(T)(S)A 2016 s 11; Private Residential Tenancies (Information for Tenants) (Scotland) Regulations 2017 SSI 2017 No 407 reg 3(1). In terms of reg 3(2), this must be done on the day that the tenancy begins, unless it only subsequently becomes a private residential tenancy, in which case this must be done within 28 days.
8 Available at www.gov.scot/publications/easy-read-notes-scottish-government-model-private-residential-tenancy-agreement/.
9 Available at www.gov.scot/publications/private-residential-tenancy-statutory-terms-supporting-notes-essential-housing-information/.
10 For example, it is not unknown for landlords to download tenancy terms from the internet. Sometimes these are intended for use in a different jurisdiction.
11 Private Residential Tenancies (Information for Tenants) (Scotland) Regulations 2017 SSI 2017 No 407 regs 2(1), 3(3).
12 PH(T)(S)A 2016 s 13.
13 Gas Safety (Installation and Use) Regulations 1988 SI 1988/2451 reg 36(6); Housing (Scotland) Act 2006 s 19A. It is not, in fact, clear that the 1998 regulations apply to private residential tenancies, as the lack of a fixed term (see para 17.28) arguably means that it is neither 'a lease for a term of less than seven years' nor 'a tenancy for a periodic term' as required by reg 36(1). It is true that PH(T)(S)A 2016 s 5 provides that references in other statutes to leases is to include agreements giving rise to private residential tenancies, but that is only '[u]nless a contrary intention appears'. Given that the 1998 Regulations appear to intend make a distinction based on length of lease, it is not clear how that interacts with the 2016 Act.
14 Energy Performance of Buildings (Scotland) Regulations 2008 SSI No 309.
15 Housing (Scotland) Act 2006 s 20. See Chapter 19.

First-Tier Tribunal's powers to draw up terms etc.

17.37   The tenant may apply to the First-Tier Tribunal where:

- the landlord has a duty to provide written terms, and has failed to do so;[1] or
- the written terms of a tenancy purport to displace a statutory term[2] in an unlawful manner.[3]

In the latter of these cases, the landlord may also apply to the Tribunal. If the Tribunal considers the ground of the application to be well-founded, it may 'draw up a document which accurately reflects all of the terms of the tenancy'.[4] Any such document drawn up by the Tribunal is 'to be regarded as setting out all of the terms of the tenancy'.[5]

Where the tenant has applied to the Tribunal on the ground that the landlord has failed to provide required information, the Tribunal has certain further powers to sanction the failure. In such an application, the Tribunal may order the landlord to pay the tenant up to three months' rent where the landlord has failed in the duty imposed by either section 10 (obligation to provide written terms) or section 11 (obligation to provide other prescribed information). Where both duties have been breached, the Tribunal may order the payment of up to six months' rent.[6]

An application by a tenant based on a failure to provide written terms, or which seeks to have sanctions imposed on the landlord, must be preceded by notice. The tenant must give the landlord 28 days to comply with the requirement beginning from the day after the landlord should have performed the duty, or beginning the day that the tenant gives notice (whichever is later).[7]

1 PH(T)(S)A 2016 s 14(1).
2 See above, para 17.29 et seq.
3 PH(T)(S)A 2016 s 14(2).
4 PH(T)(S)A 2016 s 15(1).
5 PH(T)(S)A 2016 s 15(2).
6 PH(T)(S)A 2016 s 16(2). In terms of s 16(3), where the application relates to a failure to perform a duty under s 10(1), this is only competent in the context of an application under s 14(1). For discussion of how the Tribunal might approach such penal provisions, see para 20.28.
7 PH(T)(S)A 2016 ss 14(3), 16(3)(c) and 17.

Rent

17.38   A private residential tenancy requires provision to be made for payment of rent.[1] PH(T)(S)A 2016 makes extensive provision regarding rent increases.

The landlord's ability to recover rent arrears from the tenant is severely restricted by the fact that the First-Tier Tribunal's consent is needed before diligence can be done in respect of any rent liability of any tenant or former tenant.[2]

The rent payable under a private residential tenancy may only be increased once in a 12-month period.[3] The rent may only be increased in accordance with the procedure laid down in chapter 2 of Part 4 of PH(T)(S)A 2016. An informal agreement to increase the rent will simply be void.[4]

1   PH(T)(S)A 2016 s 4(b), however, provides that a tenancy does not cease to be a private residential tenancy merely because the rent obligation has been removed or in some other way ceased to have effect.
2   PH(T)(S)A 2016 s 21. This includes any liability under s 31 for underpaid rent. On this, see below, para 17.39.
3   PH(T)(S)A 2016 s 19. Reductions in rent, however, are not limited in this way. The parties are free to agree any reduction.
4   This would appear to be the case even if the tenant begins paying the agreed increased rent. On their face, the terms of PH(T)(S)A 2016 s 44 appear to exclude even novation operating to terminate the original tenancy and create a new one with the increased rent. See further para 17.42.

17.39   *Procedure for rent increase*   The landlord initiates the process for increasing the rent by giving the tenant a rent-increase notice.[1] The notice must give the tenant at least three months' notice of the increase, unless the parties have agreed a longer period.[2] The date on which the rent increase is to take effect is known as the 'effective date'.

Unless the landlord rescinds the notice before it takes effect,[3] one of three things will happen. First, the landlord and tenant may agree to modify the rent increase notice.[4] Second, if the tenant wishes to object, they may, within 21 days of receiving the notice, refer the increase to a rent officer.[5] If neither of these things happens, the notice will take effect on the effective date.[6]

The rent officer is to make a determination of the rent increase (if any), based on an open market rent for a private residential tenancy between a willing landlord and a willing tenant, on the same terms as the actual tenancy, and beginning on the date that would have been the effective date under the rent-increase notice.[7] As the new rent is to be based on an open market rent, the rent officer's determination may, in fact, result in the rent staying the same or decreasing. In reaching this determination, there is to be disregarded any work done by the tenant that has increased the property's rental value (other than work the tenant was required to carry out under the terms of the tenancy) and any reduction in rental value that arises from a failure by the tenant to comply with the terms of the tenancy.[8]

Before making a final order, the rent officer is to issue a provisional order.[9] The parties then each have 14 days to ask the rent officer to reconsider the proposed rent.[10] If such a request is received, the rent officer must consider it before making a final order.[11]

The rent officer will then make an order determining the rent to be paid.[12] Where this is done 14 or more days before the original effective date, ie the effective date under the rent-increase notice, the order takes effect on the original effective date. Otherwise, it takes effect as of the first payment date falling at least 14 days after the making of the order.[13] In cases of error, the rent officer may correct the final order within 14 days of making it.[14] This may change the effective date of the order.

Either party may appeal to the First-Tier Tribunal within 14 days of the order being made.[15] The date on which the Tribunal's order takes effect depends on when it is made. If it is made on or before the original effective date, it takes effective on that date. Otherwise, it takes effect on the first payment date on or after the date on which the Tribunal makes its order.[16] There is no further appeal against this decision, though the Tribunal may review its order to correct minor errors, either at its own instance or at the request of one of the parties.[17]

Although the order of the Tribunal or of the rent officer cannot take effect before it is made, this must be qualified in one respect. If the outcome of the process is a change in rent, and the final order is made after the originally proposed effective date, ie the date in the rent-increase notice, the change is retrospective to that date. Accordingly, any such change in rent will result in a liability on the part of landlord or tenant for the difference between new and old rents for the intervening period.[18]

Rent officers and the First-Tier Tribunal are obliged collectively to make publicly available information about their determinations.[19]

1 This should be in the form provided for by the Private Residential Tenancies (Prescribed Notices and Forms) (Scotland) Regulations 2017 SSI 2017 No 297 Sch 3.
2 PH(T)(S)A 2016 s 22(3)–(6).
3 PH(T)(S)A 2016 s 22(3)(a).
4 PH(T)(S)A 2016 s 23.
5 PH(T)(S)A 2016 s 24. This procedure is not available if the property is in a rent pressure zone, on which see below, para 17.40. On rent officers, see para 17.3.
6 PH(T)(S)A 2016 s 22(3).
7 PH(T)(S)A 2016 s 32(1).
8 PH(T)(S)A 2016 s 32(2).
9 PH(T)(S)A 2016 s 26(1). This should identify both the proposed rent and which sum, if any, is to be attributed to the provision of services.
10 PH(T)(S)A 2016 s 26(2), (3).
11 PH(T)(S)A 2016 s 26(4).
12 PH(T)(S)A 2016 s 25(2), (4).

13 PH(T)(S)A 2016 s 25(1). In terms of subsection (3) of that section, the order is to include 'the amount of the rent that is fairly attributable to the provision of services, unless the amount is negligible or no amount is so attributable.'
14 PH(T)(S)A 2016 s 27.
15 PH(T)(S)A 2016 s 28.
16 PH(T)(S)A 2016 s 29.
17 PH(T)(S)A 2016 s 30.
18 PH(T)(S)A 2016 s 31.
19 PH(T)(S)A 2016 s 34; Private Residential Tenancies (Information for Determining Rents and Fees for Copies of Information) (Scotland) Regulations 2017 SSI 2017 No 296.

17.40   *Rent pressure zones*   PH(T)(S)A 2016 makes provision for areas to be designated as rent pressure zones, in which rent increases are restricted. At the time of writing, no such zones have been designated.

The procedure begins with an application by the local authority into whose areas the proposed rent pressure zone falls.[1] The Scottish Ministers may lay down requirements that must be met for such an application to be valid.[2]

The next step is for the Scottish Ministers to respond to the application. Within 18 weeks, the Scottish Ministers must lay before the Scottish Parliament either a draft Scottish Statutory Instrument designating the rent pressure zone, or else a document explaining why this has not been done.[3] Before laying draft regulations before the Scottish Parliament, the Scottish Ministers must consult persons appearing to them to represent the interests of landlords and tenants in the area.[4] The draft regulations must be accompanied by a document laying out the justification for designating the rent pressure zone.[5]

Where the decision is taken to designate a rent pressure zone, rent increases are limited to a specified number of percentage points over the consumer prices index.[6] This is subject to an exception, however. Where improvements have been made to the property which justify a higher rent increase, the landlord may apply to the rent officer to have the rent increased accordingly.[7]

The designation of a rent pressure zone will expire after five years, unless the regulations are revoked or a shorter duration is provided for.[8] If a rent pressure zone is to be extended beyond this, a further application by the relevant local authority will be needed.[9]

1 PH(T)(S)A 2016 s 35(1). In terms of s 39(1), no rent pressure zone may be designated without an application having first been made by the relevant local authority.
2 PH(T)(S)A 2016 s 35(2).
3 PH(T)(S)A 2016 s 36.
4 PH(T)(S)A 2016 s 40(2).
5 PH(T)(S)A 2016 s 40(3).
6 PH(T)(S)A 2016 ss 37–38. The number specified must be at least zero, but need not be a whole number. In terms of s 39, the Scottish Ministers may substitute a different prices index to be used for these purposes.

7 PH(T)(S)A 2016 ss 42–43.
8 PH(T)(S)A 2016 s 39(3).
9 PH(T)(S)A 2016 s 39(2).

PRIVATE RESIDENTIAL TENANCIES: ASSIGNATION AND SUB-LETS

17.41   As we have seen,[1] one of the statutory terms in every private residential tenancy provides that assignation and subletting are prohibited without the landlord's consent. There is, however, nothing preventing the tenant assigning or subletting *with* the landlord's consent, if that can be obtained.

There is some protection for subtenants. The head landlord is entitled to give a sub-tenant a notice to leave at the same time as giving the head tenant notice, this being called a 'sub-tenancy notice to leave'.[2] However, where the property has been lawfully sublet by the tenant[3] and the head tenancy has been terminated on the grounds of the head tenant's conduct[4] the sub-tenancy is converted to a new tenancy.[5] The result will be that the sub-tenant can only be removed in such cases if he or she falls within one of the eviction grounds. The First-Tier Tribunal may disapply this protection where it considers it reasonable to do so.[6]

1 See para 17.32.
2 PH(T)(S)A 2016 s 61.
3 PH(T)(S)A 2016 s 46. A sublet will be unlawful if it was granted without consent (express or implied) and in breach of a term of the tenancy: PH(T)(S)A 2016 s 46(3).
4 As we will see below (para 17.45), the grounds on which a tenancy can be terminated at the instance of the landlord are divided into four groups. One of these, containing grounds 10–15, relates to the tenant's conduct. It is these grounds that are relevant here. The protection does not apply in the case of termination on other grounds.
5 PH(T)(S)A 2016 s 46(2).
6 PH(T)(S)A 2016 s 53. The Tribunal may only do this after giving the sub-tenant the opportunity to make representations.

PRIVATE RESIDENTIAL TENANCIES: TERMINATION

17.42   PH(T)(S)A 2016 provides that a private residential tenancy may only come to an end in accordance with the provisions of that Act.[1] This is the case even if the parties expressly agree to bring the tenancy to an end, if that agreement does not satisfy the requirements of the Act. This provision does raise the question of the effectiveness of the ways in which the common law recognises that a lease or other contract may be brought to an end prematurely, such as frustration, confusion or novation.[2] However, given that the purpose of the provision is simply to prevent the parties contracting out of the rules on termination, there is good reason to think that at least some of these common law grounds of termination will nonetheless be effective. Presumably, though, it will not be possible for the landlord to rescind a private residential tenancy on the grounds of a material breach of the terms of the tenancy, as termination on the grounds of breach of tenancy terms is directly dealt with by the termination provisions of the 2006 Act.

The means by which a private residential tenancy is brought to an end vary depending on whether it happens at the instance of the tenant or of the landlord.

1 PH(T)(S)A 2016 s 44. For a review of the termination grounds and case law on them, see Peter Robson and Malcolm M Combe, 'The first year of the First-tier: private residential tenancy eviction cases at the Housing and Property Chamber' 2019 Jur Rev 325.
2 See generally Chapter 10 and, for confusion, para 2.24 et seq.

Termination by tenant

17.43 The tenant may bring the tenancy to an end by giving at least 28 days' notice[1] in writing[2] to that effect. The 28 days' notice is counted from the date that the landlord receives the notice.[3] The notice must state the date on which the tenancy is to end.[4] The landlord may agree in writing to a date that is less than 28 days from the date of receipt of the notice, with the result that the notice will be effective notwithstanding the lack of 28 days' notice.[5] Where there are two or more joint landlords, it is enough to give notice to one of them.[6]

The notice will only be effective if given 'freely and without coercion of any kind'.[7] The parties are at liberty to agree a shorter notice period,[8] but this must be done in writing and cannot validly be done before the tenancy becomes a private residential tenancy.[9] Similarly, the tenant may only validly give notice after he or she has begun occupying the property.[10] Accordingly, any attempt to agree a specific date for the end of the tenancy or to vary the notice period will be ineffective if done before the tenant has moved into the property.

The tenant may withdraw the notice if the landlord agrees to that.[11]

1 PH(T)(S)A 2016 s 49(3)(b)(ii).
2 PH(T)(S)A 2016 s 49(1)(b).
3 PH(T)(S)A 2016 s 49(3)(a). In terms of the Interpretation and Legislative Reform (Scotland) Act 2010 s 26, notice sent electronically or by post is rebuttably presumed to have been received 48 hours after sending.
4 PH(T)(S)A 2016 s 49(1)(c).
5 PH(T)(S)A 2016 s 49(2).
6 PH(T)(S)A 2016 s 49(5).
7 PH(T)(S)A 2016 s 49(1)(a)(i).

8   PH(T)(S)A 2016 s 49(3)(b)(i).
9   PH(T)(S)A 2016 s 49(4).
10   PH(T)(S)A 2016 s 49(1)(a)(ii).
11   PH(T)(S)A 2016 s 48(3).

Termination by landlord

17.44   The landlord[1] may also seek to bring the tenancy to an end. Notice should be given in the form of the notice to leave prescribed by regulations.[2] The tenant is 'assumed' to receive the notice 48 hours after it is sent.[3]

The notice to leave must give the required amount of notice, and will identify the first date on which the landlord may seek an eviction order from the First-Tier Tribunal.[4] The required notice period will depend on the situation. We will see below that there are different grounds on which eviction may be sought. Some of these (grounds 10 to 15) relate to the conduct of the tenant. Where eviction is sought on one of those grounds, or the tenant has been entitled to occupy the property for not more than six months,[5] the notice period will be 28 days. Otherwise, it will be 84 days.[6] Note that temporary alterations have been made to the notice periods by the Coronavirus (Scotland) Act 2020.[7]

Where the tenant receives a notice to leave, one of two things will happen. Either the tenant will leave voluntarily or they will not. Where the relevant notice period has expired *and* the tenant has ceased to occupy the property, the tenancy comes to an end.[8] Otherwise, it will be necessary to seek an eviction order from the First-Tier Tribunal.

1   Where there are joint landlords, any of them may give the notice to leave (PH(T)(S) A 2016 s 62(2)). References to the landlord include, for these purposes, a heritable creditor who is entitled to sell the property (PH(T)(S)A 2016 s 63).
2   PH(T)(S)A 2016 s 62(1); Private Residential Tenancies (Prescribed Notices and Forms) (Scotland) Regulations 2017 SSI 2017 No 297 Sch 5.
3   PH(T)(S)A 2016 s 62(5).
4   This date is the day after the expiry of the notice period (PH(T)(S)A 2016 s 62(4)).
5   On the interpretation of this period, see PH(T)(S)A 2016 s 64.
6   PH(T)(S)A 2016 s 54(2), (3).
7   Coronavirus (Scotland) Act 2020 Sch 1 para 2.
8   PH(T)(S)A 2016 s 50. Nothing here prevents the tenant bringing the tenancy to an end himself or herself at an earlier date, however: PH(T)(S)A 2016 s 50(3).

17.45   *Application for eviction order*   The landlord may not apply for an eviction order until the relevant notice period has expired,[1] and has six months from that date to apply.[2] Before applying, the landlord must notify the local authority in whose area the property is situated.[3] The Tribunal has discretion to waive the notice period where it considers it reasonable to do so.[4] The application must be accompanied by a copy of the notice to leave.[5]

An eviction order may only be sought on one of a number of grounds. Any contractual provision purporting to bring the tenancy to an end in some other way, for example an irritancy clause, will be void.[6] The ground on which eviction is sought must have been satisfied at the time of service of the notice to leave. It is not enough that the ground subsequently came to be satisfied.[7] The order brings the tenancy to an end.[8]

The account here follows the numbering in Schedule 3 to PH(T)(S) A 2016, where the grounds are listed. Schedule 3 divides the eviction grounds into four parts depending on whether: the let property is required for another purpose; the tenant's status justifies eviction; the tenant's conduct justifies eviction; or there is a legal impediment to the let continuing.

Some grounds of eviction are mandatory, meaning that the Tribunal must grant the eviction order on application being made for it to do so, assuming that the eviction ground applies to the facts as proved. Others are discretionary, and the Tribunal is only to grant the eviction order if it considers it reasonable to do so.[9] At the time of writing, however, this is subject to temporary provision made by the Coronavirus (Scotland) Act 2020, in terms of which all grounds are discretionary while the relevant provisions are in force.[10]

Part 1 of Schedule 3 (grounds 1 to 7) contains eviction grounds that apply where the let property is required for another purpose. These grounds are all mandatory, except for ground 5, which is discretionary.

Part 2 (grounds 8 and 9) contains eviction grounds based on the tenant's status. Ground 8 has a mandatory and a discretionary strand, and ground 9 is discretionary.

The part 3 eviction grounds (grounds 10 to 15) are based on the tenant's conduct. Ground 12 has a mandatory and a discretionary strand. Grounds 10 and 13 are mandatory. Grounds 11, 14 and 15 are discretionary.

The part 4 eviction grounds (grounds 16 to 18) are based on there being a legal impediment to the tenancy continuing. These grounds are all discretionary.

1 PH(T)(S)A 2016 s 54(1).
2 PH(T)(S)A 2016 s 55.
3 PH(T)(S)A 2016 s 56. The form of notice is prescribed under the Homelessness etc (Scotland) Act 2003 s 11(3), and is found in the Notice to Local Authorities (Scotland) Regulations 2008 SSI No 324.
4 PH(T)(S)A 2016 s 52(4).
5 PH(T)(S)A 2016 s 52(3).
6 *Royal Bank of Scotland v Boyle* 1999 Hous LR 63.

7   *Majid v Gaffney* [2019] UT 59.
8   PH(T)(S)A 2016 s 51.
9   The Act gives no explicit guidance on what is meant by 'reasonable' in this context. However, some guidance can be obtained from the equivalent test in relation to Scottish secure tenancies. See para 18.55.
10 Coronavirus (Scotland) Act 2020 Sch 1 para 1.

Part 1: let property required for another purpose

17.46   *(1) Landlord intends to sell*   The First-Tier Tribunal must grant an eviction order where the landlord is entitled to sell the property, and intends to sell it for market value or put it up for sale within three months of the tenant ceasing to occupy. This paragraph gives as examples of evidence of such an intention a letter of engagement from a solicitor or estate agent concerning the sale of the property, or a recently prepared document that would be required to form part of a home report under section 98 of the Housing (Scotland) Act 2006. These examples are non-exhaustive and non-prescriptive, so it would be competent for the Tribunal to find this ground established even in the absence of either of them. Equally, the Tribunal would be free to find the ground not established if it considered the evidence offered did not reflect a genuine intention. This is a mandatory ground.

17.47   *(2) Property to be sold by lender*   It is a mandatory ground that the house is subject to a heritable security granted before the creation of the tenancy and, as a result of the debtor's default, the creditor requires to sell the house with vacant possession. The obvious example of this is where the house is repossessed because of the landlord's mortgage arrears.[1]

1 See *Tamroui v Clydesdale Bank* 1997 SLT (Sh Ct) 20, 1996 SCLR 732.

17.48   *(3) Landlord intends to refurbish*   The third eviction ground is that the landlord 'intends to carry out significantly disruptive works to, or in relation to, the let property', as long as the landlord is in fact entitled to carry out such work. Work is significantly disruptive if 'it would be impracticable for the tenant to continue to occupy the property given the nature of the refurbishment intended by the landlord'. Evidence of such an intention might include planning permission for the work or a contract with an architect or builder concerning the intended refurbishment. As with ground 1, neither of these examples is conclusive if the Tribunal considers that it does not reflect the landlord's genuine intentions. Equally, alternative evidence will be sufficient if accepted by the Tribunal. An intention will not be considered to be genuine if it is only formed to justify removing the tenant.[1]

1 *Charlton v Josephine Marshall Trust* [2020] CSIH 11, 2020 SLT 409.

17.49 *(4) Landlord intends to live in property* It is an eviction ground that the landlord (or at least one of them, where the property is co-owned) intends to live in the property as his or her only or principal home for at least three months. Where the landlord is a trustee, this eviction ground is to be understood as referring to the beneficiary.

An affidavit by the landlord stating this intention is given as an example of evidence of intention and will be sufficient assuming that the Tribunal accepts it as genuine. It has been held that the suitability of the property for the landlord's occupation is relevant only in assessing the credibility of the landlord's claim to intend to live there.[1]

1 *Ortega v Lopez* [2019] UT 57.

17.50 *(5) Family member intends to live in property* It is also an eviction ground that a member of the landlord's family intends to live in the property for at least three months. Unlike ground 4, the Tribunal may only grant an eviction order on this ground if satisfied that it is reasonable to do so. This is accordingly a discretionary ground.

As with ground 4, an affidavit expressing this intention is the example given of evidence of intention. Where the family member is incapable of having or expressing such an intention, it is enough that the landlord and (if different) a person entitled to make decisions about the family member's residence has this intention.

Membership of the landlord's family is defined very specifically for these purposes. The central concepts are the 'qualifying relative' and the 'qualifying relationship'.[1] A qualifying relative is a parent, grandparent, child, grandchild, brother or sister, including relationships of the half blood, and including stepchildren as children. A qualifying relationship is one in which the parties are married to or in a civil partnership with each other, or in which they are 'living together as though they are married'.[2]

For the purposes of this eviction ground, a family member is anyone who is:

- in a qualifying relationship with the landlord;
- a qualifying relative of the landlord;
- a qualifying relative of anyone in a qualifying relationship with the landlord; or
- in a qualifying relationship with a qualifying relative of the landlord.

1 The same terms are used in relation to rights of succession to private residential tenancies. See below, para 17.149.
2 For some general discussion of the definition of cohabitation, in a number of different contexts, see Scottish Law Commission, *Aspects of Family Law: Discussion Paper on Cohabitation* (Scot Law Com DP No 170, 2020) paras 3.1–3.101. It is clear from the case law that more than merely living under the same roof is required, and that regard

must also be had to the nature of the relationship between the parties. See also paras 17.33 and 17.149.

17.51   *(6) Landlord intends to use for non-residential purpose*   An eviction order is to be granted if the First-Tier Tribunal is satisfied that the landlord intends to use the property for any purpose other than providing a person with a home. This paragraph gives the existence of any necessary planning permission for the landlord's intended purposes as an example of evidence of intention. This is, of course, not exhaustive, if for no other reason than that planning permission may not be required for what the landlord intends. This is a mandatory ground.

17.52   *(7) Property required for religious purpose*   Where the landlord holds the property so that duties can be performed from it in relation to the work of a religious denomination, it is a ground of eviction that the property requires to be let for that purpose. It is important to understand that this does not allow for the conversion of the property to a religious purpose. If that is the intention, it will be necessary to seek removal of the tenant on some other ground. This ground applies only where the property was already held for a religious purpose.

Part 2: eviction based on tenant's status

17.53   *(8) Tenant not an employee*   It is an eviction ground that the tenancy was granted in consequence of the tenant being an employee of the landlord, or in expectation of the tenant becoming an employee of the landlord, and tenant is not, in fact, employed by the landlord. This may be either because the tenant never became an employee of the landlord, or because the tenant did become an employee of the landlord and has ceased to be. The application for an eviction order must be made within 12 months of the tenant ceasing to be an employee or, if the tenant never became an employee, within 12 months of the tenancy being granted. The Tribunal may waive the 12-month time limit if it considers it reasonable to grant the eviction order nonetheless. Thus, this ground of eviction is mandatory for the first 12 months and is discretionary thereafter.

17.54   *(9) Tenant no longer in need of supported accommodation*   This ground applies where the tenancy was granted in consequence of the tenant being assessed under section 12A of the Social Work (Scotland) Act 1968 to have needs calling for the provision of community care services. An eviction order will be granted if the latest assessment of the tenant's needs would not have led to the granting of the tenancy, and the Tribunal considers it reasonable to issue an eviction order. This is a discretionary ground.

Part 3: eviction based on tenant's conduct

17.55   *(10)   Tenant not occupying let property*   The Tribunal is to grant the eviction order if the property is not being occupied under the tenancy or any lawfully granted sub-tenancy[1] as long as the non-occupation is not attributable to a breach by the landlord of the repairing standard.[2] Temporary absences will not be sufficient to satisfy this ground.[3]

1 For the requirements of a lawfully granted sub-tenancy, see para 17.41.
2 See paras 19.13–19.34.
3 *Monklands DC v Gallacher* 2000 Hous LR 112; *Mackay v Leask* 1996 Hous LR 94.

17.56   *(11)   Breach of the tenancy agreement*   The Tribunal may, if it considers it reasonable to do so, grant an eviction order if the tenant has failed to comply with a term of the tenancy. This does not apply to failure to pay rent, which is dealt with separately under paragraph 12. The fact that this is a discretionary ground suggests that the breach would normally have to be relatively serious.

17.57   *(12)   Rent arrears*   It is a ground of eviction that the tenant is in arrears with rent. In fact, this ground is divided into two, as sometimes it is subject to a discretion on the grounds of reasonableness, and sometimes it is not.

First, if the tenant has been in arrears of rent to any extent for three or more consecutive months, the Tribunal may grant the eviction order if it considers it reasonable to do so. In considering the question of reasonableness, the Tribunal is to take into account whether the tenant's failure to pay the rent in full is to any extent a consequence of delay or failure in benefit payments.[1] Presumably if the Tribunal was satisfied that the benefit, when paid, would cover the full rent for the future, itwould be unlikely to be easily persuaded that eviction was reasonable. After all, the rent arrears would not then increase, and eviction would not assist the landlord in recovering any existing arrears that would not be covered by the benefit payment.

Second, the Tribunal *must* grant the eviction order if the tenant has been in rent arrears for at least three consecutive months, and the arrears equal at least a whole month's rent at the beginning of the first day on which it considers the application on its merits, unless the arrears are wholly or partly attributable to a delay in a benefit payment.

While the Coronavirus (Scotland) (No 2) Act 2020 applies, special pre-action requirements apply where at least part of the rent arrears relates to the period during which the relevant provisions are in force.[2]

1 For what qualifies as a 'relevant benefit', see para 12(5).
2 Coronavirus (Scotland) (No 2) Act 2020 Sch 1 para 5; Rent Arrears Pre-Action Requirements (Coronavirus) (Scotland) Regulations 2020 SSI No 304.

17.58 *(13) Criminal behaviour*   The Tribunal must grant an eviction order where the tenant (or any tenant, if there is more than one) receives a 'relevant conviction'. This is a mandatory ground. Application for eviction must be made within 12 months of the tenant's conviction, unless the Tribunal is satisfied that the landlord has a reasonable excuse for not applying within that period. Even if the Tribunal is so satisfied, this ground of eviction remains mandatory.[1]

A relevant conviction is one for an offence that falls into one of the following two categories:

• it is committed by using, or allowing the use of, the let property for an 'immoral or illegal purpose'; or
• it was committed within the let property or in the locality and is punishable by imprisonment.

It is not clear what would nowadays count as an 'immoral purpose'. The most obvious example of an 'immoral purpose' is perhaps use for the purposes of prostitution. However, the difficulty largely disappears when it is borne in mind that the eviction ground is not made out simply by using the property for an immoral purpose. Instead, the tenant must be *convicted* of using or allowing such use. Accordingly, an immoral purpose will only be relevant if it is also an illegal one.[2]

Even though this is a mandatory ground of eviction, it must be remembered that the category of 'illegal' purposes may include some relatively minor conduct. Nonetheless, the Tribunal will have no discretion to refuse eviction if this ground is made out.

Whether an activity takes place in the 'locality' of the property will be considered on the facts of the specific case, but the term is capable of being interpreted broadly. For example, in *South Lanarkshire Council v Nugent*,[3] where the conduct complained of included drug-dealing in a pub a mile away from the property, no objection was made to this being described as being in the locality of the property.

A conviction is only relevant if it is received after the tenancy is granted. Accordingly, a conviction received before the tenancy is granted will not give grounds for eviction.[4]

It is not necessary that there should be a specific reference to using the premises in the criminal charge, provided that sufficient evidence is produced to show that the house was in fact used for the crime.[5]

1 It thus contrasts with ground 8, above.
2 See *S Schneiders and Sons Ltd v Abrahams* [1925] 1 KB 301.
3 2008 Hous LR 92.

4 Presumably a conviction received after the tenancy is agreed, but before it becomes a private residential tenancy, will be relevant, as it is the date of *granting* of the tenancy that is the important date.
5 *Abrahams v Wilson* [1971] 2 QB 88, [1971] 2 All ER 1114, CA.

17.59 *(14) Anti-social behaviour* It is a discretionary eviction ground that the tenant has engaged in 'relevant anti-social behaviour'. This means that the tenant has acted in an anti-social manner, or pursued a course of anti-social conduct, in relation to a person, and the Tribunal considers it reasonable to grant the eviction order on the basis of this anti-social behaviour. Unlike the equivalent ground for assured tenancies, there is no requirement for the conduct to relate to a person residing, visiting or otherwise engaged in lawful activity in the area.

'Anti-social' means causing or likely to cause alarm, distress, nuisance or annoyance, or which amounts to harassment in terms of section 8 of the Protection from Harassment Act 1997. 'Conduct' includes speech and 'a course of conduct' must involve conduct on at least two occasions.

As with paragraph 13, application for eviction must be made within 12 months of the tenant's conviction, unless the Tribunal is satisfied that the landlord has a reasonable excuse for not applying within that period.

Unlike paragraph 13, there is here no express requirement for the anti-social behaviour to have taken place in or near the property, or to have taken place since the tenancy was granted. The decision in *Raglan Housing Association Ltd v Fairclough*[1] (in relation to the equivalent English ground) is suggestive that previous behaviour will be considered relevant. In that case, a tenant had been convicted of downloading and possessing indecent photographs of children while occupying a previous (though nearby) house. It was held that the ground did not apply only to offences committed by the tenant during the period of his tenancy of the dwelling house in question but also applied if the offences were committed before the tenancy commenced. Presumably, though, the Tribunal's decision on whether it is reasonable to grant the order will be influenced by the anti-social conduct having no connection to the property. Moreover, the time limit for applying under this paragraph will exclude any conduct that is more than a year old unless the Tribunal can be persuaded, exceptionally, to take account of it.

1 2008 HLR 21, 2008 L&TR 19.

17.60 *(15) Association with person who has relevant conviction or engaged in relevant anti-social behaviour* This ground applies where a person has a relevant conviction or has engaged in relevant anti-social behaviour (as defined in paragraphs 13 and 14), and that person resides or lodges in the let property, has sub-let the property (or part of it) from the tenant, or has been admitted to the let property by the tenant on more than one occasion. Where someone other than the tenant has been responsible for the anti-social behaviour, it may not always be necessary for the tenant to have been aware of it, eg behaviour by the tenant's wife while he was in prison.[1]

As with paragraphs 13 and 14, application for eviction must be made within 12 months of the tenant's conviction, unless the Tribunal is satisfied that the landlord has a reasonable excuse for not applying within that period.

This is a discretionary ground of eviction. The Tribunal is only to grant the eviction order if it considers it reasonable to do so.[2]

1   *Scottish Special Housing Association v Lumsden* 1984 SLT (Sh Ct) 71.
2   See para 18.60 and the four relevant factors set out in *City of Glasgow Council v Lockhart* 1997 Hous LR 99. This concerned a secure tenancy, but the same test was accepted in relation to assured tenancies in *Kirk Care Housing Association v Clugston* 2000 Hous LR 106.

Part 4: legal impediment to let continuing

17.61   *(16) Landlord is not registered*   It is an eviction ground that the landlord is not registered by the relevant local authority as required by the Antisocial Behaviour etc (Scotland) Act 2004,[1] whether this is because the local authority has refused to register the landlord or because the local authority has removed the landlord from the register.

This is a discretionary ground of eviction. The Tribunal is only to issue the eviction order if it is satisfied that it is reasonable to do so. In this and the following two grounds, the Tribunal will need to balance the public interest in the proper oversight of private residential landlords with the effect on the tenant of eviction for reasons outside his or her control.

1   See para 20.8 et seq.

17.62   *(17) HMO licence has been revoked*   It is an eviction ground that the property has been licensed for use as a house in multiple occupation in terms of Part 5 of the Housing (Scotland) Act 2006,[1] and this licence has been revoked.[2]

This is a discretionary ground of eviction. The Tribunal is only to issue the eviction order if it is satisfied that it is reasonable to do so.

1   See para 20.16 et seq.
2   In terms of H(S)A 2006 s 139(1) or s 157(2).

17.63   *(18) Overcrowding statutory notice*   It is an eviction ground that an overcrowding statutory notice has been served on the landlord in respect of the let property.[1]

This is a discretionary ground of eviction. The Tribunal is only to issue the eviction order if it is satisfied that it is reasonable to do so.

1 In terms of the Private Rented Housing (Scotland) Act 2011 s 17(3). See para 20.22 et seq.

Wrongful termination

17.64   Where the First-Tier Tribunal or the tenant is misled into agreeing to the termination of the tenancy,[1] the tenant may apply to the Tribunal for a wrongful termination order. In making a wrongful termination order the Tribunal may order the payment of the landlord (or any or all of the landlords, in the case of joint landlords) to the former tenant of a sum not exceeding six months' rent.[2] The termination of the tenancy is nonetheless effective.

Where the Tribunal makes a wrongful termination order, it is to send a copy of the order to any local authority with which the person against whom the order is made is registered as a landlord.[3] This may influence the local authority's decision as to whether the landlord is a 'fit and proper person' to be permitted to be registered as a landlord.[4]

1 PH(T)(S)A 2016 ss 57 (wrongful termination by eviction order), 58 (wrongful termination without an eviction order).
2 PH(T)(S)A 2016 s 59.
3 PH(T)(S)A 2016 s 60.
4 See para 20.12

ASSURED TENANCIES: GENERAL

Definition

17.65   As we saw earlier, new tenancies that would formerly have been regulated tenancies, will be classified as assured tenancies if they were created after 2 January 1989, when Part II of the Housing (Scotland) Act 1988 came into force and before 1 December 2017, when the Private Housing (Tenancies) (Scotland) Act 2016 came into force.

In the sections that follow, the statutory provisions described will generally apply both to 'normal' and to short assured tenancies, unless the contrary is indicated. The distinctive features of short assured tenancies are described in a separate section.[1]

1 See para 17.104 et seq.

17.66   *Separate dwelling*   The general qualification for an assured tenancy is that a house is let as a separate dwelling.[1] The meaning of the term 'separate dwelling' was discussed earlier, in relation to private residential tenancies. [2] Where land is let along with the house (other than agricultural land of more than two acres), the land will be included within the assured tenancy provided that the main purpose of the letting is the provision of a home for the tenant.[3]

1 Housing (Scotland) Act 1988 s 12(1).
2 See above, para 17.12. For provision specific to assured tenancies, however, see H(S) A 1988 s 14 (1); see also ss 14(2) & (3) and s 21 for situations where the right to shared accommodation may be terminated or varied.
3 H(S)A 1988 s 13 and Sch 4 para 5.

17.67   *Only or principal home*   It is also a requirement for an assured tenancy that the tenant (or at least one of them if there are joint tenants) must occupy the house as his or her only or principal home.[1] Again this requirement has been discussed above, in relation to private residential tenancies.[2]

1 Housing (Scotland) Act 1988, s 12(1).
2 See above, para 17.13.

Excepted categories

17.68   There are thirteen categories that do not qualify as assured tenancies.[1] These are all largely carried over from the category of tenancies that were excluded from regulation under the Rent (Scotland) Act 1984,[2] and so many of the cases on regulated tenancies are likely to be highly persuasive. They are also substantially identical to the list in the Private Housing (Tenancies) (Scotland) Act 2016, discussed above.[3] Specific differences are noted in that discussion.

1 These are contained in Sch 4 to the Housing (Scotland) Act 1988.
2 See para 17.111.
3 See para 17.15 et seq.

ASSURED TENANCIES: SECURITY OF TENURE AND RECOVERY OF POSSESSION

Statutory assured tenancies

17.69   An assured tenant's right to remain in occupation of the dwellinghouse will not initially derive from the statutory provisions; as with any other tenant, it will depend upon the contractual terms of the lease, and any extension to it by the process of tacit relocation. It is only when the landlord has attempted to terminate the tenancy by sending a notice to quit that the statutory provisions for security of tenure come into force. When the notice expires, the tenancy will become a statutory assured tenancy, which will give the tenant the right to stay on in the property indefinitely unless the landlord can establish one of the stated grounds of removal.

It may be noted that there appears to something of a dearth of recent case authority in relation to the grounds of removal. This probably reflects the fact that in the case of the short assured tenancy, which was the dominant type of tenure, the ability to terminate the tenancy at the ish means that the other grounds, although competent, are less likely to be necessary.

Short Assured Tenancies

17.70 Although these security of tenure provisions superficially appear to offer a similar degree of protection to that enjoyed by regulated tenants and by Scottish secure tenants,[1] in the case of assured tenancies this protection was considerably weakened by the landlord's option of granting a short assured tenancy instead. Before the introduction of private residential tenancies, short assured tenancies were by far the most common type of assured tenancy to be found in practice[2] and did not give the tenant any security of tenure at all beyond the contractual term of the lease, which could be as little as six months.

The distinctive features of short assured tenancies are discussed in a separate section below,[3] although some of the provisions described in the immediately following section also apply to short assured tenancies.[4]

1 See ch 18.
2 See para 17.4.
3 See para 17.104 et seq.
4 Eg some of the grounds of removal.

Notice to quit

17.71 The contractual period of an assured tenancy (the period specified in the lease document) can normally only be terminated by the landlord serving a notice to quit at least four weeks prior to the termination date.[1] This notice will be invalid unless it contains certain specified information informing the tenant of his or her legal rights.[2]

A tenant under an assured tenancy who remains in possession of the house after the contractual period of the lease has been thus terminated, will continue to have the assured tenancy of the house.[2] He or she can only be removed if the landlord obtains an order from the First-Tier Tribunal, based on one of the grounds set out in Schedule 5 to the Act.[3]

1 Assured Tenancies (Notices to Quit Prescribed Information) (Scotland) Regulations 1988 SI 1988/2067.
2 H(S)A 1988 s 16(1) (as amended).
3 H(S)A 1988 s 16(2).

Termination during contractual period; irritancy

17.72   The termination grounds primarily apply to statutory assured tenancies, usually after the contractual period of the tenancy is brought to an end at the ish by service of a notice to quit upon the tenant. However, the lease may include an irritancy clause, giving the landlord the power to terminate the lease prematurely because of the tenant's breach.[1] If the irritancy provision is in normal form, it will probably be ineffective, as the lease can only be terminated on one of the grounds set out in Schedule 5.[2]

It is specifically provided that certain of these grounds (numbers 2 or 8 of the mandatory grounds, or any of the discretionary ones other than grounds 9, 10, 15 or 17)[3] may, in fact, be used during the contractual period of the lease, though only if the lease provides for it to be brought to an end on the ground in question.[4] Such a lease term is effectively an irritancy provision, though the eviction process is the same as for statutory assured tenancies and will not be competent if the provision does not echo the relevant statutory ground.

In *Royal Bank of Scotland v Boyle*[5] it was held that an irritancy clause in normal form was not enforceable as its terms were substantially different from those of the statutory grounds of possession for rent arrears. It was also held that incorporating the words of the statute by reference into the lease was probably not sufficient, though neither was it necessary to repeat them verbatim provided that their substance was included. However, it is believed to have been common practice for landlords to reproduce the relevant statutory terms verbatim in assured tenancy agreements, and this was probably the safest policy.[6]

If the contractual period of the lease has been terminated by notice to quit and superseded by a statutory tenancy, any lease provision allowing for termination of the lease (which would include irritancy) is no longer effective.[7]

An irritancy provision (apart from one that echoes one or more of the permitted statutory termination grounds) may also be considered to be an unfair term under the Consumer Rights Act 2015.[8]

1 See Ch 5.
2 H(S)A 1988 s 18(1).

3 See paras 17.77 and 17.86 et seq.
4 H(S)A 1988 s 18(6)(b).
5 1999 Hous LR 63.
6 See editors' note to *Royal Bank of Scotland v Boyle* 1999 Hous LR 63.
7 H(S)A 1988 s 16(1)(b)(i).
8 See para 21.16.

Notice of proceedings for possession

17.73   The tenant must also be given prior written notice of the proceedings for recovery of possession and the notice must state and give particulars of the relevant ground.[1] The period of notice depends upon the ground that is being used. In respect of grounds 1, 2, 5, 6, 7, 9 and 17 below it is two months, and in the case of all the other grounds it is only two weeks.[2] At the time of writing, however, temporary provision applies in terms of Coronavirus (Scotland) Act 2020, extending these notice periods.[3] The required form of the notice is laid down by the Rent Regulation and Assured Tenancies (Forms) (Scotland) Regulations 2017.[4]

It will be noted that two separate notices are involved, a notice to quit, which has the function of bringing the contractual period of the lease to an end and preventing the onset of tacit relocation, and another notice intimating the landlord's intention to raise proceedings for recovery of possession.

A Notice of Proceedings for Possession is not required in the case of short assured tenancies, though a notice to quit remains necessary.[5]

1 H(S)A 1988 s 19(2) (as amended).
2 H(S)A 1988 s 19(4). In certain circumstances the First-Tier Tribunal has discretion to dispense with the need for a notice (H(S)A 1988 s 19(1)).
3 Coronavirus (Scotland) Act 2020 Sch 1 para 4.
4 SSI No 349.
5 Private Rented Housing (Scotland) Act 2011 s 34. See also para 17.106 et seq.

Notice to local authority

17.74   The landlord is also required to give notice of the raising of the proceedings to the local authority in whose area the house is situated, unless the landlord is that local authority.[1]

1 H(S)A 1988 s 19A (added by the Homelessness etc (Scotland) Act 2003 Sch 1 para 3); the form and manner of the notice should be given in the form and manner prescribed in s 11(3) of that Act.

Position of subtenants

17.75   If a property subject to an assured tenancy has been lawfully sublet, also under an assured tenancy, then the subtenant's tenancy will not be terminated along with that of the head tenant; instead the subtenant will take the head tenant's place under the main tenancy.[1]

1 H(S)A 1988, s 28. This is an exception to the position at common law – see para 7.35.

Human Rights Act

17.76   The possible application of the Human Rights Act 1998 to the eviction of assured tenants was considered earlier in the chapter.[1]

1 See para 17.8 et seq.

Mandatory grounds of possession[1]

17.77   In these cases, the First-Tier Tribunal, if satisfied that the ground exists, must give possession back to the landlord.[2]

There is one limited exception to this mandatory rule: in the case of ground 8 (three month's rent arrears) the First-Tier Tribunal has the discretion not to grant possession if the arrears have been caused by a delay or failure in the payment of housing benefit or universal credit.[3]

Note also that, in terms of the Coronavirus (Scotland) Act 2020, all grounds have (at the time of writing) temporarily been made discretionary.[4]

In respect of grounds (1) to (5) the tenant must have been given prior written notice that possession might be required under the ground in question; however, in the case of the first two of these grounds, the First-Tier Tribunal has the discretion to dispense with the need for such notice if he or she thinks it reasonable. As noted above, grounds 2 and 8 may also be used during the contractual period of the lease, though only if the tenancy terms provide accordingly.[5]

The numbers of these mandatory grounds (and of the discretionary ones below) correspond to the paragraph numbers in Schedule 5 to the Housing (Scotland) Act 1988.

1 H(S)A 1988 Sch 5 Pt I.
2 H(S)A 1988 s 18(3).
3 H(S)A 1988 s 18(3A) (added by the Homelessness (Scotland) Act 2003 s 12(3)).
4 Coronavirus (Scotland) Act 2020 Sch 1 para 3.
5 Section 18(6); see also para 17.72.

17.78 (1) *Occupancy by landlord* The landlord formerly occupied the house as his or her only or principal home, or did not formerly occupy it, but it is now required for the landlord or for the landlord's spouse or civil partner[1] and he or she did not buy the property subject to the sitting tenancy. Where there are joint landlords these requirements only apply to one of them. This ground is similar to, but narrower than, ground 4 for private residential tenancies, which requires simply that the landlord intends to occupy as his or her only or principal home.[2]

1 Added by the Civil Partnership Act 2004 Sch 28(4) para 17.
2 See para 17.49.

17.79 (2) *Mortgage default* This is, in substance, identical to ground 2 for private residential tenancies,[1] except for the requirement of notice to the tenant that this ground might apply.[2]

1 See para 17.47.
2 See para 17.77.

17.80 (3) *Holiday property* The subjects are holiday premises that have been let off-season for a period not exceeding eight months. To qualify under this category, the property must have been occupied for holiday purposes within the period of 12 months immediately prior to the commencement of the tenancy. This ground is presumably now redundant. At any rate, it is difficult to envisage circumstances in which it might plausibly now apply.

This should be distinguished from holiday lets, which are not assured tenancies at all.[1]

1 See para 17.21.

17.81 (4) *Student accommodation* The reasoning here is similar to that in the immediately previous ground. The subjects have been let between student lettings for a period not exceeding 12 months.

This would cover lets during vacation time of properties normally let to students by their educational institution; as we saw above, the actual lets to the students themselves are not assured tenancies.[1]

1 See para 17.20.

17.82 (5) *Ecclesiastical lets* The house is required for a minister or a full-time lay missionary of any religious denomination as a residence from which to perform the duties of his or her office. This is in substance identical to ground 7 for private residential tenancies.[1]

1 See para 17.52.

17.83   (6) *Redevelopment* The landlord intends to demolish or reconstruct the whole or a substantial part of the house, or to carry out substantial works on the house, or a building of which it forms part.

This ground will not apply where the landlord or the landlord's predecessor bought the property for value after the creation of the tenancy. In other words, a landlord who bought the house subject to the sitting tenancy with the purpose of redeveloping the property will not be able to get vacant possession under this ground.

It is also a condition of the ground applying that the work cannot be done without the tenant vacating the property; alternatively, it will apply if it is necessary in order for the work to be done for the tenant to accept a tenancy of only part of the house, or some other variation of the tenancy terms, and the tenant has refused to agree to this. Where a tenancy is terminated under this ground (or under ground (9) below) the landlord is required to pay the tenant's removal expenses.[1]

1 H(S)A 1988 s 22. Compare ground 3 for private residential tenancies (para 17.48).

17.84   (7) *Inherited tenancy* The tenant inherited the tenancy from a former tenant. The proceedings for recovery of possession must be begun not later than 12 months after the death of the former tenant, or within 12 months after the date when (in the First-Tier Tribunal's opinion) the landlord became aware of the former tenant's death.

Mere acceptance of rent by the landlord after the death of the former tenant will not create a new tenancy, unless the landlord has agreed in writing to change the level of rent, the duration of the let or some other term of the tenancy. This ground was first introduced for assured tenancies, since assured tenants have more restricted succession rights than regulated tenants.

17.85   (8) *Three months' rent arrears* Both at the date of the service of the notice for recovery of possession and at the date of the hearing, the tenant is at least three months in arrears with rent.

In the case of regulated tenancies, rent arrears is always a discretionary ground, but it is normally mandatory for assured tenancies, provided that there are at least three months owing.

As already noted, the only possible exception, where the First-Tier Tribunal does have discretion, is where the arrears have been caused by a delay or failure in the payment of housing benefit.[1] However, in other cases, even where there may be other mitigating circumstances, the Tribunal has no power to delay the proceedings to give the tenant time to pay. The only leeway allowed the tenant is the opportunity to bring the arrears below the three months level during the period between the service of the landlord's notice and the date of the hearing; however, since this is one of the grounds where only two weeks' notice is required before the landlord can begin proceedings, this is not giving the tenant very much room for manoeuvre.

While the Coronavirus (Scotland) (No 2) Act 2020 applies, the Scottish Ministers are empowered to make regulations specifying pre-action requirements to be followed where at least part of the rent arrears relates to the period during which the relevant provisions are in force.[2]

1 See para 17.77; see also *Razack v Osman* [2001] CLY 4149, which preceded this amendment.
2 Coronavirus (Scotland) (No 2) Act 2020 Sch 1 para 4.

Discretionary grounds

17.86   Where one of the grounds in Part II of Schedule 5 is established, the First-Tier Tribunal is not to grant an order for possession unless it is reasonable to do so.[1]

The Tribunal has the power in the case of a discretionary ground to delay the proceedings, including the power to adjourn the case.[2] In such a case the Tribunal is generally required to impose conditions with regard to the payment of any rent arrears, and also with regard to payment of rent or other payments relating to the tenant's occupation of the property after the termination of the tenancy, or any other conditions the Tribunal thinks fit; however, the Tribunal has the discretion not to impose such conditions if to do so would cause exceptional hardship to the tenant or would otherwise be unreasonable.[3]

In the case of controlled tenancies, it has been held that the court has a duty to take the question of reasonableness into account even if the issue was not pleaded or raised by the tenant.[4] As noted above, all of the following grounds other than 9, 10, 15 or 17 may also be used during the contractual period of the lease, though only if the tenancy terms provide accordingly.[5]

The possible application of the Human Rights Act 1998 to the discretionary grounds for recovery of possession has already been considered.[6]

1 H(S)A 1988 s 18(4); see also *Trustees of Kinrara Estate v Campbell* 1999 Hous LR 55.
2 H(S)A 1988 s 20.
3 H(S)A 1988 s 20(3).
4 *Smith v Poulter* [1947] KB 339, [1947] 1 All ER 216.
5 Housing (Scotland) Act 1988 s 18(6); see also para 17.72.
6 See para 17.8 et seq.

17.87   (9) *Alternative   accommodation* Suitable   alternative accommodation is available for the tenant or will be available when the order for possession takes effect.

What is meant by suitable alternative accommodation is set out in Part III of Schedule 5.[1] Factors to be taken into account include the proximity to the tenant's place of work, the rent level and the extent and character of the accommodation. The alternative accommodation must be under a private residential tenancy or one giving an equivalent degree of security of tenure.

Where a tenancy is terminated under this ground (or under ground (6) above) the landlord is required to pay the tenant's removal expenses.[2]

In relation to regulated tenancies, it has been held that environmental factors such as noise or smell may make a property unsuitable.[3]

On the other hand, alternative accommodation will not be unsuitable merely because it is less convenient for the society of the tenant's friends or the tenant's cultural interests.[4]

Moreover, the alternative accommodation only requires to be reasonably suitable to the needs of the tenant, and it is not necessary for the tenant to be kept in the style to which he or she has become accustomed. Thus in *Hill v Rochard*[5] the tenants, an elderly married couple, had the tenancy of a period country house with many spacious rooms, a staff flat, outbuildings, a stable, and one-and-a-half acres of land, including a paddock, where the tenants kept a pony. It was held that a house with a mere four bedrooms, occupying a paltry eighth of an acre and having no stable or paddock, was nevertheless suitable alternative accommodation, and the landlords were granted possession.[6]

1 H(S)A 1988 Sch 5 (as amended).
2 H(S)A 1988 s 22.
3 *Redspring v Francis* [1973] 1 All ER 640, [1973] 1 WLR 134, CA.
4 *Siddiqui v Rashid* [1980] 3 All ER 184, [1980] 1 WLR 1018, CA.
5 [1983] 2 All ER 21, [1983] 1 WLR 478, CA.
6 But see also *Trustees of Kinrara Estate v Campbell* 1999 Hous LR 55.

17.88   (10) *Tenant's notice to quit*   The tenant has given a notice to quit to the landlord and has remained in possession of the house after the expiry of the notice.

Proceedings must be begun by the landlord within six months of the expiry of the notice. Also, the landlord will be precluded from using this ground if the tenant has been granted a new tenancy of the house in the meantime.

In the case of regulated tenancies there was a requirement that the landlord, on the strength of the tenant's notice, must have undertaken some form of commitment, eg by contracting to sell or relet the house. In the case of assured tenancies there is no such requirement.

17.89 (11) *Rent persistently late* The tenant has persistently delayed paying rent which has become lawfully due.

This ground applies whether or not there are actually any rent arrears due on the date when proceedings for recovery of possession are begun. In deciding whether or not it is reasonable to make an order for possession in relation to this ground and ground 12 below, the First-Tier Tribunal should take into account the extent to which delay or failure in the payment of the rent may have been affected by the delay or failure in the payment of housing benefit or universal credit.[1]

1 H(S)A 1988 s 18 (4A and (8) (added by the Homelessness etc (Scotland) Act 2003 s 12(4) and (5)).

17.90 (12) *Rent arrears* Some rent is unpaid on the date when proceedings are begun.

There must also have been unpaid rent on the date when notice of the proceedings was served on the tenant, unless it is a case where the First-Tier Tribunal has used its discretion to dispense with such a notice.[1]

As noted above, the Tribunal should take into account any delay or failure in the payment of housing benefit or universal credit.[2]

1 H(S)A 1988 s 19(1)(b); see also para 17.77.
2 See para 17.89.

17.91 (13) *Other breach*[1] Any other obligation of the tenancy has been broken or not performed. The fact that this is a discretionary ground suggests that the breach would normally have to be relatively serious.

In *Cadogan Estates Ltd v McMahon*[2] it was held that the tenant's bankruptcy, even if, strictly speaking, it does not amount to breach of a lease obligation, may justify recovery of possession under this ground.

In *Govanhill Housing Association Ltd v Palmer*[3] the tenant obtained an assured tenancy by fraudulent misrepresentation with regard to her housing needs. It was argued on behalf of the landlords that if the contract was reduced on this ground it should be considered void *ab initio*, that accordingly there would never have been any lease contract that could terminate and transform into a statutory tenancy, and that therefore the tenant could be evicted by an action of summary ejection.

While this reasoning appears sound, the court took the view that reduction of the lease for fraud was a termination of the contract within the meaning of section 16(1) of the Housing (Scotland) Act 1988, which would transform the contractual tenancy into a statutory one.[4] However, the landlord might be able, subject to the First-Tier Tribunal's discretion, to recover possession under ground 13 on the basis that the tenant's fraud was a breach of the lease. This seems theoretically suspect, but has the pragmatic advantage of allowing the eviction to be kept within the Tribunal's discretion.

1 Compare ground 11 for private residential tenancies (para 17.56).
2 [2001] 1 AC 378, [2000] 4 All ER 897.
3 1998 SLT 887, 1997 Hous LR 133.
4 See para 17.69.

17.92   (14) *Deterioration of house*   The condition of the house or any of the common parts of the building has deteriorated because of the neglect of the tenant, or any one of joint tenants, or anyone living with the tenant. The tenant may only be removed for the act or default of a lodger or subtenant where he or she has failed to take any steps that could reasonably have been taken to remove the person concerned.

In relation to regulated tenancies, this ground has been held to include neglect of a garden attached to the house.[1]

1 *Holloway v Povey* (1984) 271 EG 195, (1984) 15 HLR 104, CA.

17.93   (15) *Criminal or anti-social use*[1]   The tenant, or someone else either living in the house or visiting it, has a criminal conviction or is guilty of anti-social behaviour, in each case relating to the house or its locality. More specifically, the person concerned has either:

(a)   been convicted of using or allowing the house to be used for immoral or illegal purposes, or of an imprisonable offence committed in or in the locality of the house; or

(b)   acted in an anti-social manner, or pursued a course of anti-social conduct, in relation to a person residing, visiting or otherwise engaged in lawful activity in the area.

The substance of this ground is found in grounds 13 to 15 for private residential tenancies.[2]

This ground was substantially extended and developed by section 23 of the Crime and Disorder Act 1998; the original version still applies in the case of regulated tenancies.[3]

1 Substituted by the Crime and Disorder Act 1998 s 23(4).
2 See paras 17.58–17.60.
3 See para 17.124.

17.94   (16) *Deterioration of furniture*   In the case of a furnished let there has been deterioration in the condition of the furniture because of ill treatment by the tenant or anyone else living in the house.

As with ground (14) above, the tenant may only be removed for the act or default of a lodger or subtenant where he or she has failed to take any steps that could reasonably have been taken to remove the person concerned.

17.95   (17) *Ex-employee tenant* (a service tenancy)[1] The house was let to the tenant in consequence of his or her employment by the landlord, or a previous landlord, and the tenant has ceased to be in that employment.

In the case of regulated tenancies, it was also necessary for the landlord to show that the house was reasonably required for another employee. In relation to assured tenancies, that requirement has been dropped.

1 H(S)A 1988 Sch 5 Pt II (as amended). Compare ground 8 for private residential tenancies (para 17.53).

ASSURED TENANCIES: OTHER PROVISIONS

Rents under assured tenancies

17.96   As we have already observed, it is in relation to the rent level that an assured tenancy differs most fundamentally from its predecessor, the regulated tenancy. A tenant no longer has the right to have a fair rent registered with the rent officer. Instead, a market rent is payable, although the First-Tier Tribunal (formerly rent assessment committees) still has a role to play in settling disputes.[1]

The provisions described here mainly apply to 'normal' assured tenancies. Rents under short assured tenancies are considered further in a later section.[2]

1 H(S)A 1988 ss 24 and 25.
2 See para 17.105.

17.97   Where the period of let specified in the lease contract is still unexpired, or where the lease is continuing on tacit relocation, the rent will be as stated in the lease document. Since it will presumably be at a level negotiated between the parties, and since the tenant will have no right to go to the rent officer to have it altered, this means that it is likely to be at a market level.[1]

In respect of the period after the lease contract has expired, when the tenancy is continuing as a statutory assured tenancy, the landlord may serve a notice on the tenant proposing a new rent; such a notice can be served at any time, even during the contractual period of the lease, but cannot take effect before that period has expired.[2]

If the length of the tenancy was six months or more, the period of notice is six months; if the length was less than six months, the period of notice will be the duration of the tenancy, though not less than one month.[3] After the rent has been increased, it may not be raised again until after a year has passed.[4]

1 A rent review clause allowing the rent to be increased by an excessive amount may be unenforceable if it is effectively a device to circumvent the legislation – see *Bankway Properties Ltd v Penfold-Dunsford* [2001] 1 WLR 1369, [2001] 26 EG 164.
2 H(S)A 1988, s 24(1) (as amended). For the prescribed form of such a notice, see Rent Regulation and Assured Tenancies (Forms) (Scotland) Regulations 2017 SSI No 349.
3 H(S)A 1988 s 24(2) (as amended).
4 H(S)A 1988 s 24(4).

17.98 The new rent will take effect unless the tenant refers the matter to the First-Tier Tribunal, or the parties negotiate a different level of rent. Section 25 sets out the Tribunal's guidelines for fixing a market rent.

Since the tenant may feel that the landlord has proposed a rent above the market level, it may well be worthwhile to refer the matter to the Tribunal. The appropriate level of rent is that at which the Tribunal considers that the house might reasonably be expected to be let in the open market by a willing landlord under an assured tenancy. It is to be assumed that the tenancy begins at the period when the new rent is to take effect and that the house has been let on terms (other than those relating to rent) that are the actual terms of the tenancy. If a notice or notices have been given that possession might be recovered under grounds (1) to (5) of Sch 5, that should also be taken into account.[1]

There should be disregarded any effect on the rent attributable to:

(a) the granting of a tenancy to a sitting tenant;
(b) an improvement carried out by the tenant or a predecessor in title, unless the improvement was carried out in pursuance of the terms of the tenancy; and
(c) the failure by the tenant to comply with any terms of the tenancy.[2]

1 H(S)A 1988 s 25(1); see also para 17.77 et seq.
2 H(S)A 1988 s 25(2); for the operation of assumptions and disregards in relation to rent reviews see para 12.56 et seq.

Other tenancy terms

17.99 *Alteration of terms*   During the contractual period of an assured tenancy, the terms will be those in the lease document. Once the tenancy has become a statutory one, the terms (other than those relating to termination of the tenancy or increasing the rent) will initially remain the same as before.[1] They will only be changed if either the landlord or the tenant, within a year after the termination of the contractual tenancy, serves a notice on the other proposing different terms.[2]

The party receiving the notice (either the landlord or the tenant as the case may be) may, within three months, refer it to the First-Tier Tribunal, which may confirm the new terms or fix other terms that it considers reasonable.[3]

If the notice is not referred to the Tribunal, the new terms will take effect three months after the service of the notice, or after such longer period as the notice specifies.[4] Either the landlord or the tenant in his or her notice, or the Tribunal if the matter is referred to it, may make an adjustment of the rent to take account of the new terms.[5]

There are prescribed forms of the relevant notices.[6]

1 H(S)A 1988, s 16(1) (as amended).
2 H(S)A 1988 s 17(2).
3 H(S)A 1988 s 17(3) and (4) (as amended).
4 H(S)A 1988 s 17(3) (as amended).
5 H(S)A 1988 s 17(5) (as amended).
6 Rent Regulation and Assured Tenancies (Forms) (Scotland) Regulations 2017 SSI No 349.

17.100 *Assignation and subletting*[1]   It is an implied term of every assured tenancy that, except with the consent of the landlord, the tenant shall not:

(a)   assign the tenancy (in whole or in part); or
(b)   sublet or part with possession of the whole or any part of the house.

This provision only applies if there is no provision in the lease dealing with assignation or subletting.

1 H(S)A 1988 s 23.

17.101 *Access for repairs*[1]   It is an implied term of every assured tenancy that the tenant will afford the landlord reasonable access to the house and all reasonable facilities for carrying out any repairs the landlord is entitled to execute.[2]

1 H(S)A 1988 s 26.
2 For the landlord's repairing obligations, see Ch 19.

17.102   *Written lease and rent book*[1]   The landlord under an assured tenancy has a duty to draw up a formal document containing or referring to the tenancy terms, and to give a copy of it to the tenant. This should all be free of charge to the tenant. If the landlord fails to draw up such a document, or to adjust the terms of an existing document where necessary, the tenant can refer the matter to the First-Tier Tribunal.

Where the rent is payable weekly, the landlord has a duty to provide a rent book, and a landlord failing to do so will be liable to a fine. The rent book must contain certain information informing the tenant of his or her legal rights.[2]

1 H(S)A 1988 s 30.
2 Assured Tenancies (Rent Book) (Scotland) Regulations 1988 SI 1988/2085 (as amended).

17.103   *Tenant information packs*[1]   The Private Rented Housing (Scotland) Act 2011 beefed up the above requirements substantially by requiring landlords to issue each new assured or short assured tenant, no later than the commencement of the tenancy, with a tenant information pack containing certain documents (the standard tenancy documents).

These include a copy of the tenancy agreement required under section 30(1) of the 1988 Act,[2] (in the case of short assured tenancies) a copy of the notice required under s 32(1)(b) of the 1988 Act (the AT5 form),[3] a copy of any gas safety record that requires to be given to the tenant,[4] and a copy of any electrical safety record that requires to be given to the tenant.[5]

The pack should also contain detailed information about the tenancy, about the property, about the landlord, the responsibilities of tenants and landlords and further advice and support, all as specified in regulations.[6]

These standard tenancy documents may be provided together or separately and must be provided to the tenant free of charge. The documents must be in hard copy, unless the tenant agrees to accept them electronically and provides an e-mail address. Where there are joint tenants only one copy is required, apart from the gas safety record, which must be supplied to each joint tenant.[7]

When providing the Tenant Information Pack the landlord must request a signed acknowledgement from the tenant that it has been provided.[8]

1 H(S)A 1988 ss 30A and 30B (inserted by the Private Rented Housing (Scotland) Act 2011 s 33).
2 See para 17.102.
3 See para 17.104.
4 In accordance with reg 36(6) of the Gas Safety (Installation and Use) Regulations 1998, SI 1998/2451.

5 In accordance with the Housing (Scotland) Act 2006 s 19A(3).
6 The Tenant Information Packs (Assured Tenancies) (Scotland) Order 2013, SSI No 20, Schedule (as substituted by The Tenant Information Packs (Assured Tenancies) (Scotland) Amendment Order 2016 SSI No 334).
7 SSI 2013 No 20 art 3.
8 SSI 2013 No 20 art 5.

SHORT ASSURED TENANCIES[1]

Nature of tenancy

17.104 As already noted, the short assured tenancy was by far the most widely used type of private sector residential let at the time of the introduction of the private residential tenancy. In a short assured tenancy, the landlord has an absolute right to recover possession of the house when the period stated in the lease contract comes to an end. The tenant is therefore denied the right to extended security of tenure enjoyed by other assured tenants and by social tenants under a Scottish secure tenancy.[2]

In order to qualify as a short assured tenancy, it was only necessary for the term of the let to be at least six months and for the tenant to have been given written notice in advance that the tenancy was to be a short assured tenancy.[3] Renewals of the lease can be for a shorter period.[4]

If the tenant is granted a renewal of the lease, or it continues by tacit relocation, no fresh notice will be required to qualify the tenancy as a short assured tenancy.[5] The 1988 Act allowed the landlord to convert such a renewed lease into an ordinary assured tenancy by serving on the tenant a notice to that effect, though it is difficult to envisage circumstances in which a private landlord might be motivated to do so.[6] There were prescribed forms for both of the above notices.[7] As noted above, it is now possible to convert a short assured tenancy into a private residential tenancy.[8]

Despite their name, there was no maximum length prescribed for short assured tenancies, apart from the maximum length of 20 years that applies to residential leases generally.[9] However, much shorter tenancies appeared to be the norm and, according to the Scottish Government, leases for the minimum period of six months were very popular with both landlords and tenants.[10]

The provisions described earlier in the chapter, unless the contrary is indicated, will normally apply to short assured as well as other assured tenancies. This section is confined to the distinctive features of the short assured tenancy.

1 H(S)A 1988, ss 32–35.

2 See Ch 18.
3 H(S)A 1988 s 32(1) and (2); see *Key Housing Association Ltd v Cameron* 1999 Hous LR 47; in England, in relation to the equivalent assured shorthold tenancy, the courts have tolerated errors in such notices, as long as they served the purpose of informing the tenant of the special nature of the tenancy – see *Ravenseft Properties Ltd v Hall*; *White v Chubb* [2002] 11 EG 156, [2002] HLR 33; but see also *Manel v Memon* (2001) 33 HLR 24, (2000) 2 EGLR 40.
4 H(S)A 1988 s 32(3).
5 H(S)A 1988 s 32(3).
6 H(S)A 1988 s 32(4).
7 Assured Tenancies (Forms) (Scotland) Regulations 1988 SSI No 2109 (now revoked) contained these forms.
8 See para 17.4.
9 Land Tenure Reform (Scotland) Act 1974 s 8; see also para 8.28 et seq.
10 The Scottish Government *Review of the Private Rented Sector* (2009) para 4.59, which includes a table showing typical lease lengths.

Rents

17.105   A short assured tenant who thinks the rent is too high has the right, during the contractual period of the lease, to refer the matter to the First-Tier Tribunal to have a market rent fixed.[1] This is different from 'normal' assured tenancies where the rent is fixed during the contractual part of the lease and can only be reviewed if the lease later converts to a statutory assured tenancy.[2]

The right of a tenant under a short assured tenancy to have a market rent fixed by the First-Tier Tribunal is qualified in two ways:

(1)   there must be a sufficient number of similar houses in the locality let on assured tenancies for the Tribunal to use as comparisons;[3] and

(2)   the right can be discontinued in particular areas, or in other specified circumstances, if the Scottish Ministers make an order to that effect.[4]

1 H(S)A 1988 s 34 (as amended).
2 See para 17.96 et seq.
3 H(S)A 1988 s 34(3).
4 H(S)A 1988 s 35.

Termination of short assured tenancies

17.106   The grounds for recovery of possession by the landlord that apply to normal assured tenancies[1] also apply to short assured tenancies. In addition, the First-Tier Tribunal is bound to give an order for possession if satisfied:[2]

(a)   that the short assured tenancy has reached its ish (its expiry date);

(b)   that tacit relocation is not operating;[3] and

(d)   that the landlord has given a notice stating that he or she requires possession of the house.

At the time of writing, temporary provision imposing an additional requirement of reasonableness applies.[4]

The period of notice is two months, or such longer period as the lease specifies.[5]

The Act does not make the function of such a notice entirely clear. It cannot be a notice to quit in the normal sense, as it is expressly stated that it may be served before, at or after the termination of the tenancy to which it relates.[6] However, the First-Tier Tribunal cannot grant the landlord possession where tacit relocation is operating, and the common law relating to notices to quit and tacit relocation is expressly saved by section 52. It will therefore be necessary for the landlord to send a notice to quit at least 28 days prior to the expiry date of the tenancy to prevent the onset of tacit relocation.[7]

The 1988 Act does not prescribe a form of notice to quit specifically for short assured tenancies, but one that conforms to the requirements of Assured Tenancies (Notices to Quit Prescribed Information) (Scotland) Regulations 1988[8] is acceptable.[9]

1 See para 17.77 et seq.
2 These are found in H(S)A 1988 s 33(1). Paragraph (c) of that subsection was repealed by the Private Housing (Tenancies) (Scotland) Act 2016 Sch 5 para 2(3)(b).
3 See *Cavriani v Robinson* 2002 Hous LR 67.
4 H(S)A 1988 s 33(1)(e), introduced by the Coronavirus (Scotland) Act 2020 Sch 1 para 3(4)(c).
5 H(S)A 1988 s 33(2).
6 H(S)A 1988 s 33(3).
7 Rent (Scotland) Act 1984 s 112; see also para 10.30.
8 SI 1988/2067.
9 *Key Housing Association Ltd v Cameron* 1999 Hous LR 47.

17.107   There is also no prescribed form for the notice requiring possession of the house, and it has now been specifically provided 'for the avoidance of doubt' that the notice of proceedings for possession prescribed for other assured tenancies (form AT6) is not required here.[1]

In theory it should be possible for this notice to be combined with the notice to quit, provided that the respective functions of the two types are met by the single notice. In *Key Housing Association Ltd v Cameron*[2] it was held that such a hybrid notice is acceptable, but a more cautious approach would be to use two separate notices.

However, if a notice to quit is sent at least 28 days but less than two months prior to the ish, tacit relocation would not operate, but the landlord would be unable to raise proceedings for possession at the ish. In such a case it would probably be preferable to send a second notice giving two clear months' notice that possession is required. As noted above, this can even be sent after the ish if the tenancy has been validly terminated at that date.[3]

1 Private Rented Housing (Scotland) Act 2011 s 34.
2 1999 Hous LR 47.
3 See para 17.106.

REGULATED TENANCIES: GENERAL

17.108   As we saw at the beginning of the chapter, the system of regulated tenancies is intended eventually to become obsolete. However, existing regulated tenancies entered into before Part II of the Housing (Scotland) Act 1988 came into force (ie 2 January 1989) continue to have protection under the Rent (Scotland) Act 1984 and to enjoy a system of fair rents. Also, in certain limited circumstances, mainly transitional in nature, new regulated tenancies could be created after that date.[1]

It is therefore still necessary to give an account of the main provisions relating to regulated tenancies.

1 Housing (Scotland) Act 1988 s 42(1).

Protected tenancies

17.109   *Rateable value limit*   The Rent (Scotland) Act 1984 can only apply to houses which had a rateable value of under £200 on 23 March 1965.[1] This historic figure is sufficiently high in relation to values at that time for only houses at the very top end of the market to have been excluded.

Regulated tenancies tended to be older properties that were in existence in 1965. However, special provision was made to determine whether properties built since that date were of comparable value and ought to qualify.[2]

If any question arises in any proceedings as to whether a dwellinghouse is within the relevant rateable value limit, it is deemed to be within that limit unless the contrary is shown.[3]

There is no equivalent rateable value limit in respect of assured tenancies.

1 This was, of course, some time before rateable values were abolished in relation to residential properties, to be replaced by the poll tax and then the council tax.
2 See the Rent (Scotland) Act 1984 s 1(1)(a), s 7; Protected Tenancies and Part VII Contracts (Rateable Value Limits) (Scotland) Order 1985, SI 1985/314.
3 R(S)A 1984 s 1(4).

17.110 *Further criteria for protection* As with assured and private residential tenancies, a house has to be let as a separate dwelling in order to be protected. As long as there is a part that is held exclusively by the tenant, it does not matter if some of the accommodation is shared with other tenants.[1]

Subtenancies fall within the Act's definition of a tenancy, and so are also protected.[2]

1 R(S)A 1984 s 97(1). On the meaning of the term 'separate dwelling', see para 17.12.
2 R(S)A 1984 s 115(1).

Excepted categories

17.111 These are mainly of historic relevance, since whether a tenancy qualified as a regulated tenancy will generally have been determined many years ago. Many of these exceptions (though there are important differences) are the same as or similar to those that apply to assured tenancies.

The exceptions include where the tenancy is an assured tenancy, where no rent is payable or the rent is very low, where the landlord is resident,[1] student lets, holiday lets etc.[2]

1 This was an earlier version of the resident landlord exception (see para 17.22), the wording of which inadvertently included cases where the landlord and tenant occupy different flats in a house that has been converted into flats.
2 See R(S)A 1984 Pt I.

REGULATED TENANCIES: SECURITY OF TENURE AND RECOVERY OF POSSESSION

Statutory tenancies

17.112 The result of a tenancy being a protected tenancy is, of course, that the tenant enjoys the benefits conferred by the Rent (Scotland) Act 1984. This means, in contrast to the situation with assured tenancies, that the tenant has the right to have a fair rent registered with the rent officer and that the terms of the lease contract will generally only be effective to the extent that they are consistent with the terms of the Act.

However, in common with assured tenancies, the tenant has a right of security of tenure and the tenancy will become a statutory one when the landlord has served a notice to quit and the period of notice has expired.[1] And, once again, the landlord can only regain possession by court order, based on one of the relevant statutory grounds.

1 See para 17.106. For the requirements and content of the notice to quit see the Rent (Scotland) Act 1984 s 112 and the Rent Regulation (Forms and Information etc) (Scotland) Regulations 1991 SI 1991/1521 (as amended), reg 4 and Sch 2.

Terms of statutory tenancies

17.113 The terms and conditions of a statutory tenancy are the same as those in the original tenancy contract, so far as they are consistent with the provisions of the Rent (Scotland) Act 1984.[1] The period of notice of termination by either party will be the same as in the lease contract except that:

(a)   if no period of notice is stated, a tenant who wants to terminate must give the landlord at least three months' notice; and

(b)   in all cases, a landlord who wants to recover possession must give a minimum of four weeks' notice.[2]

1 R(S)A 1984 s 15(1).
2 R(S)A 1984 s 15(3) and (4); s 112.

Notification of local authority

17.114 A landlord who raises proceedings for possession must give notice of this to the local authority in whose area the dwellinghouse is situated. The notice should be given in the form and manner prescribed in section 11(3) of the Homelessness etc (Scotland) Act 2003.[1]

1 R(S)A 1984 s 12A (added by the Homelessness etc (Scotland) Act 2003 Sch 1 para 2).

Assignations and sublets

17.115 A statutory tenant is entitled to assign the tenancy, subject to the landlord's consent, and the assignee will take over a statutory tenancy.[1] Subletting is not allowed without the landlord's consent if it is against the terms of the original tenancy. Otherwise the tenancy may be sublet in whole or in part. If the head tenancy is terminated, the subtenant will be allowed to stay on as a statutory tenant.[2]

1 R(S)A 1984 s 17.
2 R(S)A 1984 s 19.

Termination of statutory tenancies

17.116   The grounds for recovery of possession by the landlord are contained in Schedule 2 to the Rent (Scotland) Act 1984 and, as with assured tenancies, consist of both discretionary and mandatory grounds. Many of these are the same, or substantially similar, to the grounds for termination of an assured tenancy, though there are significant differences that will be noted below.

Note that, at the time of writing, temporary provision in terms of the Coronavirus (Scotland) Act 2020, making all grounds discretionary and extending the relevant notice periods while these provisions are in force.[1]

The possible application of the Human Rights Act 1998 to the grounds for recovery of possession has already been considered.[2]

1 Coronavirus (Scotland) Act 2020 Sch 1 paras 5 and 6.
2 See para 17.8 et seq.

Discretionary grounds of possession[1]

17.117   In these cases, the court will not grant a landlord an order for possession of the premises unless it considers that it is reasonable to do so and either:

(a)   there is suitable alternative accommodation available; or
(b)   there exists one or more of the grounds specified in Part I of Sch 2.

In the case of these discretionary grounds (but not the mandatory ones) the court has power to delay the proceedings in various ways, including adjournment of the case.[2] This power would normally be used in cases of rent arrears in order to give the tenant time to pay.

1 R(S)A 1984 s 11 and Sch 2 Pt I, cases 1–10.
2 R(S)A 1984 s 12.

17.118   The grounds for deciding whether or not suitable alternative accommodation is available are set out in Schedule 2, Part IV, and are virtually the same as in the case of assured tenancies.[1] It has been held that alternative accommodation that is held under an assured tenancy is suitable as regards security of tenure,[2] and it may be assumed that the same would be the case with a private residential tenancy.

1 See para 17.87 and the case authority referred to there.
2 *Laimond Properties Ltd v Al-Shakarchi* (1998) 30 HLR 1099, [1998] L&TR 90.

17.119   The grounds specified in Part I of Sch 2 are rent arrears or other breach, nuisance, deterioration of the house, deterioration of the furniture (if it is a furnished let), the tenant's notice to quit, unauthorised assignation or subletting, the house is reasonably required for the landlord's employee, ie a service tenancy, the house is reasonably required for occupancy by the landlord or the landlord's family, subletting at an excessive rent, and overcrowding.

Mandatory grounds of possession[1]

17.120   As with assured tenancies, these are situations where the court does not have discretion and must grant an order for recovery of possession if the ground is proved to exist. In the case of all these grounds (except case 20, which applies where the house has been designed or adapted for occupation by a person with special needs), the tenant must have been given advance written notice that the landlord might require possession on the ground in question. In respect of cases 11 (property required for occupation by landlord), 12 (landlord acquired property as retirement accommodation) and 21 (landlord a member of the armed forces), however, the court has discretion to dispense with this notice.[2] The onus of proof that the ground exists is on the landlord.

1 R(S)A 1984 s 11 and Sch 2 Pt II, cases 11–21.
2 But see *Bradshaw v Baldwin-Wiseman* (1985) 49 P&CR 382, (1985) 274 EG 285, CA.

17.121   The mandatory grounds are the requirement of the house by an owner who has formerly occupied it, the requirement of the house by the owner as his or her home on retirement, off-season lets of holiday property not exceeding eight months, lettings of student accommodation not exceeding 12 months, short tenancies,[1] ecclesiastical lets, requirement of the house for the landlord's agricultural employee, requirement of an adapted house for a person with special needs, and in certain circumstances where the owner was a member of the regular armed forces, ie the army, navy or air force.

1 See para 17.128.

Contrast with assured tenancies[1]

17.122   The above grounds for recovery of possession were used as the basis for those applicable to assured tenancies, with the result that many of them are identical or substantially similar to the latter. In such cases the observations made above in relation to assured tenancies, as well as the case law (much of which is derived from regulated tenancies), will also be relevant here. However, there are important differences, the general effect of which is to make recovery of possession more difficult for the landlord of a regulated tenancy than it is for the landlord of an assured tenancy. Only selected cases with significant differences from those applying to assured tenancies are considered here.

1 See para 17.77 et seq.

17.123 *Rent arrears* This is always a discretionary ground, and there is no equivalent of the assured tenancy ground of persistent late payment, or of the mandatory ground where three months' rent is owing.

17.124 *Nuisance etc* This is defined as: 'Where the tenant or any person residing or lodging with him or any sub-tenant of his has been guilty of conduct which is a nuisance or annoyance to adjoining occupiers, or has been convicted of using the dwelling-house or allowing the dwelling-house to be used for immoral or illegal purposes.'[1] The equivalent ground for assured tenancies was originally identical, but has now been considerably extended and developed by the Crime and Disorder Act 1998.[2] In relation to regulated tenancies the ground remains unchanged.

1 R(S)A 1984 Sch 2 case 2.
2 See para 17.93.

17.125 *Occupation by landlord* This is where the house is reasonably required for the landlord or the landlord's family to live in. This is only a mandatory ground in the case of an owner who formerly occupied the house, or who bought it to live in after retirement, or was a member of the regular armed forces when it was bought and the lease was granted. Otherwise this ground is discretionary in the case of regulated tenancies, and in addition the landlord must have owned the house at the beginning of the tenancy, as opposed to having bought the property subject to the sitting tenancy.[1]

In the case of assured tenancies, this ground is always mandatory (though it also does not apply at all if the landlord bought the property subject to the sitting tenancy).

The words 'reasonably required' mean more than just that the landlord desires the property, but something less than absolute necessity will do.[2]

In relation to this ground only, the court is given further discretion by the application of a greater hardship test. It is provided that the court should not grant possession if it 'is satisfied that, having regard to all the circumstances of the case, including the question of whether other accommodation is available for the landlord or the tenant, greater hardship would be caused by granting the order than by refusing to grant it'.[3]

If it turns out after a tenant has been evicted on this ground that the landlord did not really require the house as a residence for himself or herself, or for a family member, but was using the ground as a pretext in order to recover possession, the tenant may be able to claim damages. If it is subsequently made to appear to the court that the order for recovery of possession was obtained by misrepresentation or concealment of material facts, the court may order the landlord to pay the former tenant compensation for damage or loss sustained by him or her as a result of the eviction.[4]

This remedy is also competent where a service tenancy has been terminated.[5]

1 *Epps v Rothnie* [1945] KB 562, CA; *Newton v Biggs* [1953] 2 QB 211, [1953] 1 All ER 99, CA. But see *Thomas v Fryer* [1970] 2 All ER 1, [1970] 1 WLR 845, CA.
2 *Aitken v Shaw* 1933 SLT (Sh Ct) 21; *Kennealy v Dunne* [1977] QB 837, [1977] 2 WLR 421.
3 R(S)A 1984 Sch 2 Pt III para 1.
4 R(S)A 1984 s 21.
5 See para 17.127.

17.126   *Tenant's notice to quit*   This ground only applies if the landlord has acted on the notice by contracting to sell or re-let the house or has taken some other step that would prejudice the landlord if the tenant changed his or her mind. In the case of assured tenancies there is no such requirement.

17.127   *Service tenancies*   As well as being let to a former employee, the house must be reasonably required for a current employee. The latter proviso does not apply to assured tenancies. As noted above, the words 'reasonably required' mean more than just that the landlord desires the property, but something less than absolute necessity will do.[1]

In the case of regulated tenancies, where the employee was an agricultural worker, the ground may be mandatory. This is not so in the case of assured tenancies.

If the landlord has misused this ground, the tenant may have a damages claim for misrepresentation or concealment of material facts.[2] This remedy is also competent where possession was granted for the landlord or the landlord's family to live in.[3]

1 *Aitken v Shaw* 1933 SLT (Sh Ct) 21; see also para 17.125.
2 R(S)A 1984 s 21.
3 See para 17.125 for a fuller account.

17.128   *Short tenancies*   This was a special type of regulated tenancy, which was the predecessor of the short assured tenancy,[1] and under which the landlord similarly had an absolute right to recover possession at the end of the lease.[2] This is why the expiry of a short tenancy gives rise to a mandatory ground for recovery of possession.

However, because of the requirement that a fair rent be registered, short tenancies were never popular with landlords. Considering, therefore, that they had a maximum length of five years and that no new ones could be created after 1989, it seems unlikely that there are many left in existence; presumably this could only be the case in respect of tenancies now continuing by tacit relocation.[3]

1 See para 17.104 et seq.
2 R(S)A 1984 ss 9, 13 and 14.
3 R(S)A 1984 s 14(3). See *William Grant & Son Distillers Ltd v McClymont* 2009 SLT 305, 2009 SCLR 388, where a short tenancy was entered into in 1988 and continued by tacit relocation until 2005; the facts are more fully set out in the judgement of the sheriff principal (reversed on appeal) reported at 2007 Hous LR 76.

17.129 *Similar grounds.*   The grounds that are identical or substantially similar for both regulated and assured tenancies are the availability of alternative accommodation, breach of the lease other than rent arrears, nuisance, deterioration of the house or furniture, ecclesiastical lets, off-season lets of holiday property and lets of student accommodation.[1] Because of their temporary nature, it is unlikely that any regulated tenancies belonging to the last two categories are still in existence.

1 See para 17.77 et seq.

17.130 *Other disparities*   The right of the landlord in an assured tenancy to recover possession of the house because of mortgage arrears, for redevelopment and from the successor of a deceased tenant has no equivalent in the case of regulated tenancies. On the other hand, other regulated tenancy grounds (for reasons not always obvious) have not survived into the assured tenancy system. These are, overcrowding, subletting at an excessive rent, mandatory possession in the case of an agricultural service tenancy and requirement of an adapted house for a person with special needs.

Unauthorised assignation or subletting is only specifically mentioned as a ground in the case of regulated tenancies, although presumably, in the case of an assured tenancy, it could qualify under the general heading of breach of a tenancy obligation.

REGULATED TENANCIES: FAIR RENTS

Rent regulation

17.131 As we saw at the beginning of the chapter, the present system of rent regulation was first introduced in 1965. The relevant Scottish provisions are now found in Parts IV and V of the Rent (Scotland) Act 1984. These allow for the fixing of fair rents for regulated tenancies by local rent officers[1] and the First-Tier Tribunal and for the registration of such rents.

Before jurisdiction was transferred to the First-Tier Tribunal,[4] the setting of fair rents was overseen by private rented housing committees, which were drawn from a large panel of professional and lay people appointed by the Scottish Ministers.

Various forms relating to rent regulation and registration of fair rents, as well as the content of rent books, are prescribed in regulations.[7]

1 On rent officers, see para 17.3.
4 By the First-tier Tribunal for Scotland (Transfer of Functions of the Private Rented Housing Committees) Regulations 2016 SSI No 337.
7 Rent Regulation (Forms and Information etc) (Scotland) Regulations 1991 SI 1991/1521 (as amended).

Registration of fair rent

17.132 Where a tenancy is a regulated one, either the landlord or the tenant, or both, may apply to the local rent officer to fix a fair rent to be registered for the house.[1] This may be done either during the contractual period of the tenancy, or after the lease has expired and it is continuing as a statutory tenancy.

After a fair rent has been registered, that rent will be the maximum that the landlord can charge, and a tenant who pays more will be entitled to recover the difference from the landlord.[2] During the contractual period of the lease, however, the tenant can hold the landlord to the rent in the lease if it is less than the registered rent. The registration takes effect from the date of registration by the rent officer, except in the case of appeals, where it takes effect from the date of the decision of the First-Tier Tribunal.[3]

Any element of the registered rent which is attributable to the use of furniture, the provision of services, the use of part of the premises as a shop or office or other business purpose, or to council tax, must be noted separately on the register if it exceeds 5 per cent of the rent.[4]

Either during the contractual or the statutory period of the tenancy, the landlord and tenant may enter into an agreement to increase the rent. However, such an agreement does not affect the tenant's right to have a fair rent registered, and unless the agreement draws attention to the tenant's statutory rights it will be unenforceable.[5]

If either the landlord or the tenant is dissatisfied with the figure arrived at by the rent officer, he or she can appeal to the First-Tier Tribunal by lodging a written objection with the rent officer within 28 days.[6]

1 R(S)A 1984 s 46 (as amended).
2 R(S)A 1984 ss 28 and 37; see also *North v Allan Properties (Edinburgh)* 1987 SLT (Sh Ct) 141, [1987] SCLR 644.
3 R(S)A 1984 s 50.
4 R(S)A 1984 s 49(2) and (3) (as amended) In relation to council tax, see also R(S) A 1984 s 49A (substituted by H(S)A 2006, Sch 6 para 5.
5 R(S)A 1984 s 34 (as amended).
6 R(S)A 1984 s 46 and Sch 5 para 6 (as amended).

Variation of rent

17.133 Once a fair rent has been determined for a property, it will remain fixed for a period of three years, unless the rent is no longer a fair one because there has been a material change in the condition of the house, eg by the carrying out of a substantial improvement,[1] or in the terms of the tenancy or in the quantity, quality or condition of the furniture.[2]

After three years have elapsed since registration, either party can apply for re-registration; if an application is made before that, the registration will not take effect until after the three-year period has elapsed.[3] If the dwellinghouse in question ceases to be let under a regulated tenancy, the landlord can apply for a cancellation of the registration.[4]

1 *London Housing & Commercial Properties v Cowan* [1977] QB 148, [1976] 2 All ER 385; *R (on the application of Haysport Properties Ltd) v West Sussex Registration Area Rent Officer* (2001) 33 HLR 71, [2001] L&TR 37.
2 R(S)A 1984 s 46(3) (as amended).
3 R(S)A 1984 s 50(2).
4 R(S)A 1984 s 52.

Phasing

17.134 When a rent is registered (or re-registered), the landlord may not be entitled to charge the new rent right away, but, depending on the size of the increase, may have to phase the increase over all or part of the three-year period.[1]

Following registration, the existing rent is increased annually by whichever is the greatest of the following amounts:

(1)   £104;
(2)   25 per cent of the existing rent; or
(3)   half the difference between the existing rent and the new registered rent.

At no point can the rent be raised above the level of the new registered rent, and so no increase can exceed the amount it takes to reach that level. The same formula is applied at the end of each year to the rent being paid in order to determine the rent payable in the succeeding year.

Under the Housing (Scotland) Act 1988 the Scottish Ministers are given power to amend these provisions for phasing or repeal them entirely.[2]

1 R(S)A 1984 s 33 (as amended); The Limits on Rent Increases (Scotland) Order 1989, SI 1989/2469.
2 H(S)A 1988 s 41.

Determination of fair rent

17.135   *Fair rent formula*   The fair rent formula is contained in section 48 of the Rent (Scotland) Act 1984 (as amended):

1. In determining a fair rent, the rent officer or First-Tier Tribunal must have regard to all the circumstances (other than personal circumstances), and in particular apply their knowledge and experience of current rents of comparable property in the area. They should also have regard to the age, character and locality of the dwellinghouse and to its state of repair. If any furniture is provided for use under the tenancy, they should have regard to its quantity, quality and condition.
2. It is to be assumed that the number of persons seeking to become tenants of similar houses in the locality is not substantially greater than the number of available houses.
3. There is to be disregarded:
    (a) Any disrepair or defect that is the fault of the tenant or the tenant's predecessor in title.
    (b) Any improvements to the property or (in the case of a furnished let) to the furniture, or replacement of any fixture or fitting, carried out by the tenant or the tenant's predecessor in title.
    (c) In the case of furnished lets, any deterioration in the condition of the furniture caused by ill treatment by the tenant or anyone else living in the house.

17.136   The key component of the fair rent formula is Part 2. It is this that requires the rent officer or First-Tier Tribunal to ignore any element in the market rent caused by housing shortages in the area. This will normally have the effect of ensuring that the fair rent for a house is substantially lower than the market rent.

When it was first introduced, the fair rent formula was criticised as being too vague. This was a deliberate policy, however, to avoid the litigation and hair-splitting that might have resulted from a more detailed formula; instead a great deal was left to the professional discretion of those charged with determining fair rents, and from this point of view the system seems to have worked reasonably well.

However, the formula has been amplified to some extent by the decisions of the courts and we will now examine some of the ways in which its wording has been interpreted.

Interpretation of formula

17.137   *All the circumstances*   Examples of relevant circumstances are:

(a)   the rents of comparable properties;[1]
(b)   the capital value of the property;[2] and
(c)   the terms of the tenancy. In the last case, the fact that a let is a furnished one will normally mean that a higher rent can be fixed.

With the increasing incidence of residential tenancies at market rents, in the form of assured and now private residential tenancies, the question arose as to whether the correct approach in fixing a fair rent is to use other registered rents as comparables, or instead to use market rents paid under assured tenancies of similar properties, with an appropriate adjustment downwards to reflect scarcity or other relevant factors. Disputes have arisen because the latter method has tended to produce higher rents.

In *Western Heritable Investment Co Ltd v Johnston*[3] it was held that either method was valid, and which was the more appropriate in a particular case was a question of fact to be decided by the rent assessment committee (or, now, the First-Tier Tribunal) rather than the court.

However, as this form of rent control becomes increasingly uncommon, it seems likely that using market rents as comparables will increasingly become the norm, and the English courts now appear to consider this to be a matter of law upon which they are competent to pronounce.[4] More recently, it has been held in the Inner House of the Court of Session that both registered and market rents should be taken account of where available.[5]

1 *Learmonth Property Investment Co Ltd v Aitken* 1970 SC 223, 1971 SLT 349.
2 *Learmonth Property Investment Co Ltd v Aitken* 1970 SC 223, 1971 SLT 349; *Skilling v Arcari's Exrx* 1974 SC (HL) 42, 1974 SLT 46.
3 1997 SLT 74, 1996 Hous LR 65; see also *Western Heritable Investment Co Ltd v Hunter* 2004 SC 635, 2004 SLT 355.

4 See *Spath Holme Ltd v Greater Manchester and Lancashire Rent Assessment Committee* [1995] 49 EG 128, CA, (1996) 71 P&CR D8; *Curtis v London Rent Assessment Committee* [1999] QB 92, [1997] 4 All ER 842; *Northumberland & Durham Property Trust Ltd v London Rent Assessment Committee (57 Ifield Road, London)* (1998) 30 HLR 1091, [1998] 2 EGLR 99; and *Northumberland & Durham Property Trust Ltd v London Rent Assessment Committee (Ealing Village, London)* (1999) 31 HLR 109, [1998] 3 EGLR 85.
5 *Wright v Elderpark Housing Association* [2017] CSIH 54, 2017 SLT 995.

17.138 *Other than personal circumstances*   The tenant's poverty or hardship are not factors that can be taken into account. Nor can the fact that the tenant is in possession of the property and enjoying security of tenure, as this is also considered to be a personal circumstance.[1]

1 *Skilling v Arcari's Exrx* 1974 SC (HL) 42, 1974 SLT 46.

17.139 *To apply their knowledge and experience of current rents of comparable properties in the area*   These words did not appear in the original fair rent formula and are still not in its English version; they were added to the Scottish version by the Tenants' Rights Etc (Scotland) Act 1980, because the Scottish courts had been taking a different line from their English counterparts regarding the need for rent assessment committees to give reasons for their decisions.[1]

The change in wording does not absolve the First-Tier Tribunal, with which jurisdiction now lies, from the need to give reasons. Rather, it allows the Tribunal to use its own judgement and skill in cases where there is insufficient evidence, eg of comparable properties.

1 *Albyn Properties Ltd v Knox* 1977 SC 108, 1977 SLT 41.

17.140 *The age, character and locality of the dwellinghouse and its state of repair*   'Locality' in this context is thought to mean the immediate locality, as that is what is likely to affect the value of the property; in relation to the scarcity element (in Part 2 of the formula) 'locality' is thought to mean a much wider area.[1]

1 See Paul Q Watchman 'Calculating Fair Rents' *Journal of the Law Society of Scotland* (Workshop Section) p 217 (July 1981).

17.141 *The quantity, quality and condition of the furniture*   There are various ways in which this could be taken into account, but the method favoured seems to be one based on a return on the capital value of the furniture.[1] In *R v London Rent Assessment Panel ex p Mota*,[2] it was held that, as long as the tenant was entitled to the use of the landlord's furniture, it could be taken into account in fixing the rent, even though the tenant, with the landlord's consent, had replaced it with her own furniture.

1 *Mann v Cornella* (1980) 254 EG 403, CA
2 (1988) 2 EG 66.

17.142   *The scarcity element*   As mentioned earlier, this part of the formula, contained in section 48(2) of the Rent (Scotland) Act 1984, is arguably the single most important element that distinguishes a fair rent from a market rent. Effectively it means that any inflationary effect on rents from housing shortages in the locality should be disregarded.

As noted above, 'locality' means not just the immediate area, but a fairly large one, ie 'the area within which persons likely to occupy this class of accommodation, having regard to their requirements and work, would be able to dwell'.[1] As there are very few, if any, areas where there is not some sort of housing shortage, it is normal for the rent to be reduced by a percentage to take account of scarcity.[2]

1 The Francis Committee and the London Rent Assessment Panel, quoted in Paul Q Watchman 'Calculating Fair Rents', Journal of the Law Society of Scotland (Workshop Section) p 217 (July 1981); *Metropolitan Property Holdings Ltd v Finegold* [1975] 1 All ER 389, [1975] 1 WLR 349, DC.
2 *Western Heritable Investment Co Ltd v Husband* [1983] 2 AC 849, 1983 SC (HL) 60.

17.143   *Tenant's improvements or disrepair caused by the tenant*   It would clearly be wrong if a tenant who added to the property's value by making improvements at his or her own expense was penalised by being charged a higher rent. Conversely, a tenant whose actions detracted from the property's value should not be able to gain from these actions. It is only improvements and not repairs carried out by the tenant that should be disregarded.[1]

It should be noted that the word 'predecessor' in this context means predecessor in title under the same lease, eg where there has been an assignation, or where the tenant has died and has been succeeded in the tenancy by a member of his or her family. Where the property is being relet under a new lease, anything done to it by the previous tenant will be irrelevant.

1 *Stewart's Judicial Factor v Gallagher* 1967 SC 59, 1967 SLT 52.

SUCCESSION TO TENANCIES

Assured and regulated tenancies

17.144   Prior to 2 January 1989, the widow or widower of a tenant under a regulated tenancy, failing which a member of the tenant's family who had resided with the tenant for six months prior to the tenant's death, had a right to succeed to the tenancy. Furthermore, there was a right to a second succession after the death of the first successor. This meant that in some cases security of tenure could span many years, covering two or even three generations of the same family.

17.145   *Assured tenancies*[1]   The Housing (Scotland) Act 1988 gives much more limited succession rights to the tenant under an assured tenancy, basically confining the right of succession to the tenant's partner who lived with the tenant at the time of his or her death. This includes the tenant's widow or widower, an unmarried partner of the opposite sex and a civil partner of the same sex.[2]

Furthermore, there is no right of succession to a tenant who has already inherited the tenancy; this means, for example, that where a partner succeeds to a tenancy and then remarries or acquires a new partner, the new partner will have no succession right. This will even be the case where:

(a)   the tenant succeeded as sole tenant on the death of the person with whom he or she had a joint tenancy, eg if the tenancy was in joint names of a husband and wife the surviving spouse will be counted as a successor and no further successions will be allowed; and

(b)   where the successor has been granted a new lease of the same house, provided that his or her occupation has been continuous.

When an individual succeeds to the tenancy, it now ceases to be an assured tenancy and becomes a private residential tenancy.[3]

1 H(S)A 1988 s 31 (as amended).
2 H(S)A s 314 (added by the Civil Partnership Act 2004 Sch 28(4)).
3 H(S)A 1988 s 31A, inserted by PH(T)(S)A 2016 Sch 5(2) para 5.

17.146   *Regulated tenancies*[1]   The succession rights of regulated tenants are now similarly curtailed, so that only the tenant's partner can now inherit a regulated tenancy.

In certain circumstances a member of a regulated tenant's family may still succeed to the tenancy, but what he or she will get is a private residential tenancy, not a regulated one. 'Family' is not defined, but a family member is thought to include not only a child but also a brother or sister of the tenant[2] and, in exceptional circumstances, a nephew or niece.[3]

1 R(S)A 1984 s 3 and Sch 1; ss 3A, 3B; Sch 1A and Sch 1B (as amended).
2 *Price v Gould* [1930] All ER 389.
3 *Jones v Whitehill* [1950] 2 KB 204, [1950] 1 All ER 389.

17.147   The circumstances where a member of a regulated tenant's family may inherit a private residential tenancy are:

(a)   on the death of the original tenant's partner, where the original tenant died on or after 2 January 1989 and the partner inherited a regulated tenancy;

(b)   on the death of the original tenant where he or she died on or after 2 January 1989 but did not leave a partner; and

(c)   where the newly deceased tenant was not the original tenant, but succeeded to a regulated tenancy under the old law prior to 2 January 1989.

In order to qualify for succession to a private residential tenancy, the family member must have resided with the tenant for two years prior to the tenant's death. Furthermore, he or she must have been a member, not only of the successor tenant's family, but also that of the original tenant at the date of his or her death. For example, this would allow a child, whose father was the original tenant and whose mother later inherited the tenancy, to succeed to the tenancy on the mother's death; however, where the original tenant's partner had remarried or otherwise acquired a new partner, it would exclude succession by the second partner or any children of the new union.

The main effect of the above amendments will be to hasten the decline of regulated tenancies. Existing regulated tenancies will not now last beyond the lifetime of the existing tenant or his or her partner.

It should be emphasised that these rather complex provisions only apply where the original tenancy was a regulated tenancy. As mentioned above, where it started life as an assured tenancy, ie after 2 January 1989, the position is much simpler: only the partner can inherit.

Private residential tenancies

17.148 PH(T)(S)A 2016 makes detailed provision for succession rights in private residential tenancies.

Where a tenant dies, the consequences for the tenancy depend on whether the deceased was a sole or a joint tenant. On the death of a joint tenant, the interest of the deceased is simply extinguished.[1] The interest of the other joint tenant or tenants is unaffected.

Where a sole tenant dies, another person may be entitled to succeed to the tenancy. This will only be the case if the deceased tenant did not inherit the tenancy himself or herself.[2] If the tenancy was inherited by the deceased tenant, the tenancy will be extinguished. Otherwise, the tenancy may be inherited by the tenant's partner, another family member or a resident carer, in that order of priority. Oddly, no provision is made for that person to opt out of inheriting the tenancy other than by giving notice in the normal way.[3] No doubt that often suits the person entitled to inherit, but equally it is not difficult to imagine a situation where that person has no wish to have the obligations of a tenant imposed on them.

1 PH(T)(S)A 2016 s 66.
2 PH(T)(S)A 2016 ss 67(2)(a), 68(1)(b), 69(1)(b).
3 See above, para 17.42 et seq. Compare the position with Scottish secure tenancies, where express provision is made for the person entitled to inherit to decline the tenancy: see para 18.85.

17.149 *Partner of sole tenant* Where a deceased sole tenant had a spouse or civil partner, or the tenant and another person were 'living together as though they were married',[1] that person may be entitled to inherit.[2] Such a relationship is called a 'qualifying relationship'.

In the case of a bereaved partner who was married to or in a civil partnership with the tenant immediately before the tenant's death, the following requirements must be met:[3]

- the tenant's interest under the tenancy was not inherited by the tenant;[4]
- the tenant told the landlord, in writing, that the let property was being occupied by the bereaved partner as the bereaved partner's only or principal home;[5] and
- the let property was in fact the bereaved partner's only or principal home at the time of the tenant's death.[6]

Where the tenant and the bereaved partner were not married or in a civil partnership, an additional requirement applies. In such a case, the bereaved partner only inherits if, for a continuous period of at least a year immediately before the tenant's death, the partner had the property as his or her only or principal home.[7] For these purposes, no account is taken of any period before the landlord was notified that the partner was living in the property.[8] For example, suppose that the partner moves in during June of one year. The landlord is notified in August, and the tenant dies the following July. Even though the partner has been living in the property for more than a year, the period up to the point at which the landlord is notified does not count. Only the period from notification to the landlord counts, and there is less than a year between that and the tenant's death. Accordingly, the partner does not inherit.

Where these requirements are met, the bereaved partner 'becomes the tenant under the tenancy'.[9]

1 PH(T)(S)A 2016 s 70(1)(a). See also paras 17.33 and 17.50.
2 PH(T)(S)A 2016 s 67(2)(c).
3 PH(T)(S)A 2016 s 67(1)(a).
4 PH(T)(S)A 2016 s 67(2)(a).
5 PH(T)(S)A 2016 s 67(2)(b). As we saw above, at para 17.33, the tenant is required to inform the landlord of anyone over the age of 16 who is living in the property. This obligation cannot be contracted out of in the case of a partner in a qualifying relationship with the tenant (or in the case of the other categories of person potentially entitled to inherit, considered below). On the definition of 'only or principal home', see para 17.13.
6 PH(T)(S)A 2016 s 67(2)(d).

7 PH(T)(S)A 2016 s 67(1)(b), (3).
8 PH(T)(S)A 2016 s 67(4).
9 PH(T)(S)A 2016 s 67(1).

17.150 *Other family members* Where there is no bereaved partner entitled to inherit,[1] another family member may be entitled to succeed to the tenancy.

The definition of a family member is a little complicated. The starting point is the concept of the 'qualifying relative'. This means a parent, grandparent, child, grandchild, brother or sister.[2] For these purposes, a relationship of half blood counts as a relationship of the whole blood.[3] A person's stepchild counts as that person's child,[4] as does anyone whom the person treats as his or her child.[5]

A person is a member of a tenant's family in the following circumstances.

- First, any 'qualifying relative' of the tenant is a member of the tenant's family.[6] Relatives not falling into that category are not members of the tenant's family.[7] For example, an uncle or aunt would not count as a qualifying relative. Nor would, say, a great-grandchild unless, on the facts of the case, the great-grandchild was treated by the tenant as his or her child.
- The second category is concerned with cases where the tenant was in a qualifying relationship with another person immediately before the tenant's death. In such a case, any qualifying relative of the partner counts as a member of the tenant's family.[8] This category is perhaps less important, because it will only be relevant if for some reason the bereaved partner does not qualify to inherit.
- Third, where there is a qualifying relative of the tenant, anyone in a qualifying relationship with that relative also counts as a member of the tenant's family.[9]

Anyone falling into one of these three categories inherits as long as the following conditions are met:[10]

- the deceased tenant was a sole tenant;[11]
- the tenant had not himself or herself inherited the tenancy;[12]
- there is no bereaved partner eligible to inherit;[13]
- the family member is at least 16 years of age at the time of the tenant's death;[14]
- the family member is occupying the property as his or her only or principal home, and has done so for at least the previous 12 months;[15] and
- at least 12 months before the tenant's death, the tenant had informed the landlord in writing that the family member was occupying the property as his or her only or principal home.[16]

497

Where more than one person is entitled to inherit as a family member, each becomes tenant jointly with the others.[17]

1 PH(T)(S)A 2016 s 68(1)(c).
2 PH(T)(S)A 2016 s 70(2).
3 PH(T)(S)A 2016 s 70(3)(a).
4 PH(T)(S)A 2016 s 70(3)(b).
5 PH(T)(S)A 2016 s 70(3)(c).
6 PH(T)(S)A 2016 s 70(1)(b)(i).
7 At least, they are not family members on the basis of that relationship with the tenant. They may conceivably qualify as family members on a different ground.
8 PH(T)(S)A 2016 s 70(1)(b)(ii).
9 PH(T)(S)A 2016 s 70(1)(b)(iii).
10 PH(T)(S)A 2016 s 68(1).
11 PH(T)(S)A 2016 s 68(1)(a).
12 PH(T)(S)A 2016 s 68(1)(b).
13 PH(T)(S)A 2016 s 68(1)(c).
14 PH(T)(S)A 2016 s 68(2)(a).
15 PH(T)(S)A 2016 s 68(2)(b)
16 PH(T)(S)A 2016 s 68(3).
17 PH(T)(S)A 2016 s 68(4).

17.151 *Carers*   The final category of person potentially inheriting the tenancy is resident carers who provide or have provided care for the tenant or a member of the tenant's family.[1] Such a person will inherit in the following circumstances:[2]

• the deceased tenant was a sole tenant;[3]
• the tenant had not himself or herself inherited the tenancy;[4]
• there is no bereaved partner or family member eligible to inherit;[5]
• the resident carer is at least 16 years of age at the time of the tenant's death;[6]
• the resident carer is occupying the property as his or her only or principal home, and has done so for at least the previous 12 months;[7]
• the resident carer had a previous only or principal home which was given up;[8] and
• at least twelve months before the tenant's death, the tenant had informed the landlord in writing that the resident carer was occupying the property as his or her only or principal home.[9]

Where more than one person is entitled to inherit as a resident carer, each becomes tenant jointly with the others.[10]

1 PH(T)(S)A 2016 s 69(5).
2 PH(T)(S)A 2016 s 69(1).
3 PH(T)(S)A 2016 s 69(1)(a).
4 PH(T)(S)A 2016 s 69(1)(b).
5 PH(T)(S)A 2016 s 69(1)(c).
6 PH(T)(S)A 2016 s 69(2)(a).
7 PH(T)(S)A 2016 s 69(2)(b).

8 PH(T)(S)A 2016 s 69(2)(c).
9 PH(T)(S)A 2016 s 69(3).
10 PH(T)(S)A 2016 s 69(4).

PROVISIONS COMMON TO REGULATED, ASSURED AND PRIVATE RESIDENTIAL TENANCIES

Protection from eviction and harassment

17.152 We saw in an earlier chapter[1] that a tenant who is unlawfully evicted may have a claim of damages against the landlord at common law. In the case of dwellinghouses, this common law remedy has been greatly reinforced by the Rent (Scotland) Act 1984 and the Housing (Scotland) Act 1988, making the landlord, or other person responsible for the unlawful eviction, liable under both the criminal and the civil law.

Moreover, these provisions apply very widely, to all residential occupiers. This means that they apply to all leases of dwellinghouses, not only those under regulated, assured or private residential tenancies. They also probably apply to residential occupation of property that is not strictly a dwellinghouse, eg a caravan or houseboat, and to forms of tenure other than a lease, eg where the property is occupied under a licence.[2]

1 See para 10.37.
2 See para 2.51 et seq.

17.153 *Criminal liability: eviction*[1] The Rent (Scotland) Act 1984 makes unlawful eviction or harassment of a residential occupier a criminal offence. There has been unlawful eviction if the landlord, or anyone else, 'unlawfully deprives the residential occupier of any premises of his occupation of the premises or any part thereof or attempts to do so'.[2]

The deprivation does not need to be permanent provided that it has the character of an eviction, but deprivation for one day and night only has been held not to be enough.[3] It is a defence if the person accused 'believed, and had reasonable cause to believe, that the residential occupier had ceased to reside in the premises'.[4]

1 R(S)A 1984 s 22 (as amended).
2 R(S)A 1984 s 22(1).
3 *R v Yuthiwattana* (1985) 80 Cr App R 55, (1984) 16 HLR 49, CA. But see also *Schon v Camden London Borough Council* (1986) 279 EG 859, (1987) 53 P&CR 361.
4 R(S)A 1984 s 22(1).

17.154   *Criminal liability: harassment*   There would appear to be, rather confusingly, two criminal offences of harassment. The first is where 'any person', ie not just the landlord, 'with intent to cause' the residential occupier to move out of the property, or relinquish any of his or her rights in connection with it, 'does acts likely to interfere with the peace or comfort of the residential occupier or members of his household, or persistently withdraws or withholds services reasonably required for the occupation of the premises as a residence'.[1]

The second offence, added by the Housing (Scotland) Act 1988,[2] is largely identical in wording, except in three significant respects:

(1)   It applies more narrowly, to the landlord and the landlord's agent only;

(2)   The words 'with intent to cause' have been dropped. Instead it is sufficient that the person causing the harassment 'knows or has reasonable cause to believe that that conduct is likely to cause' the occupier to move out or relinquish any of his or her rights. This will presumably be easier to prove, as it substitutes a more objective test for the subjective one of 'intent'; and

(3)   There has been added a defence if the person causing the harassment can prove 'that he had reasonable grounds for doing the acts or withdrawing or withholding the services in question.'

The second offence reads as if it was intended as a substitute for the first one, and it is not clear what has been gained by having the two left lying side by side. If it is an error, it is one that has been repeated by the English legislation.[3]

It has been held in England that an action or actions by the landlord can constitute a criminal offence of harassment even if the landlord is not in breach of contract or otherwise liable under the civil law.[4]

1 R(S)A 1984 s 22(2) (as amended).
2 H(S)A 1988 s 38, inserting new subsections (2A) and (2B) into R(S)A 1984 s 22.
3 Or perhaps the other way round. See the Housing Act 1988 s 29.
4 *R v Burke* [1991] 1 AC 135.

17.155   *Penalties*   A conviction for either unlawful eviction or harassment can result in a fine or imprisonment for a maximum of two years.[1]

1 R(S)A 1984 s 22(3).

17.156   *Civil liability*   Under the Housing (Scotland) Act 1988, a landlord who harasses a tenant or other residential occupier or unlawfully deprives the residential occupier of occupation may be liable in damages.[1] 'Harassment' here has a similar meaning to that applying to the second of the two criminal offences considered above.[2] As we have seen, 'occupation' is not interrupted by temporary absences.[3] For example, in *Anderson v Cluny Investment Service Ltd*,[4] the tenant was held still to be the residential occupier even though she had temporarily left so that renovation work could be carried out. However, she ceased to be a residential occupier when the landlord attempted to insist on her agreeing a new lease, on terms less advantageous to the tenant, as a condition of her moving back into the property. The landlord therefore became liable at this point for unlawfully depriving her of occupation.

Any action to enforce this liability must be brought in the First-Tier Tribunal, unless it arises from a Scottish secure tenancy or Scottish short secure tenancy.[5] The liability is stated to be a delictual one, and is in addition to any other liability arising under delict or contract or otherwise,[6] An interesting feature of this additional provision is that the measure of damages is not the usual one in delict, ie the loss suffered by the claimant. Instead it is the difference in value between the landlord's interest subject to the sitting tenancy, and the value of that interest with vacant possession.[7]

In other words, the landlord stands to forfeit any gain that evicting the tenant is likely to bring. Without this provision, it might in some cases have been in the landlord's interest to unlawfully evict a tenant if damages based on the tenant's loss were likely to be less than what the landlord would gain by obtaining vacant possession.

Liability may be avoided if the residential occupier is reinstated;[8] however, this would appear to apply only to the additional liability imposed by subsection (3) and would not preclude any common law liability arising from delict or breach of contract.[9]

Damages may be mitigated by the court or Tribunal:

(a) as a result of the conduct, prior to the eviction or harassment, of the residential occupier or anyone living with the occupier; or

(b) in certain circumstances where reinstatement has been offered by the landlord.[10]

1 H(S)A 1988 s 36(1) and (2) (as amended); see also *Fairweather v Ghafoor* [2001] CLY4164; *Scott v Thomson* 2003 SLT 99, 2002 Hous LR 114.
2 See para 17.154.
3 See para 17.13.
4 2004 SLT (Sh Ct) 37.
5 H(S)A 1988 s 36(4A) (inserted by Housing (Scotland) Act 2014 Sch 1).
6 H(S)A 1988 s 36(4).
7 H(S)A 1988 s 37(1).
8 H(S)A 1988 s 36(6) (as amended). On the meaning of reinstatement, see the English case *Tagro v Cafane* [1991] 1 WLR 378.
9 H(S)A 1988 s 36(4)(b).
10 H(S)A 1988 s 36(6B) (added by the Housing Act 1988 Sch 17).

17.157   *Where the tenant's right to occupy has ended*[1]   The above provisions apply to situations where the tenant or other occupier still has the right to occupy the property, ie where the lease has not yet ended, or where he or she has the right to extended security of tenure as a regulated or assured tenant. However, the Rent (Scotland) Act 1984 also makes provision for cases where the tenancy or right to use the property has come to an end and the occupant has not moved out. In such cases, the owner of the property must obtain an order from the First-Tier Tribunal in order to recover possession.[2]

This reinforces the common law principle applicable to all leases.[3] The provision does not apply to lodgers, temporary occupants without title, occupiers under holiday lets, occupants of hostels owned by local authorities etc, asylum seekers or displaced persons.[4] It does, however, apply to a person occupying under a gratuitous licence.[5]

Rather curiously, these provisions do not specify the consequences incurred by a landlord for evicting without an order from the Tribunal in such circumstances. It might be thought that the landlord would be liable to the civil and criminal sanctions for unlawful eviction referred to above, but the definition of a residential occupier whose eviction can give rise to such liability seems to be confined to those who have a contractual or other legal right to occupy, or a statutory right to security of tenure under a regulated or assured tenancy.[6] Presumably, however, these provisions have the effect of reinforcing the civil right at common law to claim damages for unlawful eviction.[7]

1 See also above, para 17.64, on wrongful termination orders.
2 R(S)A 1984 s 23 (as amended by H(S)A 1988, s 39). This amendment extends the protection to occupants other than tenants, but fails to make it clear whether it also extends it to assured as well as regulated tenants; fortunately, the common law will fill any gap.
3 See para 10.37.
4 R(S)A 1984 s 23A (added H(S)A 1988 s 40 and as amended).
5 *Reid v Redfern* 2019 GWD 15-239. On licences, see paras 2.51 et seq.
6 R(S)A 1984 s 22(5); H(S)A 1988 s 36(8)(a).
7 See para 10.37.

Prohibition of premiums[1]

17.158   These provisions, in relation to regulated, assured and private residential tenancies, make it an offence for the landlord or anyone else to require the payment of any premium or the making of any loan (whether secured or unsecured) as a condition of the grant, renewal or continuance of a tenancy. A premium is defined as 'any fine, sum or pecuniary consideration, other than the rent, and includes any service or administration fee or charge'.[2] Payments to obtain an assignation (which could be made either to the landlord or the existing tenant) are also an offence.

In each case the person receiving the premium is liable to a fine and to repay the sum involved. The sale of furniture to an incoming tenant at an excessive price may be considered a premium.

It is also illegal for a landlord to charge rent for a rental period that has not yet started, or to demand an advance payment of rent for a period of more than six months.[3] Breach of this will render the landlord liable to a fine and the rent for the prohibited period will be irrecoverable from the tenant.[4]

It has been specifically provided that any payments towards energy efficiency improvements under a green deal plan within the meaning of chapter 1 of the Energy Act 2011 are not to be treated as a premium for the purpose of these provisions.[5] Similarly, a deposit paid by the tenant and returnable at the end of the tenancy is not a premium, as long as it does not exceed two months' rent.[6]

1 R(S)A 1984 Pt VIII; H(S)A 1988 s 27; PH(T)(S)A 2016 s 20.
2 R(S)A 1984 ss 90(1) and 115(1) (as substituted by the Private Rented Housing (Scotland) Act 2011 s 32(3) and (4)).
3 R(S)A 1984 s 89. See also H(S)A 1988 s 27.
4 R(S)A 1984 s 89(2) and (3).
5 The Rent (Scotland) Act 1984 (Premiums) Regulations 2012, SSI No 329 para 2.
6 R(S)A 1984 s 90(3).

Repairs

17.159 We saw in Chapter 3 that a landlord has an obligation at common law to provide and maintain the leased subjects in a tenantable or habitable condition.[1] Although this is contracted out of in most commercial leases, in relation to residential tenancies it is substantially reinforced by statute. This is covered in detail in a separate chapter, where we will also consider the possible application of the Human Rights Act 1998.[2]

1 See para 3.26 et seq.
2 See Ch 19. See also Ch 21 as to whether an attempt to exclude the landlord's liability could be considered an unfair lease term.

Chapter 18

Social tenancies: Scottish secure tenancies

INTRODUCTION

Public sector and other social tenancies

18.1   We saw in Chapter 17 that the tenants of most privately let dwellinghouses have enjoyed protection of one kind or another since the early years of the 20th century. At the beginning of that period, the private let was still the most common type of tenure for householders. After the 1939–1945 war, however, the emphasis was increasingly on the public sector, mainly in the form of council lets, and in recent years it has shifted again to other forms of social tenancy with the growth and increasing importance of the housing association movement. More recently, housing stock transfers from local authorities to housing associations have shifted this balance further.

Initially, tenants in this sector did not have the legal protection from eviction enjoyed by their private sector counterparts. This was changed by the Tenants' Rights Etc (Scotland) Act 1980 which created the secure tenancy, giving public sector tenants a statutory right to security of tenure at the end of their leases, along with a number of other rights, including the right to buy. These provisions were later consolidated in the Housing (Scotland) Act 1987. These did not initially apply to all social tenancies, many of which were assured tenancies (including housing association tenancies entered into after 2 January 1989). However, on 30 September 2002, secure tenancies and housing association assured tenancies were converted to a new form of social tenancy, the Scottish secure tenancy.[1]

1 Housing (Scotland) Act 2001 s 11(1); Housing (Scotland) Act 2001 (Commencement No 5, Transitional Provisions and Savings) Order 2002 SSI No 321.

18.2   As mentioned above, in 1980 a right to buy the property they tenanted was introduced for local authority and other public sector tenants.[1] These sales were subject to a generous level of discount, which increased on a sliding scale according to the tenant's period of occupation.

The Housing (Scotland) Act 2001 extended the right to buy to social tenancies generally, but at the same time modified the provisions by substantially reducing the level of discount in the case of new tenancies. The Scottish Government, in order to preserve the social housing stock, subsequently decided to phase out the right to buy entirely, with the result that the Housing (Scotland) Act 2010 abolished the right in the case of new tenancies which commenced since that Act came into force.[2] The right to buy has now also been abolished for existing tenants, with effect from 1 August 2016,[3] except where a valid application to exercise the right to buy was made before that date.[4] Where no such application was made, the right to buy is extinguished and cannot be revived, including in the case where a valid application was made and subsequently withdrawn.[5]

1 Under the Tenants' Rights etc (Scotland) Act 1980. These tenants were known as 'secure tenants'. This Act and its various amendments were consolidated in the Housing (Scotland) Act 1987.
2 H(S)A 2010 Pt 14.
3 H(S)A 2016 s 1.
4 See eg *Taylor v North Lanarkshire Council* 2019 GWD 18-290.
5 *Davidson v Bridgewater Housing Association Ltd* 2019 GWD 34-550.

The Housing (Scotland) Act 2001

18.3   The Housing (Scotland) Act 2001 made wide-ranging changes to housing law in Scotland. Among other things, it provided a revised strategy for homelessness (including the regulation of hostel accommodation),[1] measures to tackle fuel poverty,[2] and a procedure for housing stock transfers.[3] In this chapter we will confine ourselves to consideration of the Scottish secure tenancy, the new single social tenancy introduced by the Act, which replaced the secure tenancy under the Housing (Scotland) Act 1987.

1 Housing (Scotland) Act 2001 Part 1.
2 H(S)A 2001 Part 5, as amended by the Fuel Poverty (Targets, Definitions and Strategy) (Scotland) Act 2019.
3 H(S)A 2001 s 76 and Sch 9.

Single social tenancy

18.4   All social tenants, including those of local authorities, housing associations, and other public sector and social landlords have a Scottish secure tenancy. This is a revised version of the earlier secure tenancy and includes all social tenancies. This unification of tenants' rights is further enhanced by a model tenancy agreement provided by the

Scottish Ministers.[1] This means, among other things, that housing stock transfers from local authorities to housing associations or other social landlords, or other changes of landlord, should not result in a weakening of tenants' rights.[2]

The main change is in the status of housing association tenants. Originally, they had secure tenancies, but those whose tenancies began on or after 2 January 1988 (when the Housing (Scotland) Act 1988 came into force) were assured tenants, on an equal footing with tenants in the private sector. Now they are back under the general umbrella of the Scottish secure tenancy.

1 Scottish Government 'Model Scottish Secure Tenancy Agreement' (revised version 2019) available at: www.gov.scot/publications/model-scottish-secure-tenancy-agreement-2019/#:~:text=1%20A%20Model%20Scottish%20Secure%20 Tenancy%20Agreement%20%5B1%5D,tenancies%20created%20on%20or%20 after%201%20May%202019.
2 See also Ch 21 (Unfair Lease Terms).

Registered social landlords

18.5   Registered social landlords are those landlords who are entitled to grant a Scottish secure tenancy, other than local authorities and water and sewerage authorities. They are non-profit organisations (of all types, but particularly housing associations) that are registered with the Scottish Housing Regulator. The Scottish Housing Regulator is an independent regulator with a large number of functions relating to housing, one of which is to keep a register of, and to monitor the performance of, social landlords.

The powers and functions of the Scottish Housing Regulator and the details of their legal relationship with registered social landlords are set out at length in the Housing (Scotland) Act 2010.[1]

1 H(S)A 2010 Parts 1–12.

18.6   *Change of landlord*   The functions of the Scottish Housing Regulator that relate to registered social landlords include overseeing the special procedures for any disposals of land and restructuring that lead to a change of landlord of secure tenants.[1] It also oversees the exercise of the right that approved persons have to acquire eligible houses from local authorities,eg houses not required for people with special needs, or not required by an islands council for people employed in education. The latter replaces the provisions in Part III of the Housing (Scotland) Act 1988 (the so called 'Tenant's Choice' provisions).[2]

It should be noted that Scottish secure tenants occupying any such properties will not lose that status as a result of the change of landlord.[3]

1 H(S)A 2010 Part 10 (amended by the Housing (Amendment) (Scotland) Act 2018.
2 H(S)A 1988 ss 56–64 (now repealed by H(S)A 2010 Sch 2 para 4(3)).
3 H(S)A 2001 s 11(8); see also para 18.21.

HUMAN RIGHTS ACT 1998

Application of the 1998 Act

18.7   *'Core' and 'Hybrid' authorities*   We saw in Chapter 1 that, where a landlord is a public authority, it is unlawful for it to act in a way that is incompatible with the European Convention on Human Rights.[1] Although the definition of public authority in the Human Rights Act does not mention local authorities, it is settled law that they *are* public authorities, and also that they are 'core' authorities, *all* of whose acts have to comply with the Convention.[2] Other social landlords may be 'hybrid' authorities, which will only be considered to be public authorities when carrying out acts of a public rather than a private nature.[3]

This means that the Human Rights Act will more often than not have a direct (or 'vertical') effect upon Scottish secure tenancies and the actions of Scottish secure landlords, giving tenants direct recourse against their landlords for breach of a convention right.[4]

Where the landlord is a local authority, therefore, the Act will always have a vertical effect. However, in relation to other types of social landlord the situation is more complex. Different types of body may qualify as registered social landlords with the right to grant Scottish secure tenancies. Not all of them can be considered hybrid authorities and, even when they are, not all of their actions in pursuit of their housing function will necessarily qualify as public acts where the Act will have a vertical effect. Some guidance can be obtained from the case law.

1 HRA 1998 s 6(1); see also para 1.29 et seq.
2 See eg Reed & Murdoch *A Guide to Human Rights Law in Scotland* (4th edn 2017) para 1.69.
3 HRA 1998 s 6(3)(b) and (5).
4 See para 1.30.

18.8   *The* Weaver *case*   In *R (on the application of Weaver) v London and Quadrant Housing Trust*[1] the tenant of a housing trust, which was a registered social landlord, sought judicial review of the landlord's eviction action. It was conceded that the trust was a 'hybrid' authority, some of whose functions were of a public nature. The main issue was whether the action to evict the tenant was of a public or of a private nature, as only in the former case would the Human Rights Act have a direct or vertical effect, allowing the tenant to raise the action of judicial review.

It was held that the housing trust's function of allocating social housing was a public act, and that this extended to an action of eviction for the purpose of ending a tenancy resulting from such an allocation. It was held that determining whether the act of a hybrid authority was of a public or of a private nature was a matter of fact in each case that depended upon a number of factors. In the present case several factors cumulatively established a sufficient public flavour to make the provision of social housing by the landlord a public function, including that the landlord:

(a) received significant capital payments from public funds to provide subsidised social housing to meet the needs of the poor, which was a publicly desirable objective and could properly be described as a governmental function;

(b) worked in close harmony with local government and helped to fulfil the latter's statutory obligations, in particular through allocation agreements which severely circumscribed the landlord's freedom to allocate properties; and

(c) was itself subject to regulations designed to further the objectives of government policy in housing the poor.[2] However, although the action of eviction in this case was a public act, this would not necessarily always be the case, for example in cases where the house had been let at a market rent.

Weaver therefore stopped short of saying (a) that all registered social landlords are hybrid authorities; or (b) that all acts by hybrid authorities in pursuance of their housing functions will necessarily be public acts. However, it seems likely that many registered social landlords will qualify as hybrid authorities (including most housing associations), and an eviction action, the most common situation where the Human Rights Act has been invoked, will generally be considered to be a public act when carried out by a hybrid authority. But much will depend upon the facts of each individual case.

1 *(sub nom London & Quadrant Housing Trust v Weaver)* [2010] 1 WLR 363, [2009] 4 All ER 865.

2 *R (on the application of Weaver) v London and Quadrant Housing Trust (sub nom London & Quadrant Housing Trust v Weaver)* at 379–80 per Elias LJ (drawing upon *Aston Cantlow and Wilmcote with Billesley Parochial Church Council v Wallbank* [2004] 1 AC 546 at para 12 per Lord Nicholls).

18.9 In contrast to *Weaver* it was held in *YL v Birmingham City Council*[1] that a privately-owned care home was not performing functions of a public nature in providing care and accommodation for residents placed with it by a local authority. *YL v Birmingham City Council* was followed in the Inner House decision in *Ali v Serco Ltd*.[2] In *Ali v Serco*, the defenders were a private company, which housed asylum seekers under an arrangement with the Home Secretary. The pursuer was a failed asylum seeker, and the defender proposed to remove her from the property that had been provided to her under this arrangement. The court held that the defenders could not be classified as a public body. The court drew a fundamental distinction:

> 'between the entity that is charged with the public law responsibility ... and the private operator who contracts with that entity to provide the service ...The fact that those services are ultimately intended to fulfil a public law responsibility is immaterial; they are still provided on a private law basis'.[3]

It should also be noted that the ground of eviction in *Weaver* was a mandatory ground, where the court had no discretion to refuse the landlord possession of the property.[4] This meant that the tenant's only way of challenging the eviction was by a separate action of judicial review in which the Human Rights Act provided the only ground of action.[5] And this in turn was only possible because the eviction qualified as a public act, giving the Human Rights Act a direct or vertical effect.

However, we will see later that a number of eviction grounds are discretionary and that, although the ground may be established, the sheriff is still entitled to refuse the landlord possession if this is not considered reasonable.[6] In such cases, the Act may have an indirect (or 'horizontal') effect, since the court, being itself a public authority, is obliged to exercise any discretionary powers in a way that is compatible with the Human Rights Act. This means that it is competent to claim a human rights breach as a defence to an eviction action in these cases.[7]

1 *(sub nom Y (on the application of Johnson) v Havering LBC)* [2008] 1 AC 95, [2007] 3 WLR 112.
2 [2019] CSIH 54, 2020 SC 182.
3 [2019] CSIH 54, 2020 SC 182 para [54].
4 For the difference between mandatory (management) and discretionary (conduct) grounds of eviction, see para 18.52 et seq.
5 This is no longer quite true, as a result of the Supreme Court decision in *Manchester City Council v Pinnock* [2010] 3 WLR 1441, [2011] 1 All ER 285 – see para 18.13 et seq.
6 See para 18.53 et seq.
7 See para 1.31.

Relevant convention rights

18.10   The most obviously relevant Convention rights in this context are the right to a fair hearing (Article 6), the right to respect for private and family life (Article 8) and protection of property (Protocol 1, Article 1). In fact, most of the case law so far has related to evictions where there is alleged to be a breach of Article 8.[1] Article 8 may also apply where a landlord has failed to maintain a house in a habitable condition,[2] and Article 6 if the alleged breach of any Convention right has not been given a fair hearing or has been subject to procedural unfairness.

1 See para 18.12 et seq.
2 See para 19.4 et seq.

18.11 *Right to life* We saw in Chapter 1 that everyone's right to life is protected under Article 2 of the Convention, and that the relevance of this right in a landlord and tenant context was highlighted by the House of Lords judgment in *Mitchell v Glasgow City Council*,[1] where an anti-social council tenant murdered a neighbouring tenant.[2]

There was a long history of anti-social behaviour by the tenant Drummond and of bad feeling between the neighbours, and Drummond had threatened to kill Mitchell on several occasions, though he had never actually been physically violent towards him. Shortly after a meeting with the council at which they announced their intention of evicting Drummond because of his anti-social behaviour, Drummond, who blamed Mitchell, assaulted him with an iron bar and killed him.

Mitchell's family alleged that, by failing to warn him of the immediate danger, they were in breach (a) of a delictual duty of care towards him at common law; and (b) as the council was a public authority, of his right to life under Article 2. The House of Lords held that, in these circumstances, the council did not have a common law responsibility to Mitchell for the actions of a third party by failing to warn the victim of the danger.[3]

In relation to the alleged breach of Article 2, it was held that a positive duty on the part of social landlords to safeguard their tenants' right to life would only arise in very limited circumstances, which did not apply here. The police force was the public authority which had an Article 2 duty to protect the lives of members of the public from criminal violence, and it was not appropriate that the council should have a duty to duplicate this function. However, Lord Rodger of Earlsferry indicated that Article 2 liability by social landlords might arise in different circumstances within the context of the landlord and tenant relationship:

> '[O]f course, if the council had allowed their housing stock to fall into disrepair, so that tenants were at risk of suffering life-threatening injuries or of becoming seriously ill, the council could have been in breach of art 2. But nothing like that is alleged here.'[4]

1 [2009] 1 AC 874, 2009 SC (HL) 21.
2 See para 1.37.

3 For a discussion of the delictual position from a Scottish viewpoint see Peter Webster 'Mitchell v Glasgow City Council: A foreseeable result' 2009 Edin LR 477; for some interesting counter-arguments about the possibility of a delictual claim in such circumstances see Faisel Sadiq and Justin Bates 'A landlord's liability for the acts of its tenants: Mitchell v Glasgow City Council revisited' 2009 JHL 48.

4 *Mitchell v Glasgow City Council* [2009] 1 AC 874, at 902 per Lord Rodger of Earlsferry; see also para 19.10.

Human rights and eviction actions[1]

18.12   Before granting an order for recovery of possession, the court may have to consider whether there is a potential breach of the European Convention on Human Rights. For example, it will be competent for it to consider whether eviction would be in breach of the tenant's right to respect for private and family life (Article 8) (which accounts for most of the case law on this subject), or the tenant's right of property in the house (Protocol 1, Article 1), or (in conjunction with either of these) the tenant's Article 6 right to a fair hearing.

The decision must be proportionate, and other considerations (such as the Convention rights of other tenants in the area) may outweigh these rights of the tenant; for this reason, the eviction of an anti-social tenant may be justified in terms of the Convention.

1 See also paras 18.43 et seq.

18.13   *Manchester City Council v Pinnock*   It is probably fair to say that, for many years immediately following the passing of the Human Rights Act 1998, it had little influence on eviction proceedings by public authorities. Although a human rights defence was raised in a number of cases, the fact that Article 8 is a qualified right meant that the other considerations mentioned above tended to prevail, with the result that very few of these cases were successful.[1] The view often emerging was that the Convention rights of tenants, such as the need for proportionality and a fair hearing, had been catered for by the relevant legislation.[2]

However, the position changed (in theory at least) as a result of the Supreme Court judgement in *Manchester City Council v Pinnock*[3] in which the council sought to evict one of their tenants because of the anti-social behaviour of his partner and their children. Although Mr Pinnock was originally a secure tenant, the council had previously succeeded, on the same grounds, in having his tenancy converted to a demoted tenancy. (Under the English legislation, anti-social tenants, as an alternative to eviction, may be transferred to a demoted tenancy, under which their security of tenure is much reduced.)

The county court, whose judgment was affirmed by the Court of Appeal, held that it had no jurisdiction to consider Human Rights issues, a view dictated by the earlier authority in the UK courts and in Europe. However, the Supreme Court held that in eviction cases the court of first instance did in fact have the jurisdiction to consider the human rights issues and assess the proportionality of making a possession order. This was more appropriate than proceeding by way of judicial review, because the court of first instance was able to consider and resolve any disputes of fact. It was also held that Mr Pinnock's Article 8 rights had not been violated and the eviction was confirmed.

1 For a very useful review of the case law, in both the UK courts and in Europe, leading up to the decision in *Pinnock* see Adrian Stalker 'Article 8 & Evictions by Public Authorities: the battle rages on …' (2009) SCOLAG 145.
2 For example, the Housing (Scotland) Act 2001, following in the wake of the Human Rights Act, was believed by the Scottish Executive at the time of its passing to be Convention compliant – see para 18.20.
3 [2010] 3 WLR 1441, [2011] 1 All ER 285.

18.14 *Pinnock* was a case where the tenant did not have a secure tenancy, and the same has been true of the cases that followed in its wake. For example, they included cases where the tenancy was an introductory tenancy (another English variant)[1] or where the tenant was effectively trespassing, such as in the case of Roma or other travelling communities.

It might have been thought, therefore, that the same principles did not apply to secure tenants, whose article 8 rights and the need for proportionality are arguably accommodated by the terms of the relevant legislation. However, it is clear from *Pinnock* that its principles are of general application, and extend to secure tenancies, including Scottish secure tenancies. As the European Court had already stated:

'The loss of one's home is the most extreme form of interference with the right for respect for the home. Any person at risk of an interference of this magnitude should in principle be able to have the proportionality of the measure determined by an independent tribunal in the light of the relevant principles under [Article 8], notwithstanding that, under domestic law, his right of occupation has come to an end.'[2]

1 The same considerations apply north of the border to short Scottish secure tenancies – see *South Lanarkshire Council v McKenna* 2013 SLT 22, 2012 GWD 34-693 and paras 18.17 and 18.104 et seq.
2 *McCann v United Kingdom* (2008) 47 EHRR 913, at para 50, quoted by Lord Neuburger of Abbotsbury in *Manchester City Council v Pinnock* [2010] 3 WLR 1441 at 1452.

18.15 Following the lead of the European court, the Supreme Court in *Pinnock* reached the following conclusions:

'(a) Any person at risk of being dispossessed of his home at the suit of a local authority should in principle have the right to raise the question of the proportionality of the measure, and to have it determined by an independent tribunal in the light of article 8, even if his right of occupation under domestic law has come to an end ...

(b) A judicial procedure which is limited to addressing the proportionality of the measure through the medium of traditional judicial review (ie, one which does not permit the court to make its own assessment of the facts in an appropriate case) is inadequate as it is not appropriate for resolving sensitive factual issues ...

(c) Where the measure includes proceedings involving more than one stage, it is the proceedings as a whole which must be considered in order to see if article 8 has been complied with ...

(d) If the court considers that it would be disproportionate to evict a person from his home notwithstanding the fact that he has no domestic right to remain there, it would be unlawful to evict him so long as [that remains the case].'

However:

'Although it cannot be described as a point of principle, it seems that the European Court has also franked the view that it will only be in exceptional cases that article 8 proportionality would even arguably give a right to continued possession where the applicant has no right under domestic law to remain.'[1]

1 *Manchester City Council v Pinnock* [2010] 3 WLR 1441 at 1454 per Lord Neuburger of Abbotsbury.

18.16 The court went on to explain and qualify this statement by acknowledging that 'exceptionality is an outcome and not a guide'. What the court seemed to be saying (though not exactly in these terms) is that exceptionality is not a principle to be applied in deciding whether an eviction is proportionate, but a prediction that successful article 8 challenges in this context are likely to be rare. Where a local authority has raised eviction proceedings, there are many considerations that may support a decision that their action is proportionate, such as the need for the authority to comply with its duties in relation to the distribution and management of its housing stock (including the fair allocation of its housing), the redevelopment of the site, the refurbishing of sub-standard accommodation, or the need to remove a source of nuisance to neighbours. In the vast majority of cases, therefore, the authority's action will be proportionate.[1]

1 *Manchester City Council v Pinnock* [2010] 3 WLR 1441 at 1456 and 1457 per Lord Neuburger of Abbotsbury.

18.17 *Subsequent cases* The Supreme Court reaffirmed its judgment in *Pinnock* and clarified a number of issues in *Hounslow London Borough Council v Powell*[1]

In particular:

'The court will only have to consider whether the making of a possession order is proportionate if the issue has been raised by the occupier and it has crossed the high threshold of being seriously arguable.' [2] And:

> '[T]here will be no need, in the overwhelming majority of cases, for the local authority to explain and justify its reasons for seeking a possession order. It will be enough that the authority is entitled to possession because the statutory pre-requisites have been satisfied and that it is to be assumed to be acting in accordance with its duties in the distribution and management of its housing stock. The court need be concerned only with the occupier's personal circumstances and any factual objections she may raise and (in the light only of what view it takes of them) with the question whether making the order for possession would be lawful and proportionate. If it decides to entertain the point because it is seriously arguable, it must give a reasoned decision as to whether or not a fair balance would be struck by making the order that is being sought by the local authority.'[3]

In *Corby BC v Scott*[4] the Court of Appeal held that it was desirable for a judge to consider at an early stage in possession proceedings whether a tenant's case on proportionality was arguable. If it was a case that could not succeed, it should not be allowed to take up further court time and to delay the landlord's right to possession.

In the Scottish case of *South Lanarkshire Council v McKenna*[5] the Court of Session, after a thorough review of the European and English cases, including *Pinnock* and *Powell*, held that section 36 of the Housing (Scotland) Act 2001 (relating to possession actions in cases of short Scottish secure tenancies) is compatible with article 8 of the European Convention. Although the statutory form of notice did not require reasons to be given for the eviction,[6] the section should be read in conjunction with section 6(1) of the Human Rights Act 1998. This meant that the authority would have to give reasons for the eviction when, but only when, their decision was being challenged on the ground of proportionality, which the tenant was entitled to raise as a defence to the action.

In the case of Scottish secure tenancies, where the eviction ground must be stated in the Notice of Proceedings for Possession[7] the authority will only be obliged to give reasons beyond what is said in the notice when the tenant is challenging the action on the basis of proportionality, and then only if their decision is based on reasons which actually go beyond those stated in the notice.[8]

1 [2011] 2 AC 186, [2011] 2 WLR 287.
2 *Hounslow London Borough Council v Powell* [2011] 2 AC 186 at 205 per Lord Hope of Craighead.
3 *Hounslow London Borough Council v Powell* [2011] 2 AC 186 at 206 and 207 per Lord Hope of Craighead.
4 [2012] HLR 23, [2012] 21 EG 100.
5 2013 SLT 22, 2012 GWD 34-693. For another Scottish application of the principles in *Pinnock* see *Glasgow City Council v Jaconelli* 2011 Hous LR 17.
6 This was the position at the time the case was decided. See now para 18.107.
7 See para 18.47.
8 *South Lanarkshire Council v McKenna* 2013 SLT 22 at 27.

18.18   It is clear from *Pinnock* and subsequent decisions that its principles will apply, not only to local authorities, but also to other public authorities which are seeking to evict a social tenant.[1] It is also evident that, in principle, it will apply to Scottish secure tenants as well as those with no security of tenure.

However, the Supreme Court in *Pinnock* also made it clear that its judgement only applied to possession proceedings brought by public authorities, and they specifically reserved their position regarding its application to eviction proceedings brought by private landlords.[2]

1 *Manchester City Council v Pinnock* [2010] 3 WLR 1441 at 1444 per Lord Neuburger of Abbotsbury.
2 *Manchester City Council v Pinnock* [2010] 3 WLR 1441 at 1456 per Lord Neuburger of Abbotsbury. See also para 17.8 et seq, particularly para 17.10.

18.19   It is difficult to escape the conclusion that an enormous amount of time has been spent at the highest judicial levels in both Europe and the UK in order to reach a conclusion that, in practical terms, will make little difference to the situation as it was before. In other words, it will remain very difficult for a human rights defence to an eviction action to succeed. However, at the time of writing, this area of law is still developing, so this conclusion may prove to be premature.

Statement of compatibility

18.20   When introducing the Bill that would become the Housing (Scotland) Act 2001, the Scottish Executive stated the opinion that its provisions were compatible with the European Convention on Human Rights.[1]

1 Housing (Scotland) Bill Policy Memorandum, December 2000, para 101 (available at: www.parliament.scot). See also para 18.17 in relation to possession proceedings in the case of short Scottish secure tenancies.

SCOTTISH SECURE TENANCIES[1]

Categories of landlord[2]

18.21   For a tenancy to be a Scottish secure tenancy, the landlord must be one of the following types of body:

(1)   a local authority;
(2)   a registered social landlord (including a co-operative housing association);[3]or
(3)   Scottish Water.

In the case of a local authority the right will also apply where the landlord is not the council itself, but an associated body, such as a joint board or joint committee of two or more local authorities or the common good of a local authority, or any trust under the control of a local authority.[4] Where the landlord is a co-operative housing association, it is an implied term of the tenancy that the tenant is and continues to be a member of the association.[5]

The above criteria apply at the beginning of the tenancy, but the tenancy will continue to be a Scottish secure tenancy even if the situation subsequently changes, eg if the landlord's interest passes to a person or body not falling within one of the above categories.[6]

1 H(S)A 2001 Part 2 ch 1.
2 H(S)A 2001 s 11(1); The Housing (Scotland) Act 2001 (Scottish Secure Tenancy etc.) Order 2002, SSI No 318, art 3 and schedule (as amended).
3 See para 18.5.
4 H(S)A 2001 s 11(3).
5 H(S)A 2001 s 11(1)(d), (7).
6 H(S)A 2001 s 11(8).

18.22   Provided that they have met the other criteria specified below, all tenancies from the above landlords entered on or after 30 September 2002 are Scottish secure tenancies. Former secure tenancies (under the Housing (Scotland) Act 1987) or assured tenancies under these landlords were converted to Scottish secure tenancies on that date.

The secure tenancies converted are mainly (a) all existing local authority tenancies; and (b) housing association tenancies entered prior

517

to 2 January 1989. The assured tenancies that are converted will mainly be housing association tenancies entered on or after 2 January 1989.[1]

No short assured tenancies became Scottish secure tenancies.

1 See para 18.1.

Other criteria[1]

18.23 For a tenancy to be a Scottish secure tenancy it is also necessary that (i) the house is let as a separate dwelling; and (ii) the tenant is an individual, ie rather than a limited company or other corporate body and the house is his or her only or principal home. It is an implied term of the tenancy that the house continues to be the tenant's only or principal home.[2]

1 H(S)A 2001 s 11(1).
2 H(S)A 2001 s 11(1)(c), (7); see also the case authority quoted in relation to the same criteria as they relate to private sector tenancies – see para 17.11 et seq.

Definition of house

18.24 The Housing (Scotland) Act 2001[1] defines 'house' as including:

(a) any part of a building, being a part which is occupied or intended to be occupied as a separate dwelling, and in particular includes a flat,[2] and

(b) any yard, garden, outhouses and pertinents belonging to the house or usually enjoyed with it.

1 H(S)A 2001 s 111.
2 In relation to the definition of a flat, see *Henderson v West Lothian Council* 2013 SLT (Lands Tr) 13, 2011 Hous LR 85.

Joint tenancies[1]

18.25 A Scottish secure tenant and one or more other individuals may jointly apply in writing to the landlord for the other person or persons to be included with the tenant as joint tenants under the tenancy. For a joint tenant to be accepted, the house must have been his or her only or principal home for at least 12 months prior to the application, and the landlord was notified before that period of 12 months began that the property was that person's only or principal home. Otherwise the landlord must consent to the joint tenancy unless it has reasonable grounds for not doing so.

1 H(S)A 2001 s 11(5)–(6B).

Definition of 'tenancy'[1]

18.26 'Tenancy' means an agreement under which a house is made available for human habitation, and 'lease' and related expressions are to be construed accordingly. A 'tenant' means a person who leases a house from a landlord and whose right in the house derives directly from the landlord, and in the case of a joint tenancy means all the tenants.

1 H(S)A 2001 s 41.

18.27 It should be noted that these definitions are broader in scope than the common law concept of a lease. In particular, there seems to be no absolute requirement for a Scottish secure tenancy to have either a rent or a duration, two of the essential requirements for a lease at common law.[1] In practice, of course, these two elements are likely to be present. However, the definition makes less clear the distinction between a 'tenancy' and an 'occupancy agreement', which is referred to in section 38(1)(a) but not defined.[2]

1 See para 2.22 et seq.
2 See para 18.28.

Appeals[1]

18.28 A person who is unhappy about the legal basis on which accommodation has been provided may appeal to the court. This applies where a person has been granted:

(a) an occupancy agreement instead of a Scottish secure tenancy or a short Scottish secure tenancy;
(b) a tenancy which is not a Scottish secure tenancy or a short Scottish secure tenancy; or
(c) a short Scottish secure tenancy instead of a Scottish secure tenancy.[2]

The court may, 'if it considers that there are good grounds for doing so, order the landlord to let the house to the person under a Scottish secure tenancy or, as the case may be, a short Scottish secure tenancy.'

1 H(S)A 2001 s 38.
2 See para 18.104 et seq.

18.29 While this may be a useful enhancement of tenants' rights, the procedure whereby the court may be ordered to grant a particular type of tenancy seems a little odd. The definition of a Scottish secure tenancy in particular suggests that it will come into being automatically if the statutory criteria are met, rather than because of the type of lease the landlord 'grants', or purports to grant. 'Occupancy agreement' is not defined, and given the broad definition of 'tenancy'[1] it is not clear what is envisaged.

If it refers to hostel accommodation where the occupant does not have exclusive possession, it could not be a Scottish secure tenancy because such accommodation would not normally count as a separate dwelling.[2] If the subjects *are* a separate dwelling, there may well be a Scottish secure tenancy by operation of law, whatever the landlord may choose to call it.

The term 'tenancy which is not a Scottish secure tenancy or a short Scottish secure tenancy', presumably refers to a tenancy falling within one of the excepted categories,[3] and a situation where the tenant disputes whether or not his or her lease falls within the category in question.

There could also be a situation where one of the other criteria has not been met,eg if the house is not the tenant's only or principal home, and this is something the tenant may also dispute. Similarly, a tenant granted a short Scottish secure tenancy may dispute whether one of the qualifying circumstances applies.[4]

It seems a little inappropriate, therefore, that the court should be given the power to 'order' the landlord to let the house on a particular basis. In some cases at least it should be able to declare that a Scottish secure tenancy already exists by operation of law, whatever the landlord may have purported to grant, and its grounds will be *legal* grounds based on interpretation of the Act.

1 See para 18.26 et seq.
2 See, though, para 17.12.
3 See para 18.30 et seq.
4 See para 18.106.

Excepted categories

18.30   Schedule 1 to the Housing (Scotland) Act 2001 specifies eleven categories of let that are not Scottish secure tenancies. In the case of secure tenancies under the Housing (Scotland) Act 1987, the Lands Tribunal for Scotland has expressed the opinion that the underlying intention is to exclude only the minimum number of houses consistent with the particular authority's functions,[1] which means that they should be interpreted fairly narrowly. The numbers below correspond to the paragraph numbers in Sch 1. Numbers 1, 2, 4, 5, 8 and 9 also applied, in similar or identical terms, to secure tenancies, though the others are new.

Much of the case law below concerned whether or not the tenancy in question was a Scottish secure tenancy (or, before that, a secure tenancy) for the purpose of determining whether or not the tenant was eligible to buy the house. As we have seen, this right no longer exists.

Where a tenancy falls into one of the excepted categories, it will either be a common law tenancy, a licence or (if it meets the relevant requirements) a private residential tenancy.[2]

1 *Barron v Borders Regional Council* 1987 SLT (Lands Tr) 36.
2 See Chapter 17.

18.31 (1) *Service tenancies* The tenant (or one of joint tenants) is an employee of the landlord, or of any local authority, and the contract of employment requires the tenant to occupy the house for the better performance of his or her duties, and this may be implied from the circumstances even if not expressly stated in the lease.[1] 'Contract of employment' means a contract of service or of apprenticeship; it may be express or implied, and (if express) may be oral or in writing.[2]

In *Archibald v Lothian Regional Council*[3] a school janitor, whose application to purchase the house was refused because his tenancy fell within the above exception, was served with a notice to quit at the time of his retirement. The notice to quit was effective because the tenancy was not secure, and a further application to purchase the house was again refused, this time because his tenancy had now been terminated.

Tenancies in this category (and in category 9 below), although not Scottish secure tenancies, are nevertheless subject to some of the same statutory provisions. The provisions that apply are those contained in sections 23 to 33, relating to the right to a written lease and information, variation of terms (including rent increases), repairs and improvements, and assignation, subletting and exchanges.[4]

1 See *McTurk v Fife Regional Council* 1990 SLT (Lands Tr) 49; *De Fontenay v Strathclyde Regional Council* 1990 SLT 605; *McKay v Livingstone Development Corporation* 1990 SLT (Lands Tr) 54; *Glasgow City Council v Torrance* 2000 SLT (Sh Ct) 32, 1999 Hous LR 120; *Smith v Dundee City Council* 2001 Hous LR 78; and *McAuslane v Highland Council* 2004 Hous LR 30, 2004 GWD 12-270. However, in *Gilmour v Glasgow District Council* 1989 SLT (Lands Tr) 74; *Little v Borders Regional Council* 1990 SLT (Lands Tr) 2; and *Jack v Strathclyde Regional Council* 1992 SLT (Lands Tr) 29, it was held that the exception did not reply, with the result that the tenancies were secure and the tenant was allowed to purchase the property.
2 H(S)A 2001 Sch 1 para 1(2).
3 1992 SLT (Lands Tr) 75.
4 See paras 18.96 et seq and Ch 19.

18.32 (2) *Police accommodation*[1] This applies to lets by local authorities for the purpose of the Police Service of Scotland. Also excluded are temporary lets to other people pending being required for the Police Service.

It should be noted that the exception in the case of Police Service lets in its present form only applies to lets on or after 11 March 2011 (when the amendment in the Housing (Scotland) Act 2010 came into force). However, prior to that there was a similar but less broad exclusion of lets that were specifically to police constables. Lets not caught up by either of these two exclusions will be Scottish secure tenancies.

1 H(S)A 2001 Sch 1 para 2 (as amended); see also *Robb v Tayside Joint Police Board* 2009 SLT (Lands Tr) 23, 2008 GWD 31-474.

18.33   (3) *Student   lets*   The   landlord   is   the   student's educational institution or another institution of a type specified in regulations.[1] A student who leases directly from any other category of landlord has, of course, the same rights as anyone else. An identical exception applies in the case of private sector tenancies, though it did not previously apply to secure tenancies.[2]

1 The Scottish Secure Tenancies (Exceptions) Regulations 2002, SSI No 314 (as amended).
2 See para 17.20.

18.34   (4) *Temporary accommodation during work*   This applies to temporary lets of alternative accommodation while works are being carried out on the tenant's usual house, to which the tenant has the right to return when the work is completed. The right to return may be by agreement with the landlord or by order of the sheriff where the landlord has recovered possession under number 10 of the termination grounds.[1] The tenant, however, does have the right to stay on in the temporary accommodation until his or her previous house is ready for occupation again.[2]

1 See para 18.70; H(S) A 2001 s 16(6).
2 H(S)A 2001 s 12(2) and (3).

18.35   (5) *Accommodation for homeless persons*   The house is being let to the tenant expressly on a temporary basis, for a term of less than six months, in fulfilment of a duty imposed on a local authority by Part II of the Housing (Scotland) Act 1987 to provide accommodation for homeless persons.[1]

1 See *Nisala v Glasgow City Council* 2006 Hous LR 66, 2006 GWD 34-703; *Falkirk Council v Gillies* [2016] CSIH 90, 2017 SC 230.

18.36   (6) *Accommodation for offenders*   Local authorities have a statutory duty to supervise and provide advice, guidance and assistance to offenders, including those put on probation and those recently released from prison.[1] A tenancy will not be a Scottish secure tenancy if it is granted for a term of less than six months to certain categories of probationer, ex-prisoners etc[2] or to a person who, within 12 months of being released from prison or other detention, has requested advice, guidance or assistance from the local authority.[3]

1 Social Work (Scotland) Act 1968 s 27.
2 Those specified in s 27(1)(b)(i), (ii) or (vi).
3 Under s 27(1)(c).

18.37 *(7) Shared ownership agreements* This is identical to the exception in respect of private residential tenancies and is explained in the relevant part of Chapter 17.[1]

1 See para 17.26.

18.38 *(8) Agricultural and business premises* The house is let along with agricultural land[1] or business premises.[2] More specifically, this means that it is let along with more than two acres of land, or along with a shop, office or premises licensed to sell alcohol, or is let in conjunction with any of these.

1 *Lamont v Glenrothes Development Corporation* 1993 SLT (Lands Tr) 2.
2 *Fleck v East Lothian District Council* 1992 SLT (Lands Tr) 80.

18.39 *(9) Residential use subsidiary* The house is within the curtilage of a building whose main use is not as housing accommodation. It is within the curtilage if it is used for the comfortable enjoyment of the other building so as to form an integral part of it.[1] Where the house and the other building are separated by a public road, the house cannot be within the curtilage of that other building.[2]

As with category 1 above, tenancies in this category are also subject to the provisions of sections 23 to 33.[3]

1 *Barron v Borders Regional Council* 1987 SLT (Lands Tr) 36. See also *Burns v Central Regional Council* 1988 SLT (Lands Tr) 46; *Allison v Tayside Regional Council* 1989 SLT (Lands Tr) 65; *MacDonald v Strathclyde Regional Council* 1990 SLT (Lands Tr) 10; *Walker v Strathclyde Regional Council* 1990 SLT (Lands Tr) 17; *Smith v Dundee City Council* 2001 Hous LR 78; *Fee v East Renfrewshire Council* 2006 Hous LR 99, 2006 GWD 27-610; and *Taylor v Renfrewshire Council* 2010 SLT (Lands Tr) 2, 2010 GWD 4-68; *Hopwood v West Lothian Council* 30 June 2017, Lands Tribunal.
2 *Fisher v Fife Regional Council* 1989 SLT (Lands Tr) 26; see also *Little v Borders Regional Council* 1990 SLT (Lands Tr) 2. Compare *Hopwood v West Lothian Council* 30 June 2017, Lands Tribunal, para 40.
3 See para 18.31.

18.40 *(10) Accommodation in property not owned by the landlord* The house is leased by the landlord from another body and the terms of the lease preclude the letting of the house by the landlord under a Scottish secure tenancy.

18.41   (11) *Displaced persons[1]*   A tenancy is not a Scottish secure tenancy if it is granted in order to provide accommodation under the Displaced Persons (Temporary Protection) Regulations 2005.

1 H(S)A 2001 Sch 1 para 11 (added by the Displaced Persons (Temporary Protection) Regulations 2005, SI No 1379 Sch 1 para 15). This paragraph is in force at the time of writing, but is prospectively repealed by the Immigration, Nationality and Asylum (EU Exit) Regulations 2019/745 sch 3 para 1(g), to come into force on 31 December 2020.

Notices[1]

18.42   In various circumstances, it is necessary for one party to give notice of something to the other. Any notice to a person may be given by:

(a)   delivering it to that person;
(b)   leaving it at that person's proper address; or
(c)   sending it by recorded delivery letter to that person at that address.

A person's proper address is that person's last known address.

1 H(S)A 2001 s 40.

SECURITY OF TENURE AND RECOVERY OF POSSESSION

General

18.43   The effect of a tenancy being secure is essentially the same as in regulated and assured tenancies in the private sector. In other words, the tenant has the right to stay on in the property even though the contractual term stated in the lease has expired. The landlord has only very limited rights to bring the tenancy to an end. Contrary to the general rule, whereby a contract may be terminated by novation when the parties agree substantially different terms,[1] an agreed variation in the terms of the tenancy does not terminate a Scottish secure tenancy.[2]

The tenant, on the other hand, can terminate the let at any time by giving the landlord four weeks' notice,[3] and a joint tenant can bring his or her interest to an end by giving the same notice to the landlord and each of the other joint tenants.[4] The tenancy may end on the tenant's death, but only where there is no relative entitled to succeed to the tenancy and who wants to take it up.[5]

Otherwise, the tenancy can only be terminated by agreement, if the tenant abandons the property,[6] if the landlord obtains a court order for recovery of possession,[7] or if the tenancy is converted to a short Scottish secure tenancy.[8]

1 H L MacQueen and J M Thomson, *Contract Law in Scotland* (5th edn 2020) para 4.87.
2 H(S)A 2001 s 24(2).
3 H(S)A 2001 s 12(1)(f).
4 H(S)A 2001 s 13.
5 H(S)A 2001 ss 12(1)(c), 22.
6 H(S)A 2001 ss 12(1)(b), 18(2). See paras 18.77 et seq.
7 H(S)A 2001 ss 12(1)(a), 16(2). See para 18.51 et seq.
8 H(S)A 2001 ss 12(1)(d), 35. See para 18.110 et seq.

Rent arrears – pre-action requirements[1]

18.44   The Housing (Scotland) Act 2010 introduced additional safeguards for Scottish secure tenants in cases where the ground for possession is that rent lawfully due from the tenant has not been paid. In such cases, the landlord must not send a notice of proceedings for recovery of possession[2] unless these substantial requirements have first been met and the landlord has confirmed to the court in the prescribed manner that they have been complied with.[3]

1 H(S)A 2001 ss 14(2A) & (4)(c) and s 14A (all inserted by the H(S)A 2010 s 155); the Scottish Secure Tenancies (Proceedings for Possession) (Pre-Action Requirements) Order 2012, SSI No 127.
2 See para 18.45 et seq.
3 The manner prescribed is that the writ submitted for warrant must include a statement of claim with an averment confirming to the court that the pre-action requirements in s 14A of the 2001 Act have been complied with. (The Scottish Secure Tenancies (Proceedings for Possession) (Confirmation of Compliance with Pre-Action Requirements) Regulations 2012, SSI No 93).

18.45   The pre-action requirements are:

(1)   The landlord must provide the tenant with clear information about the terms of the tenancy agreement, and also outstanding rent and any other outstanding financial obligation of the tenancy.

(2)   The landlord must make reasonable efforts to provide the tenant with advice and assistance on the tenant's eligibility to receive housing benefit and other types of financial assistance, eg other benefits or grants.

(3)   The landlord must provide the tenant with information about sources of advice and assistance in relation to management of debt.

(4)   The landlord must make reasonable efforts to agree with the tenant a reasonable plan for future payments to the landlord,

including proposals in respect of future payments of rent, as well as outstanding rent and any other outstanding financial obligations of the tenancy.

18.46   The landlord must not serve a notice of proceedings for recovery of possession in any one of the following situations:

(a)   an application for housing benefit for the tenant has been made but has not yet been determined and is, in the opinion of the landlord, likely to result in the benefit being paid at a level allowing the tenant to pay, or reduce by an amount acceptable to the landlord, the outstanding rent and any other outstanding financial obligation of the tenancy;

(b)   the tenant is taking other steps which, in the opinion of the landlord, are likely to result in the payment to the landlord within a reasonable time of any outstanding rent and any other outstanding financial obligation of the tenancy; or

(c)   the tenant is complying with the terms of a plan agreed in accordance with (4) above.

The landlord (unless it is itself the local authority) must encourage the tenant to contact the local authority in whose area the house is situated.

In complying with the above pre-action requirements, the landlord must have regard to any guidance issued by the Scottish Ministers. Guidance has been given in The Scottish Secure Tenancies (Proceedings for Possession) (Pre-Action Requirements) Order 2012,[1] which spells out in some detail precisely how the landlord should go about complying with each of the above requirements.

1 SSI 2012 No 127.

Notice of proceedings for recovery of possession

18.47   Before it can raise court proceedings for recovery of possession, the landlord must give the tenant written notice, stating the ground of termination and specifying a date on or after which the landlord may raise proceedings for recovery of possession. A verbatim repetition of the relevant statutory ground may be inadequate if it fails to explain properly the reasons for the eviction.[1] A minimum of four weeks' notice must be given, and the date specified in the notice cannot be earlier than the date on which the tenancy would have been brought to an end by a notice to quit had it not been a Scottish secure tenancy, ie the ish.[2] The notice must be in the form prescribed by regulations.[3]

Note that, at the time of writing, temporary provision has been made by the Coronavirus (Scotland) Act 2020, altering the notice period.[4]

Unlike the situation in the case of assured and regulated tenancies, there appears to be no need to send a notice to quit in addition to the above notice. This is because, unlike these other two types of tenancy, the legislation does not distinguish between a contractual and a statutory period of the tenancy.[5]

The provision that the notice cannot take effect before the ish raises the question of what the landlord's position would be if a termination ground arose during a lease with a long contractual term at a point when the ish was still some time in the future. This is theoretically possible, as the 2001 Act does not specify a maximum length for Scottish secure tenancies.[6] In such a case would the landlord have to wait until the lease was due to expire before the tenant could be removed? This problem can be avoided, however, by having a suitably short contractual term.

The situation is different in the case of short Scottish secure tenancies.[7]

1 *Glasgow Housing Association Ltd v Du* 2009 Hous LR 91, 2009 GWD 40-692.
2 H(S)A 2001 s 14(2) and (4).
3 H(S)A 2001 s 14(4); The Scottish Secure Tenancies (Proceedings for Possession) (Form of Notice) Regulations 2012, SSI No 92; see also *Govan Housing Association v Kerr* 2009 Hous LR 25.
4 Coronavirus (Scotland) Act 2020 Sch 1 para 7.
5 See para 17.69.
6 Apart of course, from the 20-year limit for all residential tenancies – see para 8.28 et seq.
7 See para 18.107.

18.48 *Notice to qualifying occupiers* The landlord must also serve notice on any 'qualifying occupier', ie a member of the tenant's family aged at least 16, or an assignee, subtenant or lodger, who occupies the house as his or her only or principal home.[1] Before serving the notice or notices, the landlord must make such inquiries as may be necessary to establish so far as is reasonably practicable whether there are any qualifying occupiers of the house and, if so, their identities.[2]

The court must grant any application by a qualifying occupier to be sisted as a party to any proceedings for recovery of possession.[3] However, it has been held that a qualifying occupier who is not sisted as a party to the action has no title to challenge an eviction decree after the proceedings have been concluded.[4]

1 H(S)A 2001 s 14(2) and (6); *North Lanarkshire Council v Kenmure* 2004 Hous LR 50, 2004 GWD 20-433; *East Lothian Council v Duffy* 2012 SLT (Sh Ct) 113, 2012 Hous LR 73.
2 H(S)A 2001 s 14(3).
3 H(S)A 2001 s 15.
4 *North Lanarkshire Council v Cairns* 2012 SLT (Sh Ct) 128, 2012 GWD 16-317, where the qualifying occupier was the defender's son. It was also held that the qualifying occupier's rights under Article 6 of the European Convention on Human Rights had not

been breached, since the correct statutory procedure had been followed. But see also *Edinburgh City Council v Porter* 2004 Hous LR 46, 2004 GWD 358, where it was held that a qualifying occupier *does* have the right to challenge a decree of possession.

18.49   *Notice to local authority*   The landlord must give notice of the raising of the proceedings to the local authority in whose area the house is situated, unless the landlord is that local authority.[1] The notice should be in the form and manner prescribed under section 11(3) of the Homelessness etc (Scotland) Act 2003.[2]

1 H(S)A 2001 s 14 (5A) and (5B) (added by the Homelessness etc (Scotland) Act 2003 Sch 1 para 4(2)).
2 Under the Notice to Local Authorities (Scotland) Regulations 2008 SSI No 324 (as amended).

18.50   *Expiry of notice*   A notice of proceedings for recovery of possession by a landlord will cease to be effective if not used within six months, or if the landlord has withdrawn it before that.[1]

1 H(S)A 2001 s 14(5); *Edinburgh City Council v Davis* 1987 SLT (Sh Ct) 33, 2002 Hous LR 136.

Proceedings for recovery of possession

18.51   Proceedings for recovery of possession may be by summary cause.[1] It has been held in relation to short Scottish secure tenancies that similar statutory wording is permissive and not mandatory, and that raising proceedings by ordinary cause instead is not precluded.[2]

The court will only grant the landlord an order for recovery of possession on certain limited grounds which are specified below. These are not quite the same as the grounds for regulated, assured and private residential tenancies, although there are similarities.[3]

1 H(S)A 2001 s 14(1). Unlike the position with private sector residential tenancies, jurisdiction has not been transferred to the First-Tier Tribunal.
2 *City of Edinburgh Council v Burnett* 2012 SLT (Sh Ct) 137, 2012 Hous LR 52. See para 18.109. Indeed, it would be necessary to proceed by ordinary cause if decree for payment of arrears of rent was sought above the level permitted for summary cause (currently £5,000).
3 See para 17.77 et seq.

Grounds for recovery of possession

18.52   The grounds entitling the landlord to recovery of possession are set out in Part 1 of Schedule 2 to the Housing (Scotland) Act 2001. There are fifteen grounds in all. In respect of grounds 1–7 and ground 15 the court has the power to adjourn proceedings with or without imposing conditions as to payment of outstanding rent or otherwise.[1]

1 H(S)A 2001 s 16(1).

18.53 *Conduct grounds* The first seven grounds (sometimes referred to as 'conduct grounds') all relate to situations where the tenant could be said to be at fault in some respect. In these cases there is no requirement that other accommodation will be available to the tenant, but the court must be satisfied that it is reasonable to make the order.[1] This therefore gives the sheriff discretion to refuse the landlord possession even where a ground of termination exists.[2]

The onus is upon the landlord to show that the ground of termination exists and that it is reasonable for the tenant to be evicted,[3] even if the tenant does not defend the action.[4] It is preferable for the landlord's claim to expressly narrate that it is reasonable to grant an order of possession, but lack of this will not nullify the action if enough information is presented to the court to enable it to make a decision, eg that the rent for almost half of a ten-year tenancy had never been paid.[5]

1 H(S)A 2001 s 16(2)(a).
2 There is a partial exception to this, in relation to ground 2, considered at paras 18.59–18.61.
3 *Midlothian District Council v Drummond* 1991 SLT (Sh Ct) 67; see also *Midlothian District Council v Brown* 1991 SLT (Sh Ct) 80 and *Renfrew District Council v Inglis* 1991 SLT (Sh Ct) 83.
4 *Gordon District Council v Acutt* 1991 SLT (Sh Ct) 78.
5 *Glasgow District Council v Erhaigonoma* 1993 SCLR 592.

18.54 *Management grounds* The remaining grounds (8–15) (sometimes known as 'management grounds') do not necessarily involve any fault on the tenant's part, but there is other good reason why the landlord should recover possession. In all of these cases the court, before it can grant an order, must be satisfied that suitable alternative accommodation is available to the tenant.[1]

In the case of ground 15 only (transfer to spouse or other partner) it is necessary for the court to be satisfied *both* that it is reasonable to make the order for recovery of possession *and* that suitable alternative accommodation is available.

1 H(S)A 2001 s 16(2)(b).

18.55 *Criteria for reasonableness*[1] In deciding whether it is reasonable to grant an order for recovery of possession, the court is to have regard in particular to:

(a)   the nature, frequency and duration of the relevant conduct;

(b)   the extent of any involvement by persons other than the tenant;
(c)   the effect of the conduct on any person other than the tenant; and
(d)   any action taken by the landlord, before raising the proceedings,
        with a view to securing the cessation of the conduct.

These criteria are not exhaustive, however, and other factors will be taken into account where appropriate.[2]

A sheriff's decision on the question of reasonableness would normally require to be fundamentally flawed before an appeal court would overturn it.[3] Where it is sought to evict a joint tenant on a conduct ground, there is no requirement to offer alternative accommodation to the innocent joint tenant, but in such circumstances it may not be reasonable for the sheriff to grant an order for possession.[4]

1 H(S)A 2001 s 16(3).
2 See eg *Fife Council v Buchan* 2008 SLT (Sh Ct) 79.
3 *Edinburgh District Council v Sinclair* 1995 SCLR 194; *Campbell v Glasgow Housing Association Ltd* 2011 Hous LR 7, 2011 GWD 13-306; *South Lanarkshire Council v Gillespie* 2012 Hous LR 45, 2012 GWD 16-334.
4 *Glasgow District Council v Brown (No 2)*1988 SCLR 679; but see also *Glasgow Housing Association v Fisher* 2008 SLT (Sh Ct) 142, 2008 Hous LR 60.

18.56   *Criteria for suitability*   The criteria for suitability are set out in Part 2 of Schedule 2. The alternative accommodation need not be provided by the landlord itself, but *must* be either under another Scottish secure tenancy or a private residential tenancy.[1]

The other criteria are not mandatory, but the sheriff must have regard to them in deciding whether or not the accommodation is reasonably suitable to the needs of the tenant and the tenant's family. They include the proximity of the new house to the tenant's (or a member of the tenant's family's) place of work, comparability with the tenant's existing house (including the terms of the let) and any special needs of the tenant or the tenant's family.[2]

1 H(S)A 2001 Sch 2 Pt 2 para 16(a); *Charing Cross & Kelvingrove Housing Association v Kraska* 1986 SLT (Sh Ct) 42.
2 H(S)A 2001 Sch 2 Pt 2 para 17; see also the case law in relation to assured and regulated tenancies – see para 17.87.

Human Rights Act 1998[1]

18.57   As discussed earlier, when exercising its discretionary powers, the court should take into account the rights of the tenant under the European Convention on Human Rights and the Human Rights Act 1998. Where the tenant defends the action on the ground of proportionality, the landlord may have to give reasons for the eviction beyond what is required in the Notice of Proceedings for Possession.[2]

1 See also paras 1.27 et seq and 18.12 et seq.
2 See *South Lanarkshire Council v McKenna* 2013 SLT 22, 2012 GWD 34-693. See also paras 18.17 and 18.47.

Conduct grounds[1]

18.58 (1) *Rent arrears or other breach* Rent lawfully due from the tenant has not been paid, or any other obligation of the tenancy has been broken.[2]

Before action can be taken by a landlord in rent arrears cases it must have complied with the pre-action requirements introduced by the Housing (Scotland) Act 2010.[3]

These provisions also require the court, in rent arrears evictions, to set a period, not more than six months in duration from the date of the decree or the disposal of any appeal, during which possession can be taken and the tenancy terminated.[4] This provision provides a 'window of opportunity' before the decree has to be implemented during which the parties may be able to reach agreement about the payment of the arrears.

1 H(S)A 2001 Sch 2 Pt 1 paras 1–7.
2 See *Angus Housing Association v Fraser* 2004 Hous LR 83, 2004 GWD 11-249; *Aberdeen City Council v Shauri* 2006 Hous LR 40, 2006 GWD 22-468; *Renfrewshire Council v Hainey* 2008 Hous LR 43; *Govan Housing Association v Kerr* 2009 Hous LR 25; *Glasgow Housing Association Ltd v Li* 2010 Hous LR 31; *Campbell v Glasgow Housing Association Ltd* 2011 Hous LR 7, 2011 GWD 13-306. In *Stirling Council v Harrower* 2013 GWD 8-180 it was held that it would not be reasonable to grant the council possession because the resulting negative effects on the tenant and her seriously ill husband outweighed the potential negative effect on the council. Note that all of the other cases listed above predate the introduction of pre-action requirements in cases of rent arrears and should be considered accordingly – see para 18.44.
3 See para 18.44 et seq.
4 H(S)A 2001 s 16(5A) & (5B) (inserted by H(S)A 2010 s 153); The Scottish Secure Tenancies (Repossession Orders) (Maximum Period) Order 2012, SSI No 128. Unlike with other grounds for recovery of possession, here the tenancy is not terminated unless and until the landlord actually recovers possession.

18.59 (2) *Criminal conviction* The tenant (or any one of joint tenants), a lodger or other person residing in the house, a subtenant, or a person visiting the house has been convicted of:

(a) using the house or allowing it to be used for immoral or illegal purposes; or

(b) an offence punishable by imprisonment committed in, or in the locality of, the house.

Unlike the other conduct grounds, this ground is sometimes mandatory. Where the notice of proceedings for recovery of possession is served within 12 months of the day that the tenant was convicted, or of the day on which any appeal was dismissed or abandoned, the court has no discretion, and must grant the order sought.[1]

1 H(S)A 2001 s 16(2)(aa) (inserted by H(S)A 2014 s 14(2)(a) with effect from 1 May 2019).

18.60 This ground (and its equivalent in relation to assured tenancies)[1] has been used in a number of cases where the tenant has been convicted of an offence relating to drugs. Even in the case of serious drugs offences, though, it is always necessary to show that eviction is reasonable on the facts, unless the ground is mandatory as outlined above.[2] There may be mitigating factors in a particular case.[3] In *Glasgow City Council v Lockhart*[4] it was held that four factors should be taken into account when determining whether it was reasonable to evict because of a drugs conviction:

(1) *Public interest.* Under this there could be considered any detrimental effect to the area caused by drug taking or drug dealing.[5]

(2) *Whether the defender knew what he or she was doing.* Here it would be relevant to consider whether the tenancy agreement specified that such a criminal conviction could lead to eviction and whether the defender was aware of this.

(3) *The gravity of the offence.* Account could be taken of the severity of the criminal penalty imposed and of whether the defender had been dealing in drugs or merely using them.

(4) *The consequences of removal.* It could affect the court's decision if eviction would make the defender homeless, particularly if there were children in the house.[6]

As this ground is now only discretionary if sought more than a year after conviction, presumably the tenant's behaviour in the intervening period will have considerable weight in such cases.

1 See para 17.93 and also the case authority referred to there.
2 See para 18.59.
3 See *Hjaltland Housing Association Ltd v Sukhram* 2018 Hous LR 100.
4 1997 Hous LR 99; see also *Glasgow City Council v Heffron* 1997 Hous LR 55; *East Ayrshire Council v Tait* 1999 SCLR 566; *Perth and Kinross Council v Gillies* 2002 SCLR 1104, 2002 Hous LR 74; *South Lanarkshire Council v Nugent* 2008 Hous LR 92, 2008 GWD 39-586; and *South Lanarkshire Council v Gillespie* 2012 Hous LR 45, 2102 GWD 116-334.
5 See *Glasgow Housing Association Ltd v McNamara* 2008 Hous LR 38. The wider community interest of combating drug dealing can override the fact that another occupant of the house is innocent of the misconduct.
6 See *Glasgow Housing Association Ltd v Hetherington* 2009 SLT (Sh Ct) 64, 2009 Hous LR 28.

18.61 In *Shetland Islands Council v Hassan*[1] it was held that it was reasonable to evict a drug dealer on this ground (and also grounds (1), (3) and (4)), even although the council intended to relet the house exclusively to his co-tenant who was a convicted rapist.

This ground has also been used to evict tenants convicted of possessing a firearm within the house.[2]

1 2012 Hous LR 107, 2012 GWD 31-631.
2 *Glasgow Housing Association v Fisher* 2008 SLT (Sh Ct) 142, 2008 Hous LR 60; *Fife Council v Buchan* 2008 SLT (Sh Ct) 79, 2008 Hous LR 74, in which the tenant was also in possession of counterfeit money.

18.62 (3) *Deterioration of house* There has been deterioration in the condition of the property or its common parts caused by acts of waste by or the neglect or default of the tenant. This will also be a ground if the deterioration was caused by a person residing or lodging with the tenant or a subtenant, unless the tenant has taken reasonable steps to have the person removed.[1]

This ground has been held to include neglect of a garden attached to the house.[2]

1 See *Paragon Housing Association v Manclark* 2013 GWD 7-161.
2 *Holloway v Povey* (1984) 271 EG 195, (1984) 15 HLR 104, CA.

18.63 (4) *Deterioration of furniture* In the case of furnished lets, there has been deterioration of the furniture due to ill treatment. There is a similar provision in relation to other residents of the house as in ground 3.

18.64 (5) *Absence from house* Both the tenant and his or her spouse or civil partner[1] have been continuously absent from the house for more than six months without reasonable cause or have ceased to occupy the house as their principal home.

A person with whom the tenant has been living as husband and wife (or in a relationship which has the characteristics of the relationship between civil partners)[2] for at least six months previously is equivalent to a spouse for the purpose of this provision.

It is important to stress here that the point is not physical absence, but rather whether the tenant can be said to have given up occupation of the house as his or her only or principal home. Thus, in *Beggs v Kilmarnock & Loudon District Council*,[3] a tenant was held still to be in occupation (for the purposes of the right to buy) even though he was serving a six-year prison sentence, as there were continued signs of occupation and there was an intention to return. The same view was reached in

Matheson v Western Isles Council,[4] in which the tenant had been hospitalised for some 15 months and would require additional support if she was to return to the house. Again, in the English case of *Crawley Borough Council v Sawyer*[5] the tenant left the house for about a year and a quarter to stay with his girlfriend, then returned after he and his girlfriend split up. During the period of his absence, he continued to pay the rent, visited the house about once a month and occasionally lived in it for periods of up to a week. It was held that the landlords were not entitled to repossess.

1 Words inserted by the Civil Partnership Act 2004 Sch 28(4) para 65(2)(a).
2 Words substituted by the Civil Partnership Act 2004 Sch 28(4) para 65(2)(b).
3 1995 SC 333.
4 1992 SLT (Lands Tr) 107. Compare *McLoughlin's Curator Bonis v Motherwell DC* 1994 SLT (Lands Tr) 31, in which the opposite conclusion was reached. In the latter case, it was accepted that the tenant's medical condition was such that he would never return home.
5 (1988) 20 HLR 98, 86 LGR 629, CA; see also *Hussey v Camden LBC* (1995) 27 HLR 5, CA and *Hammersmith and Fulham LBC v Clarke* (2001) 33 HLR 77, (2001) 81 P&CR DG20, CA. Compare *Johnston v Dundee City Council* 2006 Hous LR 68.

18.65 (6) *Misrepresentation* The landlord was induced to grant the tenancy by a false statement made knowingly or recklessly by the tenant.[1]

1 See *Falkirk District Council v McLay* 1991 SCLR 895.

18.66 (7) *Anti-social conduct or harassment* This ground should be considered in conjunction with ground 8 below. It includes conduct, not only of the tenant or one of joint tenants, but also of any other person residing or lodging in the house, or a subtenant, or even a person visiting the house.[1] It can include anti-social behaviour by the tenant's children, which the tenant has failed to control.[2]

As with the other conduct grounds, the court must be satisfied overall that it is reasonable to grant an order for recovery of possession; also the landlord must satisfy the court that it is not reasonable in all the circumstances for it to provide other accommodation for the tenant.[3]

To qualify under this ground the person concerned must have:

(a) acted in an anti-social manner in relation to a person residing in, visiting or otherwise engaged in lawful activity in the locality; or
(b) pursued a course of conduct amounting to harassment of such a person, or a course of conduct which is otherwise anti-social conduct in relation to such a person.

Certain definitions are given. 'Anti-social' means causing or likely to cause alarm, distress, nuisance or annoyance. 'Conduct' includes speech, and a course of conduct must involve conduct on at least two occasions. 'Harassment' is to be construed in accordance with section 8 of the Protection from Harassment Act 1997, which, inter alia, provides that 'harassment' of a person includes causing the person alarm or distress.[4]

1 *Scottish Special Housing Association v Lumsden* 1984 SLT (Sh Ct) 71; *Edinburgh City Council v T* 2003 Hous LR 74, 2003 GWD 29-821; *City of Edinburgh Council v Dougan* 2006 GWD 23-629.
2 *Kensington and Chelsea RLBC v Simmonds* [1996] 3 FCR 246, (1997) 29 HLR 507, CA; *Newcastle upon Tyne City Council v Morrison* (2000) 32 HLR 891, [2000] L&TR 333, CA; *Edinburgh City Council v Watson* 2002 Hous LR 2, 2002 GWD 2-76; *Edinburgh City Council v T* 2003 Hous LR 74, 2003 GWD 29-821.
3 See *Edinburgh City Council v Watson* 2002 Hous LR 2.
4 Protection from Harassment Act 1997 s 8.

Management grounds

18.67   (8) *Nuisance and harassment*   This should be considered in conjunction with ground 7 above. Like that ground it includes conduct by the tenant, a joint tenant, a lodger or other resident, a subtenant or a visitor.

The main difference is that, unlike the situation with ground 7, the landlord believes it is appropriate in the circumstances to require the tenant to move to other accommodation. The court will have no discretion to refuse an order on grounds of reasonableness, but will require to be satisfied that suitable alternative accommodation is available; for this reason, although the ground relates to conduct, it is more convenient to list it with the other 'management' grounds, where the same rules apply.[1]

1 See para 18.54.

18.68   In the provisions of the Housing (Scotland) Act 1987 in relation to secure tenancies, these two grounds, apart from this essential distinction, were originally identical and referred mainly to nuisance. However, in subsequent amendments to that Act and in the Housing (Scotland) Act 2001, they have been developed, for no obvious reason, along slightly different lines; in particular, in ground 8, the original concept of nuisance has not been expanded into the broader concept of anti-social behaviour.

Accordingly, to qualify under ground 8 the person concerned must have:

(a)   been guilty of conduct in or in the vicinity of the house which is a nuisance or annoyance; or

(b)   pursued a course of conduct amounting to harassment of a person residing in, visiting or otherwise engaged in lawful activity in the locality.

'Conduct' and 'harassment' are assigned the same meanings as in ground 7.

18.69 (9) *Overcrowding* The house is overcrowded in such circumstances as to render the occupier guilty of an offence. The criteria for overcrowding and the responsibility of the occupier are contained in Part VII of the Housing (Scotland) Act 1987.

18.70 (10) *Demolition etc* It is intended within a reasonable period of time to demolish, or carry out substantial work on, the building or a part of the building which comprises or includes the house, and this cannot reasonably take place without the landlord obtaining possession of the house.[1]

If the landlord intends that the tenant should return to the house afterwards, the court will make an order that the tenant is entitled to do so.[2] The tenant will have security of tenure in the alternative house until such time as the original house is ready for occupation again.[3]

It has been held in England that, before the landlord can regain possession, it must show a settled and clearly defined intention to carry out the works and also to show that the works cannot be reasonably carried out without obtaining possession.[4]

1 'Demolition' is to be construed in accordance with s 338(3) of the Housing (Scotland) Act 1987.
2 H(S)A 2001 s 16(6).
3 See para 18.34.
4 *Wansbeck District Council v Marley* (1988) 20 HLR 247; see also *Edinburgh City Council v Middlemiss* 2007 Hous LR 70, 2007 GWD 38-670.

18.71 (11) *House specially designed or adapted* The house has been designed or adapted for a person with special needs. This applies only if there is no longer anyone in the house with such needs and the landlord requires the house for someone who has.

18.72 (12) *House part of a group* The house is part of a group of houses designed or with facilities for persons with special needs. This is subject to a similar proviso to that in 11.

18.73 (13) *Lessee landlord* The landlord is itself a lessee under a lease that has terminated or will terminate within a period of six months from the date of raising of proceedings for recovery of possession.

18.74 (14) *Educational let by Islands Council* The landlord is Orkney Islands, Shetland Islands or Western Isles Council[1] and the house is reasonably required for an employee of the council in the exercise of its function as education authority. This applies only if the existing tenancy was granted to a similar employee whose employment has now ended.

1 Western Isles Council now operates under the name Comhairle nan Eilean Siar. H(S) A 2001 continues to refer to the original name, however.

18.75 (15) *Transfer to spouse or other partner* The landlord wants to transfer the tenancy to the tenant's spouse or civil partner, or former spouse or civil partner,[1] or to a person with whom the tenant has been living as husband and wife (or in a relationship which has the characteristics of the relationship between civil partners)[2] for a period of six months immediately prior to the date of the application for transfer.

This only applies if the other person has applied for the transfer of tenancy, and one of the parties (either the tenant or the other) no longer wants them to live together. As mentioned above,[3] in respect of this ground only, the court has to be satisfied *both* that it is reasonable to make the order for recovery of possession and also that suitable alternative accommodation is available.

1 Words substituted by the Civil Partnership Act 2004 Sch 28(4) para 65(3)(a).
2 Words substituted by the Civil Partnership Act 2004 Sch 28(4) para 65(3)(b).
3 See para 18.54.

18.76 In October 2020, the Domestic Abuse (Protection) (Scotland) Bill was introduced to the Scottish Parliament. If passed, section 18 of the Bill (as introduced) will add a new ground of eviction, prospectively numbered 15A. It applies where:

- a person (T) is either sole tenant, or is a joint tenant along with another person (P);
- P and T are partners or former partners;
- T has engaged in abusive behaviour towards P (as defined in sections 2 and 3 of the Bill);
- the house is P's only or principal home; and
- P wishes to continue living in the house.

The landlord may apply for T's interest in the tenancy to be terminated. In the case of a sole tenancy, this would be done with a view to entering into a new tenancy agreement with P.

In the Bill as introduced, this is a discretionary ground, with eviction only to be granted if the court considers it reasonable. To this there is one exception, namely where, in the previous 12 months, T has been convicted of an offence which is punishable by imprisonment, in respect of the abusive behaviour. In that case, the court must grant the order sought if satisfied that the grounds exist.

Abandonment of tenancy

18.77   We saw above[1] that the tenant's absence from the house for more than six months can be a ground for a court order terminating the tenancy. However, if the tenancy has been abandoned, the landlord may be able to recover possession without waiting six months or obtaining a court order. If it has reasonable grounds for believing that a house let under a Scottish secure tenancy is unoccupied and that the tenant does not intend to occupy it as his or her home, the landlord may take possession of it.[2]

The landlord must first serve four weeks' written notice on the tenant of its intention to repossess unless the tenant replies within that time that he or she intends to reoccupy the house.[3] If the tenant fails to reply, the landlord may, after making any necessary enquiries, serve another notice terminating the tenancy. After that it is entitled to take immediate possession without further proceedings.[4] Pending such termination, the landlord is entitled to enter the house, by force if necessary, to secure it against vandalism.[5]

Provisions for the disposal of any property left behind in the house are contained in regulations.[6]

1 See para 18.64.
2 H(S)A 2001 s 17.
3 H(S)A 2001 s 18(1).
4 H(S)A 2001 s 18(2) and (3).
5 H(S)A 2001 s 17(2) and (3).
6 H(S)A 2001 s 18(4); The Scottish Secure Tenancies (Abandoned Property) Order 2002, SSI No 313.

18.78   In *Lech v Highland Council*[1] the landlord served the requisite four weeks' notice of its intention to repossess the tenant's house on the ground that it had been abandoned. The tenant replied within a matter of days stating her intention to re-occupy and there was other evidence that she was serious in her intent, including that her rent was up-to-date and that she had spent significant amounts of money redecorating the house. It was held that the landlord was not entitled to serve a second notice and to terminate the tenancy.

1 2010 Hous LR 52, 2010 GWD 26-506.

18.79   *Appeal by the tenant*[1]   The tenant may appeal to the court within six months to have the tenancy restored, or be granted suitable alternative accommodation.[2] The grounds of appeal are that the landlord failed to carry out the prescribed procedure or that the tenant had good reason, such as illness, for not replying to the landlord's notice.[3]

Where the tenancy is restored, it is not clear whether it is to be considered a new tenancy or a continuation of the old tenancy. On the one hand, section 19(1) refers to a tenant who is 'aggrieved by termination of the tenancy by the landlord'. This implies that the tenancy is brought to an end by the landlord's notice, even if it was not in fact justified. On the other hand, the tenant's remedy in terms of section 19(3) is a 'declarator that the notice under section 18(2) is of no effect'. If the notice is 'of no effect', that implies that the tenancy has continued notwithstanding the notice. This is particularly so, given that the remedy is a declarator. In other words, the court is declaring something to be the case already, rather than depriving the notice of effect. The only way of reconciling these provisions would seem to be to read section 19(1) as referring to the *purported* termination of the tenancy by the landlord.

1 H(S)A 2001 s 19.
2 For the criteria for suitable alternative accommodation, see para 18.56 and Sch 2 Pt 2.
3 See *Tannoch v Glasgow City Council* 2000 Hous LR 64.

18.80   *Abandonment by joint tenant*[1]   There are similar provisions, and appeal rights, regarding the termination of the interest of a joint tenant who has abandoned the house. However, there are two significant differences:

(a)   After the service of the landlord's second notice, the joint tenant's interest will not come to an end immediately, but only after a further period of eight weeks; and

(b)   Any appeal to the court by the joint tenant must be made within the same eight-week period.

1 H(S)A 2001 ss 20 and 21.

SUCCESSION TO TENANCY[1]

General

18.81   On the death of a Scottish secure tenant, the tenancy will pass by operation of law to a person who is qualified to succeed the tenant. On the death of that successor a second succession is allowed, but not a third.

The tenancy will terminate on the death of the tenant, or of the first successor, if there is no-one qualified to succeed or those who are have declined the tenancy. Otherwise, it will terminate on the death of the second successor, unless there was a joint tenancy; in the latter case, the joint tenant will succeed provided that he or she is continuing to use the house as his or her only or principal home. Any other qualified person, after the death of the second successor, may continue as tenant for up to six months, but the tenancy will no longer be a Scottish secure tenancy.[2]

Where a tenant has been moved to suitable alternative accommodation under another Scottish secure tenancy, following recovery of possession by the landlord under one of the management grounds (other than ground 15),[3] both the original and the new tenancy will be treated as a single tenancy for the purpose of succession.[4] Presumably this is so that the tenant's succession rights will not start afresh where there has already been a first or a second succession to the original tenancy.

1 H(S)A 2001 s 22 and Sch 3.
2 H(S)A 2001 s 22(9).
3 See paras 18.67 et seq.
4 H(S)A 2001 s 22(10).

Qualified persons[1]

18.82   There is a hierarchy of those entitled to succeed to a tenancy. In all cases the house must have been the person's only or principal home at the time of the tenant's death:[2]

1.   The tenant's spouse or civil partner[3] or an unmarried partner (including one in a relationship which has the characteristics of the relationship between civil partners),[4] or a surviving joint tenant. In the case of an unmarried partner, there is a further residential requirement that the house must have been that person's only or principal home throughout the period of 12 months immediately prior to the tenant's death.

2.   A member of the tenant's family aged at least 16 years who has had the property as his or her only or principal home for a period of at least 12 months immediately prior to the tenant's death. A family member is a parent, grandparent, child, grandchild, brother, sister, uncle, aunt, nephew or niece.[5] These relationships are to be interpreted very broadly as the following further provisions make clear:[6]

   (a)   a relationship by marriage or by virtue of a civil partnership[7] is to be treated as a relationship by blood;

   (b)   a relationship of the half-blood is to be treated as a relationship of the whole blood;

   (c)   the stepchild of a person is to be treated as that person's child; and

   (d)   a person brought up or treated by another person as if the person were the child of the other person is to be treated as that person's child.

3. A carer of the tenant or of a member of the tenant's family, who has had the property as his or her only or principal home for a period of at least 12 months immediately prior to the tenant's death. The carer must be at least 16 and have given up his or her previous only or principal home to live with the tenant.

In all cases where there is a qualifying period of residence at the property, ie all cases except for spouses and civil partners, the landlord must first have been notified.[8]

1 H(S)A 2001 Sch 3 paras 2–4.
2 See *Hamilton District Council v Lennon* 1989 SCLR 193; *Roxburgh District Council v Collins* 1991 SLT (Sh Ct) 49, 1991 SCLR 575; *East Lothian Council v Skeldon* 2004 Hous LR 123, 2004 GWD 32-666; and *Edinburgh City Council v Johnston* 2005 SLT (Sh Ct) 100, 2005 Hous LR 80.
3 Words inserted by the Civil Partnership Act 2004 Sch 28(4) para 66(a).
4 Words substituted by the Civil Partnership Act 2004 Sch 28(4) para 66(b).
5 H(S)A 2001 s 108(1).
6 H(S)A 2001 s 108(2).
7 Words substituted by the Civil Partnership Act 2004 Sch 28(4) para 64(3).
8 H(S)A 2001 Sch 3 para 4A.

Order of succession[1]

18.83 A person in category 2 can only succeed to a tenancy where there is no qualified person in category 1 or if all such persons have declined the tenancy, and someone in category 3 can only succeed to a tenancy if the same is true of the other 2 categories. A spouse, partner or joint tenant, therefore, has preference over another family member and all of them have preference over a carer. If there is more than one qualified person in the same category, they should decide by agreement upon who is to succeed to the tenancy; if they fail to so agree within four weeks of the tenant's death, the landlord will decide.

1 H(S)A 2001 Sch 3 paras 6–9.

Notification by landlord[1]

18.84 If those in the first category (a spouse, partner or joint tenant) have all declined the tenancy, the landlord must, as soon as possible, use its best endeavours to ascertain whether there is a family member, failing which a carer, to succeed to the tenancy, and if so must notify each such person in writing. If there is a family member, the responsibility to find out about and notify the carer only arises if all family members have declined the tenancy.

1 H(S)A 2001 Sch 3 para 10.

Declining a tenancy[1]

18.85   A qualified person who is entitled to succeed may decline the tenancy by giving the landlord notice in writing within four weeks of the tenant's death or, where the person has been notified by the landlord,[2] within four weeks of the landlord's notice. Such a person must vacate the house within three months of the notice declining the tenancy. He or she will be liable to pay the rent due for any period while still in occupation, but not otherwise.

1 H(S)A 2001 Sch 3 para 11.
2 See para 18.84.

Specially adapted houses[1]

18.86   The succession rights are slightly different where the house has been designed or substantially adapted for occupation by a person with special needs. Here a distinction is made between a first and a second successor. In the case of a first successor, a person in the first category (a spouse, partner or joint tenant) may succeed to the tenancy in the normal way, but not another family member or a carer, unless he or she has the same special needs. However, a second successor is not allowed at all unless the successor has the same special needs.

This will make no difference where the second successor would have been a child or other family member, which will often be the case. However, if the spouse or partner who succeeded the original tenant has remarried or acquired a new partner, it may prevent the latter from acquiring the tenancy after the first successor's death.

Where a qualified person is denied the tenancy in such circumstances, the landlord must make other suitable accommodation available to that person.[2] The criteria for suitability are the same as those which apply when the landlord is seeking a court order for recovery of possession.[3]

1 H(S)A 2001 Sch 3 para 5.
2 H(S)A 2001 s 22(6).
3 See para 18.56 and Sch 2 Pt 2.

Co-operative housing association[1]

18.87   Where the landlord is a registered social landlord which is a co-operative housing association, any successor must apply for membership of the association. This must be done within four weeks of the tenant's death or, where the person was notified by the landlord,[2] within four weeks of the landlord's notice. If a person qualified to succeed to the tenancy fails to make such an application, or if the application is turned down, that person will be treated as having declined the tenancy.

1 H(S)A 2001 Sch 3 para 12; for the definition of a co-operative housing association, see s 41.
2 See para 18.84.

LEASE TERMS AND THEIR VARIATION

Tenant's right to a written lease[1]

18.88   The landlord under a Scottish secure tenancy must draw up a tenancy agreement stating the terms of the tenancy. The terms may be contained expressly in the agreement or be adopted by reference to another document. The agreement must be subscribed or authenticated by the landlord and the tenant in accordance with the Requirements of Writing (Scotland) Act 1995,[2] and the landlord must ensure that this is done before the commencement of the tenancy. The landlord must also supply the tenant with a copy of the agreement, and the tenant is not liable to pay any fees for this or anything else mentioned above.

The Scottish Ministers have the power to issue guidance as to the form and content of a tenancy agreement and to this end have provided a model tenancy agreement.[3]

1 H(S)A 2001 s 23(1)–(3).
2 See para 2.3 et seq. This is required by H(S)A 2001 s 23(1)(b) even though the 1995 Act does not otherwise require writing for leases of less than one year.
3 Scottish Government 'Model Scottish Secure Tenancy Agreement' (revised version 2019) available at: www.gov.scot/publications/model-scottish-secure-tenancy-agreement-2019/#:~:text=1%20A%20Model%20Scottish%20Secure%20Tenancy%20Agreement%20%5B1%5D,tenancies%20created%20on%20or%20after%201%20May%202019.

Tenant's right to information

18.89   *Right to buy*[1]   Before the creation of a Scottish secure tenancy, the landlord *must* provide the tenant with information about the right to buy. This provision has not been altered since the phasing out of the right to buy was introduced by the Housing (Scotland) Act 2010, but presumably in the case of new tenancies the tenant will now normally be informed that he or she does not have the right to buy at all.[2]

1 H(S)A 2001 s 23(4) and (5).
2 See Ch 20.

18.90   *Complaints procedure*[1]   The landlord must provide the tenant
with information about its complaints procedure.

1 H(S)A 2001 s 23(6).

18.91   *Additional information*[1]   The landlord must also provide
information about the following matters if the tenant requests it:

(a)   the terms of the tenancy;
(b)   the landlord's policy and procedure in relation to setting of rent
      and charges;
(c)   the landlord's policy and rules in relation to—
      (i)   admission of applicants to any housing list;
      (ii)   priority of allocation of houses;
      (iii) transfer of tenants between houses owned by the landlord;
      (iv)   exchanges of houses owned by the landlord with houses
             owned by other bodies;
      (v)   repairs and maintenance;
(e)   the landlord's tenant participation strategy. This only applies to
      local authorities and registered social landlords;
(f)   the landlord's arrangements for decision making in relation to
      housing management and services.

1 H(S)A 2001 s 23(6). Paragraph (d), which was concerned with the tenant's right to buy,
  has been repealed.

Variation of lease terms[1]

18.92   The terms of a Scottish secure tenancy may not be varied except
in one of the three ways specified below. This cannot be contracted out
of by any provision in the tenancy agreement. A variation in the terms of
a tenancy does not terminate the agreement. As well as being forbidden
by section 24(1) of the 2001 Act, any such provision would be deemed
unfair in terms of the Consumer Rights Act 2015.[2]

1 H(S)A 2001 s 24(1) and (2).
2 See para 21.14, including the discussion of *Peabody Trust Governors v Reeve*
  [2009] L&TR 6, [2008] 3 EGLR 61.

18.93   *Variation by agreement*   The tenancy terms may varied by
written agreement between the landlord and the tenant. The landlord
must draw up such an agreement and ensure that it is subscribed or
authenticated by the parties in accordance with the Requirements of
Writing (Scotland) Act 1995.[1]

1 See para 2.3 et seq.

18.94   *Increase in rent or charges*[1]   The landlord may increase the rent or any other charge payable under the tenancy by giving the tenant at least four weeks' notice before the beginning of any rental period. Any such notice must be in writing.[2]

If the rent is due to be paid earlier than the beginning of the rental period, the notice must be given at least four weeks prior to that earlier date. Where a notice of increase is given as above, it takes effect for every subsequent rental period also. 'Rental period' is defined as 'a period in respect of which an instalment of rent falls to be paid.'

There is no provision for a tenant or tenants to legally challenge such an increase. However, where a landlord proposes an increase payable by all, or any class of, its tenants it must, before giving notice, consult those of its tenants who would be affected by the proposal, and have regard to the views expressed by those consulted.

There are transitional provisions that affect:

(a)   housing association tenancies entered prior to 2 January 1989; and

(b)   tenancies that convert from assured tenancies (mainly housing association tenancies entered *on or after* 2 January 1989). These may still be subject to the provisions relating to rent increases (or rent control) that apply to regulated or assured tenancies.[3]

1 H(S)A 2001 s 25.
2 H(S)A 2001 s 41.
3 See the Housing (Scotland) Act 2001 (Scottish Secure Tenancy etc.) Order 2002, SSI No 318 art 5.

18.95   *Variation by court order*[1]   If either the landlord or the tenant wants to change any terms of the lease (other than rent or other charges),[2] but cannot get the other to agree, the party wanting the change may apply to the sheriff court by summary application for a variation of the terms. The court may make such variation as it thinks reasonable in all the circumstances, taking particularly into account the safety of any person or the likelihood of damage to the house or of any premises of which it forms part.

Where it is the tenant who makes the application for a variation, there are additional criteria to be met. The court must be satisfied that the term or terms sought to be varied are unreasonable, inappropriate, unduly burdensome or impeding some reasonable use of the house. In *Taylor v Moray District Council*[3] it was held that it was not unreasonable, inappropriate or unduly burdensome for a lease to contain a prohibition against keeping animals without the landlord's consent, merely because a neighbour who had exercised the right to buy was not subject to a similar restriction.

The tenant may be ordered to pay compensation to the landlord for any loss caused by the variation. Also, the tenant may be required to serve a copy of the application on the owner or tenant of any land who benefits from the term in its existing form, or who would be adversely affected by the change.

1 H(S)A 2001 s 26.
2 In *Shetland Islands Council v Fisher* 2014 SLT (Sh Ct) 107, it was held that s 26 could not be used to remove an obligation to pay a service charge for electricity even though, not being an increase in sums payable, this variation could not be effected through s 25. The local authority's reason for wanting to remove the service charge was so that the tenant would be paying electricity charges (the cost of which had come to exceed the service charge) directly to the electricity supplier.
3 1990 SCLR 551.

ASSIGNATION, SUBLETTING AND EXCHANGES

Assignation and subletting etc[1]

18.96   The written consent of the landlord is required before a Scottish secure tenant can give another person possession of the house or any part of it. This specifically includes assignation, subletting or taking in a lodger.

Assignation is only allowed where the house has been the only or principal home of both the tenant and the assignee throughout the period of 12 months immediately prior to the application for the landlord's consent. The landlord must have been notified that the property was the only or principal home of both parties before that 12-month period can begin to run.

Subletting is only permitted where the house has been the tenant's only or principal home throughout the period of 12 months immediately prior to the application for the landlord's consent, as long as the landlord was notified that the house was the tenant's only or principal home. The 12 months do not begin until that has been done.

Where the landlord is a registered social landlord which is a co-operative housing association, the assignee, subtenant or other person must be a member of the association at the time of the transaction.

1 H(S)A 2001 s 32 and Sch 5 Pt 2; see also generally Ch 7.

18.97   *Procedure*   The procedure is set out in Schedule 5 Pt 2 of the Housing (Scotland) Act 2001. The tenant must make a written application to the landlord giving details of the proposed transaction, including any payment made or to be made to the tenant. The landlord must intimate its decision (including its reasons should consent be refused) within one month of receipt of the application, failing which it will be deemed to have consented to the application.

A tenant aggrieved by a refusal may appeal to the court by summary application and the court, unless it considers the refusal to be reasonable, must order the landlord to consent to the application.

18.98 *Criteria for reasonable refusal* The following are declared, in particular, to be reasonable grounds for refusal.[1] The list is not declared to be exhaustive, and no doubt other reasonable grounds for refusal may emerge in particular circumstances. For example, in *Docherty v Tollcross Housing Association Ltd*,[2] it was held that under-occupancy could have been used as a ground of refusing consent to assignation, even before this was introduced as a specific ground of refusal (ground (g), below).[3]

(a)   The landlord has served a notice for recovery of possession, specifying one of the statutory termination grounds.[4]

(b)   A court order for recovery of possession of the house has been made against the tenant.

(c)   It appears to the landlord that the tenant has or will receive a payment in return for the assignation, subletting or other transaction. This does not apply in the case of a reasonable rent or a returnable security deposit that is reasonable.

(d)   The transaction would lead to overcrowding of the house in such circumstances as to render the occupier guilty of an offence. The criteria for overcrowding and the responsibility of the occupier are contained in Part VII of the Housing (Scotland) Act 1987.

(e)   The landlord proposes to carry out work on the house or on the building of which it forms part that would affect the accommodation to be used by the new occupier.

(f)   In the case of consent to an assignation by a local authority or registered social landlord, the proposed assignee is not a person to whom the landlord would be required to give a reasonable preference when selecting tenants in terms of the Housing (Scotland) Act 1987 s 20.

(g)   In the case of consent to an assignation, the assignation would in the landlord's opinion result in the house being under-occupied.

It has been held that, where the landlord's decision is challenged by the tenant, the court is to consider whether the landlord's decision was reasonable on the facts before it at the time of refusal of consent, rather than considering the matter anew as at the point when the court considers the case.[5]

1 H(S)A 2001 s 32(3). See also *East Lothian Council v Duffy* 2012 SLT (Sh Ct) 113, 2012 Hous LR 73.

2 2020 Hous LR 45, paras [69]–[70] (sheriff); [2020] SAC (Civ) 16, para [24] (Sheriff Appeal Court).
3 Grounds (f) and (g) were introduced by s 12(2) of the Housing (Scotland) Act 2014, with effect from 1 November 2019.
4 See para 18.47 et seq.
5 *Docherty v Tollcross Housing Association Ltd* [2020] SAC (Civ) 16, paras [26]-[28], reversing the sheriff on this point (though reaching the same conclusion on the facts).

18.99 *Subsequent rent increases* If the tenant later proposes to raise the rent paid by a subtenant or lodger from its initial amount, he or she must notify the landlord and must not go ahead with the increase if the landlord objects.[1]

1 This, at any rate, would appear to be the intention of the rather muddled wording of s 32(6); however, the preamble purports to include assignees, who would normally pay their rent directly to the landlord. Clarity is not helped by the wide definition given to 'subtenant' in subsection (8) to include assignees, lodgers or anyone else granted possession or partial possession under s 32.

18.100 *Status of assignees etc*[1] It is specifically declared that an assignation, subletting or other transaction will not create a regulated, assured or private residential tenancy.[2] This provision would appear to be redundant in the case of assignations, since the assignee would presumably enjoy a Scottish secure tenancy directly under the original tenant's landlord. Subtenants and lodgers, however, would appear to have no statutory protection as regulated, assured or Scottish secure tenants.[3]

1 H(S)A 2001 s 32(7).
2 See Ch 17.
3 Unless the misleading definition in s 32(8) is equating assignees with subtenants rather than conforming to the normal definition – see the footnote to the immediately preceding paragraph and Chapter 7 generally.

Exchanges[1]

18.101 A Scottish secure tenant is entitled to exchange his or her house for another house that is the subject of a Scottish secure tenancy. It is not necessary for both tenancies to be under the same landlord. The written consent of the landlord (or, where applicable, of both landlords) is required.

Where one of the landlords is a registered social landlord which is a housing association, the exchange tenant must be a member of the association when the exchange takes effect.

The procedure set out in Schedule 5 Part 2 of the 2001 Act regarding a written application, deemed consent and right of appeal apply to exchanges as well as assignations, sublets etc.[2] The application must give details of the other house.

1 H(S)A 2001 s 33 and Sch 5 Pt 2.
2 See para 18.97.

18.102 *Criteria for reasonable refusal*[1] As with assignations etc the landlord may only refuse consent if it has reasonable grounds for doing so. Particular examples of reasonable grounds are given, some identical, some different from those that apply in the case of assignations etc. As with those other grounds, it does not appear that the list is intended to be exhaustive:

(a)   A notice for recovery of possession has been served. This is the same as ground (a) in paragraph 18.98.

(b)   A court order for recovery of possession has been granted. This is the same as ground (b) in paragraph 18.98.

(c)   The house was provided in connection with the tenant's employment with the landlord, ie a service tenancy.

(d)   The house has been designed or adapted for a person with special needs, and such a person would no longer occupy the house if the exchange took place.

(e)   The accommodation in the other house is substantially larger than that required by the tenant and the tenant's family or is unsuitable for the needs of the tenant and the tenant's family.

(f)   The exchange would lead to overcrowding. This is the same as ground (d) in paragraph 18.98.

1 H(S)A 2001 s 33(3).

18.103 *Additional considerations* A number of matters are not clearly spelled out. Presumably the correct approach is for each tenant to submit a separate application to his or her own landlord, though this is not stated. If they both have the same landlord, can they make a joint application? Presumably also when one of the criteria for reasonable refusal applies it need only be present in respect of one of the two houses.

In the case of an appeal against refusal it is possible that the two houses may be situated within different sheriffdoms. If only one landlord has refused consent, it would seem sensible for the tenant concerned to appeal to the sheriff court for the area in which his or her house is situated. If both landlords have refused consent, it would also seem sensible for the two tenants to make a joint application to a court in either sheriffdom. Since the subject matter of the action would comprise both houses, this would normally give either court jurisdiction.[1]

1 Help and guidance to tenants seeking an exchange may be obtained from *Homeswapper* at www.homeswapper.co.uk

SHORT SCOTTISH SECURE TENANCIES

Nature of tenancy[1]

18.104 The short Scottish secure tenancy is a social tenancy which may be of a temporary nature. It is modelled on the former private sector short assured tenancy,[2] and like short assured tenancies it is for a fixed term at the end of which the landlord has an absolute right to terminate the tenancy without the tenant having the right to extended security of tenure.

However, unlike the short assured tenancy, which was generally available as an alternative to a normal assured tenancy, the short Scottish secure tenancy may only be granted in certain specified circumstances where a temporary let is thought to be appropriate. It should not, therefore, have the same effect as its private sector equivalent of seriously undermining tenants' security of tenure rights.[3]

The Scottish Government has produced a model short Scottish secure tenancy agreement.[4]

1 H(S)A 2001 s 34.
2 See para 17.104 et seq. Note that it is no longer competent to create an assured or short assured tenancy.
3 See para 17.70.
4 Scottish Government 'Model Short Scottish Secure Tenancy Agreement' available at: www.gov.scot/publications/model-short-scottish-secure-tenancy-agreement-grounds-unrelated-antisocial-behaviour-2019/#:~:text=1%20A%20Model%20Short%20Scottish%20Secure%20Tenancy%20Agreement,tenancies%20created%20on%20or%20after%201%20May%202019.

Qualifying circumstances[1]

18.105 As noted above, a short Scottish secure tenancy may only be created in certain limited circumstances where this type of tenancy is thought to be appropriate. There are two broad scenarios that potentially apply. First, the tenancy may have been converted from a Scottish secure tenancy.[2] Second, the tenancy may be a new one.

In the latter case, a short Scottish secure tenancy may only be created where one of a number of limited circumstances applies. These are specified in Schedule 6, the numbers below corresponding to the paragraphs in that schedule.

The first three cases are in various ways treated differently from the others. Most importantly, it is only in these three cases that the tenancy may later convert to a normal Scottish secure tenancy.[3]

(1) *Previous anti-social behaviour.* Within the period of three years preceding the service of the landlord's notice, a court action for recovery of possession has been granted against the prospective tenant (or any one of prospective joint tenants) in respect of an earlier tenancy. If the previous tenancy was a Scottish secure tenancy, the possession ground must have been either ground 2 (a criminal conviction) or ground 7 (anti-social behaviour).[4] This paragraph also applies where the prospective tenant was evicted for similar reasons from a private residential tenancy, an assured tenancy, a secure tenancy under the Housing (Scotland) Act 1987 or from certain categories of tenancy elsewhere in Britain.

(2) *Anti-social behaviour order.*[5] An anti-social behaviour order has been made against the prospective tenant, any proposed joint tenant, or another prospective resident in the house.[5]

(2A) *Other anti-social behaviour.* Within the previous three years, the proposed tenant or any visitor or other person to be resident at the property has acted in an antisocial manner in relation to another person engaged in lawful activity in the locality of a house occupied by the tenant or someone who it is proposed will reside with the tenant, or has harassed such a person.[6]

(3) *Temporary letting to person seeking accommodation.* The house is to be let expressly on a temporary basis to a person moving into the area in order to take up employment there, and for the purpose of enabling that person to seek accommodation in the area.

(4) *Temporary letting pending development.* The house is to be let to a person expressly on a temporary basis, pending development affecting the house. 'Development' has the same meaning as in s 26 of the Town and Country Planning (Scotland) Act 1997.

(5) *Accommodation for homeless persons.* The house is to be let to a person expressly on a temporary basis, for a period of not less than six months, in fulfilment of a duty imposed on a local authority in relation to homeless persons.[7]

(6) *Accommodation for person requiring housing support services.* The house is to be let expressly on a temporary basis to a person in receipt of housing support services.[8]

(7) *Accommodation in property not owned by landlord.* The house to be let is leased by the landlord from another body and the terms of the lease preclude the letting of the house by the landlord under a Scottish secure tenancy. As we saw earlier, this is one of the circumstances where a normal Scottish secure tenancy cannot be granted.[9]

(7A) *Temporary letting where other property owned.* The house is to be let expressly on a temporary basis to allow arrangements to be made for the proposed tenant's housing needs to be met by property owned by the proposed tenant or another person who it is proposed will reside with him or her.

1 H(S)A 2001 s 34(2) and Sch 6.
2 See para 18.111.
3 See para 18.112.
4 See paras 18.59 and 18.66.
5 H(S)A 2001 Sch 6 and para 2 (as amended).
5 See *South Lanarkshire Council v McKenna* 2010 Hous LR 36, 2010 GWD. 40-808.
6 The term 'harassment' is to be interpreted in accordance with the Protection from Harassment Act 1997 s 8.
7 By Part II of the Housing (Scotland) Act 1987.
8 The term 'housing support services' is defined in H(S)A 2001 s 91(8) to include 'any service which provides support, assistance, advice or counselling to an individual with particular needs with a view to enabling that individual to occupy, or to continue to occupy, as the person's sole or main residence, residential accommodation other than excepted accommodation'. Excepted accommodation is any specified in regulations made by the Scottish Ministers (s 91(9)).
9 See para 18.40.

18.106 In order to be a short Scottish secure tenancy, a tenancy must fulfil all of the conditions required for the existence of a normal Scottish secure tenancy.[1] In addition, there are two further requirements:

(a) The tenancy must be for a term of not less than six months.[2] As with the short assured tenancy, there is no upper limit, but short Scottish secure tenancies are unlikely to be granted on a long-term basis.[3] In the case of a converted Scottish secure tenancy or one created on the basis of paragraphs (1), (2) and (2A) of Schedule 6, the tenancy has a term of 12 months.[4]

(b) Before the creation of the tenancy, the landlord must serve a notice on the prospective tenant. The notice *must* be in the form prescribed by regulations.[5] It must state that the tenancy is to be a short Scottish secure tenancy, specify the relevant paragraph of Schedule 6 that qualifies it as such a tenancy,[6] and specify the term of the tenancy.

The security of tenure provisions and those relating to succession do not apply to short Scottish secure tenancies. Otherwise, short Scottish secure tenants have the same rights as other Scottish secure tenants.[7]

1 See generally paras 18.21 et seq.
2 See *South Lanarkshire Council v McKenna* 2010 Hous LR 36, 2010 GWD. 40-808 and para 18.17.
3 Otherwise, premature termination of the lease could be a problem – see paras 18.47 and 18.107.
4 H(S)A 2001 s 34(6A).
5 The Short Scottish Secure Tenancies (Notice) Regulations 2018, SSI No 154.
6 See para 18.105.
7 H(S)A 2001 s 34(6).

Recovery of possession[1]

18.107 *Notice* Before it can recover possession of the house, the landlord must serve written notice on the tenant in the form prescribed by regulations.[2]

The notice must state that the landlord requires possession of the house and specify a date on or after which the landlord may raise proceedings for recovery of possession. This date cannot be earlier than the date on which the tenancy could have been brought to an end by a notice to quit had it not been a short Scottish secure tenancy, ie it cannot be earlier than the ish. The minimum period of notice is two months, or such longer period as the tenancy agreement may provide.

There is an additional requirement where a former Scottish secure tenancy has been converted to a short Scottish secure tenancy in the circumstances described below,[3] or where it originated as a short Scottish secure tenancy because of the circumstances described in paragraphs 1, 2 and 2A of schedule 6 (relating to anti-social behaviour).[4] In such a case, the landlord may only serve the notice if it considers that an obligation of the tenancy has been broken.[5]

In all cases, the notice must state the reason why the landlord is seeking recovery of possession.[6]

The landlord's notice ceases to be effective if not used within six months, or if the landlord has withdrawn it before that.

A notice for recovery of possession in the prescribed form cannot double as a notice to quit, and a separate notice to quit will also be required in order to prevent tacit relocation from operating.[7] The reason for this is that a notice for recovery of possession may never actually be enforced by an application to the court.

1 H(S)A 2001 s 36.
2 The Short Scottish Secure Tenancies (Proceedings for Possession) Regulations 2018, SSI No 155.
3 See para 18.111.
4 See para 18.105.
5 H(S)A 2001 s 36(2)(aa) inserted by H(S)A 2014 s 11(a).
6 H(S)A 2001 s 36(3)(aa) inserted by H(S)A 2014 s 11(b).
7 *Aberdeenshire Council v Shaw* 2012 SLT (Sh Ct) 144, 2011 Hous LR 56. See requirement (b) in para 18.109.

18.108 *Notice to Local Authority*[1] The landlord must also give notice of the raising of the proceedings to the local authority in whose area the house is situated, unless the landlord is that local authority. The notice should be in the form and manner prescribed under section 11(3) of the Homelessness etc (Scotland) Act 2003.[2]

1 H(S)A 2001 s 36 (6A) and (6B) (added by the Homelessness etc (Scotland) Act 2003 Sch 1 para 4(3)).
2 Under The Notice to Local Authorities (Scotland) Regulations 2008 SSI No 324 (as amended).

18.109   *Court hearing*   Proceedings for recovery of possession may be by summary cause, but this is not mandatory and another type of court action,eg an ordinary cause, is not precluded.[1] The court must make an order for recovery of possession if it appears to it that:

(a)   the tenancy has reached its ish;
(b)   tacit relocation is not operating;[2]
(c)   no further contractual tenancy (whether or not a short Scottish secure tenancy) is in existence; and
(d)   the landlord has served the necessary notice, the proceedings were raised on or after the date specified in the notice, and the notice is still in force.

Any court order must appoint a date for recovery of possession. This has the effect of terminating the tenancy and giving the landlord the right to recover possession of the house at that date.

1 H(S)A 2001 s 36(1); *City of Edinburgh Council v Burnett* 2012 SLT (Sh Ct) 137, 2012 Hous LR 52.
2 For the meaning of tacit relocation see para 10.18 et seq. There appears to be some doubt regarding the operation of tacit relocation in the case of short Scottish secure tenancies –see para 10.21. See also Simon Halliday 'Tacit Relocation' 2001 Jur Rev 201 at 205–6 and P Robson and S Halliday 'Annotations to the Housing (Scotland) Act 2001, s 36' in *Current Law Statutes* 2001.

Conversion of tenancies

18.110   In certain circumstances a Scottish secure tenancy may be converted to a short Scottish secure tenancy and vice versa.

18.111   *Conversion to short Scottish secure tenancy*[1]   If the tenant under a Scottish secure tenancy, or another occupant of the house, is subject to an anti-social behaviour order the landlord may serve a notice on the tenant converting the tenancy to a short Scottish secure tenancy. The tenant may appeal to the court by summary application against such a notice. Also, in certain circumstances the tenancy may convert back to a normal Scottish secure tenancy.[2]

In *South Lanarkshire Council v McKenna*[3] it was held that when a Scottish secure tenancy had been converted to a short Scottish secure tenancy, the tenancy now had a new term of not less than six months, irrespective of the term of the earlier tenancy. A termination notice to take effect from the new ish at the end of the six-month period was therefore valid.

1 H(S)A 2001 s 35 (as amended).
2 See para 18.112.
3 2010 Hous LR 36, 2010 GWD. 40-808.

18.112 *Conversion to Scottish secure tenancy*[1] This provision only applies where a former Scottish secure tenancy has been converted to a short Scottish secure tenancy in the circumstances described above,[2] or where it originated as a short Scottish secure tenancy because of the circumstances described in paragraphs 1, 2 and 2A of Schedule 6 (relating to anti-social behaviour).[3] If the landlord has not served a notice for recovery of possession within the period of 12 months following the creation of the tenancy, the tenancy will automatically become a Scottish secure tenancy on the expiry of that period. Where the tenancy has previously been converted from a Scottish secure tenancy, the new Scottish secure tenancy will have the same term as the one that preceded the creation of the short Scottish secure tenancy.[4]

The landlord may extend the 12-month term of the tenancy by a further six months, by serving a notice on the tenant informing the tenant of the extension and the reasons for it. This must be done at least two months before the day that would otherwise be the expiry date of the tenancy, and may only be done where the tenant is in receipt of housing support services.[5] The tenancy may only be extended in this way once.[6]

Where the landlord *has* served a notice for recovery of possession, the tenancy will still convert to a Scottish secure tenancy if either:

(a)   the landlord's notice has been allowed to lapse because proceedings have not been raised within six months; or
(b)   the notice has been withdrawn by the landlord without proceedings having been raised; or
(c)   the court decides in the tenant's favour.

In all of these cases, the conversion will not take place until at least 12 months have elapsed since the creation of the tenancy.

If a conversion takes place, the landlord must notify the tenant of that fact, specifying the date on which the tenancy became a Scottish secure tenancy.

1 H(S)A 2001 s 37.
2 See para 18.111.
3 See para 18.105.

4 *South Lanarkshire Council v McKenna* 2010 Hous LR 36, 2010 GWD 40-808.

5 The term 'housing support services' is defined in H(S)A 2001 s 91(8) to include 'any service which provides support, assistance, advice or counselling to an individual with particular needs with a view to enabling that individual to occupy, or to continue to occupy, as the person's sole or main residence, residential accommodation other than excepted accommodation'. Excepted accommodation is any specified in regulations made by the Scottish Ministers (s 91(9)).

6 H(S)A 2001 s 35A.

Chapter 19

Repairs and improvements

INTRODUCTION

Repairs

19.1   Landlords of all residential property have extensive repairing obligations. Many of these obligations are the same for both private sector and social tenancies, though the statutory obligations derive from different sources. It is therefore convenient to consider the obligations for both categories of tenancy together in the same chapter. However, since the passing of the Housing (Scotland) Act 2006, which introduced the Repairing Standard for private sector tenancies, the obligations of private landlords are much more extensive.

The landlord's repairing obligation in relation to residential leases derives from a number of sources, both under the common law and from statute. Usually the landlord's obligation will be a contractual one derived from the lease contract and the housing legislation, though sometimes, eg under the Occupiers' Liability (Scotland) Act 1960, it will be delictual.[1] The Human Rights Act 1998 may also be relevant.

There is a substantial amount of overlap between these different sources of the landlord's obligations, which means that many actions can proceed on alternative grounds. For example, many cases involving dampness have proceeded on a combination of the landlord's common law and statutory duties.[2]

Sometimes (particularly in the case of social tenancies) the landlord's obligation may be extended by the terms of the lease agreement, and in individual cases it is always necessary to consult the lease terms as well as the relevant law.[3] Sometimes the lease may attempt to contract out of the landlord's statutory obligations by substituting different terms, but such contracting out will not always be legally effective.

---

1 See para 19.35 et seq.
2 See eg *Fyfe v Scottish Homes* 1995 SCLR 209; *Docherty v Inverclyde District Council* 1995 SCLR 956; *Burns v Monklands District Council* 1997 Hous LR 34
3 See eg *Campbell v Aberdeen City Council* 2007 Hous LR 26.

Improvements and other works by tenant

19.2   A Scottish secure tenant also has the right, in certain circumstances, to carry out necessary repairs and recover the cost from the landlord.[1] In addition, a Scottish secure tenant is sometimes entitled to compensation for alterations or improvements he or she has carried out with the landlord's consent.[2]

In some circumstances, a disabled tenant of a private landlord may be entitled to adapt the house in order to accommodate his or her disability.[3]

1 See para 19.50 et seq.
2 See para 19.55.
3 See para 19.56.

Structure of chapter

19.3   The chapter will therefore be divided into the following topics:

(1)   Human Rights Act 1998.[1]
(2)   The landlord's common law obligation.[2]
(3)   The landlord's statutory obligations, including the Repairing Standard.[3]
(4)   Occupiers' liability: Landlords' liability.[4]
(5)   Statutory nuisance.[5]
(6)   Tenants' right to repair etc.[6]

1 See para 19.4 et seq.
2 See para 19.11 et seq.
3 See para 19.13 et seq.
4 See para 19.35 et seq.
5 See para 19.41 et seq.
6 See para 19.50 et seq.

HUMAN RIGHTS ACT 1998[1]

Application of Act

19.4   We saw in Chapter 1 that the Human Rights Act 1998 adopted the European Convention on Human Rights into the domestic law of the United Kingdom, making it enforceable in the British courts. Where the landlord is a public authority in terms of the Act (or is a 'hybrid authority' exercising a public function),[2] it may have a direct or 'vertical' effect, which would allow a tenant to raise proceedings against a landlord for a breach of human rights under the Convention. Landlords in this category include local authorities, housing associations and many other registered social landlords when exercising the public function of housing. This means that Scottish secure tenants generally will be entitled to take direct action under the 1998 Act.[3]

1 See also paras 1.27 et seq, 17.8 et seq and 18.7 et seq.
2 On this, though, see *Ali v Serco Ltd* [2019] CSIH 54, 2020 SC 182, discussed at para 17.10.
3 See para 17.8 et seq.

19.5   In the case of tenancies from private landlords, the influence of the Act is less obvious. However, since the courts are public authorities in terms of the Act[1] and are therefore required to act in a way that is compatible with it, there may be situations where the Act has an indirect (or 'horizontal') influence in a case between a landlord and tenant that has been raised in court on some other legal ground. For example, the courts are thought to have a duty to develop the common law in a way that is compatible with the European Convention; a case based upon the landlord's common law repairing obligation might therefore be influenced by human rights issues.[2]

1 Human Rights Act 1998 s 6.
2 See para 17.8 et seq.

Relevant convention rights

19.6   The following Convention rights could arguably apply in cases relating to repairs.[1] However, as the human rights case law on repairs, so far as it has been reported, is sparse and mostly English, much of what follows is speculative:

1 See also Derek O'Carroll *A Brief Guide to the Human Rights Act 1998 in relation to Housing* (2000), para 3.10. Mr O'Carroll argues that the ineffectiveness of specific implement and other tenants' remedies could be a breach of Article 6 (right to a fair hearing). In relation to specific implement see paras 4.2 et seq, 4.21 et seq and 19.29.

19.7   *Right to respect for private and family life* (Article 8) T h i s Article could apply in the case of severe breaches of the repairing obligation, for example if the house is uninhabitable because of severe dampness. This was argued in *Lee v Leeds City Council* and *Ratcliffe v Sandwell Metropolitan Borough Council*,[1] two English cases that were heard together in the Court of Appeal. Although the tenants' action failed, it was confirmed that Article 8 could apply in cases where a house's state of repair was sufficiently severe; however an individual tenant's rights had to be balanced against the needs of the community as a whole and it was not a function of the courts to determine the housing priorities of a democratically elected council.

This case is important in that it at least confirmed that landlords can have a positive obligation under Article 8 and not just a negative duty to refrain from acting in a way that might interfere with a person's private and family life. The decision also took into account the fact that the tenant had an alternative remedy on the ground of statutory nuisance; this argument might have less force in Scotland, where actions on the basis of statutory nuisance have met with less success than they have south of the Border.[2]

On the other hand, in that case the landlord did not have a statutory repairing obligation. Scottish private sector landlords have a statutory obligation and so tenants do have an alternative remedy.

1 [2002] L&TR 35, 1 WLR 1488.
2 See para 19.41 et seq.

19.8   *Prohibition of discrimination* (Article 14)   In *R (on the application of Erskine) v Lambeth London Borough Council*[1] a local authority tenant claimed that there was a discriminatory enforcement regime under the Housing Act 1985, since private and housing association tenants could request a housing authority to serve a repairs notice, but not a tenant of the authority itself. However, since Article 14 can only be enforced in conjunction with another Article (such as Article 8), the tenant's action failed.

The court did not consider that the disrepair in question was severe enough to amount to a breach of Article 8; however, the crucial point was that, for Article 14 to apply, it was necessary that the legislation alleged to be discriminatory should have as its purpose the furthering of the rights under Article 8 or of another right protected by the Convention. This was not the case with the relevant part of the 1985 Act, whose purpose was to protect and promote public health and improve the condition of low-cost housing stock.

This case suggests that Article 14 can apply in principle, perhaps in other situations where a local authority's statutory functions result in its own tenants being treated differently from those of other landlords.

1 [2003] NPC 118, EWHC 2479.

19.9   *Protection of property* (Protocol 1, Article 1)   Everyone is entitled to the peaceful enjoyment of his or her possessions and may not be deprived of them. A lease confers a right of property upon the tenant, though this of course must be balanced against the property right of the landlord. Arguably, a tenant's right would be infringed if the condition of a house rendered it uninhabitable. Lesser breaches of the landlord's repairing obligation might have the effect of depriving the tenant of other property or possessions which were contained in the house.

19.10 *Right to life* (Article 2)   In the leading case of *Mitchell v Glasgow City Council* (which mainly concerned whether a local authority had a duty under Article 2 to protect a tenant from the actions of an anti-social fellow tenant), Lord Rodger of Earlsferry suggested obiter that a severe case of disrepair which rendered a property dangerous could possibly amount to an infringement of a tenant's right to life.[1]

1 *Mitchell v Glasgow City Council* [2009] 1 AC 874 at 902 per Lord Rodger of Earlsferry, 2009 SC (HL) 21; see also para 18.11.

LANDLORD'S COMMON LAW OBLIGATION

19.11   We saw in Chapter 3 that all landlords have a duty at common law to provide and thereafter maintain a property that is in a tenantable or habitable condition. The obligation to provide tenantable or habitable subjects is also expressed as an obligation on the part of the landlord to provide subjects that are reasonably fit for the purpose of the let. The common law duty involves a number of separate elements, including an obligation to provide and keep the property wind and watertight, free from damp and in a safe condition.[1]

We also saw that in the case of commercial leases the landlord's obligation is invariably contracted out of, the tenant's FRI (full repairing and insuring) lease being the norm. However, this is *not* the case with residential leases where the landlord's common law repairing obligation generally still applies. It would, in any case, be difficult to contract out of it in view of the extent to which it has been repeated and reinforced by statute in relation to residential tenancies.

There is much case law, old and modern, on the landlord's common law obligation as it applies to dwellinghouses.[2] In modern times, it has been applied in a number of cases where houses have suffered from dampness.[3]

Under the initial obligation the landlord has a duty to inspect the property prior to entry to ensure that it is in a tenantable or habitable condition.[4]

1 See para 3.26 et seq.
2 See para 3.29 et seq.
3 See para 3.31.
4 See para 3.35.

19.12   Once the tenant has moved into a tenantable or habitable property, the landlord is thereafter obliged to maintain it in a similar condition throughout the duration of the lease. However, this continuing obligation is not a warranty. This means, in effect, that the obligation does not arise until the tenant has drawn the need for the repair to the landlord's attention. There is therefore no breach of contract merely because the repair has become necessary, but only after the landlord has been notified and has failed to act.

Once notification has been made the landlord must carry the repairs out within a reasonable time. Otherwise the tenant will be entitled to rescind and/or claim damages.[1]

1 On the landlord's repairing obligation, see further para 3.40 et seq.

THE LANDLORD'S STATUTORY OBLIGATIONS; THE REPAIRING STANDARD

Introduction

19.13   In relation to Scottish secure tenancies, the landlord's statutory obligations derive from the Housing (Scotland) Act 2001. In the case of private sector tenancies (including assured, short assured, regulated and private residential tenancies) they derive from the Housing (Scotland) Act 2006. These repairing obligations of private landlords are collectively known as 'the Repairing Standard'.[1] They partly duplicate the provisions of the 2001 Act in relation to social tenancies, but also extend much further.

1 These currently do not apply to houses forming part of agricultural holdings. However, the Scottish Government has indicated that it intends to have the repairing standard apply to such houses by March 2027: see www.gov.scot/publications/agricultural-holdings-and-tenant-farming-guide/pages/housing-standards/.

Habitability

19.14   The obligations regarding habitability derive from identical provisions in the Housing (Scotland) Act 2006, and the Housing (Scotland) Act 2001, the former applying only to private sector lets and the latter only to Scottish secure tenancies.[1] There is an implied condition that:

- the house is wind and watertight and in all other respects reasonably fit for human habitation at the commencement of the tenancy; and
- the house will thereafter be kept so by the landlord during the tenancy.[2]

We may conveniently call these, respectively, the 'initial obligation' and the 'continuing obligation'. The word 'reasonably' refers to the condition of the house; whether the landlord has acted reasonably is irrelevant.[3]

1 H(S)A 2006 Pt 1 chr 4; H(S)A 2001 Sch 4.
2 H(S)A 2006 ss 13(1)(a) and 14(1); H(S)A 2001 Sch 4 para 1; see also *Summers v Salford Corporation* [1943] AC 283; *MacLeod v Alexander* 2000 Hous LR 136; *Mearns v Glasgow City Council* 2002 SLT (Sh Ct) 49, 2001 Hous LR 130.
3 *Docherty v Inverclyde District Council* 1995 SCLR 956.

19.15 *Need for notification* The continuing obligation to repair only arises after the tenant notifies the landlord, or the landlord otherwise becomes aware of the need for repair. Thereafter the landlord must carry out the work within a reasonable time and make good any damage caused in the process.[1]

The position is less clear with the initial obligation to provide subjects reasonably fit for human habitation. While the continuing obligation to repair is expressly triggered only by the landlord becoming aware of the need for repair, there is no such provision in relation to the initial obligation. In *Todd v Clapperton*,[2] it was held that the initial obligation was breached even by latent defects that could not have been discovered by any reasonable investigation.

1 H(S)A 2006 s 14 (2) and (4); H(S)A 2001 Sch 4 para 3.
2 [2009] CSOH 112, 2009 SLT 837. For further discussion of this issue, see paras 3.34–3.49

19.16 *Meaning of 'unfit for human habitation'* A house is considered unfit for human habitation if it falls short of building regulations by reason of disrepair or sanitary defects;[1] 'sanitary defects' includes lack of air space or ventilation, darkness, dampness, absence of adequate and readily accessible water supply or of sanitary arrangements or of other conveniences, and inadequate paving or drainage of courts, yards or passages.[2]

1 H(S)A 2006 s 13(2); H(S)A 2001 Sch 4 para 5(1).
2 H(S)A 2001 Sch 4 para 6; for some reason this definition has not been repeated in the 2006 Act, but presumably a similar definition will apply in relation to private sector tenancies.

19.17 *Comparison with common law obligation* The statutory provisions in relation to habitability largely mirror the common law obligation to provide and maintain the property in a tenantable or habitable condition, though they extend and clarify it to a considerable extent. They should, therefore, be considered in conjunction with each other.

It will be seen that there is some discrepancy between the phraseology traditionally adopted for the common law obligation and the statutory provisions. This is probably due to the fact that the statutory provisions, which evolved from earlier legislation, originated in part from the equivalent English provisions. However, essentially the common law and the statutory provisions regarding habitability provide the same thing, and there is no significant discrepancy between them, except for the fact that the statutory provisions extend much further and include relatively minor defects that do not prevent the house being lived in. The Scottish courts have approved the following definition, given by the House of Lords in *Summers v Salford Corporation*, in relation to the same wording as it appears in the English legislation:

> 'If the state of repair of a house is such that by ordinary user damage may be caused to the occupier, either in respect of personal injury to life or limb or injury to health, then the house is not in all respects reasonably fit for human habitation.'[1]

In *Summers*, the tenant was injured by a falling window, which already had one broken sash cord. This was enough to prevent the house being reasonably fit for human habitation.

1 Lord Atkin in *Summers v Salford Corporation* [1943] AC 283 at 288, citing his own judgment in *Morgan v Liverpool Corporation* [1927] 2 KB 131, adopted in *Haggerty v Glasgow Corporation* 1964 SLT (Notes) 95; see also *Christian v Aberdeen City Council* 2006 SCLR 448, 2005 Hous LR 71.

19.18   In the much more recent Scottish case of *Mearns v Glasgow City Council*[1] the same was held to be true because a pipe had been liable to burst since before the tenant took entry, even though she subsequently occupied the house for 15 years without knowledge of any danger before a burst finally occurred. The landlords had, nevertheless, failed to deliver a habitable house at the beginning of the lease. Again, it has been held that a glass pane in an internal door, which did not comply with relevant safety standards and which as a result could break without use of excessive force, resulted in a property being unfit for human habitation.[2]

1 2002 SLT (Sh Ct) 49. See also para 3.37.
2 *Todd v Clapperton* [2009] CSOH 112, 2009 SLT 837.

19.19   As mentioned above[1] many cases have proceeded on a combination of the common law and statutory duties of the landlord regarding habitability, and indeed in some cases the court has not entirely made it clear on which of these grounds its decision has been based.[2] This combination of grounds is particularly prevalent in the many cases involving dampness.[3]

1 See para 19.1.

2 See eg *Mearns v Glasgow City Council* 2002 SLT (Sh Ct) 49.
3 See eg *Fyfe v Scottish Homes* 1995 SCLR 209; *Docherty v Inverclyde District Council* 1995 SCLR 956; *Burns v Monklands District Council* 1997 Hous LR 34; see also the coverage of this topic and authority cited in paras 3.31 et seq.

Obligation to inspect

19.20 The landlord is obliged to inspect the house at the commencement of the tenancy in order to identify any work necessary to bring it up to the required standard and to notify the tenant of the result.[1]

1 H(S)A 2006 s 19; H(S)A 2001 Sch 4 para 2.

Right of access[1]

19.21 Landlords under a Scottish secure tenancy and private sector landlords both have a right of access for the purpose of viewing the state and condition of the house and for carrying out any necessary work. The landlord, or any person authorised by the landlord in writing, may exercise this right at a reasonable time, on giving 24 hours' notice to the tenant or occupier.

A private landlord may apply to the First-Tier Tribunal for assistance in gaining entry in order to comply with the repairing standard in cases where the tenant has been uncooperative.[2]

1 H(S)A 2006 s 181(4) and s 184(3) and (4); H(S)A 2001 Sch 4 para 4.
2 H(S)A 2006 s 28A et seq (inserted by the Private Rented Housing (Scotland) Act 2011 s 35 and amended by the First-tier Tribunal for Scotland (Transfer of Functions of the Private Rented Housing Panel) Regulations (SSI 2016/338)).

Exceptions to landlord's repairing obligations (private sector tenancies)[1]

19.22 A private landlord is not required to carry out repairs:

(a) which are the responsibility of the tenant, though only in the case of leases of three years or more, ie those cases where contracting out of the repairing standard is allowed;

(b) which would normally be required by virtue of the tenant's duty to use the house in a proper manner, even where the landlord has agreed to relieve the tenant of this duty;

(c) where the house is to be rebuilt or reinstated in the event of destruction or damage by fire or by storm, flood or other inevitable accident; or

(d)   which involve the repair or maintenance of anything that the
tenant is entitled to remove from the house.

1   H(S)A 2006 s 16.

The repairing standard: further requirements

19.23   The provisions in the 2006 Act apply only to private sector
tenancies and not to Scottish secure tenancies. As well as repeating the
above provisions regarding habitability which apply to Scottish secure
tenancies, the 2006 Act develops the obligation considerably, adding
even more detail and clarification.

In relation to private sector tenancies only, therefore, it is further
provided that a house meets the repairing standard if:

(1)   The structure and exterior of the house (including drains, gutters
and external pipes) are in a reasonable state of repair and in
proper working order.[1] In determining this, regard should he had
to the age, character and prospective life of the house and to the
locality in which the house is situated.[2] In the case of flats, it
includes the common property, but only where the tenant's use
of the property is adversely affected by the disrepair or failure in
maintenance.[3]
In *Hastie v City of Edinburgh District Council*[4] it was held that
the exterior of the building included windows and the tenant
was entitled to recover from the landlord the cost of repairing a
window broken by vandals.

(2)   The installations in the house for the supply of water, gas and
electricity and for sanitation, space heating and heating water
are in a reasonable state of repair and in proper working order.[5]
This includes installations outwith the house which, directly or
indirectly, serve the house and which the owner is responsible for
maintaining, either solely or in common with others.[6] In relation
to this and the remaining requirements below, regard is to be had
to any guidance issued by the Scottish Ministers.[7]

(3)   Any fixtures, fittings and appliances provided by the landlord
under the tenancy are in a reasonable state of repair and in proper
working order.[8]

(4)   Any furnishings provided by the landlord under the tenancy are
capable of being used safely for the purpose for which they are
designed.[9]

(5)   The house has satisfactory provision for detecting fires and for
giving warning in the event of fire or suspected fire.[10]

(6) The house has satisfactory provision for giving warning if carbon monoxide is present in a concentration that is hazardous to health.[11]

(7) The house meets the "tolerable standard".[12]

(8) Any common parts pertaining to the house can be safely accessed and used.[13]

(9) The house has satisfactory provision for, and safe access to, a food storage area and a food preparation space.[14]

(10) Where the house is in a tenement, common doors are secure and fitted with satisfactory emergency exit locks.[15]

The above provisions have been developed from provisions in Schedule 10 to the Housing (Scotland) Act 1987, which was repealed by the 2006 Act. However, these earlier provisions applied to *all* residential tenancies, both social and private sector, of less than seven years. Since the replacement provisions of the 2006 Act only apply to private sector tenancies, the repairing obligations of social landlords would appear to have been diminished.

1 H(S)A 2006 s 13(1)(b).

2 H(S)A 2006 s 13(3).

3 H(S)A 2006 s 15.

4 1981 SLT (Sh Ct) 92; see also *Edinburgh District Council v Laurie* 1982 SLT (Sh Ct) 83. Note that these cases were heard at a time when a similar provision, not repeated in the 2001 Act, applied to social tenancies – see the end of this paragraph.

5 H(S)A 2006 s 13(1)(c).

6 H(S)A 2006 s 13 (4).

7 H(S)A 2006 s 13(7). For Scottish Government guidance, see www.gov.scot/publications/repairing-standard.

8 H(S)A 2006 s 13(1)(d).

9 H(S)A 2006 s 13(1)(e).

10 H(S)A 2006 s 13(1)(f). This is prospectively repealed (Housing (Scotland) Act 2006 (Modification of the Repairing Standard) Regulations 2019 SSI No 61 reg 3(2)(b). This requirement is in any case included in the 'tolerable standard', included below.

11 H(S)A 2006 s 13(1)(g). This is prospectively repealed (Housing (Scotland) Act 2006 (Modification of the Repairing Standard) Regulations 2019 SSI No 61 reg 3(2)(b)). This requirement is in any case included in the 'tolerable standard', included below.

12 H(S)A 2006 s 13(1)(h). This is defined in the Housing (Scotland) Act 1987 s 86. There is some overlap between the tolerable standard and the repairing standard, but the former also includes, for example, adequate water supply, toilet facilities and drainage system.

13 H(S)A 2006 s 13(1)(i). This is added by the Housing (Scotland) Act 2006 (Modification of the Repairing Standard) Regulations 2019 SSI No 61 reg 3(2)(d), due to come into force on 1 March 2024 (reg 1(4)).

14 H(S)A 2006 s 13(1)(j). This is added by the Housing (Scotland) Act 2006 (Modification of the Repairing Standard) Regulations 2019 SSI No 61 reg 3(2)(d), due to come into force on 1 March 2024 (reg 1(4)).

15 H(S)A 2006 s 13(1)(k). This is added by the Housing (Scotland) Act 2006 (Modification of the Repairing Standard) Regulations 2019 SSI No 61 reg 3(2)(d), due to come into force on 1 March 2024 (reg 1(4)).

Contracting out

19.24 In respect of private sector tenancies, the provisions of the Housing (Scotland) Act 2006 in relation to repairs may be contracted out of in the case of tenancies 'for a period of not less than three years'.[1]

In the case of tenancies for less than three years, there is a general prohibition against contracting out, as well as against penalising the tenant for enforcing the landlord's compliance with the repairing obligation by terminating the lease or in any other way.[2] However, in such cases either party can apply to the First-Tier Tribunal to have the landlord's repairing obligation excluded or modified.[3] The Tribunal may not grant such an order unless both the landlord and the tenant give their consent to the change and the Tribunal considers it to be reasonable. It is not immediately obvious why a tenant would normally agree to this.

It is not clear how this is to apply with private residential tenancies which, as we have seen, do not have a specific term.[4] Presumably, such a tenancy not being 'for a period of not less than 3 years' (or indeed for any specific period at all), it will not be competent to contract out of these provisions.

1 H(S)A 2006 s 16(1)(a) and (2).
2 H(S)A 2006 s 17.
3 H(S)A 2006 s 18.
4 See para 17.28.

19.25 In relation to Scottish secure tenancies, there is no prohibition against contracting out of the landlord's repairing obligation contained in the Housing (Scotland) Act 2001. However, social landlords are probably less likely to want to do this, especially if they have adopted the model tenancy agreement for Scottish secure tenancies recommended by the Scottish Government.[1]

Common law obligations, of course, can generally be contracted out of. However, this will not normally now be possible in relation to private sector residential tenancies, since the statutory provisions duplicate the common law provisions.

1 See para 18.88.

Enforcement

19.26 A tenant has a number of enforcement remedies against a landlord who is in breach of the repairing obligation, some of these being more effective than others.

19.27 *Damages*[1] A tenant may recover damages in respect of any loss incurred as a result of the landlord's breach. This may include damages for any patrimonial loss caused by the lack of repair, including (where the tenant has been forced to move out of the subjects) removal costs and rent for alternative premises,[2] damage to furniture, clothing and other personal effects,[3] redecoration costs,[4] or loss of earnings in cases where the disrepair has caused illness.[5] *Solatium* may be awarded in respect of illness, personal injury or death.[6]

1 See para 4.37 et seq.
2 *Welsh, Walker & Macpherson v Sowter* (1890) 6 Sh Ct Rep 130.
3 *Gunn v National Coal Board* 1982 SLT 526; *McArdle v City of Glasgow District Council* 1989 SCLR 19; *Galloway v Glasgow City Council* 2001 Hous LR 59.
4 *Little v City of Glasgow District Council* 1988 SCLR 482.
5 *Lawless v Glasgow Police Commissioners* (1892) 8 Sh Ct Rep 195; *Gunn v National Coal Board* 1982 SLT 526.
6 *Lawless v Glasgow Police Commissioners* (1892) 8 Sh Ct Rep 195; *Sinclair v Fullerton's Trustees* (1894) 10 Sh Ct Rep 256 (funeral expenses were also awarded in this case); *Morrison v Stirling District Council* 1996 Hous LR 5.

19.28   Damages may also be claimed in respect of the inconvenience caused to the tenant because of the lack of repair.[1] They may be awarded, for example, in cases where a tenant has continued to live in a house that is not in a tenantable or habitable condition pending the landlord's rectification of the problem, most notably in those cases where the house has been affected by dampness.

In a number of cases this has been described as *solatium*, in contrast to claims for patrimonial loss. However, it has now been held that this head of damages is distinct from *solatium* for personal injury and, unlike the latter, is not subject to the three-year prescription.[2]

1 *Gunn v National Coal Board* 1982 SLT 526; *McArdle v City of Glasgow District Council* 1989 SCLR 19; *Quinn v Monklands District Council* 1995 SCLR 393, 1996 Hous LR 86; *Galloway v Glasgow City Council* 2001 Hous LR 59; *Mack v Glasgow City Council* 2006 SC 543, 2006 SLT 556.
2 *Mack v Glasgow City Council* 2006 SC 543, 2006 SLT 556.

19.29   *Specific implement*   It is competent for a tenant to obtain a court order *ad factum praestandum* to compel the landlord to carry out whatever repairs are necessary in order to comply with the repairing obligation. However, as we saw earlier, the use of specific implement for this purpose has in the past been problematical.[1]

On the other hand, a repairing standard enforcement order (RSEO)[2] is effectively a statutory form of specific implement, and RSEOs appear to be operating successfully. However, they only apply to private sector tenancies and not to social tenancies.

1 See para 4.21 et seq.
2 See para 19.34.

19.30 *Retention* If a landlord is in breach of contract, the tenant has the right to withhold rent until the breach is remedied. This remedy has been discussed in depth in Chapter 4.[1] As also noted before, in the case of residential tenancies the right of retention should perhaps be exercised with some caution, particularly against private landlords.[2]

1 See para 4.39 et seq.
2 See para 4.44 et seq.

19.31 *Abatement* This is where the tenant is entitled to a refund of rent as a result of having been partially or wholly deprived of beneficial enjoyment of the subjects for which rent is paid. Abatement is also considered in depth in Chapter 6.[1]

The granting of a rent relief order is effectively a statutory rent abatement.[2]

1 See para 4.47 et seq; for authority on abatement in relation to residential tenancies see *Renfrew District Council v Gray* 1987 SLT (Sh Ct) 70; *MacLeod v Alexander* 2000 Hous LR 136.
2 See para 19.34.

Statutory enforcement of the repairing standard

19.32 In relation to private sector lets, the Housing (Scotland) Act 2006 provides a statutory mechanism for enforcement of the landlord's repairing obligation. If a tenant believes that the landlord has failed to comply with the repairing obligation, the tenant can apply to the First-Tier Tribunal.[1] The local authority may also apply to the First-Tier Tribunal for a determination that the landlord has failed to comply with this obligation.[2]

1 H(S)A s 22.
2 H(S)A s 22(1A), (1B). The Scottish Ministers may also make an order specifying further persons to have this right.

19.33 *Procedure* Before a tenant can apply to the First-Tier Tribunal, he or she must have notified the landlord that work requires to be carried out for the purpose of complying with the landlord's repairing obligation.[1]

Consideration of the application by the First-Tier Tribunal is not automatic and the Chamber President has the discretion to reject the application if it is vexatious or frivolous, if the applicant has previously made an identical or substantially similar application in relation to the same house and there has not been a reasonable period of time between the applications, or if the dispute has been resolved.[2]

The President must normally reach this decision within 14 days and thereafter notify the applicant (and the tenant, if different) if the application has been rejected, as well the applicant's agent (if the latter's name and address is known), setting out the reasons for the rejection and explaining the procedure for appealing against it.[3]

The procedure to be followed by the Tribunal is set out in Schedule 2 to the 2006 Act.

On receipt of a tenant's application the First-Tier Tribunal must pass on certain information from it to the local authority, in order to help the local authority to identify unregistered landlords.[4]

1 H(S)A 2006 s 22(3).
2 H(S)A 2006 s 23(1) and (2).
3 H(S)A 2006 s 23(3), (4), (4A) and (5).
4 H(S)A 2006 s 22A (inserted by the Private Rented Housing (Scotland) Act 2011 s 11; see also para 20.14.

19.34 *Repairing standard enforcement orders/rent relief orders* If the Tribunal decides that a landlord has failed to comply with the repairing standard obligation, it may issue a repairing standard enforcement order ('RSEO') requiring the landlord to carry out any necessary work and make good any damage caused by it, within a reasonable deadline of at least 21 days.[1]

If the Tribunal determines that the landlord has failed to meet such an order, it may make a rent relief order, granting the tenant a rent abatement of up to 90%.[2] This may be revoked later if the work is carried out to a satisfactory standard, but the tenant will have no retrospective obligation to repay the balance of rent for the period during which the order was in force.[3]

A landlord who fails to comply with a repairing standard enforcement order without a reasonable excuse has also committed a criminal offence and may be subject to a fine.[4] Examples of a reasonable excuse would be where access has been denied, or the repairs would endanger someone. It is also an offence for the landlord to re-let the house while an RSEO is still in force.[5]

The existence of an RSEO does not prevent the landlord seeking to terminate the tenancy, for example to demolish the property. The RSEO, however, would remain in force even after the tenant was removed, until the property was actually demolished or the Tribunal was satisfied that the requirements of the RSEO have been complied with.[6]

In the comparatively short time since the 2006 Act has been in force, a considerable number of repairing standard enforcement orders have so far been made.

1 H(S)A 2006 s 24.

2 H(S)A 2006 ss 26 and 27.
3 H(S)A 2006 s 27(5).
4 H(S)A 2006 s 28.
5 H(S)A 2006 s 28(5).
6 *Charlton v Josephine Marshall Trust* [2020] CSIH 11, 2020 SLT 409.

OCCUPIERS' LIABILITY[1]

1960 Act

19.35   If the leased premises are rendered dangerous by the landlord's failure in a repairing obligation, the landlord may be liable in damages to anyone who is injured or whose property is damaged as a result. The landlord owes a delictual duty of care which extends, not only to the tenant, but also to anyone else who comes on to the property. This responsibility for dangerous premises normally falls upon an occupier, but extends to a landlord where the failure in a repairing obligation has caused the problem; in other words, whereas in a commercial lease, which is likely to be in FRI terms, any liability under the 1960 Act would normally fall upon the tenant as occupier, in the case of residential leases it is the landlord that is potentially liable and the actual tenant may, in fact, be the pursuer in the action rather than the defender.

As a result, all of the sparse case law, to the extent that it has been reported, relates to residential tenancies. Usually the claim is by the tenant or a member of the tenant's family,[2] but occasionally also by a third party visiting the house.[3]

1 The current law is found in the Occupiers' Liability (Scotland) Act 1960. This, in broad terms, restores the general approach of the law as it stood before the decision of the House of Lords in *Dumbreck v Robert Addie & Sons (Collieries) Ltd* 1929 SC (HL) 51. Accordingly, authorities older than that case will often be found to be useful.
2 *Lamb v Glasgow District Council* 1978 SLT (Notes) 64; *Murray v Edinburgh District Council* 1981 SLT 253; *Hughes Tutrix v Glasgow District Council* 1981 SLT (Sh Ct) 70; *Scott v Glasgow City Council* 1997 Hous LR 107; *Guy v Strathkelvin District Council* 1997 SCLR 405, 1997 Hous LR 14; *McCallie v North Ayrshire Council* 2002 SCLR 178; *Kerr v East Ayrshire Council* 2005 SLT (Sh Ct) 67 (sub nom *Nimmo v East Ayrshire Council* 2005 Hous LR 35); and *Kirkham v Link Housing Group Ltd* 2012 Hous LR 87, 2012 GWD 24-500.
3 *Muir v North Ayrshire Council* 2005 SLT 963, 2005 GWD 30-582; *Bell v North Ayrshire Council* 2007 Rep LR 108, 2007 GWD 25-444.

19.36   Such an action can result from a breach of the landlord's common law obligation, one imposed by the lease, or of the statutory duties imposed on residential landlords. Although, therefore, liability under the 1960 Act is delictual, the extent of the obligation is determined by the landlord's contractual obligation.

The situations in which an action under the Occupier's Liability (Scotland) Act 1960 is competent are those where the disrepair caused by breach of the landlord's obligation has led to the death, personal injury or illness to, or damage to the property of, the tenant or some other person on the property, such as a member of the tenant's family. If the tenant is seeking damages for some other kind of loss, eg inconvenience, or is seeking a remedy other than damages, eg to have the repairs carried out, then the only remedy would be an action for breach of the lease contract.

Breach of contract claims

19.37 In *Cameron v Young*[1] the tenant of a house and his wife and children all contracted typhoid as a result of the house's insanitary condition. It was held that only the tenant himself could claim damages for breach of the landlord's repairing obligation and that neither his wife nor his children had a title to sue for breach of the lease contract.[2]

Although it is now rather an old case, *Cameron v Young* has never been overruled, and appears still to be good law, though it is generally thought to have been made redundant by the passing of the Occupiers' Liability (Scotland) Act 1960.[3] However, it should be remembered that section 2 of the 1960 Act superimposes a duty of care on top of the landlord's repairing obligation; in other words, it is necessary to prove that the landlord has been negligent. As it is not always necessary to establish negligence in a breach of contract action, this may be the preferable option in cases where the actual tenant has been injured.[4] The fact that nowadays the lease is much more likely to be in the joint names of both partners should make the application of *Cameron v Young* much less restrictive.

1 [1908] AC 176, 1908 SC (HL) 7.
2 Of course, the contract would also be enforceable by a third party who had a relevant right to do so in terms of the Contract (Third Party Rights) (Scotland) Act 2017 or under the previous common law of *jus quaesitum tertio*.
3 See eg *Scott v Glasgow City Council* 1997 Hous LR 107. Certainly, the implication in *Cameron* that the landlord would not even be *delictually* liable to an occupier other than a tenant (in contrast with a neighbour) is no longer correct as a result of the 1960 Act, even if it was at the time the case was decided.
4 See the analysis of *Huber v Ross* 1912 SC 898 at para 3.15 et seq.

Volenti non fit injuria

19.38 We saw in Chapter 3[1] that the strict line taken in the case of *Webster v Brown*[2] meant that a tenant who continued to live in a property containing a known danger could be barred from an action for breach of the lease contract on the ground that he or she had consented to the danger. The appropriate remedy for a tenant in such a case was to rescind and claim damages.

However, although in an action under the Occupiers' Liability (Scotland) Act 1960 a defence of *volenti non fit injuria* ('to one consenting no wrong is done')[3] is also competent,[4] it has been argued that in such a case the court would not be bound by *Webster* and so be free to take a more liberal line when applying the doctrine.[5]

Moreover, there is authority that is contrary to *Webster*, even in breach of contract cases. We already saw that in the years following the decision in *Webster v Brown* there were many attempts to distinguish that case,[6] and there is both English and Scottish authority to the effect that mere knowledge of a danger does not imply consent in situations where the tenant has no real choice.[7]

1 See para 3.48.
2 (1892) 19 R 765.
3 *Trayner's Latin Maxims* (4th edn 1894), W Green/Sweet and Maxwell, p 633.
4 OL(S)A 1960 s 2(3).
5 See Walker *Delict* (2nd edn 1981) pp 347–48; A McAllister 'Occupiers' Liability' in *Delict* (ed Thomson), W. Green/SULI, 2007/8, 17.78.
6 See para 3.49.
7 See *Thomas v Quartermaine* (1887) 18 QBD 685, per Bowen LJ at 696, approved by the House of Lords in *Smith v Baker* [1891] AC 325 and in turn in the Inner House judgment in *Cameron v Young* 1907 SC 475 at 482–33 per Lord Kinnear.

19.39   In *Hughes' Tutrix v Glasgow District Council*[1] a council tenant raised an action against her landlords under section 3 of the 1960 Act on behalf of her child, who was injured by catching her hand on a broken toilet bowl. The pursuer had made several complaints to the landlords about the condition of the bowl. The defenders submitted a plea of *volenti non fit injuria*, contending that by continuing to reside in the premises while knowing of the bowl's condition, the pursuer had accepted the danger.

It was held that the plea of *volenti* could not be sustained because the child herself could not be considered to have accepted the risk. However, Sheriff Gordon also held that the pursuer had not accepted it either. The fact that *Webster v Brown* and the subsequent cases that had applied it had been decided on the basis of contract meant that he could distinguish them and decide the delictual claim under the 1960 Act in accordance with the less strict line indicated above.

Sheriff Gordon also felt that the view, expressed in *Webster v Brown*, that the tenant's proper remedy was to repudiate the contract and move elsewhere was socially unrealistic in modern times, particularly in the case of a council tenant whose only alternative might be to obtain another lease from the same landlords:

> '[W]hat the defenders are in effect saying is: "If you do not tell us about the defect we cannot be liable; if you do tell us and we do nothing, or a fortiori, we repudiate our obligations and make it clear that we are going to do nothing, we cannot be liable either, because if you stay on in the house you are volenti; but, of course, we are the only people who are really in a position to give you any other accommodation".'[2]

1 1982 SLT (Sh Ct) 70.
2 1982 SLT (Sh Ct) 70 at 72.

Scope of the 1960 Act

19.40 The wording of section 3 of the Occupiers' Liability (Scotland) Act 1960 (which specifically refers to 'maintenance and repair') does not make it entirely clear how much of the landlord's obligation has been incorporated, in particular whether it encompasses the landlord's initial obligation to provide subjects that are in a tenantable or habitable condition, as opposed to the continuing obligation to maintain them in such a condition.[1] However, among the sparse case authority there is at least one decision where it appears to have been assumed that the landlord's initial obligation *is* included.

In *Lamb v Glasgow District Council*[2] the tenant's wife had an epileptic fit and fell, striking the front of a coal fire. The fire was not properly fastened to the hearth and tipped forward, spilling burning coal on to her. This was due to a failure in the installation of the fire, which had been made by a previous tenant. The current tenant had not notified the landlords of any deficiency. In finding the landlords liable under section 3 of the 1960 Act, Lord Grieve observed:

> 'It is reasonable that the tenant in possession should alert his landlord to actual or suspected defects. A landlord, however, is obliged by the common law to put urban subjects in habitable or tenantable condition at entry and that must entail an inspection of the subjects at that time.'[3]

It was held that such an inspection would have revealed a reasonably foreseeable danger in the way the fire was fitted.

Lord Grieve therefore made it clear that the landlords' liability stemmed from their initial obligation. Moreover, the duty of inspection upon them at the beginning of the let (which is imposed by statute as well as common law) absolved the tenant of the need to notify them of any defect that the inspection should have revealed.[4]

In an action under the 1960 Act which is based upon the landlord's continuing obligation it is of course always necessary that the landlord should have been notified, or deemed to have been notified, of the need for the repair.[5]

1 For a more detailed discussion of this see A McAllister 'Occupiers' Liability' in *Delict* (ed Thomson), W Green/SULI, 2007/08, 17.66–17.72.
2 1978 SLT (Notes) 64.
3 1978 SLT (Notes) 64 at 64.
4 But see also *Murray v Edinburgh District Council* 1981 SLT 253 which suggests a contrary view.
5 *Bell v North Ayrshire Council* 2007 Rep LR 108, 2007 GWD 25-444; *Kirkham v Link Housing Group Ltd* 2012 Hous LR 87, 2012 GWD 24-500.

STATUTORY NUISANCE

Introduction

19.41   Under sections 79 to 82 of the Environmental Protection Act 1990[1] a tenant may be able to force the landlord to carry out repairs if it can be established that the state of the leased property amounts to a statutory nuisance.[2] This may provide an alternative enforcement mechanism to specific implement, which in the past has presented practical difficulties.[3]

1 Adopted into Scots Law by the Environment Act 1995 s 107 and Sch 17, and amended with respect to Scotland by the Public Health etc (Scotland) Act 2008 Pt 9.
2 For a useful overview of the procedure involved and for further case authority see Mike Dailly 'Enforcing Housing Repairs in Scotland' (1998) SCOLAG 67.
3 See para 4.21 et seq. Note, however, that since the cases cited in this section were heard, though in relation to private sector tenancies only, the tenant now has the option of applying for a repairing standard enforcement order, which is effectively a statutory form of specific implement – see para 19.32 et seq.

19.42   Section 79(1) of the 1990 Act lists a number of things that will constitute a statutory nuisance if they are prejudicial to health or a nuisance. 'Prejudicial to health' means injurious, or likely to cause injury, to health.[1] The situations most relevant here are where the nuisance relates to the state of any premises[2] and where it relates to noise emitted from premises (for example where the landlord has failed to provide premises that are sufficiently soundproofed).[3] Local authorities have a duty to inspect their area for nuisances and to respond to complaints and (under section 80) have the power to serve an abatement notice upon the person responsible for the nuisance. The 'person responsible' means 'the person to whose act, default or sufferance the nuisance is attributable'.[4] Where the nuisance arises from any defect of a structural character, the notice is to be served on the owner of the premises.[5] Contravention of an abatement notice is an offence.[6]

1 Environmental Protection Act 1990 s 79(7).
2 EPA 1990 s 79(1)(a).
3 EPA 1990 s 79(1)(g).
4 EPA 1990 s 79(7) (as amended).
5 EPA 1990 s 80(2)(b).
6 EPA 1990 s 80(4).

Remedy

19.43 A tenant may, therefore, report a private or registered social landlord to the local authority if the condition of the house constitutes a statutory nuisance. However, this will not be possible in cases where the local authority is also the landlord, as it cannot serve an abatement notice upon itself. In such a case, or with any landlord, the tenant may raise proceedings instead. Under section 82, a person aggrieved by a statutory nuisance may make a summary application to the sheriff court for an order against the person responsible (in the case of defects of a structural character, the owner).[1]

1 EPA 1990 s 82 (as amended).

Case law

19.44 In *Oakley v Birmingham City Council*,[1] the House of Lords held that the 'state' of premises that would amount to a statutory nuisance should be interpreted fairly narrowly and did not extend to the layout of the premises and any use of them that layout might impose; in that case there was no nuisance where the lack of a washbasin in the WC meant that those in the house (including children) had to wash their hands in the kitchen or cross the kitchen to use the washbasin in the bathroom.

The history of the legislation showed that it was 'directed to the presence in the house of some feature which in itself is prejudicial to health in that it is a source of possible infection or disease or illness such as dampness, mould, dirt or evil-smelling accumulations or the presence of rats'.[2]

1 [2001] 1 AC 617 1 All ER 385; the construction in *Oakley* was adopted in *Robb v Dundee City Council* 2002 SLT 853 at 855 per Lord Cameron of Lochbroom.
2 *Oakley v Birmingham City Council* [2001] 1 AC 617 at 627 per Lord Slynn of Hadley.

19.45   In *Anderson v Dundee City Council*[1] and *Robb v Dundee City Council*,[2] both cases involving dampness, the tenants failed to obtain orders against the landlords.

In *Robb*, it was held that the state of the house was both prejudicial to health and a nuisance in terms of the 1990 Act. However, both cases failed because the persons responsible for the nuisance were held not to be the landlords but the tenants themselves for not heating their houses adequately, even although in both cases the court acknowledged that the reason for this was that the tenants could not afford the additional heating. Nor could the landlords as owners be held liable on the ground that there was a 'defect of a structural character' since inadequate insulation was not enough on its own to constitute such a defect.

The first of these reasons seems a little odd in view of the fact that there is authority to the effect that the mere failure of the tenant to apply excessive heating in order to alleviate dampness does not necessarily mean that there is no breach of the landlord's repairing obligation.[3]

1 2000 SLT (Sh Ct) 134, 1999 SCLR 518.
2 2002 SC 301, 2002 SLT 853.
3 See para 3.31.

19.46   In neither of the above cases was it alleged that the landlord was in breach of its repairing obligation under the lease. Where the dampness is so severe that it does amount to such a breach, or where it results from something more than poor insulation that *is* a defect of a structural nature, eg lack of damp proofing, then the tenant's chances of success should be greater.

Noise

19.47   In relation to noise, the results have been more encouraging for tenants (in Scotland at least). In both *Pettigrew v Inverclyde Council*[1] and *Adams v Glasgow City Council*[2] it was held that noise from a neighbouring flat where there was poor soundproofing could amount to a statutory nuisance.

1 1999 Hous LR 31.
2 2000 Hous LR 3; but see also *R (on the application of Vella) v Lambeth London Borough Council* [2006] Env LR 33, [2006] HLR 12.

Guidance from the case law

19.48   From these and other cases further guidance as to the interpretation of the legislation has emerged:

(1) The tenant of a house whose state is alleged to be a statutory nuisance is a 'person ... aggrieved' in terms of the legislation.[1] It has been held in an English case that a person who is in occupation notwithstanding the termination of his or her right to occupy may also qualify in appropriate circumstances.[2]

(2) It is possible for a nuisance to exist in terms of the legislation without there being a breach of the landlord's repairing obligations.[3]

(3) That the state of the house is prejudicial to health and that it amounts to a nuisance are distinct factors that have to be separately established.[4]

(4) In order to be prejudicial to health, it is only necessary to prove that the house's condition is likely to be injurious to health, not that the health of the tenant or anyone else there has actually suffered as a result.[5]

(5) As the Act does not define 'nuisance', the common law definition should be applied. This means that for there to be a nuisance the problem must be *plus quam tolerabile*, ie it must be substantial and intolerable to the ordinary person.[6]

(6) If a tenant refuses an offer of alternative accommodation to allow repairs to be carried out, there is a danger that an action on the basis of statutory nuisance may be precluded on the ground that the tenant and not the landlord is the person responsible for the nuisance.[7]

(7) A non-technical approach should be taken to notices sent by aggrieved persons under section 82, which should only be required to indicate broadly the nature of the complaint, even where legal advice has been taken. Over-technical requirements might act to deter members of the public from raising proceedings.[8]

(8) There could be difficulties enforcing an order where the house is in a block of flats that is partly owner-occupied, eg where council tenants have exercised their right to buy. This is because the landlord cannot be compelled to carry out works involving the common property that would require the consent of third parties.[9]

(9) In noise cases it is permissible to have alternative pleadings under section 79(1)(a) as to the state of the premises, eg poor sound proofing, or under section 79(1)(g) as to noise emitted from the premises.[10]

1 *Oakley v Birmingham City Council* [2001] 1 AC 617.
2 *Watkins v Aged Merchant Seamen's Homes* [2019] Env LR 2.
3 *Oakley v Birmingham City Council* [2001] 1 AC 617 at 625 per Lord Slynn of Hadley.
4 *Anderson v Dundee City Council* 2000 SLT (Sh Ct) 134, 1999 SCLR 518; *Robb v Dundee City Council*, 2002 SLT 853.
5 *Anderson v Dundee City Council* 2000 SLT (Sh Ct) 134, 1999 SCLR 518; *Robb v Dundee City Council*, 2002 SLT 853.

6 *Anderson v Dundee City Council* 2000 SLT (Sh Ct) 134, 1999 SCLR 518; *Robb v Dundee City Council*, 2002 SLT 853.

7 *Carr v Hackney LBC* (1996) 28 HLR 747, [1995] Env LR 372; *Quigley v Liverpool Housing Trust* [2000] EHLR 130, [2000] Env LR D9; *Jones v Walsall MBC* [2003] Env LR 5, [2002] EHLR 17.

8 *Adams v Glasgow City Council* 2000 Hous LR 3, applying the ratio in *East Staffordshire BC v Fairless* [1999] Env LR 525, (1999) 31 HLR 677 and *R v Birmingham City Council ex p Ireland* [1999] 2 All ER 609, (1999) 31 HLR 1078.

9 *Anderson v Dundee City Council* 2000 SLT (Sh Ct) 134.

10 *Adams v Glasgow City Council* 2000 Hous LR 3.

19.49 *Financial considerations* Finally, it should be noted that in the case of some statutory nuisances, mainly those involving industrial or other business premises, the person responsible may have a defence to any criminal proceedings under sections 80 or 82 of the 1990 Act that the best practical means were used to prevent, or to counteract the effects of, the nuisance. 'Practical' is defined in section 79(9) as meaning reasonably practical, having regard, inter alia, to the financial implications.

However, this defence is *specifically excluded* in respect of statutory nuisances falling under section 79(1)(a) and (g) (the situations considered here) where residential property is involved or in cases where the nuisance has rendered the premises unfit for human habitation.[1]

The only reason for mentioning this is that the specific exclusion of nuisances involving houses seems to imply that financial considerations should not be taken into account in these cases. And yet the financial restraints upon local authority landlords undoubtedly were taken into account in some of the above decisions, including *Anderson* and *Oakley*. In future cases it could perhaps be argued that financial considerations are not legitimate in terms of the legislation.

1 EPA 1990 s 82(10)(a) and (d).

RIGHT TO REPAIR[1]

Introduction

19.50 With one exception,[2] the provisions described in this section only apply to Scottish secure tenancies, not to tenancies granted by private landlords.

A right to repair was introduced in 1994 in relation to certain categories of secure tenancy under the Housing (Scotland) Act 1987. It did not add to the categories of repair that were the landlord's responsibility. Instead, it was designed to strengthen the mechanism for enforcing the landlord's obligations by allowing a tenant, if the landlord did not respond urgently, in certain cases to take the matter into his or her own hands by instructing the repair and charging it to the landlord.

The Housing (Scotland) Act 2001 preserved the right to repair in relation to Scottish secure tenancies. The right only applies to 'qualifying repairs' and the maximum amount payable for any qualifying repair is £350.[3]

1 H(S)A 2001 s 27(2) and (3).
2 See para 19.56.
3 The Scottish Secure Tenants (Right to Repair) Regulations 2002, SSI No 316, reg 5. These regulations also list the types of repair that are qualifying repairs (reg 6 and Sch).

Alterations and improvements[1]

19.51 *Landlord's consent to work* A Scottish secure tenant may not carry out work in relation to the house, other than interior decoration, without the written consent of the landlord, which must not be unreasonably withheld. 'Work' is defined as:

(a) alteration, improvement or enlargement of the house or of any fittings or fixtures;
(b) addition of new fittings or fixtures; or
(c) erection of a garage, shed or other structure.

However, it does *not* include repairs or maintenance of any of these.

1 H(S)A 2001 s 28.

Procedure

19.52 The procedure is set out in Schedule 5, Part 1 to the Housing (Scotland) Act 2001. The tenant must make a written application to the landlord, giving details of the proposed work. The landlord must give its written decision within one month of receipt of the application, or it will be deemed to have consented. If the landlord refuses consent, it must give reasons. It may also grant consent subject to conditions, and in considering whether to impose a condition it must have regard to the age and condition of the house, the cost of complying with the condition and any guidance issued by the Scottish Ministers.

Tenant's right of appeal[1]

19.53 A tenant aggrieved by a refusal or the imposition of a condition may appeal to the court by summary application. In reaching its decision, the court is to have particular regard to:

(a)   the safety of occupiers of the house or of any other premises;

(b)   any expenditure which the landlord is likely to incur as a result of the work;

(c)   whether the work is likely to reduce the value of the house or of any premises of which it forms part, or to make the house or such premises less suitable for letting or for sale;

(d)   any effect which the work is likely to have on the extent of the accommodation provided by the house; and

(e)   any relevant code of practice issued by the Commission for Equality and Human Rights

If the effect of the work is to add to the value of the house, the tenant cannot be charged extra rent to reflect that added value.[2]

1 H(S)A 2001 Sch 5 Pt 1, paras 6–8 (as amended).
2 H(S)A 2001 s 31 (as amended).

Discretionary compensation[1]

19.54   If improvements carried out with the landlord's consent by the tenant or by the tenant's predecessor under the same tenancy, have added to the value of the property, the landlord has a discretionary power to make a payment to the tenant at the end of the tenancy.

1 H(S)A 2001 s 29.

Right to compensation

19.55   In addition to the landlord's discretionary power, tenants who carry out improvements have a *right* to compensation in certain circumstances when the tenancy comes to an end, including on assignation and when there is a change of landlord.[1] This right (which has been enjoyed since 1994 by certain categories of secure tenant under the Housing (Scotland) Act 1987) only applies to 'qualifying improvement work'. The types of improvement that qualify and other details of the scheme are contained in regulations.[2]

Compensation may be paid, not only for improvements carried out by the tenant but also by an earlier joint tenant, or the tenant's predecessor under the same tenancy.

Compensation may not be paid under this heading in respect of an improvement for which a discretionary payment has been made.[3]

1 H(S)A 2001 s 30.
2 The Scottish Secure Tenants (Compensation for Improvements) Regulations 2002, SSI No 312.
3 See para 19.54.

Disabled tenants' right to adapt rented housing

19.56 The Housing (Scotland) Act 2006[1] gives tenants of private landlords the right to adapt their house in order to accommodate a disability that they or any other occupant has. The consent of the landlord, which should not be unreasonably withheld, is required. Relevant factors to be considered in determining whether the granting of consent is reasonable include factors such as safety, cost, whether the proposed work is likely to reduce the value of the property for letting, and how easily it could be reinstated.

This right has been extended to include a right to make adjustments to common parts in which the tenant has an interest, for example common parts of a tenement building in which the disabled tenant rents a flat.[2] The exercise of this right requires the consent of a majority of the owners of the common parts (which should not be unreasonably withheld), which failing that of the sheriff.

1 H(S)A 2006 ss 52–54.
2 Relevant Adjustments to Common Parts (Disabled Persons) (Scotland) Regulations 2020 SSI No 52, made under the Equality Act 2010 s 37.

Chapter 20

Private landlord regulation

INTRODUCTION

20.1 Under the general umbrella of the regulation of private landlords, this chapter will provide an overview of six topics in particular:

(1) Antisocial Behaviour Notices (Antisocial Behaviour etc (Scotland) Act 2004, Part 7);

(2) Registration of Private Landlords (Antisocial Behaviour (Scotland) Act 2004, Part 8);

(3) Licensing of Houses in Multiple Occupation (HMOs) (Housing (Scotland) Act 2006, Part 5 (as amended, inter alia, by the Private Rented Housing (Scotland) Act 2011, Part 2));

(4) Overcrowding (Housing (Scotland) Act 1987, Part VII; Private Rented Housing (Scotland) Act 2011, Part 3);

(5) Tenancy Deposit Schemes (Housing (Scotland) Act 2006, Part 4); and

(6) Control of short-term lets (Town and Country Planning (Scotland) Act 1997 s 26B, inserted by the Planning (Scotland) Act 2019 s 17; Civic Government (Scotland) Act 1982).

ANTISOCIAL BEHAVIOUR NOTICES

General

20.2 Part 7 of the Antisocial Behaviour etc (Scotland) Act 2004 is designed to tackle antisocial behaviour by making private landlords responsible for curbing any antisocial behaviour by their tenants or by their tenants' visitors. The local authority may serve an antisocial behaviour notice on such a landlord, failure to comply with which can have criminal and civil consequences.

'Landlords' affected

20.3 The provisions do not only apply to landlords in the strict sense of the term, ie under a tenancy agreement that qualifies as a lease at common law, or as a regulated, assured or private residential tenancy under the housing legislation.[1] It also applies to 'landlords' under other types of occupancy arrangement, in the widest sense of the word. 'Landlord' in relation to such an occupancy arrangement is defined as 'the person who under the arrangement permits another to occupy the building or, as the case may be, the part of the building'.[2] An 'occupancy arrangement' is defined as 'any arrangement under which a person having the lawful right to occupy a building or part of a building permits another, by way of contract or otherwise, to occupy the building or, as the case may be, the part of it; but does not include a lease'.[3]

This very wide definition means that the provisions extend to 'landlords' where the contract is a licence,[4] as well as cases where the property is used as hostel or bed and breakfast accommodation, or where there is a resident landlord. In addition, arrangements are included that are not contractual in nature and there is no requirement for the payment of rent. Arguably, therefore, the provisions could be invoked against a parent in relation to the antisocial behaviour of their child. The argument would be stronger in the case of an adult child, or any other child towards whom the parent does not have parental responsibilities.[5] It is doubtful whether a parent can be said to be 'permitting' a younger child to occupy the family home.

This breadth of scope also means that the provisions are not limited to those landlords who are required to register with the local authority.[6] There are certain exemptions, not only of social tenancies generally, eg lets by local authorities and other registered social landlords), but also care home services, school care accommodation services, independent health care services, secure accommodation services and houses used by a religious order.[7] However, some other categories that are exempt from landlord registration[8] may be the recipient of antisocial behaviour notices, eg resident landlords.

1 See Ch 2, Ch 17 and Ch 18.
2 AB(S)A 2004 s 81(1).
3 AB(S)A 2004 s 81(1).
4 See para 2.50 et seq.
5 In terms of the Children (Scotland) Act 1995 s 1.
6 See para 20.8 et seq.
7 AB(S)A 2004 s 81(1) and (3).
8 See para 20.8 et seq.

Definition of antisocial behaviour

20.4   For the purpose of these provisions a person engages in antisocial behaviour when that person acts in a manner or pursues a course of conduct that causes or is likely to cause alarm, distress, nuisance or annoyance to someone residing in, visiting or otherwise engaging in lawful activity at or near a relevant house.[1] In the case of Scottish secure tenancies, this is also a ground for eviction of the tenant.[2]

1 AB(S)A 2004 s 81(4).
2 See para 18.66.

Service of notice[1]

20.5 Where it appears to a local authority that the occupant of or a visitor to a relevant house in its area is engaging in antisocial behaviour at or in the locality of the house, it may serve an antisocial behaviour notice on the landlord, inter alia, describing the antisocial behaviour and specifying the required action and the deadline for carrying it out.[2] However, before serving a notice, the local authority must first give the intended recipient advice and assistance about antisocial behaviour notices and the management of the antisocial behaviour in question, at the same time warning the recipient of the consequences of failure.[3]

A copy should be sent to the landlord's agent if known.

A notice may also be served where a house is being used as a holiday home.[4]

1 AB(S)A 2004 s 68.
2 For a full list of requirements for a notice see AB(S)A 2004 s 68(3).
3 The Antisocial Behaviour Notice (Advice and Assistance) (Scotland) Regulations 2005 SSI No 563.
4 AB(S)A 2004 s 68(1A) (inserted by the Antisocial Behaviour Notices (Houses Used for Holiday Purposes) (Scotland) Order 2011 SSI No 201 Art 3(a)).

Review of notice

20.6 A landlord served with an antisocial behaviour notice may, within 21 days of it being served, require a review of the notice.[1] The reviewer must have had no involvement with the decision to serve the notice, be senior to the person ultimately responsible for that decision, and may confirm, vary, suspend the effect of, or revoke the notice.[2]

1 AB(S)A 2004 s 69.
2 AB(S)A 2004 s 70.

Failure to comply with notice

20.7 If a landlord fails to comply with an antisocial behaviour notice there are several steps that the local authority may take. It may apply to the sheriff for an order suspending the requirement for the payment of rent or any other payment in respect of the house.[1] The validity of the lease or occupancy arrangement is not affected in any other way. It may also apply to the sheriff for an order transferring the landlord's rights and obligations under the tenancy or occupancy arrangement to the local authority for a period not exceeding 12 months.[2] The passing of such an order does not affect the rights or liabilities of the tenants.

A local authority also has the power to take direct action by itself taking any necessary steps to deal with the situation and to recover any resulting expenditure from the landlord.[3]

A landlord who fails to comply with an antisocial behaviour notice is guilty of a criminal offence.[4] It is a defence for a landlord charged with such an offence to show that there was a reasonable excuse for the failure.

1 AB(S)A 2004 s 71 et seq.
2 AB(S)A 2004 s 74 et seq and Sch 3.
3 AB(S)A 2004 s 78; see also the Antisocial Behaviour Notice (Landlord Liability) (Scotland) Regulations 2005 SSI No 562.
4 AB(S)A 2004 s 79.

LANDLORD REGISTRATION

Introduction

20.8   Under Part 8 of the Antisocial Behaviour etc (Scotland) Act 2004 local authorities are required to keep a register of landlords renting out houses in their area.[1] Only those deemed fit and proper persons to act as a landlord are allowed to register, and it is a criminal offence for unregistered landlords to let out property and to collect rent. It is also possible for a landlord to be struck from the register in certain circumstances. Any member of the public may apply to a local authority for information about entries on their register about a particular house or a particular landlord.[2]

1 AB(S)A 2004 s 82(1) as amended.
2 AB(S)A 2004 s 88A (added by H(S)A 2006 s 176(7) and as amended); members of the public can also search all of the registers by means of the Scottish Government's Landlord Registration central online system at www.landlordregistrationscotland.gov. uk

20.9   The legislation was widely criticised for the amount of bureaucracy it created, and for having incurred much expense to very little effect, eg in weeding out 'rogue landlords'.[1] Part 1 of the

Private Rented Housing (Scotland) Act 2011 tightened up the system considerably, inter alia, by increasing penalties, strengthening the powers of local authorities and making more information available to prospective tenants.

1 See eg Robin Bennett 'Landlord Registration – Needless Red Tape' (2008) SCOLAG 278 or Kate Berry *Private Rented Housing Bill*, SPICe Briefing, available at: www. parliament.scot/parliamentarybusiness, p 6.

Landlords affected

20.10   The definitions of 'landlord' and 'occupancy arrangement' are identical to those in relation to antisocial behaviour notices.[1] In other words, the scope of the provisions is also very wide, applying not only to landlords under leases and other contractual arrangements, but all types of occupancy arrangement, including lodgers. One significant difference is that the provisions only apply to occupancy arrangements with 'unconnected persons', in other words those who are not members of the 'landlord's' family.[2] Essentially, therefore, the provisions extend mainly to commercial arrangements (though, technically, an unrelated lodger living rent free would also fall within the definitions).

A number of other exceptions are listed, eg where the house is being used as a care home, by a religious order, an independent hospital or a holiday house.[3]

1 AB(S)A 2004 s 101(1); see para 20.3.
2 AB(S)A 2004 ss 83(8) and 84(3)(c).
3 AB(S)A 2004 s 83(6) (as amended).

Registration

20.11   *Applications*   The landlord's application is required to contain a substantial amount of information which is prescribed by the 2004 Act and by regulations,[1] including the landlord's name and address, the addresses of the relevant house or houses, the landlord's agent (if any) and any criminal convictions of the landlord, among other things.[2] A fee is normally payable.[3] The local authority may then either enter the applicant in the register or, if not satisfied that the applicant is a fit and proper person to be a landlord, refuse to do so.[4] Registration will normally last for three years, after which a fresh application will be required.[5]

In reaching its decision (or in carrying out any other of its landlord registration functions) a local authority has the power to obtain information from certain parties, including the owners of houses or the agents of owners or tenants.[6]

20.12 *Private landlord regulation*

Once registration has been completed the local authority must give the landlord a landlord registration number.[7] All written adverts of properties to let must include the registration number, or the words 'landlord registration pending' if the landlord's application for registration has yet to be determined.[8]

1 AB(S)A 2004 s 83(1) (as amended); The Private Landlord Registration (Information) (Scotland) Regulations 2019 SSI No 195.
2 Landlords can apply for registration with all local authorities in Scotland on the Landlord Registration central online system at www.landlordregistrationscotland.gov.uk.
3 Private Landlord Registration (Fees) (Scotland) Regulations 2019, SSI No 160.
4 AB(S)A 2004 s 84.
5 AB(S)A 2004 s 84(6).
6 AB(S)A 2004 ss 97A and 97B (inserted by PRH(S)A 2011 s 9).
7 AB(S)A 2004 s 84(5A) (added by PRH(S)A 2011 s 3(1)).
8 AB(S)A 2004 s 92B (added by PRH(S)A 2011 s 6).

20.12 *Fit and proper persons* Section 85 of the 2004 Act[1] specifies a number of factors which a local authority should take into account when deciding whether or not an applicant is a fit and proper person to be a landlord, and the amendments in the 2011 Act elaborated upon these as well as increasing their number. They include whether the applicant has committed any offence involving fraud or other dishonesty, violence or drugs (to which the 2011 Act added firearms and sexual offences), or whether the applicant has contravened the law in relation to housing or landlord and tenant law, eg unlawful eviction or breach of the repairing standard.[2] Equally, past dishonesty in the applicant's conduct as a landlord may lead to the conclusion that the applicant is not a fit and proper person. Thus, in *Thomson v Aberdeen City Council*,[3] it was held that a local authority was entitled to reach the conclusion that a landlord was not a fit and proper person, after he tried to claim exemption for a lease to six unrelated students by falsely claiming that they were part of a religious order who lived as one family.

Applicants must declare any convictions for any of the relevant offences and any antisocial behaviour orders against them.[4] The 2011 Act also gave local authorities the power to require a landlord to provide a criminal record certificate if it deems this to be necessary when applying the fit and proper person test.[5] Failure to provide this may result in a landlord being removed from the register, or in a new application being refused.

1 AB(S)A 2004 s 85 (as amended).
2 *Coyle v Glasgow City Council* 2012 SLT 1018, 2012 GWD 16-332.
3 2011 SLT (Sh Ct) 218, 2011 Hous LR 12.
4 The Private Landlord Registration (Information and Fees) (Scotland) Regulations 2005, SSI No 558, Sch 1 (as amended).
5 AB(S)A 2004 s 85A (inserted by PRH(S)A 2011) s 2.

Changes in circumstances

20.13 A landlord must notify the local authority in writing of any relevant changes in circumstances, eg if a new house or houses have been let, or generally if any information supplied at the time of the application for registration has become inaccurate) and failure to notify the local authority is an offence.[1]

If a house is subject to a repairing standard enforcement order by the First-Tier Tribunal, the Tribunal's decision imposing that order is to be noted against the landlord's registration.[2] Where such an order is in force, it is an offence for the landlord to re-let the property unless with the Tribunal's consent.[3]

1 AB(S)A 2004 s 87.
2 AB(S)A 2004 s 87A (added by H(S)A 2006 s176(6)).
3 Housing (Scotland) Act 2006 s 28.

Enforcement

20.14 A local authority may remove a landlord from the register if it considers that the landlord is no longer a fit and proper person to be a landlord.[1] Breach of the legislation, eg where a lease is entered by an unregistered landlord, can lead to criminal prosecution and a fine of up to £50,000 may be imposed.[2] The court may also disqualify a convicted person from being registered as a landlord for up to five years.[3] Civil consequences include the power of the local authority to serve a notice suspending a tenant's obligation to pay rent or any other consideration in relation to the houses concerned. In addition, in the case of a private residential tenancy, the fact of the landlord having been removed from the register is a ground on which the First-Tier Tribunal has the discretion to terminate the tenancy.[4] However, apart from this the validity of any lease or occupancy arrangement will remain unaffected.

When the First-Tier Tribunal receives an application from a private tenant regarding a landlord's failure to meet the repairing standard, it must pass on certain information from the application to the local authority, in order to help the local authority to identify unregistered landlords.[5] The same applies where the Tribunal makes a wrongful termination order against a landlord[6] or where, in proceedings before it, the Tribunal learns or is given cause to suspect that a landlord is not registered.[7]

1 AB(S)A 2004 s 89.
2 AB(S)A 2004 s 93 (as amended).
3 AB(S)A 2004 s 93A (inserted by PRH(S)A 2011 s 8).
4 See para 17.61.
5 H(S)A 2006 s 22A (inserted by PRH(S)A 2011 s 11); see also para 19.33.

6 See para 17.68.
7 Private Housing (Tenancies) (Scotland) Act 2016 s 72.

Advice and Assistance

20.15 A local authority must provide advice and assistance about good letting practice to applicants for registration and, where registration is refused or a landlord removed from the register, about how to remedy the situation.[1] In such cases, and also where an order has been made suspending rent payment, the local authority must also advise the tenant or tenants concerned, including (where appropriate) advice (including financial advice) on their situation in the event of their lease being terminated.[2] Local authorities must also, if approached by prospective tenants, give advice on landlord registration and letting practice.[3] They must also publish on their website such information about registration fees as they consider appropriate.[4]

1 AB(S)A 2004 s 99; the Private Landlord Registration (Advice and Assistance) (Scotland) Regulations 2005 SSI No 557 (as amended), regs 2 and 3.
2 PLR(A & A)(S) Regulations 2005 SSI No 557 (as amended), reg 4.
3 PLR(A & A)(S) Regulations 2005 SSI No 557 (as amended), reg 4.
4 PLR(A & A)(S) Regulations 2005 SSI No 557 reg 3A (inserted by Private Landlord Registration (Fees) Scotland) Regulations 2019 SSI No 160.

LICENSING OF HOUSES IN MULTIPLE OCCUPATION ('HMOs')

Requirement for Licensing

20.16 The law regulating houses in multiple occupation ('HMOs') is now contained in Part 5 of the Housing (Scotland) Act 2006.[1] Every house in multiple occupation ('HMO') must be licensed by the appropriate local authority unless it falls within the statutory exemptions.[2] Every local authority must keep a register containing information about HMO licences for living accommodation situated in its area.[3]

1 As amended, inter alia, by PRH(S)A 2011 Pt 2.
2 H(S)A 2006 s 124. See also para 20.18.
3 H(S)A 2006 s 160.

Meaning of 'house in multiple occupation'[1]

20.17 A house is an HMO if it is living accommodation occupied by three or more persons who are not all members of the same family, or of one or other of two families, and it is their only or principal home.[2] It must form part of premises owned by the same person and the occupants must share one or more of the basic facilities, namely a toilet or personal washing or kitchen facilities. A person does not share a basic facility if the living accommodation has more than one of that facility, and the person has the exclusive use of one of those, eg where a bedroom has an *en suite* toilet in addition to the shared one.

The provisions would therefore apply in a situation where three or more students shared a house or flat, but not normally hotel residents, unless they were long-term residents.

The Scottish Ministers have power to designate additional categories of HMO, which need not necessarily meet all of the above criteria.[3]

1 H(S)A 2006 s 125 (as amended by PRH(S)A 2011 s 13).
2 For definitions of the relevant relationships see H(S)A 2006 s 128.
3 H(S)A 2006 s 125(1)(b) (inserted by PRH(S)A 2011 s 13); at the time of writing no such further designations have been made.

Exemptions

20.18 Exemptions from licensing include situations where the owner or owners occupy the property along with members of their own families, or other families not exceeding three families in total, care home accommodation, prison accommodation and armed forces accommodation.[1] The Scottish Ministers have the power to designate further exemptions.[2] An owner may be granted a temporary exemption order in order to take steps that would mean that a licence was no longer required, eg by reducing the number of tenants or to carry out works necessary to improve the safety or security of the occupants.[3]

1 For the full list see H(S)A 2006 s 126.
2 H(S)A 2006 s 127; at the time of writing, no such further exemptions have been designated.
3 H(S)A 2006 ss 142 and 143.

Applications[1]

20.19 An application for an HMO licence may only be made by an owner of the living accommodation concerned. The local authority may either grant the licence (with or without conditions)[2] or refuse it.[3]

An application may be refused because of the unsuitability of either the applicant (or the applicant's agent) or of the living accommodation. The applicant or agent will be unsuitable if either have been subject to a disqualification order as a result of an offence under section 154 of the 2006 Act[4] or if either is not a fit and proper person.[5] The criteria for determining the latter are the same as those that apply to the registration of landlords under the Antisocial Behaviour etc (Scotland) Act 2004.[6]

In determining whether the accommodation is suitable (or can be made so by the imposition of conditions) the local authority should consider its location, condition and amenities, whether any rooms have been subdivided or adapted in a way that has resulted in an alteration to the situation of the water and drainage pipes within it, the type and number of persons likely to occupy it and their safety and security, and the possibility of undue public nuisance.[7]

The local authority may refuse an application if it believes that use of the property as an HMO would constitute a breach of planning control.[8] It also has the discretionary power to refuse to grant a licence if it considers that there is, or that the grant of the licence could result in, an overprovision of HMOs in the locality.[9] The local authority must, of course, act reasonably in reaching its decision.[10]

Where an application has been refused, the local authority may not normally consider a further application by the same applicant within one year for a house considered unsuitable, or (if it was the applicant who was unsuitable) for any house at all.[11]

A licence will be granted for a minimum period of six months and a maximum of three years; it may be renewed thereafter after a fresh application.[12]

A landlord may appeal against a local authority's decision to refuse an HMO application, or other HMO-related decision, by summary application to the sheriff within 28 days.[13]

1 H(S)A 2006 s 129.
2 See H(S)A 2006 s 133.
3 For the procedural requirements relating to an application see the H(S)A 2006 Sch 4.
4 See para 20.21.
5 H(S)A 2006 s 130.
6 See para 20.12.
7 H(S)A 2006 s 131 (as amended by PRH(S)A 2011 s 13(3)).
8 H(S)A 2006 s 129A (inserted by PRH(S)A 2011 s 13(2)).
9 H(S)A 2006 s 131A (inserted by PRH(S)A 2011 s 13(4)).
10 See eg *A v City of Edinburgh Council* 2018 Hous LR 106, in which the landlord's Asperger's syndrome necessitated reasonable adjustments in the decision-making process.
11 H(S)A 2006 s 132.
12 H(S)A 2006 ss 134 and 135.
13 H(S)A 2006 s 159. On the sheriff's powers on appeal, see *Fieldman v City of Edinburgh Council* 2020 SLT (Sh Ct) 220; *Valente v Fife Council* [2020] DUN 38.

Changes of circumstances

20.20   A HMO licence may terminate if ownership of the property in question changes, or a sole owner dies (though the licence may transfer temporarily to the new owner or executor as the case may be).[1] It should not simply be assumed that the new owner will be able to get a licence on the same terms, where the local authority considers that there has been a relevant change in circumstances.[2] In certain circumstances the licence may also be varied or revoked by the local authority.[3] It may also be cancelled at the request of the licence holder.[4]

1 H(S)A 2006 ss 136 and 137.
2 See *Them Properties LLP v Glasgow City Council* 2010 SC 690, 2010 Hous LR 69.
3 H(S)A 2006 ss 138 and 139.
4 H(S)A 2006 s 141.

Enforcement

20.21   Local authorities have wide enforcement powers to deal with situations where an HMO is operating without a licence, or where a condition of a licence has been breached. The civil consequences which an owner may incur include the suspension of the tenants' obligation to pay rent and the service of a notice requiring the owner to remedy any breach, including an amenity notice requiring the owner to carry out work necessary in order to make the premises fit for occupation.[1] Owners and others in breach are also criminally liable, and those convicted may not only have their HMO licence revoked, but also be disqualified from holding a licence (or acting as an agent for a licence holder) for up to five years. They may also incur a fine of up to £50,000.[2]

1 H(S)A 2006 ss 144–153.
2 H(S)A 2006 ss 154–157 (as amended).

OVERCROWDING

Introduction

20.22   Part VII of the Housing (Scotland) Act 1987 contains measures to address problems of overcrowding in housing, including the private rented sector.[1] The problem of overcrowding in this sector is of course largely addressed by the requirement for the licensing of houses in multiple occupation.[2] The present provisions, however, catch overcrowding situations that have fallen through the net of the licensing arrangements, eg where the occupants claim to be members of the same family, thereby making it difficult for the local authority to identify that the house is an HMO.

In addition, Part 3 of the Private Rented Housing (Scotland) Act 2011 contains measures to assist local authorities in tackling problems of overcrowding in the private rented sector. It does so by giving local authorities the power to serve an overcrowding statutory notice on the landlord of a house which is overcrowded. At the time of writing, however, most of Part 3 has yet to come into force, and the regulations empowered by this part of the Act have yet to be passed.

1 The provisions in the 1987 Act relate to overcrowding in relation to all tenures, but have apparently been little used because of lack of resources – see Kate Berry *Private Rented Housing Bill*, SPICe Briefing, pp 14–15, available at: www.parliament.scot/parliamentarybusiness.
2 See para 20.16 et seq.

Definition of overcrowding

20.23 The definition of overcrowding is contained in Part VII of the Housing (Scotland) Act 1987,[1] and the 2011 Act adopts this definition. A house is regarded as overcrowded if it fails to pass one of two tests, the room standard test or the space standard test.[2]

The room standard is contravened when the number of persons sleeping in a house and the number of rooms available as sleeping accommodation is such that two persons of opposite sexes who are not living together as husband and wife must sleep in the same room. Children under the age of 10 are left out of account.

The space standard is contravened when the number of persons sleeping in a house exceeds the permitted number, having regard to the number of rooms of the house available as sleeping accommodation and their floor area. No account is to be taken of a child under the age of one, and a child above that age but under the age of 10 is reckoned as one half of a unit. Section 137 provides two tables for calculating these limits.[3]

In relation to both tests a room is considered to be available as sleeping accommodation if it is of a type normally used in the locality either as a living room or as a bedroom.

It is an offence for the occupier of a house to cause or to permit it to be overcrowded.[4] It is also an offence not to give written notice to a prospective tenant of the permitted number of occupants.[5]

1 The provisions in the 1987 Act relate to overcrowding in relation to all tenures, but have apparently been little used because of lack of resources – see Kate Berry *Private Rented Housing Bill*, SPICe Briefing, pp 14-15, available from the Scottish Parliament website at www.parliament.scot/parliamentarybusiness.

2 H(S)A 1987 ss 135–137.
3 H(S)A 1987 s 137(2).
4 H(S)A 1987 s 139. For defences, see ss 140–143.
5 H(S)A 1987 s 144.

Overcrowding statutory notices[1]

20.24   The 2011 Act prospectively gives a local authority the power to serve an overcrowding statutory notice on the landlord of a house which is overcrowded, where the local authority considers that the overcrowding is having an adverse effect on the health or wellbeing of any person or on the amenity of the house or of its locality. 'Landlord' means an owner who is required to register with the local authority under the private landlord registration scheme.[2] The notice should set out the steps to be taken by the landlord to rectify the situation and the time limit (not less than 28 days) within which the notice must be complied with. The conditions are that the landlord must not cause the house to be overcrowded in the future and take reasonable steps to prevent this from happening,[3] as well as any steps necessary in order to achieve this.

The Scottish ministers are given the power to prescribe the form of such a notice and the persons to whom copies should be sent.[4] Section 28 sets out in some detail the various types of service of the notice (which include electronic service) considered to be appropriate.[5]

The local authority has the power to obtain information from anyone who appears have an interest in the house for the purpose of enabling it to discharge its functions.[6]

1 PRH(S)A 2011 s 17.
2 PRH(S)A 2011 s 31; see para 20.10.
3 PRH(S)A 2011 s 20.
4 At the time of writing regulations to this effect have still to be passed.
5 PRH(S)A 2011 s 17.
6 PRH(S)A 2011 s 27.

20.25   *Matters to be considered*[1]   There are several matters which a local authority must take into account before serving a notice. They must assess whether serving the notice is reasonable and proportionate in the circumstances. They must weigh up the nature of the adverse effect, and the degree to which the overcrowding is contributing or connected to it, as well as the likely effects of serving the notice, and whether there are other means to address the problem. The local authority must also take account of the views of the landlord, the occupier and others living in the house, their particular circumstances and the likely effects upon them. They must consider whether the overcrowding is causing homelessness or, conversely, whether service of a notice may have that effect.[2]

At the same time as serving the notice the local authority must provide information and advice to the occupier by means of a separate notice, the contents and form of which are to be prescribed by the Scottish Ministers. They may also provide such other information as they consider appropriate and comply with any reasonable requests for further information from the occupier.[3]

1 PRH(S)A 2011 s 18.
2 Whether a person is homeless or threatened with homelessness, is to be determined in accordance with H(S)A 1987 s 24 (PRH(S)A 2011 s 18(4)).
3 PRH(S)A 2011 s 19. At the time of writing, the necessary regulations have still to be passed.

20.26 *Effects of notice* A notice is effective for the period stated in it, which must be not less than one or more than five years.[1] The recipient of a notice may make representations to the local authority within seven days with a view to having the notice revoked or varied, and failure by the authority to respond within a further seven days can lead to the notice being automatically revoked.[2] The local authority may itself later decide to vary or revoke a notice.[3] The landlord has the right to appeal against a notice to the sheriff.[4] Failure to comply with a notice is an offence.[5]

1 PRH(S)A 2011 s 21.
2 PRH(S)A 2011 s 22.
3 PRH(S)A 2011 ss 24 and 25.
4 PRH(S)A 2011 s 23.
5 PRH(S)A 2011 s 26.

TENANCY DEPOSITS

Introduction

20.27 The law on tenancy deposits and tenancy deposit schemes is contained in the Housing (Scotland) Act 2006, Part 4 and The Tenancy Deposit Schemes (Scotland) Regulations 2011.[1] After a number of delays, the provisions are now fully in force.[2]

The purpose of the legislation is to tackle the problem of deposits that are unfairly held by landlords, to ensure that deposits are safeguarded throughout the duration of the tenancy, eg in the event of the landlord's insolvency, and to ensure that deposits are returned quickly and fairly, particularly in the event of a dispute.

Deposits must be paid into a tenancy deposit scheme which has been approved by the Scottish Ministers. To date there are three approved schemes in Scotland.[3]

A tenancy deposit is defined as a sum of money held as security for (a) the performance of any of the occupant's obligations arising under or in connection with a tenancy or an occupancy arrangement; or (b) the discharge of any of the occupant's liabilities which so arise.[4] The scheme only applies to private sector tenancies and not to council, housing association or other social tenancies, ie lets from other registered social landlords. In other words, it mainly applies to private residential tenancies.

1 SSI 2011 No 176.
2 There were a number of transitional provisions, but the final deadline by which all pre-existing tenancy deposits must have been paid into an approved scheme was 15 May 2013 – see TDS(S)R 2011, SSI No 176, reg 47(b).
3 These are SafeDeposits Scotland (www.safedepositsscotland.com), The Letting Protection Service Scotland (www.lettingprotectionscotland.com) and MyDeposits Scotland (www.mydepositsscotland.co.uk). Further information about tenancy deposits and schemes can be obtained from the Scottish Government website at www.gov.scot/policies/private-renting/tenancy-deposit-schemes.
4 H(S)A 2006 s 120(1).

Landlords' duties

20.28 A landlord who has received a tenancy deposit must, within 30 working days of the beginning of the tenancy, pay the deposit to the scheme administrator of an approved scheme and ensure that it remains in such a scheme until it is repaid at the end of the tenancy.[1] In addition, the landlord, also within 30 days, must supply the tenant with the following information:[2]

(1) Confirmation of the amount of the deposit and the date on which it was received by the landlord.
(2) The date on which the deposit was paid to the scheme administrator.
(3) The address of the property to which the deposit relates.
(4) A statement that the landlord is, or has applied to be, entered on the local register of private landlords.[3]
(5) The name and contact details of the administrator of the scheme to which the tenancy deposit was paid.
(6) The circumstances in which all or part of the tenancy deposit may be retained at the end of the tenancy, with reference to the terms of the tenancy agreement.

If any of the above information becomes inaccurate over time, the landlord is required to update it.[4]

As noted above, landlords must be registered, or in the process of becoming registered, with the relevant local authority in their register of private landlords[5] and must provide information of this to the administrator of the tenancy deposit scheme.[6]

A tenant may apply to the First-Tier Tribunal where a landlord has failed to comply with any of the above duties.[7] Where the Tribunal is satisfied of the landlord's failure to comply, it will order the landlord to pay the tenant an amount not exceeding three times the tenancy deposit.[8] In *Fraser v Meehan*,[9] it was said that the purpose of this was 'to punish the defender's behaviour and to express condemnation of or indignation at the enormity of the offence'. In that case, an award was made of the maximum permitted, in circumstances where the landlord had professional experience in residential letting and had provided insufficient evidence of the purported damage for which he had made a deduction from the deposit. By contrast, in *Jenson v Fappiano*,[10] a sum equivalent to only one-third of the deposit was awarded in the case of an amateur landlord who had complied with the requirements as soon as he had become aware of them. The amount awarded is a matter of discretion, subject to the maximum permitted and taking account of the seriousness of the breach, and will not readily be interfered with on appeal.[11] Application must be made within three months of the end of the tenancy. However, in one case, even though this deadline was not met, it was held that the tenant was entitled to have his deposit returned without any deduction, on the grounds that it was 'contrary to public policy to entertain the [landlord's] assertions of the [tenant's] breach of the tenancy agreement when he has unlawfully failed to place the deposit into the hands of the Tenancy Deposit Scheme administrator'.[12]

1 TDS(S)R 2011 SSI No 176 reg 3.
2 TDS(S)R 2011 SSI No 176 regs 3 and 42.
3 See paras 20.8 et seq.
4 TDS(S)R 2011 SSI No 176 reg 43.
5 See para 20.8 et seq.
6 TDS(S)R 2011 SSI No 176 reg 44.
7 TDS(S)R 2011 SSI No 176 regs 9 and 10.
8 TDS(S)R 2011 SSI No 176 reg 10.
9 2014 SLT (Sh Ct) 119 at para [13]. For discussion of this and of the equivalent English provisions, see James Hurford, '"Condemnation and indignation": What should the courts consider in awarding damages under the tenancy deposit scheme?' 2014 *Journal of Housing Law* 50.
10 2015 GWD 4-89. See also *Kirk v Singh* 2015 SLT (Sh Ct) 111.
11 *Tenzin v Russell* 2015 Hous LR 11.
12 *Omale v Barcenas* [2015] SC FORT 13 para 13.

Tenancy Deposit Schemes

20.29 Regulation 6 sets out a number of conditions which a tenancy deposit scheme must meet before it can be approved by the Scottish Ministers:[1]

(1) The proposed scheme administrator must be a fit and proper person to act as such, and in particular must declare if he or she has been convicted on any offence involving fraud or other dishonesty, has been declared bankrupt or has been disqualified from being a director of a company.[2]

(2) A scheme must be based on the model set out in the Regulations.[3] This means, inter alia, that no fees should be payable by landlords, that deposits should be paid into a special account, that all landlords should be able to participate in the scheme and make use of its dispute resolution mechanism, that an appropriate customer service facility should be available to landlords, tenants and the general public, that the scheme should be self-financing, eg from interest on the investment of deposits and that there must be procedures to safeguard deposits from the failure of the scheme.

(3) The scheme must comply with the accounting requirements set out in the Regulations.[4]

(4) It must comply with the procedure for payment, holding and repayment of deposits.[5]

(5) It must have a dispute resolution procedure in conformity with the Regulations.[6] In particular, the procedure must be free of charge to both landlords and tenants and adjudicators must be independent of both parties.

The Scottish Ministers have power to provide financial assistance by making payments or giving guarantees or other assistance in connection with the creation, administration or operation of an approved scheme, and the resolution of disputes relating to an approved scheme.[7]

Scheme administrators are required to provide annual and quarterly performance reports to the Scottish Ministers.[8]

1 TDS(S)R 2011 SSI No 176 reg 6.
2 TDS(S)R 2011 SSI No 176 reg 7.
3 TDS(S)R 2011 SSI No 176 Part 3.
4 TDS(S)R 2011 SSI No 176 Part 4.
5 TDS(S)R 2011 SSI No 176 Part 5.
6 TDS(S)R 2011 SSI No 176 Part 6.
7 TDS(S)R 2011 SSI No 176 reg 8.
8 TDS(S)R 2011 SSI No 176 regs 45 and 46.

Publicity[1]

20.30 Once a scheme has been approved, the administrator must ensure that it is publicised across Scotland for the purposes of informing landlords about the tenancy deposit scheme and the services it provides, making landlords, tenants and the general public aware of the date on which the scheme will become operational, and promoting tenants' understanding of landlords' duties in relation to tenancy deposits.

The publicity should take place as soon as reasonably practicable after the scheme has been approved, and also immediately prior to the scheme becoming operational and for a reasonable period of time thereafter. Prior to a scheme becoming available, the administrator must make available an information leaflet.

1 TDS(S)R 2011 SSI No 176 regs 40 and 41.

REGULATION OF SHORT-TERM LETS

Introduction

20.31 The Scottish Government has announced plans to introduce new forms of regulation for what it calls 'short-term lets'. The purpose of these plans is to address problems raised by the letting of property through platforms such as Airbnb, such as the causing of disturbance to neighbours and the impact of such lettings on the availability of residential property.[1] As we shall see, however, the definition of 'short-term let' is significantly broader than this suggests.

At the time of writing, draft legislation to implement these plans has not been produced. It is therefore only possible to give an outline of what is intended. It is envisaged that these changes will come into force in April 2021.[2]

It is proposed to regulate short-term lets in two ways. First, it is proposed to allow local authorities to restrict the granting of short-term lets through planning law. Second, it is intended to introduce a licensing system for short-term lets.

1 Scottish Government, *Short Term Lets: Consultation on a licensing scheme and planning control areas in Scotland* (September 2020) para 3.3, available at: www.gov.scot/publications/short-term-lets-consultation-licensing-scheme-planning-control-areas-scotland/. For discussion of some of the issues arising from short-term lets, see Gillian Mawdsley and Alison McNab, 'Whose Legal Problems are Short-term Lets?' 2020 SLT (News) 1 (published before the Scottish Government's consultation document).
2 Scottish Government, *Short Term Lets* para 3.10.

What is a short-term let?

20.32 The Scottish Government has proposed a number of criteria for determining whether an arrangement is a short-term let for these purposes. According to these proposals, an arrangement will be a short-term let if it meets all the following criteria:[1]

- The let is for residential purposes.
- The accommodation is 'all or part of a house or flat or serviced apartment'. There is no requirement for the guest to have exclusive occupation of any part of the property.
- The let is temporary, the property not being the guest's only or principal home. Accordingly, any let that is a private residential tenancy is automatically excluded.[2] The Scottish Government does not intend to specify a maximum length for the let. Accordingly, a short-term let may in fact be for a lengthier term than the name would suggest. The Scottish Government gives the specific example of a worker on a three-month contract to work away from their principal home, and there is nothing in principle preventing even longer arrangements qualifying as short-term lets.
- The let is 'for commercial consideration'. This need not be a monetary consideration, a benefit in kind being enough.
- The let is not to a member of the host's immediate family.

1 Scottish Government, *Short Term Lets* para 4.8.
2 See paras 17.11 et seq.

Control area regulations

20.33 Some, but not all, short-term letting requires planning permission as a change of use.[1] The Town and Country Planning (Scotland) Act 1997 has now been amended to allow a planning authority to designate all or part of its area as a 'short-term let control area'.[2] In a short-term let control area, any use of a dwellinghouse for the purpose of providing short-term lets is deemed to involve a material change of use, requiring planning permission.[3]

The Scottish Ministers are empowered to make further provision by regulations for the designation and operation of short-term let control areas, including procedures to be followed by planning authorities, exclusions, and the definition of 'short-term let' for these purposes.[4] With regard to the last of these, the definition of short-term lets is not to include private residential tenancies or any tenancy of a dwellinghouse (or part of it) where all or part of the dwellinghouse is the only or principal home of the landlord or occupier.[5] At the time of writing, the relevant regulations have not been produced. However, the Scottish Government has provided an outline of its proposals.[6]

1 Scottish Government, *Short Term Lets* para 5.3.
2 TCP(S)A 1997 s 26B(1). In terms of subsection (4), this includes the power to vary or cancel a designation as a short-term let control area.

3 TCP(S)A 1997 s 26B(2).
4 TCP(S)A 1997 s 26B(5).
5 TCP(S)A 1997 s 26B(3).
6 Scottish Government, *Short Term Lets* Chapter 5.

Licensing of short-term lets

20.34   The Scottish Government also proposes to introduce[1] a system of licensing for short-term lets. The intention is that each local authority will implement a licensing scheme of their own from 1 April 2021 and must have done so by 1 April 2022.[2] There will be transitional arrangements for existing providers of short-term lets, but all providers will be required to have a licence by 31 March 2024 at the very latest.[3]

At the time of writing, the regulations to allow for this licensing system have not yet been produced. However, the Scottish Government has published an outline of its proposals.[4] There will be several mandatory requirements for licensees, mirroring, to a significant extent, those already applicable to other lets of residential property. For example, the licensee will be required to comply with the repairing standard.[5] However, local authorities will be able to impose further requirements on licensees. Failure to comply with the requirements will be an offence, punishable by a fine.[6]

1 Under the Civic Government (Scotland) Act 1982 s 44.
2 Scottish Government, *Short Term Lets* para 6.4.
3 Scottish Government, *Short Term Lets* paras 6.84–6.89.
4 Scottish Government, *Short Term Lets* Chapter 6.
5 Scottish Government, *Short Term Lets* paras 6.10–6.13. On the repairing standard, see para 19.13 et seq.
6 Scottish Government, *Short Term Lets* paras 6.114–6.121.

Chapter 21

Unfair lease terms

CONSUMER RIGHTS ACT 2015

21.1   Terms in residential leases that are unfair to the tenant may be invalid and otherwise subject to attack under the Consumer Rights Act 2015. This applies to leases entered into from 1 October 2015 and replaces the Unfair Terms in Consumer Contracts Regulations 1999, which made similar provision.[1] These regulations implemented an EC Directive and themselves replaced earlier regulations passed in 1994.[2]

There was initially some uncertainty as to whether contracts relating to heritable property fell within the scope of the Directive and the resulting regulations. It is now established, however, that these did extend to contracts relating to heritable property.[3] The same may be assumed of the 2015 Act, given that it is equally intended to implement the Directive.[4]

The 2015 Act applies to unfair terms in contracts concluded between a trader and a consumer.[5] A consumer is defined as 'an individual acting for purposes that are wholly or mainly outside that individual's trade, business craft or profession'.[6] This means that a residential tenant qualifies as a consumer in terms of this definition. Equally, commercial and other non-residential tenants fairly obviously fall outwith the definition of 'consumer' and so outwith the 2015 Act.[7]

A 'trader' is 'a person acting for purposes relating to that person's trade, business, craft or profession'.[8] This means that not only assured, regulated and private residential tenancies are affected, but also *all* residential tenancies, including lets from local authorities and other social landlords.[9]

---

1 SI 2083 (as amended, inter alia, by The Unfair Terms in Consumer Contracts (Amendment) Regulations 2001 SI 2001/1186).

2 Directive 93/13/EEC; SI 1994/3159 (now revoked).

3 See Jon Holbrook 'Unfair terms in leases and mortgages' (2000) 4 L&T Review, 38; *Camden LBC v McBride* 11 November 1998 (unreported); digested (1999) CLY 3737.

4 This is the case even though the definition of 'trader' in the Consumer Rights Act 2015 s 2(2) does not expressly extend to landlords.

5 Consumer Rights Act 2015 s 61(1).

6 CRA 2015 s 2(3).
7 However, see Susan Bright 'Protecting the Small Business Tenant,' 2006 Conv 137, which presents a cogent argument for extending consumer protection to small business tenants.
8 CRA 2015 s 2(2).
9 For an analysis of this and of the application to residential tenancies generally, see Susan Bright 'Unfair Contract Terms and Local Authority Tenancies' [2004] JHL 2; see also *Starmark Enterprises Ltd v CPL Distribution Ltd* [2002] 4 All ER 264 at 279 per Lady Justice Arden. For confirmation that the regulations do apply to local authorities see *Newham LBC v Khatun* [2005] QB 37, [2004] 3 WLR 417; see also *Peabody Trust Governors v Reeve* [2009] L&TR 6, [2008] 3 EGLR 61.

CMA guidance

21.2   The Competition and Markets Authority has produced general guidance on the 2015 Act.[1] Specific guidance (pre-dating the 2015 Act, but updated since) has also been produced for the use of lettings professionals.[2] In relation to previous published guidance (produced by the then Office of Fair Trading), it has been held that the courts should take account of this guidance.[3] The guidance is intended to apply to all jurisdictions of the UK.

There is no space here for a comprehensive discussion of the guidance, but many of its recommendations are incorporated in the overview that follows. The guides are easily obtained from the UK Government website, and are highly recommended to anyone wanting to investigate this topic in more depth.

1 *Unfair Contract Terms Guidance: Guidance on the Unfair Terms Provisions in the Consumer Rights Act 2015* (Competition & Markets Authority, July 2015, CMA37); available at: www.gov.uk/government/publications/unfair-contract-terms-cma37.
2 *Guidance for Lettings Professionals on Consumer Protection Law: Helping You Comply with Your Obligations* (Competition & Markets Authority, June 2014, updated October 2019, CMA31); available at: www.gov.uk/government/publications/consumer-protection-law-for-lettings-professionals#history.
3 *Peabody Trust Governors v Reeve* [2009] L&TR 6; [2008] 3 EGLR 61, considered in para 21.14

Unfair terms[1]

21.3   A contractual term is unfair if 'contrary to the requirement of good faith, it causes a significant imbalance in the parties' rights and obligations under the contract to the detriment of the consumer.' Unlike the position before the Consumer Rights Act 2015, it is not relevant that a term was individually negotiated by the parties. In other words, these rules apply to leases negotiated by the parties just as much as they do to standard form leases. That said, an individually negotiated term is perhaps more likely to be seen as fair, especially where the parties have similar bargaining strengths and, even more so, when the tenant has been legally represented.

Fairness includes the notion of good faith, and landlords are expected not to take advantage of a tenant's weaker bargaining position, or lack of experience, in deciding what their rights and obligations will be.[2]

Some kinds of term are automatically unenforceable (the CMA uses the term 'blacklisting' for this).[3]

1 CRA 2015 s 62.
2 *Unfair Contract Terms Guidance* paras 2.10–2.41.
3 An example is the bar on excluding liability for death or personal injury contained in CRA s 65. On blacklisting generally, see *Unfair Contract Terms Guidance* ch 4.

Transparent language[1]

21.4   The landlord must ensure that any written term of a contract is expressed in plain, intelligible language. Transparency is paramount, and in cases of doubt, the interpretation most favourable to the tenant will prevail.

This is similar to the common law rule of construction *contra proferentem*,[2] but goes further: a term that is legally unambiguous may still fail the transparency test, particularly where legal terminology is used. In the view of the CMA, much standard legal terminology (eg 'indemnity', 'joint and several liability', 'lien', 'time is of the essence' etc) could be open to objection, unless it is accompanied by a clear explanation of its meaning.[3]

1 CRA 2015 s 68.
2 See *Peabody Trust Governors v Reeve* [2009] L&TR 6; [2008] 3 EGLR 61, considered in para 21.14.
3 *Unfair Contract Terms Guidance* paras 2.54–2.56.

Core terms[1]

21.5   As long as they are in plain, intelligible language, the 2015 Act does not apply to core terms, such as the definition of the main subject matter of the contract or the amount of the price or remuneration, as long as they are transparent and prominent. This means that they may not apply to rent,[2] the description of the property or the length of the lease, but may apply to other provisions.[3]

1 CRA 2015 s 64.
2 But see Dermot McKibbin 'Housing stock transfer and unfair contract terms' [2003] JHL 78, which suggests otherwise.
3 See *Unfair Contract Terms Guidance* paras 3.2–3.33.

Effect of unfair terms[1]

21.6 If a term in a lease is unfair in terms of the 2015 Act it will not be binding upon the tenant. However, the rest of the lease may be binding upon the parties if it is capable of continuing in existence without the unfair term, ie if the unfair term is severable from it.

1 CRA 2015 s 67.

Enforcement[1]

21.7 The rules contained in the 2015 Act may be enforced by the courts in the normal way. In addition, a complaint may be made to the Competition & Markets Authority, or one of the qualifying bodies specified in Schedule 3. (In the case of leases, the CMA is probably the most relevant recipient for complaints.) The CMA will often negotiate with particular suppliers (or landlords) to have unfair terms removed from their contracts, but also has backup powers, including interdict and the right to obtain documents and information.

The court has a duty to consider the fairness of terms, even if neither party raises this as an issue.[2]

1 CRA 2015 Sch 5, and see generally *Unfair Contract Terms Guidance* ch 6.
2 CRA 2015 s 71.

LEASE TERMS THAT MAY BE UNFAIR

21.8 Schedule 2 to the 2015 Act gives a list of examples of contractual terms that may be regarded as unfair. The list is declared to be indicative only and not exhaustive.[1] In some cases a term may already be legally ineffectual, eg an attempt to contract out of the landlord's statutory repairing obligations. Such a term may nevertheless be considered unfair under the Act, as it may mislead a tenant who is unaware of his or her legal rights.

1 CRA 2015 s 63(1). For an in-depth discussion of potentially unfair terms (including some not discussed below) in the context of housing stock transfers, see Dermot McKibbin 'Housing Stock Transfer and Unfair Contract Terms' [2003] JHL 78.

Unfair disclaimers

21.9 Part 5 of the CMA guide[1] comments at considerable length upon Schedule 2, para 1 of the 2015 Act, which relates generally to exclusion or limitation of liability. The many types of disclaimer that the CMA believes may be attacked as unfair under this heading include exclusion of liability for death or personal injury (including liability under the Occupiers' Liability (Scotland) Act 1960),[2] exclusion of liability for poor service,[3] terms requiring the tenant to pay a call-out charge if the landlord was called out to make repairs for which the landlord was legally responsible,[4] exclusion of liability for delays in carrying out services,[5] or exclusion of liability for failure to perform contractual obligations,[6] or even binding the tenant while allowing the landlord to provide no service at all.[7] Exclusion of liability for failure to perform contractual obligations could be fair in some circumstances, eg to protect landlords from circumstances outwith their control, but unfair if an exclusion clause goes further than is strictly necessary to achieve a legitimate purpose.

The above survey is only an overview and not exhaustive, and readers are referred to the guidance itself for further details.

1 *Unfair Contract Terms Guidance.*
2 Paras 5.3.1–5.3.4.
3 Paras 5.5.1–5.5.10.
4 Paras 5.9.1–5.9.7.
5 Paras 5.10.1–5.10.5.
6 Paras 5.6.1–5.6.11.
7 Paras 5.12.1–5.12.3.

Repairing obligations

21.10   In addition to the landlord's common law repairing obligation, landlords of residential premises have a number of statutory repairing obligations.[1] A clause attempting to transfer the landlord's repairing obligation to the tenant may be unfair (and will generally be excluded by statute in the case of a private sector tenancy anyway)[2] as may any attempt by the landlord to exclude liability for the state of the property furnishings[3] or exempting the landlord from any delay in carrying out repairs.[4]

Tenant declarations in a standard form lease that may not relate to reality are open to attack.[5] This could potentially apply to the standard clause that the tenant accepts the property as being in good repair at the beginning of the lease if, in fact, the tenant has not been given an opportunity to check this out properly.

1 See paras 19.11 et seq and 19.13 et seq.
2 See para 19.24.
3 An obligation to supply goods of satisfactory quality would appear to be implied in relation to the furnishings (CRA 2015 s 9, read with the definition of 'hire' in s 6(1)). Any attempt to exclude liability in respect of this is void in terms of CRA 2015 s 31(a).
4 See para 21.9.
5 See *Unfair Contract Terms Guidance* paras 5.34.1–5.34.4

Rent retention

21.11 A term may be unfair if it prevents the tenant from offsetting a debt owed to the landlord against any claim he or she had against the landlord.[1] This would presumably include any attempt to contract out of the tenant's common law right to retain the rent when the landlord is in breach of contract.[2]

The CMA guide suggests that the equivalent English right of set-off would fall under this heading.[3]

1 CRA 2015 Sch 2 para 2.
2 See paras 4.31 et seq above.
3 *Unfair Contract Terms Guidance* paras 5.8.1–5.8.11.

Rights of entry to the property

21.12 A term allowing the landlord on giving the tenant reasonable notice to enter the property for the purpose of inspection, or allowing prospective new tenants to view the property, may be reasonable. However, a term allowing an excessive right of entry may be an unfair exclusion of the landlord's common law duty to maintain the tenant in full possession and not to derogate from the grant,[1] and may also be void under the 2015 Act.[2]

1 See paras 3.10, 3.11 at 3.14 et seq.
2 *Unfair Contract Terms Guidance* paras 5.32.2–5.32.3.

Financial penalties

21.13 A term may be considered unfair if it requires 'a consumer who fails to fulfil his obligations under the contract to pay a disproportionately high sum in compensation'.[1] This could cover a requirement to pay unreasonable interest on arrears of rent, or a term that would allow a tenant to forfeit a security deposit for a relatively minor infringement.

1 CRA 2015 Sch 2 para 6; *Unfair Contract Terms Guidance* paras 5.14.1–5.14.10.

Variation of terms etc

21.14 A term may be unfair if it allows the landlord without a valid reason to vary the terms of the lease or make any changes in the characteristics of the property.[1] This could cover making changes to the building or the furniture, or moving the tenant to another property.

In *Peabody Trust Governors v Reeve*[2] the landlords claimed that they were entitled to make unilateral variations to their tenancy agreements in accordance with the procedure under section 103 of the Housing Act 1985 (not applicable to Scotland). This was permitted by one clause in the tenancy agreement but contradicted by another. The landlords argued that the tenancy agreement had to be interpreted to take account of the fact that, because of the large number of tenants and properties under their control, they needed to have a unilateral method of varying tenancy agreements in order to manage their housing stock. They also argued that, in any case, the ability to unilaterally alter the terms was fair.

It was held that:

(a)   although such a power would be useful to the landlords and help to prevent their housing stock becoming unmanageable, this was nevertheless a risk that the legislature had chosen to allow social landlords to run on the basis that they would be able to manage without such powers. Also, because the terms of the agreement were unclear and contradictory, the court was obliged to adopt the interpretation most favourable to the tenant. There could therefore be no variation of the tenancy agreement without the written consent of both parties;

(b)   the landlords' attempt to enforce only one of two contradictory clauses was unfair, and there was no reason to suppose that the landlords absolutely required such variation powers; and

(c)   in order to satisfy the requirements of the Regulations, any such unilateral variation clause would need at a minimum to take full and proper account of the guidance set out by the Office of Fair Trading. This of course should now be read as referring to the 2015 Act and to the CMA guidance.

1 CRA 2015 Sch 2 paras 11–13; *Unfair Contract Terms Guidance* paras 5.21.1–5.21.13.
2 [2009] L&TR 6, [2008] 3 EGLR 61.

Rent reviews

21.15   A rent review clause may be unfair if the lease allows the rent to be increased without the tenant's consent, or without reference to independent criteria.[1]

1 CRA 2015 Sch 2 paras 14–15; *Unfair Contract Terms Guidance* paras 5.23.1–5.23.7.

Irritancy

21.16   We saw above that an irritancy clause in a residential lease is limited in its application.[1] None of the examples given in Schedule 2 specifically covers this; however, in terms of the general criteria for fairness (in particular the requirement for good faith) an irritancy provision may be considered unfair, as it may mislead the tenant regarding the landlord's powers to terminate the lease prematurely.

1 See para 17.45.

Unreasonably excluding the tenant's right to assign or sublet

21.17 As mentioned above,[1] the list of potentially unfair terms in Schedule 2 to the 2015 Act is indicative only and not exhaustive. In principle, a term limiting assignation or subletting by the tenant might be subject to the 2015 Act.[2] However, as we have seen, the tenant of residential property has very limited rights to assign in most cases anyway.[3]

1 See para 21.8.
2 *Unfair Contract Terms Guidance* paras 5.33.1–5.33.5.
3 See para 17.41.

Landlord's right to assign or sublet without consent

21.18 While a term conferring such a right upon a landlord, eg allowing a stock transfer, is not necessarily unfair, it might be considered so if it seemed to reduce the tenant's contractual rights, or misrepresented the tenant's legal position.[1] Even if such a term was held to fall foul of the 2015 Act, however, it is doubtful whether that would make much practical difference. After all, the landlord's right to sell the property or to grant an interposed lease (with the effect of making the tenant a sub-tenant) arises from the general law, not from any term in the lease.[2]

1 *Unfair Contract Terms Guidance* paras 5.28.1–5.28.4.
2 On interposed leases, see para 7.40 et seq.

21.19 The above is only a selection of examples of the ways in which the 2015 Act may apply to unfair terms in residential leases.

Appendix 1

Law Reform (Miscellaneous Provisions) (Scotland) Act 1985

(1985 CHAPTER 73)

An Act to amend the law of Scotland in respect of certain leases, other contracts and obligations; certain courts and their powers; evidence and procedure; certain criminal penalties; the care of children; the functions of the Commissioner for Local Administration; solicitors; and certain procedures relating to crofting and the valuation of sheep stocks; and to make, as respects Scotland, certain other miscellaneous reforms of the law.

[30th October 1985]

Provisions relating to leases

4 Irritancy clauses etc. relating to monetary breaches of lease.

(1) A landlord shall not, for the purpose of treating a lease as terminated or terminating it, be entitled to rely—
  (a) on a provision in the lease which purports to terminate it, or to enable him to terminate it, in the event of a failure of the tenant to pay rent, or to make any other payment, on or before the due date therefor or such later date or within such period as may be provided for in the lease; or
  (b) on the fact that such a failure is, or is deemed by a provision of the lease to be, a material breach of contract,
  unless subsection (2) or (5) below applies.

(2) This subsection applies if—
  (a) the landlord has, at any time after the payment of rent or other payment mentioned in subsection (1) above has become due, served a notice on the tenant—
    (i) requiring the tenant to make payment of the sum which he has failed to pay together with any interest thereon in terms of the lease within the period specified in the notice; and

        (ii)   stating that, if the tenant does not comply with the requirement mentioned in sub-paragraph (i) above, the lease may be terminated; and

    (b)   the tenant has not complied with that requirement.

(3)   The period to be specified in any such notice shall be not less than—

    (a)   a period of 14 *days* [weeks]¹ immediately following the service of the notice; or

    (b)   if any period remaining between the service of the notice and the expiry of any time provided for in the lease or otherwise for the late payment of the sum which the tenant has failed to pay is greater than 14 *days* [weeks]¹, that greater period.

[(3A) The Scottish Ministers may, by regulations, amend the period referred to in paragraphs (a) and (b) of subsection (3).

(3B)   Regulations under subsection (3A) are subject to the negative procedure.]²

(4)   Any notice served under subsection (2) above shall be sent by recorded delivery and shall be sufficiently served if it is sent to the tenant's last business or residential address in the United Kingdom known to the landlord or to the last address in the United Kingdom provided to the landlord by the tenant for the purpose of such service.

(5)   This subsection applies if the tenant does not have an address in the United Kingdom known to the landlord and has not provided an address in the United Kingdom to the landlord for the purpose of service.

[(5A) This section applies regardless of whether the circumstances referred to in paragraph (a) or (b) of subsection (1), in which a landlord is entitled to terminate a lease, occurred before or after the date on which paragraph 7 of schedule 7 of the Coronavirus (Scotland) Act 2020 came into force.

(5B)   A notice served under subsection (2) before the date on which paragraph 7 of schedule 7 of the Coronavirus (Scotland) Act 2020 came into force becomes void if, by that date, the time period specified in the notice has not yet expired.]²

Amendments

1 Word in square brackets substituted for word in italics (temporarily) by the Coronavirus (Scotland) Act 2020, s 8, Sch 7, para 7(a).

2 inserted (temporarily) by the Coronavirus (Scotland) Act 2020, s 8, Sch 7, para 7(b), (c).

5 Irritancy clauses etc. not relating to monetary breaches of leases.

(1)   Subject to subsection (2) below, a landlord shall not, for the purpose of treating a lease as terminated or terminating it, be entitled to rely—

(a)   on a provision in the lease which purports to terminate it, or to enable the landlord to terminate it, in the event of an act or omission by the tenant (other than such a failure as is mentioned in section 4(1)(a) of this Act) or of a change in the tenant's circumstances; or

(b)   on the fact that such act or omission or change is, or is deemed by a provision of the lease to be, a material breach of contract,

if in all the circumstances of the case a fair and reasonable landlord would not seek so to rely.

(2)   No provision of a lease shall of itself, irrespective of the particular circumstances of the case, be held to be unenforceable by virtue of subsection (1) above.

(3)   In the consideration, for the purposes of subsection (1)(a) or (b) above, of the circumstances of a case where—

(a)   an act, omission or change is alleged to constitute a breach of a provision of the lease or a breach of contract; and

(b)   the breach is capable of being remedied in reasonable time, regard shall be had to whether a reasonable opportunity has been afforded to the tenant to enable the breach to be remedied.

6 Supplementary and transitional provisions relating to sections 4 and 5.

(1)   The parties to a lease shall not be entitled to disapply any provision of section 4 or 5 of this Act from it.

(2)   Where circumstances have occurred before the commencement of sections 4 and 5 of this Act which would have entitled a landlord to terminate a lease in reliance on a provision in the lease or on the ground that the circumstances constituted a material breach of contract, but the landlord has not before such commencement given written notice to the tenant of his intention to terminate the lease in respect of those circumstances, he shall, after such commencement, be entitled to terminate the lease in respect of those circumstances only in accordance with the provisions of section 4 or 5 (as the case may be) of this Act.

(3)   Nothing in section 4 or 5 of this Act shall apply in relation to any payment which has to be made, or any other condition which has to be fulfilled, before a tenant is entitled to entry under a lease.

7 Interpretation of sections 4 to 6.

(1)   In sections 4 to 6 of this Act 'lease' means a lease of land, whether entered into before or after the commencement of those sections, but does not include a lease of land—

      (a)   used wholly or mainly for residential purposes; ...[1]

      (b)   comprising ...[1] a croft, the subject of a cottar or the holding of a landholder or a statutory small tenant[; or

      (c)   where the lease is an agricultural lease.][2]

(2)   In subsection (1) above—

['agricultural lease' means a lease constituting a 1991 Act tenancy within the meaning of the Agricultural Holdings (Scotland) Act 2003 (asp 11) or a lease constituting a short limited duration tenancy[, a limited duration tenancy, a modern limited duration tenancy or a repairing tenancy][3] (within the meaning of that Act);][4]

'cottar' has the same meaning as in section 28(4) of the Crofters (Scotland) Act 1955;

'croft' has the same meaning as in section 3 of the Crofters (Scotland) Act 1955; and

'holding' (in relation to a landholder or statutory small tenant), 'landholder' and 'statutory small tenant' have the same meanings as in the Small Landholders (Scotland) Acts 1886 to 1931.

Amendments

1 Repealed by the Agricultural Holdings (Scotland) Act 2003, s 94, Schedule 1, para 7(a)(i).

2 Inserted by the Agricultural Holdings (Scotland) Act 2003, s 94, Schedule 1, para 7(a)(ii).

3 Substituted by the Land Reform (Scotland) Act 2016, s 129(2), Schedule 2, para 2.

4 Substituted by the Agricultural Holdings (Scotland) Act 2003, s 94, Schedule 1, para 7(b).

Appendix 2

Tenancy of Shops (Scotland) Act 1949

(1949 CHAPTER 25)

An Act to make provision with regard to tenancies of shops in Scotland.

[29th March 1949]

1 Provision for renewal of tenancies of shops.

(1)   If the landlord of any premises consisting of a shop and occupied by a tenant gives or has given to the tenant notice of termination of tenancy taking effect after the passing of this Act, and the tenant is unable to obtain a renewal of his tenancy on terms that are satisfactory to him, he may, at any time before the notice takes effect and not later than the expiry of twenty-one days after the service of the notice or after the passing of this Act, whichever is the later, apply to the sheriff for a renewal of his tenancy.

(2)   On any application under the foregoing subsection the sheriff may, subject as hereinafter provided, determine that the tenancy shall be renewed for such period, not exceeding one year, at such rent, and on such terms and conditions as he shall, in all the circumstances, think reasonable, and thereafter the parties shall be deemed to have entered into a new lease of the premises for that period, at that rent and on those terms and conditions.

(3)   Notwithstanding anything in the last foregoing subsection, the sheriff may, if in all the circumstances he thinks it reasonable to do so, dismiss any application under this section, and shall not determine that a tenancy shall be renewed, if he is satisfied—

(a)   that the tenant is in breach of any condition of his tenancy which in the opinion of the sheriff is material; or

(b)   that the tenant is notour bankrupt or is divested of his estate by virtue of a trust deed for behoof of creditors, or, being a company, is unable to pay its debts; or

(c)   that the landlord has offered to sell the premises to the tenant at such price as may, failing agreement, be fixed by a single arbiter agreed on by the parties or appointed, failing such agreement, by the sheriff; or

(d)   that the landlord has offered to afford to the tenant, on terms and conditions which in the opinion of the sheriff are reasonable, alternative accommodation which, in the opinion of the sheriff, is suitable for the purposes of the business carried on by the tenant in the premises; or

(e)   that the tenant has given notice of termination of tenancy and in consequence of that notice the landlord has contracted to sell or let the premises or has taken any other steps as a result of which he would in the opinion of the sheriff be seriously prejudiced if he could not obtain possession of the premises; or

(f)   that, having regard to all the circumstances of the case, greater hardship would be caused by determining that the tenancy shall be renewed than by refusing so to do.

(4)   Where a tenancy has been renewed under subsection (2) of this section, the tenant shall have the like right to apply for further renewals as if the tenancy had been renewed by agreement between the landlord and the tenant, and accordingly the foregoing provisions of this section shall, with any necessary modifications, apply to a tenancy which has been renewed under the said subsection (2) or under this subsection.

(5)   If on any application under this section the sheriff is satisfied that it will not be possible to dispose finally of the application before the notice of termination of tenancy takes effect, he may make an interim order authorising the tenant to continue in occupation of the premises at such rent, for such period (which shall not exceed three months) and on such terms and conditions as the sheriff may think fit.

(6)   ...[1]

[(7)   An application under this section shall be made by way of a summary cause within the meaning of the Sheriff Courts (Scotland) Act 1971][2].

Amendments

1 Repealed by the Tenancy of Shops (Scotland) Act 1964, s 1(2).
2 Substituted by the Sheriff Courts (Scotland) Act 1971, s 46(1), Sch 1, para 3.

2 Application to Crown property.

The foregoing section shall apply to any such premises as are mentioned therein in which the interest of the landlord or tenant belongs to His Majesty in right of the Crown or to a government department or is held on behalf of His Majesty for the purposes of a government department, in like manner as the said section applies to any other such premises.

3 Citation, extent, interpretation and duration.

(1)　This Act may be cited as the Tenancy of Shops (Scotland) Act, 1949, and shall extend to Scotland only.

(2)　In this Act the expression 'shop' includes any shop within the meaning of the Shops Acts, 1912 to 1936, or any of those Acts.

(3)　...[1]

Amendment

1 Repealed by the Tenancy of Shops (Scotland) Act 1964, s 1(1).

Index

[References are to paragraph number]